Hoover vs. Roosevelt

Also by Hal Elliott Wert

Hoover the Fishing President:
Portrait of the Private Man and His Adventurous Life Outdoors
Paperback Edition 2020

George McGovern and the Democratic Insurgents:
The Best Campaign and Political Posters of the Last Fifty Years
2015

Hope: A Collection of Obama Posters and Prints
2009

Hoover the Fishing President:
Portrait of the Private Man and His Life Outdoors
2005

"Years of Frustration: Herbert Hoover and World War II" in
Uncommon Americans:
The Lives and Legacies of Herbert and Lou Henry Hoover
2003

"Military Expediency, the 'Hunger Winter,'
and Holland's Belated Liberation" in
Victory in Europe 1945: From World War to Cold War
2000

Hoover vs. Roosevelt

*Two Presidents' Battle over Feeding
Europe and Going to War*

Hal Elliott Wert

STACKPOLE
BOOKS

*Essex, Connecticut
Blue Ridge Summit, Pennsylvania*

STACKPOLE BOOKS
An imprint of Globe Pequot, the trade division of
The Rowman & Littlefield Publishing Group, Inc.
4501 Forbes Blvd., Ste. 200
Lanham, MD 20706
www.rowman.com

Distributed by NATIONAL BOOK NETWORK

Copyright © 2023 by Hal Elliott Wert

All rights reserved. No part of this book may be reproduced in any form or by any electronic or mechanical means, including information storage and retrieval systems, without written permission from the publisher, except by a reviewer who may quote passages in a review.

British Library Cataloguing in Publication Information available

Library of Congress Cataloging-in-Publication Data
Names: Wert, Hal Elliott, author.
Title: Hoover vs. Roosevelt : two presidents' battle over feeding Europe and going to war / Hal Elliott Wert.
Other titles: Two presidents' battle over feeding Europe and going to war
Description: Essex, Connecticut : Stackpole Books, [2023] | Includes bibliographical references and index. | Summary: "The story of how the U.S. entered World War II as seen through the lens of Herbert Hoover, 'Hoover vs. Roosevelt' brings a fresh perspective to a time in our nation's history when our country was deeply divided over what now seems a 'done deal.'"—Provided by publisher.
Identifiers: LCCN 2022025377 (print) | LCCN 2022025378 (ebook) | ISBN 9780811739726 (cloth) | ISBN 9780811769709 (epub)
Subjects: LCSH: World War, 1939–1945—United States. | Neutrality—United States. | World War, 1939–1945—Civilian relief—Europe. | Roosevelt, Franklin D. (Franklin Delano), 1882–1945. | Hoover, Herbert, 1874–1964. | United States—Politics and government—1933–1945. | United States—Foreign relations—1933–1945. | Isolationism—United States—History—20th century.
Classification: LCC D753 .W47 2023 (print) | LCC D753 (ebook) | DDC 940.53/2273—dc23/eng/20220624
LC record available at https://lccn.loc.gov/2022025377
LC ebook record available at https://lccn.loc.gov/2022025378

∞™ The paper used in this publication meets the minimum requirements of American National Standard for Information Sciences—Permanence of Paper for Printed Library Materials, ANSI/NISO Z39.48-1992.

For

Grandmother, Cora Mae Davis Shadle
Mother, Frances Mary Shadle Wert

You Never Faltered in Your Love and Sacrifice
For Your Three Unruly Boys

"For I was hungry and you gave me something to eat,
I was thirsty and you gave me something to drink,
I was a stranger and you invited me in,
I needed clothes and you clothed me,
I was sick and you looked after me,
I was in prison and you came to visit me."

—Matthew 25, 34–36

Contents

Foreword by Justus D. Doenecke ix
Acknowledgments xv
Introduction 1

Chapter 1　The End of All Wars 11
Chapter 2　The Contenders: Hoover and Roosevelt 25
Chapter 3　The Liars' League: The World Turned
　　　　　　Upside Down! 49
Chapter 4　War 65
Chapter 5　Crushed 83
Chapter 6　The Rapprochement That Failed: The Battle
　　　　　　over Aid Begins 145
Chapter 7　Rescue in Romania, Hungary, and Lithuania 189
Chapter 8　Embargo Repeal, Politics, and Negotiations in
　　　　　　the Garden of Beasts 239
Chapter 9　In the Jaws of the Soviet Bugbear 299
Chapter 10　Finnomania: A Cause Célèbre 331

Conclusion 385
Notes 389
Bibliography 453
Index 497

Foreword

"No other twentieth-century American statesman has had his range of interests and breadth of understanding of domestic and foreign problems."[1] So wrote historian Joan Hoff Wilson in 1975 as she stood in the vanguard of those who sought to rehabilitate the reputation of Herbert Hoover. Gary Dean Best was only slightly less laudatory concerning America's thirty-first president, writing in 2013 that "few could grasp—as Hoover did with consummate skill—all the pieces in the intricate chessboard that made up the American and world economies."[2] Most historians would probably differ with Wilson and Best, finding the thirty-first president inadequate during the Great Depression, which began in 1929. Almost as important, scholars perceive Hoover as too "isolationist" during World War II and much of the Cold War. (The word *isolationist* itself, usually used in pejorative fashion, does little justice to the complexity and context of this political stance, with *anti-interventionist* being the more accurate term.)

Over the decades, few historians of "isolationism" fail to put the Hoover of 1939–1941 among the ranks of those unwilling to risk war in order to defeat the Axis powers. From 1957 to 2020, the most prominent historians of anti-interventionism have included Hoover as one of the movement's most prominent leaders.[3] Ted Galen Carpenter is more subtle, making penetrating distinctions among the anti-interventionists. Carpenter sees some, such as Senator Hiram Johnson (R-CA) and "fascist" commentator Lawrence Dennis, as "doctrinaire isolationists," always maintaining the need for a unilateral and cautious approach to foreign affairs. Others, such as Senator Robert A. Taft (R-OH) and Representative Daniel A. Reed (R-NY), were "pragmatic isolationists," willing to concede that modern circumstances limited the applicability of rigid nonentanglement. Still others, such as Congressman John Taber (R-NY) and law professor Clarence Manion, were "marginal isolationists," a diverse and amorphous group who usually supported the prevailing foreign policy while dissenting on foreign aid and military alliances. Carpenter places Hoover in the third camp, finding him opposing the major measures of Franklin Roosevelt until 1941 but taking a more moderate stance until 1949, when—with the fall of Nationalist China—he became an adamant critic of Harry Truman's foreign policy.[4]

Hal Elliott Wert's extraordinarily well-researched book is very much in Carpenter's vein, for in 1939 and 1940 Hoover revealed himself as one of the more restrained anti-interventionists. In this work, Wert thoroughly describes how, once World War II broke out in Europe on September 1, 1939, Hoover mobilized massive efforts to feed its war-torn countries, beginning with Poland that September and Finland in December. By so doing, Hoover introduced the human tragedy of the global conflict to an ignorant and self-absorbed American public.

In his postpresidential years, Hoover was a prolific writer, in general quite aware of his prominence on the world scene and particularly conscious that the world should learn of his relief efforts in World War I and its immediate aftermath. Yet, increasingly realizing that his years were numbered, he neglected what Wert sees as "a critical portion of the story of American intervention into World War II" (6). His volume covering the period from 1939 to 1963 devotes only eleven pages to his early World War II endeavors.[5]

In this extensively documented account, Wert has combed scores of manuscripts, memoirs, diplomatic dispatches, master's and doctoral theses, scholarly works and articles, and contemporary books and journalistic accounts. He has even gone so far as to consult narratives in the Polish and Lithuanian languages. Certain features of this book make the story particularly vivid. The use of color posters from Color Blaze and Stanford's Hoover Institution enlivens the account, as do little-used photos of wartime Poland.

Some aspects of Wert's narrative bear particular attention. The author shows not only how the British blockade operated but also how Hoover perceived the role of the Hague and Geneva Conventions in such matters.

Foreword

He offers much fresh material on the Molotov-Ribbentrop pact, which triggered Hitler's invasion of Poland, and ably captures the lethargic atmosphere in Britain, France, and Germany as these countries all suddenly realized that they were at war. Extensive material is presented on America's Neutrality Act of May 1939 (which involved an arms embargo of nations at war) and its replacement by legislation that November. The new law permitted arms shipments, provided the belligerent nations transported these munitions and paid cash for them. Hoover, coordinating with aviator Charles A. Lindbergh, sought an alternative to the bill, one that would ban shipment of such offensive weapons as bombers, submarines, and poison gas. Their effort failed, as did other attempts to amend "cash and carry."

Wert offers a moving account of Poland's defeat, graphic enough to draw parallels to Vladimir Putin's invasion of Ukraine in February 2022. Few students of history have been aware of the postinvasion activities of such Polish leaders as President Władysław Raczkiewicz, Prime Minister Felicjan Składkowski, Foreign Minister Józef Beck, and military commander in chief Edward Śmigły-Rydz. Wert has also offered little-known details on the Russian invasion of eastern Poland on September 17, 1939, an event that further traumatized the population. He likewise covers the little-known role played by Rumania, Hungary, and Lithuania in coping with the plight of Polish refugees.

Equally moving is Wert's account of the Russian invasion of Finland, an event that began on November 30, 1939, and ended on March 12, 1940. As in the case of Poland, Wert discusses the immediate prewar diplomacy leading to the Soviet attack, debates within the Roosevelt administration over a proper response, and Hoover's spearheading of the Finnish Relief Fund (FRF). Wert ably describes the "Finnomania" involved in the nationwide publicity campaign to aid the Finns, a movement far greater in scope than any effort to assist the Poles. (One photograph shows Hoover accepting a contribution from Popeye the Sailor—see page 331.)

In some ways the story of Hoover's forays into Polish and Finnish humanitarian work shows him as a skillful bureaucratic entrepreneur, one who could rival such classic prototypes as Admiral Hyman Rickover, J. Edgar Hoover, or Robert Moses. He maneuvered dexterously amid a hostile Roosevelt administration and a rival relief administrator, Norman Davis, whom Roosevelt had appointed head of the American Red Cross in 1938. He also crossed swords over turf with novelist Dorothy Canfield Fisher, who (with Marion G. Canby) in October 1939 created the Children's Crusade for Children.

One ends up with great admiration for certain individuals who did all possible to aid the crushed Poles, among them Charlotte Kellogg of Hoover's Commission for Polish Relief (CPR); Paul Super of the Polish Young Men's Christian Association; Clare Hollingworth, cub reporter for London's *Daily Telegraph*; and Anthony J. Drexel Biddle Jr., US ambassador to Poland. Gilbert Redfern spent twenty-seven months in Vilnius, Lithuania, on behalf of the CPR. Wall Street banker Lewis Strauss played a vital role in Hoover's efforts in both Poland and Finland. Strauss had been Hoover's personal secretary in 1917 when Woodrow Wilson created the Food Administration and in 1919 assisted him in running the American Relief Administration.

Though slighted in most accounts of Hoover, the former president's efforts to aid the Poles and Finns—writes Wert—were most successful. Finland received $3.5 million from the FRF alone and, under Hoover's prodding, $2.3 million from the Red Cross; $3 million was spent on Polish refugees and those under direct German occupation. For the only time in his life, Hoover had been able to bend FDR's foreign policy to his goals.

Wert portrays Hoover as one who in private was relaxed and gracious, in the process puncturing the stereotype of a rigid, aloof, impersonal figure. The author does concede, however, that in many ways Hoover's personality was not suited for the presidency, particularly in his woeful inadequacy in reaching a mass audience (33–34). Wert devotes considerable space to Hoover's quixotic effort to win over the delegates to the Republican convention of 1940, hoping to do so by delivering a speech powerful enough to accomplish that goal.

Yet, though revealing great respect for Hoover the man, Wert is not involved in hagiography. He finds that in Hoover's initial passion for wealth, "his business practices were often questionable and sometimes illegal" (35–36). He concedes Hoover's negative qualities, for the former president could be "ruthless and unforgiving and at times, like [Franklin] Roosevelt, an SOB." Trying his hand at a bit of psychohistory, Wert writes, "At the center of it all was a defensive orphan boy in pursuit of legitimacy—a man in need of acceptance and love" (36). Hoover was lackadaisical as a father, relegating his children "to the sidelines" (41). Wert finds that Hoover's humanitarian impulse was not solely altruistic, as both the ex-president and FDR realized his relief efforts enhanced his presidential aspirations. Hoover hoped that a deadlocked Republican convention in 1940 would turn to him and fully realized that spearheading relief efforts would keep his name before the public.

Ironically, the anti-interventionist Hoover's humanitarian efforts, by putting the spotlight on Nazi and Soviet aggression, made Americans highly sympathetic to the cause of the European Allies. Surely the attention he gave to refugees and the starving supplied more ideological fuel for William Allen White's Committee to Defend America by Aiding the Allies and the more militant Fight for Freedom Committee than to the No Foreign War Committee and the far more potent America First Committee.

Wert's definitive study involves far more than the efforts of one of America's most prominent citizens to relieve suffering in two European countries. He offers a unique window onto both Europe and the United States during the first months of the greatest conflagration in centuries.

—Justus D. Doenecke

Acknowledgments

WHILE A BOOK HAS AN AUTHOR'S NAME ON THE COVER, IT TOOK THE talent and skill of many people to bring it to fruition. The list of those who made possible *Hoover vs. Roosevelt: Two Presidents' Battle over Feeding Europe and Going to War* is a long one, as the book is a culmination of over twenty-five years of research. I was pleased that when I asked Justus D. Doenecke to write a foreword, he agreed. Few, if any, know more about the political battles between the interventionists and noninterventionists from September 1939 to the attack on Pearl Harbor on December 7, 1941, and the German declaration of war a few days later, on December 11. Of his many articles and books, *Storm on the Horizon: The Challenge to American Intervention, 1939–1941* is indispensable. Thank you. Much is owed as well to George Nash, a longtime friend and dean of the Hoover scholars, who took the time to read chapter after chapter and call me on the phone to discuss Hoover, his policies, and his judgment and, of course, to correct my mistakes. In addition, George agreed to write one of the shoutouts on the back of the dustjacket. Thank you, George. Iwona Korga, president of the Piłsudski Institute of America, read the chapters on Poland and helped ensure that I made fewer mistakes with Polish orthography. Thank you, Iwona. Her assistant, Malgorzata Skrodzki, located a fine photo of General Kazimierz Sosnkowski preparing to escape Poland in September 1939.

Mary Anne Demeritt deserves special praise for carefully proofreading the entire manuscript, as she has done for nearly all my past books and articles. We have had many long discussions over coffee on what she thought I should add and should delete, and I have listened. Thank you, Mary Anne. My brother Frank, also an academic, read all the chapters and offered succinct advice on how I should proceed. Thank you, Frank.

My many research trips to Washington, DC, were generously supported by longtime friends Ron and Cecil Deaton, who lived just across the river in Springfield, Virginia, and offered not only a place to stay but also enjoyable companionship. On weekends, Ron and I would explore the Civil War battlefields that surrounded the capital. I wish to offer a tribute to another fine friend, Glen Jeansonne, a prolific writer who did pioneering work on radicals in the 1930s and 1940s, Huey P. Long, Gerald L. K. Smith, and Leander Perez, and later produced two fine volumes on Hoover. Glen passed away in 2018, and I sorely miss our many discussions on Hoover and Roosevelt.

Two people at the Hoover Presidential Library and Museum in West Branch, Iowa, deserve special praise. The talented Lynn Smith, audiovisual archivist, was diligent in helping me obtain exactly the photo needed to match a particular event or speech. For the last several years, I have emailed her at least once a week. Diligent and as necessary to the book's completion was Spencer Howard, archivist technician, who has a thorough knowledge of the library's collections and whom, like Lynn, I emailed at least once a week with a specific request. Over the years both Lynn and Spencer have been essential, but due to the Covid lockdowns they went the extra mile. In fact, Covid threw a monkey wrench into my progress as nearly all the archives and libraries in the country closed their doors. Spencer and Lynn would be in the library only on occasion, but, when there, they invariably found what I needed. Lynn and Spencer, thank you. Craig Wright, the supervisory archivist, was extremely helpful during the lockdowns. At their sister institution, the Franklin D. Roosevelt Presidential Library, Patrick Fahy, archivist, was able to achieve the same feat. Thank you, Patrick. Tom Schwartz, director of the Hoover Presidential Library and Museum, has been supportive of my research and generous in having me participate in programs open to the public on facets of Hoover's life. These sessions have always been delightful affairs. The color plate section would not have been possible without half a dozen images from the massive poster collection at the Hoover Institution in Stanford, California. Several photos are also from their collections. Sarah Patton helped with locating documents and Chris Marino with poster images and photos. Importantly, the *Historian*, the *Polish Review*, and

Acknowledgments

the Siena College Research Institute all granted permission for me to freely use material previously published. Special thanks also go to Don Davis, archivist with the American Friends Service Committee Archives in Philadelphia. The document, photo, and poster collection is extensive and especially rich in material on the German Children's Feeding Program in the 1920s. Thanks go as well to Ryan Bean, reference and outreach archivist, at the Kautz Family YMCA Archives at the University of Minnesota. The photo of Charlotte Kellogg was located by Jessica Dooling and Michael Frost, Manuscript and Archives, Sterling Library, Yale University. Eric Huber, librarian and archivist, Queens Borough Library, New York, manages the photo morgue of the *New York Herald Tribune*, an indispensable source for Hoover photos. Jill Livingston, Siskiyou County Museum, Yreka, California, furnished my favorite Hoover fishing photo. Lee Arnold, senior director of Library and Collections, Historical Society of Pennsylvania, helped in locating photos of Ambassador Tony Biddle. A treasure trove of photos documenting Biddle and his staff's race across Poland in front of the Germans came from the photo album of Mary McKenzie, located in the Ossolinski National Institute in Wrocław, Poland. Agata Janiak of the Manuscript Department generously provided two dozen of the photos. Renata Banaszczyk, chief specialist, data sharing, Narodowe Archiwun Cyfrowe (National Digital Archives), provided several photos from the extensive collection of historical photographs. Assistance and necessary direction in my search for photos in Poland was aided by Paweł Banaszczyk at Ośrodek KARTA, who sent a collection of the Poles in Romania—*Rumuński Azyl: Losy Polaków, 1939–1945* (*Romanian Asylum: The Fate of the Poles, 1939–1945*). Izabella Mościcka, Museum of Independence in Warsaw, also provided information and photos of the famous radio musical group, the Lwów Wave, that entertained interned Polish soldiers in Romania. Thanks go as well to the Romanian National Archives for two photos of interned Polish soldiers. Thank you, Dr. Liviu-Daniel Grigorescu, Dr. Claudiu-Victor Turcita, and Elena Cirjan. In this country the collections of the Polish Museum of America and the Balzekas Museum of Lithuanian Culture were essential.

My hat is off to the staff of the Kansas City Art Institute Library: M. J. Poehler, director; Lora Farrell, catalog and digital services; Megan

Channel, circulation; and Elizabeth Davis, visual and archival research. In the last few years, Elizabeth rounded up at least fifty academic articles I felt compelled to read. Thank you, Elizabeth.

Special thanks go to Stackpole publisher Judith Schnell and to Stephanie Otto for once more overseeing photos and illustrations. David Reisch, my patient editor, has, I am sure, aged considerably through this overlong process. Thank you, Dave. To long suffering family and friends, I know, don't talk about the book. My mistakes are mine alone.

Introduction

Hoover at work at one of his desks, 1960 (courtesy of Herbert Hoover Presidential Library and Museum [hereafter HHPLM]).

Year after year, the lights burned far into the night in Apartment 31-A of the luxurious art deco Waldorf-Astoria Hotel towering high above Manhattan. The apartment's sole inhabitant, former president Herbert Hoover, the "Chief," sat at his writing table for hours on end, rapidly scribbling away with a sharpened pencil on foolscap. If, on occasion, he was in bed at a reasonable time, he would often awaken in the middle of the night, walk down the hall, and plunge back into one of the four books he was simultaneously writing. Hoover, a veritable writing machine, cranked out thousands of words a day. Material for each book was placed on a separate table. Come morning, regardless of how many hours he had slept, he was up around 5:30 a.m., left his night's work on his secretary's desks to be typed, looked over his calendar to check on the day's visitors, ate breakfast promptly at 9:00 a.m. (usually with guests), and returned to his office. There he reviewed the proofs of his previous day's work, which arrived each morning by a special delivery courier. Corrections and additions followed, and then—back to writing.[1] Soon a nonstop parade of callers began to arrive. The day-to-day logistics of Hoover's Waldorf world were ruled with an iron hand by his longtime secretary, Bunny Miller. If you didn't have direct access to the Chief (and few did), you had to go through her. Lunch was at 1:00 p.m. and dinner at 7:30 sharp. On occasion he lunched with friends at the Dutch Treat or University Club. Lowell Thomas quipped that the University Club was so stuffy that a man couldn't take his mistress there unless she was the wife of a member. A night out was usually a concert, a movie, or the Old-Timers' Game at Yankee Stadium. On evenings home alone, taking a break from writing, he would smoke his pipe, watch a baseball game, listen on the radio to Ray Henle's *Three Star Express* or join sixteen million listeners to hear NBC's commentator, Fulton J. Lewis, hold forth on events unfolding in Washington, DC.

Dinner nearly every night included a variety of guests, as he disliked dining alone. He was as dedicated to his cocktail—a martini—as he was to his routine. This gin and vermouth California concoction with a lemon twist was normally accompanied by macadamia nuts and cheddar cheese—what he liked to call "rat cheese." He enthralled dinner guests with his stories of adventures worldwide; a favorite was his encounter with a tiger in a Burma cave. His guests were all ears as he related Hu-Hua and Hoo Loo's madcap brush with the Boxers in 1900 during the siege of Tientsin in the crumbling empire of the Chinese dowager empress Cixi.[2] Sure to gain his listeners' rapt attention were political battles won and lost through seven presidential administrations, including his own. His devilish shtick on Calvin Coolidge always brought smiles, grins, and laughter. And then there was Franklin Delano Roosevelt, a source of endless invective. If his guests could be enticed, he loved to play canasta. Energized by these evening affairs, he saw his guests to the door, returned to his writing tables, and pushed on into the night. If a midnight snack was in order and he could find nothing of interest in his small kitchen, he sent out to the nearby Horn & Hardart automat for baked beans.

In the first years of the 1950s, Hoover's three-volume memoirs were published. The first volume, *Years of Adventure*, largely focused on the relief organizations he had created that saved millions of lives, the Commission for Relief in Belgium (CRB), and his work for President Woodrow Wilson as head of the US War Food Administration.[3] Volume 2, *The Cabinet and the Presidency*, briefly covered aid rendered through the American Relief Administration (ARA), and the third volume was largely Hoover's explanation of the Great Depression—much akin to a Socratic apology.[4] But by the late 1950s, Hoover was an octogenarian in declining health. He reasoned that time was not on his side and had his eye on the clock. But with the time that remained, he was determined to tell his story—to secure his legacy. As long as he was alive, his critics would not have the last word. Reviewing his lifetime of achievement, he decided that his relief efforts were his most important contribution and needed to be thoroughly documented. He would not be remembered as a great American president, but he wished to ensure that he would be remembered as the "Great Humanitarian." It was a story that only he could tell. With this goal in mind, in the late 1950s, he undertook a massive four-volume explication of those achievements. He titled it *An American Epic*, and what a story it is. His work on the *Epic*, however, was interrupted by other projects: manuscripts sitting on the other three tables. The former president was disciplined, but he always kept a number of balls in the air simultaneously so that he could give in to his whims and move back and forth between projects as he chose.

One of those balls, his magnum opus, titled *Freedom Betrayed*—a searing indictment of the Roosevelt administration and the failure of liberalism—became his great obsession, a book that would not be published until decades after his death.[5] An overnight guest, returning from the bathroom long after midnight, noticed a light burning in his host's office. Poking his head through the door, he asked what in the world the Chief was doing. Looking up, Hoover snapped, "I'm making my Roosevelt book more pungent."[6] A further distraction, *The Ordeal of Woodrow Wilson*, chronicled his close association with the president as war food administrator and his role as advisor to the president at Versailles. This new undertaking had emerged when his voluminous "Wilson" material would not fit into the *Epic*. His Wilson book was his best literary effort, largely because his friend, literary executor and journalist Neil MacNeil, pushed him through revision after revision. Hoover managed to avoid what a friendly critic called his tendency to beat the life out of any sentence he wrote. An American president writing a biography of another American president would be a first; the book would have great appeal and promised a broad audience.[7] Hoover knew Wilson and the events going on at Versailles, a pivotal moment in history, in ways not previously revealed. To read *The Ordeal of Woodrow Wilson* is to see how much the two presidents had in common. Hoover's own ordeal clearly mirrors Wilson's. The story of one is the story of the other. The book's publication to acclaim in 1958 freed the workaholic Hoover to return to *An American Epic*.[8]

The work's first three volumes relate in great detail his tremendous relief accomplishments from 1914 to 1923, though the story is often burdened by a reliance on facts and figures. The books read more like dry government reports; only the determined reader can stay the course. But for the vigilant, the magnitude of Hoover's accomplishments becomes clear. Underneath the facts and figures are the millions of lives that Hoover saved. The lessons of Hoover's CRB experience also emerge: how to organize vast relief undertakings; how to garner political, private, and public support; and how to overcome stringent opposition, abilities that became the touchstone for all his future relief efforts. The CRB and the ARA determined his thinking on relief, forming a "how-to manual" in his mind. His successes with these enormous undertakings made his reputation; his vast experience became a deep well on which he would continue to draw.

It is revealing that Volume 4 gives pride of place to his creation on November 18, 1940, of the National Committee on Food for the Small Democracies (NCFSD) and his work under Harry S. Truman in the first years after World War II in feeding the hungry in thirty-eight countries. He titled a later chapter "We Began World Organization to Meet the

Famine."[9] Hoover saw his life as a great drama unfolding on a world stage in which he often played the starring role. The NCFSD likely stood out for Hoover, as it chronicled his two-year battle with Roosevelt and Prime Minister Winston Churchill to win support for his European feeding plan. His work for Truman celebrates his return to center stage, even if in a supporting role. A few months before his death, on August 10, 1964, while celebrating his ninetieth birthday, he posed with his publisher Henry Regnery and his completed *Epic*—a major accomplishment. But in Volume 4, a careful reader may wonder why Hoover's relief efforts for Polish refugees, for aid to Poland and Finland in 1939 and 1940, received a mere eleven pages. The "Great Humanitarian" passed up the opportunity to elucidate the part he played in this critical period when the country debated how to respond to this latest European catastrophe. Could war be avoided? Could the victims of Nazi and Soviet aggression be aided, and, if so, how? It was unlike Hoover to pass over

Hoover and his publisher Henry Regnery celebrate the release of *An American Epic* (photograph by Ivan Dmitri; courtesy of HHPLM).

such an important story, but the reason he did is simple. Time was running out, and to complete the *Epic*, Hoover had to cut corners. Left out was a critical portion of the story of American intervention into World War II. While his successes in aiding the Poles and the Finns in 1939 and 1940 were never on a scale matching the feats of the CRB and the ARA, they deserve more than honorable mention, as he had once again rescued tens of thousands from hunger and starvation.

Less than a week into the Nazi invasion of Poland, which began on September 1, the Poles' need for assistance of every kind was glaringly obvious. In mid-September, Hoover answered Poland's cri de coeur. Plunging into the fray, he promised aid and challenged President Roosevelt's provision of limited emergency assistance, while simultaneously working tirelessly to prevent American entry into the war. For Hoover, feeding the Poles did not necessitate American intervention; it need not be a backdoor to war. Feeding the hungry and avoiding US participation in the European fray were positions Hoover had advocated for some time. But in attempting to feed those in Nazi-occupied Europe, he faced greater obstacles than when undertaking aid to Belgium during World War I or as war food administrator or those faced by his ARA. To this array of obstacles, another factor was added. Hoover had begun discreetly seeking out pockets of potential political support for another run at the presidency, convinced that he had a chance to capture the Republican nomination in 1940. Hoover's aspiration to regain the presidency tainted his struggle to assist the Poles and gave his political opponents and the public an opening to question his motives.

The wily Roosevelt immediately assumed that Hoover's push to aid Poland was not motivated solely by humanitarian concerns. With the 1940 presidential election a little over a year away, both political parties were beginning to look over potential candidates. Any Hoover relief achievements would result in his name being splashed across the pages of American newspapers. The gimlet-eyed Roosevelt possessed an extremely sensitive political antenna. The appearance of a threat, no matter how unlikely, garnered the president's attention. Roosevelt's suspicions proved right; Hoover indeed had his eye on the White House, and, of course, Roosevelt did as well. Would the president break the two-term tradition

Introduction

and stand again for reelection? It was anybody's guess, as Roosevelt, elusive, even duplicitous, was silent on the issue. But in the fall of 1939, neither Democrats nor Republicans possessed an heir apparent. Moreover, Hoover was counting on his current Polish relief effort and his later effort on behalf of Finland to evoke his successful track record from World War I and remind the public of how well he had handled relief during the great Mississippi flood of 1927—an achievement that had helped propel him to the White House.[10] These memories would help to roll the rock from his political tomb and secure for him the Republican nomination. Like Lazarus, he would walk again among the living. Saul Bellow once observed that "to be a celebrity is like picking up a high-voltage cable which you can't release,"[11] which captures Hoover's determination to once more be in the public eye. He passionately wished for a rematch with his great nemesis, FDR, "That Man." Combative by nature, he was spoiling for a fight, sure that, if given this second chance, he could defeat Roosevelt. Hoover was as duplicitous as was Roosevelt and longed to taste the sweetness of redemption, of vindication, of revenge. He confided to trusted aides that feeding the Poles and Finns might well be a backdoor to scoring a victory in "his crusade against collectivism," a way to strike a blow against the detested New Deal.[12] The "Great Humanitarian" was driven by animosity and altruism. His aides attempted to convince him that if he were nominated, his election was unlikely. This was a message the modern-day Don Quixote would not hear. But despite his cocky rhetoric, Hoover did not ardently pursue the Republican nomination; he dabbled, perhaps glimpsing that his political chances were near zero, though he continued to dream, clinging to hope that things would swing his way.

Hoover's desire to render aid to the desperate in Poland and Finland, however, was far more than a stalking horse for the office he sought. He was sincere in his efforts to aid those in need. For him, it was a moral obligation. From fall 1939 until December 1941, he skillfully marshaled considerable resources on behalf of his relief efforts and persistently argued against any US direct intervention into the war. His actions were hampered at every turn by the Roosevelt administration.

Volume 4 of the *Epic* also fails to tell the story of Hoover's representatives sent to negotiate with the British and the Germans. It neglects the teams sent to survey need in what remained of Poland, a truncated, war-devastated mishmash that the Nazis called the Government General. Missing in action are those on the ground who rendered aid to the refugees and Polish soldiers flowing by the tens of thousands into Romania, Hungary, and Lithuania. Theirs is a story filled with danger, hardship, and dogged determination to assist those who suffered the need of nearly everything—people whom Clarence E. Pickett, executive secretary of the American Friends Service Committee, called "Nobody's Nothings."[13] The names of those brave individuals are in essence lost to history: William McDonald, Homer Morris, Maurice Pate, Arthur Gamble, Howard W. Elkinton, Father Justin Figas, Edgar Rhoads, and Frederic Walcott in Poland; Paul Super and James W. Brown in Romania; and Gilbert Redfern and Dorsey and Zora Stephens in Lithuania. Some were from the Young Men's Christian Association, which proliferated in Central Europe after the Great War, while others were veterans of Hoover's CRB and the ARA. Others included Quakers, Mennonites, and the Church of the Brethren, who had been involved in the German Children's Feeding Program in postwar Weimar Germany. Still others possessed hard-won experience in the Spanish Civil War. These men and women were guided by their deep religious beliefs to serve those in need, and most spoke German, Polish, or both.

Against heavy odds, Hoover managed to provide critical aid to fleeing refugees in countries on Poland's fluid border and some to Poland, Finland, Lithuania, and (briefly) occupied Belgium. Relief agencies that organized in big cities and small towns nationwide found creative ways to mobilize Americans who worked tirelessly to raise millions of dollars. Many donated to Hoover relief agencies and to the American Red Cross. Thousands of women throughout the country interrupted their busy lives as wives and mothers to spend thousands of hours rolling bandages, knitting garments, collecting clothing, and holding an endless variety of fund-raising events. The relief story is not one of courage in combat or of the dropping of bombs, rattling of machine guns, or bursting of artillery shells; rather, it is the story of those individuals motivated to do something about the carnage and chaos left behind when the din of battle subsided and the armies had moved on—a persistent humanitarian push underneath the headlines. The relief efforts, in addition to aiding those in need, played a critical role in educating citizens about the deplorable conditions existing in these war-torn countries, developed considerable empathy for the victims, helped to encourage support for Great Britain and France, and pushed the country closer to some form of intervention. As the gathering storm broke, US avoidance became less possible.

The burgeoning Roosevelt-Churchill relationship and the political battle between the Roosevelt administration and its anti-interventionist opponents are well known, but the complex, exciting, and important story of the Hoover-Roosevelt struggle over aid, Hoover's success in rendering it, his halfhearted effort to regain the presidency, his fight against American intervention, and his attempts to harness the war's combatants to international law has remained the last unrevealed piece of the larger story of US entry into World War II. The relief story is shot through with multiple plotlines attached to larger issues like earmarks to an appropriation bill. The arguments put forward by Hoover and Roosevelt in these years are forever linked to the present, as the debate over the ethical legitimacy of new weapons and military strategies continues to rage, as does the debate over the level of American support for small countries facing an aggressor. The wartime distinction between combatants and civilians remains as murky as ever, much like heated debates over sanctions. Responsibility for millions of refugees—the result of intrastate and interstate wars, international wars, collapsed economies, and drastic changes in weather—have driven the politics of the developed countries. If and when the United States should engage militarily remains a hotly debated, divisive topic. The use of food as a weapon of war continues unabated despite persistent efforts to cleave to the moral precepts of the Geneva and Hague Conventions. *Hoover vs. Roosevelt* examines how Americans wrestled with these questions in 1939–1940. Doing so demanded broad and deep research in an array of rarely used secondary and primary sources, both domestic and international, to bring forth voices from the era and reveal the story that an aging president in failing health omitted from his *An American Epic*, a story that surely further enhances his legacy.

I

The End of All Wars

National League for the Limitations of Armament, Armistice Day 1926 (courtesy of National Photo Company Collection, Library of Congress).

HERBERT HOOVER'S CHALLENGE TO PRESIDENT FRANKLIN ROOSEVELT'S policy on emergency aid rested on a bedrock of principles to which he held fast—a moral framework that found expression in the laws of war codified in the Geneva Convention of 1864 and the Hague Conventions of 1899 and 1907. Hoover arrived at his commitment to the Geneva and Hague Conventions as a result of his four-year struggle to feed civilians in Belgium and northern France under a harsh German occupation during

World War I. He was an eyewitness to the devastation wrought by the war of attrition viciously fought in the trenches for over four years. Ten million men were killed in battle and thousands of civilians displaced and rendered dependent. His experience in feeding millions at war's end through the American Relief Administration (ARA) and the German Children's Feeding Program served to reinforce this commitment. Throughout, he was particularly troubled by the suffering of women and children.

The Hague Conventions that so influenced the former president were ratified by twenty-six countries and spelled out the responsibilities of occupying powers, defined war crimes, forbade the bombardment of undefended towns, recognized noncombatant status, barred the use of chemical weapons, established rules for blockade and siege, provided for protection of prisoners of war, and outlawed the use of certain types of weapons. Two years later, in 1909, the British attempted to further expand the rules of naval warfare aimed especially at blockade, contraband, and prize in the Declaration of London. Ten nations signed, but none ever ratified, the agreement.[1]

Hoover adamantly opposed a blockade that denied the import of food to occupied countries or to neutrals. His Commission for Relief in Belgium had worked hard to wring blockade concessions from the British and French. Lord Kitchener and Winston Churchill (whom Hoover would always intensely dislike) led a military faction that regarded feeding the Belgians as a "positive military disaster," since it released the Germans from the obligation.[2] Churchill called the stubborn Hoover a "son of a bitch."[3] But for Hoover, not feeding the hungry was a violation of his Quaker upbringing and of international humanitarian law. When World War I came to an end, his commitment again brought him into conflict with the British and the French. "The Allied tight blockade on food and other supplies to all Europe," said Hoover, "had ample justification during the war."[4] But Hoover demurred, "Despite the promise made in the Armistice Agreement, and despite every American effort, the food blockade on Germany was continued for months after the Armistice ... a most insensate wicked action."[5] Sir Adrian Carton De Wiart described the Germans in 1919 as "starved and pitiful. ... [T]he whole population seemed to consist of old men, miserable women and sick children."[6]

German accounts were filled with the horrors of starvation visited on their country. "Civilians were being forced to eat cats and dogs, the latter known as 'roof rabbits.' Bread was made from a mixture of potato peelings and sawdust."[7] The *Frankfurter Zeitung* maintained that 763,000 civilians had died due to the hunger blockade by January 1919.[8] A policy of starving women and children was wrong and might lead to the collapse of Germany. "It was," Hoover proffered, "a crime in statesmanship against civilization as a whole. It sowed dragon's teeth of war, which two decades later again enveloped most of mankind."[9] To Hoover, hunger was one of the central destructive forces in human history. He eloquently put his thoughts in verse:

> I am the stalking aftermath of all wars.
> Pestilence is my companion.
> Tumult and revolution rise around my feet
> We kill more than all of the guns.
> I breed fears and hates that bring to man more wars,
> From me comes no peace to mankind.
> My legacy is to Children of Famine—
> Stunted bodies and twisted minds.[10]

Four months into the post-armistice blockade, Churchill acknowledged that German women and children were starving. Evidence from the War Office demonstrated that "the German people are suffering."[11] British troops occupying the Ruhr were so moved by the hunger and despair surrounding them that they shared their rations with German women and children. "There were children wandering around the streets half-starved."[12] This situation risked, according to Churchill, "the ... collapse of the entire structure of German social and national life under the pressure of hunger and malnutrition." He continued, "Now is the time for action. Once Germany has accepted the terms to be imposed upon her—and until that moment all of our forces must be held in the strongest condition of readiness—the revictualling of that country and the supplying of it with necessary raw material can be begun and pushed forward with energy."[13] But Hoover did not wait, organizing a German Children's Feeding Program. Millions of German and Austrian children were shepherded through the critical food shortages caused by the blockade and by the lack of resources of the new Weimar government. By 1921, a million children a day were fed. The Hoover program continued to operate until 1923 and was then continued by the American Friends Service Committee until 1928. Thankful German recipients christened the aid *Hooverspeisung* (Hoover Supplies) or *Quakerspeisung*, words that became familiar to nearly all Germans. After Churchill became prime minister in May 1940, he and Hoover would again lock horns over blockade.

Throughout the 1920s, strenuous efforts were made to seek disarmament and to revive and expand the laws of war agreed to at The Hague. Rapid advancement of technology—the airplane, the tank, the submarine, and poison gas—further complicated the issues.[14] Prior to the outbreak of war in the 1930s, arguments swirled over the meaning, the implementation, and the soundness of these earlier agreements. Air attack was greatly feared, spurred by the earlier writing of Italian airpower theorist Giulio Douhet, who predicted the coming of strategic bombing in his widely read 1921 book *The Command of the Air*.[15] Imaginations had

German Children's Feeding Program, 1921 (courtesy of American Friends Service Committee).

been stimulated as well by German airship and Gotha bomber raids on Britain in World War I that had killed and wounded over five thousand, "the beginning of a new epoch in the history of warfare."[16]

The matter was not whether Douhet was right, but rather that a great many people, both in and out of power, believed him. British cabinet member and former and future prime minister Stanley Baldwin, speaking to Parliament in 1932, warned, "I think it is well for the man in the street to realize that there is no power on earth that can protect him from being bombed, whatever people will tell him."[17] His conclusion struck fear in his listeners: "The bomber will always get through. This is what is waiting for them when the next war comes."[18] Armageddon was in the air, so to speak. Ironically for Baldwin, in March 1941 the horrors of bombing touched him personally when a German bomber tragically destroyed London's famous Café de Paris, frequented by the smart set. His youngest daughter suffered severe facial injuries and was among the eighty wounded. Thirty-four others were killed, some blown to smithereens. One of them was the famous Jamaican bandleader Ken "Snakehips" Johnson, who was decapitated.[19]

Repeated violations of the Geneva and Hague Conventions—the Italian and Japanese use of poison gas; the bombing attacks on Spanish cities by the German Condor Legion and Italian Aviazione Legionaria; Italian atrocities in Ethiopia; the Japanese air attack on Shanghai and horrifying rape of Nanjing in the 1930s—fueled ongoing debates on how to respond. The League of Nations' attempts to address these aggressions ended in failure.[20]

The belief was commonly held that any coming wider war threatened a descent into barbarism. Newly elected International Committee of the Red Cross delegate Marcel Junod, in the opening days of the German campaign in Poland in September 1939, wrote,

> And we knew that in the past twenty years the means of destruction had made terrifying progress, and that during the desperate struggle itself they would make still further and still more terrible advances. We knew too that the war which had just begun, and whose end no man could foresee, would not spare the noncombatants; that, on the contrary,

it would cause them terrible sufferings, inspired and exacerbated by the flood tide of passion whipped up by every ideological war: police inquisitions, internment camps, forced service, confiscation, and mass persecutions.[21]

Junod went on to acknowledge that this new war would be a hundred times worse than the horrors that had occurred in Ethiopia and Spain. But sketchy information seeping out of Poland that fall indicated that the atrocities being committed by the Nazis exceeded Junod's worst anticipation. As the war widened, civilians in the cities of Warsaw, Helsinki, Rotterdam, Coventry, and Belgrade were bombed. Occupying powers failed in their responsibility to the populations they controlled, and atrocities against noncombatants were routine. International humanitarian law was trampled underfoot, and yet it remained one of the few options available to those who attempted to limit the violence and protect civilians.

At the outbreak of war, the moral and legal questions over how it was to be fought quickly led to the question of whether a country could strictly adhere to the laws of war and still win. Did survival trump principle if opponents waged a savage war that discounted prior conventions? Was a commitment to "by any means necessary" a principle? Whether or not a government justified its tactics, they were cathected to larger questions of morality and the conduct of war—questions running like rivulets through the British and American public debates over how to respond to the unprecedented violence promised by this new war. Many citizens asked whether there was a US obligation. Were we or our allies "our brothers' keepers"? The moral arguments over obligation and the use of particular weapons, tactics, and strategies, like the debate over aid, were elements of the all-prevailing battle with the anti-interventionists. A popular view held that in World War I, all sides had lost, and surely that would be the outcome of a second worldwide conflict. Occam's razor often provided the solution to these vexing dilemmas, as the Allies did what was necessary to win and then later came to regret it. In the words of that Machiavellian H. L. Mencken, who opposed US entry into the war, "In politics [war] man must learn to rise above principle.... [W]hen the water reaches the upper decks, follow the rats."[22]

The blockade, declared by Britain on its first day at war on September 3, was of grave concern to those in countries soon overrun by the Nazis. The governments of Belgium, Greece, Holland, Luxembourg, Norway, Poland, Yugoslavia, and the Free French, which had fled to the relative safety of London, took exception to the British absolutist approach. After all, it was their duty to attempt to aid their fellow citizens under German occupation in any way possible. This legitimate conflict of interest caused continuous difficulties and posed a tragic dilemma for the governments-in-exile. They understood, but were reluctant to accept wholesale, that winning the war would require their civilian populations to undergo extreme hardship, often resulting in large numbers being starved, killed, or wounded. German occupation took a heavy toll, but any future liberation dependent on an invasion of the Continent would also be costly.

Much of the time overseas governments accepted these harsh realities and generally assented to blockade and strategic bombing. They realized full well that their countrymen's efforts at sabotage, espionage, and reconnaissance would invite German reprisals. Blockading food, however, stirred considerable backlash. In the first few years of the war, these governments fought hard, especially the Belgians, as they were heavily dependent on food imports and quickly encountered serious deficits. The London-based overseas governments would not accept the British argument that the denial of food to their civilian populations was a legitimate war tactic, countering that it instead constituted a violation of the Hague Conventions. Allowing food imports into German-occupied countries, they argued, would not impede the British war effort. How could Allies starve Allies? The US ambassador to Belgium, John Cudahy, heir to a Milwaukee meatpacking fortune, spoke out strongly against the British barring imports into occupied Europe. He was recalled by President Roosevelt in August 1940 for his public statements advocating food imports into Belgium but returned to Brussels as a journalist in June 1941. He discovered for himself the severity of the food shortage caused by German military occupation and by the British blockade when he first visited a ten-year-old boy named Rene Colin, whom he had known when ambassador. He remembered Rene as "a robust juvenile specimen with cheeks the same pigment as that apple from Washington State we call 'delicious,' and sturdy legs with bulging old-fashioned piano supports."[23] Shocked by what he found, Cudahy wrote,

> It was not that the high color in his sunken cheeks had turned to pasty gray and that he had grown so thin that his neck resembled a *pipestem*, nor was it the heavy smudged shadows under his eyes, nor his limbs like those of a tree withered by the blight. No, it was complete metamorphosis of the hearty, happy Belgian boy I had left only ten months before into the dejected tired little old man that stood before me now, spiritless as a wounded bird, all the bloom gone from him as light fades from the ending day.[24]

Relief organizations, which abhorred the conditions described by Cudahy and other onsite observers, sided with the overseas governments in their opposition to blockade as these efforts to provide food and a broad array of other necessities were continuously stymied. Nothing could be sent to blockaded countries without British permission.

The blockade met more resistance even after precision and area bombing greatly increased. Starvation threatened entire populations rather than individuals who had the bad luck to live near selected targets. Later in the war this attitude would change somewhat as the occupied countries feared that the burgeoning concept of total war, which embraced mass bombing of civilian populations, would be applied to them—a tactic used on the Germans and later the Japanese and described by historians Peter Calvocoressi and Guy Wint as "the inevitability of the deplorable."[25] Importantly, while German cities were "firebombed," cities occupied by the Nazis were spared the horrors of sweep conflagration and subjected to the bombing of selective military and industrial targets, though the result inevitably was the unintended killing of civilians—which the air forces deemed "collateral damage." Tragic mishaps did occur. On April 5, 1943, a flight of seventeen US Army Air Force B-17s attacked the Erla Motor Works in the town of Mortsel outside Antwerp. All but two of the bombs missed their target. The rest, twenty-four tons, pummeled the city, killing 936—including 209 children, whose school took a direct hit. In addition, 1,600 sustained minor to serious wounds.[26]

Officials in Belgium and in the overseas government in London protested, as did outspoken anti-Nazi Cardinal Jozef-Ernest van Roey. However, the Nazis approved of the cardinal and other voices across occupied Europe who spoke out against the bombing campaign, claiming it was the fault of the Allies and a violation of international law. As the D-Day landings approached, bombing raids and strafing missions greatly increased, and so did civilian casualties. The raid on Marseille on May 27, 1944, killed 1,752, while the bombing of Caen a week later killed an estimated 1,000. By war's end, 68,778 Frenchmen had been killed by Allied bombers.[27] Numerous books on the subject, especially by German authors, conclude that the bombing was and remains "indefensible."[28] Aaron William Moore, in *Bombing the City: Civilian Accounts of the Air War in Britain and Japan, 1939–1945*, called strategic bombing "an equal opportunity murderer." George Orwell, on May 9, 1944, in his regular column for the *Tribune*, wrote of the bombing campaign, "The immunity of the civilian has been shattered."[29]

British historian Andrew Roberts, however, rightly characterized the bombing campaign waged against German cities as a "cruel reality," adding that "for most in the west at the time it was considered a perfectly legitimate way to bring a satanic enemy to its knees once Total War had been unleashed by Hitler, but for some—especially after the war had been safely won—it was a morally unacceptable war crime."[30] Historians later berated a number of aspects of the war deemed acceptable at the time.

On those occasions, however, when the governments-in-exile did not go along with Allied military plans for their countries, or before most were fully persuaded of the necessity of particular policies, these governments could count on the moral and sometimes political support of members of the political opposition, peace committees, pacifist antiwar groups, certain religious organizations, isolationists, noninterventionists, and outspoken individuals who dissented from the prevailing strategies for winning the war. Lofty humanitarian pronouncements put forth as war aims by both the United States and Great Britain also served to bolster arguments for relaxing the blockade and limiting bombing to military targets. In the United States, Herbert Hoover, while no pacifist, spoke the loudest and most effectively in support of feeding occupied Europe and admitting refugees and against the bombing of civilian populations. The former president opposed "the inevitability of the deplorable." A chorus of voices in opposition to evolving tactics of total war included peace activists Dorothy Detzer of the Women's International League for Peace and Freedom; Dr. Rufus Jones, American Friends Service Committee (AFSC) chairman; AFSC executive secretary Clarence Pickett; Frederick J. Libby of the National Council for Prevention of War; and Norman Thomas, the pacifist head of the American Socialist Party and presidential candidate in 1928, 1932, and 1936.

In Great Britain, Dr. George Bell, the bishop of Chichester, repeatedly questioned the conventional wisdom of blockade and bombing, as did outspoken writer and pacifist Vera Brittain, who had lost her fiancé, her brother, and two close friends in World War I.[31] In 1944, she published a widely circulated pamphlet titled "Massacre by Bombing."[32] In the British Parliament, on August 20, 1940, the lone voice of Dick Stokes, Labour member and socialist from Ipswich, challenged Churchill's affirmation of a stringent blockade, pleading, "Surely you can hold out some hope to our own friends in Europe who, according to the Ministry of Economic Warfare, will suffer the most appalling privation of famine and plague during this coming winter."[33] Stokes often spoke out against mass bombing and was particularly vexed late in the war by the firebomb destruction of Dresden. But Great Britain's transition from strong support and sympathy with a pacifism articulated by the Peace Pledge Union in 1936 to full engagement in total war occurred quite rapidly in 1939 and 1940. C. E. M. Joad, a popular philosopher, earned great acclaim for his impassioned speech in support of pacifism during the "King and Country" debate at the Oxford Union in 1933, when the motion "that this house in no circumstance will fight for King and country" passed by a vote of 275 to 153.[34] By September 1940, Joad had come full circle, publicly announcing, "There can be something worse even than war, and that is the Nazi domination of Europe."[35]

War or not, dissent did not evaporate in either Great Britain or the United States or in the overseas governments. Leading indigenous figures in the Nazi-occupied countries continued to speak out. Cardinal Roey, in a May 1944 radio address from Belgium, pleaded of the Allies, "Stop bombing us," admonishing, "Spare the private possessions of the citizens, as otherwise the civilized world will one day call to account those responsible for the terrible treatment dealt out to an innocent and loyal country."[36] The cardinal's superior, Pope Pius XII, had much earlier spoken out strongly against bombing after the devastating Luftwaffe raid, Operation Retribution, on Belgrade on April 6, 1941. His Holiness also spoke up for refugees and condemned the bombing of civilians. Hoover, Bell, Brittain, Stokes, Detzer, Jones, Pickett, Thomas, and Roey all spoke passionately for a segment of the public that shared their support of the humanitarian laws of war, opposed the blockade, and abhorred the mass bombing campaigns. The horrors of the First World War were ever present in their minds. Now they were daily exposed to the evolving horror of a second.

In the United States, as in Great Britain, clashes were driven by government policy, the desire to provide aid, and the expectations of those in need. From 1939 through 1941, the fiercely divisive two-year brouhaha was a crucial factor in the nation's journey from preparedness to participation.[37] Arthur Schlesinger Jr. noted that the battle was "the most savage political debate of my lifetime. There have been a number of fierce national quarrels—over communism in the late Forties, over McCarthyism in the Fifties, over Vietnam in the Sixties—but none so tore apart families and friendships as this fight."[38] Hoover later reflected in his magnum opus, *Freedom Betrayed*, "One of the saddest products of these years of our national debate on peace or war was the passions aroused among our people. There were sincere persons on both sides, but emotion everywhere clouded reason."[39]

No matter how momentous the decisions surrounding intervention were within the domestic political arena, in a worldwide context they remained largely symbolic and even rhetorical as the "gathering storm" in Europe and the Pacific burst into war. Movement toward intervention progressed unevenly, and many saw aid of any kind as a potential backdoor into the conflict, as a step that would not prevent America's entry but rather propel the country toward war itself. "I believed in mandatory neutrality and in staying out of Europe's wars under all circumstances," voiced Frederick J. Libby, chairman of the National Council for Prevention of War.[40] Democrats also spoke out: "If the world is to become a wilderness of waste, hatred, and bitterness," judged Pennsylvania governor George Earle, "let us all the more earnestly protect and preserve our own oasis of liberty."[41] Military or civilian aid sent to Ethiopia, China, Spain, Poland, Finland, or Vichy France was small, though often of critical importance. Aid rendered to Greece after the Nazi conquest saved the population from starvation, while Hoover aid to refugees and interned Polish soldiers in Romania, Hungary, and Lithuania was critical to them and, importantly, to the reformation of the Polish army in France and then Scotland. Escaped Polish pilots contributed mightily to winning the Battle of Britain. The famous 303 Spitfire Squadron defending the approaches to London shot down German aircraft at a rate three times the average of other Royal Air Force (RAF) units.[42] Hoover aid facilitated the worldwide Polish and Jewish diaspora and provided a waystation for Jews as they fled Poland and undertook the treacherous journey to Palestine.

The long, rancorous debate over aid, however, did work to crystallize and solidify positions and shape policy but did not result in increased assistance from the Roosevelt administration.[43] Frustration among Roosevelt's advisers who wished to aid struggling underdogs caused the president on several occasions to break the law on their behalf. However, belated recognition that aid to those in occupied countries threatened unwanted entanglements and potential political and legal consequences, particularly in the case of Finland, caused the White House to retreat to its policy of emergency aid only. A national timidity won the day as advocates of limited aid, largely liberal internationalists, prevailed. Nonetheless, these advocates' persistent lobbying in the media did much to inform and to educate a nation not too keen on learning about events transpiring overseas, humanitarian responsibility, or threats to American interests. William Allen White's Committee to Defend America by Aiding the Allies, a group of modern Paul Reveres, and those in the America First Movement well understood that Americans preferred war projected on screens in their neighborhood theaters in four-minute Movietone newsreels narrated by Lowell Thomas. Moviegoers could turn to one another and exclaim, "My God, how awful." Ironically, the hit film of August and September 1939 was the now classic *Wizard of Oz*. While the film's allegory was more about populism, viewers might conclude that a world mired in war would necessitate Dorothy's courage.

Throughout the stormy debate, Roosevelt, convinced that Adolf Hitler and Benito Mussolini posed a direct threat to the United States, maneuvered in a toxic political environment to construct a consensus for support for the Allied cause.[44] In September 1939, when the Gallup Poll asked, "Do you think the United States should declare war on Germany and send our Army and Navy to fight abroad," 94 percent said no. A year and half later, in July 1941, 79 percent responded, "Stay out!"[45] The horrific meat-grinder trench warfare of the First World War was vividly alive in the American collective memory. Most Americans forty and older had powerful memories, and tens of thousands of others had direct experience witnessing "donkeys leading lions to slaughter." The horror of World War I was alive in the minds of many Americans. Who could forget the huge number killed, those grotesquely maimed, and those permanently disabled by poison gas? The attitude that the war was not worth its price was prevalent. Dissatisfaction with the Treaty of Versailles, skepticism about the League of Nations, and opposition to schemes of collective security all played a role. Newly minted senator Robert Taft of Ohio, like Hoover, "shrank from intervention in European affairs out of disillusion with the experiences of 1918–1919."[46] The war art of Otto Dix, the poetry of Wilfred Owen, and, in 1929, the publication of Erich Maria Remarque's sensational *All Quiet on the Western Front*, followed by the movie, were a part of American popular culture. Owen, killed in battle a week before the armistice, penned one of the strongest antiwar lines ever written—"The old Lie: Dulce et decorum est / Pro patria mori"—the conclusion to a poem taught and often memorized by students in high schools and colleges across the country.[47] Others were disturbed that the war had been one of choice, and a smaller number saw no clear and present danger. Intervention was simply a second liberal crusade.[48] Conspiracy theories were in vogue. Those opposed to direct participation in the war in support of Great Britain and France were in one of two camps: those who could abide the piles of arms and legs outside the surgeon's tent and those who could not. Those holding dozens of differing explanations for World War I found expression in one simple exhortation: "Never Again!"

In the late 1930s, the metastasizing European crisis pushed Hoover and Roosevelt further apart. Hoover became more critical of Roosevelt's foreign policy pronouncements. Their disagreements came full circle, as

Otto Dix, *Shock Troops Advance under Gas* (courtesy of Artists Rights Society).

Hoover had long fiercely criticized Roosevelt's New Deal policies. In conjunction with the ongoing animosity between Hoover and Roosevelt, the outbreak of a second world war set in motion new disagreements and opened old wounds, engendering a pitched battle over the extent of US participation in the widening conflict and a growing debate over what to do with its victims. The aid debate was often relegated to the back pages of American newspapers due to a shocking series of military catastrophes that were front-page headlines: the German invasion of Poland, the Winter War in Finland, the fall of France, the Battle of Britain, the mammoth Nazi attack on the Soviet Union, and the Japanese attack on Pearl Harbor. The world seemed to hang in the balance. On occasion, Hoover and Roosevelt's disagreements received front-page attention. Regardless of the headlines reporting battlefield news, the debate over aid claimed persistent public interest.

Much of the story revolves around the personalities and the histories of the two contenders—Hoover and Roosevelt—and their radically different approaches to politics, war, neutrality, and blockade.

2

The Contenders
Hoover and Roosevelt

Hoover and Roosevelt (open source).

"I'M NOT JESUS CHRIST, I'M NOT GOING TO RAISE HIM FROM THE DEAD," snapped Franklin Roosevelt to startled Wall Street financier and presidential advisor Bernard Baruch, who had the temerity to suggest that now that Europe was at war, Herbert Hoover's vast experience might be of use.[1] The former president had earned such a fusillade, as Roosevelt and the Democrats had successfully tagged him with responsibility for the Great Depression and considered him politically moribund, an opponent successfully buried but useful as a foil. The charge that he and his Republican colleagues were responsible for the Great Depression maintained great political appeal. The Democrats' campaign theme "Off the rails with Hoover," buttressed by an unrelentingly critical press and endless gallows humor from comedians, proved an endless wellspring of votes. Will Rogers quipped, "When Wall Street took that tailspin, you had to stand in line to get a window to jump out of, and speculators were selling space for bodies in the East River."[2] Eddie Cantor cracked, "Now-a-days, when a man walks into a hotel and requests a room on the nineteenth floor, the clerk asks him, 'For jumping or sleeping.'"[3]

Hoover might have parried Roosevelt's characterization of him, as did Mark Twain to a similar claim: "The report of my death was an exaggeration."[4] Much to the president's chagrin, Hoover proved to be quite alive—a persistent, outspoken critic of all things Roosevelt. From his perspective, the president had it wrong both at home and abroad. Hoover's outcries little affected Roosevelt's policies, and his opinions were not shared by many in the Republican Party; however, he was an articulate spokesman for a new conservativism of his own invention.[5] Roosevelt kept the "Great Humanitarian" off balance and at arm's length, hoping that if he shut his eyes, Hoover would be gone when he opened them. To his disappointment, his efforts could not make the scrappy Hoover go away. Hoover's power was not based on a wide acceptance of his political views; rather, it lay in his ability as a former president to get his message out to a huge number of people. How did these two powerful men arrive at such an impasse?

The bitter rivalry that festered was freighted by a history that grew steadily after Hoover's defeat in the 1932 presidential election. Both men, though loath to admit it, privately respected each other's talents, even as their relationship progressed from friendship early in their public careers to acrimony and then to enmity. The two men could not have been more different. Nevertheless, when they first met while serving in President Woodrow Wilson's cabinet, they shared a number of friends, some of whom hosted Sunday evening suppers for eight to ten guests. The Roosevelts were regulars, whereas the Hoovers attended only occasionally. Oddly, at these gatherings the meal ended with scrambled eggs served from a chafing dish.[6] Later, on two occasions in the early 1920s, the Hoovers dined at the Roosevelts' quarters on R Street.[7] The elegant home of the Hoovers and the spacious apartment of the Roosevelts were places of intellectual excitement that overflowed with guests with an assortment of ideas on how to fix the problems facing the nation and the world. All were caught up in the world's reordering then underway in the palace of Versailles. Realization of Wilson's intoxicating promise that the recent conflict had been "the war to end all wars," to be followed by an enduring peace, seemed imminent. Roosevelt, enamored of Hoover's talents and awed by his achievements with the CRB and the ARA, wrote to Hugh Gibson, then serving as minister to Poland, "He is certainly a wonder, and I wish we could make him President of the United States. There could not be a better one."[8] Regardless of this early friendship and shared hope for the future, as their careers advanced both men bowed to political expediency, distanced themselves from one another, and recalled their Washington acquaintanceship differently.

Differences aside, Hoover and Roosevelt were both profoundly influenced by Wilson. Internationalists, Wilsonian in their worldview, they came of age in the progressive political era that dominated the exciting first years of the new century. Roosevelt's exuberant, big-game-hunting, trust-busting "Uncle Teddy" held the White House and ushered in significant reforms. For Franklin, he served as a role model, the kind of man of action he wished to be. Finley Peter Dunne's Irish barkeep, Mr. Dooley, speared Uncle Teddy, calling him "Tiddy Rosenfelt," and claimed that his book about his Rough Rider days should have been titled *Alone in Cuba*.[9] TR's braggadocio aside, Franklin longed for a San Juan Hill of his own and the accolades for military prowess that would follow. In 1978, Franklin Roosevelt Jr. observed, "My father spent his whole adult life competing with T.R."[10] Elected to the reform-minded New York Assembly in 1910, the future president had his eyes opened to the deplorable working conditions in factories throughout the Empire State, prodded on by his future secretary of labor, Frances Perkins. His social consciousness raised, Roosevelt as governor and president followed in his uncle's footsteps by pushing potential government solutions to the problems of unemployment and poverty.

Hoover, new to public service in the opening days of World War I, was also drawn to Teddy Roosevelt and his commitment to reform. The future president, like TR, was a microburst of energy. Hoover followed the Rough Rider when, in 1912, he abandoned the Republican ticket to run as a Bull Moose progressive, thereby guaranteeing that a progressive of a different stripe, Woodrow Wilson, would win the presidency. The long shadow of the reform era colored the thinking of both future presidents throughout their lives. The Wilsonian idealism that ran through Hoover's veins, undergirded by his Quaker heritage, was captured by Sumner Welles, later Roosevelt's undersecretary of state, when he wrote, "We had been thrilled to the depths of our emotional and intellectual being by the vision that Woodrow Wilson held out to us of a world order founded on justice and on democracy."[11] Later in life, in his best-selling book *The Ordeal of Woodrow Wilson*, Hoover wrote admiringly of the prince of peace: "He was a man of staunch morals. He was more than just an idealist; he was the personification of the heritage of idealism of the American people. He brought spiritual concepts to the peace table. He was a born crusader."[12] Wilson was the future Republican president's mentor. The aging Hoover liked to flatter himself by saying that had the Virginia schoolmaster lived, he would have looked approvingly on many of his decisions.

Hoover knew well the back corners of the unjust and undemocratic world, having globe-trotted to remote mining locations for several dozen years. He witnessed the abysmal conditions in which millions lived, especially in China. Herbert and his wife, Lou Henry, shared a first taste of war in summer 1900 when caught up in the Boxer Rebellion ravaging northern China, a country being torn apart by a riot of international competition. The arrival in Tianjin of the US 9th Infantry Regiment, transported from the Philippines, was the necessary reinforcement that allowed soldiers from a half dozen foreign armies to mount a final assault on the Boxers. A marine officer knew Hoover was familiar with the shell-pocked two-mile stretch of open ground "honeycombed with ponds and water-filled ditches" that had to be crossed to reach the Boxer-defended city walls.[13] The captain asked the twenty-six-year-old geologist to guide his troops across the no-man's-land. Hoover agreed. As the skirmishers neared the wall, the Boxers opened up with a hail of gunfire. As no cover was available other than the shell holes and the fresh grave mounds of Boxers, a terrified Hoover nearly panicked—"I could scarcely make my feet move forward," he recalled.[14] He asked for a rifle, and when it was passed to him, he managed to get control of himself. That night, before the rise of a full moon, the units retreated to a safe position. Later, Hoover commented, "I can recommend that men carry weapons when they go into battle—it is a great comfort."[15] Hu-Hua and Hoo Loo (as they were called by their Chinese servants) were lucky to have survived, but Lou Henry recalled the experience in a letter to a friend, exclaiming that "she had missed the most interesting siege of the age."[16] She bragged that the Boer War sieges of Kimberly, Mafeking, and Ladysmith were "trifling affairs."[17] Some years later, in the stiflingly hot summer of 1916, in the midst of World War I, Hoover, who was feeding millions of Belgians and Frenchmen and had witnessed the destruction wrought by war, had a second view of combat when he observed fighting on the Somme. Standing on an observation platform on the German side of the trenches, he was shocked by the ant-like choreography of modern industrial warfare as thousands of soldiers plodded dutifully onto the field of battle. At war's end, ten million soldiers had been killed, and millions more maimed. His brush with the Boxers and his observation of modern war were lodged deep within him, as were his long years of work with those overtaken by war who found themselves homeless, hungry, and diseased.

Roosevelt, in his youth, had experienced several grand tours of Europe, as was expected of one of his class. These were a chance to connect with important people in the hope of advancing a future career. In the summer of 1918, as assistant secretary of the navy, he toured battlefields along the western front—the Marne, Château-Thierry, Belleau Wood, Verdun—horrific engagements all. There the young secretary witnessed what Lord Byron called the "brain-splattering, windpipe-slitting art."[18] Roosevelt demanded to get as close to the action as possible, yearning for his TR moment. In the village of Mareuil, destroyed by artillery fire, he worked his "way past water-filled shell holes" and the detritus of battle—"rusty bayonets, broken guns, emergency ration tins, hand grenades, discarded overcoats, rain-stained love letters, crawling lines of ants" and in one place a pile of dead Germans "awaiting burial."[19] Eagerly he fired a French 155mm shell into the German positions.[20] His desire for action, affirmation of his manliness, collided with the inescapable horror of the battlefield.

Later, in February 1933, Roosevelt confronted a situation that demanded courage under fire. The president-elect was vacationing in Miami, Florida, shortly before his inauguration, a tension-filled time when the nation seemed at a standstill in the midst of a collapsing economy. In Bayfront Park, surrounded by thousands, he gave a short speech from the backseat of an open car and was talking with Chicago mayor Anton Cermak perched on the running board. Giuseppe Zangara, an Italian immigrant who had suffered an up-and-down existence, concluded that his predicaments were caused by plutocrats running an exploitive capitalist system. Zangara imagined the solution to be the assassination of a president. Hoover was his original target, but Roosevelt was at hand. Pushing his way through the crowd surrounding Roosevelt's car, Zangara stood on a wobbling metal folding chair and yelled out "Too many are starving to death!" as he began firing.[21] Lillian Cross, standing next to Zangara, hit his arm after his first shot, causing the four other bullets fired from his eight-dollar .32-caliber pistol to miss his intended target. Tragically, his first shot lodged in the breast of Mayor Cermak. His four wild shots hit five other people. The Secret Service at once ordered the driver to speed Roosevelt to safety, but the president-elect ordered the car stopped and had the bleeding mayor loaded into his car. Roosevelt remembered, "He was alive, but I didn't think he was going to last. I put my left arm around him and my hand on his pulse, but I couldn't find any pulse."[22] Speeding to the hospital, Roosevelt continued to hold the mayor, talking to him all the way to keep him from going into shock. Hours after the incident, Roosevelt, among friends and advisors, seemed unfazed by the attempt on his life or by his calm heroics in attending to Cermak. Raymond Moley, then a member of the soon to be president's brain trust, observed that there was "not so much as the twitching of a muscle, the mopping of a brow, or even the hint of a false gaiety—to indicate that it wasn't any other evening in any other place. Roosevelt was simply himself—easy, confident, poised, to all appearances unmoved."[23] Nineteen days later, two days after Roosevelt was sworn in, Cermak died. Zangara, convicted of murder, received the death sentence. On March 20, in a North Florida prison, the defiant Italian immigrant was strapped into an electric chair named "Old Sparky." Just before the sheriff threw the switch, Zangara called out, "Pusha da button! Go ahead, pusha da button!"[24]

While both men's exposure to killing was limited, each demonstrated courage under fire, and what they observed and experienced deeply impacted them, permanently shaping their attitudes toward war. Roosevelt, while heavily influenced by Wilson and Uncle Teddy, was not a crusading idealist. Frances Perkins, who worked closely with Roosevelt during her Albany years, wrote, "Wilson's high intellectual quality and complete devotion to his program of the 'New Freedom' evoked lasting admiration in young Franklin Roosevelt."[25] Later, when president, he described himself as pragmatic and as a juggler, a fiddler, a keen observer, and a quick study. All true, but in a Wilsonian mold. Hoover, much more the idealist, was guided by his principles. Given their differences, both men saw the United States as a redeemer nation and had absorbed British foreign secretary George Canning's view that the new world had to be called into existence "to redress the balance of the old."[26] Hoover's and Roosevelt's ears caught the words of John Winthrop's sermon aboard the *Arbella* on April 8, 1630: "Wee shall be as a citty upon a hill, the eies of all people are uppon us."[27] They were missionaries in the service of that city—evangelists for America's errand in the wilderness. Both in their own way pushed the idea of American exceptionalism, self-sufficiency, and self-restraint, embracing the words of Ralph Waldo Emerson: "Our day of dependence, our long apprenticeship to the learning of other lands, draws to a close. The millions that around us are rushing into life, cannot always be fed on the sere remains of foreign harvests."[28] During World War II, their desire to secure the peace on Wilsonian principles, a second chance to correct the failures of Versailles, blinded them to the hard political realities emerging from this new war. Regardless of their efforts, spheres of influence would triumph over collective security, a concept Wilson held was the key to ending war. So impacted were they by World War I, they often appeared to be marching backward into the future.

Hoover, when president, framed the spiraling economic downturn in the fall of 1929 that became the Great Depression internationally and, on leaving office, convinced himself he had put in place a solution to the collapse. Not long after, he abandoned what remained of his Teddy Roosevelt progressivism, moving to the right and embracing a more classic liberalism. Roosevelt, as president, in his search for solutions to the ongoing economic crisis, veered to the left but embraced economic nationalism by backing away from international solutions and taking the United States off the gold standard. The Roosevelt administration, employing a bootstrap solution, attempted to weather the economic hurricane by going it alone. FDR, demonstrating his leftward drift and long-standing commitment to government as the answer to economic and social problems, quipped, "If war does come, we will make it a New Deal war."[29]

As Europe plunged into conflict, both men recognized the twin evils of fascism and communism, but Roosevelt thought fascism the greater threat, while Hoover saw communism as a worldwide calamity. The Soviet Union, he said, "is one of the bloodiest tyrannies and terrors ever erected in history. It destroyed every semblance of human rights and human liberty; it is a militant destroyer of the worship of God. It brutally executes millions of innocent people without the semblance of justice. It has enslaved the rest."[30] Roosevelt was more circumscribed in his public utterances; in April 1939, he sent public messages to Hitler and Mussolini asking that they seek peaceful solutions to international questions, but privately he agreed with Ambassador William Dodd in Berlin, who characterized Hitler as "a throwback to primitive medieval rapaciousness and simply not open to reason."[31] He also agreed with his secretary of agriculture, Henry Wallace, who judged the two dictators as "madmen" who "respect force and force alone."[32] In 1939, both Hoover and Roosevelt opposed American intervention, and both supported revision of the neutrality laws and expenditures for military preparation to ward off growing threats. Both worked assiduously to sell their version of America and its future to the public: Roosevelt, a government-centered New Deal approach, and Hoover, a New Day built on voluntary cooperation—a third way.[33] Hoover codified his ideas in book after book, while Roosevelt relied on his speeches and the radio, although in the first two years of his administration Roosevelt published two best sellers, *Looking Forward* and *On Our Way*. His Sunday evening fireside chats were faithfully embraced by millions of listeners, who were assured that they had "nothing to fear but fear itself."[34] He exuded utter confidence that the nation, "we the people," would pass safely through the dark waters that presently engulfed them. A frustrated Republican belatedly acknowledging the president's radio skills blurted out "all Roosevelt had to say was 'My friends.'"[35]

The president, in office since 1933, held a much stronger hand than the former president, as he controlled the levers of power, but against the odds Hoover challenged his nemesis's foreign policy. Hoover had overcome great odds since childhood and did not shy from challenges that others would not embrace. His challenge to Roosevelt and his political ambition were also hindered by aspects of his character. Hoover, taught modesty in the Quaker tradition, hesitated to put himself forward because self-interest was wrong. To satisfy his ambition, of which he was slightly embarrassed, he maneuvered others to carry his flag. In public he appeared cold and uncomfortable in his own skin. He cared deeply about people, the country, and the future, but he failed to communicate those sympathies publicly. He wore his insecurities on his shirtsleeves. He disliked politics and yet was a successful politician. His either/or rhetoric was a detriment; many just tuned him out. His need to embellish his successes seemed beyond his control. He lent truth to the insight that "bad news always comes with an exaggeration of the difficulties faced." He was a lamentable speaker but gave hundreds of speeches. He struggled unsuccessfully throughout his life to manage his public persona, a difficult balancing act for a private man. Ethan T. Colten, one of the founders of the YMCA, wrote in his memoir, "He is a shy person in public, almost impassive, but privately jovial and free."[36] The tale of the two Hoovers seemed at times like an Agatha Christie mystery. Peggy Noonan, speechwriter for presidents Ronald Reagan and George H. W. Bush, once wrote of Pat Buchanan that she had "never seen such a gap between public persona and private personality."[37] She never met Herbert Hoover.

Privately, Hoover was a different man. He loved to hold court; he was a raconteur and fond of jokes, especially ones involving a minister, a priest, and a rabbi—euphemistically, he called them "Eskimo jokes." On occasion, Hoover, demonstrating his wry sense of humor, landed a well-targeted *bon mot* (his best perhaps in the 1932 campaign, when, in response to Roosevelt's frequently changing and seeming contradictory positions, he described his opponent as "a chameleon on plaid"). The evening cocktail hour included a "martini and a half." On occasion he drank the version invented by his friend, diplomat Hugh Gibson, who dispensed with the olive and replaced it with a pearl onion.[38] When secretary of commerce, he rediscovered his affection for baseball, a game he had played poorly at Stanford and so became the team's manager. During his presidency he attended several World Series games, but on leaving office he was in the ballpark much more often. In all, he attended thirty-two World Series games, more than any other president.[39] While Hoover enjoyed football and other sports, baseball was to him America's greatest game.

Starting in 1920, after his return from the byzantine negotiations conducted at Versailles, Hoover rarely missed the yearly gathering of rich and powerful men at the Bohemian Grove. "For Hoover the ritualistic ceremony and the companionship found underneath the spectacular giant redwoods gave him much satisfaction, a feeling of being accepted and at home both with nature and with other people."[40] In love with the outdoors since a boy, he mastered nearly every kind of fishing and found spiritual renewal in the woods and streams throughout America. Hoover thirsted for the tonic of the wilderness, the excitement felt on entering and the contentment felt when leaving. Ansel Adams said of Yosemite, one of Hoover and Lou Henry's favorite places, that it was "the heart of earth speaking to us."[41] John Steinbeck, who wrote of his and Hoover's California, penned in *Cannery Row*, "Our father who art in nature." After political setbacks—and he suffered many—he retreated to his favorite trout streams in the American West or to Key Largo, Florida, to chase bonefish. Toward the end of his life, he shared a charming meditation on the enchantments of the piscatorial art in a short book titled *Fishing for Fun and to Wash Your Soul*. Sadly, to know the affable Hoover, you had to be there. Unfortunately, the public never was.

Hoover's deep desire to help people abandoned by the world was likely tied to his own abandonment as a child, an orphan boy from Iowa and Oregon. Hoover lost his father at age six and his mother at nine. Consequently, he was taken under the wing of surrogate mothers: Mollie Brown in Iowa and Evangeline "Vannie" Martin and Jenny Grey when he was coming of age in Oregon. After his parents' death, he was shuffled from one household to another, finally ending up under the stern hand of his mother's brother, Dr. Henry Minthorn. Hoover spent most of his life running from his troubled childhood. His rise to the top paralleled the best Horatio Alger tales; it was a story based on suffering that produced

Trophy fish on the Klamath River, Brown's Camp, California, October 1933 (courtesy of Siskiyou County Museum, Yreka, California).

a largely detached individual. Hoover embodied the nineteenth-century myth of the self-made man whose fortunes would be secured by dint of industry, prudence, and perseverance.[42] He was a workaholic and the living embodiment of the American creed, as described by Michel Chevalier in his prescient nineteenth-century book *Society, Manners and Politics in the United States*: "The habits of life are those of an exclusively working people. From the moment he gets up, the American is at his work, and he is engaged till the hour of sleep. Even mealtime is not for him a period of relaxation. It is only a disagreeable interruption of business which he cuts short as much as possible."[43] Witnesses remarked that Hoover could consume a five-course meal in eleven minutes, and lunch and dinner were often working affairs.[44] At his cottage at the Key Largo Anglers Club, he would eat more leisurely, but once the meal was completed, he plunged back into his work. When out on the water, if the fish would not bite, he scribbled away on a legal pad. Hoover's maniacal drive for success was partially about earning money—lots of it—and during his scramble to the top, his business practices were often questionable and sometimes illegal. His ability to assay abandoned and failing mines, raise sufficient venture capital, and make these enterprises profitable mirrored the business techniques of J.P. Morgan. In acquiring his fortune, Hoover encountered many failures, but he possessed, despite his insecurities, a deep belief in himself that allowed him to take incredible risks that produced substantial rewards. "He had always considered himself the most capable man in any room, and with rare exceptions he was right. He had supreme confidence in his ability to draw up a grand scheme, map it out in the smallest detail, and execute it in every dimension."[45] He could be ruthless and unforgiving and at times, like Roosevelt, an SOB, but at the center of it all was a defensive orphan boy in pursuit of legitimacy—a man in need of acceptance and love.

Hoover rarely spoke of his father, and it was nearly thirty years before he visited the scene of his childhood in either Iowa or Oregon. Perhaps he had taken the advice of the great Kansas City Monarch's pitcher, Satchel Paige, who cautioned, "Don't look back. Something may be gaining on you."[46] He commented to Helen d'Oyle Sioussat, director of the CBS TALKS Department, "Look how I have risen. You have dreams. You have to rise to your dreams."[47] His ninety-year journey from a little house on the prairie in West Branch, Iowa, to a five-room suite in one of America's most luxurious hotels, the Waldorf-Astoria, was a long, serpentine road, but "Hoover's extraordinary achievements came with a cost."[48] His saving grace was his generosity and his sincerity—especially his efforts to aid children, which inspired a number of men and women to devote their lives and fortunes to helping him achieve his goals. Hoover family friend Allan Campbell remarked that he had "never known a man with as many devoted friends, the 'do or die' kind who would follow him anywhere no matter how difficult the chore or how little the personal reward."[49]

Hoover approached the world as an engineer; he loved numbers and reveled in data. He was a wholehearted empire builder and thought in terms of the "giantism" that dominated the engineering and architectural projects of the age—the Panama Canal, the Blue Ridge Parkway, the Hoover Dam, the Empire State Building, the Golden Gate Bridge. As an outspoken advocate of modernization in the early twentieth century, Hoover applauded these projects and, of course, was the father of

Warsaw 1946, signed by Hoover to Maurice Pate (courtesy of HHPLM).

two: the Blue Ridge Parkway and the Hoover Dam. Frank Lloyd Wright and Austrian architect Adolf Loos declared the new engineering projects art.[50] Henry van de Velde of Germany's famous Bauhaus proclaimed, "The engineers stand at the entrance to the new style—the architects of the age."[51] What is needed, he proclaimed, is "a logical structure of products, uncompromising logic in the use of materials, proud and frank exhibition of working processes."[52] Van de Velde's conclusion was one Hoover surely embraced: "A great future is prophesized for iron, steel, aluminum, linoleum, celluloid, cement."[53] French architect Anatole de Baudot observed, "A long time ago the influence of the architect declined and the engineer, *l'homme modern par excellence*, is beginning to replace him."[54] The new fields of sociology and social work and the science of home economics also piqued Hoover's interest. He was influenced by Frederick Winslow Taylor, the efficiency advocate of scientific management, the time and motion man who claimed, "In the past man has been first. In the future the System will be first."[55] Hoover, a budding social engineer in his own right, brought his Taylorism into the Warren Harding administration as secretary of commerce, transforming a sleepy department into a powerful force for efficiency, standardization, and innovation. He was driven to quantify, to measure, to organize—everything from a standard size for lumber to a scheme for radio call signs—a determined effort to impose order on the world. But in truth, Hoover was a Taylorite before Taylor, wholeheartedly committed to efficiency, and had internalized the admonition "Waste not, want not." A reporter, observing Hoover at work in the mines in the godforsaken broiling hell of western Australia in the late 1890s, commented that nothing escaped his notice and that he took in "every level, dive, stope, and winze."[56] His approach to economics—classic liberalism—was in line with much of what was written by Frederick Hayek and Ludwig von Mises, but it is unlikely that he read either. Like so many of Hoover's theories and ideas, they came from his own experience. He agreed with John Maynard Keynes's negative assessment of the Treaty of Versailles. But regarding great economist's overall theories, Hoover had gone to Stanford, not to "Keynesbridge." He disdained politics, as he saw solutions to problems in organizational terms. The organization, the system, was the solution. As secretary of commerce and president, Hoover was committed to engineering the good life, the paving on the road to the city on a hill.

Hoover's management style, among those who called him the "Chief," allowed for open discussion in hashing through decisions—sessions that encouraged argument for differing points of view. Sometimes, though, when an explanation or a question annoyed him, Hoover puffed up his round cheeks, dropped his head, and uttered an emphatic "HUMPH."[57] A longtime friend of Lou Henry, in response to a question about Hoover's conversational skills, remarked, "He was not a very affable dinner partner. . . . [H]e didn't have any small talk at all."[58] Hoover had nothing on Silent Calvin Coolidge, whom he often called "that little man," who usually answered question with a "Yep," "Nope," or "Humph." Conversational skills aside, once a consensus was reached, Hoover would not allow further disagreement or opposition to his position in public, and he was willing to crush those who stood in the way of his plans. He could be an authoritarian. He recognized that there were other ways of approaching a problem but was sure that his was the best way forward. "Had Hoover approached things differently, not top down," wrote historian Kendrick A. Clements, "his ideas and plans might have gotten further—caught fire so-to-speak."[59] In return he was loyal, sometimes overly so, to those who served him. He rarely lost his temper, but when he did, he would slam the table with his fist and display his extensive four-letter-word vocabulary learned in the mines of western Australia, where, he claimed, water was more expensive than beer. Hoover, principled, was often stubborn to a fault, and when challenged he had a tendency to double down. In defeat he could be petulant and defensive, and later in life he sometimes appeared the curmudgeon. But William C. Green, who had known Hoover since his time in the CRB and then went on to a long career in the state department, observed that Hoover "mellowed in his older period. His manners improved, his consideration of others improved, his realization of the importance of little things in social intercourse improved as the years went on."[60]

The future president applied his organizational skills to the creation of the Commission for Relief in Belgium. For his success, he was brought into the Wilson administration in August 1917 to head the War Food Administration. Hoover convinced the women of America that food conservation was a selfless cause. Willa Cather wrote in an article for the *American Red Cross Magazine*, "'Who is this Hoover? What is he? That all our wives obey him?' I doubt if the name of mortal man was ever uttered by so many women, so many times a day, as was his. An old German farmer-woman told me, 'I chust Hoovered and Hoovered so long I lose my appetite. I don't eat no more.'"[61] In February 1919, the Congress approved the American Relief Administration (ARA), with Hoover as its head. The ARA expanded exponentially, spanning the Wilson and Harding administrations. From 1919 until 1923, thousands of relief workers dispensed "four million tons of supplies to twenty-three countries," including war-ravaged Soviet Russia.[62] For his outstanding accomplishments, as a man who saved nearly one hundred million human beings, Hoover earned the sobriquets "Great Humanitarian" and "Master of Emergencies."

ARA relief column on the frozen Volga, Tsaritsyn, now Volgograd (courtesy of ARA, Russian Operation Records, Hoover Institution Library and Archives).

Hoover viewed the huge technological leaps of the 1920s as a "New Day" that promised an answer to many of the problems associated with the rise of mass man. His landslide victory in the 1928 presidential election had attracted many from the rising class of professional elites—those whose technical skills justified a rapid social mobility—who looked forward to a comfortable slide into modernity. In the booming consumer and leisure economy that he enthusiastically supported, the new president understood that conservation was imperative: resources consumed by a burgeoning population were fast disappearing. He served as the honorary president of the Izaak Walton Club from 1926 to 1932 and, as president, transferred several million acres of public lands to the forest service, helping to lay the groundwork in conservation for a "consciousness of equilibrium and an ethics of restraint."[63] Hoover would likely be happy in the Silicon Valley that blossomed in the 1990s just a few miles from his former residence on the Stanford campus. But he would surely grouse about its environmental impact, as he would no longer be able to see San Francisco Bay or Mount Tamalpais on the northern horizon through the large plate-glass windows in his studio.

He considered his wife, Lou Henry, an equal partner, and they prided themselves on their progressive, modern marriage as they traversed the world together, always involved in one project after the other. Their partnership culminated in the translation and publication of a famous 1556 Latin treatise on mining, *De re metallica* by Georgius Agricola. After Hoover went into government service, the marriage of their younger years became far more traditional, and they experienced long periods of forced separation due to the demands of Hoover's various undertakings and appointments and his unbridled ambition. Gone were the long sojourns to exotic places, partnerships in literary enterprises, collaborations in collecting, and explorations of their beloved Yosemite National Park. Wife and children were relegated to the sidelines. His two sons were fatherless for years. These extended separations caused Lou Henry a great deal of pain, as did living in Washington, DC. She was not enamored of politics. Her heart was always in California, where she treasured weeklong horseback camping trips with female friends into the Sierra Nevada. She once quipped that she wished Washington, DC, was in California.[64]

Hoover's opponent—the affable, charismatic Roosevelt, a blue blood born to wealth and privilege, often devious and disingenuous—was as hard internally as the steel that braced his legs. He doggedly pursued his policies, carefully crafting his rise to the top. He believed deeply in his own superiority, wrote Lynn Olson, "and had a sense of being endowed with a special purpose . . . determined to do things [his] own way."[65] The way in which the "Squire of Hyde Park" held his cigarette holder and thrust his chin upward affirmed his patrician heritage. Some fellow aristocrats deemed the Democrat Roosevelt a traitor to his class. He was a master politician, possessed of a sunny disposition and a disarming boyish charm used to beguile his opponents and get what he wanted from supporters. This appeal, coupled with his use of humor, produced the illusion in many who left the Oval Office that he agreed with them, to their later disappointment. Philip La Follette, governor of Wisconsin and a member of a famous family of progressives, said that others were led astray when talking to the president as he nodded his head, saying, "Yep, yep," throughout the conversation.[66] Describing the president's attributes, historian Wayne S. Cole wrote,

> Roosevelt was intuitive rather than systematic, artful rather than scientific, and innovative rather than doctrinaire. He was highly flexible and shied away from rigid formulas or systems. He liked to play with ideas, to explore alternative approaches, without irrevocably committing himself to any single policy or approach. He was not troubled by inconsistencies. He had the emotional self-confidence and political realism that allowed him to abandon policies that did not work or methods that proved ineffective. He kept his options open.[67]

While Cole illuminated much of Roosevelt's character, it would be a mistake to assume that the president did not know what he wanted; his flexibility and explorations were tactics in pursuit of specific aims.

Nonagenarian justice Oliver Wendell Holmes, after a birthday visit by the new president and his wife on March 8, 1933, less than a week after the inauguration, turned to his clerk, Donald Hiss, and offered his unsolicited judgment: "A second-class intellect. But a first-class temperament!"[68] Roosevelt, on May 15, 1942, in a conversation with his Hyde Park neighbor, longtime friend, and treasury secretary Samuel I. Rosenman, unabashedly revealed himself: "You know I am a juggler, and I never let my right hand know what my left hand does.... I may have one policy for Europe and one diametrically opposite for North and South America. I may be entirely inconsistent, and furthermore I am perfectly willing to mislead and tell untruths if it will help win the war."[69] This is perhaps as close as the president ever came to explaining himself—as being radical and retrograde simultaneously. Unlike Hoover, Roosevelt distrusted "the organization," the chain of command, and the bureaucracy. The president clearly understood what we today call the "deep state": a bureaucracy with its own agenda that would attempt to maneuver the president to favor its goals. While Hoover banked on organization, Roosevelt banked on people, routinely bypassing those in official positions. To govern, he developed personal relations with individuals in whom he had confidence. His administration, to the frustration of those who served him, was erratic, even chaotic, which enabled persistent internecine warfare among his lieutenants, a Lincolnesque team of "jostling, bickering" rivals he rarely reined in.[70] Many were critical of "this style," and Roosevelt did pay a heavy cost for his approach. Those who served him loyally but found themselves humiliated by him in public could be forgiven for thinking him an SOB. "Those who lasted longest in his inner circle were persons willing to subordinate their own ambitions and egos to the president's."[71] While he wished to maintain vitality and openness to new ideas, his unorthodox style was a way to maintain power and ensure he was in control. "Whether or not his physical infirmities strengthened that desire, his administrative style invariably worked to limit the power and authority of any individual or agency he worked with."[72] The president found a way to impose his will. Future president George W. Bush echoed Roosevelt's approach when he declared, "I'm the decider, and I decide what's best."[73] Those who advised Roosevelt or attempted to influence his decisions learned he was a man who kept his own counsel.

Isaiah Berlin put his finger on Roosevelt's character, observing that he "had not left us his own account of his world as he saw it; and perhaps he lived too much from day to day to be temperamentally attracted to the performance of such a task."[74] Roosevelt rarely wrote anything down and forbade cabinet members to take notes during meetings. Much of the president's day-to-day business was conducted on the telephone, and transcripts were a rarity. But his two best-selling books, written early in his presidency (*Looking Forward* and *On Our Way*), clearly laid out the policies he wished enacted to realize the New Deal. His death in April 1945 precluded any memoirs. Hoover, on the contrary, was prolific, cranking out his memoirs in three volumes, plus several dozen books on a variety of subjects, including several best sellers and the four-volume *An American Epic*, a disputation on his humanitarian accomplishments. But, like Roosevelt, Hoover also conducted much of his business on the telephone. No telephone log was kept, and conversations were rarely recorded or transcribed.

Roosevelt, as a young man, had mastered sailing and engaged in feats of swimming. He was athletic, tall, and handsome. Uncle Teddy may have tested himself in the Badlands of North Dakota, raced up San Juan Hill, foolishly plunged into the Amazon River basin, and shot animals in Africa, but adventuresome Franklin and friends sailed the coast from New York in his sixty-foot schooner, the *Half Moon II*, to the family's summer home on Campobello Island. Roosevelt often undertook long, strenuous swims in the icy waters of the Bay of Fundy. His crippling bout with polio was his greatest test. His handicap radically changed his life, severely limiting him physically and rendering him permanently dependent on others. He magisterially transcended the terrible blow that had struck him. In love with the sea since boyhood, he relished cruising on the presidential yacht and fishing off the stern. Demonstrating his pluck, the first summer in the White House, to the horror of the Secret Service, he sailed with his three sons, a first mate, and a small armada of accompanying ships and boats to Campobello in a yawl named *Amberjack II*. On arrival, the Roosevelts hosted a beach party for the officers of the naval vessels, who were served hot dogs roasted by Eleanor over an open fire.[75]

Competitive, Roosevelt loved to win. An ardent card player, he excelled at poker. Saturday nights in the White House often featured four or five close friends, political insiders, perhaps a carryover from his days at Harvard living on the "Gold Coast." He mixed cocktails, told jokes and stories, did vicious impressions of rivals that produced howls of laughter, teased the other players, and thrived on being the center of attention. Hoover was often the butt of his pantomimes and jokes. The Tates, Democrat contributors, joined the Roosevelts for dinner on the evening of February 12, 1944. It was a small dinner party, and the president was in an ebullient mood. The conversation flowed from topic to topic: oil resources in the future, the Berlin-to-Baghdad railway, and the origin of the shad. During speculation over the shad, Roosevelt asked whether any of his guests knew how "my distinguished predecessor Mr. Hoover" fished. The guests were delighted, as they knew that the president loved to do imitations of friends and enemies alike, mimicking the voices and gestures of his targets. As background to his story, Roosevelt recalled that Hoover had built a camp at Rapidan, Virginia. On weekends, Hoover drove to the camp, Roosevelt maintained, "at 80 miles an hour, pushing all the people off the road as he went." "Now Frank," Eleanor interjected, giving her husband the green light, "that is a mean story." "I know," quipped Roosevelt, who relished telling it. The camp, he told his listeners, who were now all ears, was built in a stream in a valley, and the Bureau of Fisheries stocked the stream. Now grinning mischievously, Roosevelt revealed that a truck from the bureau arrived just ahead of Hoover and released a dozen trout into the stream, "pet trout: all of them with pet names." "There was a bridge across the stream and the trout were dumped under the bridge. Just above and just below the bridge nets were placed so that they could not get out; then an armchair was brought out and President Hoover would come and sit in the armchair while someone handed him a rod and fixed a fly on the hook which he would cast and pull in the trout one by one." The president's story, punctuated with hand motions and pantomime, was "quite malicious and very funny."[76]

Harry Hopkins, Roosevelt's doppelganger-like key advisor who lived in the White House, knew the president's daily routine well: "Dinner at seven. The ceremonial cocktail with the President doing the honors. He makes a first rate 'old fashioned' and a fair martini. . . . After dinner he retreats to his stamps—magazines and evening paper. Missy [Marguerite LeHand, the president's longtime private secretary who lived on the third floor of the White House] and I will play Chinese checkers. George Fox [medical assistant] comes in to give him a rub down and the President is in bed by ten."[77] Holding court was his forte, and he loved being the center of attention. He thrived on the accolades of the crowd, but, except to a very few, he was inaccessible. Eleanor's cousin, Corrine Robinson Alsop, observed that Roosevelt "had a loveless quality, as if he were incapable of emotion"[78] His daughter, Anna Boettiger, said of him, "He doesn't know any man and no man knows him. Even his own family doesn't know anything about him."[79]

During the couple's time in Washington, Eleanor discovered a cache of letters that revealed her husband's affair with her secretary, Lucy Mercer. Together they negotiated a complex arranged marriage, avoiding divorce, managing to maintain respect for one another, and stumbling forward largely leading independent lives. Despite the barrier between them, they were a very successful political team. Eleanor, deeply hurt by her husband's affair, suffered a wound that never healed, but she prevailed by becoming one of the most influential women in the world. Throughout all but the last few years of his life, Roosevelt had suffered a dominating mother who controlled the purse strings. He did not rebel against her tyranny, nor did he come to dislike women. Rather, he flourished in their company.

After his polio diagnosis, he surrounded himself with a harem of women dedicated to his needs. He loved to picnic with them on the grounds at Hyde Park and at his southern White House in Warm Springs, Georgia. Roosevelt never gave up Lucy, the love of his life, and she was with him when he died in Warm Springs, as was Margaret "Daisy" Suckley, with whom Roosevelt was entranced for a number of years.[80]

Like Hoover, Roosevelt was stubborn; unlike Hoover, he was patient in getting his way. Al Smith, mentor, friend, competitor, and vehement critic, said of Roosevelt in 1944, shortly before their deaths, that he "was the kindest man who ever lived but don't get in his way."[81] His attorney general, Francis Biddle, saw the president as "an Old Testament Christian who believed that his friends should be rewarded and retribution visited upon his enemies, for . . . once his will was marshalled behind as vision it became sinful for others to interfere with the fruition."[82] Both Hoover and Roosevelt, while wildly different as administrators, picked men of

FDR and Fala at picnic in Hyde Park, August 1940 (photo by Margaret Suckley; courtesy of Franklin D. Roosevelt Library).

talent for their organizations, and both commanded loyalty from subordinates and from large segments of the population. Both men were also often reviled and scorned; Roosevelt was characterized as "That Man," and Hoover was tagged as the "Pariah from Palo Alto." Hoover, who never fully escaped blame for "causing the Great Depression," partially inhabited a psychological "Hooverville" of guilt that fueled a deep need for public redemption. It was sometime before he realized that he owned it—an albatross around his neck. Lou Henry wrote to their son Allen that her husband was "utterly brain tired," that his presidency had been "a long dull deadly grind." She opined, "It will be a slow process getting back to normal," much like "recovering from an illness."[83] In seeking redemption, he made up an enemies list of those who remained loyal and those who had defected.[84] The famous German poet Heinrich Heine captured Hoover's lust for revenge: "One must, it is true, forgive one's enemies—but not before they have been hanged."[85] He paced back and forth in his den, played solitaire, read stacks of eastern newspapers, railed against Roosevelt and the New Deal, attempted to fish, and drove eight thousand miles throughout the West in his V-16 Cadillac. Those who knew him well marveled that, through perseverance, he outwardly came to terms with the opprobrium heaped on him, but they failed to realize it was an art Hoover had mastered in his difficult childhood—it was something he knew how to do.

Roosevelt also wrestled with the raging economic beast that threatened to destroy capitalism, had destroyed his predecessor's presidency, and hung like an eidolon over his own administration. Both men often failed to find solutions to the daunting problems of war and peace that faced the nation but were major architects in shaping the America being swept into war. The differences in their character and politics and their long history with one another would be central to their decisions as they were caught up in the rush of events in the crisis year 1939. Regardless of their inimical personalities, Hoover and Roosevelt proved worthy opponents.

In the early morning hours of August 24, the roof fell in on the long-simmering European crisis. The chickens, so to speak, had come home to roost. The signing of the Nazi-Soviet nonaggression pact caught most world leaders off guard, leaving them stunned by Hitler's *coup de théâtre*. This seemingly impossible union between two malevolent countries espousing antithetical ideologies assured the destruction of Poland and precipitated the outbreak of World War II.[86] Hoover and Roosevelt scrambled to adjust to this radical geopolitical shift and could not know that a midnight cabal in faraway Moscow would bring the two of them into a protracted, hard-fought conflict over aid to the hungry of Europe and going to war—a battle royale.

3

The Liars' League

The World Turned Upside Down!

Adolf Hitler (open source).

Joseph Stalin (open source).

HEAVY SNOW HAD SLOWED THE WEHRMACHT UNITS THAT MARCHED into Prague on March 15, 1939. Czechs that lined the streets saluted, some cried, most stared, apprehensive for their future. Hitler, not content with the award of the Sudetenland, tore up the Munich Agreement and partitioned what remained of his small democratic neighbor.[1] Hitler later justified his stiletto maneuver, exclaiming, "We could not possibly tolerate the existence in the heart of Germany of however small an abscess in the form of an independent Czechoslovakia. We accordingly lanced that abscess."[2] To the German people, their Führer pontificated,

"Czechoslovakia has ceased to exist."[3] Across Europe apprehension rose dramatically.[4] Debate over Hitler's intentions ended with the absorption of Bohemia and Moravia into the Reich and the creation of the satellite state of Slovakia.[5] Support in Great Britain for appeasement, which had dwindled considerably during and after Munich, shifted rapidly away.[6] Most British citizens recognized that the overrunning of Czechoslovakia was substantially different from Hitler's earlier territorial acquisitions.[7] The Führer had tipped his hand, revealing that his ambitions were larger than his oft-stated goal of gathering all Germans into the Reich. Nothing could change the fact that the Czechs were not German.

Great Britain, France, the Soviet Union, and other European countries haltingly accepted the implications of Hitler's territorial grab: war was in the offing. Thus ensued a sequence of halfhearted, clumsy, and ultimately ineffectual responses as each nation pushed the other to attempt to bell the German cat. British prime minister Neville Chamberlain was despondent, feeling that his life's work, his dream of peace, was imperiled. He would come to regret his hubris in quoting Shakespeare after emerging from the British Airways Lockheed 10 Electra at Heston Airfield that September morning on his return from Munich and his rendezvous with Hitler: "Out of this nettle danger, we pluck this flower, safety."[8] Recognizing Hitler had deceived him at Munich, Chamberlain clung to the belief that the Nazi leader might still be stopped by stratagems short of war.[9] In his view, the Führer's ravenous appetite for territory, his desire for Danzig and Danzig's desire for the Führer, might ignite war at any moment, but he "simply could not and would not accept the view that war was inevitable."[10] The prime minister and his cabinet, with some grousing, doubled down on the failed policy of appeasement. Chamberlain was not alone in his sense of Hitler's betrayal. Conservative member of Parliament Henry "Chips" Channon, Chamberlain enthusiast and peace advocate, wrote in his diary, "No balder, bolder departure from the written bond has ever been committed in history."[11] Across Britain, newspapers and periodicals expressed outrage: the *News Chronicle* termed the invasion "naked and unashamed aggression"; the *Observer* called it "most shameful and ominous page in the modern annals of Europe"; and the *Daily Telegraph* announced that Hitler "had dropped the mask."[12]

In response, the governments of Britain and France hoped to erect a barrier to check Hitler, a move that would bring about a negotiated settlement. This "line in the sand," drawn on March 31, 1939, was the Anglo-French guarantee of Poland's territory just sixteen days after Hitler had dismembered what remained of the Czechoslovak state. The British and the French did not intend to fight for Poland; rather, they counted on gaining time to convince the Poles to give up Danzig and avoid a European war.[13] Herbert Hoover, to the end of his life, believed that the British and French were emboldened to offer the guarantee to Poland by Franklin Roosevelt's implied secret support.[14] Ambassador William C. Bullitt, close to the president and a loose cannon, may have promised American support to the British and the French if they guaranteed Poland's border. Proof of these charges was gleaned from Polish and French documents captured by the Germans—a collection of materials released as *The German White Paper*.[15] Bullitt "vigorously denied these allegations and even had the French Premier Edouard Daladier write Roosevelt denying the allegations."[16] The State Department and the Polish ambassador, Jerzy Potocki, an aristocrat from a powerful landowning family in eastern Poland, also denied the legitimacy of the documents but later told Hoover that the State Department had requested the denial. In a January 16, 1939, dispatch to Warsaw, Potocki laid out a detailed conversation in which Bullitt implied he spoke for the president and would present the pledge of support to the Quai d'Orsay: "[The British and French] have the moral assurance that the United States will leave the policy of isolation and be prepared to intervene actively on the side of Britain and France in case of war. America is ready to place its whole wealth of money and raw materials at their request."[17]

Regardless of ringing denials, Ambassador Bullitt's intemperate remarks did misrepresent Roosevelt's position, misleading the Poles and the French as to America's intentions. Just how seriously they were taken is a matter of conjecture, although the French press and American correspondents in Europe had done much to mislead the French public into thinking they had an American commitment to their defense.[18] Roosevelt clarified his position to a French visitor, exclaiming that his country could count on "everything except troops and loans."[19] Responding to the British and French guarantee of Poland's borders on March 31 and to Hitler's recent acquisition of Memel, Roosevelt that same day held a press conference outside his cottage in Warm Springs, Georgia. Before taking questions, he emphasized that his remarks were off the record. The British and the French had made it clear that German aggression had to stop. "The world is being put on notice as to where the responsibility will lie if there is war."[20] For Roosevelt, events in Europe were an alarm bell that could not be ignored.

For the Poles, the guarantees had the opposite effect of what the British and French intended. The Polish government felt emboldened by a commitment from powerful (if distant) allies. Józef Beck, Poland's foreign minister, a colonel who had been one of the most trusted aides to strongman Józef Piłsudski, believed the guarantees would prevent a German attack, though the British informed him toward the end of May, during joint staff talks, that "no action was envisaged to aid them and that none would be considered, since priority must be given to the defence of the British Isles and communication routes with the empire. Nor would the Royal Air Force bomb German military installations, since that might lead to retaliatory raids on Britain."[21] But if the British guarantee failed to shield Poland, then perhaps an entente cordiale with the Germans was possible. So, in May and again in July, Beck attempted to present diplomatic solutions to the German government. Hitler's foreign minister, Joachim von Ribbentrop, however, refused to meet with the anxious Polish envoy.[22] Throughout the summer the Nazis engaged in a propaganda blitz, loudly beating war drums that should have sent a clear warning to Beck, the British, and the French that Hitler was intent on destroying Poland. On the contrary, in early August the Polish leadership was brimming with confidence, likely a psychological response to their untenable situation—a bravado of the damned. "The foreign policy of Poland," wrote journalist John Gunther, "since [World War I] has been that of a nut in the nutcracker."[23] Ambassador Potocki confided to Undersecretary of State Sumner Welles that if war came, the Polish army would conduct an offensive into Germany, unleashing its mobile cavalry divisions. Beck, too, shared Potocki's unshakeable blindness, claiming the British and French guarantees so threatened Germany that if no war came, Hitler would be overthrown by the following spring.[24] Delusions aside, Potocki and Beck's fatal mistake was believing that their recent British and French allies would come to Poland's defense if attacked. Perhaps the Polish leadership repressed the fear that they might once more be the victim of great power expediency and that their twenty years of independence were coming to an end, that the nut was about to be cracked.

The Anglo-French guarantee and negotiations with the Soviets, as well as the Polish attempts at negotiation, infuriated Hitler and pushed him to adamantly restate his commitment to the invasion of Poland. The Führer flew into one of his infamous "carpet-chewing" rages, shrieking at Admiral Wilhelm Canaris, chief of German intelligence, "I'll cook them a stew that they'll choke on."[25] Hitler had long thought that Britain and France would not fight, but once he realized that they were likely to declare war, he pushed on, aware of the risks and the potential negative consequences.[26] If the Allies attacked the German West Wall, it would quickly become a stand-off. Reverting to his colorful storehouse of front soldier trench talk, Hitler declared it would be a *Kartoffelkreig* (a potato war). He welcomed war, though this was not the one he wanted, nor was Germany prepared for it. But at heart the Nazi leader was a gambler. Having taken repeated risks to become the chancellor of Germany, he again rolled the dice. For Hitler to fulfill his promise to Canaris, he needed a way around Germany's traditional geographical dilemma of a possible two-front war. The Führer had promised his generals this would not happen, and, as a solution, he prudently undertook a rapprochement with the Soviet Union: an audacious, pragmatic move on the part of both Hitler and Joseph Stalin, as each leader's country was anathema to the other. The two had hurled vicious propaganda at one another for years; Stalin called it "buckets of shit." Hitler had further aggravated Stalin by liquidating much of Germany's large Communist Party.[27] Dachau, Hitler's first concentration camp near Munich, which opened in April 1933, quickly filled with ten thousand Communists and other enemies of the regime.[28]

But beginning in May 1939, Hitler flirted with the idea of a nonaggression treaty with the Soviets. Ribbentrop planted the bug in his ear, convinced that the Soviets had been dropping hints of a possible rapprochement for some time.[29] His proof was Stalin's long March 10 speech on foreign policy to the Eighteenth Congress of the Bolshevik Party. His intention "not to allow our country to be drawn into conflicts by warmongers who are accustomed to get others to pull the chestnuts out of the fire for them" signaled that an agreement with Germany, as opposed to one with Britain and France, was possible.[30] Ribbentrop, a former champagne salesman and the Führer's epigone, pushed Hitler to seek an agreement. Slow to respond, often equivocating, Hitler finally came to see the wicked irony of the stratagem. Ribbentrop, receiving a green light, now worked assiduously to bring about his master's diplomatic coup. So began a clever game of diplomacy infused with all the intrigue and conspiratorial features of a John le Carré novel. Its success depended on shrewd assessments and skillful timing.

Stalin, usually addressed as *Vozhd* (leader), deciding that nothing was to be gained through the ongoing negotiations with the British and French mission that had encamped in Moscow in mid-August, now warmed to Hitler's overtures, inviting the Nazis to treat. Hitler, when he received the news from his foreign minister, broke into a wide smile. His brilliant personal photographer, Heinrich Hoffman, recorded the moment:

> "Chaps," he cried, "Stalin has agreed! And we are to fly to Moscow, to conclude a pact with him! And won't that just make the world sit up again!" And in a mood of complete abandonment, such as I have seen on only one other occasion—and that was later when France capitulated—he slapped himself delightedly on the knee. "That," he exclaimed, "will really land them [the Western powers] in the soup!"[31]

Another eyewitness to the occasion, Walther Hewel, a Foreign Ministry adjutant, described the Führer's "complete abandonment" in more detail: "Hitler began to hammer on the wall with his fists, uttering inarticulate cries, and finally shouting exultantly 'I have the world in my pocket.'"[32] To celebrate, champagne was brought in. "We were all tremendously excited and pleased," wrote Hoffman. "Joyously we clinked glasses and drank a toast to this great diplomatic coup. Hitler, obviously delighted at our enthusiasm, became more expansive than ever, though he touched no drink."[33]

The door to an accord now open, the Nazis rushed in, insisting they arrive days earlier than the Kremlin wanted. Stalin relented. Ribbentrop and his team boarded two four-engine Focke-Wulf Condors in Berlin and flew to Königsberg, where they spent much of the night drinking in the Deutsches Haus Hotel's newly opened bar. Ironically, Königsberg was the birthplace of Immanuel Kant, the philosopher who laid out the necessary and sufficient conditions for perpetual peace. The following day, August 23, after a short flight, the team alighted in the paranoid capital of world revolution at 1:00 p.m.[34] The Nazi flags that welcomed the visitors had been found at the last minute in a Moscow film studio making anti-Nazi propaganda films.[35]

Foreign Minister Ribbentrop had long grasped that a Nazi-Soviet pact would be a stunning achievement for Hitler and for himself. The fate of Poland and much of the territory around it was squarely in the two dictators' hands.[36] In prenegotiations, the Germans had made clear that they welcomed spheres of interest and indicated that those areas were open for discussion. At Ribbentrop's insistence, talks began immediately between himself, Stalin, Soviet foreign minister Vyacheslav Molotov, and German ambassador to the Soviet Union Count Friedrich-Werner von der Schulenburg. But on the way to Molotov's office in the "Little Corner" of the Kremlin, Ribbentrop, escorted in one of Stalin's bulletproof black ZiSes, stopped off at the German embassy for champagne and caviar. Arriving at the Kremlin, the German delegation wove its way through the Kremlin labyrinth. Entering the appointed meeting room, they were surprised to find Stalin "in Party tunic and baggy pants tucked into his boots."[37] Ribbentrop's fears that nothing of substance would be decided melted away; the Soviets were eager to come to an agreement. Part of Stalin's enthusiasm was due to word from the Far East that General Georgy Zhukov, in a battle at Khalkin-Gol/Nomonhan begun on August 20, using a combined arms assault, had inflected on the Japanese casualties as high as sixty-one thousand and was heading for victory.

The details of the nonaggression pact, to last ten years, were quickly decided. Stalin, lusting for the return of territory lost in the collapse of the czarist empire, suggested a separate secret protocol that carved up Central Europe between the two ambitious despots. Ribbentrop, in the role of generous plenipotentiary, offered the *Vozhd* eastern Poland, Bessarabia, Finland, Estonia, and "Latvia, up to the river Dvina [Daugava]."[38] Not satisfied with three-fourths of Latvia, holding to the adage that more is better, Stalin demanded the whole country, with the border on the Niemen rather than the Dvina. Stalin may have recalled that the Niemen was the starting point for Napoleon's invasion of Russia in 1812, and the river would make a good defensive line in case Hitler double-crossed him. Equivocating, Ribbentrop replied that he would have to consult with Hitler and returned to the German embassy in an ebullient mood, "telling everyone the Pact was in the bag."[39]

Nervously waiting for some word from Moscow, Hitler walked back and forth across the terrace of his Obersalzberg *Berghof*. When the call came, Hitler listened as his minister explained Stalin's demands. The Führer hung up, consulted a map, and returned Ribbentrop's call a short time later: "Yes, agreed."[40] The protocols were finalized around midnight and sent to the secretaries to type the official copies for signature. Rounds of drinks and toasts, vodka and champagne, followed one after the other; then Stalin raised his glass, quieting the room. "I know how much the German nation loves its Führer. I should therefore like to drink to his health."[41] When speaking about Hitler, Stalin used the Russian slang word *molodetz*, meaning "a fine fellow."[42] For several hours the reverie continued, marked by self-congratulations and more drinks on both sides. For the German delegation, the price of the agreement came due, as it was impossible to refuse toast after toast that demanded a shot of vodka. Ribbentrop, feeling the effects, pleaded dyspepsia, but Stalin would have none of it. "Drink!" he bellowed. "Drink now! It is for your country!"[43] "One of the young Germans, a six-foot SS officer named Richard Schulze, noticed Stalin was drinking his vodka from a special flask and managed to fill the glass from it, only to discover it contained water. Stalin smiled faintly as Schulze drank it, not the last guest to sample his little secret."[44] The cunning Koba (Stalin's favorite nickname from his revolutionary days) was the master of political theater. Around 2:00 a.m. the protocols were ready for signing, while photographers prepared to capture the moment. Hitler had ordered Heinrich Hoffman, a hard drinker tagged with the moniker *Reichssaüffe* (state drunk) by those who envied his close friendship with the Führer, to photograph Stalin's ears while recording the protocol's historic signing. Ear shape in Nazi racial theory would determine whether the Communist leader was a Jew. Hitler suspected that Stalin, as a Communist, was a Jew, but he needed proof: loose ears meant Aryan, while attached, prominent lobes were Jewish.[45] Hoffman's flash bulbs popped as Molotov and Ribbentrop took turns signing the protocol, while Stalin stood back looking on.[46] For the group photo, the Russian photographer placed a large outdated camera on a tripod and fused black powder on a tin plate for the flash that produced a loud bang and cloud of smoke.[47]

Included in the agreement was a clause that read, "This protocol shall be treated by both parties as strictly secret."[48] Verbally, both pledged to deny that any secret deal had been reached. Nazi Germany and the Soviet Union had just set an international record in negotiating and concluding a world-altering protocol in a mere thirteen hours. With the strokes of their pens, Hitler and Stalin had struck the match that would set Europe ablaze. The liars' convention disbanded with great satisfaction to all its participants. Stalin, seeing Ribbentrop to the door, imparted, "I can guarantee on my word of honor the Soviet Union will not betray its partner."[49] Ribbentrop, on returning to Berlin, was greeted by Hitler, who flew from his Bavarian redoubt to hail his foreign minister as "a second Bismarck."[50] Hitler, viewing Hoffman's stack of photos, was relieved to see that Stalin's ears were loose—he had not concluded an agreement with a Jew.

In Washington, the response to the pact varied from shock to complacency. Roosevelt, after the killings during the Night of the Long Knives on June 30, 1934, suspected that the Soviets and the Germans might find common ground, and on August 4, 1939, in a move to maintain the peace, conveyed to the Soviets that any agreement they made with Hitler would "simply delay a German attack . . . until after a French defeat."[51] Secretary of State Cordell Hull, lowballing the pact, wrote in his diary, "Berlin's announcement . . . that the German-Russian accord had been reached did not surprise us. Nevertheless, it was alarming."[52] Hull had long thought war was coming but did not reveal the truth behind his lack of surprise. Charles Bohlen, the senior Russian-language

After midnight in the Kremlin, Molotov signs the Hitler-Stalin pact as Ribbentrop and a smiling Stalin look on (courtesy of United States Holocaust Memorial Museum).

officer at the US embassy in Moscow, regularly reported to Foggy Bottom on the progress of the Soviet-German rapprochement. His source: the second secretary of the German embassy, Johnny Herwarth. Beginning in mid-May, Herwarth provided Bohlen with the details of the burgeoning pact. On August 16, he confided that an agreement was imminent and that Ribbentrop would possibly fly to Moscow to conduct negotiations. As Herwarth could not be certain, Bohlen tempered his telegram to Washington, reporting only the details of which he was confident. Washington received the news with a good deal of skepticism, but Hull prudently warned the British and French that the Russians and Germans were poised to reach an agreement. From August 16 to the signing of the Nazi-Soviet pact, all went black, as Herwarth's intelligence was absent. He was on a courier mission to Berlin but arrived back in Moscow while Ribbentrop and Stalin were dividing Eastern Europe. The following morning, he called Bohlen and asked him to come to the German chancellery. On his arrival, "while Ribbentrop was upstairs sleeping off a long night of successful negotiations and festivities at the Kremlin," Bohlen wrote, "my friend gave me the details of the ten year pact."[53] Herwarth passed on an overview of the secret protocols, telling Bohlen that Hitler and Stalin had agreed to spheres of influence but not that they had agreed to the transfer of territory.

There were other points of view on the significance of the pact. Adolf Berle, assistant secretary of state and member of the president's brain trust, caustically penned in his diary, "The last couple of days have produced exactly the sensation you might have waiting for a jury to bring in a verdict on the life or death of about 10,000,000 people."[54]

Hoover spoke up in an article in *American Magazine* in midsummer, warning that America must not take "a seat at the table where power politics is being played." He characterized Roosevelt's policy of "something more than war and less than words" as a sure means of dragging the country into war.[55] For him, the Nazi-Soviet pact, while surprising, was simply a last step toward what he thought had been coming for some time. Later, reflecting on the dog days of summer in *Freedom Betrayed*, Hoover penned a summation of the two dictators:

The audience was all the nations in the world—two billion terrified human beings. The leading parts were acted by Hitler, a consummate egoist, the incarnation of the hates of a defeated nation, cunning, intent on conquest, without conscience or compassion; and Stalin, intent on spreading Communism over the world, a ruffian, cold, calculating, an Ivan the Terrible and Genghis Khan reborn. Boiling with hatred of each other, and despising the free nations, they were united only in a determination to destroy free men—and then each other.[56]

Later he wrote, "When the two greatest dictators on earth joined in an alliance on August 23, 1939, not only did they launch the Second World War, but another world-wide famine became inevitable."[57] Perversely, Hitler and Stalin had provided Hoover with an opportunity for his resurrection, a return to the corridors of power.

On the other side of the Atlantic, perhaps too close to events, the news of the protocol's signing stunned the unsuspecting Allies, whose intelligence agencies had deemed an agreement all but impossible. Chamberlain affirmed Britain's commitment to Poland in the House of Commons but wrote to his sister that "he felt like a coachman negotiating a carriage down a difficult path on the edge of a very steep cliff." Revealing his refusal to see that the pact meant war, he continued, "There were times when one's heart appeared to skip a beat until ultimately the crisis passed and one was still on the road."[58] Winston Churchill recalled that "the sinister news broke upon the world like an explosion."[59] Harold Macmillan, a member of the "Eden Group" of antiappeasers in Parliament, then yachting along the coast of France, put into Poole Harbour to learn "for the first time the news which had so shaken the world. For the Russo-German treaty meant either another easy victory for Hitler or was under the worst possible conditions, with Russia neutral, Czechoslovakia already overwhelmed, and France and Britain powerless to bring any effective aid to Poland, whose independence they had guaranteed."[60] As Macmillan so clearly recognized, the last impediment was removed from the path of a German invasion. Chips Channon caustically responded to the news in his diary: "Then I realized that the Russians have double-crossed us, as I always believed they would. They have been coquetting secretly with Germany, even as our negotiations proceeded. They are the foulest people on earth."[61] Channon continued, "The Russians have decided the Germans are the best bet," and "Ribbentrop is flying to Moscow to conclude their death alliance."[62] Stunned by the turn of events, he concluded in his August 22 entry, "But I cannot bear to think that our world is crumbling to ruins. I refuse to admit it."[63] Had the Western powers not moved through the 1930s in a somnambulistic fog of peace, their leaders might have remembered that the two pariah nations had cooperated after signing the Rapallo Treaty in the early Weimar years.[64] The Nazi-Soviet pact, long on the table of possibility, when realized, was a crippling blow to Allied strategy politically, militarily, and economically. Before a first shot was fired, the Germans had punched a hole in any blockade. British-French high hopes that blockade would strangle Germany dimmed. "Coming as a veritable thunderbolt," wrote French minister of finance Paul Reynaud, "the agreement stupefied public opinion equally in Britain and France. In the opinion of [Gustave] Gamelin, French Army Commander-in-Chief, for example, the *volte-face* of Russia, by leaving us practically alone to face Germany, made us powerless."[65] France was hardly militarily powerless, but General Gamelin's remark did reveal an attitude that would contribute to France's coming defeat.

Poland, not France or Britain, would suffer the immediate consequences of the midnight meeting in Moscow. When the details of the agreement reached Warsaw, it is easy to understand why the Poles thought history had repeated itself. In Warsaw, Józef Lipski, the Polish ambassador to Berlin, a lawyer who had been in the Polish Ministry of Foreign Affairs since 1925, away from his post for consultations with Foreign Minister Beck, awoke in his hotel to news of the pact. "This was a terrible moment for me. The two adversaries shook hands against us."[66] Polish professor Alexander Polonius, visiting family on leave from his teaching post in Great Britain, penned in his diary on August 23, "This evening it was definitely confirmed on the wireless that a German-Soviet pact had been signed in Moscow, and that the two countries had found a common language." Ignorant of the secret protocols, Polonius speculated, "What could this language be, if not the partition of our country?"[67] Poland was to be divided up, as in 1793 and 1795.[68] "The news was the signal for everybody to cut their holiday short and go."⁶⁹ His mother, who had been reading *Gone with the Wind*, confided that she felt "war cannot be avoided and that she had a dream that our family will be scattered."⁷⁰

Ivan Maisky, the Soviet ambassador to Great Britain, in the dark as to the secret protocol agreed to in Moscow, witnessed air raid precautions underway in London. "Tension is growing, along with the expectations of something frightful, menacing and unavoidable. Is this serious? Or are these just psychological preparations for a new Munich? There's no doubt," Maisky observed, "that Chamberlain would like a second Munich very much. We'll see."⁷¹ Later in Moscow, Anastas Mikoyan, at a reception celebrating the Russian Revolution, confided to Johnny Herwarth's wife, Pussi, "The combination of Soviet natural resources and German know-how opened prospects that simply took his breath away." Warmed to his subject, he continued, "The treaty marked one of the most important moments in all history, and the alliance that it brought into being was unbeatable."⁷² For Communist Party members worldwide, the pact was an incredible betrayal. Numbers of fellow travelers, disillusioned, fell away from the Bolshevik experiment. Stunned, Ruth von Mayenburg, a Sudetenland member of the Comintern residing in the Lux Hotel in Moscow, along with six hundred other foreign Communists in exile, recalled, "It seemed to us as though the clock on the Kremlin tower stopped."⁷³ Later she explained, "We were so shocked that we couldn't talk for a few hours. It was actually shameful, and we weren't able to overcome this feeling of shame for a long time. One had to mobilize one's Marxist concepts of imperialism, of international struggles, of *everything*, in order to deceive oneself about this matter of conscience."⁷⁴

Hitler ventured that party members would see the pact as expedient, but "the next morning in the garden of the Brown House, the Nazi party headquarters in Munich where many SA troopers congregated, many hundreds of party badges were lying on the ground where they had been pitched by enraged and disillusioned members."⁷⁵ Higher up in the Nazi pecking order, news of the pact came as a shock to Propaganda Minister Joseph Goebbels, as he "had been told nothing about any deal with the Soviet Union." Despite "having been convinced for so long that the destruction of Bolshevism was the great mission of National Socialism,"

Goebbels, a master of expediency, "quickly convinced himself that this 'brilliant coup' was one more example of the Führer's genius, and issued instructions to the German press that it was to concentrate on this 'sensational turning point' in European politics."[76]

Whether shocked, complacent, or unsurprised, nearly all observers agreed that the Hitler-Stalin pact moved Europe irrevocably toward war. In the United States, in response to this looming catastrophe, the American Red Cross and private relief agencies that traditionally provided medical supplies, food, and financial assistance for war's victims considered the magnitude of what another widespread conflict might necessitate.[77] The Roosevelt administration anticipated no direct participation in a European conflagration. Relief matters were officially the responsibility of the Red Cross, a semiautonomous organization with a military cast that operated under a congressional charter and whose director was appointed by the president of the United States. Red Cross personnel wore US Army uniforms, albeit bearing different buttons and insignia, and were encouraged to abide by military regulations. In wartime the Red Cross's traditional mission was to aid the sick and wounded in military hospitals, to help prisoners of war, and to provide a bridge for soldiers between civilian life and military duty.[78] In the twentieth century, the Red Cross's mission had expanded exponentially, especially during World War I, to include aid for civilians victimized by war. In past wars, private agencies had proliferated in response to immediate and specific needs. Organizations such as the International Committee of the Red Cross, the League of Red Cross Societies, the American Friends Service Committee, the American Jewish Joint Distribution Committee, the Mennonite Central Committee, Bundles for Britain, the British War Relief Society, the Unitarian Service Committee, Catholic Relief, the International YMCA, and the China Relief Fund were already actively at work. Assistance was rendered to refugees pouring into France from Francisco Franco's Spain, Adolf Hitler's Germany, and Benito Mussolini's Italy, as well as to those forced to flee or left destitute by Japanese aggression and to British citizens who suffered the dislocations of evacuations.[79]

Norman H. Davis, chairman of the American Red Cross, a longtime diplomat, financier, and top advisor to FDR, circulated a memorandum to his central committee on August 28, 1939, outlining the Red Cross's response to a European war. Davis believed war was imminent and that the United States might eventually participate, but he claimed that "the overwhelming sentiment of the American people" was for noninvolvement and neutrality.[80] The Red Cross, Davis said, in planning to aid Europe, ought to stay well within the limits set by public opinion and by the Roosevelt administration. This meant that the Red Cross position must be one of extreme caution, ambiguously tiptoeing forward, as the organization feared accusations of spearheading any American meddling in European affairs that would drag the country into war. World War I relief also served as a warning, as some argued that Hoover's feeding programs through the Commission for Relief in Belgium had helped persuade Americans to enter that conflict.

After lengthy deliberation, the Red Cross's central committee decided that a prudent first step was to increase the organization's size through an enrollment campaign. Once this aim was accomplished, Davis argued, the Red Cross could better assist in the repatriation of American citizens abroad and assist soldiers in what would likely be a greatly enlarged American army. The question of mass relief for civilians in worn-torn countries was discussed, as was medical aid for wounded soldiers in foreign armies. Though the committee reached no final decision, there was general agreement that Red Cross aid should be of short duration and limited to medical supplies—a continuation of its traditional role. If asked by individual governments or by foreign Red Cross organizations, the American Red Cross agreed it would do what it could to alleviate suffering. As a cautionary measure, a three-man investigative team was sent to Europe to make contacts and be available to survey possible needs. Given the parameters under which it agreed to operate, the Red Cross was as prepared as it could be. Any further policy decisions awaited the commencement of war, which arrived before Norman Davis's letter explaining recent changes in Red Cross policy reached chapter chairmen throughout America.[81]

4

War

Citizens of the nation's capital learn of war (Harris and Ewing; courtesy of Library of Congress).

September was "always the happiest month in Poland," claimed Dominik Wegierski, an academic living in Kraków. "Vacationers were returning from the beaches and the mountains, students were returning to schools and crops were ripening in the fields."[1] It looked to be a bountiful harvest. Varsovians escaped the mounting tensions by flooding the city's restaurants, movie theaters, and night clubs. Music floated onto the shores of the Vistula from the decks of cruise boats that plied the river. Famous recording star Hanka Ordonówna entertained at the Tip Top Club, and couples danced the latest rage: the Lambeth Walk. For a night at the movies, viewers could catch Loretta Young starring in two different films: her latest hit, *Wife, Mother and Friend*, or an older musical, *Caravan*. For those with a more European taste, French actress Viviane Romance starred in *Imprisoned Woman*.[2] Distractions aside, the merrymakers could not help but see the hundreds of soldiers thronging the streets and packing the city trams, bus stations, and rail depots. "All night the troops passed through—artillery, cavalry, infantry—until the streets rang with the monotonous sound of marching feet."[3] The Polish army was mobilizing. Perhaps a few more days, perhaps a few weeks—the hour was at hand. They were coming.

At 3:30 a.m. on September 1, 1939, "the happiest month in Poland" but a few hours old, Paul Super, secretary of the Polish YMCA, finished his broadcast to America on the NBC network. He had pleaded for American support for Poland in its struggle with Germany. As he walked out "onto the silent and deserted street no artificial light of any kind was visible; complete blackout."[4] With no taxi or *doroszki* in site, Super decided to walk the mile to his home on Mokotowski Street, as "it was so lovely a summer night, almost as bright as day under the full moon. The balconies and windows of the long rows of apartment houses of the average six stories were in many places green with vines and flowering plants; the streets were so strangely quiet, so gloriously moonlit, so beautiful."[5] Super arrived home about 4:00 a.m. and headed for bed, unaware that he had witnessed Poland's last hours of peace. He could not have possibly dreamed that in a few short weeks he would be in Bucharest working for Hoover's newly created Commission for Polish Relief, scrambling to provide aid to the thousands of soldiers and civilians streaming into Romania. Hitler too—the attack order given, accompanied by an exhortation to his commanders to "close their hearts to pity" and employ "the greatest brutality and without mercy"—slept soundly in his bed in the old chancellery in Berlin.[6] The coming dawn would shatter Poland's happiness for over a generation, as fall's fair weather had for centuries also proved an opportune time for campaigning.

In Danzig Harbor, the fog had not lifted when the outdated visiting German battleship *Schleswig-Holstein* opened fire with its 11-inch guns at 4:45 a.m. on a small unit of Polish soldiers stationed on the Westerplatte Peninsula. Forty-five minutes later, the telephone rang in the American embassy in Berlin. William Russell, along with the chargé d'affaires, Alexander Kirk, had kept watch throughout the night in case something happened. Russell answered, and Kirk signaled for him to pass the phone over. He listened without saying a word as he jotted a note on a piece of white paper. Hanging up, he pushed the paper across his desk. "Russell, will you wake the code clerk. That was the British Embassy. The first German bombers left for Poland ten minutes ago."[7] Hermann Göring's feared Luftwaffe had taken off in semidarkness. "A beautiful sight must have greeted the invaders when they saw the mountains at dawn and flew over the forest of Żywiec," reaching their bombing targets at the moment many were crawling out of bed, brushing their teeth, or sitting down to breakfast.[8] Within the hour, huge German armies, sixty divisions, crossed the Polish frontier from three different directions; the Luftwaffe pounded Polish cities—perfect *Jadgwetter*.[9]

"The guns began to bark."[10] It was on! Hitler had his war, a triumph of the will, and Poland was to be the victim of the Führer's unbridled ambition.

Clare Hollingworth, cub reporter for the *London Daily Telegraph*, had the luck of the Irish, for she struck Kilkerry gold being close to the German border.

> As the first light of dawn pierced the sky over Katowice ... I was awakened by explosions. Distant gunfire created a noise like banging doors. Aircraft roared over the city.
>
> More heavy explosions.... There was a lightening burst in the park, then another ... then another....
>
> I woke up [British consul John Anthony] Thwaites and dashed off to telephone Robin Hanky, second secretary at the British Embassy in Warsaw. "Robin," I shouted, "The war has begun!"
>
> "Are you sure, old girl?" he asked.
>
> "Listen!" I held the telephone out of my bedroom window. The growing roar of the tanks encircling Katowice was clearly audible. "Can't you hear it?" I cried.[11]

Clare Hollingworth, August 1939, Katowice, in front of Consul Thwaites's car, which she used to scout German troops massed on the Polish border; to her right are her assistant and the consul's driver (courtesy of Patrick Garrett).

He could. Hollingworth had a scoop that would make her famous as the first journalist to report the beginning of a second world war.

Poland's twenty-eighth prime minister, Felicjan Składkowski, a doctor and general who had studied medicine at Jagiellonian University, had decided to sleep in the Interior Ministry as a precautionary measure. His prudence was rewarded when the phone rang in his half-lit office. It was the provisional governor of Kraków reporting that the main railroad station was being bombed. Składkowski hung up the phone, intending to alert President Ignacy Mościcki, but before he could dial the secure phone line, it rang again. Poznań this time. Then Lublin, then Toruń, then Kutno, all under attack. A few minutes later he was on the phone with the president and then with the Polish commander in chief, Marshal Edward Śmigły-Rydz, a World War I and Polish-Soviet War cavalry hero, painter, and poet, christened Śmigły (Speedy) for his military prowess.[12] On receiving the news, Rydz and his staff officers hurried to the stuffy basement command center to realize Poland was under massive attack. As the shock dissipated, he issued Communique Number 1, which ended with a rousing call to arms: "Soldiers! Germany—our everlasting foe—has violated our borders. The time has come to fulfill our duties. Soldiers! Fight for the existence and future of Poland. For each step taken into Poland, the enemy must pay dearly with his blood. . . . The ultimate victory will depend on us and our allies."

Air raid sirens whaled across the capital. It was 6:15 a.m. Concert pianist Magdalena Lipkowska was still awake, having been home for only a short while after a night of enjoyable dancing. She remembered that she had been designated as a fire watcher for her apartment building and was to be on lookout on the roof when the sirens went off. She raced to the roof in her evening gown.

> It was an exciting spectacle—bombers flying in formation and dog fights between the Luftwaffe and our few planes that had escaped destruction on the ground. Some planes went down, leaving trails of smoke behind; I was certain they were the enemy's and I was pleased. I could see smoke from whatever was set on fire and wondered what had been hit. This spectacle lasted for about an hour and then everything was as quiet as if nothing had happened. I returned to my apartment and turned on the radio.[13]

Announcer Zbigniew Świętochowski confirmed for his audience that Poland was at war. Throughout the day, Świętochowski interrupted patriotic music, Chopin, and coded messages to announce, "*Uwaga, uwaga* [attention], this is an alarm warning for the city of Warsaw. . . . Be on the alert!"[14] Later that afternoon, during a second German bombing raid, American ambassador Anthony Joseph Drexel Biddle Jr. reported, "From the courtyard of our Chancery we watched maneuvers between Polish pursuit planes and German bombers."[15] German press and radio reports claiming that the Polish air force had been destroyed on the ground were false.

Those who lived in Wieluń, 125 miles to the southwest of Warsaw near the German border, were not as lucky as their Varsovian cousins when the air raid sirens commenced on the first day of war. Wieluń, a small town of sixteen thousand, had no strategic value but was one of the first Polish cities to be attached by the Luftwaffe. The first bombs fell minutes after the sirens blared at 4:35 a.m. and just a few minutes before the first shells fired from the battleship *Schleswig-Holstein* in Danzig Harbor smashed into the Polish garrison on Westerplatte. But why Wieluń?

Ambassador Biddle and embassy staff observe planes over Warsaw (photo by Julien Bryan; courtesy of United States Holocaust Memorial Museum).

Perhaps Wolfram von Richthofen of Condor Legion fame selected the city as an experiment to test the effectiveness of carpet bombing or simply to terrorize the Poles and spread panic. Jan Tyszler recalled that when the bombing began, "we fled to the yard next door where my father had a garage. He was a mechanic. We sat trembling in the car inspection pits. By afternoon, our house was the only one left standing. All the other buildings were in ruin."[16] From the first wave of Luftwaffe bombers in the gray dawn until 2:00 p.m., 70 percent of the city was destroyed and twelve hundred of its citizens killed. Nearly all those lucky enough to have survived joined the tens of thousands from other Polish cities fleeing to the east. In less than a day, the German army entered the ruins to find only a few hundred remaining. Carpet-bombing experiment or instrument of terror, the raid was effective. Richthofen began the Polish campaign by violating the Hague Conventions and committing a war crime. He had, however, satisfied his Führer's order to be brutal. It was the first of hundreds of crimes to follow, many on this very first day of combat.

Both Britain and France likewise teetered on the brink of war, as they had promised to come to the aid of Poland if Germany invaded. While German armor pushed into Poland, her two great allies dithered. In Paris, late that morning, Georges Bonnet, the French foreign minister and a leader of the Radical-Socialist Party, assured Polish ambassador Juliusz Łukasiewicz, an early Piłsudskite, that France would act. At 12:30 p.m., Bonnet called Łukasiewicz to his office after a meeting of the Council of Ministers, saying that he "did not have the slightest doubt that it would be impossible to halt the course of events." Łukasiewicz recalled, "He was sure that France and England would declare war on Germany, but he could not inform me exactly when and in what form this would take place. In view of this talk, I still had no cause for worry about the time England and France would declare war on Germany."[17] The French course of action, clear in the morning, was muddled by evening. The following morning, to the Polish ambassador's chagrin, the French had still not declared war, hoping to stall action until an Italian proposal for an international conference could be fully explored.[18] Benito Mussolini's self-serving proposals provided the excuse for the French to continue to dither and gave Hitler the jump in Poland.

The British, too, were slow to react. Word of the German invasion reached Whitehall some three hours after the initial attack. Winston Churchill, sleeping soundly at Chartwell, was awakened at 7:30 a.m. by a call from the Polish ambassador, Edward Raczynski, a landowning aristocrat related to the House of Hapsburg, who broke the news that the German invasion was underway.[19] The cabinet did not meet until 11:30 a.m., some six hours after the outbreak of war. Prime Minister Neville Chamberlain opened the session by saying that "the event against which he had fought so long and so earnestly had come upon us."[20] Chamberlain, like his French allies, hoped that an Italian proposal for an international conference would bear fruit. Late on September 2, Chamberlain, thought to be shillyshallying by some in his cabinet and by many in the House of Commons, was forced to present an ultimatum to Germany at 9:00 a.m. the following day or face an outright revolt that threatened to bring down the government. Leo Amery, Conservative member of Parliament and antiappeaser, claimed everlasting fame when Arthur Greenwood rose in the House to speak for Labour. Amery called out to him, "Speak for England." In his memoirs he vividly captured the push against delay.

> The House was aghast. For two whole days the wretched Poles had been bombed and massacred, and we were still considering within what time limit Hitler should be invited to tell us whether he felt like relinquishing his prey! And then these sheer irrelevances about the terms of a hypothetical agreement between Germany and Poland and the non-recognition of the annexation of Danzig.
>
> Was all this havering the prelude to another Munich? A year before the House had risen to its feet to give Chamberlain an ovation when he announced a last-moment hope of peace. This time any similar announcement would have been met by a universal howl of execration.[21]

Chamberlain, bowing to the inevitable, issued the ultimatum. Unless Hitler withdrew troops by 11:00 a.m., a state of war would automatically exist between Great Britain and Germany.[22]

Finally, the French faced the inevitability of war and sent an ultimatum to the Germans, although it would expire at 5:00 p.m., six hours later than Britain's. To no one's surprise, the attack on Poland continued after the British and the French time limits expired.[23] Anatole Monzie, a prolific writer, ardent pacifist, and director of public works, fought hard in the cabinet against a declaration of war and confided in his diary the following day, "France at war does not believe in the war."[24] "The hesitations of France's generalissimo [Gustave Gamelin] began in the very first hour of the war."[25] From the Munich Agreement to the Vichy armistice, the French leadership would prove to be a graveyard of carnival barkers.

At 11:15 a.m. on September 3, Chamberlain, strode to the BBC microphone in No. 10 Downing Street, informing the nation that Great Britain was at war. British writer and pacifist Vera Brittain wrote, "The hour comes near. With a sense of precipitating the advance of doom, I turn the knob of the radio. In a moment the silence of the little room is broken by a familiar voice—an old voice, harsh and arrogant, though now it trembles."[26] At noon, in a speech to the House of Commons, Chamberlain revealed the depth of his despair: "You can imagine what a bitter blow it is to me that all my long struggle to win the peace has failed.... Everything that I have worked for, everything I have hoped for, everything that I have believed in during my public life, has crashed into ruins."[27] The prime minister's remarks, an exercise in self-recrimination, did not constitute a war speech that would rally the nation to meet its new responsibilities. Churchill later pitilessly speared his opponent: "Chamberlain had been given the choice between shame and war. He chose shame and got war!"[28] Blanche Dugdale, Lord Balfour's niece, wrote in her diary, "The shame is over. We were at War with Germany at 11:00 a.m. today and France at 5 p.m."[29]

Unlike in August 1914, no crowds thronged the Potsdamerplatz on September 1 or packed Piccadilly Circus on September 3, joyfully greeting their country's announcement of war.[30] Duff Cooper, who had resigned his post as first lord of the Admiralty after Munich, observed, "There was no enthusiasm. If any had existed it would have been dimmed by the black-out which descended upon us even before the declaration of war."[31] In Warsaw and in cities throughout Poland, things were quite different. The Poles celebrated joyfully in the streets, singing enthusiastically and cheering in front of the British and French embassies. Sir Howard Kennard, Britain's ambassador, obviously embarrassed, occasionally stepped out on the balcony to wave to the crowd.[32] "Thus far, in France," Ambassador Bullitt wrote from Paris, "there is a curious unreality about the war. The whole mobilization was carried out in absolute quiet. The men left in silence. There were no bands, no songs. There were no shouts of 'On to Berlin' and 'Down with the Kaiser!' as in 1914. There was no hysterical weeping of mothers, and sisters and children."[33] Alone with her husband, Margot Asquith captured in 1914 what many felt on September 3, 1939: "'So it is all up' I said. He answered without looking up at me. 'Yes, it's all up.' I sat down beside him with a feeling of numbness in my limbs.... I got up and leant my head against his; we could not speak for tears."[34]

From a Berlin suburb, the anti-Nazi Jochen Klepper wrote, "How can a people cope with a war without any enthusiasm whatever, so downcast?!"[35] From Dresden, Victor Klemperer, a Jewish academic managing a tenuous existence with his wife, recorded in his diary the confusion surrounding the war's start. The butcher boy brought the first news declaring the Polish invasion and claiming Britain and France remained neutral. Klemperer said to his wife, Eva, "Then a morphine injection or something similar was the best thing for us, our life was over." Later, going to the city, he asked about Allied neutrality and heard from "an intelligent salesgirl in a cigar shop in Chemnitzer Platz . . . 'No—that would really be a joke!'"[36]

Soviet ambassador Maisky, in London, reflected, "So, war has begun. A great historical knot has been loosened. The first stone has rolled down the slope. Many more will follow. Today, the world has crossed the threshold of a new epoch. It will emerge from it much changed. The time of great transformations in the life of humankind is nigh. I think I'll live to see them unless, of course, some crazy incident cuts my days short."[37] Maisky knew that being recalled to Moscow might just be one of those crazy incidents.

In Washington, President Franklin Roosevelt, roused from his sleep at 2:50 a.m., picked up the phone to hear William Bullitt calling from Paris, reporting that he had just spoken with Tony Biddle, the American ambassador to Poland. The president could guess what he was about to hear, as the likelihood of war had been hanging in the balance for months and especially since the Nazi-Soviet pact had been signed a week earlier.

"Who is it?"

"This is Bill Bullitt, Mr. President."

"Yes, Bill."

"Tony Biddle has just got through from Warsaw, Mr. President. Several German divisions are deep in Polish territory, and fighting is heavy. Tony said there were reports of bombers over the city. Then he was cut off."[38]

"Well, Bill," the president said, "it has come at last. God help us all."[39]

Roosevelt hung up, propped himself up on his pillow, lit a cigarette, and immediately phoned Secretary of State Cordell Hull.[40] Hull recalled in his memoir, "The phone rang stridently beside my bed. Tense from days of preparing and waiting, I wakened and turned on the light. It was already three o'clock in the morning of Friday, September 1, 1939. I picked up the receiver, 'Cordell, Bullitt has just been on the phone. The Germans have invaded Poland.'" Though the secretary expected war at any time, it "was none the less a shock." He added, "There flashed through my mind the thought that here perhaps was the end of civilization as we knew it. Here was untold death, suffering, destruction."[41] After speaking with Hull, Roosevelt telephoned the secretaries of war and the navy. Throughout the long night, telephones rang and lights came on all over Washington as word of war spread throughout the capital like a drop of black ink splashed on a piece of cotton rag paper.

As dawn approached, the president, at 4:00 a.m. took his first official action of the war in an appeal to Great Britain, France, Italy, Germany, and Poland:

> The ruthless bombing from the air of civilians in unfortified centers of population during the course of the hostilities which have raged in various quarters of the earth during the past few years, which has resulted in the maiming and in the death of thousands of defenseless men, women and children, has sickened the hearts of every civilized man and woman, and has profoundly shocked the conscience of humanity.
>
> I am therefore addressing this urgent appeal to every Government which may be engaged in hostilities publicly to affirm its determination that its armed forces under no circumstances, undertake the bombardment from the air of civilian populations or of unfortified cities, upon the under-standing that these same rules of warfare will be scrupulously observed by all opponents. I request an immediate reply.[42]

At 5:00 a.m., Roosevelt called Eleanor, asleep at the family home in Hyde Park, to deliver the news. She and her houseguests—Mrs. George S. Huntington, an old friend, and journalist Dorothy Thompson, an outspoken anti-Nazi—wakened to the ringing phone to learn that "Hitler's troops had gone into Poland."[43] Upset by the news, none "could go back to bed, for a sense of impending disaster was upon us. The thing we had feared had finally come, and we seemed to know that sooner or later we would be dragged into the vortex with all the European countries."[44] Alerted by the president, the three women clicked on the radio to listen through the "hiss and crackle of static interference" to Hitler's announcement speech from the Kroll Opera House in Berlin.[45]

The president, demonstrating his sangfroid, went back to bed and slept until 6:30, when another call from Bullitt related the latest news from Paris and Warsaw. So began a long day of meetings on the first day of the war. At 10:40 a.m., Roosevelt held a press conference and went over the night's events. At the conclusion of his remarks, Phelps Adams, Washington correspondent for the *New York Sun*, posed the first question: "I think probably what is uppermost in the minds of all the American people today is, 'Can we stay out?' Would you like to make any comment at this time on that situation?" "Only this," said the president, "that I not only sincerely hope so but I believe we can and that every effort will be made by the Administration to do so." Adams queried, "May we make that a direct quote?" The president said, "Yes."[46] A few more questions followed, and Roosevelt was then quickly wheeled to a meeting with the nation's military leaders: Secretary of War Harry H. Woodring, Assistant Secretary of War Louis A. Johnson, Acting Secretary of the Navy Charles Edison, Chief of Naval Operations Admiral Harold R. Stark, and Army Chief of Staff George Marshall. Marshall had been promoted to the permanent rank of major general and chief of staff earlier that morning.[47]

Later that afternoon, at an emergency cabinet meeting, the president more fully articulated his thoughts on the early-morning call from Bullitt. Roosevelt had forbidden note taking at cabinet meetings, but naval secretary Charles Edison, convinced of the historical importance of the president's response on the news of war, returned to his office and wrote down what he remembered the president having said.[48] To his assembled cabinet, Roosevelt maintained that he had initially been startled, but then a feeling came over him that he had been through it all before. His "mind raced back" to his time as assistant secretary of the navy during the Great War, when he often received tragic messages in the middle of the night, and now history looked to repeat itself. Edison continued to hurriedly record the president's words:

> Twenty-five years ago, due to similar causes, the people of this country, excited by the war in Europe, allowed themselves to be drawn into a frenzy of increasing prices, of increasing the cost of living. The result of this mistake we all know to our sorrow. Whether the temptation comes from abroad, excessive profits and sky-rocketing prices of materials and labor are paid for out of human misery. True patriotism, in this hour of crisis, includes the determination that no warlike events shall be

permitted to disturb the peaceful and orderly pursuits of the American people. Our defense, geographically and in a military sense, and particularly in a financial and economic sense, remains adequate only to the degree that we soberly and earnestly refuse to ... neglect the task that lies before us—to defend our country and our people.[49]

Edison immediately sent his expanded notes over to the White House, hoping the president might find them useful in his upcoming Sunday night fireside chat. Roosevelt did not. His off-the-cuff remarks were clearly intended only for the ears of his inner circle.

On the far side of the Pacific Ocean, in his quarters in Manila, Lieutenant Colonel Dwight Eisenhower, who labored with General Douglas MacArthur to train the Philippine army, recorded in his diary his thoughts on the developing catastrophe. The future supreme commander of the Allied armies in Europe wrote, "It's a sad day for Europe and for the whole civilized world. ... If the war, which now seems to be upon us, is as long, drawn out and disastrous, as bloody and costly as was the so called World War, then I believe the remnants of nations emerging from it will be scarcely recognizable. ... [I]t doesn't seem possible that people that proudly refer to themselves as intelligent could let this situation come about."[50] Eisenhower was right that the long war would transform his country, but not in the way he envisioned.

Herbert Hoover, like Roosevelt, shared memories of the horrors that attended the Great War and for months had spoken out to his audiences against participation in any new European conflict. He greeted the arrival of war with a heavy heart, describing that first week of September 1939 as "one of the saddest weeks that has come to humanity in one hundred years."[51] On a radio broadcast that originated in San Francisco, Hoover elaborated on the meaning of the new conflict and what he thought should be America's response. The invasion of Poland, he said, was "senseless war," an apocalypse, one that would widen. He foresaw a war of attrition that would result in the deaths of millions and bring "another quarter of a century of impoverishment to the whole world. There may come a time of desperation when all restraints go to the winds—the most barbarous war we have ever known."[52] Hoover concluded his remarks emphatically:

America must keep out of this war. The President and Congress should be supported in their every effort to keep us out. We can keep out if we have the resolute national will to do so. We can be of more service to Europe and to humanity if we preserve the vitality and strength of the United States for use in the period of peace which must sometime come. And we must keep out if we are to preserve for civilization the foundations of democracy and free men.[53]

Resignation widely prevailed in all four capitals, Washington, London, Paris, and Berlin, where the outlook on the widening conflagration mirrored those of President Roosevelt: "Yes, I was almost startled by a strange feeling of familiarity—a feeling that I been thru it all before."[54] That familiarity was shared by millions. Vera Brittain, depressed over the turn of events, said of her two children that "they are spared the memories of an older war generation. They cannot see the pictures haunting my mind—the waiting darkness of a long-ago August midnight suddenly broken by excited voices crying that England's ultimatum to Germany has expired."[55]

Having only recently arrived in America and drinking alone in the Dizzy Club, a gay bar on Fifty-Second Street in New York City, British poet W. H. Auden agonized over the outbreak of war by penning "September 1, 1939," which captured the feeling of failure that permeated what appeared to be a crumbling West: the 1930s were "a low dishonest decade."[56] Beautiful British seventeen-year-old Joan Wyndham, reacting to the news, wrote in her diary,

> The posters say "HITLER INVADES POLAND". Everywhere children are waiting in expectant noisy herds, but the mothers are quiet, grey and some of them crying. Passing a side street I saw a Punch and Judy show playing to an empty road. Everything tilted at a slightly grotesque angle, like surrealist film. Mummy and Sid went to church so I sat in my room and got completely drunk for the first time in my life—on rum. It was a very nice experience indeed. I no longer cared a damn what happened to anybody.[57]

From Paris came the voice of narcissistic expat writer James Joyce proclaiming the outbreak of war a "personal affront . . . part of fate's conspiracy against him."[58] Europe, reminiscent of a Pablo Picasso or perhaps a Salvador Dali painting, had "entered some fractured cosmos . . . assembled from broken pieces."[59] Beneath the panic and gloom was the forced acknowledgment that the policy of containment through appeasement had failed miserably. Chips Channon, who had championed appeasement, wrote, "There is a settembrile feeling in the air—going is the summer, going indeed, is almost everything."[60] Britain, France, and Germany warily slipped into war for the second time in twenty-five years. The suicide of Europe was about to occur. Watching these events unfold in Europe, Americans undertook a great debate about how to respond or how to avoid once again being pulled into what Eleanor Roosevelt called the vortex of Europe.

The Allies, having finally declared war but in a state of psychological denial, still clung to the hope of a negotiated peace, a chance to wiggle out of their commitments and therefore only symbolically fulfill their commitment to Poland. The Polish government pleaded for Britain and France to provide immediate military assistance. The ever-cautious Allies did as little as possible. The British loaned Poland £5 million, and the French loaned F600 million. On the night of September 3, British bombers began the so-called confetti war by dropping 5.4 million leaflets over Hamburg, Bremen, and the Ruhr and, according to Oliver Harvey, secretary to Lord Halifax, "reconnoitered."[61]

No British bombers appeared to aid Polish ground units in the struggle with the Wehrmacht. Harvey noted, "When it was suggested that the RAF might bomb the Ruhr, the Air Minister, Sir Kingsley Wood, declared with affronted decency that factories were private property."[62] At this point, the naive air minister was hopelessly unprepared for the coming demands of economic warfare and the totality of the conflict. General Gamelin, on September 7 and 8, ordered several divisions to cross the German border into the Saarland, where they encountered a few small towns abandoned by the Germans and some surrounding acreage but did not assault the lightly defended positions along the West Wall—the Siegfried Line some eight miles inside the border. French sappers, loath to enter the German minefields, instead drove herds of pigs in front of them. The Royal Air Force and the French air force bombers were nearly all on the ground. As Hitler had clearly foreseen, it was all quiet on the western front.[63] Unlike the hesitant British and the French, the Nazis, within hours of the Allied declarations of war, attacked their new enemies at sea.

The Battle of the Atlantic began immediately and tragically. On the evening of September 3, some 250 miles off the northwest coast of Ireland, the U-30, commanded by Lieutenant Fritz-Julius Lemp, observed the passenger liner SS *Athenia*, blacked out, navigation lights dimmed, sailing west on a zigzag course in the hope of warding off a submarine attack and reaching the port of Montreal safely.[64] The *Athenia*'s captain had informed the passengers of Britain's declaration of war around noon. Fear aboard the liner was palpable. Against the possibility of attack, the passengers and crew had only the guarantees codified in the 1936 British-German agreement that prohibited submarines from attacking passenger ships. Would prowling German subs respect the pledge? This was the question in the minds of nearly everyone aboard. That hope was quickly shattered. The 1,103 passengers, including 300 Americans and 500 Jewish refugees, three-quarters of whom were women and children, had finished dinner and were beginning to settle in for their second night at sea when, at approximately 9:00 p.m., the U-30 fired two torpedoes from point-blank range. One missed, but the other struck the ship dead center, destroying the engine room and allowing water to pour in through the gaping hole. The ship stayed afloat, the lifeboats were launched, and the listing ship was abandoned in an orderly manner.[65] The *Athenia* did not slip beneath the waves until 10:00 the following morning. Loss of life was limited to 118, including 28 Americans, but those killed died gruesome deaths. Some perished when the torpedo slammed into the ship; a few were crushed between the lifeboats and the ship's side; others without life jackets drowned in the frigid waters when their lifeboats capsized.[66] A small fleet came to the rescue; the first responders were maritime ships nearby on the busy sea lane, but three Royal Navy destroyers soon joined them. One of the lifeboats alongside the Norwegian rescue ship *Knut Nelson* drifted to the stern and was pulled into the propellers, killing those on board.[67] Survivors, many landing in Ireland, captioned their traumatic experience "marvelous crew, heroic passengers, perfect morale."[68]

In America, the sinking of the *Athenia* shared the front pages of newspapers across the country with the British declaration of war, stirring a hornet's nest among readers who instantly recalled the sinking of the *Lusitania*. German propaganda minister Joseph Goebbels, realizing the dastardly error of his U-boat commander, claimed the British had actually sunk their own ship in order to win support from neutrals (i.e., the United States). Hitler ordered that all attacks on passenger ships stop as he clung to the illusion that Britain would eventually seek a negotiated peace. In his diary, Goebbels confided, "We received a report from a certain ... at just the right time, which finally unveils the secret of the *Athenia*. According to this account Churchill had holes bored in her bottom."[69] In response to the tale of the prevaricating "master of propaganda," Hoover commented, "It is such poor tactics that I cannot believe that even the clumsy Germans would do such a thing." Propaganda aside, Lieutenant Lemp in his small submarine had touched off one of the greatest struggles in World War II, the Battle of the Atlantic—one the British had to win if they were to survive. While Lemp had the *Athenia* sighted in his periscope, Chamberlain "invited the sixty-five-year-old hawk and political exile Winston Churchill back into the government" as first lord of the Admiralty.[70] To all in the Royal Navy worldwide, the message was flashed: "Winston is Back!" Back indeed, but the sinking of the *Athenia* signaled that this new war had little or no regard for past conventions at sea or on land.

While British destroyers and civilian rescue ships dealt with the sinking of the *Athenia*, Chamberlain ordered the British navy to immediately implement a blockade, a tactic that many in the Allied camp felt would force the Germans back to the negotiating table. Churchill later wrote, "Besides protecting our own shipping, we had to drive German commerce off the seas and stop all imports into Germany." His Majesty's navy snapped into action and began to round up ships throughout the Atlantic Ocean. The first case considered involved a neutral Dutch steamer loaded with ore that was headed for Germany. The British navy intercepted the vessel at sea and escorted it into a British port to determine the future of its cargo.[71] Quickly, the Royal Navy cleared the seas around Great Britain and sought to expand the blockade into the

Mediterranean. Ships were brought into contraband-control points at Weymouth, Ramsgate, Kirkwell, Gibraltar, and Haifa.[72] An irate Ray Brock, a *New York Times* correspondent, observed firsthand the scope and effectiveness of the British efforts at control of the seas. He and his wife, Mary, were on their way to Europe aboard the American freighter *Black Eagle*. Mid-Atlantic when Britain declared war, the crew kept vigilant watch for U-boats and mines, a task nearly impossible in the dark of night. On September 4, just off the Cornish coast, the ship was hailed by a British destroyer and forced into port. Brock later wrote,

> Then, like a picture coming into focus, the incredible scene ahead leaped into view through the thick mist. Seventy-six ships—we counted them later—were rocking in the Channel chop, their anchor balls hoisted, lights out, stacks dead. They were like ghost ships in some ocean graveyard. But these were no ghost ships. In my glasses, I picked out the fine lines of Dutch merchantmen, Swedish passage-cargo boats, a listing Turkish lumberman, Greek freighters, Belgium Channel packets, the breath-taking close-up sweep of the huge *Nieuw Amsterdam*—big ships and medium sized ships, rolling at anchor in the grey rain.[73]

British officials sealed the *Black Eagle*'s radio room with a piece of red tape and took away the radio operator, "Sparks," along with the ship's papers. Eight days later, the British finished processing the American vessel, and the *Black Eagle* was allowed to sail on to Antwerp. During the entire episode, the British did not inform the US government of the ship's detention. The American press reported that the *Black Eagle* had been sunk or possibly lost at sea.[74] The Royal Navy continued to clear the seas of ship traffic, while ten boats from the German submarine fleet and two German pocket battleships, the *Admiral Graf Spee* and the *Deutschland*, hunted targets in the North and South Atlantic. In the first fourteen days of the war, they bagged twenty-one British ships.[75]

5

Crushed

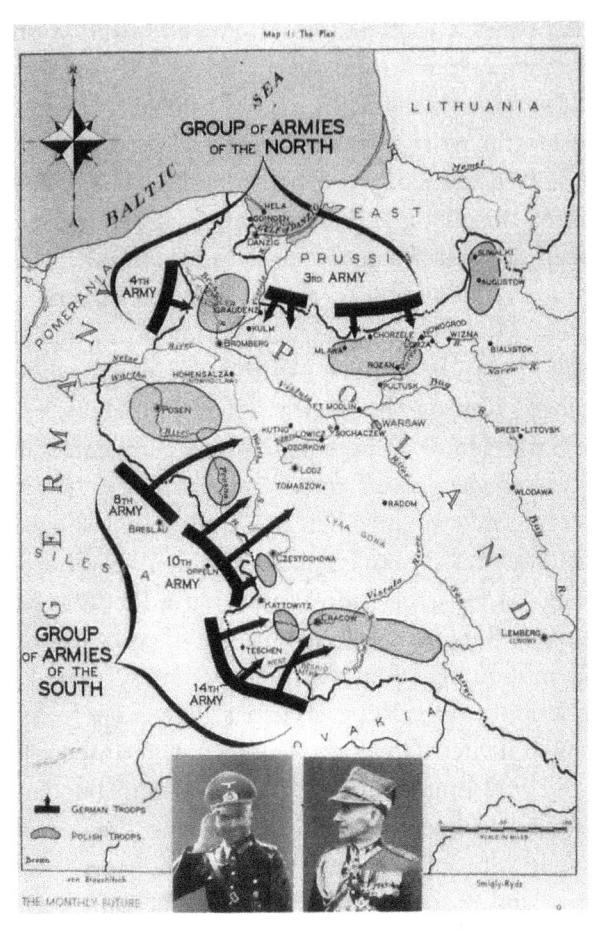

Bottom photos: German general Walther von Brauchitsch (left); Polish general Śmigły-Rydz (right) (courtesy of *The Monthly Future*, 1939).

It was a mistake, General Adrian Carton De Wiart, head of the British Military Mission, warned Marshal Edward Śmigły-Rydz, "to fight the Germans as soon as they had crossed the frontier into Poland."[1] If Rydz would listen to anyone, it was De Wiart, who had headed the British Military Mission to Poland in 1919, served as advisor to Józef Piłsudski before he became the Polish chief of state, and distinguished himself in combat on numerous occasions. Wounded eight times, three times having been shot in the head, he had lost an eye and a hand. His reward was the coveted Victoria Cross and a chest full of other ribbons. In 1915, suffering a wound in France, he wrote, "My hand was a ghastly sight; two of the fingers hanging by a bit of skin, all of the palm was shot away and most of the wrist. For the first time, and certainly the last, I had been wearing a wrist-watch, and it had been blown into the remains of my wrist. I asked the doctor to take my fingers off; he refused, so I pulled them off myself and felt absolutely no pain in doing it."[2] His comrades considered him an indomitable spirit, an unkillable soldier. Fitted with a glass eye, he found it disgusting and, while riding in a London cab, pulled it out and tossed it out the window. "With his drooping white moustache and a black shade over one eye," wrote Clare Hollingworth, "he looked like a Japanese war-idol."[3] Tall and handsome, he radiated authority and looked as if he had stepped off an adventure film set. It was said of De Wiart and his multiple wounds that "he simply survived and got on with it." The first military mission to Poland ended in 1924. Shortly thereafter, De Wiart resigned his commission following a kerfuffle with the War Office. What now? His aide-de-camp, Prince Charles Radziwill, had inherited a half-million-acre estate bearing the family name Mankiewicze located in the middle of the Pripet Marshes a few miles from the Russian border. Radziwill invited De Wiart to join him to inspect the property. Taken with the wild isolation of the place and the abundance of game, he casually remarked that he would enjoy living there. Not long after, Radziwill offered him a handsome wooden house forty miles from the manor on an island reachable only by boat. Enchanted, De Wiart accepted and for the next twenty years lived the life of a warrior monk in his Walden-like paradise. To avoid the bitter cold, he wintered for three months each year in London.

De Wiart, in his conversations with Rydz, continued to try to persuade him that the Z Plan, the positioning of Poland's armies on its borders, would fail. He emphasized that "the country west of the Vistula was terrain admirably suited to tanks at any time, but now, after a long, long spell of drought, even rivers were no longer obstacles.... I did not see how the Poles could possibly stand up to the Germans in country so favorable to the attacker."[4] Rydz refused the advice, claiming that if he did not defend the borders, he would be accused of cowardice. Regardless of the military consequences, he must stand firm. But given the Wehrmacht's overwhelming strength in both men and matériel, it probably mattered little what defense strategy the Poles adopted, as the outcome would be the same: defeat. Positioning his armies on the borders would hasten guaranteed defeat.

Poland's ability to defend itself was likewise crippled by British and French insistence that Rydz delay mobilization so as not to provoke a German attack. But clearly an attack was coming, and when it did, the Polish army paid a heavy price for heeding its allies' self-serving advice. Caught in the midst of moving large numbers of men and equipment

Śmigły-Rydz and his wife, Marta Thomas-Zaleska, in 1939 (courtesy of Getty Images).

to various fronts, units were strung out across the country and further hindered by the first crush of fleeing refugees jamming the roads. Hollingworth, driving from Katowice to Kraków on the second night of the war, witnessed terrified people determined to stay ahead of the advancing Germans: "The road for miles was a jostle of peasant wagons; and the blue lights of my car brought out the humped figures, the carts overpiled, and everywhere the white discs of children's faces, with the vague radiance of a blue-period Picasso."[5] In Kraków, noted Professor Wegierski, "an improvised committee for assisting these unfortunates could hardly deal with the increasing numbers. It was not a matter of finding accommodations, food or clothes but of people to distribute and handle them. The population of Cracow helped as best it could, but the wave soon increased beyond control—a horrible wave of misery that I pray to God never to see again."[6]

Communication between military formations was rendered all but impossible. Many units were understrength, had no reserves, and were not in position to blunt the invaders. Regardless, the Polish army, with strong support from the population, went to battle reflecting the optimism of its leadership. All summer long the government had conducted a full-on propaganda campaign geared to convince the country that Poland was determined to defend itself and could repel a German invasion. Patriotic posters were plastered to walls and kiosks in every Polish city. Soldiers on the march or packed into train cars sang patriotic songs and shouted, "On to Berlin!"

From the initial clash with the German army, contrary to the rapidly deteriorating military situation, rumors of Polish battlefield successes circulated wildly: the army had pushed into Germany; the cavalry had entered Danzig; the German attack was not a surprise; the British had bombed Berlin.[7] Misinformation was rife. History returned with a vengeance. The ceding of German territory to the new Polish state created at Versailles in 1919 had caused continuous ethnic conflict, resulting in a war within a war. Polish paramilitary groups fell in to support the army. Activist German-Poles in Nazi paramilitary units (*Selbstschutz*) indulged in sabotage, sniping, spying, disinformation, and direct combat with the Polish soldiers and militia. Poles widely accepted greatly exaggerated rumors about the scale of "fifth columnist" actions, creating an atmosphere of suspicion that became an explanation for every military setback. Unfortunately, a number of innocent ethnic Germans fell victim to these rumors and lost their lives. Those captured who had too soon declared their political allegiance by wearing Nazi armbands were rounded up and executed. Gestapo, *Einsatzgruppen*, and Abwehr detachments following in the wake of the army's advance carried special investigation books (*Sonderfahndungsbuch*), compiled in Berlin, listing those most wanted by the Nazis. It was a time to settle old scores. Thousands were arrested, tortured, and murdered.[8]

By the end of the next day, September 2, regardless of wishful thinking or rumor, the Wehrmacht began to push aside the Polish resistance; a breakthrough occurred to the southwest of Czectochowa, home of the sacred Black Madonna, and made rapid progress.[9] The battle of the borders was lost. Reeling, the Łódź army attempted to form a line behind the river Warta. Bombing raids on Warsaw increased. "Many people, against strict orders, gathered in doorways, at windows, and even on the roofs to watch despite the incredible danger," drawn to these aerial duels like moths to a kerosene lantern.[10] Those on the ground cheered at each Nazi plane that plunged to earth in a fiery crash. Cries of "No, no" rang out when Polish planes fell from the sky. All eyes were glued to the downward spirals; people prayed, fingers crossed, waiting for a parachute to open.

Amid the air raid warnings, restaurants, bars, and cafés outfitted for the blackout thrived, catering to thousands seeking safe harbor and to those who had spent long hours at hard labor, exhausted by preparing a defense system for the city. "Everyone digs trenches," wrote newsreel cameraman Harrison Forman in his diary recording the opening month of the war, "men, women and children."[11] "Cabarets open," he noted, "but no gaiety. In critical days no longer checked gas masks with hats and coats when entering restaurants, etc. Even danced with masks. For knew you'd have no time or strength to fight someone who'd picked up your mask at an alarm."[12] The Ali Baba Theatre provided a modicum of relief from the rising tensions by featuring a comedian who mocked Hitler, an act in the cabaret revue's premiere of *Pakty i Fakty* (Pacts and facts). Disappointingly, a small crowd was on hand to appreciate the opening night performance.[13] The show, however, did not go on, despite enthusiastic reviews, for two days later a bomb destroyed the theater. Hard drinkers congregated in the Crooked Lantern, famous for macho drinking bouts. Like gunfighters in the Old West, challengers came from everywhere to take on the reigning champ. "Army officers were very proud of their capacity for vodka and measured it in terms of meters. The measurement was made by placing the liqueur glasses in a straight line and then checking the distance covered."[14] Many drinking games were played. A favorite of Polish soldiers, the Russian game, began with as many as six sitting around a table. Each rapidly quaffed three shots of vodka, "then crawled under the table to places on the other side and had three more, continuing to go back and forth under the table until only one was left to drink the last three vodkas and claim the championship over his comrades, sprawled in drunken stupor in a mass of bodies under the table."[15] Likely apocryphal, officers touted the record as just short of ten feet. The city's artists, actors, writers, and journalists still flocked to their favorite haunt, the famous coffeehouse Ziemiańska (the Landed Gentry Café), known for its pastries in a classic Viennese style, where a heated debate on what was happening and what would happen never ceased. Martha Osnos, an upper-middle-class Jewish patron, described the babble as "blind people discussing color."[16]

The YMCA building too was alive with activity of a different sort. Paul Super spent a hectic day training hundreds who volunteered to assist the army and the growing number of refugees to obtain water, food, toiletries, and shelter. Two of the first to offer their services were Countess Teresa Lubieńska and Countess Joseph Potocka, both of whom had been active for years in relief work and were members of the authentic landed gentry. Air raids interrupted planning sessions. "Yet, for a few days," Super observed, "Warsaw was rather calm and we got our work started."[17] In the field, things were different. The army, though outgunned and outmanned, fought valiantly, killing and wounding many German soldiers, and for a short time slowed the German advance. Historians have hotly debated how much blitz was in the Nazi blitzkrieg, but "there was only one way for the German army to achieve its objective operationally: keep moving"—and keep moving it did.[18]

The Wehrmacht's combined arms operations executed a war of movement (*Bewegungskrieg*) that the Poles were unprepared to counter.

"Indeed, there were always signs that the war was moving too fast for the Poles; like a second-rate boxer, they were being 'beaten to the punch.' Everything happened before they expected it; one saw this in little things."[19] Those retreating from the battle described flotillas of aircraft that were "followed by endless waves of tanks, while infantry is hardly seen at all. This technique seems at first to have bewildered our officers and soldiers, who expected the good old, respectable trench warfare they knew so well from the Great War."[20] Case White (the German designation for the campaign in Poland), while not without command and operational difficulties, was a huge success, "proof of a military revolution."[21] Major Percy Black, US military attaché in Berlin, was invited to accompany the staff of the 228th Infantry Division commanded by General Hans Sutter in its assault on Poland from East Prussia. Black witnessed the destruction of the Modlin Fortress by a "massed close battle division" of 160 Stuka dive-bombers. "No longer, as in previous campaigns, did armies have to pause while heavy siege guns rolled up," said Black, though in fact, in the assault on Warsaw, the Germans did bring up heavy artillery in addition to employing the Luftwaffe.[22] Black went on to witness the fall of the capital and, on returning to the United States, gave a series of talks in military circles on the effectiveness of the German use of aircraft and tanks: blitzkrieg. Black's trips to the front, made after battle, were carefully chosen by his hosts, though he did see the fighting unfold from the position of a staff officer so that his comment to the *New York Times* that he "did not believe any of the atrocity stories" had no basis in his "frontline experience."[23]

To the southwest of Warsaw, the Wehrmacht soon reached the edge of Kraków. "We counted the time we might still hold out in hours, not days—and the news from the West mentioned only preparations, but nothing more."[24] Punishing air attacks crippled morale. "Thus Cracow, defenseless against air attacks, began to give way to dark thoughts," as thousands fled the imperiled city.[25] Among the multitude moving eastward were the young Jagiellonian University scholar Karol Józef Wojtyła (the future Pope John Paul II) and his father.[26] "The elder Wojtyła, weak and in poor health, would occasionally ride in a cart or a truck. Lolek [Karol's nickname] and his father sometimes found themselves in a ditch, trying to shelter from strafing Luftwaffe aircraft."[27] The JU-87 Stukas often had a siren, nicknamed a "Jericho trumpet," attached to the fixed landing gear or the front edge of the wing. In a steep dive, the plane dropped from the sky like a bird of prey, perhaps more like Południca, the noon witch of Polish folklore, emitting an eldritch scream that caused panic among those on the ground. For those thousands terrorized by such attacks, it was a sound not to be forgotten.

On September 3, Polish spirits were buoyed as the British and then the French declared war. Varsovians by the hundreds, then by the thousands, gathered outside the British and French embassies, cheering wildly, singing, and hoisting homemade banners expressing thanks. Sir Howard Kennard, Britain's ambassador, obviously embarrassed, occasionally stepped out on the balcony to wave to the crowd.[28] Super commented, "We felt we were saved."[29] Diarist Alexander Polonius, thinking of the Polish soldiers valiantly hanging on in Westerplatte and how he might serve his country, stepped out into his sunlit garden of flowers, where in the distance he could hear the playing of "God Save the King":

> That could only mean on thing. She declared war on Germany. Everybody was mad with joy. "Long live Britain! Long live King George!" Their bombers will be here any moment to help us. And with us the whole street exulted, the whole town, the whole of Poland. France will come in any time now; she is still giving Hitler the chance to stop; a narrow thread is still left uncut; peace can still be restored if the Germans decide to withdraw from our country immediately. Now we cannot possibly lose the war. We can be assured as to our future.[30]

Hollingworth and British consul John Anthony Thwaites, in their hotel in Kraków, hurriedly packed up their things, preparing to escape the German army by retreating east to Lublin. Walking down the stairs, Hollingworth heard "God Save the King" on the radio, followed by an announcement that Great Britain was at war. "A porter approached me and kissed my hand as the radio switched to the 'Marseillaise.'"[31] A thousand miles from London, Hollingworth shared with Prime Minister Neville Chamberlain and thousands of other Britons a similar reaction:

Karol Józef Wojtyła, the future pope John Paul II (second on the right), Academic Legion Military Training, June 1939 (courtesy of Alamy).

It was the worst moment of the war for me and I felt slightly sick. I steadied myself against the wall and thought of my years on the staff of the League of Nations Union and the organizing of the Peace Ballot. All that we had worked for seemed lost. London would be bombed and friends and buildings I loved destroyed. And now neither Britain nor France could prevent all these people around me from falling into German hands.[32]

Amid the jubilation, later that day Rydz confronted "a terrible irony. At the very time that Britain and France were officially joining the war, his own front had just broken."[33] In briefing the missions leaving for Paris and London, the distraught commander told his anxious listeners, "The front is breaking down everywhere. It is left to us to retreat behind the Vistula to the extent it will still be possible."[34] There a defensive line might be established that would hold out until equipment and supplies arrived from the West. The Polish high command reasoned the French and British would honor their commitments by assaulting the German West Wall. The missions must use every means at their disposal to convince the Allies that immediate assistance was essential. In the meantime, the important thing was to stay in the war. The site chosen for the government's new headquarters was the city of Brześć (Brest-Litovsk), situated on the Bug River in eastern Poland. The city might be defendable, as "it had been one of the largest fortresses of the Old Russian Empire," and to the south "the vast primeval forest at Białowieża, Hermann Goering's favorite hunting retreat . . . offered concealment."[35] Brześć had long played an important part in Poland's history, and in 1918 it was the site of the treaty between the new Bolshevik government of Russia and the Central Powers, an agreement in which the Bolsheviks surrendered a large slice of the former czarist empire—a concession that helped open the road to an independent Poland. The city held out the faint possibility that it would be the place where the German advance might be halted. Much of the government and a number of military units began to train and caravan the 120 miles. Some ministries were of necessity sent to other towns.

The German battle plan, a classic double envelopment treasured by German staff officers since Frederick the Great and invented by Hannibal at Cannae, managed in the first few days of the campaign to break through and overrun swaths of territory and encircle huge numbers of Polish soldiers. *Kesselschlacht* (cauldron battle) carried the day. Hollingworth had observed the first wave of refugees on the second day of the war, but now, to the west of Warsaw, floods of frightened people crowded the roads. Wehrmacht panzers "were advancing so rapidly that the refugees, if they were lucky, were simply pushed aside into the fields. The less fortunate were strafed by Stuka dive bombers."[36] Nothing now stood between German general Walter von Reichenau's army and the capital. Worse, the Poles, though few reckoned with the fact, were all but out of time. "My friends of the local command," observed Hollingworth, "did not realize that they would never be able to fall back fast enough, never unify their front on the Vistula or anywhere. In a few days their army would be split into fragments."[37] Hugh Carleton Greene of London's *Daily Telegraph* reported, "People still believed that rivers were defensible."[38] None in the press corps were "then thinking in terms of ultimate retreat . . . and common to all was the belief that the Poles would hold fast all winter east of the river Vistula, among the Pripet Marshes."[39]

Monday morning, only four days into the war, many government workers found they had a new assignment: pack and await orders to move. To their amazement, the order arrived later that same afternoon. Loaded into trucks, cars, and buses, the motorcade of office workers took hours to cross the jammed bridge over the Vistula into the suburb of Praga and make its way to the east Warsaw rail station, arriving at 10:00 p.m. By 11:00, exhausted, all had boarded the trains, but, to their frustration, the trains did not leave the station. No one knew why: perhaps plans had changed; perhaps military trains had priority; perhaps the tracks were under repair after being bombed; perhaps the high command was undecided. Finally, after a trying night, at 5:00 a.m. the first of the Warsaw government evacuees set off on the journey east, some for Lublin and others for Brześć.[40] Word that the government was leaving quickly spread throughout the city, while many inhabitants could see for themselves that ministries were striking their tents.

The sun was not yet up on Tuesday morning, September 5, when the phone rang in Super's apartment at 5:15 a.m. Awakened by the maid, he picked up the receiver to hear the YMCA general secretary on night duty claim "that for hours young officials living in our building had been quietly departing, with suitcases, and it was evident that some sort of exodus from the city was on. He advised us to get up, dress and prepare to join the exodus."[41] The director, reacting to events around him, did not know that, during the night, German armored columns had threatened Modlin to the north and that Rydz, fifteen minutes earlier, had ordered the government and the Diplomatic Corps to evacuate. Heeding the unexpected advice, Super awoke his wife, Margaret. Now dressed, along with their two maids they considered what to pack. Forty-five minutes later the phone rang again. This time it was his secretary claiming that a friend in the upper echelon of the government had warned that a large air and ground attack was about to commence. Offering more startling advice, she said they "should pack such things as they could easily carry across the fields and take to the open country."[42] Their selection of what would be necessary was guided by their ages and his heart condition. In an overnight bag for her, a dispatch case for him, and two very small leather cases, Super recalled, "the little we then took from our home was all we saved of our many beautiful and valuable things."[43]

The Supers arrived at YMCA headquarters to discover a good deal of confusion and their safety and future unclear. "So we went into our restaurant, ate breakfast, and waited."[44] A staffer just back from Great Britain brought hopeful news: a committee to aid the Poles through the YMCA had been formed, and the Swedish YMCA was exploring how it might be of assistance. Soon the decision was made that all would decamp to Lublin. The Supers were to travel with the YMCA leadership and with officials from the Ministry of Social Welfare in a caravan of five cars and trucks. Younger staff and office workers were instructed to follow in any way they could, including shank's mare. Super told himself, "There was the relieving fact; we all believed that our departure was a few days only, a week or ten days at most, by which time British and French aid would reach us and make our return to Warsaw possible."[45] Ready by 11:00 a.m., the nervous evacuees sat for hour after hour in the office of YMCA chairman Dr. Tadeusz Dyboski, waiting for word to get underway, which did not come until 6:00 p.m.; half an hour later, the Supers squeezed into their assigned car.

Paul Super, late 1930s, at the port of Gdynia (courtesy of Narodowe Archiwun Cyfrowe [Polish National Digital Archives]).

Earlier that same day, concert pianist Magdalena Lipkowska wrote in her diary, "About seven in the morning, I was on my way to the Malta Corps office"—she had volunteered to train auxiliary nurses for the Knights of Malta—"and for the first time I saw dive bombing. It was as if silver butterflies in formation came noiselessly down out of the transparent and pale daytime moon. Although they were enemies, I could not help but admire the masterly hands guiding the craft."[46] A few blocks further on, she witnessed the beginning of one of the more intriguing stories of the war. The Polish gold, some eighty tons, along with bags of currency and the banknote printing plates, were carried from the treasury and "loaded by anyone who could give a hand into several city buses, which were then driven away, escorted by a handful of men who were not even civil servants."[47] The famous Halina Konopacka—gold medal winner in the discus at the 1928 Olympic Games and wife of the treasury minister, known as the First Lady of the Second Republic—drove one of the forty red buses on the harrowing night journey across Poland to a freight yard in Śniatyń, where the gold was loaded onto a train for Constanta, Romania. The gold, nearly five years later, ended up in vaults in New York, Ottawa, and London, but not before having traveled to Istanbul, Syria, Beirut, France, Mali, and Dakar.[48]

The Supers' small caravan was caught up within minutes in the rush to leave the city and slowed for several hours by the traffic on the bridge over the Vistula. The couple was shocked by what they witnessed on the road in the few hours of remaining light:

> Recall now all you have read and all the pictures you have seen depicting the flight of refugees before a powerful and brutal army. Apply those words and pictures to that of which Margaret and I now became a part. From our car we looked about us upon the hastening stream of trucks, private autos of every conceivable size and age, horse drawn vehicles, push-carts, bicycles, baby buggies, toy express wagons, people afoot, single or in groups, all loaded to the very limit, the vehicles with people and baggage, the pedestrians laden with suitcases, bundles of all sizes and shapes, and carrying a most miscellaneous assortment of valued personal property and household effects. For all knew only too well that whatever they left behind was probably gone forever.[49]

As the darkness descended, the cars, with lights out, were forced to reduce speed and move at a crawl. Super reflected on the historical significance of what was transpiring and recalled how he and his family had ended up spending long years in Poland. The YMCA had arrived in 1919, as during the Great War it served the American, French, Polish, and Polish American troops in General Józef Haller's Polish regiments attached to the French army. When Haller's army, fifty thousand strong, left for Poland, it requested that the YMCA come along. Y workers struggled to build an organization from the ground up, while Herbert Hoover's American Relief Administration (ARA), partially staffed by the army's loan of doughboys, fed the new nation. Among those who came to assist the resurrected Poland were a small group of volunteer Polish American women, the Grey Samaritans. From Polish communities around the country, hundreds applied, but few were selected by the YMCA to train in nursing and social work in New York City. From among those trained,

Polish Grey Samaritans arrive in Warsaw, 1920 (courtesy of Polish Grey Samaritan Records, Box 1, Folder 1, Hoover Institution Library and Archives).

thirty were sent to Poland, where they braved war and typhus as they crisscrossed the devastated countryside in cars donated by the Ford company, distributing clothing and food while providing medical attention and teaching hygiene.

Super's long tenure in Poland began when he was asked to serve as YMCA general secretary by John R. Mott, general secretary of the international committee of the YMCA, a Christian Evangelist who had built YMCA organizations worldwide and a future recipient of the Nobel Peace Prize. Mott chose Super because of his vast experience, boundless energy, and commitment to Christianity and the goals and practices of the Y. Super had no interest in Poland, but given Mott's prestige and religious authority, it was impossible to tell him no. Reading several books on Poland and talking with Y staffers who had served there, he learned the country was overwhelmingly Catholic. Super had one condition: "I will go to Poland, but the Polish YMCA which I shall help develop will be a Catholic YMCA."[50] Mott, a Methodist committed to ecumenism, approved. Super arrived in Poland on March 22, 1922, assuming his stay would be of short duration.

The Poland in which Super alighted that March was a tough place. Returned to the map of Europe at Versailles in 1919, the new nation was beset with tremendous problems. Its borders with the newly independent Lithuania and Czechoslovakia were contested, as were its borders with the Soviet Union and Germany. Hoover, an ardent supporter of a Polish state who provided millions in aid through the ARA, described the country at its birth under its new president, the world-famous pianist Ignacy Paderewski:

> Many hundreds of thousands had died of starvation. The homes of millions had been destroyed and the people were living in hovels. Their agricultural implements were depleted, their animals had been taken by armies, their crops had been only partly planted and even then only partly harvested. Industry in the cities was dead from lack of raw materials. The people were unemployed and millions were destitute. They had been flooded with rubles and kronen, all of which were now valueless. The railroads were barely functioning. The cities were

almost without food; typhus and diseases raged over whole provinces. Rats, lice, famine, pestilence—yet they were determined to build a nation.[51]

The country, already a wrecker's yard, was further destroyed by the outbreak of the Polish-Soviet War, which raged until spring 1921. The Poles prevailed with the help of Ukrainian nationalists and by winning a great victory to the west of Warsaw, but the non-Polish citizenry of the region would never successfully integrate, and victory created a wound that, for the Soviets, would never heal. Afflicted by war, pestilence, famine, and political chaos, a large swath of Central Europe, the remnants of collapsing empires, became known as the bloodlands.[52] Norman Davies aptly titled his two-volume history of Poland *God's Playground*.[53]

Super, in his memoirs, recalled that he had his work cut out for him, work he was in no way sure he wished to undertake. The cold winds of March sweeping through Warsaw's streets captured his doubts. But April promised spring and, for all Christians, Palm Sunday and Easter. He and his colleague Arthur Taylor were pleased to accept the invitation of General Listowski, liaison officer to the YMCA, to attend the Easter Eve service in the city cathedral. Toward the end of the service, Christ is declared risen and flowers are rushed to the altar. Cardinal Hlond, followed by priests and parishioners, paraded through the church singing, "Halleluiah, He is risen!"[54] Streaming from the cathedral, the crowd continued to sing as it moved through the old town to the palace square. "Suddenly," Super wrote, "it sweeps over me that the song really in many hearts, as most surely in mine, is '*Poland* is risen!' The resurrection of a nation which has been in a tomb almost one hundred and fifty years, and now living and free! No words that I can write can convey my profound emotion as the idea filled my mind. That was many years ago, but that memory still stirs me. It was then, I think, that Poland began to possess me."[55]

Following his epiphany, throughout the summer and fall Super worked to build a YMCA facility to the north of Kraków at Szyce, a place he called "our" village. Here, and with his travels to the Tatras, among the summer "profusion of flaming red poppies and bright blue corn-flowers,"

Super became enmeshed in Polish rural life. "I felt my heart begin to burn with desire to serve this people and this land, and a love for Poland began to grow in my breast that will prepare me for what was soon to come, a call to that service."[56] That fall Super's wife and two sons arrived. All eventually learned Polish, and over the next seventeen years the couple would come to know every region of their adopted country. The Supers wrote several books on Polish history and culture, she under the pen name Ann Su Cardwell. Old Polish prints and documents signed by Polish kings lined their apartment walls, and they passionately collected rare books published in the sixteenth and seventeenth centuries. Both also fancied Polish cuisine. They understood the country's weaknesses and its political and social problems. They shied away from the anti-Semitism enacted economically that erupted occasionally in violence and was often heard in Polish social circles, enthusiastically carrying water nonetheless for the country they had come to love.[57]

Not long after midnight, Super's reminiscences were interrupted as the seven-and-a-half-hour trip to Lublin ended when the line of cars and trucks arrived intact. Worn out, both physically and mentally, the Supers climbed the stairs of the Social Insurance building and found two couches on which to attempt sleep. Over a fitful night, the couple shared thoughts on their traumatic past few days and tried to make sense of the tragedy. The momentous events were humbling. Super wrote, "A state of 35,000,000 inhabitants being crushed. Cities and towns bombed. Thatched-roofed villages set afire and reduced to heaps of ashes. Streams of refugees on the open roads strafed and bombed from the air. Millions on the move. An army disrupted. Chaos. The sadness of it all overwhelms us. Virgil's words, 'All of which I saw, a part of which I was.'"[58] How to understand a country torn apart and seventeen years of hard work gone in five days?

The Supers, relieved by the coming dawn, found breakfast and, soon after, a place to stay and a promise they would be fed. At the same time the Luftwaffe found Lublin. On the way back to the Social Insurance building, between raids, the couple bumped into three young YMCA workers from Warsaw. Plans were hatched for how to serve the hundreds of soldiers streaming through the city. The following morning, before any plans could be put into action, the bombing resumed. A decision was reached to move farther east to Chelm. The caravan arrived in the dark, and all hoped to set up operations in the morning, but once again, on the following day around noon, scout planes overhead ensured that bombs would soon fall. Polish officials selected Dubno, as a city of last resort. It was but thirty-five miles from the Soviet border. Not long after they left Chelm, the Luftwaffe scored a direct hit on the Social Insurance clinic and dispensary. Once again on the road, the column of vehicles proceeded slowly. Super, frustrated with the pace, asked Dyboski why they were not going faster. He was stunned by the response: "The slower we went the less far we would go, and the nearer to Warsaw we would be when the signal came to return."[59] Many in the Polish leadership could not grasp what was happening and that the signal they were counting on would likely never be sent. Late that night, they reached Włodzimierz without incident. One of the travelers knew the location of a restaurant, but in the blacked-out city "we had to feel our way along the walls" of buildings to find it.[60]

Risking daytime travel, the following morning the Y leadership continued through Łuck and on to Dubno, again without being bombed. The Ministries of the Interior and Social Welfare, along with army staff, had converged on the city to again try to function. The army's task was to re-form units from retreating soldiers, reserves, and new recruits. Super was charged with "welfare work for the refugees and for soldiers."[61] As in Lublin, experienced Y personnel had found their way to Dubno and shortly had a canteen set up in the railroad station assisting needy Polish soldiers. That evening the leadership met and decided that a mission to America headed by someone of stature, someone who could plead Poland's cause and explain her needs, had to be undertaken. Władysław Raczkiewicz was selected. He met with Super on the morning of September 12 and asked for letters of introduction and a list of people with whom he should talk. Raczkiewicz never made the trip, as the rapidly changing military situation forced him to accompany the Polish government on its hopscotch-like retreat to Kuty on the Romanian border.

For the Supers, the next two days were filled with work, but the nights, without lights, in their ramshackle, Jewish-owned hotel left much time for reminiscence, speculation, and self-reflection. Both were grateful that they only experienced one air raid and that bombs were dropped some distance away. Super's heart condition worried him, and he was unsure whether he could survive the tension, the emotional and physical strain that accompanied twelve- to sixteen-hour days in a topsy-turvy war zone. He wrote that sometime during the night he found his "directive and support" from several sources. One was a particular quote attributed to Hendrik Hudson in Henry Van Dyke's *Northwest Passage*: "We'll hold the honor of a certain aim amid the perils of uncertain ways, and sail ahead, and leave the rest to God." Reassured, he concluded, "I sailed ahead and left the rest to God."[62]

Early in the morning of September 14, it happened again. Just after breakfast, a staffer hurried to the Supers, telling them to quickly pack and report to the local Social Insurance headquarters. Was German armor approaching? Had they information on a large air attack? To their dismay, the radio reported that the Soviet army was amassing on the Polish border, poised to enter the country. If they did not leave immediately, they would be trapped between the Germans and the Soviets, captured by one or the other. Poland's southeast corner narrowed like a funnel, and the only chance for the Supers and the Social Insurance leadership, as well as for thousands of others moving across Poland, was to pour through that funnel into Romania. Ironically, the breakup of Czechoslovakia provided a second avenue of escape for Poles, as Hungary, a friendly state, established a border with Poland by annexing Transcarpathia in March 1939 and a sliver of Slovakia a month later. Mountainous and perilous, it was nonetheless one of the few paths open to many.

The three-car caravan, unlike previous evacuations, sped through town after town, arriving in the dark at Czortkov. Car seats and park benches served as beds. At first light, the three packed cars drove to the frontier town of Śniatyń on the river Prut. The following morning, September 17, the Social Insurance caravan, having left Warsaw on September 5, arrived at the border crossing near Śniatyń at 2:00 p.m. and pulled into a long line of vehicles, trucks, carts, refugees, and soldiers waiting to cross the bridge into Romania. While waiting, Super discovered the general secretary of the Łódź YMCA, Aloisy Trypka, and the two immediately began planning relief work for the refugees and soldiers working out of the Bucharest YMCA. "We had no money," wrote Super, "the total fortune in my purse being five dollars."[63] The two relief plotters were unfazed, as they had long experience in finding money. The Buick carrying the Supers crossed the bridge into Romania at midnight. During a lengthy holdup in Suciava, Polish air force pilots and crews marched through on the way south toward Bucharest. Super, in his memoirs, wrote, "We were told by the Romanians to proceed to Pascani. There we were interned."[64]

"The foreign diplomats, journalists and officials were still sitting in Warsaw's fashionable cafes talking about a long war when they learned that they too must pack and depart within a few hours. The evacuation order came the morning of September 5."[65] "Very few managed to take anything with them."[66] The Diplomatic Corps's flight across Poland paralleled that of the Supers and the Ministry of Social Welfare. Polish foreign minister Józef Beck confidentially told US Ambassador Tony Biddle in late August that if war came and it became necessary to evacuate the capital, he would provide a large truck to haul whatever the embassy wished to take and that the motorcade would be guarded. A special train would also be available for staff. The train was tempting, as the Biddles possessed a private railroad car, but driving, though still risky, seemed safer. Skeptical that Beck would be able to provide what he promised, Biddle went ahead and purchased the needed truck, filling it with "canned goods, kerosene lanterns, candles, et cetera," fearing that he and his family and staff might be forced to spend the winter somewhere in eastern Poland, likely in the palace the Biddles rented from the Potockis east of Lwów in the small town of Pomorzany.[67] If forced to leave Warsaw, they would not be staying this time at Łancut, another opulent estate of the Potockis in southern Poland where they often spent weekends, as it was too close to Warsaw.

Nałęczów, a spa town to the southwest near Lublin, was the destination. Here the Polish Foreign Ministry and the Diplomatic Corps were to set up shop. Biddle called his wife, Margaret, at 7:00 a.m., telling her to pack what she could and come immediately to the embassy. The Biddles' home, one of the most beautiful in the city, was in the "leafy suburb of Konstancin," where the couple frequently entertained lavishly.[68] Margaret's father, Boyce Thompson, had made a fortune in mining and left his only daughter approximately $85 million. In her diary, she wrote, "No taxis were available so I took a drosker [*sic*] and arrived with my gas mask, fur coat and bags in time."[69] In truth, there was little to take, as she had earlier sent her jewelry and "valuables out of the country, and had packed practically everything else which was not in everyday use. In addition she had stocked not only the embassy but also their place in the suburbs ... as well as the country palace outside Lwów. At each place there were gas masks, provisions and drums of gasoline enough to carry them through for three months if necessary."[70] At the embassy, "hustle-bustle" described the staff as they packed "official and personal equipment and prepared to move out. Cars were loaded till the springs threatened to flatten; a truck striped with camouflage paint was crammed to bursting."[71] Biddle, taking an extra precaution, painted "U.S.A." atop his yellow Cadillac and on the roofs of the six cars and truck that made up what *Life* magazine described as a "caravan of death." The lead car flew an American flag.[72] The dapper ambassador and his wife dressed to the nines and, accompanied by Biddle's stepdaughter, Peggy Schulze, a large black-and-white Great Dane named Okay, and a number of secretaries, left the embassy in late afternoon to undertake the dangerous drive. Code clerk Eugenia McQuatters, driving Biddle's station wagon, hauled the four secretaries, one male Polish citizen, and drums of gasoline, following closely behind the Biddles.[73] Other embassies and consulates in the neighborhood throughout the day made their own preparations for the move. All assumed they would likely be back in Warsaw in a few days, a week or so at the most.

Throughout the day, while the Americans prepared to leave, a train at the East Station composed of fourteen carriages awaited Polish ministry officials, their families, diplomatic personnel, and a smattering of journalists all bound for Lublin. Arrival was delayed by the difficulty of crossing the Vistula bridges. One of the journalists, J. Crang of the *London News Chronicle*, traveling with his family, described the bedlam in the station as it took nearly three hours to ascertain the right train and the right carriage before night descended and the station plunged into darkness: "Mothers shouting in the dark for their children, husbands for wives, children weeping for their parents, all fearing a repetition of the raids which a day earlier had bombarded the same station, killing many."[74] The economic counselor of the Foreign Office, Jan Wrszlacki, and the assistant counselor, Count Potulicki, in charge, sometime in the predawn hours finally got the train underway.[75] Not far from Warsaw, a message arrived to say that the rail junction at Deblin had been destroyed and the train would have to seek an alternative route. Nicknamed the "Phantom Train," it began its journey traveling north but over and over again was forced to detour and subjected to long delays in its efforts to reach its new destination, Krzemieniec. The fifteen hundred men, women, and children aboard were to suffer an unimaginable ordeal.[76]

Late that same afternoon, those on the street in Warsaw stared, mouths open, at a large Rolls-Royce moving in a line of cars and trucks preceded by half a dozen motorcycle outriders. In the backseat, barely visible, sat the white-haired Ignacy Mościcki, Poland's president of thirteen years. The column moved slowly through the streets before joining the throng crossing the landmark Prince Poniatowski Bridge. Hours later the president and his retinue disappeared into the oncoming night. Whether they would safely reach Brześć was an open question, but no question remained as to whether the government was abandoning the capital. The following day, Boruch Spiegel, a Jewish tailor and Bundist (a Jewish socialist labor movement), wrote, "He had never witnessed such chaos before—a national government dismantling itself overnight and running for dear life, so all that remained of once-powerful ministries were the charcoal embers of hastily burned documents" and the promise of return when the war was won.[77] The citizens of Warsaw now realized that the wolf had been called from the forest and they must either flee to the southeast accompanied by the migratory storks that roosted on their rooftops or stay and fight.[78] Rydz and the Polish high command would soon learn that the decision to move east destroyed any pretense of command and control. Poland was to be "crushed like a soft-boiled egg."[79]

The Americans' convoy safely made the short trip to Nałęczów but discovered that the city's railroad station had been bombed earlier in the day. The house assigned to Biddle and his family was filled with wounded women and children: "On the back porch, one woman who was due shortly to give birth had had her leg severed at the knee."[80] With an acute shortage of medical supplies, all were attended to as best as possible and then sent off to a nearby Lublin hospital. The wounded gone, the house became the working headquarters of the embassy. After morning meetings, Biddle spent the afternoon working on a cable to Washington. He had, from war's first shot, attempted to keep Washington up to date on the rapidly unfolding military and political situation. His analysis was trusted, and through the State Department and his friend and fellow Mainline Philadelphian, Ambassador Bill Bullitt in Paris, his views reached Franklin Roosevelt's ears. Biddle copied Bullitt on all his Washington cables, and they frequently talked on the phone.[81] The respite in Nałęczów provided an opportunity to reflect on the German air campaign and attacks on open cities, as Roosevelt, with the outbreak of war, had asked that all belligerents "in no event, and under no circumstance, undertake the bombardment from the air of civilian populations or of unfortified cities. I request an immediate reply."[82] Earlier, Hitler, the British, and the French had agreed on this principle. Biddle was the president's eyes on the ground to confirm whether the Führer had kept his word. Given what he observed, Biddle questioned whether it was possible to attack military targets from the air and not kill civilians. After all, Western European armies billeted troops in towns and villages, and military production factories "were usually surrounded by densely populated communities of employees."[83] Biddle's experience confirmed the earlier anxieties of Prime Minister Stanley Baldwin—"the bomber always gets through"—and Marcel Junod's assertion that any new war "would not spare the noncombatants."[84] An air attack, even if aimed at military targets, would result in civilian casualties, as targets were difficult to hit and required saturation bombing. And just as Junod had feared, the Nazis used the Luftwaffe as a propaganda tool and a terror weapon, gunning refugees on the roads and in trains and bombing towns and villages regardless of their military value. Biddle questioned the collateral human cost attached to air warfare. In wrestling with this dilemma, he had witnessed firsthand "the inevitability of the deplorable."[85]

That same day, seventy-one miles west of Lwów, a fifteen-year-old Jewish girl, Renia Spiegel, put on a brave face, knowing her town would soon be bombed. In her diary, she wrote,

Enemy planes keep flying over Przemśyl, and even now and then there is an air-raid siren. But, thank God, no bombs have fallen on our city so far. Other cities like Krakow, Lwów, Częstochowa and Warsaw have been partially destroyed. But we are all fighting, we are all fighting, from young girls to soldiers. I've been taking part in female training—digging air-raid trenches, sewing gas masks. I've been working as a runner. I have shifts serving tea to the soldiers. I walk around and collect food for the soldiers. In a word, I'm fighting alongside the rest of the Polish nation. I'm fighting and I'll win.[86]

In Nałęczów, shortly after dinner that evening, the Polish vice minister for foreign affairs, Count Jan Szembek, an experienced diplomat close to Foreign Minister Beck, met with Biddle, French ambassador Léon Noël, and British ambassador Sir Howard Kennard. German armor was less than twelve miles away, and there was no time to waste. Nałęczów, proving an unsafe location for the Foreign Ministry and the Diplomatic Corps, served as only a thirty-hour layover. The ministry, said Szembek, would retreat to Łuck to meet up with the prime minister and the president, who were forced from Brześć. The Diplomatic Corps would now join the "Phantom Train" and a horde of refugees in attempting to reach Krzemieniec, nearly three hundred miles to the east and within eighteen miles of the Soviet border. If the diplomats reached the Volhynian city, "a picturesque little town of bright painted fretwork houses on the side of a hill," it would be the end of the line, as further retreat was not possible.[87] At 11:00 p.m. the first small group of cars left the lovely spa town, with the rest following at intervals. Headlights covered in blue cloth, a waning moon, blacked-out towns, large Polish army movements, and clouds of white dust from the long summer drought that covered the windshields made driving a challenge.[88] Regardless of the difficulties, travel was safer than during the day, as the Luftwaffe did not fly at night. Refueling in Łuck, in the early morning on the outskirts of Dubno, the "death caravan" sought shelter in a grove of trees as the Luftwaffe attacked the city's railyards.[89] The daily bombing runs occurred roughly every two hours as the planes flew from bases in Slovakia and East Prussia and created intervals of relative safety. Now not far from their destination, the diplomats and accompanying journalists pushed on, hoping not to be killed by Stuka strafing runs or by Dornier bombers nicknamed "flying pencils." Someone in the caravan realized that when aircraft approached, the car radios would make a clicking sound. A quick glance out the window would confirm the early warning if the refugees or those working in the fields looked to the sky. When they did, the passengers would scramble from the vehicles and race to the woods or lie on their backs in the ditches alongside the road to "keep an eye on the plane. If the plane went on, we would immediately shift backwards or forwards from our positions in case the pilot returned with the idea of machine-gunning the spot whereat he had originally marked us."[90] Biddle and his charges, sleepless and covered in dust, arrived in Krzemeiniec intact at 10:30 a.m. on the morning of September 7. Margaret Biddle recalled, "Peg and I curled up on the floor on a blanket, used our jackets for pillows and our fur coats over us and slept for an hour and a half in spite of carpenters fixing doors that wouldn't shut, chairs being brought in, floors being washed, and our Jewish landlords issuing orders in Yiddish! I can truthfully say I've never slept better or enjoyed anything more!"[91]

While Margaret and Peggy slept in the arms of Morpheus, Julien Bryan, in Warsaw, was wondering why he'd decided to come to Poland. A photographer who, for the past several summers, had made documentary films, photos, and slides of rural life in Europe, he found he still had a large amount of film and time before the *Queen Mary* sailed for the States. War would likely soon break out in Poland, but he reasoned that he could slip in, capture a city on the edge, and leave before he was in danger. Departing Venice by train on September 1, Bryan was in Cernăuți on September 3 when he learned the Germans had invaded Poland and the British and French had declared war. The train had been in Poland but fifteen minutes when it was first bombed.[92] As the passengers scrambled into ditches and hid behind trees, they were not "frightened, but only thrilled and excited."[93] After several more raids, the passengers decided it was safer to stay inside the steel rail cars and lie on the floor. The rush of excitement had dissipated—all aboard realized that if the planes scored a direct hit, many would be killed or wounded. A trip that usually took twelve hours now took seventy-two. No food was available on the train, but "at every station pretty girls from the Polish Red Cross came out with tea and soup and bread and sometimes fruit. The food was for the soldiers, yet because we were hungry they generously gave it to us. We tried to pay them, but they laughed and shook their heads. This was a gift of the Red Cross. They could take no money."[94]

By the time the train's occupants arrived on the outskirts of the city at 1:00 a.m. on September 7, the East Station was blanketed in darkness. What light there was came from "small oil lamps . . . covered with dark blue paper," which cast eerie shadows on the wall and floors.[95] Luckily, a Polish soldier commanded a droshky to take Bryan to the posh Hotel Europejski, a favorite haunt of the Biddles, other diplomats, Polish elites, journalists, and tourists. Rooms were available, and when Bryan asked the price, the desk clerk shrugged his shoulders. He was in a hot bath for just a few minutes when the air raid sirens went off, forcing him to hurry to the basement shelter. In the morning, with no taxis or droshkies available, he managed the long walk to the American embassy. Bryan, always keen to note the ironies of war, passed a bookstore with a Polish copy of *Mein Kampf* displayed in the window. Inside the embassy compound, he asked the secretary whether he might see the ambassador. Shocked, he learned that Biddle and the government had left the city two days before.[96] The news photographers and cameramen had gone with them. Bryan pondered his predicament but then realized, "Here I was, face to face with the kind of scoop every photographer and newspaperman dreams about."[97] Like Clare Hollingworth, he would make the most of his opportunity and luckily live to tell the story.

Needing permission to shoot photographs and to film or risk being shot, he walked into Mayor Stephan Starzyński's office, pitched his proposal to the secretary, and was granted an audience. The mayor was excited to have what was happening in Warsaw be documented and shown to the world. Throughout the siege the plucky mayor broadcast daily to his fellow Varsovians, encouraging them—reassuring them that Warsaw would not surrender: "Destiny has committed to us the duty of defending Poland's honor."[98] The British *Daily Mail* honored his determination with the nickname "Stubborn Stephan."[99] To accomplish his task, Bryan was given a "little German car, camouflaged with mud and silver paint" and a Polish officer to serve as guide and interpreter.[100] Later, he would be assisted by two Polish American college exchange students who had moved into the basement of the embassy: Stanley Kubicz and John Petrowski. Assistance likewise came from William C. McDonald, an American engineer who for seven years had managed road construction projects for the Warren Brothers Company of Cambridge, Massachusetts. He had volunteered his services shortly after the war began—he spoke fluent Polish, possessed a car, and was well connected to Polish wholesalers and suppliers. He was so valuable that he was added to the staff as a "dollar-a-year" man.[101] Fearless, McDonald, who knew the city well, made forays from the embassy under shell fire to obtain food. Consul staffer Douglas Jenkins Jr. oversaw the embassy commissary and, with the aid of McDonald and his Polish helper Talmant, built up reserves of flour, rice, and butter. On a September 15 food run, McDonald and Talmant "barely escaped a shell that landed only fifty feet behind their car. But they brought back a barrel of butter."[102] Consul General John K. Davis, in his written report on the first twenty-one days of the war, commended McDonald's bravery and asked the department to recognize his contributions.[103]

Traveling through the city, Bryan and his assistants encountered one horrific scene after another. On photographing an apartment building hit by a five-hundred-pound bomb, he scribbled in his notebook, "Bodies are not pleasant sights under any circumstances, and when they are of young women, torn to pieces . . . and sometimes without heads or arms or legs, they are horrible to behold."[104] In front of another bombed-out apartment building, he witnessed a surreal scene: "A mother was sitting on the ground peeling potatoes. A girl of seventeen had found a mirror and was primping beside the ruins of her home. Two little boys were reading a Polish edition of a Mickey Mouse Sunday color supplement. Fourteen dead horses were lying in the middle of the street. Volunteer brigades were coming to cover them with lime and then drag them away and bury them. Twenty feet from the horses lay ten people."[105]

The daily nightmares visited on the city recorded by Professor Polonius in his diary, *I Saw the Siege of Warsaw*, added to the work undertaken by Bryan, though Polonius's experiences were captured in words rather than photographs. In the Frascati Gardens, a woodland housing development that became an emergency cemetery, he had volunteered for a burial detail, describing what he called the hecatomb of Warsaw:

> To-day we had a consignment of some seventy corpses of both sexes. They were brought in wheelbarrows and carts, heads and limbs dangling and shaking as the carts jolted over the uneven ground. Some were badly mangled, others without heads, and each load was tipped unceremoniously on the ground. The most disgusting part of the job was the identification of the victims. We had to search through the pockets of their blood-soiled coats and in the women's handbags. About two-thirds passed straight from the morgue into the collective grave unidentified. . . . So nauseating was the stench of the bodies that one of the digging party put on his gas mask, and it was a real relief when we had finished and could walk off hurriedly and sit down to recover and to forget.[106]

On the way home, Polonius commented that the new YMCA building was in the neighborhood and that it was due to Paul Super, whom he called "an American friend of Poland and especially of the younger generation."[107] Polonius would not be surprised to learn that Super, the American friend, had a few days earlier crossed into Romania and was hard at work setting up a relief program for Polish military and civilian refugees. Occasionally, when in need of a respite from his tortured environment, he stopped by the well-known Ziemiańska café, a remnant of its former splendor, for tea, ersatz coffee, and whatever the management could still offer, to exchange information, gossip, speculate when the British bombers would arrive, and discover whether friends and acquaintances were still alive.[108]

The air attack on Warsaw now intensified and was accompanied by a twenty-four-hour-a-day artillery barrage that was reducing the city to rubble. The German ring closing in on the capital was anything but rosy, but the Poles contested the Germans at every point. Strategically positioned, their antitank guns took a fearsome toll on Nazi armor. Nevertheless, the noose tightened. An additional source of injury threatened those moving about the city, as they were sometimes injured or burned by shrapnel from the exploding antiaircraft shells fired from Polish flak guns. Worse, the city was running out of food. "Hunger was already staring out of people's eyes."[109] Humans and animals suffered alike. Horses killed in the action were set on by people with knives and stripped to the bone. Large flocks of disoriented pigeons could find no safe space to roost and sometimes ended up on a dinner plate. Lost or abandoned dogs that roamed the railroad stations and streets in search of their owners began to disappear. Families were forced to decide whether they could maintain themselves and their pets when the order came that allowed only one dog per household. The Polonius family chose to leave their aunt's center-city apartment to avoid the concentrated bombing attacks and return to their home in the southern suburbs, even though they would be close to the defensive trench line. On arrival, they soon learned that of their three much-loved dogs, two had been destroyed: Orla, a white sheepdog, and Pecca, an Airedale. No chloroform or poison was available, and the gardener had refused to kill the dogs. Finally, a man had been found who hanged them for ten shillings.[110]

Amid the ongoing battle, Bryan and his team covered every corner of the city and, between September 9 and 20, recorded the horrors inflicted by the relentless bombing. Many of his photographs have become some of the most widely viewed images from the war. Perhaps his most famous is the photo of ten-year-old Kazimiera Mika attempting to grasp the death of her older sister, who was machine-gunned by a Stuka while digging potatoes in a field. Day by day Bryan came to realize that the night he had arrived at the East Station, the droshky had not carried him across the Vistula, but rather across the river Styx into a macabre underworld of fire and death.

Evacuated during a truce on September 21, walking across a no-man's-land among twelve hundred other evacuees, including McDonald, Bryan put down his suitcase to help a woman with a baby. Turning back, he found his suitcase with his photographs was gone. Miraculously, a day later in Königsberg, the missing suitcase was in the hotel lobby. In an effort to secure his treasures, he hid three rolls of film he thought the most important in the canister of another passenger's souvenir gas mask. Bryan took off his shirt and wrapped the processed reels of film around his waist,

Kazimiera Mika (ten) grieves over the body of her sister Andzia (fourteen) (photo by Julien Bryan; courtesy of United States Holocaust Memorial Museum).

though his suitcase still contained a wealth of photos that included ten Kodachrome slides, the only color photos of the siege.[111] Confronting the German sergeant minding the evacuees, he demanded his passport, saying he had to catch a train that would soon leave for Stockholm. Much to his surprise, it was handed to him. Bryan stopped over in Riga and, with the help of the embassy, dictated his Warsaw story, sending a portion by cable to the United States; in Stockholm he sent the rest. Sailing from Bergen on a Norwegian ship, Bryan realized while lounging on the ship's deck that he had never received a bill for his hotel stay. His good fortune continued, as his ship was not torpedoed by a German submarine. He landed in New York on October 7, his incredible journey over. It would be many years before Bryan returned to Poland.

Bryan's photographs were an instant success, as was his lecture tour. His photos and films documented the siege of Warsaw and supported reports made by Biddle and others. Biddle's American "death caravan" included several photojournalists and cameramen who captured the destruction of Polish cities and the plight of the refugees. Combined with Bryan's photos and films of Warsaw's systematic destruction, these images ensured no one could doubt the atrocities Germans had visited on the Poles right from the start. Nor could one doubt Poland's dire need of assistance, which was clear for all to see. It also took little imagination for those viewing Bryan's photos and listening to his talks to comprehend what would happen to the Allies if Hitler attacked in the West. The visual record was like an update of Francisco Goya's *The Horrors of War* and H. G. Wells's predictions of disaster in his novel *The Shape of Things to Come*.

Meanwhile, in Lublin, British consul Thwaites and his journalist companion Hollingworth received word from Nałęczów on the evening of September 6 that the embassy was leaving for Krzemieniec. They were to follow. Early the next morning, their two cars got underway. For hours they maneuvered through the peasant carts and pedestrians until, once beyond the tangled mass, they were able to increase their speed. Ahead was car traffic. To her relief, Hollingworth saw the Union Jack and the flags of other nations flying from vehicles enmeshed in the slow-moving column. Reaching Łuck, Hollingworth left the caravan and "found a bed in a monastic college." She planned to cable her stories to London, but the next morning she was forced to relinquish her scarce accommodations when the Polish General Staff arrived from Warsaw.[112] Her stories would have to wait. Thwaites found her a place on an estate some distance from the city. After two days, Hollingworth returned to Łuck, a city being blown apart by repeated bombing attacks. The citizenry blamed the destruction on the British, who had failed to come to Poland's aid. Attempts to wire her stories to London were unsuccessful. She suspected sabotage.

Word that the panzers were closing in again persuaded her to join fellow journalists and diplomats who had reached Krzemieniec. Undertaking the journey during daylight hours was risky, but aside from a bombing in Dubno, Hollingworth arrived safely at her destination. Irrepressible and fearless in her determination to get the news, she floated the idea of making a run back to Warsaw over dinner on her first night in Krzemieniec. "You're nuts" was the reaction of the listeners, but the more she talked, the more they came around to the daring proposal. Several British citizens had been left behind. Would she attempt to bring them back with her? The answer was yes. Several hours later, after rounding up a sufficient reserve of gasoline, Hollingworth set forth in the dark, driving west through the hordes of refugees to a Warsaw under siege.

Unbeknownst to Hollingworth, the German panzers had crossed the Vistula at several points and were rapidly moving east. Her chances of evading these spearheads depended once more on her "luck of the Irish." The retreating Polish army in desperation attempted to establish a defensive line on the Bug River. All along the potential line from Lublin north to Białystok, thousands filed into the roads, blending in with the masses moving east to avoid the coming battle and escape the advancing Wehrmacht. At Adampol, fifty miles northeast of Lublin, the large, aristocratic Zamoyski family, which traced its ancestry and land grant back to 1331, was offered refuge by Isabella Radziwill, a visiting cousin, on the huge Mankiewicze estate near the Russian border, the same estate in the Pripet Marshes where De Wiart had spent many happy years. The family, fifty in number, including servants, formulated a strategy for making the three-hundred-mile trip. The old and the young were to travel in the family's four cars and leave as soon as it was dark. The remaining thirty adults were to leave at first light in a caravan of horse-drawn wagons. The four-car motorcade left as scheduled, drove all night, and in the morning continued on rather than seek shelter. The cars slowed and then came to a stop, as ahead a large truck had overturned, blocking the road. While stuck in the line of waiting vehicles, Christine Zamoyska-Panek recalled that there came "from the sky, a crescendo of roaring motors."[113] As all scrambled from the cars seeking shelter, she continued,

> I turned my head just enough to see the German planes descend; they almost touch the church steeple. I cover my head. Now only sounds. *Tatatatatatatata*, machine guns. They stop for a moment, and then *tatatatatata*. After the second pass the sounds diminish; the planes, decreasing in size, fly toward the horizon. Silence, then a broken sob. I look. Red stains on her white dress, a little girl is lying very still. She was too small to run. I have never seen a dead child before.[114]

Five days later, the harried Zamoyskis reached Mankiewicze to find that the situation was very much like the one they had left at Adampol: "The palace filled beyond capacity with refugees, boxes and homeless dogs."[115] There was no word of the wagon caravan.

Throughout the evacuation to Krzemieniec from Nałęczów, Biddle demonstrated initiative and leadership as he arranged for accommodations for his staff, scouted a location for the embassy to halfway function, and assisted others in the Diplomatic Corps. He emerged as a spokesperson for the corps in dealing with the Polish Foreign Office, "the only person consulted by all."[116] In his cables to Washington over the next several days, he continued to document incidents of Luftwaffe bombing of civilians. His compilation included a refugee train bombed; a bomb that destroyed a Girl Guide hut, killing twelve young girls near the East Station in Warsaw; and a hospital train with red crosses painted on the roof that was bombed while unloading the wounded.[117]

Colonel Stansilaw Sosabowski, later commander of the First Polish Independent Parachute Brigade, told of another attack on a hospital train as described by his doctor son aboard a Red Cross train on its way to Warsaw in the first two weeks of the war. German bombers had intentionally attacked the train "in broad daylight, in spite of the large red crosses painted on the tops and sides. It had been hit at one end and the chief doctor had run off in frenzy and disappeared. A few of the staff, including some nurses, had been killed, but the train and the medical supplies were mostly all right."[118] The rails in front and behind the train were destroyed, but fortunately engineers managed to repair the track, and the train proceeded to Warsaw.

Biddle, sincere in his efforts, had only scratched the surface of the atrocities being committed by the Wehrmacht and the Schutzstaffel (SS). The ambassador was yet unaware of the destruction of Wieluń in an aerial assault on the opening day of the war. He could not know that while he was preparing cables to Washington, hundreds were being executed in Bydgoszcz, and in Końskie a group of Jews were rounded up to dig a grave for German soldiers whose bodies had been mutilated. A German major intervened on seeing the Jews being beaten and mistreated as they worked and ordered them released. As the Jews left, a different officer fired two shots. "General firing broke out, and in the chaos twenty-two Jews were killed."[119] By chance, the famous movie director Leni Riefenstahl (maker of *The Triumph of the Will* and *Olympiad*) and her crew, there shooting a documentary on the Polish campaign, witnessed the murders. A photo captures their horrified reaction as they are forced to see the true nature of the Third Reich. While the film was never produced, Riefenstahl and her crew clearly knew they were not in Kitzbühel anymore. To the Wehrmacht's credit, the lieutenant who fired the first shot was court-martialed and received a prison sentence, but the question remains as to why atrocities like those at Końskie and Bydgoszcz persisted throughout the Polish campaign. Soldiers, new to combat, were urged on by propaganda and admonished by Hitler to show no mercy, and there was no uniform response on the part of commanders to violence and looting. In some units there was an overall lack of discipline, whereas other units intentionally took part in murder; in short, the army was out of control, indoctrinated with hatred of the Slavs and taught that most of the territory invaded was rightfully theirs.

Leni Riefenstahl and crew witness killing of Jews at Końskie (courtesy of Alamy).

For the next several days, Biddle and his staff were able to communicate with Washington, look for missing Americans still thought to be on the roads, and gather information about the German advance. Early in the morning on September 10, Biddle "walked to the heighth of the mountain adjacent to and overlooking the town of Krzemieniec."[120] Gazing down into the village, he noticed that the sunlight reflected off the roofs and chrome trim of the diplomats' cars—an invitation to a Luftwaffe attack. He descended the hill and ordered a lean-to constructed to shelter the vehicles. All were painted gray and, for a good measure, further camouflaged by scattering buckets of dust on the wet paint.[121] The yellow "U.S.A." remained on the roof of his once-yellow Cadillac.

The camouflage job completed, Biddle lunched with Soviet ambassador Nikolai Charanov, his wife and two children, and his military attaché. They were joined by Estonian minister Marcus. Charanov revealed he had received a report that the Wehrmacht was approaching Lwów and that large-scale Soviet mobilization was taking place along the Polish border. Biddle asked whether the Soviets feared that the city, on capture, would be declared the capital of an independent Ukrainian state, a vassal of Berlin. Charanov answered off the record that was probably the reason. The Russian ambassador may not have known that Hitler and Stalin had already agreed on partition when the two dictators signed the Nazi-Soviet nonaggression pact, or he simply misled Biddle. Biddle, too, did not know the secret details of the Machiavellian agreement.

Later that afternoon, the "Phantom Train" miraculously arrived. Counselor Wrszlacki recounted to eager listeners that the "ghost train" had been attacked seventy-two times, and no one had been injured. Crang, in a piece for the *News Chronicle*, wrote of the price paid by those onboard the train:

> Time after time the passengers left the carriage in terror and hid in the fields and woods and ditches. Once, when the bombers reappeared overhead, women and children escaped by lying down in swamps inches deep in water until the planes had passed. So terrified became the passengers that the slightest noise caused people to jump from the train. At each station one saw passengers, unable to bear the strain any longer, disappear into the woods and not emerge again. A judge in Poland's highest tribunal, who travelled in the same carriage with me, left the train with his wife, preferring to remain in the fields rather than continue his journey. After each bombing fewer passengers remained in the train. Those who remained had their nerves shattered, particularly women and children. Food and water were completely unobtainable, and people were fainting from exhaustion. The most pitiable sight was the little white faced, terror stricken children trying to hide themselves to escape bombing. Their cries are still ringing in my ears. For four days the trains wandered from place to place . . . finally [getting] to Krzemieniec.[122]

On hearing the gruesome tale of the "ghost train," the Biddles and the embassy staff knew that the decision to caravan, risky as it was, had been the right one.

Foreign Minister Beck arrived mid-morning on September 11 to brief diplomats on the military situation. He and Mrs. Beck had had a nightmarish trip from Brześć, as each town they passed through was bombed. Beck's wife swore the Germans always knew where they were and were trying to kill them. Beck told the assembled diplomats that Germany had violated its agreement of September 2 not to bomb open cities and nonmilitary targets. In a conversation jointly with British ambassador Kennard and French ambassador Noël, he asked them to push their governments to start bombing German "aircraft factories or railway junctions."[123] In a meeting with Biddle, Beck admitted that Poland was on its last legs and that, without the support of Britain and France, time was running out. The Polish high command hoped to establish a defensive line across the funnel of Poland, a redoubt, a Romanian bridgehead, into which army units could pour. Scattered and partially destroyed units and as many as seventeen intact divisions were moving toward the southeast corner. But that line, if established, could hold only if supplied from Romania and if the British and French attacked in the West in sufficient force to draw off some of the German units. During the night word arrived from Lwów that Wehrmacht armored columns were moving south and east in an effort to cut off the government and keep Polish troops from reaching the Romanian border. "As a result, Minister Beck gave orders to mobilize all government officials for a conference in the morning."[124]

The next day, Biddle and the Diplomatic Corps had an undeniable answer as to whether the Luftwaffe had intentionally bombed open cities and villages. Four bombers started their run on the edge of town and laid down a string of bombs as they followed Krzemieniec's main street. The damage was horrific: sixteen killed, including several children; forty seriously injured; and the town ablaze and without water to fight the spreading fires. Hollingworth, back in Krzemieniec, had not reached Warsaw and barely escaped capture by a German infantry company by driving "madly across the fields … running over farm meadows, bumping across maize-stubble, rolling into rutted tracks, with springs creaking."[125] As she drove down the main street, the damage she observed was horrid: "The ballet-set was broken, the gay sugar-stick fronts were cracked, balconies sagged, roofs had been beaten in. Some of the houses were a pile of sticks and stones, where people were still digging for their dead."[126] Shortly after the bombing, Edward J. Thrasher, the military attaché's code clerk, and Vice Consul Morton arrived amid the devastation, having survived a horrendous drive from Polish military headquarters in Brześć. Guided to the community hall, in the basement of a school, where the diplomats of all nations dined together, the code clerk recalled, "Ambassador Biddle welcomed me warmly . . . and I sat down . . . at the [c]rude table with him, Mrs. Biddle, their daughter, and Okay, their huge mastiff. All, including Okay, dined off tea, black bread, and *kassa* [kasha]."[127] For Thrasher, it was good to be back with the embassy personnel under the firm hand of Ambassador Biddle, a man he much admired.

The outspoken papal nuncio Monsignor Phillippe Cortesi, outraged by the German bombing attack on a declared open city, approached Biddle and requested his support for a meeting of all the neutral mission chiefs, who would compose a letter of protest to be sent to the pope and to their heads of state. Biddle concurred, pledging his support as long as the protest was not political and stating that he was an "objective observer of what had taken place and on humanitarian grounds."[128] At the meeting held in the bleachers of a soccer field, Monsignor Cortesi explained his proposal and asked each of the neutral diplomats to sign the collective statement, which Cardinal Hlond would deliver to the pope. Biddle spoke on behalf of the papal nuncio's proposal and urged all in attendance to sign. The Turkish ambassador vouched his support as well and had barely concluded his remarks when, one after another, the Italian ambassador and the Spanish, Bulgarian, and Swiss ministers all forcefully stated they would not support such a document. The opposition of the Italian and Spanish ministers surprised no one participating in the meeting, but Biddle was particularly perturbed by the comments of the Swiss minister and lost his temper, berating him for his failure to join in the protest. Hollingworth, observing the mashup, thought that, given Bulgaria's precarious international position, its objection was understandable, but she agreed with Biddle that the Swiss vote was unacceptable. "Switzerland," she wrote, "is the home of the Red Cross, the habitat of the League. Switzerland leads the world in good works. Indeed, the Swiss now tell us that only neutrals can do relief work in war-time, and that they are the only neutral equipped to do it. Just our money is needed, and that of the Americans."[129] Ironically, on two occasions during the debate, the would-be protesters were driven into air raid trenches by low-flying German aircraft, though no bombs were dropped. The Swedish minister, embarrassed, recounted, "We crawled out together, when the all-clear siren sounded, like dirty and naughty schoolboys, trying to look as though we were not afraid."[130] The question put to a vote was approved. Afterward, in conversations with a number of the diplomats, Hollingworth "heard no praise" for Switzerland, "one of the most pharisaical nations on earth."[131] The protest letter failed to achieve unanimity, but it was important as a first collective step on record by neutral nations to protest the bombing of declared open cities and aerial assaults on civilians, which were clearly violations of international law and of Germany's pledge not to do so. The letter's authenticity derived from the signers' firsthand experience of being bombed and witnessing the destruction of Polish cities on their cross-country trek. Exposing Germany's brutal conquest also countered its propaganda to the contrary and warned of what could be expected if the war continued. "Because the diplomats were there," Hollingworth explained, "this became the *bombardment célèbre* of the war. It was one of Hitler's affronts to the world, meant to daze and stun, to kill incipient opposition by a blow to the face. The poor diplomats did not understand; but the method had been known to drinkshop bullies for centuries."[132] The Germans surmised that the diplomats would soon cross into Romania, taking with them a lesson on what German armed forces were capable of delivering.

After the tense meeting, when the chatter had died down and the participants drifted away, Hollingworth sought out her friends in the rump British embassy, who huddled together in a barely lit room drinking gin mixed with cherry jam to hear her story of the failed attempt to reach Warsaw. One of those friends eager to hear of her adventures was the wife of Counselor Clifford Norton, Nöel Evelyn Hughes, who went by the name of Peter. It is said that in the dark the stars come out, and throughout the anxious days of retreat one of those stars was Peter Norton. Like Hollingworth, she was unafraid and possessed of seemingly endless stores of energy. Like Biddle, she assumed a leadership role among the diplomats helping to organize the caravan, driving the couple's Plymouth on the bombed-out roads at night and making sure everyone had food, and she was resourceful in caging supplies in Polish cities and villages and tending the wounded after the bombing raid on Krzemieniec. Peter Norton was everywhere all at once. Prior to going to Poland with her husband in 1938, she was one of the women art gallerists who brought Modernism to London—the Bauhaus to your house. She shared with Hollingworth a deep concern for the refugees she witnessed daily as the diplomatic caravan worked its way through the crowded roads. Both women were self-assured and unflappable.

The gin and cherry jam heightened expectations. Hollingworth did not disappoint. She opened her wild tale with graphic accounts of the refugees being machine-gunned by the Stukas:

> Two fighters came into view, diving at the road. The peasants hurled themselves desperately to either side, a confusion of running figures, of flinging skirts, overturned carts and prams and baggage. Flat in the fields, they covered their heads in a fold of coat or sacking, with the ostrich-impulse of terror. The gallant fliers roared over, raking the road and fields with fire. A horse dropped and lay kicking. When most of the peasants returned to the road, ten minutes later, I noticed that half a dozen lay on their sides, their heads under a fold of sacking.[133]

Hollingworth continued to hold the rapt attention of her listeners as she described the refugees she encountered on every road:

> There were few carts on the road now, but I must have met thousands of refugees, most of them travelling on foot. There are signs which anyone who has been concerned with refugees knows well, when the cost of flight becomes too high. The individual feels that the events have overwhelmed him. He has given up all hope of reaching safety; as a person he hardly exists at all, but as a human mechanism he goes on functioning, dragging, in the mass, blindly on. There were still children among those I saw, loaded two and three into prams, dragging further and further behind and becoming lost or abandoned.[134]

From the beginning of the war, Hollingworth's reportage paid particular attention to the plight of the refugees. In Katowice, she briefly mentioned that evacuating British subjects was not comparable to the all-but-impossible task before Mrs. Dougan, who had come from Prague to protect more than a thousand refugees from throughout the expanding territories of the Third Reich. Hollingworth's concern for their welfare and her knowledge of their suffering, the heartbreaking decisions of life and death, were acquired firsthand, as a month earlier the job had been hers.[135] The British Committee for Refugees from Czechoslovakia (BCRC) had asked her to go to Gdynia to aid 451 refugees hustled aboard the last train out of Prague hours before the Germans swept in on March 15, 1939.[136] The BCRC wanted Hollingworth, as her reputation preceded her. She was well known and well spoken, an experienced writer, who had long worked with the League of Nations Union (LNU) and its "peace ballot" project. Her politics were solidly leftist, and, through the organization's refugee committee, she had successfully lobbied for aid to German and Austrian refugees seeking safety in German-speaking areas of Czechoslovakia. Hollingworth agreed to help the desperate people in Gdynia and immediately left by train for Brussels. There she was given money, plus 180 Belgian visas and a hodgepodge of others for a number of countries. Back on the train, she arrived in Berlin and then flew to Gdynia. On arrival she made sure the refugees on her list had all arrived, been fed, and found a place to stay. All but two, who would have to wait for additional visas to arrive within the week, boarded ships to various ports.[137]

Successful, she was asked to go to Katowice, close to the German border, a city in which Czech, Austrian, and German refugees congregated, begging for rescue. Each night a hundred or more escapees avoided detection and slipped into Poland. Kraków, too, faced a refugee crisis, so Hollingworth asked London for help, and the committee sent Hermann Field, of the notorious Field family of Communists.[138] Over the next four months, she worked tirelessly, helping three thousand people to pass through Poland. Her ongoing registered list of approximately one thousand refugees, supplied with identification cards with her signature and that of British consul general Thwaites, provided some protection against Polish raids and deportations back to Germany. This list functioned much like Oskar Schindler's did later in the war. To arrange a rescue, Hollingworth would go to almost any lengths. She dressed refugees in various disguises, had them carry chickens aboard trains, and created a code to confuse those who listened to her telephone conversations or read her mail. The British press tagged her the "Scarlet Pimpernel."[139] Unlike the average relief worker, Hollingworth, due to her years in the LNU, had a wide array of official, political, and press connections in many countries. She persuaded the LNU's deputy high commissioner for refugees, Dr. G. Kullmann, to come to Poland and observe the situation. He met with Polish officials and arranged for refugees not to be deported and for the BCRC to be allowed to give them aid, a gentleman's agreement.[140]

By July, Nazi agents had infiltrated Hollingworth's organization; her zealous tactics threatened the operation of BCRC in Prague, as the Gestapo wanted to know how those in her care got to Katowice. MI-5 and MI-6 were concerned about the large number of Communists and Social Democrats granted visas and the escape of nearly the entire leadership of the Sudeten Communist Party through Poland; the Passport Control Office found block visas to be a scandal. While she had succeeded magnificently, her return to London was demanded. Amazingly, in her bull session with friends that night in Krzemieniec, she held forth on her close encounters with the Germans and on the vicious and senseless attacks on Polish cities and fleeing refugees, but no mention was made of her previous humanitarian work within Gdynia and Katowice. That silence continued later in several books, which barely mentioned her relief work.[141] Only after her death did her nephew and biographer, Patrick Garrett, reveal the names of Communists working in the relief organizations in Katowice, Kraków, and Prague, a subject she did not talk or write about and a discovery he made by examining MI-5 and MI-6 records in the British National Archives.

To the Poles and the diplomats' dismay, the military situation continued to deteriorate. The Foreign Office, in the promised morning briefing on September 13, ordered the corps to evacuate to Zaleszczyki, 155 miles to the south on the Dniester. This warmest city in Poland was a resort famous for its beaches, fine restaurants, cafés, wines, and fruits, especially apricots, all celebrated in poetry and prose—a place of ample sunshine for "healers, frail, lightly ill with chest, physical and nervous weakness, seeking peace and rest."[142] Well-heeled vacationers clambered aboard the fastest train in Poland, the Luxtorpeda, which traversed the

375 miles in four and a half hours. In September 1939, the city of sun and fun was jammed with refugees—perhaps as many as one hundred thousand—waiting to cross the international bridge into Romania. Preparing to leave for this resort on the Dniester, Biddle, as he had done on previous evacuations, carefully organized the American motorcade, ensuring sufficient gasoline before leaving at night.

For those in eastern Poland now facing the rapidly advancing German army, it was their turn to join those from the western and central provinces in making a run for the Romanian border, to tread the road to Zaleszczyki. Later, Poles who had stayed behind would say of all those who fled the Germans and the Soviets, usually accusingly, that they had taken "the road to Zaleszczyki." To the northwest of Lwów, on the family estate near Rawa Ruska, Princess Virgilia Sapieha, an American woman married to a titled Polish aristocrat, was one of many landed gentry who opened their villas and castles to voluntarily feed and house soldiers and refugees moving east. Eventually they were overwhelmed by those in exodus, their resources depleted. In the evening, she, her mother-in-law, the chatelaine, and the estate manager pondered the fates of those filling the roads. "Where could they go? Who would feed them? The still, bright night came, and the shadows of the forest closed around us. Deep in there, the hares and foxes, the deer and wild boar cuddled down among the warm leaves in the underbrush. Even when winter came, they would know what to eat and where to sleep. But these new inhabitants of the forest, these restive human families moving among the trees, were helpless."[143] A few nights later, her disheveled husband burst in, telling her she must wake the children, pack, and leave immediately. A little after 10:00 p.m., in two cars, the family drove toward Lwów. Later, she recalled,

> At first the night concealed everything. We had to drive without lights, so the familiar road and fields were a black blur against which I could distinguish nothing. Then I began to see that the night was alive. People shuffled along on foot, carrying bundles. Trucks stood still at the sides of the road, piled high with the gray shapes of sleeping figures. Small cars crept along with branches strewn over their roofs as camouflage. Everywhere, something moved in the dark.[144]

As they approached Lwów, the sky was red from the burning buildings. In the city, though it was the middle of the night, the streets were crowded. Her husband awakened the Romanian consul and retrieved their visas. Saying good-bye, he kissed the children, ordered the chauffeurs to drive straight through, and left to join his military unit. As the car sped south, they were forced to stop at checkpoints. Looking out the window, Sapieha saw "people about us, lying under bushes and in the ditches."[145] By mid-morning they had reached the frontier and safety. Not long after, the German conquerors left Rawa Ruska, turning it over to the Russians. With the arrival of the Red Army, Ukrainian peasants looted the estate.

The American convoy leaving Krzemieniec reached Tarnopol in the middle of the night to discover the city had been heavily bombed earlier in the day. The blackout, recalled Biddle, was "so intense that I found it necessary to walk in front of the car, with one hand on the radiator cap, and feel my way along, calling back directions to Mr. Moszczyński at the wheel of my car. It took us well over an hour to traverse the comparatively small city."[146] At 2:30 a.m. on September 14, without further incident, the motorcade arrived at its destination to find no accommodations available. In a park, relatively safe under trees, the Americans hunkered down in their cars for the night. The location was actually a part of an old estate and stood empty. After permission was obtained, beds were rounded up, staff quartered, and an outdoor embassy established. The following morning, after three and a half hours of sleep, the "embassy on the lawn" enjoyed breakfast prepared on a kerosene stove. Beck and the Foreign Office, after leaving Krzemieniec, changed plans, passed up Zaleszczyki, passed up Śniatyń, and drove on to Kuty farther to the west. The bridge spanning the Dniester in Zaleszczyki was an inviting target. If it was brought down, the Foreign Office and the Diplomatic Corps risked capture. An added threat was the massing of the Red Army on the Polish border only a short distance away. The low wooden bridge on the Czeremosz river in Kuty, built in the early 1930s by the Polish army, was much more difficult to hit from the air. Just as important, Rydz and his general staff, struggling to organize the bridgehead, were headquartered much closer in Kołomyja, twenty-seven miles to the north.

Ambassador Anthony Biddle and the "Death Caravan" prepare to leave Zaleszczyki (photo by Mary McKenzie; courtesy of Ossolinski National Institute, Wrocław).

Early in the morning, Hollingworth and a car crammed with British diplomats and staff left Krzemieniec, stopped in Tarnopol to breakfast with the British Military Mission and pick up what news they could, and drove on to Zaleszczyki. Ambassador Kennard was to follow but by evening had not shown up. The following morning, all were gravely concerned that the worst had happened. Just before lunch, to the relief of all, news arrived with Beck's aide that the British ambassador was safe. He had decided midway not to come to Zaleszczyki but to veer off, following Beck and the Polish Foreign Office to Kuty. He had had no way to communicate his decision and regretted having caused such anxiety as to his safety.

While Beck's aide brought news of the British ambassador, he was there to ask Biddle whether he would cross the border and establish a communication relay center in Cernăuți and then come to Kuty, and not bring his staff, as food and lodging were in short supply. Soon after, the first of the Diplomatic Corps, including much of the American staff, crossed the bridge and traveled on to Cernăuți and Bucharest. That afternoon, Biddle prepared a cable for Washington outlining the horrific examples of German bombing and strafing conveyed to him the previous day by Beck. He added his wife's experience and that of American military attaché Maj. William H. Colbern, a fearless redheaded Missourian, who had left Warsaw several days after Biddle and seen the damage inflicted on the cities of Siedlce and Brześć. The ambassador speculated on how towns and cities of the future would have to "undertake a radical re-vamping in terms of physical layout" in an attempt to avoid destruction from the air.[147] As in his past cables, Biddle, information starved, gave only a glimpse of the partial damage done to Polish cities. Julien Bryan's caustic suggestion that the destruction of Warsaw be presented to German gymnasium students in algebra word problems framed what Biddle had continually reported to Washington:

> *Question*: If in a Polish town there are ten thousand civilians and five hundred soldiers defending the town, and the German fliers drop a hundred bombs, each killing five people, and if the bombs are dropped indiscriminately over the town, killing the same proportion of civilians as soldiers—how many dead people will there be when the German pilots return to their base?
>
> *Answer*: Four hundred and seventy-five dead civilians, including fifty babies, and only twenty-five soldiers.[148]

That evening the ambassador dined with those few remaining on his skeleton staff. The next day, the last in Zaleszczyki, Biddle and Colbern collaborated on a cable warning that Poland's chances of establishing defensive positions along the Romanian border were thin. A later cable reported what updated military information they possessed. As the two of them labored on their report, in Przemyśl, the Einsatzgruppe von Woyrsch and Wehrmacht soldiers from the Seventh Infantry Division drove Jews through the street to the village of Pikulice on the edge of the city. Pushed up a hill and into a cemetery, they were murdered by a spray of machine-gun fire.[149] Margaret Biddle and Vice Consul Morton, fresh from Brześć, spent much of the day securing visas from the Romanian chargé d'affaires. Between cables, her husband ensured that all was ready for staff driving to Kuty to set up yet another embassy headquarters, the fourth in ten days. That afternoon, the Biddles crossed the international bridge into Romania. Margaret described the joy on their arrival in Cernăuți and checking into the Zum Schwarzer Adler (Under the black eagle), a hotel with a garden restaurant and a gypsy orchestra: "You can have a comfortable bed, a bath, and delicious food."[150] After no bath for six days and a diet of bread, butter, cheese, and beer, she applauded that the caviar "certainly did taste good."[151]

That same afternoon, Hollingworth had not yet left Krzemieniec. Walking to her assigned quarters in a hillside military hospital, she was hailed by *London Times* reporter Patrick Maitland. She was surprised he was in Zaleszczyki, as he and much of the foreign press had left Warsaw for Bucharest on September 5. Maitland was accompanied by Hugh Carleton Greene from Hollingworth's paper, the *Daily Telegraph*, and Sonia Tomara, who spoke Russian and worked freelance for the *New York Herald Tribune* and the *Chicago Tribune*. They were among a gaggle of reporters who descended on the city sensing the end for the Polish government. They had boarded a plane, flown to Cernăuți, and arrived at the international bridge in a fleet of taxis. Most were going back to Cernăuți later in the day to file their stories—the taxis were waiting. Greene, Hollingworth's boss, convinced her she needed to do the same: "For Christ's sake come along now."[152] If she crossed the river, she would have to leave the car behind that had served her so well, but with her mind made up, she stuffed her few belongings into a dirty pillowcase and walked across the bridge accompanied by Greene, who lugged his large typewriter.[153] As they were being hassled at the border, British Consul Thwaites, with whom Hollingworth had worked closely in Katowice and whose telephone she had used to alert Warsaw that the German invasion was underway, happened by and bartered the four journalists' entry into Romania. Pound notes sealed the deal.

That night in Cernăuți, Hollingworth was as pleased as the Biddles with a decent bed and good food. She and her fellow journalists went out on the town and wandered into a night club, a place she described as the kind the Romanians love—small, and full of black paint and mirrors, against which the blondes nodded their plumes. The cabaret was lively. ... [I]t was good to be somewhere warm and gay and full of light again. It was very good. Then why didn't I feel more cheerful, I wondered? There was a chill, a weight, a feeling of vague guilt. I found that I was calling up the faces of the peasants as they had fled so desperately before the machine guns. How sentimental.[154]

Yes, sentimental, but how like her to continue to show compassion, haunted by those millions of Poles whose lives had been destroyed by war.

Invigorated by good food and a comfortable night in Cernăuți, the Biddles left early the next morning, September 16, for Kuty. Tony Biddle had succeeded in fulfilling Beck's request to establish an information relay station and had secured the cooperation of the American minister to Romania, Franklin Mott Gunther, who sent Counselor Fred Hibbard to help set up the operation. Arriving in Kuty, they were pleased to learn that a small house near the town center and close to both the British and the French ambassadors had been reserved for them. Meeting with a group of Polish officials, Biddle was updated on the military situation, which for the Poles had momentarily changed dramatically in their favor. News of the previous night's victories of General Kazimierz Sosnkowski was on everyone's lips throughout the day. Perhaps the Poles did have an angel on their shoulder. To the north of Kołomyja, with sixteen thousand infantry, the general counterattacked overextended, exhausted German units. His small force, without artillery or tanks, retook village after village. A few miles farther on, the Poles caught the third battalion of the SS-Germania Division, spread out and resting in a wooded area. "Men of the Polish 49th Hutsul Rifle Regiment stormed the German positions in a night-time bayonet assault, 'slashing and stabbing ... at anything that moved.'"[155] No doubt, the mad rush into aggressive smashmouth infantry combat produced the victory. The battle over, the delighted Poles discovered the village chock-full of abandoned equipment. The proud Germania had lost over one thousand men, with thousands more captured. Pushing ahead, the spent soldiers reached the Janów Forest.

Word of the success arrived the following morning in Kuty and Kołomyja. For the battered Polish high command, it was like a shot of adrenaline. Prime Minister Felicjan Składkowski wrote in his diary, "*Radosne wiadomości* (joyful news), at last something good in this war."[156] Additional reports further bolstered Polish spirits: captured German prisoners were exhausted; tanks were running out of gas. Perhaps, as the Polish national anthem proclaimed, Poland was not yet lost. If only the rains would come and turn the roads into a sea of mud, then maybe, just maybe! Shortly after Sosnkowski's push, the weather favored rain.

The same day, Hollingworth, accompanied by fellow journalists Greene and Tomara, decided to return to Kuty for a scheduled interview with the British ambassador and gather what news they could on the military situation. Navigating the Dniester bridge was no mean accomplishment, as the walkway was missing planks, often leaving considerable gaps. Clinging to the railing and inching along, Greene slipped and dropped into the shallow river. No damage was done, but his bridge plunge produced no end of ribbing. The British ambassador was found at lunch in the back of a grubby restaurant. After a pleasant interview and a meal of bread and tomatoes, the three walked to the Polish Foreign Office sequestered in a farmhouse on the outskirts of town. On the way, an officer from the British Military Mission stopped them to convey the astounding news of Sosnkowski's success. Arriving at the Foreign Office, Beck was not to be found, but "one of the Under-Secretaries . . . was tremendously excited over the Polish victories." Hollingworth recalled, "I really believed that at this moment the most pessimistic of the Poles believed the tide of war had turned against the enemy."[157] For Hollingworth, Greene, and Tomara, it was mission accomplished. They hurried back to Kuty to file their stories.

That evening, Biddle met with Beck, who frankly stated that even if Poland set up a defense perimeter, it would possibly last no more than three weeks unless the British and the French provided supplies and undertook military operations in the West. While buoyed by Sosnkowski's accomplishments, Beck confided that fear was palpable among officials and the military because the Soviets massing on the southern border might invade at any moment, thereby cutting off the option of escape to Romania.

Surprisingly, Beck did not bring up the reports of the additional threat posed by widespread looting by Ukrainian and Byelorussian peasants, as well as attacks on Polish villages and Polish military units by armed bands of the Organization of Ukrainian Nationalists. The Ukrainian militias and those seeking revenge were akin to the ethnic German *Selbstschutz* militias and the uprisings occurring in the west of Poland—wars within the war. Perhaps, overwhelmed with larger problems, Beck considered that situation moot.

The conversation between the two diplomats switched first to Romania and King Carol, then to American aid to Britain and France. Finally, the foreign minister warily suggested that if aid was being considered, he hoped Poland would be considered as well. Biddle made no reply.[158] Beck then turned to the rush of Polish officers and their families entering Romania, who would soon run out of everything. Of great concern was that Poland's collapse would render its currency worthless. Biddle promised to cable President Roosevelt the next day when in Cernăuți and to take steps to secure aid for the refugees from sources in Romania; then he would return.

Dawn was breaking on the morning of September 17 when the Soviets crossed Poland's six-hundred-mile border at dozens of locations, an action sanctioned by the liars' league, the Hitler-Stalin nonaggression pact signed twenty-five days earlier. Two Russian independent tank brigades, the twenty-third and twenty-sixth, were selected to move across southern Poland as quickly as possible, cutting off escape routes over the bridges in Zaleszczyki and Śniatyń and pushing on to Kuty to capture the Polish government. When Rydz answered his phone at 5:00 a.m., a border guard officer informed him that the feared invasion by the Red Colossus was underway. He bellowed into the phone, "*Bić się!* [Fight!]"[159] But as the border was lightly manned, there was no chance of serious resistance.

The Soviet tank columns came forward under large propaganda banners proclaiming "Russia to the Aid of Poland." Through loudspeakers they shouted that they had come to help fight the Germans. When the news reached Rydz, he knew immediately that the gains made by Sosnkowski, the blessing of any rain, and the attempt at a Romania bridgehead would make no difference. His chief of staff maintained there were no illusions, no "doubts about the character of such a Soviet incursion. It was clear to us that we had received an insidious stab in the back which finally settled the fate of the whole campaign."[160] Rydz reminded himself of how many times he had heard Piłsudski ask, "Who will look reality in the face?"[161] Just before noon, Rydz, Beck, and Składkowski did just that and concurred that the only option was to accept the French offer of right of residence. It was time to cross into Romania. There they could continue the fight. The decision made, the government moved to the small spa town of Kosów, closer to the border, and made preparations to ensure that in France the *Sanacja Junta* remained in power. A threat to the government's future materialized at once as General Władsław Sikorski walked into the Kosów headquarters. The general had opposed the 1926 Piłsudski coup and remained on the political fringe. Twice since the start of the German invasion, he had requested a combat command, and twice Rydz had failed to respond. He wanted, he said, to cross the frontier as a part of the general staff. While Rydz discussed Sikorski's petition with his generals, Beck drove to the wooden bridge a half mile south of Kuty in an effort to work out the transit details with recently appointed Romanian ambassador Gheorghe Grigorcea.[162] Grigorcea assured the worried minister that the passage to Constanta would be smooth. Relieved, Beck carried the news back to those waiting in Kosów, where he learned that, under pressure from subordinates, Rydz had relented, admitting Sikorski to the inner circle.[163]

In Cernăuți, Biddle awoke on the morning of the September 17 and, after breakfast, sent the cable he had promised Beck. As concerned as Beck was regarding the fate of the huge number of Poles successfully crossing into Romania, he called Paris to discuss with Bullitt how to alert "relief organizations in the United States of the increasing plight of reportedly accumulating Polish refugees."[164] It is not surprising that Bullitt responded favorably, for Hubert Earle, clerking for Bullitt in the summer of 1939, revealed, "Many times [he] spoke of the refugee problem, and praised France for its generosity in taking them in, particularly in the case of the Spanish refugees."[165] Relief organizations in America, some of them already rendering overseas aid, were gratified to have recognition from the two ambassadors that a humanitarian crisis was happening in Poland and countries on her borders. At midday, Biddle was preparing to return to Kuty, when Major Colbern knocked on his door, bringing news that the Soviet army had crossed into Poland and that the government would leave for Romania that evening. Colbern's information was firsthand, as that morning, reconnoitering east of Śniatyń, he had run into a column of Russian heavy tanks.[166] Biddle showed no surprise at Colbern's information, as it only confirmed what he already knew. An hour before, Bullitt had started their phone conversation with the news that French radio was reporting the Soviet invasion.

Biddle and Colbern's conversation was interrupted when British ambassador Kennard, fresh from Kuty, stopped by, bearing the same news of the Russian invasion. That morning, he said, Beck had asked him to come by the farm that headquartered the Foreign Office. Neither had a car available, so Beck took what he had: a motorcycle with a sidecar. With some effort, the lanky ambassador managed to squeeze in his legs. On arrival, Beck walked out to welcome him and calmly said, "My dear Ambassador, I must tell you that the Russian forces have crossed our frontier and are marching into the country. There will be a complete and speedy breakdown. I advise you to leave immediately."[167] Taking the foreign minister at his word, Kennard returned to the small house that served as an embassy, packed, and left in his Rolls-Royce for the border. Several vehicles carrying his staff trailed behind. Trouble occurred when the Romanian border guards would not let them pass. Stuck in the late morning heat in a line of vehicles surrounded by refugees and soldiers, Kennard sat like a granite monument in the rear of his stately car. He did not move, exhibiting the stoicism that had built an empire. Finally, the order came from Bucharest to allow his party entry. An American journalist captured the moment: "without a change of face, without a look behind the ambassador passed into Roumania."[168]

Later, walking into the hotel lobby, Biddle was inundated by a swarm of reporters asking about the spiraling events and told that the bridges at Zaleszczyki, Śniatyń, and Kuty were jammed with lines, miles long, of evacuees waiting to cross. The roads on the Romanian side were also snarled with traffic. There was no way the ambassador could navigate the massive congestion and reach Kuty. In truth, things throughout Poland were far worse than the reporters knew. Panic gripped those pushed against the frontier by the advancing German and Soviet forces. All of the bridges across the southern frontier were packed. At dozens of places, rafts pulled by rope or cable carried soldiers, refugees, and vehicles across, though some simply swam or waded. In the air, Polish military aircraft flew low, winging their way to landing fields. Some, running out of fuel, put down in pastures. The planes had been on the ground but a few hours before eager crews counted their bounty, painting over the Polish markings with the Romanian colors. Along Poland's other frontiers, thousands crossed into the Soviet Union, especially Jews, and also across the short border with Hungary. A smaller number escaped into Lithuania and Latvia. A massive Polish diaspora was underway.

As they could not return to Kuty, the Biddle's traumatic eleven-day ordeal was over. Unbeknownst to the couple, a company of Polish soldiers holed up inside their rented palace in Pomorzany fought fiercely until the Red Army forced their surrender. As the couple boarded the train for Bucharest in the late afternoon, they looked up and counted forty planes of the Polish air force flying into Romania. They were witnessing the end of Poland's Second Republic. The Biddles had well represented their country since 1937 and had made many friends and gained the trust of many in government. The ambassador was especially close to Foreign Minister Beck. As the train wound through the colorful wooded hills on its way south, the question of Poland's future, the refugees' fate, and whether a new government would be established and an army raised in France hung in the air.

Julian Bussgang and his family, having fled Lwów on September 14, reached Kosów after moving slowly for two days in a river of humanity and vehicles. "In the morning," Bussgang wrote in his memoir, "we arranged a cart to the border town of Kuty."[169] There they witnessed the spectacle of thousands crossing the bridge, while thousands more waited their turn, a wait that grew to more than twelve hours. The bridge master, Colonel Stefan Soboniewski, megaphone in hand, "possessed a great roaring voice," but hoarse from hours of yelling, he still managed to call out units and groups assembled in the pastures beside the bridge.[170] "People crossed in a continuous stream. No one knows how many. Maybe 15 thousand people, maybe 30 thousand, maybe 50 thousand. They walked in complete silence, a dense mass without faces, without gestures. Even the children didn't cry."[171] "As the day wore on, the civilian refugees were held up to allow the government and army to cross. Ministry after ministry and embassy after embassy were called out over a megaphone to cross over the little border bridge, heading into Rumania. . . . It took the better part of a day for the Government motorcade to cross."[172] Unable to bring their weapons into Romania, the soldiers tossed them over the side of the bridge into the river. By early evening, the piles of rifles, carbines, machine guns, and pistols reached high above the waterline. The silence was broken only by the sound of a few vehicles, the occasional whinny of a cavalry horse, and the roaring engines of Polish fighter planes overhead.

It was late afternoon when Hollingworth and Greene, after earlier learning of the Soviet invasion, hurried once more to Kuty, recognizing this could be a last chance. The roads packed, Hollingworth did what she had done several times before. Veering off the main highway, she navigated the rutted side roads and drove cross-country. Correspondent Cedric Salter described her "as the most foolhardily brave journalist of all the Anglo-Americans in Poland."[173] Nearing Wyżnica, a small village near the river's bank, they ran into a two-mile traffic jam, abandoned the car, and walked toward the frontier. On the roadway were people who had fled from all parts of their country. A large bus that traveled all the way from Soznowiec in southwest Poland "was full of wild-haired mothers and exhausted children, of bundles and blankets and remains of food; a trim green-post van . . . was filled with postal officials, their blue uniforms and their eyes gaping, streaked with dirt, and huddled together like chickens."[174] Darkness was setting in, and already on the Polish side, with the lights out, it was difficult to be certain of what they were seeing. On their walk across the bridge, the two journalists talked with soldiers and refugees about what they expected on the Romanian side: an internment camp, a quick trip to a ship in Constanta Harbor, or a train to France through Yugoslavia and Italy. None were sure, and each held their own hopes. Up the bridge ramp came a car with a man hanging on the running board. Once again it was Consul Thwaites, this time waving a flashlight and shepherding the British Military Mission out of the country. It would take some ingenuity to keep them from being interned, as once on the soil of neutral Romania they were enemy combatants. As they turned to walk back across the bridge, with the Military Mission disappearing toward the lights of Wyznica, one of the greatest ironies of the war occurred. It began to rain!

Then, at about 9:30 p.m., with headlights on, a large Rolls-Royce drove up the approach ramp onto the bridge. "Two bareheaded young men in raincoats on the running-boards" guarded the white-haired former chemistry professor, Polish president Ignacy Mościcki.[175] Those accompanying and those in the president's car handed over their weapons as they reached the Romanian side of the bridge. Half an hour later, in the second car, Beck and his wife, stepdaughter, and aide, Count Michael Lubieński, followed the same routine. The foreign minister had spent years trying to steer his county between Germany and the Soviet Union, and in the end he failed to avoid either Scylla or Charybdis. The prime minister, Felicjan Składkowski, a medical doctor and in office as the compromise appointee between political factions after Piłsudski's death in 1936, was the next to exit his country. Dozens of prominent members of the government and trucks loaded with baggage followed closely behind. In the rain, the line of cars proceeded to Cernăuți, where a train waited for the Polish heads of state. Each was assigned a private sleeping car. After 1:00 a.m. on September 18, the marshal of Poland, Śmigły-Rydz, crossed the Czeremosz. For him, leaving Poland while his army was still fighting in a number of locations was the end of his sterling reputation. Major Zygmunt Wenda, his adjutant, recalled that "the Marshall was terribly depressed. He even refused to drink the tea that I had brought."[176] Still standing on the bridge in the rain, Hollingworth and Greene had witnessed the calamity, the end of the Second Republic. Exhausted, they walked the two miles back to their car to spend an unpleasant night sleeping in wet clothes.[177]

Rydz reached the VIP train waiting in Cernăuți at 4:00 a.m. For him, "there was a special salon car at the head of the train."[178] Rydz's suspicions were right: the Romanians had caved under tremendous pressure from the

Germans and Soviets. The train at last was underway by 4:40 in the afternoon. Twenty-four hours later, it arrived not in Bucharest or Constanta but in the city of Craiova in the southwest corner of the country. "When Rydz and his staff stepped from the train, the cars bearing the other Polish leaders had disappeared, decoupled during the night. President Mościcki had been taken to the city of Bicaz in the extreme northwest of Romania and Beck to Slanic, also in the east."[179] Unable to communicate with one another, the *Sanacja Junta* was at an end—*Vae Victis*. Their French allies were not unhappy with this turn of events, nor were the British, as they wished the new Polish government forming in Paris under their auspices to be a broad-based coalition. That the Piłsudski leadership was interned in Romania served Allied interests.

With most of the army and the government now in Romania, it was the turn of the civilian refugees who had waited so long. "Thus in the early hours," wrote Julian Bussgang, "my parents and my sister, and I left our native Poland. We crossed the border on foot, walking across the bridge, knapsacks on our backs, small suitcases in hand, making our way in the darkness, apprehensive about what lay ahead."[180]

Around noon, dried out, the two enterprising journalists were determined to cross back into Poland. Romanian soldiers guarding the bridge barred their entry. But Hollingworth's persistency prevailed. The streets were nearly empty; few signs remained of the crush of humanity that only a few hours earlier had filled the roadways leading into the city. "At a cross-road, a lorry was drawn up with two machine-guns mounted on it covering approach roads."[181] Greene asked a group of air-raid wardens when the Russians would be there and whether they would resist. The wardens answered that the Russians were expected at any moment and that the machine guns were to prevent them from being killed by Ukrainians.[182] Shots were heard in the distance, and over the rise of hill Russian tanks came into view. Hollingworth and Greene shook hands with those around them, wished them good luck, and headed for the bridge.[183] As she stepped off the bridge into Romania, Hollingworth, who had been on the job for barely a month, was the only foreign journalist on the front on the war's first day, and she was the last foreign journalist to leave. It was an incredible to start to an amazing career.

The Polish army crossing the bridge over the Czeremosz into Romania, September 17, 1939 (illustration by John D. Bindon; courtesy of John D. Bindon).

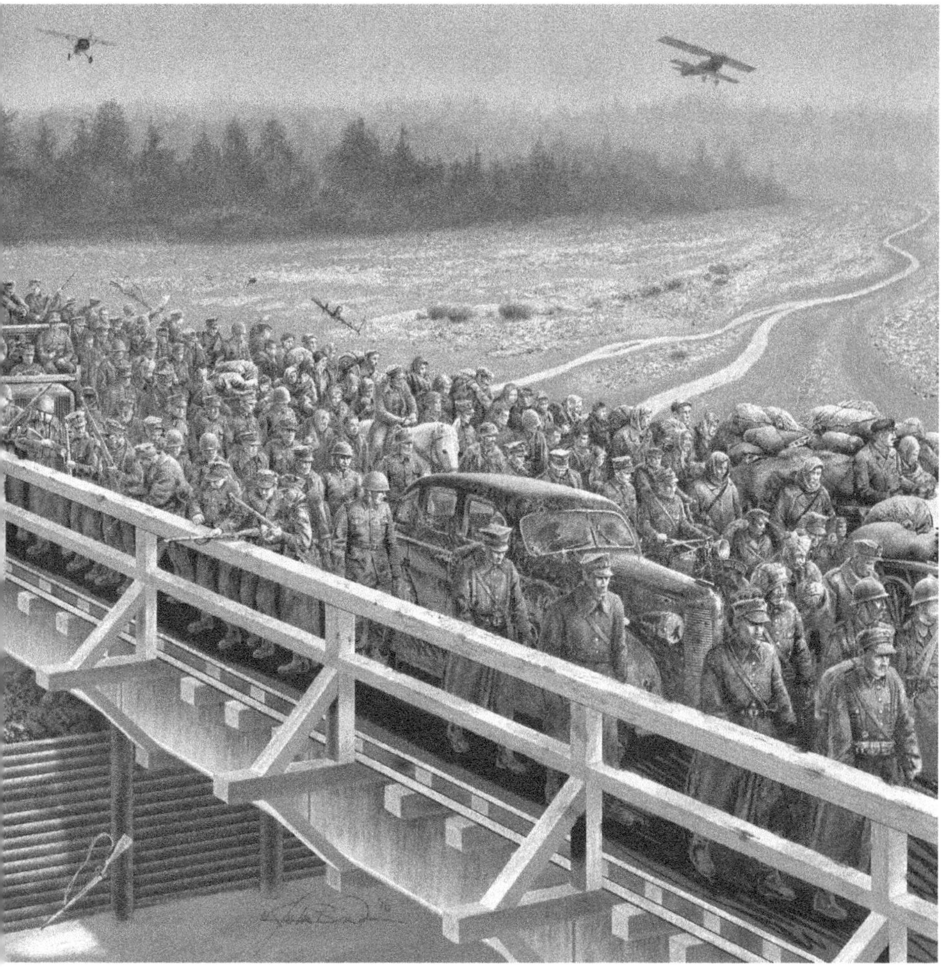

While Hollingworth and Greene had not met the Bussgangs on the bridge, they shared their apprehensions about the future. On the way back to Cernăuți, Hollingworth wrote, "We encountered the inevitable refugees, mainly families of soldiers and airmen threading their way into Rumania as Polish warplanes continued to fly out of their defeated country. I counted seventy-four and then gave up."[184] Perhaps the only good news for the throng of Polish soldiers that waited for orders while in Cernăuți was being greeted by the young women of the city with open arms. "The girls would 'adopt' a Polish soldier and take him along, one on each side."[185] That they did not speak the same language was of no consequence. "One girl would run into a shop and buy bread, or chocolate, or bananas. Then the two would more or less feed him."[186]

Hollingworth and Greene had ample time to ponder Poland's fate on their two-day drive through the Carpathian Mountains to Bucharest. Poland was finished, but they concluded that what lay ahead for those who had fled their country would be determined by several interrelated factors. What would happen to huge number of refugees, a number growing larger by the day? What kind of treatment would the soldiers being sent to internment camps receive? What pressure would be brought to bear by the Germans and the Soviets regarding the soldiers and refugees? Paul Super, from the war's start, had broadcast appeals to the United States for assistance, as had William C. McDonald, broadcasting from a Warsaw under siege. Ambassador Bullitt recommended aid, and, from Bucharest, Biddle reported to Roosevelt of the refugees' dire needs. Would the president heed his ambassador's advice? Would Americans support a relief effort to aid the stricken Poles? Hollingworth's dispatches to the *Daily Telegraph* spelled out to her readers the catastrophes that overtook those jamming the roads of Poland in search of safety. Would British relief agencies come to their aid?

On the roads, detours, sections under construction, and military checkpoints (and often a total lack of roads) created challenges for the two journalists. As they drove, they went miles without running into anyone, but then they would pass hundreds strung out in lines walking along the side of the roads; at other spots, there would be larger groups that seemed to band together for safety. Occasionally they passed abandoned cars, trucks, buses, and carts, either broken down or out of gas. "In the surrounding countryside," wrote Hollingworth, the refugees "slept in cars or in open fields, the rich buying food in the villages, the poor begging their way through a poor country."[187] Many slept against buildings or lay down in the fields. But amid this human suffering, the travelers could not help but admire the beauty of the mountains as they passed through isolated villages that harkened back to another age: "The meadows seemed a wash in sienna, an expanse of pale colour, with the beech woods blotting it, showing whitish on the outcroppings of rock. Blocky white houses, with roofs of brown, were piled up to Byzantine churches, their towers visible for fifty miles."[188]

6

The Rapprochement That Failed

The Battle over Aid Begins

September 5, 1939, Roosevelt signs neutrality proclamation (open source).

SATURDAY, SEPTEMBER 2, 1939, THE SECOND DAY OF WAR, FOUND THE president in a series of meetings discussing the American response. "A huge map of Europe was hung on the wall in the White House executive office. Army and Navy intelligence officers stuck pins in it to keep the President up to the hour on the fighting."[1] The declaration of neutrality demanded by 1937 law was drawn up and ready to be issued, and the general declaration of neutrality in conformity with international law was drafted, but the two documents awaited the British and French response to the fighting in Poland. Due to uncertainty regarding whether and when the British and the French would declare war, meetings at the White House and the State Department were filled with speculations and educated deducements in the absence of hard evidence.[2] One of the president's meetings was with Breckinridge Long, who had earlier arrived from Saint Louis, called back from semiretirement by Roosevelt to head a special division of the State Department "created to handle emergency matters arising out of the war situation."[3] Roosevelt and Long had not met for a number of years, so after catching up with his former ambassador to Italy, the president confided that he found the European situation "very involved . . . and somewhat mystifying" and that it seemed the Germans had not staged a "full-force" invasion.[4] It was likely, he speculated, that they were bluffing, looking to acquire Danzig, a part of the corridor, and Silesia, and then make peace. What, the president asked, did Long think? Long answered that if the president's scenario was correct, then Poland, Britain, and France would likely agree to an international conference hosted by Italy to work out the details.[5]

After meeting with Long, the president, back to business, issued an invitation for all nations with representation in the World's Fair, which had opened on April 30, to continue operating into the next year. The Poles might be defeated, but they would continue to exist on the fairgrounds in Flushing Meadows. The rest of Saturday afternoon he spent preparing remarks for his Sunday night address to the nation, "fireside chat" number fourteen. He likewise asked that Secretary Cordell Hull and his team at the State Department prepare a draft. In preparing his speech, Roosevelt did not use the off-the-cuff remarks he had made the day before at the cabinet meeting, written down and forwarded to him by Charles Edison. Clearly those thoughts were only for the ears of his inner circle. Hull and Assistant Secretary of State Adolf Berle completed their draft and sent it to the White House by 1:30 p.m. Roosevelt would, he informed the State Department, send over the speech for Secretary Hull to make any changes he thought necessary. Berle was pleased that the president had written the first draft himself. In his diary, he wrote, "Of this I am extremely glad. When the President really can take the time to draft, he can do a better job than anyone can do for him; when he uses other people's drafts, it is commonly because of lack of time."[6] Berle was also quite pleased that Roosevelt was sending the draft over to Hull for a final look, as he thought that was the correct way to respond to the war crisis. He recalled "how Wilson had done his speeches without telling Lansing [Wilson's secretary of state] anything about it, so that the White House and the State Department were virtually cut off."[7] Late in the afternoon, the president changed his mind and asked those working on his speech to come to the White House. At 4:45 p.m., Hull, Berle, Undersecretary of State Sumner Welles, and Assistant Secretary of War Louis Johnson met the president in the Lincoln Study. Roosevelt, "in his shirt-sleeves," noted Berle, "went over the draft, which was a tremendous improvement over anything I had done; we took out a couple of phrases which, the President readily agreed, indicated bias against the German method (how could any sane person draw any other conclusion?)."[8] "Late that afternoon," the speech complete, Hull decided "to get a little relaxation in preparation for what I knew lay ahead in the following week. I took three of my associates with me for a game of croquet on the lawn of 'Woodley,'" home of Herbert Hoover's former secretary of state, Henry Stimson, being rented by Berle.[9] Woodley, built in 1801, had been the home of former presidents Martin Van Buren and Grover Cleveland. After croquet, Berle met his wife, Beatrice, and the two of them went for a swim in the pool of the Hungarian minister, John Pelenyi.[10]

Roosevelt, also in need of relaxation, prepared to enjoy the evening. Eleanor was at her cottage Val-Kill with female friends on the estate at Hyde Park, a place the president called the "Honeymoon Cottage." War or not, Roosevelt eagerly awaited the planned stag dinner and night of cocktails and poker after two extraordinary days. Secretary of the Interior and close political advisor Harold Ickes, Assistant Attorney General Robert Jackson, Roosevelt's doctor Ross McIntire, military advisor and secretary Edwin "Pa" Watson, and secretary Steve Early "made a congenial crowd, and cocktails in the Oval Room before dinner put us all in a friendly and relaxed mood. After a simple but good dinner we went back to the Oval Room for poker."[11] Seven-card hands, dollar limit, were standard, with "Woolworth," fives and tens wild, the favorite game. Several times during the evening, an aide handed the president dispatches. About 11:00 p.m., after reading one, he looked up and said, "War will be declared by noon tomorrow."[12] All were pleased, as they agreed that Britain and France had finally faced the inevitable. "We played," said Ickes, "until about half past twelve, when we broke up because the president was tired, having had his sleep interrupted for two or three nights by flash news from Europe. Dr. McIntire put his foot down on a really late party and I was glad because I like early parties myself."[13] The president was not dealt winning hands, losing $35, approximately $650 in 2022 dollars. Ickes was the big winner, raking in $53.50 ($992).[14]

Roosevelt, in bed only a few hours, had his sleep interrupted once again. Sometime after 4:00 a.m., Ambassador Joseph Kennedy called from London to tell him that Britain and France would declare war later that day. The president woke Secretary Hull at 4:45 a.m. He "dressed, had a brief breakfast, and went to the State Department."[15] Britain's war declaration reached East Coast newsrooms fifteen minutes later. In Baltimore, where Ickes's wife was about to have a baby, the *Sun*'s early special edition beat sunup by nearly an hour. Delivery trucks tossed bundles in front of newsstands by 5:30 a.m. Soon city newsboys flooded the streets holding the paper high and crying out the banner headline: "ENGLAND DECLARES WAR ON GERMANY."[16] In city after city the pattern was the same: editors rushed to headline the front pages of their thick Sunday editions. Some in Baltimore could be forgiven for not rising early, as they had attended the sold-out Glenn Miller concert the night before at the Hippodrome.[17] Throughout the country many people were slow to get the news, as they were enjoying the three-day weekend, grabbing the last days of summer however they could—at the lake, the beach, or a picnic in the park, in the woods, on the front porch, or driving in the country. As Monday was Labor Day, others were decorating floats for parades, frying chicken, baking pies, or practicing a stump speech. Americans were not shocked by the news but were apprehensive about what this latest European war meant for them and their country. One thing was certain: the vast majority were determined to stay out. The economy was finally picking up. There was so much to do to come back from ten years of depression. The last thing needed was war.

On Sunday at noon, Roosevelt issued a Labor Day statement and then returned to rehearsing his fireside chat. At 4:00 p.m., Hull, Welles, Berle, and Johnson returned to the White House to listen to the president read his speech and offer suggestions. The president understood the mood of the country, and that evening, as he assured millions of listeners that America's role was that of peacemaker, he stressed, "Passionately though we desire detachment, we are forced to realize that every word that comes through the air, every ship that sails the sea, every battle that is fought, does affect the American future. Most of us in the United States," he continued, "believe in spiritual values" and hold to the New Testament, which teaches us to oppose "the use of force, of armed force, of marching armies and falling bombs. The overwhelming masses of our people seek peace—peace at home, and the kind of peace in other lands which will not jeopardize our peace at home."[18] The president would, he said, issue a neutrality declaration, "but I cannot ask that every American remain neutral in thought as well. Even a neutral has a right to take account of facts. Even a neutral cannot be asked to close his mind or his conscience. I have said not once, but many times, that I have seen war and that I hate war. I say that again and again."[19] To many listeners, this was the "most striking sentence in the broadcast," as it "underscored by contrast with Woodrow Wilson's words in 1914" that "the United States must be neutral in fact, as well as in name, during these days that try men's souls. We must be impartial in thought as well as action, must put a curb upon our sentiments as well as upon every transaction that might be construed as a preference of one party to the struggle before another."[20] Roosevelt concluded that he "hoped the United States will keep out of this war. I believe," he said reassuringly, "that it will. And I give you assurance and reassurance that every effort of your government will be directed toward that end.... There will be no black-out of peace."[21] Yet a feeling of resignation hung over Washington, as it did over London, Paris, and Berlin, where the outlook on the widening conflagration mirrored that of President Roosevelt: "Yes, I was almost startled by a strange feeling of familiarity—a feeling that I had been thru it all before."[22]

In America, Monday morning, September 4, was Labor Day, but all through the long holiday weekend, the president had met a parade of key personnel facing the outbreak of war. In the Oval Office at 10:37 a.m., he conducted several short meetings, lunched with navy brass, and ordered ships to patrol five hundred miles out to sea, "thereby putting into effect," Berle noted, "the substance of a suggestion that was made clear back in Jefferson's time."[23] Searching for a legal precedent, Berle discovered that during World War I, "several Latin American nations had proposed such a concept."[24] At 2:00 p.m. Roosevelt met with his cabinet. The wide range of topics under discussion included how to protect the Americas, gather citizens strung out across Europe, and ensure freedom of the seas.

The president further sought his cabinet's advice on issuing an emergency declaration and suggested that it too might come a week or so later, after—as was typical of the president—he had had a chance to gauge public opinion. Secretary of Agriculture Henry Wallace argued strongly that the president should wait, but if he did not, the intent should be made clear so as not to cast doubt on the president's commitment to neutrality.[25] Hull likewise counseled caution and the careful use of language. Heeding the advice, the president eventually compromised and issued a limited emergency declaration several days later that still gave him control over the "anchorage and movement of vessels to and from the territorial waters of the United States. He had the authority over traffic in arms and could prevent the departure of vessels engaged in the conduct of hostilities. He could expand the list of materials for American security and stop the sailing of ships carrying them."[26]

One of Roosevelt's more fanciful Labor Day ideas was his suggestion that the United States buy the French luxury liner *Normandie*, which was docked in New York indefinitely to avoid being sunk by a U-boat on a return to France. The president thought $20 million a fair price. Treasury Secretary Henry Morgenthau was just back in his office; he had been vacationing in Norway as the crisis over Danzig moved toward war. The coast guard cutter *Campbell* picked up Morgenthau on August 28 in Bergen and sailed for Newfoundland at full steam in rough seas. On arrival, the secretary boarded a flight to Washington.[27] Roosevelt tasked the tired secretary with broaching the subject of the sale with the French ambassador and approaching the British on selling the *Queen Mary*. Neither the French nor the newly appointed British ambassador, Lord Lothian, warmed to the suggestion. The volatile Ambassador William C. Bullitt sent off a cable from Paris, claiming he was mortified by the suggestion that the French might even consider selling the grand liner. Luxury liners aside, a main concern was when to call a special session of Congress to amend the neutrality laws—the president's top priority.

Hull characterized the unending discussions between the president, his cabinet, and his advisors as they struggled to move forward: "Over and above all the questions that confront us with the outbreak of war hung the predominant one—how were we to conduct ourselves as a neutral, and what were we to do with the neutrality legislation on our books embracing the arms embargo."[28] Throughout the discussions Hull was confident that the State Department had answers for many of those questions and was well prepared for war in Europe. The department had begun planning in 1936, and detailed evacuation plans for Americans existed by the time of the Munich crisis in 1938.[29] That same year, Roosevelt ordered the newly created "Special Division" under Long to begin operations on the second day of war. The division was tasked with handling refugees, provide relief, locate American citizens, and arrange their transportation home. In 1939, several interdepartmental meetings were held to coordinate evolving plans. Roosevelt's wise but unneutral suggestion to his cabinet was to wait a few days so that the British and the French would have time to purchase munitions, load their ships, and clear port. Once he declared neutrality and named belligerents, the export of munitions would be illegal. How many British and French ships managed to load arms and ammunition in that five-day window of opportunity remains unknown. Debate swirled around whether to include Canada as a belligerent. Roosevelt settled the issue by phoning Prime Minister McKenzie King and asking his intentions. King stated that Canada would not be at war automatically but only when "Parliament had so voted."[30]

Late that afternoon, the president met with Norman Davis to discuss Red Cross procedures on how best to bring home Americans stranded in Europe, what constituted emergency aid, and what to do about the growing number of refugees.[31] During the discussion Roosevelt broached the subject of consulting Hoover. Several friends and a few top advisers had suggested he consider bringing leading Republicans to Washington for consultation. The president, who read a stack of newspapers daily, was keenly aware of columnists who "had been harping on the idea that there should be taken into the administration such men as Herbert Hoover, [Arthur] Vandenberg, [Robert A.] Taft, young [Henry Cabot] Lodge, and 'even [Thomas E.] Dewey.'"[32] Eleanor's friend and confidante Marie (Missy) Meloney, editor of *This Week Magazine*, a pioneering woman journalist with a long track record in progressive causes, was "quietly campaigning to have Herbert Hoover take over the government's relief enterprises."[33] She was as well connected among Republicans as she was among Democrats and had supported Hoover's efforts feeding the Belgians in World War I, founded the Better Homes in America movement in 1922, and been onboard with Hoover in advancing the home economics revolution that gathered steam in the 1920s. Meloney wrote to Eleanor lobbying for Hoover and advocating for a "conference of leading women from all over the country" to advise him.[34] Young volunteers would assist the relief effort. Meloney's was a voice Eleanor would listen to, but Eleanor had reasons of her own. For the First Lady, Hoover's track record on aiding millions made his advice indispensable. She admired his concern for children, which she shared, and was especially moved by his success in feeding German children in the aftermath of war. A portion of her sympathy may have come from her knowledge that Hoover himself was an orphan and, like her, had experienced a difficult childhood. Then, too, her conception of European relief was more in line with Hoover's than it was with her husband's. Siding with Meloney, she held high hopes that Hoover would consent to run such an organization as she imagined.[35] Eleanor pushed her husband to bite his tongue and explore the possibility of bringing Hoover to Washington. The president, relenting, said that if Hoover agreed, he would consider hosting a conference of leading women that might serve as a prelude to a more general relief program.[36]

Roosevelt sought Davis's advice on how best to approach the prickly Hoover. Roosevelt selected Davis as head of the Red Cross because he understood the burgeoning refugee crisis and was a trusted advisor, a New York financier turned diplomat. But, equally important, he knew Hoover well, having served as his assistant in the last years of the Wilson administration. Later, when Hoover was president, he had appointed

Marie Mattingly Meloney, circa 1925 (Bain News Service; courtesy of Library of Congress).

this ardent Anglophile as chief negotiator at the 1930 London Naval Conference and at the 1931–1932 General Disarmament Conference at the League of Nations in Geneva.[37] Historian Wayne S. Cole described him as "skilled, energetic, persistent, realistic, and cautiously optimistic."[38] Critically, Davis had the unenviable job of serving as go-between for Hoover and the president-elect during the tension-filled, calamitous interregnum that lasted from shortly after the November election in 1932 until the inauguration the following March. For his years of accepting difficult assignments, the press dubbed him "Uncle Sam's handy man."[39] Though Davis was an ardent Democrat, Hoover was well disposed toward the genial former diplomat; however, the enmity between the president and the former president was palpable and only increased after Roosevelt was reelected in 1936.

Given this acrimonious history, the president did not wish to risk approaching Hoover directly by inviting him to the White House, as doing so would, at the very least, generate headlines like "Roosevelt Seeks

Hoover's Advice" or, worse, "Roosevelt Courts Hoover." As the outcome of any meeting was up in the air and the political risks seemed high, Roosevelt, ever cautious, and Davis, the consummate diplomat, conspired to feel Hoover out by tiptoeing through the back door, even though both knew that strategy risked offending the former president. Myron Taylor was selected for this mission improbable, the instrument of their strategy. Taylor, former head of U.S. Steel, an ambassador without portfolio, friend, and adviser to the president, was also immersed in problems of the refugee crisis sweeping Europe. Taylor had represented the United States at the Evian Conference in 1938, where he failed to persuade the thirty-two participant countries to take in more refugees—particularly endangered Jews. Ironically, his own country was among those that said no to the proposed increases. The question of how to approach Hoover resolved, Roosevelt moved quickly by summoning Taylor to meet with him two days later, on Wednesday, September 6. If Hoover refused to meet, the president (if pressed) could tell his wife, his advisors, and the press that he had tried. Any rebuff would come from Hoover. However, the eighteen days between September 6 and 24 saw a bizarre series of meetings, exchanges, memos, letters, and telephone conversations. Neither Hoover nor Roosevelt likely imagined that what transpired would have enormous consequences, triggering an intense three-year battle over aid to Europe—the pebble that presaged the avalanche.

The next day, Ambassador Jerzy Potocki and his aide, prior to the US declarations of neutrality, descended once more on the State Department seeking information and launching an effort to keep open current supply chains and secure the possibility of future purchases, especially of arms and ammunition, by pleading that the proclamations should not name Poland as a belligerent. While the German army was driving the Polish army back toward Warsaw, it was still held by the Poles, and most military observers thought they would be able to establish a defense somewhere east of the Vistula. Potocki cleverly posited that while Great Britain, France, and Germany were officially at war, Poland and Germany had not declared war on one another; therefore, the embargo should not apply. The invasion of Poland, said Potocki, was similar to the Japanese invasion of China in 1937: the United States did not impose an embargo as under the law because Roosevelt did not find a war. To attempt to get the president's ear, the two diplomats asked Jay Pierrepont Moffat, head of the European desk, to send their request to Berle at the White House.[40] To clarify the situation, Moffat invited both of them to join him in the office of the department's legal adviser, Green H. Hackworth, who maintained that, as Poland was allied with Great Britain and France, their request was without merit. Any favoritism shown, Moffat said, brought into question whether the United States was complying with the neutrality laws and politically could damage the president's desire to amend them. Potocki pushed Moffat to ascertain whether he spoke for the administration. Equivocating, Moffat maintained that the president's Sunday night radio address and Hull's remarks in the months leading up to the war made clear where the administration stood on neutrality. The Poles left disappointed, but Moffat, covering his bases, sent the request to Berle, who read it to the president. Roosevelt "agreed that the Polish Ambassador's point had no validity as a practical proposition."[41] Potocki was disappointed but not dissuaded. In the coming months he would use all the means at his disposal to obtain aid for his country, as would Ambassador Edward Raczynski in London and Ambassador Juliusz Łukasiewicz in Paris.

After Roosevelt talked with Prime Minister King, the neutrality proclamation was amended so as not to name Canada. Secretary Hull, just before 1:00 p.m. on September 5, affixed the great seal, "in a battery of Klieg lights," in a ceremony held at State.[42] A few minutes later, the president signed the proclamation, as did Hull. The 1937 Neutrality Act required the president to declare that arms and ammunition could not be sold to named belligerents in a second declaration defining the terms of neutrality. Later that afternoon, Hull, Berle, and Undersecretary of State Sumner Welles walked the document to the White House. Roosevelt, winding up a press conference, signed in front of a "huge throng" of reporters. It was done: the United States had declared its neutrality in the burgeoning European war and was legally prohibited from selling war materials to Britain, France, or Poland (if it survived). Berle noted the glumness among Roosevelt's inner circle of advisors, as all recognized the president's hands were tied. That glumness, however, quickly turned into a determined push to secure changes in the neutrality laws. While

From left: Secretary Cordell Hull, Undersecretary Sumner Welles, and Assistant Secretary Adolf Berle on their way to neutrality legislation signing (courtesy of United States Holocaust Memorial Museum).

the president did not publicly reveal his strategy, he intended to defend America by aiding the Allies.

On Wednesday, Ickes met with Roosevelt, seeking his reaction to the columnists clamoring for him to take into his administration key Republicans like Herbert Hoover, Arthur Vandenberg, Robert Taft, and even neophytes like Henry Cabot Lodge Jr. and Thomas E. Dewey.[43] Roosevelt replied he was aware of the clamor but noted that there was no talk of bringing in the 1936 Republican candidates Alf Landon and Frank Knox. "Of course," the president said, "I know what this means."[44] Ickes interrupted; it was an effort on the part of the press "to build up a Republican candidate for next year." "Exactly," said the president.[45] But bringing in two Republicans was advantageous for several reasons, and bringing in Landon and Knox was a safe choice, as the foxy Roosevelt knew neither Republican was a political threat. Landon would be surprised to learn that he was politically moribund, as he harbored the hope that a path to a second nomination might open for him, but the president would be proved right in his judgment. Ickes spoke up for Knox and pointed out that his foreign policy views were in line with the administration's, suggesting he would do well at Navy and that such a move would strengthen the president's hand. In a time of crisis, a "unity cabinet" deflected criticism, increased the chances for changes in the neutrality laws, and allowed for shedding members of his cabinet whom the president wished to show the door: Harry H. Woodring at War, as he disagreed on policy with the president, and Edison at Navy because "he was too deaf to be effective."[46] The two Republicans would be offered War, Navy, or Commerce. Ickes's meeting with Roosevelt was short but important, as he needed advice on sorting through and selecting Republicans who would be a good fit. It is unlikely Roosevelt revealed to Ickes the strategy that he and Davis had concocted to approach Hoover, but later, over lunch, the president met with Sumner Welles and Myron Taylor to decide how to proceed. Taylor was to call Hoover, arrange a meeting, and invite him to the White House to discuss a relief plan for war victims in Europe. On Friday, Taylor telephoned mining engineer Edgar Rickard, Hoover's business manager and longtime friend, explaining that he was "anxious to see H. H. soon after his arrival" back in New York.[47]

For Hoover, the German invasion of Poland, a country he had helped to bring into existence and championed for so long, weighed heavily. In his address delivered from San Francisco on the first night of hostilities, he had spoken out about the tragedy of war's return to Europe and stressed that America must keep out. But relief was on the Chief's mind when, on the second day of the war, in Palo Alto, he met with Charlotte Kellogg, an old friend, fellow relief worker, and political ally. Their discussion dealt with war news and the obvious assistance Poland would immediately need. Charlotte and her entomologist husband, Vernon, had been deeply involved with the Commission for Relief in Belgium (CRB) in World War I. Vernon Kellogg's book *Headquarter Nights* chronicled his interaction with the German High Command while in continuous and often contentious negotiations to keep food arriving in Belgium. With Hoover's American Relief Administration (ARA) in the aftermath of the war, he served as chief of mission to Poland and Russia, witnessing the horrors of the great Soviet famine of 1921 while guiding "the first food train to the Volga."[48] Charlotte, a prolific writer, having spent time in both Belgium and Poland, penned *Women of Belgium*, *Bobbins for Belgium*, *Poland's Women*, and *Jadwiga: Queen of Poland*. Her assignment in Belgium was to supply forty thousand women lace makers with thread and "to sell some of their finished products abroad, a task at which she admirably succeeded."[49] For Hoover and Kellogg, it was a given that if Poland was in need, they would attempt to provide aid in whatever way possible. Their fingers, as the expression goes, were deep in the Polish pie. Both understood that the spiraling war, no matter how tragic, was a political opportunity for Hoover to advance his quest for the looming Republican presidential nomination by generating a wave of favorable publicity. Hoover did not enter the relief arena in September 1939 solely to advance his presidential candidacy, but relief and his candidacy were like conjoined twins—partially separate but clearly attached. Throughout the summer, Hoover had stumped in California to win the allegiance of key Republicans to his policies. Meeting with dozens of party leaders, he distributed copies of his speeches and position papers, along with a newsletter titled *Republican Circles*, which was highly critical of Roosevelt's policies at home and abroad.[50] Kellogg's job was to write, speak, and glad-hand in support of Hoover. The summer of retail politics was the first step in Hoover's two-step crypto candidacy campaign, an effort to ensure an uncommitted California delegation to next year's convention and encourage his rivals to seek the nomination. Robert Taft, the newly minted senator from Ohio and son of former president William Howard Taft, had declared himself a candidate for the nomination in August. Hoover was sure that others would throw their hats into the ring—notably New York City district attorney Thomas E. Dewey, Senator Arthur Vandenberg of Michigan, and perhaps even Frank Gannett, the Buffalo, New York, media mogul. The more, the merrier. As the field of candidates increased, Hoover's hope for a brokered convention showed promise.

Kellogg, after her meeting with Hoover, continued to talk up his candidacy and also worked toward forming a Polish relief campaign with support from her California Republican colleagues and from a field rich with past players from Hoover's relief organizations. Hoover continued to confer his blessings on Kellogg's efforts, telling her she "could be of real service."[51] His business concluded in the Golden State, he left for fishing and politicking in Montana and Wyoming. The hopeful candidate had the wind at his back. He was bolstered by Republican victories in the 1938 election—a seventy-two-seat pickup in the House and seven seats gained in the Senate—as well as successes in California, an overwhelming number of citizens favoring peace, and the political possibilities presented by the war. The nomination and his longed-for vindication seemed within reach. The year 1940 looked to be a grand one for the Grand Old Party. To Hoover, the Houdini in the White House was vulnerable.

Arriving in Chicago on Saturday, Hoover received a call from Rickard informing him that Myron Taylor, acting at the behest of Roosevelt, wished to meet and explore his thoughts on relief. The Chief's initial surprise was tempered by skepticism and suspicion, for he possessed "an intense, almost pathological distrust" of the president.[52] Why would Roosevelt send an emissary? What did he really want? Hoover wondered whether this was an effort to derail his potential candidacy, an attempt to co-opt him. Still, his desire to see what might be offered, alongside his wish to be recalled to service and the opportunity to school his great rival, led him to agree to meet Taylor on Monday at his Waldorf apartment. After all, maybe Roosevelt really did just want his advice. Part of Hoover's reluctance was rooted in his hostility to bipartisanship, as he believed it was unhealthy for a vigorous political climate. However, at the heart of his reluctance was a wariness of any olive branch held out by Roosevelt, as he harbored a hurt inflicted by years of vindictive attacks. *Newsweek* reported, "Few administrations in U.S. History ever went to greater lengths to smear a predecessor than the present one, and the former president had every right to question the sincerity of a sudden peace gesture."[53] The faults that beset America, according to Roosevelt, the wrenching Depression that had paralyzed the country, lay at the feet of Hoover and his two predecessors, Calvin Coolidge and Warren Harding. Hoover was a failed president, Coolidge a do-nothing president, and Harding a corrupt president, a trifecta of disaster. Kicking off the Second New Deal in a campaign speech on October 31, 1936, Roosevelt did not name these past presidents but launched into his standard stem-winding rant against a failed era of wrongheaded, niggardly ideas about the role of government:

> For twelve years the nation was afflicted with hear-nothing, see-nothing, do-nothing government. The nation looked to government but the government looked away. Nine mocking years with the golden calf and three years of scourge! Nine crazy years at the ticker and three long years in the breadlines! Nine mad years of mirage and three long years of despair! And, my friends, powerful influences strive today to restore that kind of government with its doctrine that that government is best which is most indifferent to mankind.[54]

That Hoover had responded in kind, hurling vitriol at Roosevelt and the New Deal, was of little consequence outside his small base, which cheered him on as Roosevelt was wrapped in a Teflon suit of armor defended by a Praetorian Guard of reporters. His narrative of who was responsible for the Great Depression prevailed; the public generally accepted his explanation. Thus, Hoover's efforts at defending himself and his administration made him look guilty as charged.

Taylor arrived at the cave of the bear at 11:00 a.m. on Monday morning with an invitation for Hoover to come to Washington on Wednesday for discussions with Roosevelt about organizing "relief measures for European countries and . . . creating a new agency to undertake the task."[55] While Eleanor had urged the president to offer Hoover the job of overseeing relief, Davis did not.[56] As to a new relief agency, Hoover advised Taylor that none was necessary, as the American Red Cross was equipped to handle the job. The Red Cross, Hoover opined, could snap into action within hours, and it had experience in overseas relief, as well as trained personnel and "committees and organizations in every city, town, and village in the country."[57]

Taylor responded that he appreciated the warning, but the president saw the Red Cross in a more limited role, as "an adjunct to military activities"; a large relief effort would demand a new agency.[58] Hoover countered that this conception of the Red Cross was dated—witness its effectiveness during the great Mississippi flood of 1927 and its earlier work in China and Japan.[59] Any new government agency, Hoover stated, would "parallel" the Red Cross and would not be workable for years. His insistence that the Red Cross undertake European relief was far more than a practical recommendation. It was his queen's gambit, a gamble that Roosevelt would not adopt a cross-blockade feeding program like his CRB operation in World War I. If the president did as he expected, the door to Polish relief was open to him. At an impasse, Hoover told Taylor that he would not come to the White House, as his doing so "would only create speculation and unnecessary discussion in the country," and that he had a responsibility to the Republican Party, but he would advise the president if he wished on relief or on any other topic.[60] Unable to resist a jibe, "with what must have been sublime pleasure," Hoover added, "I wish to devote my whole energies to keeping the United States out of war."[61] If that were Roosevelt's policy, said Hoover, Republicans would surely support it.

Taylor left empty-handed, keenly aware that the president and ex-president were, unsurprisingly, far apart. But he carried with him back to Washington direct evidence of the enmity that separated the two men, as Hoover, during their conversation, divulged what he considered an unpardonable act committed against him by FDR. How exactly Hoover told the story is unknown, but the gist was that he and Lou Henry, on leaving Roosevelt's inauguration late in the afternoon of March 4, 1933, arrived by motorcade at Union Station to be greeted by five thousand people, all supporters from various Hoover organizations and clubs from the DC area, who shouted their support and encouragement. Hoover, as did Roosevelt, worried about an assassination attempt, as the mood in the country was fearful, angry, dark, and threatening—"there had been heavy security at the inaugural, including machine-gun nests up and down Pennsylvania Avenue."[62] The shots fired at Roosevelt by Giuseppe Zangara in Miami a week earlier were still news. Chicago mayor Anton Cermak, hit by one of Zangara's bullets, lay in a hospital bed fighting for his life.[63] Hoover knew he had been the assassin's first choice. The fates of Abraham Lincoln, James Garfield, and William McKinley could not have been far from his mind. Larry Richey, secretary and mother hen to

Hoover, ruminated over the potential dangers his charge might face on the four-hour trip to New York, as security was but four railroad agents.[64] Colonel Edmund W. Starling, head of the Secret Service, was nearby as the Hoover entourage climbed one by one onto the rear platform of the train. Thinking a solution was at hand, Richey asked the colonel to order his detail to accompany Hoover. He was shaken by the response: "I'm sorry, Larry, but you are now a private citizen with no authority to order anyone to do anything."[65] Starling was following the law, but Hoover blamed Roosevelt. Surely the new president had given the order. "I had," Hoover said, "all the security in the world going to the inauguration." He then added, revealing the pathos of his fall from grace, "The moment Roosevelt was sworn in, I was nothing."[66]

Hoover and Lou Henry arrived in New York safely. No assassination attempt or other threat materialized. The protective Richey called ahead to the police commissioner, a Democrat, who sent 125 men in blue and 25 detectives to escort the Hoovers through the crowd of well-wishers in Pennsylvania Station to their Midtown East apartment in the Waldorf.[67]

Taylor, hearing this story, was surely bewildered. Hoover, however, was adamant and remained so for the rest of his life, saying Roosevelt had turned the screw. The supposed Secret Service slight was one of the larger stones in the foundation that supported Hoover's hatred of the president. Hoover added an additional insult to his injury, telling Taylor that he found it disrespectful that Roosevelt had not contacted him directly. With the conversation ended, Taylor had an earful from the cantankerous bear. Hoover, in unloading his grievances, could not know whether he would hear more from the White House. In their lengthy discussion on relief, Hoover held back from his guest that Kellogg had already set in motion an effort to aid the Poles that he supported. Later that same day, Hoover confirmed his intentions, telling Rickard that the Polish relief effort would be headed by Kellogg, who was continuing to round up volunteer leadership across the country from among the Chief's faithful and what newcomers she could corral.[68] But the aid question now took on a new urgency for Hoover, as the reports of Polish defeat after defeat convinced him the "resistance [would] vanish."[69] Regardless of what might transpire in Washington or the outcome of the battle being waged in Poland, the "Great Humanitarian" had already made up his mind. He would move forward with a relief campaign of some sort for the people of a nation he held so closely. "It was obvious," Hoover later wrote, "that if I set up any relief machinery, Davis and his colleagues in the Red Cross would fight it, and I would be at the tender mercies of Roosevelt, whose loyalties were worth nothing, and fighting against a New Deal drive behind Davis. It seemed to me a terrible thing to project this sort of a situation, when the lives of so many would be at stake."[70]

Taylor had been gone from Hoover's apartment but a few minutes when Rickard, Richey, journalist and close friend Mark Sullivan, and friend and adviser Arch Shaw came together to discuss over lunch the question that was as important to them as were the overtures emanating from Washington. What should be the Chief's response on the "neutrality question [soon] to come before Congress"?[71] Later in the afternoon Hoover met with Perrin Galpin and discussed the Polish situation and the possibility of conducting a Polish relief campaign. Galpin had served as secretary to the CRB and the ARA and as president of the Belgian American Educational Foundation created from the CRB's remaining funds in the aftermath of World War I. He recounted his experience in his *Reminiscences*, writing of his close association with Hoover, Hugh Gibson, and American ambassador Brad Whitlock and of the daily challenges faced in feeding millions in Belgium and northern France. The Belgians, for his successes, rewarded him with honorary degrees from the Universities of Brussels and Louvain. Galpin was well versed in how to organize and run a massive feeding program and would be a welcome addition to Kellogg's burgeoning relief committee. Having worked together in Belgium and Poland, Galpin and Kellogg were close friends. Toward the end of their meeting, after Galpin had agreed to assist Kellogg, Hoover invited him to join the "neutrality revision team" for dinner. With Galpin in attendance, Polish relief was a subject likely touched on, but the discussion focused on how the neutrality laws should be revised. All soon agreed that when the legislation was formalized, Republicans should insist that a preamble "state without equivocation the U.S. would not enter the war, and not simply 'hope' it would not, as the president stated."[72]

Hoover and his advisors feared the president was hiding his intentions and, given his "impulsive temperament," "what he might do."[73] The discussion continued late into the evening, finally concluding that Hoover should not enter the debate; it should not be a party issue. The following day at lunch, at dinner, and into the evening, the discussion continued on how to support ending the arms embargo and ensure America stayed out of war. Hoover sought middle ground, falling back on a position he had backed during the Geneva Disarmament Conference, which took place late in his term as president. The United States, he reiterated, should be restricted to selling only defensive weapons, a list that forbade guns over 75mm, submarines, bombers, and poison gas. The embargo should be rescinded, yes, but not without qualification.

Hoover, having for some time feared that a wider European war was on the horizon, had put forth a proposal in July outlining rules that he hoped belligerents and neutrals would adopt: blockade should not apply to food ships and there should be "no bombing of civilian populations [or] anywhere except in the field of actual fighting men on land or sea, and at works devoted strictly to munitions."[74] The Geneva and Hague Conventions and his own long experience contributed to his original thinking on preventing and limiting war. He was outraged that the Japanese in China, the Italians in Africa, and the Germans and Italians in Spain had violated the precepts he advocated and wantonly flaunted international agreements. He continually sought tools that would harness aggressors and articulated methods of enforcement. When the Japanese overran Manchuria in 1931, creating the puppet state of Manchukuo, Hoover, then president, opposed economic sanctions for the damage inflicted on the innocent, stating, "We will not go along on war or any of the sanctions either economic or military, for those are the roads to war."[75] Working with his secretary of state, Henry Stimson, who argued for economic sanctions, Hoover prevailed and originated the idea of nonrecognition. The "Hoover-Stimson Doctrine" was adopted "virtually verbatim" by the League of Nations. While nonrecognition did not curtail Japanese aggression, it became one more way of pressuring nations that violated international law and today remains in use, although critics then and now charge the doctrine amounts to no more than "spears of straw and swords of ice."[76]

Taylor, back in Washington, reported to Davis that Hoover had rejected the idea of a new relief agency, maintaining it was the job of the Red Cross. Davis brought Roosevelt news of the Taylor meeting later that same afternoon. The president, peeved by Hoover's rejection of his offered rapprochement, was encouraged by Eleanor to try again and so instructed Davis to arrange another meeting, even though he recognized that Hoover's recommendations required a change in policy. Hoover, eager for Roosevelt's response, was willing to hear more. He agreed to meet with Davis. The next day, September 13, Roosevelt and Davis met again and decided they would try to bring Hoover around by offering him leadership of relief operations.

Prior to Davis's arrival on September 14, earlier in the day, Hoover met with Maurice Pate, who had been a part of the CRB and after the war played a leading role in the ARA in Poland, which fed over one million children. Pate spoke fluent Polish, worked for Standard Oil in Poland in 1920s, had married a Polish socialite, and was a business partner of William C. McDonald, who had distinguished himself during the siege of Warsaw. Hoover revealed that he was moving toward forming an independent Polish relief organization that would feed the Poles and asked him to join Kellogg and Galpin, both of whom Pate had worked with in the past, in putting together an organization. Pate agreed to serve.

That evening, Davis joined Hoover, Edgar Rickard, and Arch Shaw, management theorists and longtime supporters, at 6:30 p.m. for dinner and cocktails.[77] The careful Hoover invited Rickard and Shaw to ensure he had witnesses. Later, as he had done after his meeting with Taylor, he wrote a memorandum of the conversation, which he later revised several times.[78] Over the course of the four-hour dinner, Davis pushed Hoover to consider Roosevelt's offer to head the proposed European relief operation. Hoover declined, but the crypto-candidate implied, as he had to Taylor, that a key reason was that "he might be directing a political campaign."[79] Hoover again emphasized that "it would be unfortunate if a large number of committees and organizations came into being . . . to collect for relief," reiterating that "all war relief from the United States should be concentrated in the American Red Cross."[80] Finally, he stressed that the Red Cross was in a position to send a relief unit to Poland almost immediately and should do so. Davis countered, explaining that the Red Cross was dependent on voluntary contributions, and in his judgment the public was not prepared to supply large amounts of money. Only Polish American groups had shown they would undertake raising money, but Davis claimed that "no substantial amounts had yet been received."[81] Hoover agreed to submit his challenging proposals in writing to the Red Cross Executive Committee and to accept Davis's invitation to come to Washington to attend the Executive Committee meeting scheduled for Monday, September 18. But he stipulated that there would be no contact with Roosevelt.[82] Davis, in response, said that the president did not understand why Hoover was unfriendly toward him. He knew nothing about any withdrawal of Secret Service protection that Hoover revealed to Taylor. While Roosevelt may not have known about Starling's rejection of Richey's request, he surely understood Hoover's "unfriendliness." Hoover, of course, found the claim of "unfriendliness" patronizing and disingenuous, and the Secret Service explanation left him incredulous. Regardless of these rough spots, Rickard, in his diary, characterized the evening as "most interesting." Hoover and Davis reminisced about their years together in the administration of Woodrow Wilson, a president both greatly admired, as well as about their disappointment that the United States had not joined the League of Nations and the failure of the General Disarmament Conference on which both worked so hard.[83] But conviviality did not break the stalemate. As promised, on the following day Hoover sent off the requested letter but continued to harbor serious reservations about Roosevelt's offer. His meetings with Taylor and Davis had not allayed his suspicion about their intentions.[84]

 Davis left Hoover's apartment late that evening for the four-hour trip back to Washington. The temperature had fallen to the mid-sixties on a beautiful fall night, the sky barely illuminated by a sliver of new moon. In the rear seat of the dark car, Davis had time to mull over his discussions with the unmovable Hoover and to consider what he would say to the president and tell Eleanor when she asked. Things were moving fast at home and abroad. The day before, Roosevelt had called Congress into an extraordinary session to amend the neutrality legislation, with the opening gavel set for September 21. The *New York Daily News* headlined General

The Rapprochement That Failed

Kazimierz Sosnkowski's successes as a victory on the way to defeat: "Poles Tottering: Report 2 Nazis Divisions Routed," and a bit farther down the page, "Lwow, an Inferno under Nazi Raids."[85] What the president might do for a stricken Poland, how to expand "emergency aid," and concerns about Hoover were all up in the air. While Davis was dining with Hoover in New York, Berle recorded in his diary a harbinger of rising tensions and tragedies yet to come:

> Last night, a quiet dinner party. . . . It was intended to be a pleasant evening. But [Finnish minister Hjalmar] Procopé came in twenty minutes late, white as a sheet. He had a cable from Helsinki saying that the Russian troops would be on the march in a few hours. His advices I think were a bit previous; I should think it would still be a couple of days; but Procopé . . . knew exactly what it meant. He plucked me by the sleeve and told me this; and I told him I had been considering the situation, and devoted the rest of the evening to trying to buck him up a little. There is not a trace of the diplomat left; merely a well-informed Finn seeing the end of one of the most valiant attempts in history to remake a nation. For undoubtedly with the Russians on the march Finland, Estonia and Latvia are gone; Lithuania I suppose will be left as a puppet state, nominally for buffer purposes.[86]

Berle was right that it would still be a few days, but Procopé's fears were justified, even if not yet realized. Soon after the Soviets had secured their share of Poland, the Finns were pressured to sign a mutual-assistance pact. The Estonian foreign minister, Karl Selter, was called to Moscow for consultation on September 24 and handed an ultimatum. The secret protocols of the Nazi-Soviet pact were now unfolding for all to see. The Soviets would defend Leningrad by grabbing the north and south shores of the Gulf of Finland, all accomplished with German connivance.

In the morning, after only a few hours' sleep, Davis called Pa Watson, Roosevelt's secretary, asking to meet with the president as soon as possible. Watson immediately sent Roosevelt a memo: "Norman Davis says that Hoover is coming Monday. He thinks it most important that he report what Hoover said yesterday to him before Hoover gets here."[87] Roosevelt, eager to hear what his adversary had to say, asked that Davis come to the White House first thing in the morning. The sleepy go-between had the first appointment of the day, when meetings regularly began around 11:00 a.m. The president asked several questions and was particularly interested in where Hoover thought the money might come from to aid the suffering Poles. Davis responded that Hoover advocated an appeal to Red Cross chapters, an idea that neither he nor Roosevelt thought possible. The cost of a feeding program would far exceed anything that might flow from the chapters. After all, the country was still in a slow economic recovery. Neither Roosevelt nor Davis seemed to consider, if the Red Cross was not likely to succeed with a fund-raising campaign, how Hoover was to fare if he were to become head of a new European relief agency. But contradiction and differences aside, the president was satisfied that the Red Cross was consulting with Hoover and that he was coming to Washington.[88] The president, however, as Hoover surmised, had no intention of reversing a major plank in his policy, which might involve the United States in a cross-blockade feeding operation, could prove a back door to war, and would require going to Congress for a large expenditure of money. Going to Congress could kick off a political football that threatened neutrality revision and could undermine his plans to make Britain and France the first line of the country's defense. Floating the idea of a new relief agency had for Roosevelt been from the start theoretical, a possible option for a future contingency. The president wished to learn what such a relief agency might look like—the Red Cross had never done a mass-feeding operation on a continuing basis—but given his current commitment to limited emergency aid, a new relief agency was out of the question. He knew, too, that even if he changed current policy, Hoover would likely never join his administration, and that was why he had made the offer. Consulting the former president might provide useful information and would allow him to better judge Hoover's political plans, satisfy critics, and mollify Eleanor and her friends, but a part of his political theater required that Hoover meet with the Executive Committee and submit a proposal that would be rejected. Ironically, with adjustments in timing and procedure, Hoover wanted the same thing. The rapprochement had turned into a quid pro quo. Later an aide quipped that with Hoover it was a matter of whether you wanted him outside the tent pissing in or inside the tent pissing out. Roosevelt never wanted Hoover at all.

As Hoover's letter traveled from New York City to Washington, he began to have second thoughts about attending the Red Cross Central Committee meeting. He called Davis on Saturday morning with the suggestion that his letter be released to the press, arguing that this would make clear his position and "avoid useless speculation."[89] He wanted the letter published to make a record that Roosevelt's relief policies would do little or nothing for the Poles. Publication also offered him protection against whatever version the committee might report of what transpired at the meeting. He feared being co-opted but also suspected that he might be being used; he smelled a trap. It would be embarrassing for him to be present if the committee rejected his proposal. He feared headlines like "Hoover Again Leaves Washington in Defeat" or "Red Cross Rejects Former President's Relief Proposals." Such headlines would kill his political future. Hoover's reluctance to travel to Washington was further complicated by his belief that protocol dictated that, as a former president, he was obligated to call on the sitting president. For Hoover, Washington was a minefield. He would not go.

Davis did not hesitate in refusing Hoover's second gambit, saying he would not publish the letter before the committee had a chance to discuss. The letter, in effect, he told Hoover, was "ringing the bell for a national campaign for funds for relief in Poland."[90] Hoover's thoughts about Davis's reference that he wished to conduct a Salvation Army red kettle street campaign are unknown. If such a campaign were to occur, said Davis, the Red Cross would be obligated to "undertake similar mass feeding relief and feeding operations when other civilian populations became destitute."[91] While Hoover feared being used, Davis well understood that his intentions were to publicly reveal that the Roosevelt administration had no intention of coming to Poland's aid. The final paragraph of the Hoover letter took Davis by surprise, for Hoover, playing the camel, made an effort to shove his nose under the tent, claiming, "In addition to acting as an Honorary Vice President of the Red Cross I should sit in the councils of the Executive and Central Committees."[92] Davis had not offered these policy-recommendation seats to Hoover and would not have done so without the prior approval of the Executive Committee and the president. Always the diplomat, Davis called it a "misunderstanding."

For a second time on Saturday, Hoover phoned Davis, interrupting an article he was drafting for the *Saturday Evening Post* on staying out of war, offering to withdraw references to Poland and replace them with a general statement that the Red Cross "should be prepared to undertake the sort of relief operations which had been carried on . . . during and after the World War." Between the first and second telephone calls, Davis met with Roosevelt to plan the way forward. Sticking with no to publishing the letter and no to an expanded relief program, they decided on a compromise. Davis offered to send Hoover a telegram inviting him to Monday's meeting, which he was welcome to release to the press. Hoover rejected the idea of a telegram as insufficient and would not be coming to Washington; there was nothing to be gained by traveling to the nation's capital. The two adversaries' attempt at securing advantage ended in deadlock. Davis, in a face-saving move, asked Hoover whether, "in the event the Red Cross should launch a national campaign for war relief funds," he would head such a committee.[93] Hoover declined but reiterated that he "would be willing to be a member of the committee" and would not give up his attempts at securing leverage over Red Cross decisions.[94] Davis, dumbfounded, was surely puzzled by the former president's chutzpah.

The rush of weekend events continued as Hoover wrestled with Davis but was interrupted by Ambassador Potocki, who formally requested that Hoover undertake relief for his embattled country.[95] While Warsaw, under siege, was holding out, the Germans had cornered the army and the government in a few square miles around the small town of Kuty on the Polish-Romanian frontier. Any plans for a redoubt evaporated. The Red Army's being strung all along the Polish border but concentrated in the south suggested a rapid thrust to capture the government. At any moment, Marshal Edward Śmigły-Rydz might be forced to give the order to abandon the country, crossing the bridge over the Czeremosz into exile. The ambassador recognized from the war's start that Poland's need for foreign assistance would be great and the possibility of receiving any was slim. He had, to no avail, persistently lobbied the State Department.

Daily he hounded Arthur Krock of the *New York Times*, asking, "What in the world is England doing about sending help to Poland; that Poland is suffering terribly?"[96] Great Britain and France would not come to their allies' aid in any substantial way, nor would neutral governments, whose only response was an outpouring of sympathy.

Potocki, rebuffed by the Roosevelt administration, reasoned that Hoover might help, though he recognized the dangers that accompanied asking a fierce Roosevelt opponent out of office and out of favor. As millions of Poles revered Hoover, Potocki wagered he might again be induced to come to Poland's aid. He approached Hoover because of his reputation, but that reputation was based on his effectiveness as a "miracle worker" in organizing huge relief operations. More important, his past achievements for Poland were an integral part of the country's history. In 1919, working through Wilson and on numerous committees at Versailles, Hoover had pushed hard for a recreated Polish state. He was friends with Poland's first president, Ignacy Paderewski, and had through the ARA provided huge amounts of food, medicine, and critical supplies, contributing mightily to the country's survival in its first few tumultuous years. He was widely respected for having overcome great odds against his success: the British efforts at blockade, Allied hostility to feeding programs, and a mountain of red tape that threatened to strangle aid. Potocki needed his talents but also his gritty determination, a persistence that caused Winston Churchill to call him a son of a bitch. Hoover's sobriquet, "Master of Emergencies," recognized his mastery of logistics. John Maynard Keynes, a prominent economist and member of the British delegation to the Paris Peace Conference, said Hoover "was the only man who emerged from the ordeal of Paris with an enhanced reputation."[97] Hoover had only recently burnished his Polish credentials when a spring fact-finding trip to Europe included a visit to Poland. In Kraków he paid tribute at the tombs of Józef Piłsudski and the American Revolutionary War hero Tadeusz Kościuszko, but, significantly for the future of Polish relief, Hoover briefly stopped in Warsaw, where he visited, among others, the American director of the Polish YMCA, Paul Super, and his wife, Margaret, honoring the role the Y had played in resurrecting Poland in its first years of independence.[98] Back in the United States, he wrote to Super, "This letter is for the dual purpose of expressing appreciation for the fine courtesy you extended to me in Warsaw, but more important than that, my admiration for the magnificent work you have carried on in Poland."[99]

The country showed its gratitude to Hoover by showering him with honorary degrees, awards, and medals.[100] Potocki could not be sure of Hoover's response to his request, but it was a certainty that Hoover needed the Poles as badly as they needed him. If Hoover could be persuaded to act, then more than emergency aid might be obtained.[101] To the ambassador's surprise and relief, Hoover revealed an aid effort had been underway since he had greenlighted Kellogg's activities on the second day of the war. Hoover must have been pleased by the ambassador's request, as the timing offered an opportunity to increase his leverage with the Red Cross; more important, it conferred legitimacy on his burgeoning relief organization and guaranteed his option to act independently. Potocki may not have realized that Hoover intended to launch his political campaign not from the heart of America but from the heart of a Europe in shambles. On reflection, this should have not been surprising, as Hoover's first reach for the presidency in 1920 had begun in the devastation of Belgium and Poland caused by the Great War. During his two Saturday telephone conversations with Davis, Hoover did not mention Potocki's plea or that he had agreed to help the Poles.

Charlotte Kellogg made her way through the black-and-white tiled corridors of the elegant State Department building on the morning of Sunday, September 17, burdened by reports that the Soviet Union had invaded eastern Poland. At 5:30 a.m., Roosevelt had his sleep interrupted yet again when Bullitt called from Paris with the news.[102] True, Warsaw still held, but it would be a matter of weeks, perhaps only days, until the end of a Poland she and her husband had worked so hard to build. The defeat was not unexpected, nor was the Soviet invasion, for reports of the Red Army massing along the Polish frontier had been arriving for days. Still, when the expected finally happened, it was a shock. The events in Poland had the State Department operational even though it was Sunday. Kellogg, on behalf of her gathering Polish relief committee, was there to send a cable, jointly written with partner Galpin, requesting information from US ambassador to Poland Tony Biddle, now in Bucharest. To judge the magnitude of the relief challenge they would face, they needed to know the number of Poles in Romania and Hungary. Reports were erratic, but large numbers of Poles had also fled into Lithuania and a smaller number into Latvia; apparently a large number sought protection from the Red Army moving through eastern Poland, especially Jews. By sheer coincidence, Kellogg crossed paths with Davis. "I going in—he on his way to see Eleanor Roosevelt on this very matter."[103] Davis told her that "Mr. Hoover, the other day, had told him that in his opinion the Red Cross should do the *whole job*."[104] Kellogg held her tongue. "I did not ask if Mr. Hoover had not mentioned the fact that he had encouraged this understanding." She went on to tell Davis that she only began to organize for the Poles after seeking the approval of Hoover and that he had encouraged her. Davis's response seemed strange to her. "I think he thought there was humor in the situation. But there was just a suggestion of something I didn't quite get!"[105] The suggestion seemed to be that her undertaking was unnecessary or at best redundant. Davis's position seemed puzzling. But the humor, or perhaps irony, that Davis found was that all the while Hoover had been insisting "the Red Cross should do the whole job," he had been organizing a relief effort. He was playing a double game.

Kellogg, cable sent, returned home to send a letter updating Galpin on what had occurred with Davis. Of her reception at the State Department, she wrote, "I can't say enough about the swift friendly, effective help I get there."[106] She reported that, the day before, a productive meeting of the relief planners had taken place but emphasized, "Our major uncertainty is the time and size of the Red Cross effort which may be made. By the end of the week the picture should be clearer. In the meantime, we have been preparing for that first meeting of the nucleus of the committee-to-be and hope it may be called for Thursday next."[107] Her committee-to-be was not, she stressed, "at all in opposition [to the Red Cross]—we have a clear understanding of our supplementary purpose, which may, at any moment become contributory, or even merge."[108] Equally strange, Kellogg, as an afterthought, wrote across the top of the letter, "Please destroy—you always do, don't you?"[109] Galpin did not.

Davis, after the brief tête-á-tête with Kellogg, walked the short distance to the White House to keep his appointment with the First Lady.

Eleanor was eager to persuade him of her point of view. "Young people of this country," Eleanor said, "were interested in doing something to help other people and ... if they could be organized for rendering relief abroad they would be satisfied and would be less inclined to become interested in fighting."[110] She told Davis that "she had talked to the President about this and had suggested that, in view of the great experience which Mr. Hoover had had, it would be a fine thing to get him to head some such a move" and "she thought that perhaps, since they might be undertaking operations that would not come within the scope of Red Cross activities, there ought to be a separate organization but in some way affiliated with or cooperating with the Red Cross."[111] Kellogg and the First Lady shared a similar vision of any new relief effort or agency. Davis responded that he had spoken with the president and talked with Hoover: "He was insistent that the Red Cross do it and what the almost insuperable difficulties were but that I was going to talk the whole thing over with the Executive Committee on Monday. Mrs. Roosevelt was very sorry and hoped we could still get Mr. Hoover interested."[112] Eleanor was not about to give up winning over her husband and Davis to a broader relief effort on behalf of the Poles and the thousands of other European refugees. With the conversation at an end, she told Davis that the president would like to see him in his study.

Davis and the president had been in touch almost daily for several weeks, so there was nothing new to report. Still, Roosevelt maintained that he wished to work something out with Hoover. Davis answered he would know more after the next day's meeting with the Executive Committee. He explained that Hoover's request to be honorary vice president and to sit on Red Cross policy committees, if granted, would mean that an invitation would have to be extended to the other honorary vice president, Chief Justice Hughes, and to Roosevelt himself as president of the Red Cross. "Jokingly," Roosevelt quipped "that if he attended, we would have to have the meetings at the White House."[113] Davis must have smiled, as both well understood that Hoover's refusal to meet with Roosevelt precluded such a meeting from happening. The solution, said Davis, was to skirt Hoover's request and, after the Executive Committee meeting, invite him to attend the next scheduled meeting. Roosevelt "entirely agreed," adding as an afterthought "that it would have been highly inadvisable to publish Mr. Hoover's letter."[114]

Davis and Roosevelt, after deciding on how to proceed, talked over the problems surrounding relief more generally. "The President said that he felt that the civilian distress was going to be terrible and that the Red Cross should, insofar as possible, extend its activities to civilian relief because whereas originally the chief victims of war were the fighting forces, the civilians were becoming more and more victims of war."[115] While Davis may have sounded ambiguous on civilian relief in his conversation with Kellogg, with the president he was clear: "We wanted to do what we could but . . . what we could do would depend largely upon what the American people were willing to have us do, but . . . to undertake mass relief on the scale that Hoover had in mind and what he had carried on before would be clearly beyond the capacity of the Red Cross and any possible private organization."[116] Polish relief alone, under Hoover, he told Roosevelt, "expended two hundred million dollars, which came largely from appropriations by Congress and by some other governments."[117] Davis and the president thought to expand emergency aid somewhat to include food relief when practical, but no large extended feeding programs would be undertaken. All money for aid would continue to be dependent on donations from the Red Cross chapters. As Davis left the White House, the president was wheeled into the dining room to lunch with British ambassador Lord Lothian, knowing that tomorrow's committee vote would go his way. For Roosevelt, the attempted rapprochement with Hoover was over. Tellingly, the president did not meet again with Davis until late September. As for Poland, the president judged that the nation was in the final throes of defeat and partition and, for all practical purposes, beyond reach. To Lothian, over their Sunday lunch, he confided that "the restoration of Poland depended upon the outcome of the war and not on the attempt to render aid strategically now, however difficult it might be to resist the piteous appeal of the Poles and public opinion."[118] For the president, the Polish crisis moved far down the list of his concerns. Now he could devote his full attention to neutrality revision. In three days, he would preside over a national unity conference. On September 20, fourteen leading Democrats and fourteen leading

Republicans gathered to discuss neutrality and peace. Former president Hoover did not receive an invitation. Roosevelt had extracted his price for Hoover's unwillingness to meet with him.[119] The special session of Congress convened the next day, September 21. In addressing the members of the House and Senate, Roosevelt asked his divided and anxious listeners to "again re-examine our own legislation."[120] It remained to be seen whether Congress would pass the changes the president proposed. Roosevelt, like Hoover, anticipated a terrific battle.

After the Sunday morning meeting with Davis, Eleanor, that evening, wrote to Missy Meloney expressing her disappointment at Hoover's rejection of her husband's offers, explaining that the reason given was that "next year he might be directing a political campaign."[121] Eleanor was far off the mark, avoiding the deep policy differences of which she was aware. But she emphasized, "I am still trying to induce them [her husband, Davis, and the Red Cross] to do something on a fairly comprehensive scale and I think after the Red Cross meeting tomorrow and by the time I get back on the 26th the gentlemen may have straightened out their thinking on this subject. I think men are slower than women under certain circumstances."[122] While Eleanor certainly had a point about men, in this case she was slow to realize that the decision on ending discussions with Hoover and limiting aid had been made that morning. When back in Washington, she further expressed her disappointment in a letter to her close friend Martha Gellhorn: "Dear Marty . . . Mr. Hoover turned us down."[123] A few weeks later, she wrote to Meloney, this time outlining the wide differences on policy between her husband and Hoover but suggesting that perhaps there was another explanation:

> I also heard from someone else that Mr. Hoover felt a little hurt that Franklin had not talked to him himself. I think he has a right to feel that way because I think Franklin should have talked to him, but many of the men around Franklin felt it was wiser to sound Mr. Hoover out first.[124]

Eleanor's source, likely Davis, who heard it from Taylor, was right that Hoover was offended by Roosevelt's indirect approach. The touchy Hoover, a stickler for protocol and protective of his status as a former president, would object to anything other than mano a mano.¹²⁵ This slight, however, does not account for the failed rapprochement.

Davis, on Monday, at the committee meeting, carefully explained his interactions with Hoover and asked for the members' advice. Following Davis's lead, all agreed that the former president should be invited to a future meeting and that Hoover's letter would delete policy recommendations if released to the press. Davis promised to inform Hoover of the committee's decision and to thank him for his advice.¹²⁶ As planned, Davis and Roosevelt got the results they wanted. The committee recognized that the Hoover courtship was at an end. Belated attempts, regrets, and recriminations would follow, but the two great adversaries' ideas on aid had reached an unbreachable gulf. Both were gratified that no reporter caught wind of this headline story throughout the shuttle diplomacy between the White House, the State Department, the Red Cross, and Hoover's Waldorf apartment.

As promised, Davis called Hoover the following afternoon, breaking the news of the committee's rejection of his proposals. It was a short conversation, but Davis divulged that Eleanor had encouraged the president to reach out to him and that his friend Marie Meloney had lobbied for him to head an enlarged relief effort. Meloney lived in the Waldorf, just a few floors above Hoover. Immediately after ending the call, he was on his way to her apartment to hear the full story, amazed that he had an ally in the First Lady.¹²⁷ Back in 31-A, Hoover told Rickard what he had learned. That evening Rickard penned in his diary, "Mrs. Roosevelt has injected herself into this business and has talked with Marie Meloney, trying to get Marie to persuade H. H. he must take over European relief problem."¹²⁸ As for Davis, Hoover thought he "was trying to give square deal" but that Roosevelt was trying to sidetrack him.¹²⁹ What Meloney told Hoover is unknown, but it was she who had first written Eleanor on behalf of Hoover, although the First Lady may have earlier reached the same conclusion. In any event, she had warmly received her friend's recommendation.

Matters were further complicated the following day when Kellogg called Rickard, "thinking H. H. trying to block formation of her independent Polish Relief but managed to clear her mind."¹³⁰ Kellogg could only have gotten that idea from Meloney, who had talked briefly with

Hoover the previous afternoon. The two had long been friends and were instrumental in 1923 in bringing Marie Curie to the United States and raising funds to purchase her needed radium. Together they had translated Madame Curie's biography of Pierre Curie, and Meloney wrote the book's introduction. It is possible that Kellogg knew all along that Meloney was asking Eleanor to push FDR to bring Hoover in as head of relief. That they may have on occasion spoken to one another, sharing information, is not surprising, as both were passionate about doing what they could for the Poles.

Later that same day, Meloney had the opportunity to explain all in her meeting with Hoover. For her, Hoover's refusal meant the grand White House relief conference, which she had imagined was to be attended by concerned, prominent American women and which Eleanor had endorsed, was not to happen. The two women were also disappointed that their effort to have Hoover head a new relief agency had failed, as had their effort to convince the president and the Red Cross to commit to more than emergency aid. Eleanor, however, did not accept defeat. When an opportunity arose, she continued to urge a role for Hoover and to advocate for a greatly expanded relief effort on the part of her husband's administration.

For Hoover, the final rejection of his proposals freed him to move forward however he chose. The White House had surrendered the initiative. If successful, he would increase his leverage, bolstering the chances of his political comeback and forcing the administration to explain why it was doing so little for Poland. The day after receiving Davis's telephone call, Hoover did not miss the opportunity to steal a march on the administration. It had to be pleasurable to write Davis, shaming the Red Cross for its moral failure to step up. "I was disappointed," he wrote, "to hear that there was any hesitancy on the part of the Red Cross in undertaking one the greatest obligations that has ever come to them. To take the leadership of American effort to allay civilian suffering in the war is a mission which no one can perform so effectively as the Red Cross."[131] Davis's answer was an insipid recitation of the problems involved as a justification of Red Cross policy.[132] A few days later, Davis again wrote to Hoover informing him that the International Red Cross, with German approval, had sent two representatives to Warsaw to survey relief needs and that the Red Cross had decided to send two delegates to Europe to investigate. To Hoover, this new information merely confirmed that the Red Cross would do little to help the Poles.[133]

Kellogg, on the morning of September 21, received a call from Moffat at the State Department informing her that the telegram she had sent to Biddle in Bucharest had received a reply.[134] The ambassador estimated there were fifteen to twenty thousand refugees, with the number "rapidly increasing."[135] As no significant relief effort was operating in Romania, Biddle recommended medical supplies, food, and shelter for those who had fled and for those in need in Poland. Later that day, Moffat sent Kellogg portions of the telegram and attached a handwritten note on larger estimates of refugee numbers from the press. Based on Associated Press and United Press dispatches, the *New York Post* reported on September 19 and 20 that over one hundred thousand had entered Romania and over thirty thousand "had reached Hungarian soil."[136] Kellogg, given the huge and growing numbers, realized that with winter coming her committee-to-be faced a humanitarian crisis. Action was immediately required.

Early on Friday evening, Kellogg met with Hoover, bringing news of the number of desperate Poles and the progress she had made organizing a relief committee. Over the weekend, Hoover decided to act. On Sunday, he wrote again to Davis that since the Red Cross Executive Committee's decision rejected his proposals, "there was no use for [him] in the picture."[137] In a note to himself rationalizing a decision he had made sometime before, he wrote, "This wound it up so far as I was concerned. If there is a relief job to be done, I will organize it myself."[138] He was confident that the next president would be a Republican, in which case relief policy would change instantly. If, however, another Republican besides himself were elected, Hoover would likely receive a position in the new administration—a cabinet post or perhaps the directorship of emergency war relief. At the very least, he would exercise considerable influence. Hoover came to know that Roosevelt's offer was a hollow gesture, that he would have overseen an agency unlikely to conduct a nationwide fund-raising campaign, serving a president unlikely to request Congress to authorize needed funding. In a hostile administration he would be stranded on a bureaucratic island surrounded by sharks—a St. Helena existence was no existence at all. With his independence intact, Hoover would, as he had in the past, go his own way. On Monday, he threw down the gauntlet, announcing he had formed a Commission for Polish Relief (CPR). He would expedite aid to the refugees and explore ways to aid those in Poland proper, depending on what unfolded. He maintained that "the voice of experience says we could not create liberty and self-government in Europe. We cannot reconstruct Europe," claiming reason told him that it was not America's war.[139] But while Europe could not be reconstructed, it could be fed. Difficult obstacles stood in the way, but to Hoover it seemed possible to replicate the achievements of the CRB and the ARA. From the large pool of loyal, experienced relief workers, he could count on volunteers to flesh out an organization and act quickly.

This "Hoover Club," on which Hoover would draw, was a lifetime fraternity whose members promoted and protected one another, recruited others with a similar outlook and background, and rose to positions of power and authority; it included, wrote Hoover, "cabinet members, judges, governors, generals, admirals, and high officials in our Foreign Service."[140] The basis for membership was professionalism and expertise, but having money was important, and having made money yourself was best. The top echelon of any Hoover organization was expected to volunteer. As the Chief, he was the commander of a private relief national guard—minutemen who had the means to put aside other commitments for immediate service. As the Paris Peace Conference wrapped up in 1919, Hoover concluded that its creation, the Treaty of Versailles, was so hopelessly flawed that Europe would assuredly face future catastrophes.[141] The terrible *Boche* banished, Parisians seemed atop the world; reveling in their victory, they enjoyed a fine summer by jamming the outdoor cafés and strolling the boulevards. Hoover, to the contrary, poured out his foreboding to Wilson's closest advisor, Colonel Edward House, who wrote in his diary,

> Hoover fairly wallowed in gloom last night. He talked to me steadily from seven o'clock until ten and there was not a ray of light to be seen in any directions. Europe is to be in chaos, according to him, within thirty days. I tried to get him to make it thirty-one, but he refused.[142]

Hoover's worst fears were confirmed by French premier Georges Clemenceau, who pulled him aside as he was about to leave Paris: "There will be another world war in your time and you will be needed back in Europe."[143] Clemenceau's assuredness was tinged with a biting irony, as the cynical premier was largely responsible for the treaty's flaws. Hoover remained in a grand funk, as did his friend, famous economist and member of the British delegation to the Paris Peace Conference, John Maynard Keynes, who shared with him the view that the treaty was seriously problematic. Keynes would tag the Versailles settlement a Carthaginian peace in a best-selling book *The Economic Consequences of the Peace*.[144] But Keynes, despite his despair, conferred on Hoover the distinction of leaving Versailles with an enhanced reputation.[145] When the CRB and ARA relief missions officially ended, these organizations did not die. Most who served with the Chief shared his belief that they would be needed in the future, and so Hoover, along with the organization's alumni, set up skeletal versions—associations and foundations that continued various forms of scaled-down philanthropy. Importantly, these shrunken agencies—organizations staffed by veterans, now minutemen of relief, who prided themselves on being called Hoovermen—could be rapidly scaled up to meet the next famine emergency. The Chief said of his ready reserves, "No other group of men in the world had comparable experiences in the administration of relief, or an understanding of the terrors and suffering from starvation."[146] When Hoover announced the forming of the CPR, all the officers and a third of the directors were old hands from the CRB and the ARA. But who were these men and women who would rescue the Poles, where had they served, and what had been their accomplishments?

Women in the Hoover Club were few in number, but one who occasionally called him Chief was Charlotte Kellogg, who was the leading force in bringing about the CPR. She had been ably assisted by Galpin, Pate, and Rickard. In the shuffle of officers and directors during the first few months of operation, Kellogg became vice chairman, the only woman at the executive level. Her friend, Hoover enthusiast Missy Meloney, may not have gotten her White House conference on relief, but she was rewarded with a seat on the CPR board of directors.[147] The men asked to

Charlotte Kellogg, Belgium War Relief speaking tour, circa 1940 (courtesy of Kellogg-Dickie Papers, Manuscripts and Archives, Yale University Library).

serve with the CPR came from different parts of the country and had varied educations, though many had attended elite universities in the United States and abroad. Hoover, who saw himself as a man of the West, favored graduates from his alma mater, Stanford, and had an affinity for Californians. Some few were the scions of the captains of industry, and others were East Coast blue bloods. Chauncey McCormick, cousin of the irascible and eccentric editor of the *Chicago Tribune*, Colonel Robert A. McCormick, served as CPR chairman. His grandfather partnered with William Deering, who founded the International Harvester Company, and Chauncey served on its board for many years. Just weeks before the outbreak of World War I, he married William Deering's granddaughter in Paris, thus merging two shares of a huge fortune into one. As a captain in the American Expeditionary Force, he was charged with providing medical supplies and food for refugees. He came to the attention of Hoover in 1918 and was sent to Poland to work with the ARA in distributing food throughout the war-shattered country. Art lovers, he and his wife amassed a huge collection that led him to become a trustee of the Art Institute of Chicago and later its president.

The president of the CPR, Maurice Pate, was assisted by Hugh W. Gibson, who had retired from the State Department a year earlier after a distinguished career and become an editor at Doubleday, Doran, where he published *Belgium*, an introduction to the small country's history and culture. As secretary of legation in Brussels from 1914 to 1916, Gibson, by chance, was present at the creation. In the office of American ambassador to Great Britain Walter Hines Page, he witnessed Page and two Belgian diplomats persuade Hoover to put aside his international mining company and organize food for Belgium's hungry. As an American diplomat, Gibson was instrumental in assuring Hoover's CRB was successful. Prescient, he and a friend formed the first Hoover for President Club in June 1915, testifying they would see Hoover in the White House within fifteen years. Gibson achieved notoriety that same year when he defended Canadian nurse Edith Cavell, who had been accused of espionage and would be executed by the Germans. Her crime was helping over two hundred British prisoners escape into Holland.[148] In 1919, he was the first American minister to Poland, appointed because of his knowledge of the country acquired during his ARA service. In 1922, he married Ynès Reyntiens, whose father had been aide-de-camp to King Leopold II, but, unlike many in the Hoover Club, the newlyweds were not fabulously wealthy. Two years later, Gibson was appointed minister to Belgium and Luxembourg. In addition to his diplomatic duties, he served on the US delegation's preparatory commission to the General Disarmament Conference from 1926 to 1932 and on the delegations to the Geneva Naval Conference in 1927 and the London Naval Conference in 1930; finally he chaired the US delegation to the General Disarmament Conference in Geneva from 1932 to 1933. As a delegate to this series of conferences, he worked closely with fellow diplomat Norman Davis. Gibson, with Hoover, shared a commitment to bringing about arms reduction and advocated solutions to international problems through the League of Nations and the International Court, though his country belonged to neither organization. Contrary to the image of the diplomat, Gibson possessed a sunny disposition and a sense of humor that embraced a love of puns and practical jokes. Gibson's humor often took aim at the stuffed shirts that inhabited the State Department, people for whom he had no regard, tagging them "the boys with the white spats, the tea drinkers, the cookie pushers."[149] Diplomat Joseph C. Grew, in his memoirs, described Gibson as a "crackerjack," a "wild Indian."[150]

W. Hallam Tuck joined the CRB in 1915 and went to work in the ARA, where he too developed a close relationship with Hoover. After the war, a chemical engineer by training, he was active in Belgian companies. Notably, in 1920 he married Hilda Bunge, whose family was one of the largest and richest grain dealers in the world and remains so today. Near Waterloo, the Tucks constructed an opulent manor house, known as Tuck's Castle, as a summer residence. As a Hoover minuteman, Tuck answered the Chief's call to help get the CPR up and running and to provide financial assistance.

Director Lewis Strauss was the son of a Virginia shoe wholesaler whose German Jewish family had come to America in the 1840s. When the war broke out, he earned a considerable amount of money working for his father. His intent had been to go to college, but instead he decided to be of humanitarian service. He traveled to Washington and met with Hoover, who admired his gumption and accepted his offer to work without pay. Hoover quickly recognized Strauss's talents. When he became head of the War Food Administration and later formed the ARA, Strauss became his private secretary and confidante. In Paris in 1919, he befriended Rudolf Holsti, who was there to lobby for Finnish independence but was scraping by on little to no money. Strauss came to his financial rescue, introducing him to Hoover and to other champions of the Finnish fight for recognition. After independence was achieved, Strauss was instrumental in arranging loans to the newly independent country, seeing Finland through its early difficult years. In working with the American Jewish Joint Distribution Committee, Strauss came to know several partners in the prestigious Wall Street investment firm of Kuhn-Loeb, which in 1919 offered him a job. In 1923, he married Alice Hanauer, the daughter of another partner, and by 1926 his salary was over a million a year. He worked in both Hoover presidential campaigns and came to share with Hoover a deep loathing for the

New Deal. Strauss did not serve long with the CPR but could be counted on for significant contributions.

But of all those involved in launching the CPR, Merian Cooper was one of the few in the Hoover Club whose adventures exceeded the globe-trotting Chief himself. His storied life began after being expelled from the Naval Academy in his senior year for "hell raising" and advocating for airpower. Volunteering for the army, he was part of the US Expeditionary Force that unsuccessfully pursued Pancho Villa. Shot down in a flaming bomber in World War I, the seriously burned Cooper was treated by the Germans and transferred to a prisoner of war camp. On release, he spent the next two years heading the Polish division of the ARA in Lwów while distributing food throughout the region. When the Polish-Soviet War commenced in February 1919, he, along with seven other Americans, formed the famous Kościuszko Squadron. In support of the Polish advance on Kiev, Cooper was once again shot down and imprisoned for nearly nine months by the Bolsheviks. His time in prison was spent writing *What Men Die For* (published in 1927), but toward the war's end he and two other prisoners escaped and in eleven days crossed the four hundred miles to the Latvian border on foot and by hopping trains. For his bravery, Piłsudski pinned on his chest the Virtuti Militari, Poland's highest medal. Cooper went on to make travel adventure films and joined the newly formed Pan America Airways, which initiated the first regularly scheduled transatlantic fights. But what would produce lasting fame for this intrepid adventurer was writing and producing the wildly successful film *King Kong*. Cooper's vivid imagination touched off an endless genre of monster dinosaur and wild animal films. In all, he produced sixty-seven features. As head of the Hollywood Committee of the CPR, Cooper recruited stars like Mary Pickford.

Theodore Abel and Frederic C. Walcott rounded out the CPR directors and officers. Abel had been born in Łódź, immigrated to the United States, and earned a doctorate in sociology from Columbia University. After Adolf Hitler was awarded the chancellorship in 1933, Abel wanted to know who had voted for the Führer and why. He offered a cash prize for the best essay on the theme "Why I Became a Nazi." Through this innovative research technique, Abel received hundreds of essays and in

1938 published a compilation of the men's responses in a book titled *Why Hitler Came to Power*. He planned on publishing the women's essays later but did not. Assumed lost, the essays turned up in the Theodore Abel Papers when they were donated to the Hoover Institution. Frederic Walcott, like so many of Hoover's ready reserves, served in the CRB and as an assistant to Hoover in the US Food Administration, as well as with the Rockefeller War Relief Commission, which donated large amounts of money to the CRB and undertook relief work in Poland. Walcott amassed a considerable fortune in finance and in cotton-cloth manufacturing. After his World War I–era work with Hoover, he retired from business at age fifty-two and dedicated himself to conservation, focusing on restoration of the Great Mountain Forest in Connecticut. Entering the political arena, he became a member of the state senate and then a US senator. At Hoover's request, he stepped forward to serve as treasurer of the CPR.

Hoover himself was more cautious, as a failed relief effort could damage his fledging presidential campaign. Seeking a buffer, he chose to serve as an honorary chairman, a "behind-the-scenes wirepuller."[151] If the CPR failed, he would bear limited liability; if it was a success, he would "step from behind the curtain and take the applause."[152] Politics also influenced his decision, as his campaign demanded attention. It was running out of money. But more important, he reserved his time for the fight over revision of the neutrality laws. For Hoover, the battle over revision centered on stopping Roosevelt from wandering down a path that would take the country into war.

Prudence was needed with regard to direct aid to Poland, as the country's future remained unresolved and the news was grim. The heroic defense of Warsaw ended in capitulation on September 27, and in the first week of October the remaining Polish forces in the field surrendered. Still, the Germans seemed approachable and might accept food aid, but for those under the thumb of their new Red master, the prospect of aid was fanciful.

As Hoover had so often articulated, feeding the hungry was a humanitarian obligation, difficulties be damned! It was a matter of will. The first tasks were to find office space, solicit donations, and seek partner organizations in Romania, Hungary, and Lithuania that could undertake a large-scale relief operation. Herbert L. Satterlee, a CPR director who was a partner in a prestigious New York law firm and the son-in-law of J. P. Morgan, provided the CPR with a large start-up donation and two floors in a building at 37 East 36th Street rent-free for a year. The first floor became a walk-in show room, festooned with posters, tables stacked with literature, and receptionists who encouraged donations. The second floor served as the operation center.[153] If Roosevelt and Davis wondered how a private relief agency could be staffed and funded so quickly, the answer was that it had all begun years ago in Belgium, and as to money, the cumulative wealth of the founding CPR officers and directors was immense.

Regardless of the outcome in Poland, the CPR asked McDonald, in Geneva since being evacuated from Poland a few weeks earlier, to go to Berlin and began talks with the German Red Cross and with the Foreign Office. He was joined by his business partner, Pate, and soon after by Walcott and John Hartigan. Hartigan, an army officer and World War I fighter pilot, served on the Saar Plebiscite Commission for the League of Nations in the 1920s and 1930s. Gilbert Redfern, a naturalized US citizen, was sent to Vilnius, where conditions were very bad. He had spent the last six years representing American companies in Poland, reporting from there for the *Manchester Guardian*, and had been a foreign attaché in the Commerce Department in the three Republican administrations that preceded Roosevelt. Soon after, he was joined by Dorsey and Zora Stephens, who first traveled to France to survey the needs of the sixty thousand Poles exiled there.

Most of the Hoover people shuffled assignments in the field, and those in the New York office also moved in and out of various positions as circumstances dictated. Hoover's "management style," his belief in flexibility and opposition to rigid organizational plans, characterized the CPR. He was committed to centralized decision making, but implementation was to occur in decentralized fashion carried out by individual initiative. A small staff would undertake limited local organization by recruiting a few key figures in the community, then rely on publicity to stimulate rapid organizational growth and raise money. The president had developed and utilized these techniques successfully in his past relief campaigns, and he was dedicated to them. Charlotte Kellogg spearheaded building organizations in key American cities and kept Hoover apprised of success by forwarding names to him of those he might personally contact. She wrote, "I promised to pass along to you these two suggestions. If you have time while at Stanford to get in touch with this splendid Hollywood Committee . . . it would do Merian Cooper and his groups a lot of good."[154]

The New York office was staffed by Columba P. Murray Jr., Colonel Joseph Kreuger, and Bernard Fraser, all veterans of the ARA. In operation for only a few weeks, McCormick stepped down as CPR chairman and was replaced by Henry Noble MacCracken, a prominent pacifist and internationalist who shared with Hoover a commitment to social work and the growing field of public health. He was the founder of the American Junior Red Cross and a founder in 1925 of the Kościuszko Foundation, named for the famous Polish engineer and general in George Washington's army. MacCracken, after a 1922–1923 visit to Poland, teamed with the Polish American scholar Stephen Mizwa, at the request of the Polish government, to form a scholarship committee to bring Polish students to study in America. MacCracken's acceptance of the chairmanship of the CPR was a coup for Hoover, as it brought into the leadership a person outside the Hoover Club. As the CPR gained in stability and prestige, the round-robin switch of officers continued.[155] Nearly every CPR "news bulletin" recorded changes as people left for Europe, returned to jobs with the home office, or were recruited to the cause. By any standard, it was remarkable how rapidly Hoover was able to assemble an organization in both this country and abroad.

The first challenge for the commission was to find a way to assist the tens of thousands who had fled into countries on Poland's borders. The key was to enlist the Polish YMCA to conduct relief in Romania and Hungary. Y officials in Geneva and New York knew that the director, Paul Super, and his wife, Margaret, had crossed the border at Śniatyń, but nothing had been heard from the couple since.

7

Rescue in Romania, Hungary, and Lithuania

Interned Polish soldiers, Comişani Army Camp No. 2 (courtesy of Romanian National Archives, Bucharest).

THE FAIR FALL WEATHER THAT HAD DOOMED THE POLES ACCOMPANIED the refugees who flooded the highways into Bucharest, but those who undertook the journey in November faced the *crivaț*, a "frost-hard wind that blew from Siberia straight into the open mouth of the Moldavian plain."[1] As winter arrived, snow would block the mountain passes leading to Romania and Hungary, allowing only the hardy and the lucky to survive the treacherous passage. But still they came. Many would freeze to death or be shot in their effort to escape. "In Bucharest they flooded into legations and consulates of the allied and neutral powers, as well as their own."[2] Mihail Sebastian, a Jewish writer, noting the ambiguity of his own situation, wrote in his journal, "a group . . . coming toward my block. They were raggedly dressed, each carrying a battered backpack, but they were alive—do you know what I mean?—alive and saved."[3] But those fleeing Poland arrived in a country already in crisis and unprepared to provide for them, a country ruled by

> a blood-stained corrupt regime, despised by everyone except the few people who profited by it. Here . . . an upper class indifferent or pro-Nazi. Here . . . a deep-seated popular antisemitism. Here . . . a fascist movement which, decimated though it was, had the halo of martyrdom. Here . . . four-fifths of the people, eleven million out of fourteen—peasants, humble, starving, inarticulate, abjectly poor—who had never enjoyed any of the privileges of democracy.[4]

Romania, like a patient on life support, lived in dread that one of its many political factions, or the Germans or the Soviets, would at a moment's notice pull the plug ending it all. With Poland crushed, Romanians speculated on what the Nazi-Soviet pact had in store for them. Surrounded by uncertainty, King Carol and Romanian officials "were playing an edgy game, trying to appease Hitler while showing some elements of respect for their erstwhile alliance with the Poles," a defense arrangement knotted in 1927.[5] Neighbors waited for the chance to strip territory gained after the Versailles peacemakers in 1919 created a greater Romania as a reward for fighting alongside the Allies. To the northeast, Bessarabians were sure that the Soviets, on their border since mid-September, would invade any day—some abandoned their belongings and joined the Poles in seeking refuge. To the southeast, Bulgaria eyed the return of the Dobruja, while to the west the Hungarians, mourning the loss of Transylvania twenty years earlier, dreamed revanchist dreams. In response, King Carol, "trapped in a ring of 'revisionism,'" and enamored of France's defensive strategy, began construction of a three-hundred-mile Romanian Maginot Line to the west and north, which wits and critics dubbed "Carol's Dyke."[6]

Tony and Margaret Biddle arrived by train into the uncertainty of Bucharest on September 19 and were met at the station by embassy staff who drove them directly to the Athenee Place Hotel, one of the few shining stars left to support the city's reputation as the "The Little Paris of the East." The writer R. G. Waldeck described the hotel as a place where

> Spies of every Intelligence Service in the world; the diplomats and military attachés of great and little powers; British and French oil men on their way out, and German and Italian on their way in; Gestapo agents and Ovra agents and OGPU agents, or men who were at least said to be agents; amiable Gauleiters and hard-headed economic experts; distinguished Rumanian appeasers and the mink-clad German and Austrian beauties who were paid to keep them happy; the mink-clad Rumanian beauties who were paid by Udurianu [King Carol's powerful protégé and watchdog] to make the Italian and German ministers talk and who were paid by the German and Italian ministers to make Udurianu talk.[7]

The lobby and the salon rooms were steeped in the history of a menagerie of the famous and the infamous. A knowledgeable guest might recall that in 1915 John Reed, before migrating to the earthquake revolution brewing in Russia, hunkered down to write *The War in Eastern Europe*. Here in this luxurious hotel, tinged with a wash of the Orient, Biddle gathered information, attending diplomatic receptions and cocktail parties. He apprised Washington of the refugee crisis, answering the questions posed by Charlotte Kellogg's committee-to-be, and sent detailed reports on German strafing and bombing of people, towns, and villages to the State Department. Roosevelt wanted to know whether the Germans were violating the pledge they had made to him not to bomb civilian targets. Biddle would assure him they were. News reports reaching Washington were not inaccurate, though neither Biddle nor the press, despite what they had witnessed, knew or imagined the extent of bomb damage, loss of life, or widespread atrocities.

But cables and reports aside, the whirlwind luxurious life at the Athenee Palace, the conspiratorial setting, was an environment in which Tony and Margaret thrived. There they ran into American journalist Virginia Cowles, who wrote for the *Sunday Times*; she had arrived too late to report on the Polish campaign but was eager to fill in Biddle on the "strange scene" unfolding at the Bucharest airport: "Nearly three hundred planes—forty twin-engined bombers and over two hundred fighters—had arrived at the aerodome. Over a hundred pilots, exhausted and unshaven, were sleeping on the floor of the waiting-room; their uniforms were torn and dirty and many of them had bandaged hands and faces."[8] Biddle shared with her his amazement at the effectiveness of the German spy network that broadcast the moves of the Polish government "an hour or so after the most secret decisions had been made. On several occasions," he revealed, "he had heard the news of his own proposed movements (even when he was going from one remote village to another) broadcast before he had started on the journey."[9]

The lobby of the hotel, a spider's web of dangerous intrigue, and the English bar, afloat in beautiful women, gossip, and tantalizing rumors, were among the few places remaining in Europe where the old order could kibbitz with the new. Café society flourished, where patrons, after strolling the boulevards, sipped Amalfi cocktails. The Romanian glitterati made their way through the Polish refugees and poor peasants who had turned to begging, intent on dining in the top restaurants, Capsa's, Cina's, Le Jardin's, and Mavrodaphne's, "the newest, the most expensive, and so, for the moment the most fashionable of Bucharest's cafés."[10] After dinner, night clubs like Maxim Zig Zag, where a few years earlier the famous American black jazz singer Zaidee Jackson had performed to a full house, remained popular. Other nightspots included Barul Melody and La Zissu Musichall, which featured "ensembles of violins, cimbalon, cobza, and accordians" accompanying the wildly popular "Magic Bird," Maria Tănase, known as the Édith Piaf of Bucharest.[11]

Just after lunch on September 21, both the old order and the new were jarred from the Athenee's straight-arm chairs and overstuffed couches as shocking news spread rapidly throughout the hotel. The prime minister, Armand Călinescu, had been shot dead in the street by eight fascist Iron Guard Legionnaires. Without accurate information, some wrote the "news" off as rumor, but as the day wore on, the truth of the story was pieced together. A timber cart had blocked the prime minister's roadway near the chicken market, his Cadillac slowed, and legionnaires opened fire. Bodyguard and prime minister were gunned down, but miraculously the chauffeur survived. Horia Sima, the banished nominal leader of the Iron Guard and key figure in the plot, had supposedly sneaked back into the country dressed as a woman and made his way to the site to watch the assassination, an act in retaliation for Carol's murder a year before of Corneliu Codreanu, the martyred leader and founder of the Iron Guard.[12]

Reveling in their success, the eight assassins stormed the studio of Radio Romania, held the staff at gunpoint, and began to broadcast. A few garbled sentences were uttered announcing their deed, but amid "some minutes of wild, confused shouting," the station went dead.[13] Quickly surrounded by police, the assassins surrendered, hardly expecting the fate that awaited them. Shaken, the diplomats and reporters gathered in the Athenee recognized that Romania had edged closer to the precipice. Late that afternoon, Clare Hollingworth and Hugh Carleton Greene arrived at the hotel, dust covered and exhausted, after a trying two-day trip from Cernăuți. They made their way through the lobby, weaving in and out through knots of guests talking excitedly about the prime minister's murder. Usually, Hollingworth and Greene would have made for the English bar and plunged into the alcohol-fueled verbal fray, but not tonight. The Călinescu story was already on the wire worldwide. Bath and bed were foremost in their minds.

In Washington, the State Department, after spirited debate, decided the Polish government did not have to be on its own territory to continue to be recognized.[14] "Our peripatetic Ambassador," noted Breckinridge Long in his diary, "would accompany that government to Paris."[15] After only three days in the lap of luxury, the Biddles prepared to leave, but while packing on September 22, a second round of violence erupted. The imprisoned legionnaires, after having spent a night of beatings and torture, were dragged from their cells and transported to the scene of the assassination. There they were machine-gunned. King "Carol's police . . . spat on the bodies and trampled them before the eyes of the populace. 'Leaving them' with their brains hanging around like calves' brains at the butcher's."[16] The dead legionnaires lying in the street attracted viewers from around the city, mesmerized by the scene before them.

Mihail Sebastian captured the mood prevailing in Bucharest, a mood that mimicked what had overhung Warsaw on the days surrounding the outbreak of war:

> It was a wonderfully sunny day. I lie on the chaise longue on my terrace and look at this city, which can be seen so well from above. The streets are full of life, cars drive along in every direction, traffic policemen direct the traffic from their boxes, the shops are open for customers—the whole machinery of this great city seems to be working normally, and yet somewhere at its heart a terrible blow had been delivered, without yet being felt. It is as if we were in a city strewn with dynamite due to explode in five minute's time—a city which, for the moment, carries on unawares, as if nothing has happened.[17]

However, much had happened, testing how long one could continue living in a burning house.

The State Department's instruction that Biddle was to accompany the Polish government to Paris and remain as ambassador, however, was no more than a rhetorical flourish, as the Polish leadership was interned on the insistence of the Germans, quartered in different parts of the country, and discredited by their military defeat.[18] President Mościcki had constitutionally transferred the government to Paris before crossing into Romania and nominated his successor. The government forming in Paris, at the insistence of the French, refused his recommendation and put forward Władyław Raczkiewicz. Important political elements in France and influential Poles in France were working to ensure a broad-based coalition including those who had been shut out of government by the *Sanacja* colonels—a slow-rolling *coup de régime* was gathering steam. Biddle was to accompany to the City of Light General Władysław Sikorski, a key player in the changes underway. Not long after midnight on September 17, Sikorski, mixed among the army brass, crossed the Czeremosz. Without aides, riding in a friend's car, the pair reached Cacica, a Polish salt-mining village, where they found bed and board. The following day, on the road to Bacău, the car ran out of gas. Fearing they were stranded, they were rescued by Premier Składkowski, whose Romanian escort found them the necessary fuel.[19]

Sikorski arrived in Bucharest in the late afternoon on September 20 and went immediately to the French embassy, there warmly greeted by his friend Ambassador Noël. Now under the protection of Noël, the general dodged any threat of internment. At meetings in the Polish consulate, Sikorski persuaded the ambassador and staff to switch to his side by assuring them there was a change in government underway in France. At 10:00 p.m. on the night of September 22, Sikorski and Noël drove to Bucharest's Gara de Nord and were met by the Biddle family, their dog Okay in tow, and British Counselor Clifford Norton and wife Peter. The party "boarded the *Sicuplou-Expres* [Simplon Orient Express] train to Paris" via Milan, one of the most luxurious and famous trains in Europe, one whose mention called up images of glittering crystal, exquisite dining, and chilled champagne served in three separate dining cars.[20] Famous passengers had included Lawrence of Arabia, Leon Trotsky, Mata Hari, Marlene Dietrich, and Agatha Christie, whose book *Murder on the Orient Express*, published in 1934, forever imbued the train with a cloak of mystery and intrigue. Sikorski's journey has received short shrift, overshadowed by Lenin's trip in a sealed train from Zurich to the Finland Station in St. Petersburg, but drama and intrigue were onboard as Sikorski's French, American, and the British escorts ensured that the general arrived safely in France.[21] For Sikorski, like Churchill in the 1930s, his years on the outside looking in were over. After two days' travel across Romania, Yugoslavia, Italy, and a large swath of France, the train arrived on September 24 at the Gare de Lyon.[22] Comically, French military sent to meet the train somehow missed Sikorski and the general checked into to a nearby hotel. The bloodless *coup*, off to a slow start, would nonetheless succeed. Within a week, first Sikorski succeeded to command of the Polish army; two days later, on September 30, he was asked to form a new government. Patching together a shaky coalition, he became prime minister of the Government of the Republic of Poland in Exile.[23] His ascent to power was soured by the news that arrived from Berlin and Moscow that the liars' league had divvied up control of Poland. Koba (Stalin), possessing an unbridled appetite for territory, first drew the proposed line as the Vistula but agreed to a line farther to the east along the Bug. Details were left to further negotiations, but, regardless of those details, Poland ceased to exist, partitioned once more. Sikorski was prime minister of a government without a country.

Sikorski's quick exit was one of many that occurred in the first days after the government and military had crossed into Romania. The Polish embassy was a madhouse of those who understood that the opportunity to get through Romania was a window that might at any moment close. Ways had to be found to locate and transport personnel considered essential to the Polish army and government being assembled in France. Thousands who had trod the road to Zaleszczyki now trod the road to Constanta. Hundreds arriving there found passage on ships heading to destinations world-wide, hoping to disembark at a ship's first port of call and from there find a way to France. The French leased several ships in Constanta, and thousands of refugees stopped in Bucharest only to secure necessary documents, change money, and then make their way to a holding camp in Babadag bulging with 19,645 internees, including twenty-five generals.[24] How long the charade could continue, with the Romanians telling the Germans they were doing their best to intern the Poles while in fact aiding the exodus, was anyone's guess. The competing road to Paris was to follow the Biddles' route by train, by car, or on foot, through Yugoslavia or to Budapest, as both countries assisted the fleeing Poles.[25] The Yugoslavs sent teams to camps in Romania to organize, guide, and accompany groups to their border. Some charged nothing but others as much as 10,000 złoty (approximately $35,000 in current US dollars). The Italians, sympathetic, contributed to the exodus by reducing rail fees and often charged nothing for the steady stream moving on to Paris and Angers, the seat of the new Polish government and reviving army.

The new government gave top priority to pilots, many of whom made harrowing escapes, but perhaps the most consequential among the escapees were three mathematicians—Henryk Zygalski, Jerzy Różycki, and Marian Rejewski. The trio had spent years reverse engineering the German enigma crypto machine and figuring out how it worked. On July 26, five weeks before the German invasion, the British and French in the Kabacki woods near the small Polish town of Pyry, the purlieu top-secret headquarters for the Cipher Bureau, were briefed on what had been achieved and amazingly witnessed the cryptologists read German ciphers intercepted early that morning. Demonstrating showmanship, the Poles turned on six machines, and as the rotors whirred, their guests' eyes widened. The importance of these breakthroughs was not lost on the astonished observers. The Poles decided to share with their visiting allies by giving them two precious enigma machines. To ensure security, one went by diplomatic bag to Paris, and the other arrived, courier escorted, in mid-August in Victoria Station.[26]

The cryptographers' journey to Paris and London began during the first week of the German invasion. Panzers quickly broke through the Polish border defenses and threatened to overrun Pyry. On September 5, the Cipher Bureau (BS4) packed highly classified equipment and documents, traveled to Warsaw, and boarded one of the first trains evacuating government employees east to Brześć. Throughout the journey their train was routinely bombed and strafed by Stukas. Neither the Cipher Bureau nor the Polish high command were in Brześć long, as they were forced south toward the Romanian border by advancing German armor. Again, now in Kołomyja, their position was threatened by both the German and the Soviet armies. Aside from two enigma machines, the cipher unit destroyed everything. On the night of September 17, the cryptologists, in a crowded truck, joined Polish army units crossing into exile. The Romanian border guards confiscated the truck, but the crypto machines must have seemed like encased portable typewriters, as they stirred no interest.[27] Separated from their military colleagues, the trio was ordered to report to an internment camp. They disobeyed and instead caught a train in Cernăuți bound for Bucharest. At the British embassy, their pleas for assistance were ignored, as the caravan of embassy employees from Warsaw had just arrived. At the French embassy, forewarned to be on the lookout for them, all was different. There they were given money and found accommodations, while necessary documents were prepared and train tickets secured. On September 23, the three cryptographers whose work promised a huge wartime advantage to the Allies, and whose escape had largely been a matter of luck, settled into a comfortable compartment bound for Paris, only a day behind Ambassador Nöel, Biddle, the Nortons, and Sikorski.[28] The two "typewriter cases" in their possession were never out of their sight. On arrival, the trio was immediately dispatched to a secret facility southeast of Paris, code named *Victor*. They were soon joined by nearly a dozen of their colleagues who had also made the treacherous journey from Pyry.

In New York and Geneva, YMCA officials continued to fret over the missing Supers, while in Bucharest, James W. Brown ("Brownie"), the director of the Romanian YMCA (ACT in Romanian), sent inquiries to Y workers in towns along the northern border: "Find the Supers!" Brownie knew that the couple had crossed the Prut River into Romania at Śniatyń just after midnight on September 18, along with two other cars from the Social Welfare Ministry.[29] After that, nothing was heard, as the Supers had no way to communicate their whereabouts. As the car the Supers were riding in pulled into the border station in Zapruttya, Paul and Margaret feared they would not be granted entry, as their passports had been sent to Kuty for entry visas and not returned. The guards assumed all the car's passengers were Polish and waved them through. The road to Bucharest seemed open, but after driving south all night and reaching Suciava (Suceava), they were held up for six hours by Romanian officials trying to decide what to do with them.[30] As they waited, Super witnessed "a long line of blue-uniformed Polish aviators, chiefly ground crews but fliers also, march past us in good order. They thought they were entering a country of an ally for re-formation and further action. They little foresaw their fate."[31] Finally, the Romanians made a decision. The Supers and the welfare officials were told to proceed to Pascani, where they would be met, checked in, and interned.[32] Arriving late, they ate dinner in the railroad station restaurant and afterward lounged around the station, waiting on instructions. While waiting, to their surprise, Foreign Minister Beck, on his way to internment, briefly stopped and attempted to talk with those he knew, but Super remarked that "he was distraught and preoccupied and did not give his attention to the things that were being said. For him these were moments of extreme tragedy."[33] For Beck, the tragedy would continue, as his internment in Romania was permanent. First held in a luxury hotel in Brasov, later in a rural schoolhouse in Stanesti, he was attended by his wife Jadwiga, his secretary, and his cat, finally succumbing to tuberculosis on June 5, 1944.[34] During internment he dictated his memoir, *Final Report*, which was published due to the perseverance of his wife.

Dutifully, the Supers and their traveling companions from the Welfare Ministry reported to the Pascani police station and found no one there. To make do, desks were cleared and used as beds, but the Supers attempted to sleep in two office chairs. In the morning, they reported their whereabouts to the legation. Three days passed before Brownie and a Romanian captain arrived on September 22 to end the Supers' internment. "A quick goodbye to our friends, a hurried packing of our few belongings, and we four were on the train en route to Bucarest, freedom, and a chance to serve."[35] The couple checked into Bucharest's other first-class hotel, the Ambassador, which Super described as a "splendid hostelry." He alerted the American press and Y headquarters in New York that he and his wife were safe. "The next few days we spent getting new passports, buying clothes, and talking with 'Brownie' about what to do for the Poles."[36] The Supers were slightly embarrassed about their comfortable quarters but remained in the Art Deco Ambassador hotel throughout their stay in Romania.

Brownie, while the Supers were interned in Pascani, had raised enough money from the American and British Communities to begin to render aid. He was able to do this because of a sterling reputation achieved in service to the young people of Romania as national YMCA secretary. Brown had arrived in Bucharest in 1920, serving two years longer than Super had in Warsaw. Like Super, his friends and contacts spanned the country. He was close to Queen Maria and King George II of Greece but focused his attention on the needy. Born in Japan, his mother and father were Presbyterian missionaries. He followed in their calling, receiving his religious training at Columbia Seminary and Princeton. His humility led to his being often referred to as the "most beloved foreigner in Bucharest."[37] Bur his status, and being an American, brought him to the attention of the German agents in the city, who kept a close watch on his activities.

Refugees had been arriving in the city in small numbers since mid-August, but day by day the trickle grew into a steady stream. By mid-September, Brown wrote to the New York Y office alerting them to the growing numbers. "Hundreds of Polish refugees are now pouring into Romania. The cities of Iassy and Cernauti have established refugee camps," and the Romanian Red Cross sent "thirty-five army wagons to the frontier, fitted with bathing and disinfecting facilities; but there were too many fugitives. All attempts to inspect them with regard to dirt and disease broke down. All attempts to register their entry broke down."[38] Bucharest was alive with rumors of the wildest kind, most predicting imminent disaster. Brownie passed on to the New York office stories circulating in the city that, if true, were horrifying.[39] A number were of the plight of Jews barred entry into the country.

Among the refugees arriving in the city were dozens of Y personnel who had made their way to Bucharest and were eager to assist. Super and Brownie gladly welcomed them and were especially pleased that the secretary of the Łódź YMCA, Aloisy Trypka, was among them; he would play a leading role in the relief effort. Trypka and Super were especially pleased, as they had sketched out a relief plan weeks earlier in Śniatyń while waiting to cross the Prut River into Romania. By merging their staffs, joint operations were underway that were coordinated as best they could with others—the Child Welfare Society, Dom Polski (Polish Home Society), the Save the Children Fund, Straja Tarii (Romanian government youth movement that included the YM and YWCA), and the Romanian Red Cross, though they insisted on operating independently. Hundreds of skilled professionals were also among the refugees—doctors, nurses, dentist, lawyers, teachers, and carpenters who volunteered to serve.

The first step was to register all, feed them, provide medical assistance if needed, and finally find a place for them to stay. The city was scoured for hotel rooms, pensions, rooming houses, and Romanians willing to take in refugees. Many welcomed the Poles and helped them as best they could. Each day, Poles queued outside the Y in long lines. Morale picked up somewhat as word excitedly spread among them, "Pan Super jest!" (Super is here!).[40] Whatever criticism may have followed him to Bucharest was brushed aside. Among the Poles, he was lionized. Optimism soon took a back seat in the last week of September as conditions worsened; "now came cold rainy days and the misery of the refugees, most of whom had left Poland in their summer clothes, was intensified."[41] "It has rained all the day long. These unhappy folks have no umbrellas, many of them have no rain coats, few have coats that really turn water. They are all wet and draggled. There are almost none who can be said to be well-dressed."[42]

Hollingworth, in the last week of September, the morning of the 24th, awoke knowing she could not stand another day, as she said, "lying soft at the Athenee Place Hotel."[43] There were no big stories to report, the kind that had produced the repeated adrenaline rushes she had lived on since the war's start. But part of her willingness to take extreme risks for the "scoop" was a commitment to detail for her readers the terrible suffering of the refugees and the destruction inflicted on Poland. Her work with the Czechs and Sudeten Germans in the previous summer had opened her eyes. Helping them had proved challenging, the risk sufficient to engage her talents. Dozens of reporters were telling the refugee story in Bucharest. She could see for herself their horrid condition, but it was time to find how many were still on the roads, or stranded in towns and villages, or pushed into camps along the frontier. Whatever she found might make good copy, but it was also an opportunity to be useful in whatever way she could. Driving north, her apprehension was confirmed. It had been a week since the high command had fled, but she "found the roads still jammed with Polish army lorries, field guns, private cars, good trucks and passenger-coaches."[44]

In New York, on September 27, the CPR adopted Professor Abel's recommendation to solicit Super to manage refugee relief in Romania and Hungary.[45] A few hours later, Abel, accompanied by Pate, sat down with International YMCA officers Frank V. Slack and E. E. "Gene" Barnett and pitched their relief plans. The Y officers were impressed, embraced the CPR plans, and agreed (if he consented) to loan Super. The meeting over, Slack and Barnett immediately cabled Brown:

PATE ABEL MEMBERS POLRELIEF COMMITTEE CHAIRMANED MACCRACKEN NOW IN OUR OFFICE WISH SEE POLISH REFUGEE RELIEF ROUMANIA UNDER WAY SOONEST POSSIBLE STOP THEY SUGGEST SUPER . . . TAKE CHARGE . . . ROUMANIA ALSO HUNGARY IS HE WILLING . . . STOP AMERICAN COMMITTEE ANXIOUS REMIT FUNDS IMMEDIATELY . . . COMPLETE DISCRETION EFFETIVE USE STOP PATE SUGGESTS CONVERSION CASH AND PURCHASE FOODSTUFFS IN EACH

COMMUNITY THROUGH LOCAL DELEGATES SELECTED BY SUPER STOP THEY DESIRE CABLE NUMBER REFUGEES ROUMANIA HUNGARY PERCENTAGE DESTITUTE POSSIBLE LENGTH THEIR NECESSARY CARE ESTIMATED WEEKLY COST AND YOUR RECOMMENDATIONS IN ORDER SECURE MAXIMUM AMERICAN CONTRIBUTIONS REFUGEES . . . IMPORTANT FIRST ALL POSSIBLE MEANS GOVERNMENT AND PRIVATE IN THESE COUNTRIES CALLED INTO ACTION SECOND THAT REFUGEES REGARD THIS AS TEMPORARY HELP THIRD THAT RELIEF BE STRICTLY NONSECTARIAN.[46]

The cable reached Brown and Super on Friday morning, September 29. The following day, Super's decision reached New York. He accepted, asking that Brown serve as treasurer. It was impossible to answer the CPR's question as to the number of refugees in Romania, as the huge wave that began on September 16 had not crested. But a number was necessary. Super estimated fifty thousand, and caring for them through the winter would require $75,000 per month ($1,411,414 in today's money). He did not estimate the number of interned Polish soldiers but was aware that many had donned civilian clothes and were among the civilian refugees. As for Hungary, Super knew only that the number was large but claimed Budapest could not be administered from Bucharest, recommending a separate organization.[47] A few days later, Super revised his estimate upward to seventy thousand civilian refugees and placed the number of soldiers interned in seventeen different places as likely twenty thousand.[48] Despite the challenge posed by the numbers, the next to the last line of the cable warned that assistance should be considered temporary, revealing CPR thinking that by spring 1940 the refugee crisis would be under control, and most would have found haven.

The CPR, pleased Super had agreed to oversee relief, cabled funds, "including $10,000 collected by M. F. Wegrzynek, owner of 'Nowy Swiat,' the leading Polish newspaper in the New York City area."[49] With money in hand, the effort to accommodate the swelling numbers accelerated.

Super recorded the hectic pace: the "staff worked most of the night. Brown till 5 a.m."[50] Super, exuberant, wrote to Barnett in New York on September 30, 1939:

> What joy they [refugees] register when they see the familiar names and faces of the Polish YMCA! It gives me some of the most stirring moments of my life as I see how they rejoice in our presence. My wife has never been so glad we are where we are. Our complete loss of everything in Poland, about $15,000, seems of no great importance. We have life and health and a magnificent chance to serve.[51]

Margaret Super, under her pen name Ann Su Cardwell, sent a stream of articles about the refugees to CPR headquarters for placement in magazines and newspapers and worked tirelessly alongside her husband, as did Sally Brown. The Cardwell articles, widely disseminated, did much to inform the American public of the plight of the Polish refugees. To comprehend more fully what the refugees had experienced and how he might meet their needs, Super spent much time circulating among those that queued to register and those at various stages of processing throughout the building. He and his wife shared with those seeking help that they had made the dangerous retreat across Poland but had not suffered the air attacks and lack of food and water, as had so many who came by train or those who walked at night and slept in the woods by day. Super was moved by these interactions, by the incredible stories, by being bombarded with questions. In a postscript in a letter to Davis, he wrote, "Two young boys. Two women. Meal ticket for lunch ... 5 men. 'Can I get something to eat?' They can. 4 more. Three more. This is a heartbreaking thing. A father and a girl of say 6. Rain. The chill of fall. A Polish girl has been helping at the north station but now she has no money on which to live. 'Can we help?' We can. Two young women. No hats. 'Where can I get clothes?' A young Man and his wife. All kinds of problems."[52] A grateful refugee told Super, "You are the only person in high authority that one can get at and talk to. All the others in other places are hid behind three secretaries."[53] Super and Brown could take pride in their accomplishments; clothing was available, and by September 30 six hundred meals a day were served in the YWCA restaurant.[54]

With the Y buildings filled, Super managed to rent a nearby house and set up a Polish headquarters and dedicate the foyer to a *świetlica*. For Super, the *świetlica* was a mandatory feature of any Y facility. A common room, a "clean, well-lighted place," served as a club with a buffet, a place to read, to play chess or checkers, hear lectures, listen to the radio, enjoy entertainment, participate in study groups and take courses offered in a variety of subjects, attend religious services, and generally socialize.[55] Returning to the refugees their dignity, improving their morale, and attending to their spiritual needs was central to the Y mission. For a hundred reasons, the relief committee needed transportation. For the Polish embassy, the problem was easily solved, as many vehicles had been abandoned, impounded, or left in the care of the embassy by those who boarded trains for foreign destinations. The CPR eventually possessed a fleet of eleven, one of which was a Packard limousine. The vehicle market was hot with bargains galore!

In Bucharest, the relief effort was coming together when Dermod O'Donovan, an Irishman and an experienced Y worker, arrived with a British Quaker relief team. O'Donovan and the two other team members, Dr. Richard Ellis and Francesca Wilson, had all worked with refugees in Spain. Ellis was to collect the team's findings, return to Great Britain, and report to the Quaker relief committee what was needed and how they might serve. Wilson was busily gathering material on children, but her work was interrupted when she was transferred to Budapest, where the relief operation was desperately short of trained workers.[56] O'Donovan joined with Super and Brown, but because he advocated "the principle of 'full coverage,' by which he meant that all refugees everywhere in Romania must be located and served," he was sent north to do just that.

Along the border, Romanian officials were collecting refugees adrift and shuffling them into improvised camps. Soon, most were moved to southern cites in Wallachia and Dobruja. Soldiers, those of lower rank, were being moved from scattered sites and sent to two large internment camps nearing completion that would each hold ten thousand, one northwest of Bucharest in Comișani near the city of Târgovista and the other farther west in Târgu Jui, and to a third large camp, to the northeast of Bucharest in Buzău. Officers, captains and below, were interned in smaller facilities away from the border, as were higher-ranking officers under close supervision in hotels and resorts. Fifteen hundred majors and above, many with families, were quartered in a resort near the city of Olt.

Hollingworth, who had been scouting conditions in the northern towns and villages for several weeks, discovered that refugees tended to band together in groups, both large and small, and took shelter wherever possible—hotels, apartments, private homes, abandoned buildings, barns, sheds, tents, cars, buses, and truck beds. Shelter ranged from very good to squalid.[57] Many were running out of money, and what money they had (usually złoty) was a currency rapidly depreciating. To compensate, the Romanian government provided a daily stipend of 100 lei for adults (approximately $14 today) and 50 lei for children, spending daily a total of $20,000 (today $375,000).[58] This large expenditure was underwritten by the Polish government-in-exile leaving behind three tons of gold when the main shipment left Constanta for France.[59] The government stipend covered the cost of food, plentiful and cheap, but places to stay were in short supply, skyrocketing in price. Civilian refugees were encouraged to move into one of forty-six government camps.[60] But regardless of the level on which the refugees lived, all counted on leaving Romania at the

Polish soldier work detail observed by Romanian officer camp inspectors, Comişani Army Camp No. 2 (courtesy of Romanian National Archives, Bucharest).

first chance, and most were willing to take visas from whatever country they were offered. Throughout the fall, numbers dwindled, many ending in places of which they had never dreamed—Kenya, India, Paraguay, Mexico, Syria. Others, less fortunate, regardless of CPR expectations to the contrary, remained in Romania.

In the soldiers' internment camps, conditions were horrific. The chilly rainy weather that welcomed October annually turned the region into what the Romanians called the autumn sea of mud (*marea de noroi toamnar*), making moving about an onerous task. It was possible that with each step you sank up to your knees. The older wooden barracks in many of the camps were much the same as those of the recently activated Romanian soldiers: poorly heated, "ill-lighted, overcrowded, with inadequate sanitation. In every camp," Hollingworth reported, "there is a desperate shortage of clothing, shoes, blankets and palliasses."[61] Food was adequate, though prepared in unsanitary conditions. Lice were rampant. Reports claimed malaria was spreading. Memories of cholera and typhus epidemics that occurred in the aftermath of the last war were alive in the minds of Romanian health officials, who feared potential outbreaks of typhus, cholera, flu, and rampant dysentery.

Hollingworth, in the third week of her explorations, crossed paths with O'Donovan on his way to organize one of the recently improvised civilian camps. After but a few hours, they recognized that they were kindred spirits, and she welcomed the invitation to join him. At the camp, they "found a slummy building and wretched people, going over their grievances, quarreling, all self-respect gone."[62] Morale had reached a new low. O'Donovan gathered all together and delivered a rousing patriotic speech emphasizing their Polish heritage and their duties as exiles and to themselves. The first thing that must be done, he insisted, was to clean the building. Handing out the necessities to accomplish the task—buckets, brooms, mops, soap, paint, and paint brushes—the sweepers, moppers, movers, and painters went to work. With most tasks completed, O'Donovan unrolled travel posters touting famous places and sites from around Poland that would hopefully connect them with home. That the paint on the walls was not yet dry was of no consideration, for the refugees enthusiastically slapped the posters up wherever possible.

The work complete, dinner was served. As people began to finish the meal, O'Donovan "pushed back his chair. 'Now let us sing some Polish songs.'"[63] It was a masterful first day's performance. Hollingworth was deeply moved. For those in the camp, their dignity and self-worth were on the mend, their living conditions much improved.

Super was taken by surprise on October 3 when "a competent looking Romanian lady of possibly 40 years can into our headquarters." The woman in question was Princess Catherine Caragea (Caradja)—famous throughout the country. Immediately, formalities were pushed aside, wrote Super; "she got down to business at once, with an offer to take all the Polish babies who needed care. I told her that might be a big order, but she replied that she was the head of St. Catherine's Crib, the Romanian branch of the 'Save the Children Fund,' and already had 2,000 orphans under her care and might as well take a few more."[64] In Cernăuți, the princess had rounded up five hundred children living on the streets who had been separated from their parents or abandoned. Her orphanage in Bucharest had the reputation of being one of the best in Europe. Hollingworth, touring the orphanage, "found the children in a splendid modern building, with sun-rooms, nurseries, balconies; and washing and cooking facilities as good as any I have seen. One half of the block was divided from the other by a 'secret' door. On one side, the newly arriving children were washed, de-loused, and put under observation for illness they might have developed en route. On the other side, they were settling down as regular residents." Mingling with the children, who were excited to see visitors, Hollingworth was "incautious enough to mention his parents. 'All gone,' he said. 'There was a bang. Mummy went like that, all in bits. Daddy too.'"[65]

Princess Caragea's actions solved Super's problem of caring for women, babies, and abandoned and orphaned children. He was grateful. Working closely with one another, the two became good friends. One evening, over dinner, Super asked her how she had become involved with orphans. "Because," she answered, "I was one."[66] When she was an infant, she said, her father had concocted a wild scheme to gain control of his wife's money. He kidnapped his daughter and hid her in an orphanage in Great Britain, passing her off as a French foundling named Jeanne

Bardin. Her family searched for her unsuccessfully for years but refused to give in to her father's demands. Her mother, deciding that she would never see Catherine again, divorced and started a new family. The young princess's mother died when Catherine turned thirteen, and her father, not about to give up, retrieved her from the orphanage, asserting that he was her legal guardian and she was entitled to a share of any inheritance. Placed in a finishing school in Paris, with the contrivance of her grandfather, she escaped to Romania on the Orient Express into the care of her maternal grandmother.[67] "What a story!" Super exclaimed. "And what a woman!" "She was a splendid coworker. Just before Christmas I went into one of our headquarters rooms and found her amidst a mountain of bundles, asking, 'What is all this?' 'Packages for my Polish orphans and other children, 700 parcels,' she said."[68]

By mid-October, Hollingworth ended her camp visits, thanked O'Donovan, and left for Bucharest satisfied with what she had seen: "It seemed to me that in Roumania everything possible was being done for the Poles."[69] The SCF, for which she had worked in Katowice, operated in Hungary before the war and was quick to arrive in Romania. Money was flowing from America. In her own country, the Quakers, the Anglo-Polish Fund, the Lord Mayor of London Relief Fund, and the Save the Children Fund (SCF), chaired by its founder, Lord Noel-Buxton, were all successfully raising money. The Anglo-Polish Relief Fund brought together various organizations under the umbrella of a Central Fund, a kind of United Way for Poland, with Count Edward Raczyński, Poland's ambassador to Great Britain, serving as honorary president. The Central Fund (a name with zero public relations appeal) was renamed the Polish Relief Fund. Super and Brown had played a role in spurring the British into action, for they had called on Sir Reginald Hoare, the British minister in Romania, "and delicately made the point that the Poles had expected a good deal from their British allies and thus far had received very little. Sir Reginald saw the point."[70] Did Super have specific requests in mind? He did, he said, have three. "Money, wool in any form, and Dr. W. J. Rose of London, who, speaking Polish, could be of great use."[71] Hoare answered, "No wool could be exported, money he would try to get," and he would see what could be done about Rose. "The money and Rose both came, other British workers followed."[72] Some Brits who contributed sought forgiveness, to escape a shame they felt for failure to aid the Poles militarily, a shame Hollingworth shared. She had originally intended to return to London and seek a new assignment as a foreign correspondent. The cub reporter's reputation as a journalist assured, she told herself, "there was something more urgent here. Besides, I felt almost a personal obligation."[73] Back in Bucharest, Hollingworth boarded the train for London to seek an assignment with a refugee organization.

Super, by mid-October, concluded (as had Hollingworth) that the first stage of the relief operation, what he called the first wave, was well underway. Super could take pride in his accomplishments. The number of meals provided daily averaged 1,300 breakfasts, 3,600 lunches, and 2,500 dinners.[74] Acknowledgment of Super's success arrived from Hoover and the CPR in New York, "from many sources and all reports which we have from Roumania are that he is doing a splendid piece of work."[75] Pate wrote to Super, "Mr Slade, who I saw one evening last week, is very proud of the work you and Mr Brown are doing. Americans and Polish-Americans all over the country admire the quick way you and Mr Brown got into action."[76]

Success in Romania now freed Super to deal with the struggling relief operation in Hungary. He and his wife left for Budapest on October 18. The couple, arriving the next day, checked into the Hotel Jagerhorn. The Supers had first visited Budapest in 1925 and remained drawn to the beautiful city cut in two by the Danube, a city that had been a crown jewel of the vanished Austro-Hungarian Empire and continued to boast fine restaurants like Gundels, the Apostles, the New York Café, and the Café EMKE. Actors, writers, and politicians favored the Café Bucsinzky while artists peopled the Café Japán. Among the famous hotels were the Astoria and the Danubius/Gellért with its Romanesque baths. The well heeled spent afternoons shopping and strolling the elegant *Váci utca*. Opera, theater, and musical performances bolstered a flourishing night life.[77] But Germany's eastward expansion threatened Hungary's future, and farther to the east the Soviet Union menaced. Hungarians well remembered Béla Kun's effort to establish a Soviet Republic in 1919. But twenty years later, in September 1939, a new element pervaded Hungary—fifty thousand

Polish civilian refugees and thirty thousand Polish soldiers streamed into the country, most over the course of a few days. Hungarian resources were not up to the task; they were desperate for assistance.

Among the tragedies that afflicted the Poles, however, was an unforeseen bright spot that greatly facilitated their escape and rescue, for they had only shared a border with Hungary since the previous March, when the Hungarians annexed Carpatho-Ruthenia from a disappearing Czechoslovakia.[78] The Magyars were pleased with the acquisition, as territory was a bitter subject for them; the Treaty of Trianon, signed at Versailles in summer 1920, had assigned a third of their territory to others. Hungary, now landlocked, was ironically ruled by an admiral. The Poles were doubly rewarded, as relations with their new neighbor to the south were cordial. On September 17, the Polish minister asked the Hungarian foreign minister, István Csáky, how Polish soldiers and refugees would be treated. Hungary would abide by the Geneva Convention, said Csáky, and the soldiers would be disarmed and interned. Civilians who possessed the means of support could stay as resident aliens, and those in need would be cared for. The following day, the border was declared open.[79] Like the Romanians, Hungarian peasants and townsmen opened their homes to these new arrivals. Small numbers crossed in the first days of September, but when the Polish army ordered its soldiers to leave the country and reassemble in France, as in Romania, the few became the many. The Hungarian Red Cross and army personnel, along with a relief worker from the Save the Children Fund, went to the border and greeted entire Polish units by playing the Polish national anthem and waving the flags of both nations.[80] Intact elements of the Carpathian Army included armored units, mountaineering sharpshooters, a heavy artillery regiment, mechanized artillery, sappers, fusiliers, light cavalry, an infantry regiment, a motorized anti-aircraft regiment, a signal corps unit, assorted militias, police, border guards, a field hospital, and the Institute of Military Cartography.[81]

But those who made their way into Hungary later were in poor condition after trekking through the dangerous Carpathian forests and valleys in the rainy fall weather, many in summer clothes. The high passes already had three feet of snow. How many were killed or captured by Soviet or

10th Armored Cavalry "Black Brigade," after crossing into Hungary (courtesy of Wikimedia Commons, Fortepan.hu/photo, source Berkó Pál).

Slovakian patrols is unknown. Among those fortunate enough to successfully make the treacherous journey were General Kazimierz Sosnkowski and three of his aides. After inflicting a series of defeats on German units on September 15 and 16, Sosnkowski's exhausted Małapolska army sought to recover in the Janów forest. Instead, air and artillery attacks were followed by a ground attack, decimating the Poles. "I had seen many a battlefield, many a time witnessed heavy and bloody combat," observed General Bronisław Prugar-Ketling, commander of the 11th Carpathian Infantry Division, "but never had I seen such a dreadful harvest of war."[82] Retreating toward Lwów, Sosnkowski judged that chances of getting into the city were better if attempted by individuals or small groups. If his soldiers did not wish to try, they should head for the Hungarian border and then to France. Sosnkowski and his aides, in civilian clothes, left Lwów on September 22, after having a photo taken in a local studio. Avoiding patrols, as "NKVD units were ... shooting Polish officers on sight," the foursome usually traveled at night and slept in safe houses, trusting their lives to guides for twelve days, who led them along forest trails and through the snowy mountain passes.[83] Reaching the border on October 4, none the worse for wear, "the Hungarian gendarmes," Sosnkowski wrote, "turned out to be kind, hospitable people. They invited us to supper and gave us four beds in the common room of the barracks."[84] Prime Minister Sikorski was pleased to learn that the general was safe, as he wished him to join his newly formed government in Paris. After a few days in Budapest, the Polish Consulate provided travel documents, and Sosnkowski was on his way to the City of Light, arriving on October 11.[85]

In the first few days in Hungary, hundreds of Poles—the necessary, the well connected, and the wealthy—followed in Sosnkowski's path. Escapes slowed but continued at a rate of approximately fifty to a hundred a day. From camps along the Yugoslavian border, escapes as large as 250 men were routinely orchestrated. Polish Military Attaché Jan Emisarski discharged hundreds of soldiers so that they could cross the border as civilians.[86] The Nazi government pressured the Hungarians to stop the getaways; German agents were thick in the country and reported daily back to Berlin. Some Hungarian officers were pro-Nazi, and in Budapest as in Bucharest, the Hungarians played the double game of assuring the Nazis that they were doing all they could to keep the Poles penned up and at the same time either ignoring or abetting the escapes. The fear of Stalin and the Bolsheviks, now on their border, also contributed to Hungarian timidity.

The goal of the soldiers and civilian refugees who crossed into Hungary was to reach the capital, check in at the Polish consulate, gauge their situation, and decide what to do, but most were intercepted by authorities and sent to centers scattered throughout the country. Civilians were sent to seventy towns and villages and soldiers to a similar number of internment sites. Forty of the internment camps held roughly four hundred soldiers, often housed in abandoned buildings that lacked facilities. Super observed that "the condition of refugees was pitiable; that of the soldiers, worse."[87] Super needed a base other than the Hungarian YMCA from which to gather information and to meet with those who might help build an organization—a Polish YMCA. To do so, he sought the help of American minister John Flournoy Montgomery. At the Legation, he

General Kazimierz Sosnkowski and aides leave for Hungary, September 22, 1939 (courtesy of Piłsudski Institute of America).

was warmly received, provided information, and offered financial advice. But the minister and his staff, eager to assist the relief effort, went further by offering an office, secretarial support (if needed), and use of the legation cable to communicate with Bucharest, Geneva, and New York. Super was delighted. In his exuberance, he cabled Pate: "I want to commend our American Minister Montgomery for his kind and efficient interest in the problem. Have the 5,000,000 Am. Poles tell him he must watch over the interests of their blood here. He will, and gladly."[88] The minister, past president of the International Milk Company, was an ardent Democrat who had enthusiastically supported Roosevelt in 1932. His campaign contributions earned for him the diplomatic post in Hungary, a country he came to love, captivated by "Budapest's Gilded Age atmosphere, old world pageantry—the elaborate costumes, and glittering semi-feudal rituals."[89] Just before leaving to take up his new assignment, Roosevelt told him, as he had many others, to feel free to contact him directly, but Montgomery later complained that the president "held him at arm's length, insufficiently" interested in his detailed reports.[90] Unable to gain the president's attention, he complained, "none of my talks with him personally or by letter have ever given me any reason to believe that he had any thorough knowledge of the subjects which he discussed or that he had much interest in getting information. He seemed to me half-baked and to have no real knowledge of his subjects. He has ideas of his own and that is sufficient."[91] Over the years Montgomery developed a wide range of friendships among Hungarians, the diplomatic corps, and prominent people from other European countries and was close to the regent, Miklós Horthy, keeping detailed transcripts of their many conversations.[92] For Super, Montgomery's experience and contacts proved invaluable.

The coalition of organizations Super assembled relied heavily on the Polish consulate; on the Hungarian Red Cross, which he maintained was better equipped and more efficient than its Romanian counterpart; and on the Hungarian YMCA/YWCA, the Hungarian-Polish Society, the British Quakers, and relief workers from the Save the Children Fund. All provided an array of services like food, clothing, housing, and registration. Some contributed money; a few were largely financially self-sufficient, while most, seriously underfunded, were struggling. Success depended on being able to build a Polish YMCA for civilian refugees and interned soldiers using Y workers who crossed into Hungary, along with obtaining money enough to support the relief effort. Two from the Ministry of Social Welfare who also served as senior Y leaders, Dr. Tadeusz Dyboski and General Stefan Hubicki, were with Super in the caravan that had outrun the Germans and dodged the Soviets. South of Dubno, the caravan split. The cars in which Dyboski and Hubicki were riding, along with other key Y personnel, drove southwest, crossing into Hungary. Hubicki, in uniform, and his wife were interned.[93] Dyboski began immediately to assemble a Y relief team but was soon called to France to "give our new government an account of all the affairs of the Social Insurance in Poland" and of assets he had transferred to Hungary.[94] Leaving Budapest on October 11, aboard a train, somewhere in Yugoslavia, exhausted, Dyboski lost consciousness and died. His wife wrote to Super, "He has found peace, and is resting now in a small cemetery situated on a hill."[95] Super, on his arrival in Budapest a week later, pressed for the release of the Hubickis. He was successful. Freed, Hubicki joined the relief team and took "charge of the cultural, educational, and publication program, and made those calls in which his personality, rank, and character were an obvious asset."[96]

Any illusion Super harbored that the CPR would be the main source of money was shattered on his second day in Budapest. "We will back you," cabled Pate, "but in view of long pull ahead and needs of Romania Lithuania Wilno Warsaw prefer first utilize all other sources in your masterful coordinating way. The American public is not so enthusiastic about war relief as it was at the time of the last war," he opined, "and we will not have an easy job raising funds. However, no stone will be left unturned to give you the support which you feel your picture merits."[97] Super knew what this meant: fund-raising was going slowly, the CPR was strapped for cash, and the desperate situation unfolding in and around Wilno took priority. Rounding up necessary amounts of money fell to him. In the next three months, the CPR sent $17,000 (today $316,290)[98]—essential but insufficient. For additional needed money, Super asked Pate "to try to get the American Red Cross to back the Hungarian Red Cross with cash in a big way."[99] Pate responded that the CPR was seeking to cooperate with the American Red Cross: "They have had a great deal of publicity in the newspapers," he wrote, "but have not been so fast in promptly meeting the emergencies abroad. This, as you know, is characteristic of the ARC. They generally do a good job in this country, but their organization is slow and heavy in foreign work."[100] Claiming the superiority of the CPR executive committee over that of the Red Cross, he explained that they were "nearly all former Hoover men who know the technique of relief from Belgium and from work in Central Europe after the war. These men, like the YMCA, handle relief and welfare work on a business basis, elastic, fast moving, selecting able men and placing confidence and authority in the hands of those men."[101] Two key issues, Pate stressed, were how to raise money and not be at cross purposes with the Red Cross and other organizations in the field and what the Red Cross intended to "do for refugees outside of Poland, and how much they will do in occupied Poland."[102] Both issues were unresolved. But, perhaps unwittingly, Pate had put his finger on an unsolvable problem between the two organizations. The CPR was largely Republican and the Red Cross top leadership Democrat, organizations overseen by two men who intensely disliked one another and were supported by loyal staff.

But the politics of relief aside, what Super intended was clear. He wrote to Pate, "In three days two American Red Cross men should arrive here. I expect to tell them they must, a. First $300,000 at once for the Red Cross, b. $200,000 before Xmas and an expert here as technical adviser and inspector and reporter to U.S.A."[103] Anxious, the next day he again wrote to Pate: "I *fear* they will propose giving supplies only. *This will utterly never suffice. The Poles will simply die of dirt and cold and disease.*"[104] But earlier he wrote to Strong in Geneva regarding his hopes that the Red Cross men "are prepared to take on a big job involving lots of money," as "the needs here are awful. They make one sick."[105] The two Red Cross men, Ernest J. Swift and Wayne Chatfield-Taylor, were presently in Bucharest as part of a European fact-finding trip sizing up relief needs and had held meetings with the various relief agencies, including Brownie and his staff. Swift, serving as vice chairman, had been with the Red Cross since the World War. Taylor had served in a variety of positions in the Roosevelt administration since 1933, including foreign policy advisor to Roosevelt, but was appointed Red Cross European delegate in 1939, resigning as assistant secretary of the Treasury after clashing with his boss, Secretary Henry Morganthau, over policy.

Super arrived at Swift and Chatfield Taylor's hotel, sure that he could persuade them to make a $200,000 cash donation to the Hungarian Red Cross. He decided the $300,000 was too high a figure; still, $200,000 would be just under $4 million in today's money—not an inconsiderable amount. Unfortunately, Super's proposal was not well received. "I got a flat turn-down. They said their agency did not send money abroad for relief, only supplies."[106] He protested that supplies were needed, but it would be months before they arrived. "The need was immediate and urgent," he reminded them.[107] No matter; it was against policy, it could not be done. Super, stung by his appeal's rejection, retorted, "Well then gentlemen, I must go over your head and appeal directly to your headquarters in America."[108] Super did not, as he threatened, appeal directly to Norman Davis, knowing it would fall on deaf ears, but instead wrote to Pate, recommending he write to Eleanor Roosevelt asking her support of Polish relief. His wife Margaret had already sent a five-page handwritten appeal on September 26, which, unknown to the Supers, had made a deep impression on the First Lady.[109] An end-run appeal to Eleanor was a good idea, as she favored an expansion of aid to Poland and its refugees, but what Super failed to appreciate was that the Hoover/Roosevelt battle over aid to Europe had landed squarely in Budapest and Bucharest. Super's experience drew him to a conclusion that Hoover had long held: the American Red Cross should jettison its policy of emergency aid only, expand its operations to include feeding, and adopt a comprehensive relief program, as it had the organization and resources to do so.

Davis wrote the president on October 25: "About a week ago this Committee [the CPR] indicated to me that they might fold up tent if we would take over their activities, and that we at least take Super, about whom I made inquiries to our delegation. Since then, however, the Polish Committee, which is apparently being backed by Hoover, has decided to try and go ahead with their relief effort."[110] However, Davis already knew that the CPR was a Hoover relief operation, as did the president, and Davis also knew that it had already accomplished much in Romania and

Hungary, though he did not tell the president. Davis might ignore CPR accomplishments, but Roosevelt surely was aware of the CPR's press coverage, given his ravenous appetite for ten newspapers a day, and he could not escape his wife's support for an expanded Red Cross relief effort. Hoover and the CPR likewise knew that the Red Cross would not reverse policy unless the political pressure to do so became unbearable. On November 14, in a second meeting of relief organizations in Washington, Davis and Pate went over the same ground, with Pate reasserting that the CPR would step aside if the Red Cross would commit to an extended relief program. Davis again said no. Frank Slack, in attendance representing the International YMCA, reported:

> On the whole, my impression was that the meeting was called to bring perhaps a bit of official pressure on the C.P.R. to prevent it from moving too fast or too far in the matter of independent financial approach to the United States. Nobody indicated that it should pass out of the picture but I thought I detected a fairly strong official attitude the R.C. should be the central organization. As far as I can see in a situation like this, an organization which assumes central control has also got to assume an equal degree of responsibility, and I do not yet have the feeling that the R.C. is willing to go that far. I think they will take what is sent to them but I don't think they will go out and definitely try to stimulate large interests in the Polish refugee situation.[111]

Clarence Pickett of the American Friends Service Committee, also in attendance, concurred with Pate's conclusions, writing in his diary, "At 11 o'clock had a meeting with Norman Davis to discuss cooperation with the Red Cross. Decided to continue negotiations for relief, but to consider the Red Cross only temporarily in the picture and open to withdrawal as soon as possible."[112] Pickett had already committed his organization to oversee any CPR relief the Germans allowed into the Government General.

The CPR needled Roosevelt (and Davis) that they had initiated relief because the administration failed to do the job, which lent credibility to their efforts and put the White House on the defensive. But the CPR jabs were disingenuous, as they had no intention of folding their tent and remained committed to aiding the Poles. Just as important, if successful, the generated publicity could bolster Hoover's chances of obtaining his party's presidential nomination, which the CPR Hoovermen executives and directors welcomed. The threat that hovered over the success of CPR's all-in strategy was that neither Charlotte Kellogg's fund-raising committees nor the efforts of the Polish-American communities would be able to raise the money needed to sustain the relief programs. At the conclusion of the November 14 meeting, none of the differences between the CPR and the Red Cross had been resolved, but Pate, later on that chilly evening, warmed when reading Eleanor Roosevelt's column "My Day" in the *Washington Daily News*. "I hope," she wrote, "that everyone who can, will help this committee. It should inspire every confidence because of past experience in this work."[113] The First Lady's endorsement of the CPR, with over four million readers in ninety newspapers, was huge, promising to increase donations to the cash-strapped organization. Pate wrote to Mrs. Roosevelt expressing his gratitude and was further rewarded a few days later when a check for $50 arrived at the New York headquarters.[114] Super's intuition of who to approach had been correct, though he had in mind a far larger amount.

A downside to Roosevelt and Davis's policy was that it pulled its practitioners in several directions simultaneously. Interned Polish soldiers and civilian refugees were receiving aid from outside agencies; this was recognized as a good thing, though downplayed, and yet was a reminder that the policy was a victory of political pragmatism over obvious need. A successful Hoover relief drive might also reward Roosevelt if it was of short duration. But Davis's Red Cross, and especially the Romanian Red Cross, concluded that the CPR was horning in on territory exclusively theirs and that they risked being co-opted. Ironically, early in September, that was what Hoover suspected Roosevelt had in mind for him. Distrust and suspicion among individuals and organizations abounded.

Swift and Taylor reported to Davis that Super, "while [an] excellent organizer, had antagonized Rumanian Red Cross officials, greatly impairing his effectiveness in that direction."[115] Earlier, Super had alienated the International Committee of the Red Cross (ICRC) delegate sent to Bucharest, Robert Brunel, who had turned down his request for aid, calling him comic and haughty, "very much a stuffed shirt."[116] The ICRC would continue to disappoint, as the decision was made not to engage in relief and not to aid interned Polish soldiers in Romania, Hungary, Latvia, and Lithuania, given that they were not prisoners of war and not entitled to the protection of the Geneva Convention. They would focus their attention on those captured by the Germans. Sometime later, the ICRC shipped clothing to Hungary. Super's overtures to the British also "brought no visible results. On the whole I felt utterly baffled so far as both coordination and money were concerned, and up against obstacles in getting Polish YMCA work organized."[117] But Super pushed ahead, supported by the American minister and by the Hungarian Red Cross, although relief proceeded at a snail's pace.

Swift and Taylor, in concluding their report, surmised that regardless of the outflow of soldiers and civilians from Romania and Hungary, the "majority will remain ... for an indefinite period, probably duration of the war. Hence relief problem will be a continuing one." Super's plan, they estimated, would cost $30,000 a month. "Therefore," they suggested, "would it not be preferable for American Red Cross to continue its policy of furnishing materials, medical supplies and other aid through Rumanian Red Cross and not attempt to engage in elaborate expensive operation unless American Red Cross is prepared to underwrite complete refugee program for indefinite period at approximate cost of $60,000 per month for Rumania alone."[118] The administration's policy of emergency aid only prevailed; the Red Cross would not be dragged into any long-term commitment that posed military and political risks or distracted from the developing strategy of defending America by aiding Great Britain and France. The Red Cross, however, soon relented on cash payouts due to press coverage of the Polish need, CPR successes, and the persistent pressure of Eleanor Roosevelt on her husband and on Davis to do more. Eleanor, on November 2, sent a copy of Margaret Super's letter to Bernard Baruch, Davis, and her husband, saying, "It would seem that the time had come when money should go to Polish relief. If nothing else can be done, or had been done, I think I will publish this letter, asking the women's organizations undertake to join together in a relief organization which shall cover all civilians as they need it, the money to be distributed through the International YWCA, YMCA, Friends Service Committee, and Red

Cross."[119] Cash payments—a small concession—were made to the League of Red Cross Societies, which passed the money on to the Romanian, Hungarian, and Lithuanian Red Cross.[120] As intended, the indirect cash transfers were a kind of hidden hand. Few involved in relief in Hungary had any idea that money from the American Red Cross was aiding their effort for the Poles. Tamas Salamon-Racz, head of the Polish-Hungarian Refugee Committee, flatly stated, "only the Hungarian and the Polish Red Cross operated in Hungary, not the American."[121] Responding to Eleanor's plea for additional aid, Davis wrote, "As you will note, we have made considerable headway in meeting the needs and we are doing everything which seems wise and practicable."[122] Surreptitiously, he acknowledged that the Poles had gotten all they were going to get. Roosevelt did not tell his wife what he had told British ambassador Lord Lothian back in September: "The restoration of Poland depended upon the outcome of the war and not on the attempt to render aid strategically now, however difficult it might be to resist the piteous appeal of the Poles and public opinion."[123] Eleanor surely suspected that her husband and Davis were the roadblock to additional aid. Despite her suspicions, she soldiered on for the Poles, an unacknowledged ally of Hoover and the CPR.

As to the CPR, Roosevelt and Davis remained convinced that it was but a screen for Hoover's political ambitions. Breckinridge Long recorded in his diary, "Of course Herbert Hoover is behind several of these organizations, and Norman thinks that they would like to provide another spring-board for him so that he could be elected to the Presidency again on account of relief in Poland like he was on account of his Belgian relief. I remarked that I thought there would have to be a great deal of spring in the board to get Hoover elected to anything."[124]

Super was recovering from his failure to persuade the Red Cross to financially step up when a telegram arrived from the International Y office in New York. Super could not believe what he read: "No Association funds available."[125] He shot back to Slack, "I am only depressed and sad. What, in God's name, am I supposed to do and do with."[126] Pouring out his heart, he added a postscript: "This means that the whole job falls on Pate. Please arrive at an understanding with him. I'll get the money; it's not that. But for the *American Y.M.C.A.* to let me down and the Polish

Y.M.C.A. down! That's a sad chapter in *their* (American Y.M.C.A.) history."[127] A third quest for additional money lay in persuading the Hungarian government to grant Super's request of an exchange rate of 9.5 pengos to the dollar, nearly four pengos over the official rate, which, if agreed to, would amount to a 40 percent increase in purchasing power.[128] The government refused. Cash strapped, Super was forced to cut back on his ambitious plans. As a solution, he approached the British relief organization, as they had received an exchange rate for their pounds 33 percent over the official rate. The British agreed to help by taking responsibility for sixty camps in the west of Hungary and leaving sixty to Super and the YMCA in the east.[129] Frustrated by the series of financial setbacks, but undeterred, Super returned to Bucharest hopeful that what he had put in motion would produce results before his next visit. In his absence, Hungarian relief was about to be invigorated. Hollingworth, making the rounds of London relief organizations, secured an appointment as honorary commissioner with her old employer, the Save the Children Fund (SCF). Apparently, her transgressions in Katowice had been forgiven by the Fund and by the foreign office, as her necessary visas were verbally expedited.[130] In Paris she was informed that the British had not yet appointed a representative to the new Polish government. The person doing the most for Poles in France was her old friend, Peter Norton, who had "raised funds and material... had opened workshops, with the approval of the French; here the exiles were making shoes, clothes, and other things which they had no money to buy. The main obstacle, amazing in view of her standing as the wife of a senior diplomat, was the obstruction of officialdom."[131] Meeting with Norton, the two women agonized over the reports of the Polish refugees' travails in Hungary. Surely, they decided, they could assist those in need. Hollingworth would go on ahead to reconnoiter, and Norton would purchase supplies and trucks and shepherd the caravan to Budapest.[132] Her driving skills, exhibited in Poland, paid dividends. Budapest is nearly due east of Paris, but, to avoid Germany, the caravan was forced to drive through Switzerland, Italy, and Yugoslavia, a three- or four-day trip interrupted by lengthy border checks.

On her arrival, Norton learned from Hollingworth that the condition of the Polish refugees was deplorable. Super's CPR was making the most headway, but, sadly, her organization, the SCF, only ventured out of the capital on weekends. Hollingworth pointed out that Francesca Wilson, with the British Quakers, was also a stumbling block, often baffled, a woman with "high ideals and little knowledge of Central Europe. The rest of the refugee bodies, Hungarians and Polish, bickered and obstructed and wrangled, while food and supplies stood in the capital, and the refugees in the camps half starved and more than half froze."[133] There was no time to waste. Hollingworth and Norton, with their truckloads of food, medicines, soap, blankets, and underclothes, became a two-woman guerilla relief operation. Some clusters of Poles they encountered—the lucky ones—had landed in convents and spas, adequate but short on supplies. Others, particularly those in abandoned houses and factories that housed hundreds, "would sleep together ... in these places, in damp cellars or filthy old machine-rooms. For bedding they would sometimes have palliasses and blankets, but sometimes vermin-ridden straw spread on stone floors. They were cut off from the world, without books, newspapers or radio; suspended in a private misery of cold, dirt and hunger, and horror-stories told over and over again."[134] Aside from money and supplies that enabled a cleanup, a Super *świetlica* was the solution to these morale-destroying environments. The government, through the Hungarian Red Cross, spent $44,000 a day on food, a hefty amount for a poor country, but the food was prepared and served in those awful facilities. At one camp, Losonc, conditions triggered a revolt that was put down shortly before Hollingworth and Norton arrived. Their truckload of supplies helped to temper tensions.

Norton added to the supplies she had brought from Paris by co-opting those stored in Budapest and taking charge of distribution. Supplies now regularly arrived at the camps. "It was due to her," Hollingworth exclaimed, that the conditions of the refugees' lives had so improved.[135] "Her pounding energy could not be held by etiquette, and she offended every committee by putting the welfare of camps above their dignities."[136] Hollingworth credited the CPR with doing fine work in Budapest, but Super, before returning to Bucharest, was hamstrung by having not yet received permission from the government to work in the refugee camps or with the interned soldiers. Hollingworth and Norton, by not seeking permission, by violating regulations and breaking protocol, made powerful enemies. Hollingworth had been charged by SCF with assessing refugee needs and writing a report on her findings and working with the SCF representatives already in Budapest. Instead, she and Norton set up an independent relief operation and drove their cache of supplies to the seventy refugee sites scattered throughout the country. Unofficial word arrived from the British embassy in Paris, heatedly supported by some of the local relief agencies, that perhaps Mrs. Norton should return and continue to work with the Poles in Paris and Angers, the cite chosen for the Polish government and army.

Leaders at SCF headquarters in London were fed up with Hollingworth's independence. She could not follow the rules and had embarrassed other SCF workers and those in other agencies. Her previous work for SCF and the British Committee for Refugees from Czechoslovakia (BCRC), while rescuing over three thousand people, had been run the same way and, worse, had initiated an investigation by MI5 and MI6 into why so many prominent Communists were granted visas.[137] The Soviet Union, an ally of Nazi Germany since the signing of the Hitler-Stalin pact, needed watching. Hollingworth's relief work career was cashiered for the second time. The six-week renegade relief program came to end in December. That she and Norton had intervened successfully to circumvent the logjam was of no avail. Norton returned to France and continued her work with the Poles. Hollingworth reserved the first seat available on the Orient Express but had a week on her hands. Not one, as she had said, to "lie soft" in a plush hotel, she used the opportunity to travel back to Romania to interview Józef Beck, languishing under house arrest in the ultra-modern Aero-Palace Hotel in Barșov. After lunch, watched over by a German agent, the small group of exiled Poles and their British guest were joined by Beck. The foreign minister, seeming distant, "looking tired and ill," answered only a few questions.[138] He had lost the savoir-faire with which he had conducted his duties. With a heavy heart, Hollingworth traveled to Cluj to talk with Marshal Józef Piłsudski's secretary, Mademoiselle Illaová, who expressed her desire to return to Poland and her hope that it would be reconstructed soon. She was surely aware that the Germans had created a truncated

Poland with the generic name General Government in late October, but Hollingworth knew her desires were an expression of Polish patriotism. "It is not the preservation of free institutions and personal liberty, as it is to an Englishmen, a Frenchmen or an American. It is not the power of the state, as to the Germans, or perhaps an Italian. It is not a system and an ideology, as to a Russian. It is simply the existence of Poland."[139] By Christmas, Hollingworth was back in London seeking to work as a journalist while writing her book *The Three Weeks' War in Poland*.[140] She would not again work in relief.

In Bucharest, Super was pleased that in his absence his Polish YMCA had reached refugees throughout the country. Thirty-seven centers were in operation, which included the two huge camps of interned soldiers. Super had visited most of them. Nearly all had *świetlicas*, had a volunteer doctor and a nurse, and (to the delight of the internees) now featured occasional entertainment by singers, musical groups, theater troupes, writers, poets, and actors, all of whom were refugees. One of the most famous entertainment groups, Wesoła Lwówska Fala (Lwów's Merry Wave), had been on the air since 1933 and was listened to every Sunday by six million fans. In between popular music and sketches, the comedians Szczpcio and Tońko performed skits in the Lwów dialect, and Adolf Fleischen parodied Yiddish and the Jewish community. Super remembered that "they and a beautiful motor bus came to us about the same time. Maybe the troupe came in the bus; I am not sure. Well, we housed them, fed them, clothed them, and started them on a service of morale-building-through-entertainment that was simply splendid."[141] The Wave, in the beautiful motor bus, drove to Buzău for their Romanian début in the huge camp of interned soldiers, a two-night performance on November 14 and 15. Only one of the Wave's five female stars, Włada Majewska, made an appearance. Super was beside himself with enthusiasm. The first half of the show featured Polish patriotic music and poetry, a trip in nostalgia that aroused emotions and brought many in the audience to tears. A former cabinet minister, caught up in the moment, fainted and was "carried from the hall."[142] The intermission was followed by over an hour of uproarious comedy accompanied by gales of laughter and outbursts of applause.

With the Wave off to tour other camps, Super surmised that his work in Romania had succeeded to the point that it was time for him to join the tens of thousands of Polish soldiers and refugees gathering in Angers. There he might be able to continue to serve. Evidence continued to pile up that reinforced his sense that it was time to move on. The *świetlica* at Tȃrgovista was so successful that it was envied by the Romanian guards, who requested one for themselves. Trypka, who had worked hard with Super to organize *świetlicas*, found a location outside the wire. Two days before Christmas, the Supers attended the opening. The fanfare included speeches by Romanians and Poles, as well as music by a Polish soldier band, and was topped off by refreshments. But the celebration was not over. All gathered outside and, led by the band, marched back inside the camp to continue festivities at the Polish soldiers' *świetlica*.[143]

In Bucharest, visitors lavished praise on Super's success in bringing together a diverse collection of relief agencies. In late November, Theodore Abel from the CPR came to report on Super's work, as did Malcolm Davis of the Red Cross, with whom Super got on well, unlike his interaction with Chatfield-Taylor and Swift.[144] Davis needed assurance that Red Cross supplies in shipment would, on their arrival, be under American control from warehouse to recipients. Brownie assured him it would be arranged.[145] Franciscan Father Justin Figas, representing the Catholic clergy of America, was next to arrive. Super escorted the priest and his secretary on a three-day inspection tour of ten camps. Coming to know Figas, he was won over by his charm and empathy, considering him a friend.[146] More important, Figas, a journalist, was impressed by the relief effort. On his return to America, his articles praising Super encouraged Catholics to contribute to the CPR.

Super, from the beginning of the relief operation, had adhered to a two-stage plan that he called the first wave and the second wave. He estimated the emergency phase would end around October 15, and then the second wave would last anywhere from six months to a year or longer. He later outlined a third wave that would continue care for those still interned.[147] The success of the first wave allowed Super in late October and early November to find solutions to other problems. An obvious problem was the difficulties faced by married women (some with children) whose husbands were missing or dead, as well as unmarried women, both young and old, who were in camps. Groups of women had gathered together for support in dozens of locations, and many others were struggling on their own. The YWCA leadership formed a women's division, persuading the wife of a Polish official, Helena Drymmer, to run the program. First, Drymmer had women in the men's camps released. Next, "amid the early snows she drove over the hills and mountains of southern Romania locating groups or large communities of women and studying their situation and needs."[148] Brought to eleven centers, outfitted with sewing machines, the women were taught dressmaking as well as how to make handbags, hats, gloves, coats, undergarments, blankets, and other necessities. As with the men, *świetlicas* were established and a variety of courses were offered, academic and practical. For the younger women, Girl Scout units were formed.

When access was granted to the soldier camps, it was discovered that young boys in school uniforms and Boy Scouts in uniform had been interned with the soldiers, a problem that needed attention. King Carol, when made aware of this situation, was furious, demanding an immediate solution. Nearly five hundred were pulled from the camps and turned over to Brown and the Romanian YMCA, which cared for the young men in a Y camp and a rented resort hotel near Brasov. Students also needed help. O'Donovan, using British funds, solved the problem by setting up a hotel to accommodate them. Room and board supported about one hundred enrolled in the university.[149]

With the second wave running smoothly, the Supers returned to Budapest, hoping that in their absence the relief effort was making progress. In Romania, the Supers had built a large and efficient relief operation. In four months, they (along with Brownie, Trypka, and Y secretaries from Poland) assembled a country-wide organization that employed 511 and depended on 679 volunteers. The relief coalition had spent $93,654 (today, 1,799,329), a third from the CPR, a third from the Polish government and the Bank of Poland, and a third from British relief organizations.[150] Tens of thousands had been fed, clothed, housed, and cared for medically and spiritually. Over one hundred thousand refugees and soldiers had passed through the two countries, the refugees landing in places all over the world. The soldiers made their way to France or were a welcome addition to the French forces in Syria. The Supers were pleased to find that the work, so successful in Bucharest, had been duplicated in Budapest. It was time to leave and prepare for the work waiting in France. Knowing CPR support to the Polish YMCAs they had created would continue pushed to the side any doubts they may have had.[151] Visas secured, friends held an afternoon farewell party at the Carlton Hotel coffeehouse. "Early the next morning, at 7:20, we left Budapest for Geneva. Our hearts were a bit heavy; our bodies weary; we looked forward with longing to a brief period of rest and recuperation in the deep snow of the Swiss mountains."[152] In a four-month period, the CPR effort to aid the Poles had been successfully accomplished by the Supers. Paul and Margaret attributed their achievement to being guided by the hand of God! To Davis and Strong, he wrote, "the Lord does not call thee into the forest to live only with a penknife."[153] For Hoover and the CPR, the Romanian and Hungarian successes were gratifying, and they were generous in praise of the Supers. With two operations running smoothly, the CPR could focus on a third: the tragedy unfolding in and around the Polish city of Vilnius.

Fog on the highway on Sunday morning, October 29, meant slow going between Kaunas and Vilnius for the five occupants and their driver squeezed into a mid-sized sedan. Even so, the distance was short, some sixty miles. Dr. Jurgis Alekna, president of the Lithuanian Red Cross; the famous writer Ignas Šeinius, serving as the Red Cross representative for the Vilnius region; American minster Owen J. C. Norem; and Gilbert Redfern and Frederick Dorsey Stephens of the Commission for Polish Relief (CPR) would soon reach their destination. Small talk prevailed, as they were apprehensive about what awaited them in the conquered city other than a desperate refugee crisis. The Soviets had invaded on September 17. Facing little resistance, large elements of the Red Army swiftly moved across Poland's narrow northern corridor. Advanced cavalry units, riding their shaggy steppe ponies, streamed through thousands of refugees bent on reaching the city or on crossing into Lithuania at any point. In two days, Vilnius was in Soviet hands.

As the car plodded along, Alekna expounded on his country's progress in its twenty years of independence. Šeinius thought he exaggerated but said nothing. The three Americans seemed to be listening to the Red Cross president's monologue, but Redfern interrupted to ask whether they were "still far away from the old border? Or demarcation line as you called it." Alekna rambled on, so Šeinius answered they would reach the line in question "in about fifteen minutes."[154] Redfern's interest was sparked, as the border dispute between Poland and Lithuania had persisted for twenty years, thereby spoiling relations between the two newly independent countries. The "old border" (known as the straw border) achieved a kind of notoriety, as the Poles had at various intervals stuck long branches in the ground with straw attached to the top. Wits, lounging in Vilnius cafés, quipped that the Poles had marked the border with brooms, and those brooms had a habit of not staying put. Across a no-man's-land of about half a mile, incidents were frequent: "Poachers, border runners, and outlaws roamed back and forth across the line drawing occasional fire from both Lithuanian and Polish guards."[155] Farmers, traders, and travelers were all subject to searches, long delays, and quibbles over documents.

Redfern pursued the question of borders and territorial claims, saying he knew that "Vilna was the ancient capital of Lithuania," but he later revealed his belief that "in October 1939 it was about as much Lithuanian as I am Turkish."[156] Redfern was right: ethnically diverse, the city of 220,000 was approximately 6 percent Lithuanian, 66 percent Polish, and 28 percent Jewish.[157] The long-established vibrant Jewish community, a center for learning and Talmudic scholarship, had been tagged by Napoleon as he passed through the city in 1812 as "the Jerusalem of the North."[158] The Jews of Vilnius took pride in the appellation. But to Lithuanians the percentages were irrelevant. The return of Vilnius was at the center of Lithuanian nationalism, a wrong to be corrected. "We shall not rest until Vilnius is ours": this call to action had been heard and repeated since the loss of the city in 1920.[159] It was a goal hardily endorsed by Alekna, an outspoken Lithuanian nationalist, who, after the Polish takeover of the city in 1920, moved his medical practice to Kaunas.[160] But the Poles were just as adamant in their claim, symbolically reinforced in 1937 with the granting of Józef Piłsudski's wish that his heart be cut out and buried in his mother's grave in the city's Rasos Cemetery and his brain go to Stephen Bátory University.[161]

The dispute over the city continued to smolder, but the Soviet occupation in September 1939 appeared to settle the issue. Then, on October 10, the Lithuanian government was stunned when informed by the Soviets that Vilnius was theirs for the taking.[162] The Lithuanian foreign minister, Juozas Urbšys, was called to Moscow, invited to the Little Corner for consultation, where in the past week the Estonian foreign minister and the Latvian foreign minister had received the full force of Stalin's velvet hammer, "like peas against a wall."[163] Faced with a Soviet fait accompli, both had agreed to bases in their countries. The Lithuanians knew that they, too, would have to bend to Stalin's demands for bases, and perhaps territorial rearrangements, but if they were persistent, they might wangle a few concessions. Stalin opened the talks with a hammer; laying a map on the table, he revealed that the Soviets and the Germans had concluded an agreement "granting to the Soviet Union a major portion of Lithuania and a narrow strip of border to Germany."[164] Recovering from the blow, Urbšys later wrote, "I refrain from saying too much: a vision of Vilnius, the city and its territory, which the government of Lithuania has sent me to regain, looms before me."[165] Stalin softened, exuding his charm, saying he did not wish to partition Urbšys's country. The Germans would likely, according to him, renounce their claims, and he offered to call in the German ambassador to affirm his assertion. Molotov attempted to break the tension by interjecting, "Any imperialist country would simply occupy Lithuania and that would be that. Unlike us. We wouldn't be Bolsheviks if we didn't search for new ways."[166] Stalin spread "out a second map of Lithuania on the table, one more felicitous to the Lithuanian heart. The line drawn on it shows Vilnius and a portion of the territory to its east ceded to Lithuania."[167] A part of Urbšys had to be elated—Vilnius would be Lithuanian—but for the Soviets the transfer of the city was simply tossing the Lithuanians a bone intended to mollify their loss of independence. The Soviets allowed the Lithuanian delegation a week of protests and heated arguments, but finally Stalin had had enough. To a final plea to not to station troops in Lithuania, Stalin's "answer is a short and unsparing, 'Nyet!'"[168] The following day, October 10, the Lithuanians signed the Mutual Assistance Treaty—twenty thousand Soviet soldiers would be stationed on four bases located at strategic palaces in the country. The infamous straw border would now be gone, the new border was well beyond Vilnius, though Stalin gifted only 20 percent of the surrounding region, keeping the rest for himself.

Lithuanians now knew that the territorial arrangements they were witnessing across Eastern Europe were sanctioned by the secret codicil to the Nazi-Soviet pact concluded a few months earlier in Moscow. What other rearrangements the liars' league had in store for their country could only be guessed, and while they suspected that they would likely not survive as a nation, they proceeded with the acquisition of Vilnius, oblivious to their pyrrhic victory.[169] Pleased at having achieved their historic goal, thousands made their way to Vilnius to celebrate. But the return of the city screened by a triumphant entry could not hide the reality that Lithuania was firmly in the grasp of the Soviets. A joke, widely circulated, went to the heart of the matter: "Vilnius belongs to us, and we belong to the Russians." What was it Urbšys wrote—"peas against the wall"?

Alekna stopped talking as the car reached the outskirts of the city, but the others may have been pleased with his oration, as it gave little chance for the tensions to surface that existed between the CPR, the Red Cross, and Norem. Norem reflected the view of Franklin Roosevelt and Norman H. Davis that the CPR was an interloper pushing its nose in where it didn't belong. Alekna also shared Norem's views, which assumed the Lithuanian Red Cross should oversee all relief activity. But any future difficulties remained dormant, as all were keen to observe what was happening in the city. Stephens, pleasantly surprised with what he saw, exclaimed, "It is an entirely European city!"[170] Redfern, with long experience in Poland, reassured him that the city was European and attractive, featuring a variety of architectural styles. Stephens's expectations were perhaps shaped by his experience in 1921 and 1922 working for the American Relief Administration in the ghastly famine-ridden Volga River area, and Vilnius, long under tsarist rule, would look more like towns in central Russia. Despite its baroque attractions, Vilnius was no Bucharest or Budapest, not a city whose hotel bars were flooded with journalists and the European upper crust; it had no famous restaurants whose tables boasted shimmering crystal and polished silverware, no nightclubs featuring sultry torch singers, no elegant fast trains that sped from Warsaw,

Vienna, Berlin, or Paris. Vilnius was the "administrative, cultural, military, economic and financial centre for northeastern Poland."[171] The city was surrounded by vast estates of the landed gentry worked by peasants bound to the land. For small farmers and the residents of small towns and villages of the Vilnius region, it was a hardscrabble life. Tracy Strong of the World Committee of the YMCA, on a visit in early spring 1940, wrote, "This proud and ancient city, with its many churches, synagogues and mosques; with a mixed population . . . with its deeply rooted traditions, prejudices and hatreds became a maelstrom of human needs and one of Europe's major relief problems."[172]

Reaching the city center, the would-be rescuers noted many more Red Army soldiers in the streets, mixing freely with Lithuanian soldiers and wary civilians in pursuit of necessities. Šeinius remarked that, unlike the sharply dressed soldiers of his country, the Bolsheviks seemed underfed, each "lost in his dark brown, wide as a potato sack and awfully long uniform."[173] Officers were harder to pick out but wore shorter jackets and jodhpurs tucked into high black boots, "creat[ing] an impression that all . . . have crooked legs."[174] The Soviets, in violation of their agreement, had not left the city as promised, but the soldiers were well behaved and treated the skittish residents respectfully. Redfern observed,

> In many respects, indeed, the Soviet soldiers in Vilna seemed as if they had come from another planet. Vilna to them was something like a new world, something which they did not even know existed. They descended on the stores like a swarm of locusts, buying everything in sight that attracted the eye, and paying in Polish złoty almost any price asked. Women's under-garments went like hot cakes—but the shop-keepers had first to explain what they were. The troops were well supplied with złoty, the Soviet authorities obtaining them from the banks in any amount desired.[175]

Contrary to the behavior of individual Red Army soldiers, the high command from the first days of the occupation indulged in looting government buildings and factories. In front of the famous Vrublevskiu Library, which possessed an extensive collection of Lithuanian history, green Soviet army trucks blocked the way. Crate after crate exited through the library door and into the trucks. Šeinius momentarily stopped breathing. "Jumping out of the car," he asked those standing around why they were allowing this to happen, but he knew the answer: there was nothing they could do.[176]

Shaken by what they were witnessing, they continued toward the hotel. On the way they passed long queues outside food distribution centers. Shops were usually not open on Sunday, but food supplies from co-ops all over Lithuania had begun arriving the day before and continued to arrive all through the night.[177] The last few blocks to the hotel were stop and start, slowed not just by the food lines but also by the crowds watching the Lithuanian and Soviet troops parading the streets, celebrating the city's transfer. Soldiers on foot, on horseback, and in tanks, accompanied by brass bands, passed under a banner stretched over the roadway that read, "Inhabitants of Vilnius Welcome the Lithuanian Army." An excited bystander exclaimed, "The street is drowning in flowers and banners. You

Lithuanian army enters Vilnius, October 29, 1939 (courtesy of Wikipedia/Kam.lt).

can hear Lithuanian speech everywhere. Today is a great day for Lithuania and its citizens."[178] Passing Lithuanian military and police units received a tepid welcome from Poles in the crowd, but the Soviets were greeted with icy stares. For the Lithuanians, the future was uncertain; however, in five weeks under Soviet rule, the Poles had experienced first defeat and then tyranny. Boxy Soviet army trucks, red stars painted on the doors, repeatedly crisscrossed the food lines and gaps in the parade, transporting booty to the central railroad station, a persistent reminder of the deadly cost of Communist rule. Worse, everyone knew or had heard of someone who had simply disappeared.

Successfully navigating the traffic, Redfern and his fellow passengers met at the hotel with Ignacy Zagórsky, a lawyer, and Dr. Maria Petrusewicz, who had organized the volunteer Committee to Aid the Refugees on September 22, as the Polish Red Cross was barely functioning and the Polish YMCA had exhausted its resources.[179] Feeding and housing the thirty thousand destitute refugees was beyond their capabilities, but they were able to aid thousands supported by donations from locals and by a gift of one hundred thousand złoty from the city's Soviet commander. The commander, having confiscated the money from the banks, had no shortage of cash. The relief committee spent the money quickly, as the złoty daily declined in value. Further, they explained that refugees had begun arriving from Danzig in the first week of the war and that Vilnius already had a refugee population composed of those who earlier fled Memel and its surrounding territory to escape the Germans. With the outbreak of war, thousands more made their way to the city, while others were strung out along the border to the south. Many were trapped in the Suwałki region, a bulge of Polish territory sandwiched between East Prussia and Lithuania now occupied by the Nazis. The Soviet invasion triggered a second huge wave that largely trekked from Warsaw and other cities to the east. Intact Polish military units, as well as stragglers from units crushed in battle, poured into Lithuania. A small number of air force personnel from the Porubanek airfield near Vilnius made a "twelve-hour dash" to the Latvian border and were interned.[180] Zagórsky and Petrusewicz assured their listeners that the refugee situation was desperate and that the fourteen thousand interned Polish soldiers were held in deplorable conditions. Unlike the soldiers interned in Romania and Hungary, the Lithuanian and Latvian governments did not aid and abet escapees. An unfavorable geography also proved an obstacle. Those few who did escape and managed to avoid recapture made their way to the coastal cities of both countries, where they begged for passage to Sweden, Norway, or almost anywhere else. Eventually, the lucky few joined the Polish forces in France and Great Britain.

Among the refugees stuck in Vilnius, a third were women and children, and fifteen thousand were Jews. As immediate action was required, it was decided that Šeinius would stay and assist Zagórsky and Petrusewicz. With sufficient information about the mounting tragedy, Alekna and the three Americans returned to Kaunas.[181] As they drove out of the city in the fading afternoon light, the parade crowds had dissipated, and the temperature was dropping. The food queues were still there, many people in summer clothing, compelled by hunger to stay in line throughout the night, as the food stores would not open until 7:00 the following morning.[182] Many suffered frostbite, and there was almost never enough food for those who had waited so long.[183] Throughout the frigid night, those in line were accompanied by one of the few sounds coming from the streets: the whirring emitted from the motors of the Red Army trucks that continued to make their runs.

Back in Kaunas, Alekna ordered the Red Cross to do all it could to support Šeinius. Redfern cabled the CPR in New York: "The situation here is tragic in the extreme."[184] A Polish countess, after walking four hundred miles from Warsaw, sobbed, "We are now a nation of vagabonds."[185] Redfern pleaded that a remittance should be sent immediately and winter clothing and shoes as quickly as possible. As time was the critical factor, he recommended that the CPR work through the committee established by Zagórsky and Petrusewicz. The CPR agreed. In just a few days, Redfern got his remittance in support of soup kitchens and assurance that winter clothing was on the way.[186] Stephens left for Paris to persuade the Polish government to send money. He was successful. Norem apprised the State Department of the burgeoning crisis and requested that the American Red Cross undertake emergency aid. The Red Cross acted immediately by sending $15,000 to the League of Red Cross Societies to purchase warm clothing and allotting $10,000 to the Lithuanian Red Cross, but it would take several months before the winter clothing arrived.[187] The American Jewish Joint Distribution Committee (JDC) contributed amounts that allowed the nearly fifteen thousand Jewish refugees to receive adequate care. The Dutch, Danish, and Swedish Red Crosses, neutrals inside the blockade, were able to ship clothing more quickly to Kaunas and Vilnius. The Danish shipments of overcoats and warm clothing were accompanied by a gift of forty thousand lits ($6,757).[188] The largest contribution came from the London-based Polish Relief Fund, which gave $100,000. By the end of the first week in November, Redfern was back in Vilnius with funds from the CPR, ensuring that the soup kitchens continued to operate.

Zagórsky and Petrusewicz were elated with cash contributions, as the Lithuanian government allowed the foreign relief agencies to purchase lits at a 50 percent discount, greatly increasing their purchasing power. The generous influx of money, however, proved a stopgap measure, as

Food kitchen in Vilnius, 1939–1940 winter (courtesy of CPR Records, Hoover Institution Library and Archives).

the number in need of assistance dramatically increased. Against overwhelming odds of success, the government was bent on Lithuanization. The first step was to move several government offices to Vilnius to replace the Polish equivalents. The dismissed Polish government workers were soon destitute. The international relief agencies protested—Redfern was most outspoken—but the process continued unabated.

To the south of Vilnius in the no-man's-land that sprang up between the newly drawn border separating Germany and Lithuania, unimaginable horrors occurred routinely. The Germans allowed the refugees to leave after being stripped of nearly all their possessions, "persecuted with all the thoroughness and brutality of the Nazi regime."[189] This often included warm clothing that the German soldiers sold on the black market for extraordinarily high prices. Because the refugees now possessed nothing, the Lithuanians refused them entry, and the Germans would not take them back. There they remained, huddled together in small groups, freezing, and starving. A JDC representative described the plight of a group of Jews in the Suwałki region:

> We found two children about twelve years of age, fourteen women and fifteen men. This was the third day they had been on the frontier in subfreezing weather, most of them were unable to talk coherently, but kept screaming to us and crying to be taken away. I learned that each day they had been visited by German guards and searched to the skin again and again to make sure they had not succeeded in hiding some money or valuables. One man with a bandaged leg had the wound opened because the Germans had ripped off the bandage to see whether he was hiding any money. With the aid of some of the peasants, some of whom I saw standing crying while we talked with the refugees, they built crude, thatched huts which offered some protection against the wind, but none against the rain. One young woman had died during the night and her body lay on a field to one side covered with a burlap bag. A small *Shtet'le* of 50 Jewish families each provided shelter for seven or eight refugees and every night the young men in this region moved through the border areas saving as many as possible. The 31 refugees previously described were finally saved after the JDC guaranteed their support after being admitted into Lithuania.[190]

Clusters of Jews with little food and no water were also trapped between the Soviet and German borders. "The Soviet authorities, which hitherto admitted refugees ... closed the frontier because the Nazi anti-Semitic measures had increased the numbers of fleeing Jews to a point where the Russians felt they could no longer cope with the problem. Barred from the Soviet area, the refugees turned back to Nazi Poland, only to find that the German frontier guards refused to re-admit them."[191] Weather, too, conspired against the refugees, as subfreezing temperatures arrived early. The winter of 1939 and 1940 was the coldest in forty-five to fifty years.[192] Throughout the Vilnius region the daily temperature reached new lows. The task for the refugees and the Vilnius victims of Lithuanization was to find a way to survive. This was made possible for most by the efforts of the Zagòrsky and Petrusewicz committee supported by the CPR, an assortment of international relief organizations, and the Lithuanian Red Cross, working with a budget of $150,000 a month. It was a day-to-day struggle to sustain the burgeoning numbers.[193] Redfern, under conditions much more difficult than those faced by Paul Super and James W. Brown in Romania, soldiered on.

8
Embargo Repeal, Politics, and Negotiations in the Garden of Beasts

Hoover and Ambassador Jerzy Potocki, all smiles at the Pułaski Memorial Day event in New York City on October 11, 1939 (courtesy of AP Images).

For both Herbert Hoover and Franklin Roosevelt, the month of October 1939 was filled with uncertainty. With Red Cross and Commission for Polish Relief (CPR) efforts underway, the organizations remained at loggerheads, with both men focused on the debate over revision of the neutrality laws before Congress. Roosevelt reasoned that after Hitler had violated the Munich agreement and the British and French had guaranteed Poland's borders, war was in the offing. To be able to protect the United States and aid Britain and France, repeal of the law's embargo provision was mandatory.

Between 1935 and 1937, as the Neutrality Acts passed Congress, Roosevelt, in line with public opinion, had no objections to what the legislation wished to accomplish. His administration was "definitely committed to the maintenance of peace and the avoidance of any entanglements which would lead [the United States] into conflict."[1] He signed each bill placed on his desk but privately pointed out the potential to drag the country into war. He was also alert, as always, to any curbs he perceived on executive prerogatives, any restrictions that would tie his hands.[2] The ink of his signature on the first piece of legislation was hardly dry when, a month later, the Italians invaded Ethiopia. Roosevelt, along with a majority of Americans, supported Emperor Haile Selassie's ragtag army. Secretary Harold Ickes wrote in his diary, "I suspect that, pretty generally speaking, the whole civilized world has the same point of view."[3] Black Americans were mobilized on a large scale for the first time on a foreign policy issue. In Harlem, Blacks were recruited to serve in the emperor's army but stopped from serving by the Justice Department. Still, well-known Chicago pilot John C. Robinson, "the Brown Condor," traveled to Ethiopia, gained the trust of Haile Selassie, and was awarded the rank of colonel in command of Ethiopia's air force. At war's end, Robinson returned to Chicago to a hero's welcome.[4] Italian Americans supported Italy, holding large rallies in New York City, Philadelphia, and Chicago, where "people [gave] their gold rings and watches, cigarette lighters and crucifixes, as well as copper postcards by the hundreds."[5] Roosevelt needed the votes of both Blacks and Italians in the coming election, and with the country overwhelmingly anti-interventionist, declaring the United States neutral was an easy call. Revelations of Italian atrocities, the bombing of cities and Red Cross hospitals, the use of mustard gas, and the execution of prisoners shocked Americans, diminished Italian American support, and tarnished Benito Mussolini's reputation. More important, the war demonstrated that the neutrality laws were anything but neutral. Clearly, they favored the stronger and better-armed Italians and prevented any assistance, no matter how unlikely, to the underdog Ethiopians.[6]

Il Duce's conquest was complete in May 1936, and a month later General Francisco Franco undertook a coup in Morocco that began the Spanish Civil War. The conflict divided Americans, and the Left put great pressure on the president and the Congress to lift the mandatory embargo of arms shipments to Spain passed in January 1937. Martha Gellhorn, writer and paramour of Ernest Hemingway, decided that if fascism was to be stopped, then Spain was the place to do it. The irrepressible Gellhorn wrote to a friend, "Me, I'm going to Spain with the boys. I don't know who the boys are, but I am going with them."[7] Once there, in lengthy emotional letters to Eleanor Roosevelt, her surrogate mother, Gellhorn apprised the First Lady with her eyewitness accounts of horrific bombings, atrocities, and suffering inflicted on children. She urged the First Lady to support sending food and arms, hoping she in turn would pressure her husband to lift the embargo. Gellhorn and Hemingway collaborated on a Republican propaganda film by Dutch filmmaker Joris Ivens, titled *Spanish Earth*. Near its completion in June 1937, she held high hopes she could convince Eleanor and Franklin to view the film. Eleanor responded in the affirmative: "How about you three coming to Hyde Park, Monday the 5th of July and showing the film there?"[8] Gellhorn was pleased by the president and First Lady's reaction: "they were sympathetic to the plight of the Spanish people" and suggested to Ivens that he could strengthen the film "by underlining the causes of the conflict."[9] Despite pressure from some of those close to the Roosevelts and from left-wing activists who fervently favored the Loyalists, the president was not persuaded to lift the embargo, as he was aware that most Americans either were neutral or had no opinion and Catholics were moving in support of Franco.[10] The war in Spain continued to rage, but the president stayed clear, letting it play out.

The Spanish Earth, a film directed by Joris Ivens and written by Ernest Hemingway, shown to Franklin and Eleanor Roosevelt by Martha Gellhorn, July 1937 (author's collection).

In late summer, the war in China escalated into a titanic struggle for Shanghai, followed in December by the conquest and rape of Nanking and the sinking of the US gunboat *Panay*.[11] Aggressions, piled one on the other, brought Republican and Democratic senators and congressmen more in line with the president. Support for revision grew as more and more Americans recognized the "dilemma of neutrality."[12] Since events had proved that neutrality laws always favored the aggressors (a popular argument supported by the Roosevelt administration), why not write the neutrality laws in such a way that they favored countries the United States approved of and wanted to see succeed in defending themselves?

Roosevelt, in a Chicago speech on October 5, 1937, responded to what he termed "the present reign of terror and international lawlessness" that had begun a few years previously and "reached a stage where the very foundations of civilization [were] seriously threatened."[13] Always innovative but circumspect in his use of language, Roosevelt advocated that the "three bandit nations," as they were called by Cordell Hull, be not embargoed, sanctioned, or boycotted but rather "quarantined."[14] "The people of the United States under modern conditions must, for the sake of their own future," he emphasized, "give thought to the rest of the world.... [T]here is no escape through mere isolation or neutrality."[15] In other words, the president was suggesting collective action to implement embargos or sanctions in order to isolate the aggressors. The response was immediate and often negative. From inside the administration, Hull and Davis "were shocked beyond words."[16] Democratic senator Burton Wheeler of Montana and Republican senators William Borah of Idaho and Gerald P. Nye of North Dakota branded the president a "warmonger."[17] Kentucky senator Alben Barkley, a few days after the speech, met with the president in his bedroom at the White House—Roosevelt as usual was in his pajamas and cloaked in his worn but treasured grey bathrobe. "Well," said Barkley, "you certainly suggested a new approach in your Chicago speech." "Yes!" Roosevelt replied, "I certainly stirred up the animals, didn't I?" "Yes," Barkley replied, "you certainly stirred 'um up."[18] Roosevelt explained to the press that he was not calling for action but only floating an idea, ringing an alarm bell, searching for "a new concept for preserving peace."[19] He was true to his word and made no moves to quarantine any country. A year later, Roosevelt disapproved of the Munich agreement but was relieved that the British prime minister had managed to avoid war. He was under no illusion that Neville Chamberlain had established "peace in our time."[20]

Six weeks after Chamberlain's triumphant return to Great Britain, Secretary Henry Morgenthau described what he called a "momentous White House meeting" on November 14, 1938: "The president pointed out that the recrudescence of German power at Munich had completely reoriented our international relations; for the first time since the Holy Alliance in 1818 the United States now faced the possibility of an attack on the Atlantic side in both the Northern and Southern Hemispheres."[21] In developing a plan to defend the United States, Roosevelt saw the southern border as a "soft underbelly" vulnerable to attack. He worried that Nazi inroads in Latin America, economic and political, might result in airfields being built with long-range bombers capable of attacking American cities. The president's fears were likely attributable to the "bomber hysteria" prevalent in the 1930s, reinforced by films like *Things to Come* and confirmed by the Condor Legion's destruction of Guernica and the Japanese bombing of Chinese cities. The unforgettable iconic photograph of baby Ping Mei in the Shanghai Railroad Station on August 8, 1937, seen by 136 million people, seemed to credit Stanley Baldwin's predictions that "the bomber always gets through," and with devastating effect.[22] Awareness of rapidly developing aviation technology brought into question the Atlantic Ocean as a guarantee against attack. The president judged Adolf Hitler's ambitions were unbridled and that further demands would soon be made. To British ambassador Ronald Lindsay, he confided the Polish corridor or even Romania would be the Führer's next target. "Somehow or other," he feared, the United States would be drawn into the war.[23] To counter Hitler, Roosevelt explained, Britain and France must be better prepared for war, both being weak in air power.

The path forward was clear: despite opposition, defense spending had to dramatically increase. The ability to defend the country demanded strengthening the navy and building a modern army and air force.[24] Fearing opposition from his own party as well as from a coalition of anti-interventionists, he announced a modest $300 million increase in defense spending.[25] But it was Hitler's violation of the Munich agreement in

March 1939 that convinced Roosevelt to push Congress to repeal the neutrality law governing embargo. He and his secretary of state were strongly opposed to US entry into the war but questioned whether the country could remain neutral, aid the Allies by large sales of aircraft, weapons, and ammunition, and "somehow or other" not be dragged into war.[26]

Roosevelt largely kept to his goal of providing all aid to Britain and France short of war by keying in only a few trusted aides as he faced a thicket of opposition in the Senate. To keep from creating more opposition, he stayed behind the curtain, meeting with targeted senators and congressmen individually or in small groups. In April, he was encouraged by opinion polls showing that more than half the country favored selling war materials to Britain and France if in a declared war.[27] A month later, New York congressman Sol Bloom, acting chairman of the House Foreign Affairs Committee, offered that passage of revision in the House was likely. In fact, he told Roosevelt he could have any bill he liked.[28] Hull, publicly and in his memoirs, presented himself as the measured diplomat, but when he lobbied members of Congress to secure embargo repeal, the Tennessean had a hard time controlling his hot, Andrew Jackson–like temper. The secretary invited senators and representatives to his apartment or met with them in the White House, where he climbed down their throats in a manner that would make future president Lyndon Johnson smile. They were "making the biggest mistake of [their] lives"; the European crisis was not "another goddam piddling dispute over a boundary"; the neutrality laws were a "wretched little bobtailed, sawed-off domestic statute" and "just plain chuckle-headed."[29]

Bloom was right; the bill passed in the House. Hull, beside himself, wrote that a real tragedy had occurred when, on June 30, the House passed the bill by a vote of 201 to 187, but only after an amendment containing a modified arms embargo had been inserted. This amendment had been slipped in suddenly by a majority of two votes—159 to 157—when over one hundred Democratic members of the House were absent, having gone home before the session ended, many to avoid going on record with their vote.[30] The amendment, a concession to Republican John M. Vorys of Ohio, prevented the sale of arms and ammunition. Once in, it was impossible to remove, as the Democrats did not have the votes. The bill as amended allowed the sale of aircraft parts and other war materials, even if on arrival reassembled fighter planes and tanks had no ammunition. But the legislation, moving to the Senate Foreign Relations Committee headed by Nevada senator Key Pittman, confirmed the adage that the upper house is where good bills go to die, as the committee voted 12 to 11 to delay consideration until the next session of Congress in January of the coming year.[31] "Pittman lamented that he had more confidence in the will of God than in the philosophy of modern statesmen."[32] The president, however, was losing confidence in the hard-drinking, silver-pistol-carrying Pittman, who obsessed about silver subsidies and was now more seriously distracted by his longtime problem with alcohol.[33]

Roosevelt, hopping mad and stung by this congressional rebuff, determined to try again at the first promising opportunity. He was not about to tie a toe tag to a change he considered essential to America's defense, convinced that after Hitler and Joseph Stalin concluded their nefarious pact on the night of August 22–23, the liars' league would embark on war. At a press conference held in his Hyde Park office, the president made his position clear. They had made a cynical bet, a gamble, said Roosevelt of the anti-interventionists, both Republicans and Democrats, who rejected his wished-for changes to the neutrality laws. They wagered that no war would come until after they returned in January, saying they would take care of things then: "I sincerely hope they are right, but if they are not right and we have another serious international crisis they have tied my hands and I have practically no power to make an American effort to prevent such a war from breaking out. Now, that is a pretty serious responsibility."[34] In a rearguard action in support of embargo repeal, the president had Louis Johnson, the aggressive assistant secretary of war, throw down the gauntlet in several hard-hitting speeches reiterating the president's judgment that the embargo "encouraged war."[35] Of those senators who had failed to repeal it, Johnson said, "however honorable may have been their intentions, they have much to answer for. They played politics when peace was in the balance, and men may die as a result."[36]

The president's opportunity arose a few days after Johnson's speeches—Hitler invaded Poland on September 1. During the first few days of the war, Roosevelt repeatedly assured Americans of US neutrality and vehemently rejected the possibility of direct American participation. At a press conference on September 1, when asked whether the United States could avoid involvement, he responded, "I believe we can; and . . . every effort will be made by the administration so to do."[37] Two days later, September 3, responding to the British and French declarations of war in a fireside chat titled "The War in Europe," the president voiced his strong support for neutrality, renouncing war with "assurance and reassurance that every effort of your government will be directed to that end."[38] The president missed no opportunity to hammer home the point. At a cabinet meeting later that day, Roosevelt reaffirmed his position. Hull reported the president as having said that there was a difference "between our preparing for war and our preparing to meet war problems. Pay attention only to the latter, because we were not going to get into the war."[39]

During the tumultuous first week of war, a public opinion poll showed the overwhelming majority of those questioned answered, "Everything possible . . . should be done to keep the nation out of war."[40] However, the poll also suggested that American opposition to engaging in a European war might be more circumstantial than the Roosevelt administration and hardcore anti-interventionists assumed. Forty-four percent responded that if Britain and France were imperiled, the United States should send its armed forces to Europe. In late August, polls also recorded that 76 percent of respondents feared that the United States would be drawn into the war.[41] George Gallup explained the polls were not contradictory but that "to a great many Americans the issue is simply one of helping England and France, without going to war ourselves."[42] Gallup might have been more truthful and acknowledged that the US desire to be involved and noninvolved simultaneously was a dilemma seemingly without answer, one that animated anti-interventionists' fears. Republican senator Arthur Vandenberg of Michigan, in his diary on September 15, called this approach an illusion that would end with the United States going to war:

> The story of 1917–18 is already repeating itself. Pressure and propaganda are at work to drive us into the new World War. . . . The same emotions which demand the repeal of the embargo will subsequently demand still more effective aid for Britain and France and Poland. . . .

It is a tribute to the American *heart* but not to the American *head*. Oh, yes, all these good people abhor the thought of our entry into the war; they are all opposed to that. President Roosevelt has given them their cue, however, in his use of the treacherous idea that we can help these countries by methods "short of war." My quarrel is with the notion that America can be half in and half out of this war . . . which—if we are really in earnest about this business of "helping the democracies"—is utterly cowardly as a public policy for a great country like ours. I hate Hitlerism and Nazism and Communism as completely as any person living. But I decline to embrace the opportunist idea . . . that we can stop these things in Europe without entering the conflict.[43]

Ed Halsey, secretary to the Senate, on September 7 told the president that his research indicated "that sixty senators will support a 'cash and carry' neutrality act; that twenty-five will stand in opposition; that the others are on the doubtful or uncertain list."[44] The brutal Nazi assault on Poland turned the heads of some senators who had voted against repeal or for postponement a month earlier. More good news arrived from Senator Pittman and Representative Bloom, who reported to the White House that the chances for repeal and revision were good, particularly in the upper chamber.[45] In mid-September, the president's twin goals of aiding the Allies and preparing for war brightened considerably. Roosevelt did not hesitate, taking full advantage of the moment when it appeared likely that the Germans would follow up the Polish campaign with an immediate attack on Britain and France and, remotely, perhaps on the United States. For the president, it was time for a decision. Texas senator Tom Connelly observed, "Roosevelt was a different man. He now spoke with sureness about foreign affairs and kept a firm grip on the reins as he detailed what he wanted of Congress."[46] Perhaps the confident president Connelly so applauded had overcome the timidity induced by his drubbing over court packing and the reemergence of depression as the administration moved forward aggressively with a campaign for embargo repeal and clarifications to the neutrality laws, vowing a bipartisan vote to demonstrate the president's "determination to keep the country out of war."[47] Though Halsey's vote count was quite solid and Pittman and Bloom were reading the shifting mood of the Congress correctly, Roosevelt worried a Senate filibuster might succeed. On September 11, judging the situation favorable, he called Congress into special session. "Nothing was left undone in planning the administration's moves."[48] The president was determined to have his way—so much so that he slowed the pace of mobilization in September and October 1939. Industry was less rapidly converted from peacetime to wartime production, and the number of servicemen was not increased to meet this "limited national emergency."[49] The slowdown was designed to deflect noninterventionists' criticism and suggested that the current level of preparedness was sufficient, or might even decrease, if embargo repeal passed through Congress. The White House further claimed that these changes would spur the economy and transfer some of the burden of the defense of the hemisphere to the Allies. The advantage to the United States would be that the Allies' chances of stopping the Germans would be greatly increased without direct US participation.

The response from the anti-interventionists was swift and sharp as they girded "their loins for bitter combat."[50] Powerful Republican senator William Borah, "the Lion of Idaho," disagreed with the president's prognosis of what would follow the end of hostilities in Poland. Rather than an expansion of the war, he and many anti-interventionists expected a German-orchestrated peace offensive designed to end the conflict and bring about a general negotiated settlement coupled with a revision of the Treaty of Versailles.[51] In that case, embargo repeal would be unnecessary. But, as Senator Barkley said, the president had "certainly stirred 'um up." From the start the anti-interventionists knew they would not be able to prevent lifting the embargo. They didn't have the votes. Privately, Borah said that he favored repeal with the proviso of "cash and carry" but that he "must make some sort of fight ... so as to keep the President from leading us into war."[52] Borah, Nye, Wheeler, and California Republican senator Hiram Johnson, proudly known as the "sons of wild jackasses," ratcheted up the pressure to generate as much support as possible for nonintervention, fighting "with all the intensity, determination, and organization they could command."[53] All four were committed to staging political theater, knowing that embargo repeal was the opening round in battles that were sure to come.

Borah, a western progressive Silver Republican and a skilled lawyer who had gone head-to-head with the famous Clarence Darrow in the murder trial of Big Bill Haywood, was a feared and admired orator with a prodigious memory:

> The rumble of his great voice resounded in the corridor of the office building as he committed a passage to memory. He also used such occasions to polish his enunciation. The models for his style were Burke, Pitt, Fox, Daniel Webster, Wendell Phillips, and Lincoln. He studied their oratorical works with care and adapted some of their allusions and exclamations to his own use. There were few thrills at the Capitol comparable to seeing and hearing Borah on the Senate floor. Word from the press gallery that "Borah is up" sent hordes of reporters scurrying to their perches and crowds of visitors to the gallery.[54]

He was also a lifetime ladies' man who earned the epithet "son of a wild jackass" in both politics and in bed. "He was not a handsome man. He was course-featured and burly, but unequivocally masculine, square-chinned—with a dimple."[55] Other than his stature and dynamism on the floor of the Senate, perhaps his full head of dark brown hair and his penchant for bow ties proved the attraction.

Well knowing Borah's escapades—he opened his law office a few doors from the red-light district—fellow Boiseans christened him "the town bull." In Washington, DC, he conducted a long affair with the married daughter of Theodore Roosevelt, Alice Roosevelt Longworth, who perhaps saw in Borah a likeness to her father. Alice was often in the front row of the Senate gallery to hear him speak. Washington gossips tagged her with the nickname "Aurora Borah Alice."[56] Supposedly, her lover was also the lover of "Cissy" Patterson, publisher of the *Washington Times*. His wife, known as "Little Borah," tolerated it all, as did Idaho voters, for throughout his career he paid no political price for his sexual peccadillos. The old Lion, now seventy-four and suffering grave illness, on September 14 displayed his slightly diminished oratorical skill, leading a bullish charge in a radio address claiming that behind the president's words was his desire to aid Britain and France. Borah asked his audience, "Is not this laying the foundation of intervention—in fact, is it not intervention—in the present European war?"[57]

"The real nub of the neutrality controversy," declared Borah's fellow son of a wild jackass and anti-interventionist, North Dakota senator Nye, was "presidential power, presidential discretion, presidential chance to commit the country in a way that makes staying out of war exceedingly difficult.... [I]f America really means to stay out of foreign war, she needs to remember how easy it is to get in. We need the neutrality law. We need restraints upon a President."[58] Nye, markedly different from his three colleagues, was "lean, youthful and energetic."[59] The senator, a small-town newspaper editor, "stood five feet, ten and one-half inches tall and kept his brown hair smoothly combed"; he was well dressed, choosing "dark double-breasted suits and colorful ties."[60] He had come a long way from his debut on the Senate floor in 1925 "wearing high-tip yellow shoes and a gaudy tie and sporting a soup-bowl haircut."[61] But those who wrote off the newly minted senator as a William Jennings Bryan–like hayseed from the frozen prairies of North Dakota were in for a shock. He avoided the Washington social scene; instead, he fished and played golf and bridge. A heavy smoker, "serious, earnest and direct, he was also considerate, generous, and had a sense of humor. He spoke in a soft, low-pitched voice and was a good listener." He also became an accomplished rhetorician.[62] Skilled and dogged in Senate investigations and in pursuit of legislation he favored, he demonstrated courage speaking "out candidly on explosive issues."[63] Imbibing the progressive spirit of "Fighting Bob LaFollette" and a touch of agrarian radicalism inherited from William Jennings Bryan, he tangled with the conservative and big business faction in his own party and supported much of Roosevelt's New Deal.

Johnson spoke out as well, agreeing with Nye and Borah that a large portion of their opposition to embargo repeal was distrust of the president. Born in 1866, a year after the end of the Civil War, he became a skilled lawyer, emerging from the reform battles in California after 1900 as a staunch progressive. In 1912, he ran for vice president on the Bull Moose ticket with Teddy Roosevelt. Like Borah, he was "square built," aggressive in style, and possessed of a dogged determination to win.[64] Biographer Richard Coke Lower wrote, "Johnson shared with his father not only a fighter's determination and an eagerness to personalize political contests and call unto the character of his foes, but also a jealous nature, a mercurial temperament, petulance, insensitivity to others, and self-absorption in any campaign he waged."[65] In open court, perhaps he did not float like a butterfly, but it was said that his voice would "sting like a bee."[66] In photographs from the late 1930s, often standing in a boxer pose, he appears pugnacious, a curmudgeon, the naysayer ready for a fight, a man who described himself as a bloc of one. Throughout the neutrality battle, Johnson's Senate office would serve as headquarters for those opposed to repeal, leaders of opposition groups, and friendly members of the press.[67]

The fourth member of the jackass mavericks was Burton K. Wheeler (known to friends as B. K.), a progressive New Deal Democrat who loathed concentrated power; he was a rabid anti-interventionist and as independent minded as his three colleagues. *Time* magazine described the Montanan as "a lanky, rumpled man who walks with a rapid shamble, smiling quizzically, his glance a friendly, direct glare through octagonal spectacles, smoking a cigar with the superb nonchalance of Groucho Marx."[68] B. K. had led the Senate fight that blocked Roosevelt's efforts to pack the Supreme Court, and the president had not forgiven him. Journalist Raymond Clapper wrote in his weekly column, "For a few weeks during the controversy," Wheeler was tagged "as a New Dealer turned tory, which is listed as a crime second only to beating your mother-in-law."[69] *Life* magazine suggested that Roosevelt bore enmity toward B. K. as a man he "detests as he detests few others."[70] The defeat, coupled with the economic downturn of 1937, knocked the president off center, killed the New Deal, and was responsible for much of the timidity Roosevelt exhibited until the outbreak of war. B. K. explained, "I dislike disagreeing with my President, I dislike it especially when he is a personal friend, but I must fulfill the duties of a senator as the constitution outlines."[71] But on other occasions, Wheeler pontificated, "I must confess that it gave me quite a thrill when we defeated the President. We could not have had a smarter or more powerful antagonist."[72]

The four outspoken anti-interventionist senators, regardless of minor differences, were suspicious of Roosevelt's intentions, as, to their way of thinking, he was leading the country toward war.[73] B. K. laid out his opposition to changes in the neutrality laws in a speech, titled "Foreign Policy and Neutrality," on *The American Forum of the Air* on April 15, 1939. He recognized that a "very grave crisis" was upon the world, but the United States must avoid becoming "the guardian of all people of the world in whatever country they may be found. I want you to know," he assured his listeners, "that I will never vote to send a single American boy to fight upon foreign soil unless this nation is attacked."[74] The four mavericks and those around them in the Senate were not alone in their judgment, as foreign policy critics on both the right and the left had been suspicious of Roosevelt's intentions, contending he had been leading the country toward war ever since his October 5, 1937, speech in Chicago urging that aggressor nations be "quarantined."[75] Roosevelt, of course, adamantly denied the charge. Later, Attorney General Robert H. Jackson clearly cataloged the president's dilemma:

> I have never doubted that the President was utterly sincere in his desire to stay out of war and that he had hoped in the early stages that he would be able to succeed with that policy. He was trying to pursue a policy that was inconsistent, in a sense, and one that looks perhaps more inconsistent than it was—one, to avoid involvement in a war, and two, to be strong defensively so that we could not be taken unawares and would be successful in case we were involved in it. Every step taken in execution of one policy tended to reflect on his sincerity in the other.[76]

Stubborn Senate opposition paled in comparison to the roar generated by a bevy of anti-interventionists from across a wide political spectrum that included militant peace groups like the Peace Section of the American Friends Service Committee (AFSC), the Fellowship of Reconciliation, the World Peace Commission of the Methodist Church, the American section of the Women's International League of Peace and Freedom, the National Council for the Prevention of War, and the War Resisters League. Senate and House mail rooms were inundated with letters and telegrams, the volume reaching half a million in one day. One organization responsible for a large share of the mail was the National Keep America Out of War Committee, which mobilized its members on September 16:

The Die is cast! Make no mistake, the significance of the Special Session is that America moves toward PEACE or WAR, depending on the ACTION of EACH OF US, now! Preservation of neutrality and peace is now dependent upon the VOLUME of protest you can generate against repeal of the Neutrality Law and its MANDITORY ARMS EMBARGO. TIME IS SHORT. Here is YOUR AMMUNITION. USE IT and organize friends to HELP YOU. DELUGE your Congressman in Washington and the local MEDIUMS OF PUBLIC OPINION *now* with demands for REAL NEUTRALITY.[77]

Handcarts were necessary to deliver the letters to senators' offices. *Life* magazine reported to the nation on October 2, "Through the great bulk of the messages—the ones typewritten on embossed stationary, the ones scrawled in pencil on cheap ruled paper, the ones from businessmen, from mothers, from veterans, from young people—ran the same passionate prayer: KEEP AMERICA OUT OF WAR."[78] Southern senators, reported the *New York Times*, "were receiving small pink slips, all apparently typed on the same typewriter but signed by a different citizen."[79] The slips read, "Keep America Out of Europe's Wars. I hereby petition you to use your influence in every way to keep the U.S. rigidly neutral, entirely free from all entangling alliances with other nations. American blood must never again flow on foreign soil."[80] Seven hundred Iowans sent their senator, Guy M. Gillette, a giant postcard with a drawing of burning ruins labeled "1918," reading, "Lest We Forget, Let's Stay Out."[81] Rallies in support of embargo retention and extension were held in numerous cities, but the citizens of Bloomington, Indiana, were surprised when an airplane dropped thousands of leaflets "opposing repeal of the Neutrality Act and 'all entanglements outside our hemisphere.'"[82]

On the evening of Friday, September 15, in a radio address, the enigmatic Charles Lindbergh, the most famous man in the world, perhaps one of the few men Roosevelt feared, warned America that intervention risked "all in the conflagration."[83] The aviator did not mention embargo repeal but said, "I speak tonight to those people in the United States of America who feel that the destiny of this country does not call for our involvement in European wars."[84] He argued, "We must either keep out of

"America, to the Starving People of Russia," 1922, Hoover Feeds the Soviet Union (courtesy of Poster Collection, Hoover Institution Library and Archives)

"Gift of the American People, ARA," 1922, Hoover Feeds the Soviet Union (courtesy of Poster Collection, Hoover Institution Library and Archives)

(courtesy of Wikimedia Commons)

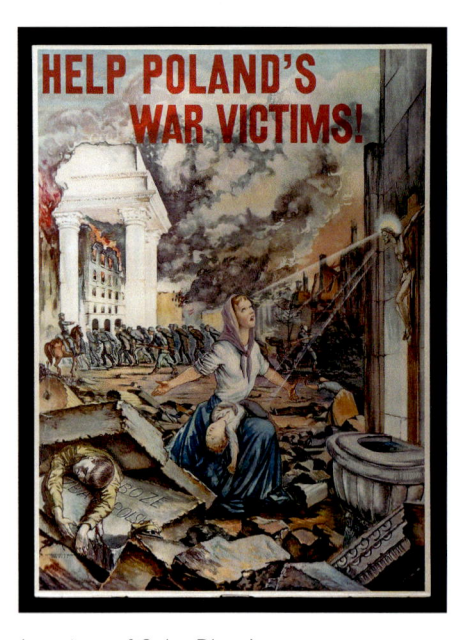

(courtesy of Color Blaze)

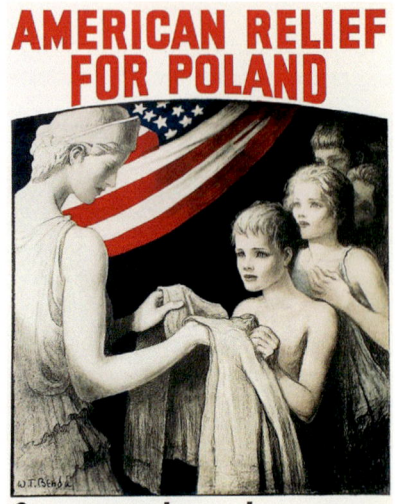

Artist, W. T. Benda (courtesy of Color Blaze)

Artist, W. T. Benda (courtesy of Color Blaze)

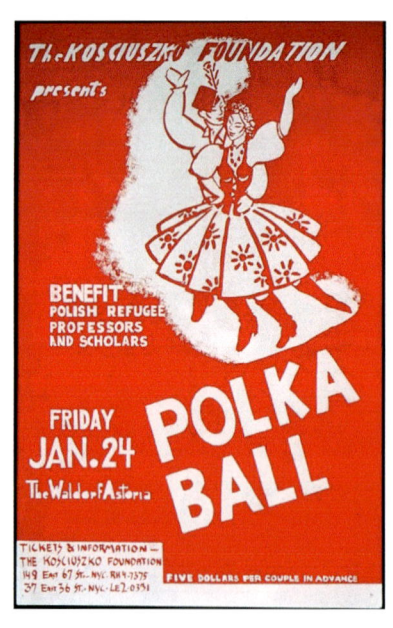

(courtesy of Poster Collection, Hoover Institution Library and Archives)

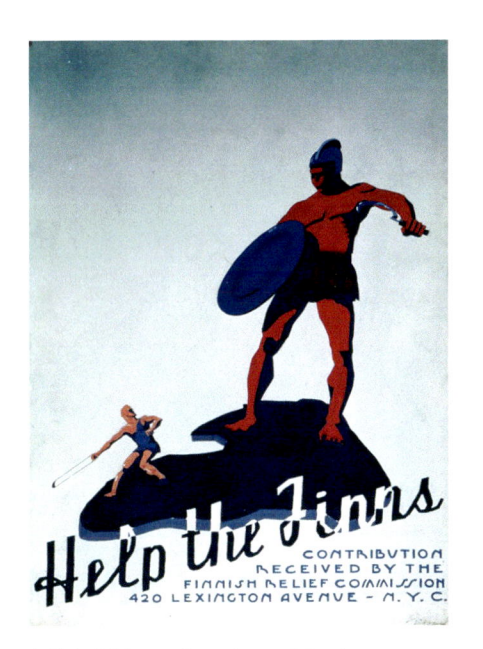

Artist, Gibbons (courtesy of Poster Collection, Hoover Institution Library and Archives)

Artist, Worden Wood (courtesy of Color Blaze)

Artist, Benedict Gropp (courtesy of Poster Collection, Hoover Institution Library and Archives)

Artist, D. Longmaid (courtesy of Poster Collection, Hoover Institution Library and Archives)

(courtesy of Color Blaze)

Postcard (courtesy of Color Blaze)

Postcard (courtesy of Color Blaze)

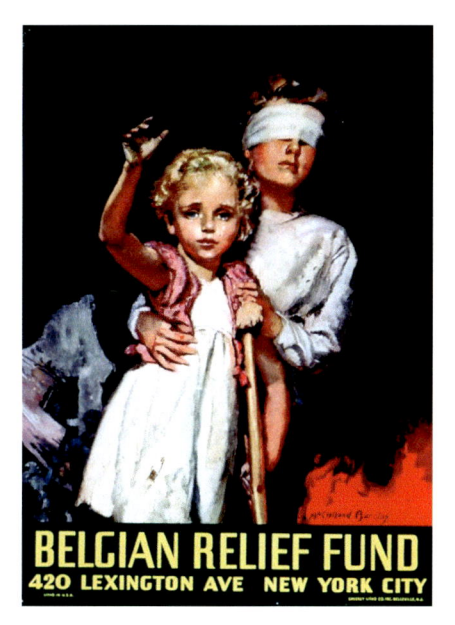

Artist, McCelland Barkley (courtesy of Poster Collection, Hoover Institution Library and Archives)

Artist, Ronay (courtesy of Color Blaze)

Artist, James Montgomery Flagg (courtesy of Color Blaze)

European wars entirely or stay in European affairs permanently." He then admonished, "We cannot count on victory merely by shipping abroad several thousand airplanes and cannon. We are likely to lose a million men, possibly several million—the best American youth."[85] Lindbergh had been reluctant to express his views but had been encouraged to do so by William Castle, Hoover's undersecretary of state, by newscaster Fulton J. Lewis, and by Colonel Truman Smith, former military attaché in Berlin now working for General George Marshall in Washington.[86]

Roosevelt, shortly before Lindbergh's speech, decided that the aviator posed a serious threat to his plans for embargo repeal and "scrambled to stop him."[87] Lindbergh, the night before his speech, arrived at his apartment at 10:30 p.m. after a long day of meetings to find a message from Smith asking him to call in the morning.[88] Early the next morning, first thing, he did so, but Smith could not meet until 10:00 a.m., and Lindbergh was in a meeting on aircraft development until 2:00 p.m. He had returned to his apartment for lunch with guests when Smith arrived. Excusing themselves for privacy, they retired to the bedroom, where Smith revealed that if Lindbergh canceled his speech, the "administration" would create a secretaryship of air, a cabinet post equal to secretary of war or the navy, which he would head. As was typically Rooseveltian, the offer came from the White House through Secretary Harry H. Woodring, who passed it on to Chief of Air Corps General Hap Arnold, who in turn sent Smith to tender the offer. Laughing, Smith said, "So you see, they're worried."[89] Lindbergh was indignant, writing in his diary, "This offer on Roosevelt's part does not surprise me after what I have learned about his Administration. It does surprise me, though, that he still thinks I might be influenced by such an offer. It is a great mistake for him to let the Army know he deals in a such a way."[90] Lindbergh eventually learned that Roosevelt would "scramble to stop him" and his fellow anti-interventionists in a different way. Days after his speech, he became the primary target of FBI director J. Edgar Hoover, who in his effort to curry favor with his master regularly reported on Lindbergh's activities to Roosevelt.[91] Hoover and his G-men were successful in building files on those in opposition to the president.

Lindbergh addresses the nation, September 15, 1939 (courtesy of Getty Images).

Lindbergh's wife, Anne Morrow, a talented best-selling author, helped her husband craft his speech and, on the weekend, was gratified the news coverage was largely positive, as were the telegrams that poured into the networks.[92] In her diary she wrote, "Read papers all morning. Very exciting. C[harles] is praised by both sides—at least each respects his integrity and sincerity. Criticism from paper in England.... That was bound to come."[93]

The speech itself, aside from Lindbergh's admiration for the German Luftwaffe and his penchant to hobnob with its hierarchy, contained little that was objectionable to many of his listeners, who shared his eugenic or culturally chauvinistic tone. Damning criticism, however, came from ardent interventionist journalist Dorothy Thompson (nicknamed the "Blue-Eyed Tornado") in her syndicated column "On the Record," carried by 170 newspapers and read by ten million people. She labeled Lindbergh "a somber cretin," a person "without human feeling," a man who "has a notion to be an American fuehrer," a man whose "inclination toward fascism is well known to his friends."[94] Thompson had lived in Germany during the rise of Hitler and had contempt for all things Nazi, having witnessed the savage brutality at the heart of the movement. It was a reciprocal relationship; the Führer had declared her persona non grata, making her the first American journalist expelled from the country and an instant celebrity.[95] But Thompson had her finger on the Lindberghs, who were enthralled by advances in German aviation and impressed by the Third Reich's ritualistic displays of power, darkly seeing fascism, as Anne later wrote, as "the wave of the future."[96]

Anne Lindbergh, who expected savage attacks, was nonetheless taken aback by Thompson's "personal, and bitter mudslinging."[97] Ickes, having always disliked Lindbergh, hardily approved, calling Thompson's comments a "smashing attack."[98] Charles and Anne's friend Castle wrote in his diary, "D. Thompson attacked him rottenly this morning, saying he [*sic*] pro-Nazi, 'but probably most reasonable people know that she is nuts anyhow.'"[99] Nuts or not, Thompson paid a heavy price for her attack. She confided to her friend Raoul de Roussy de Sales, correspondent for *Paris Soir* and *Paris Midi*, that her Lindbergh article had "provoked such an avalanche of insulting and threatening letters and telephone calls that she [was] afraid."[100]

Powerful critics of the administration on the far right included Father Charles Coughlin, the radio priest and leader of the National Union for Social Justice, whose nationwide Sunday broadcast, *The Hour of Power*, emanating from the National Shrine of the Little Flower in Detroit, tallied thirty million listeners a week. The radio priest pedaled anti-Semitism (the Jews as conspiratorial international bankers), anticommunism, and Nazi propaganda, successfully cultivating the paranoid fringe. Coughlin, two days after Lindbergh's speech, called for a march on Washington to protest any changes in the neutrality laws and demonstrate for peace. Coughlin backed off on the march, but hundreds of his supporters descended on Washington, pushing their way into congressional offices, demanding that their voices be heard.[101] "Cash and carry," Coughlin thundered, would soon be "credit-and-carrion."[102] "The dripping, menacing hand of war," he warned, "draws ever nearer to our heart."[103] Few anti-interventionists, however, were galvanized by the crude nativism expressed by Coughlin or attributed to them by the foreign policy establishment; rather, they were motivated by religious convictions, by trench warfare's smashmouth combat in World War I, by the horrific cost of the war and the loss of civil liberties, by disappointment in Woodrow Wilson's failure to make the world "safe for democracy," and by the ubiquitous antiwar art, literature, poetry, songs, plays, and films that had emerged from the Great War. Hemingway's popular novels *The Sun Also Rises* and *A Farewell to Arms* captured the disillusionment and sense of failure felt by many who became known as the "Lost Generation." Coughlin's archenemy, entertainer, Jewish activist, Democrat, and Roosevelt supporter Eddie Cantor, used his microphone to carefully denounce the radio priest but credited nonintervention by singing Tin Pan Alley writers Howard Johnson and Willie Raskin's "If They Feel like a War, Let Them Keep It over There."[104] Cantor only sang the song on a few occasions, but the sheet music had been on sale since 1935 and had found an audience. Aside from Coughlinites and other fringe groups, however, most anti-interventionists, Republican and Democrat, were international in all ways but one: they refused to sanction US participation in the new war.

In the political hubbub occurring during the week before Roosevelt addressed Congress, Hoover saw an opportunity to advance his own plan

Father Coughlin (courtesy of Getty Images).

for neutrality revision, a plan he had arrived at with his political team on September 11 after meeting with Myron Taylor about the role of the Red Cross in relief. The plan, arrived at late that evening, was the result of an exchange of letters and several meetings with Castle that began shortly after the outbreak of war as the two of them hashed out a response on how to proceed. With the outline of a plan formed, Castle wrote to Hoover asking that he "put down on paper the plan for dealing with the 'Neutrality' question." Hoover obliged, explaining, "Both sides sincerely believe that the course they propose is best designed to meet our major issue of keeping out of war."[105] The huge chasm between the opposing sides was creating bitterness that denied a united national resolution. The former president continually searched for a middle ground regarding the embargo law that guaranteed the country would not end up being dragged into war. FDR's policies, he claimed, were dangerous because they gave the European democracies confidence that the United States would at some point come to their rescue.[106] He argued this encouraged those nations to abandon appeasement, to abandon conciliation toward Germany and Italy, which generally increased the risk of war.[107] As a leader of the Republican opposition, Hoover considered it his job to define issues, develop criticism, and offer viable alternatives to the Democrats. "We need to keep our feet on the ground and arm our nation fully for defense."[108] Either solution, Hoover argued, posed great dangers, making it necessary to find a middle way that dampened down the bitterness and quelled the turmoil. Both arguments, Hoover contended, ignored humanitarian concerns, but he overstated when he claimed that, had the three principles proposed in June 1932 at the General Disarmament Conference in Geneva been ratified, "this present war would have been impossible."[109]

Toward the end of the memorandum, he reconsidered, writing, "I have never believed that war could be prevented by regulation, although there are many regulations which decrease the danger of involvement by removing causes that arouse the war spirit. A democratic nation gets into a war because of popular demand."[110] Over the years, since his World War I experience in Belgium, Hoover had continually supported an expansion of the laws of war and now urged that the three principles become a part of the revised neutrality laws. To Castle, he reiterated the first principle or regulation stipulating the United States would "not sell aggressive weapons to anybody at any time, whether they be at war or peace." Guns over 75mm, submarines, bombers, tanks, and poison gas would continue to be embargoed.[111] The second principle posited that all nations had a right to defend themselves and could freely purchase defensive weapons—"pursuit planes, small arms, anti-aircraft, etc."[112] The third further explained why the first principle prohibited the sale of aggressive weapons, as "they are the instruments by which attacks are made upon civilians. America should not be, even by sale, an indirect or possible party to the killing of women, children, or civilians in general."[113] For Hoover and his team, deeply trustful of the president, it was necessary to tie his hands. Any plan for repeal was dependent on acceptance of a preamble, an "emphatic declaration" that "without equivocation" pledged the United States would not enter the war. Castle responded favorably to the memorandum and its preamble, saying he welcomed the "high moral basis ... making it something of which the United States can be proud and showing the world that neither now nor at any latter time shall we be in any way a party to the destruction of non-combatants which is one of the horrible aspects of modern war."[114] He concluded by urging Hoover to soon announce his plan publicly, assuring him that it would receive "a warm response everywhere" and that he was "willing to fight like the devil for Hoover's suggestion if it became clear that repeal was not possible."[115] Regardless of merit, it was all but impossible for Hoover to line up votes for a compromise, as both Roosevelt loyalists and those in league with the sons of wild jackasses were irreconcilable. Borah and Johnson, along with other western progressives, had never cottoned to anything Hoover and, while he was serving as president, had bedeviled his legislative agenda.[116]

Roosevelt, the day before the opening of the joint session on September 21, met with key leaders of both parties, nine Democrats and six Republicans, who gathered first at the Willard Hotel among a gaggle of reporters to discuss national unity, neutrality, and peace.[117] Republican senator Warren Austin of Vermont remarked, "The cash-and-carry policy involves partiality to Britain and France and was not even handed but actually a qualified neutrality," and he would vote to enact it.[118] Later that day, at the White House, those circled around the president's desk in a half-moon mostly embraced the idea of cash and carry; though Roosevelt preferred total repeal, he knew he would have to compromise with the Senate.[119] The president, apparently not fearing leaks, revealed his intent to aid Britain and France, but none of the six Republicans present were among Roosevelt's fiercest critics. Conspicuous by their absence were the obstreperous and acerbic Borah in the Senate and Hamilton Fish in the House, "who loudly continued to insist that Americans regarded the Atlantic and Pacific as walls not worth scaling, divinely erected to safeguard the New World from the Old's polluting influence."[120] Roosevelt, on the contrary, thought the Atlantic and the Pacific were highways. Referring to Borah's September 14 radio address laying out the argument against embargo repeal, Roosevelt attempted to discredit them, "as he had done earlier and ... was to do many times later [using] the guilt-by-association device," remarking that if the German press gave extensive coverage to their speeches, then it must see benefit in their isolationist position. In fact, it did, as did the Italian and Japanese press.[121] Borah, however, had long before spoken out clearly on those spreading Nazism in the United States, calling them "evangels of the swastika" and saying that Nazis and Communists were "whelps from the same kennel barking at the same thing, constitutional government."[122] But Roosevelt supporters approved of turning the word "isolationist" into a pejorative, a political weapon, and of tagging anti-interventionists as Nazis or Communists.

Two of the six Republicans, Alf Landon and Frank Knox, the 1936 Republican standard-bearers, bore with equanimity the president's attack on their fellow Republicans. Landon, before the meeting, told the press he supported "Roosevelt's wish to revoke the embargo provisions of the Neutrality Act ... so the United States could conduct a cash-and-carry trade with European nations during war."[123] When the Republicans realized "they had been invited to a conference on legislative strategy, they grew somewhat restive. The House leader, Joe Martin, whispered to Landon at one point, 'I'd like to know what we're here for,' and both Landon and Knox were annoyed at having been asked to travel so far to act as mere window-dressing."[124] But by the end of the two-hour session, Landon, backpedaling, declared himself neutral on revision, pending the progress of further debate in Congress.[125] Knox stayed after to chat with Roosevelt and learned the president was warming to the idea of a "wartime coalition cabinet," an idea Knox was pushing on the opinion page of the *Chicago Daily News*.[126]

Among those missing at the Willard and the White House were not just Borah and Fish; also conspicuous by his absence was Hoover. Roosevelt had extracted his price, snubbing the former president for his unwillingness to meet with him to discuss the Red Cross role in Polish relief.[127] Privately, Hoover may have been miffed by the slight, though he would not have accepted any invitation from the president in any circumstance, especially to a bipartisan affair, as he distrusted the very idea, seeing it, in Roosevelt's hands, as a means of co-optation or an attempt to splinter the Republican Party (or both).[128] Landon and Knox were perturbed about being used as window dressing, but in Hoover's view that was what Roosevelt thought Republicans were for.

Given his animosity, Hoover imagined there were no restraints on what Roosevelt might do to get his way. He was disheartened to learn that in the days following the conference, Roosevelt won support for repeal from two prominent Republicans in addition to Landon and Knox: Henry Stimson, Hoover's secretary of state, and his longtime friend, Kansan William Allen White, "the Sage of Emporia." White, however, upset that Roosevelt had not invited Hoover, expressed his displeasure to Knox, writing, "I realize that Hoover is poison, that he is a sort of political typhoid carrier, but he is honest, intelligent and courageous. And intellectually the Democratic party cannot afford to slight him, and the nation cannot afford to ignore that type of man."[129] But Roosevelt did continue to slight him. More damning, however, was White's judgment that Hoover was "poison," a "political typhoid carrier." Clearly he thought his friend had no chance of obtaining the 1940 Republican nomination he so arduously sought.

Adolf Berle, the night before Roosevelt's address, arrived at the White House at 8:30 to finalize the president's speech, to find Judge Samuel I. Rosenman and Hull already there. Rosenman, "the President's oldest literary advisor . . . the last member of the original brain trust still in occasional active service, had been summoned from New York to be present, as he is commonly summoned when the President feels that a state paper has great import."[130] Roosevelt was making a few changes suggested by Rosenman, when Hull, echoing Woodrow Wilson's 1914 absolute declaration of neutrality, "pointed out the political expediency of making a commitment that we would never, under no circumstances and whatever happened, go to war. Quizzically, the president looked at him," Berle confided in his dairy, "and there was dead silence for some seconds. Then he said: 'Can you guarantee that? Can I guarantee it?' Nobody said anything."[131] The tension was broken when Berle, reading Roosevelt correctly, had the last word: "All we can do is to say that until the Atlantic line is seriously threatened or crossed, we will not go to war." The president concurred—the United States would do what it could to avoid war but recognized war might not avoid the United States. The hour was late when the speech was agreed on. Berle accompanied Roosevelt to his bedroom, where they "talked a little as the president was turning in—very sleepy—for the night. He was mulling over the subject which was most in his mind: what kind of a threat to the United States was the war going to be?"[132] As the president speculated about what might unfold, he drifted off. "It was a hard night's work for him and he was tired."[133]

The tension between Roosevelt and Hull resolved, the next morning Roosevelt and Rosenman went over the speech one more time before the president left for Capitol Hill. The president was set to speak at 2:00 p.m., but tension in and around the Capitol remained high, as many demonstrators were on hand. Elements of the Far Right and Far Left posed a danger, as both ends of the political spectrum opposed embargo repeal. Elaborate precautions beyond any since Roosevelt's inauguration were taken, as a second attempt on his life was thought possible. Between the White House and the Capitol grounds, the streets had "the appearance of an armed camp. The corridors of the House wing where the President was to speak were barricaded at strategic points and a Secret Service agent guarded every entrance to the chamber."[134] Ironically, overseas events barged their way into Washington as early-morning news of the assassination of Romanian premier Armand Călinescu brought about an increase in security. "Every Treasury agent available was pressed into service."[135] Regardless of stepped-up security, several hundred members of the Philadelphia Committee for the Defense of Constitutional Rights, a far-right, anti-Semitic, anti-Communist organization led by Thomas A. Blisard, pushed their way through Capitol police into the rotunda.[136] The senators, to reach the House side of the Capitol, were forced to walk a gauntlet of agitated protestors, bombarded by the pleas and shouts of those opposing repeal. A group of women, many with American flags in hand, "attempted to storm the entrance to the House wing, and several women became enraged at Capitol policemen who barred their way."[137] Shouts rang out: "We're mothers" and "We don't want our boys to go to war." One, pointing, yelled, "Have six, she has seven."[138] Representative Luther A. Patrick, an Alabama lawyer elected in 1936 on no platform, having made no promises to anyone, with an admission that he had no understanding of complex economic issues, emerged from the House chamber to confront the protesters as the senators filed in.[139] "What did Congress do to you," he asked, "that wronged you?"

Several mockingly responded they hoped Congress would not do anything to wrong them. Another (likely Blisard's mother, Anne) asked Patrick whether he was a Communist. "No," he emphatically replied. Studiously looking him up and down, she replied, "You sure look like one."[140] Luckily, the senators passed through the crowd without serious incident, and no arrests were made.

Under heavy police and Secret Service protection, Roosevelt entered the House chamber to a somber scene. Wheeled to the speaker's rostrum, he began his nationally broadcast speech in his confident, rhythmic style. He smoothly sidestepped his real intent—aid to Britain and France in their fight against Germany.[141] In this way the foxy Roosevelt could not be accused of opening a front door to war. The back door, his restrictive policies on emergency aid only to refugees and to Poland, he had already closed. Roosevelt asked his divided and anxious listeners to "again re-examine our own legislation."[142] Embargo repeal, he said, was necessary to bring US law into conformity with traditional international law.[143] "I regret that Congress passed that Act. I regret equally that I signed that Act."[144] He proposed policies restricting American ships from war zones, not allowing citizens to travel on belligerent ships, and denying credit to belligerents; most important, though, he endorsed cash and carry. Taking these positions lent credibility to FDR's statements that the country would avoid war and specifically addressed anti-interventionists' bugaboos arising from the interpretation of how the United States ended up going to war in 1917. Some could take consolation that the president had compromised and not asked for an unqualified repeal. "I should like to be able to offer the hope that the shadow over the world might swiftly pass. I cannot. The facts compel my stating, with candor, that darker periods may lie ahead."[145] But the president persistently offered "assurances and reassurances" to his listeners while aiming at his opposition. "Let no group assume the exclusive label of the 'peace bloc.' We all belong to it."[146] Embargo repeal, he asserted, would lessen America's chances of being drawn into the conflict. In its adoption, Roosevelt argued, "lies the road to peace," concluding, "In such circumstances our policy must be to appreciate in the deepest sense the true American interest."[147]

Hoover did not listen to the president's speech, instead attending to a busy afternoon schedule. A few days earlier he had been buoyed by Castle's enthusiastic response to his neutrality memorandum, deciding to move aggressively. To stick to his strategy of maintaining a low profile and yet put his plan forward, Hoover needed surrogates—those who would adopt his position and argue for it without using his name. He began to court supporters and arranged with Senator Charles W. Tobey of New Hampshire that, when appropriate, his arguments for repeal would be introduced into the Senate debate.[148] Several times Castle suggested that Hoover talk with Lindbergh, with whom he had been friends ever since Lindbergh conquered the Atlantic by air and whom he had been courting as an ally in the fight against intervention. The intrepid "Lucky Lindy" just might be the important voice Hoover needed. Hoover had some acquaintance with the Lindberghs, having, as president in August 1929, invited the couple to spend the weekend at his hideaway, Camp Rapidan, in the Appalachian Mountains southwest of Washington, DC.[149] There, he and Charles, while playing horseshoes and spending evenings in front of a fire, had an opportunity to discuss aviation and world problems.

Hoover decided to heed Castle's advice, writing the famous flyer on September 20, "I just want to let you know how much I was impressed with your really great address and what a help it has been to the American people. Sometime if you have the time, I would be delighted to have an opportunity to talk with you in confidence."[150] But before the letter was mailed, Hoover decided the talk could not wait. Later that afternoon, Edgar Rickard called Lindbergh and asked that he come by the Waldorf the next morning at 11:00, just hours before the president's speech.[151] Lindbergh agreed to Hoover's impetuous request. In their forty-minute conversation, the two found themselves comfortable with one another and in agreement on the view that Britain was in decline and that German expansion was inevitable, "either peacefully, or by fighting, if necessary."[152] Hoover claimed he had told British foreign secretary Lord Halifax "sometime ago that the only way to avoid a European war was to permit German economic expansion in Eastern Europe."[153] Embargo was not of "fundamental importance in keeping the country from war," he told Lindbergh, and "after the embargo controversy was over," a nonpolitical committee or organization determined to keep the country out of war should be formed.[154] Hoover offered that Lindbergh should take part, and the aviator replied that he "would be much interested and would like to learn more about it," though he wrote in his journal that he was "very skeptical about the effectiveness of most committees."[155] Hoover did not bring up his compromise embargo repeal plan. Leaving the Waldorf, Lindbergh walked to the Engineers Club, where he read the papers, and then lunched with Juan Trippe, head of Pan American Airways, at the exclusive Cloud Club atop the Chrysler Building.[156] He, like Hoover, did not listen to the president's speech.

Anti-interventionists in every corner of the country who heard or read the president's speech were not "assured and reassured." They did not believe a word the president said.[157] Nor did Rickard: "Listened to F.D.R. opening special session of Congress and can agree with him in his antiwar declaration, but I do not believe him."[158] Even if Roosevelt believed his policies would not lead to war, his repeated denials of US involvement echoed Woodrow Wilson's declaimers of noninvolvement prior to entry into World War I. Regardless of what the president said, inevitably war would be the result.[159] Knowing embargo repeal would pass, the anti-interventionists in Congress and their allies in a myriad of opposition groups—ranging from the Communists, Trotskyites, and Socialists on the far left to keep-America-out-of-war groups and the German American Bund on the far right, plus a large number of peace groups and activists—had worked hard to broaden their bases of support and raise the political temperature to new heights. In this they were successful, firing the opening round of what was to be an ongoing pitched battle. In the weeks following Roosevelt's speech, this assortment of anti-interventionists held rallies and demonstrations across the United States, pigeonholing members of Congress in their home states and in Washington, DC. The National Council for Prevention of War held a mass meeting of peace groups in Washington on September 29 that featured speakers Senator Champ Clark of Missouri, Arthur Capper of Kansas, Robert La Follette of Wisconsin, and David Walsh of Massachusetts.[160] The deluge of mail, running 10 to 1 against repeal, arrived daily on the desks of those in Congress. Frustrated as to their effect, however, Father Coughlin wrote, "I wish to report to you that many Senators and some Representatives have paid no heed to the millions of letters which you mailed to Washington."[161]

One of the more audacious peace actions was undertaken by the rambunctious daredevil pilot Laura Ingalls, the first woman to fly the Andes Mountains. She held innumerable records for stunt flying and speed records, having proclaimed, "I'd rather fly than eat, drink, or run around; and I mean it."[162] Joining the newly formed Women's National Committee to Keep the U.S. Out of War, she agreed to fly to cities along the East Coast opposing embargo repeal and advocating peace with Germany, as she admired Nazi efficiency and "Hitler's Ideology and Aryan supremacy."[163] She kicked off her blitz for peace by flying over Washington for two hours, dropping leaflets on the Capitol and surrounding neighborhoods that implored Congress to stay in session and to think carefully before approving Roosevelt's requests and asserted, "American women do not intend to again have their sons sent to die on foreign soil."[164] Arrested on landing for violating the airspace over the White House, she claimed leaflets that landed there must have been blown by the wind. She was hauled before the Civil Aeronautics Board, but her prominence as a leading aviatrix, nearly as famous as Amelia Earhart, resulted in the suspension of her pilot's license for one week. Undeterred, the next day she and a companion tried to barge into a closed session of the Senate Foreign Relations Committee.[165]

The battle lines over embargo repeal hardened, but Roosevelt assuaged his opponents by agreeing to a conditional repeal and fielding a string of prominent Democrats and Republicans to speak on behalf of his plan. One of his more successful tactics was to form a bipartisan coalition of supporters for all aid short of war. Republicans Frank Knox, Alf Landon, Henry Stimson, Clark Eichelberger, and William Allen White helped effectively combat hardline anti-interventionist opposition. White and Eichelberger formed an effective organization cumbersomely named the Non-Partisan Committee for Peace through Revision of the Neutrality Law, which effectively campaigned for repeal.[166] White telegraphed his longtime friend Hoover, asking him to join.[167] He was disappointed when Hoover declined. Republican lawyer and foreign policy guru Allen Dulles, in a talk to New York Young Republicans on October

4, supported embargo repeal and cash and carry.[168] Dulles and his partner, New York representative Hamilton Armstrong Fish, entered the debate when their book *Can America Stay Neutral?* was released a few days after Roosevelt's September 21 speech. At the last minute, their publishers at Harpers included a copy of the president's address obtained from the *New York Times*. Dulles and Fish argued it was not possible to legislate neutrality or to keep America out of war through legislation. A response to conflict was a matter of policy, and policies changed in addressing ever-changing situations. As proof they detailed the failures of neutrality in the face of the ongoing crises of the previous ten years. Their comprehensive review, laced with appendices that provided a basis of support for repeal, sold well.[169]

For Roosevelt Democrats in Congress, Republican support was welcome, as they maintained the initiative and kept the opposition off balance. Key Pittman advised the president after his address that he should stay away from Congress and permit him to steer the legislation through the Senate.[170] Roosevelt agreed and already had his head down. A few days after Congress had been called into special session, Interior Secretary Ickes approached the president, seeking approval of a speech he was soon to give on *America's Town Meeting of the Air*. The topic was a third term. "The President was distinctly of the opinion that I ought not to speak on the third term at all. He feels that sentiment in Congress is going along quite well so far as neutrality legislation is concerned and, of course, he does not want to do anything to disturb that. He said: 'Wait until we get this neutrality legislation before we discuss any political subject.'"[171] Poor Ickes found that the president's caution left him no speech at all, forcing him to scramble for what to say on the looming broadcast. Just how carefully and thoroughly Roosevelt heeded Pittman's advice can be seen in a letter he wrote to Lord Tweedsmuir, governor general of Canada, who had requested a brief visit to Hyde Park in early October. Invoking the three Japanese monkeys, Roosevelt wrote, "I am almost literally walking on eggs, and having delivered my message to Congress, and having good prospects of the bill going through, I am at the moment, saying nothing, seeing nothing and hearing nothing."[172] Roosevelt feared a filibuster or, worse, an inadvertent Vorys-like amendment that would limit his options. The president had "nothing to fear but fear itself," as the votes in the Congress were safe. But he was not alone in his tiptoeing. Unlike Lord Tweedsmuir, Prime Minister Mackenzie King also "walked on eggs." Already at war, he was counting on an embargo repeal to bolster Canadian defenses. Invited to attend the New York Chamber of Commerce annual dinner, he wrote to his old boss and close friend John D. Rockefeller Jr.,

> Apart, however, from the necessity of my being continuously at the Ottawa end of the trans-atlantic cable, I have, quite frankly, been a little doubtful in my own mind as to the wisdom of making, at this time, any public utterances in the United States. Were I not to speak of the war, would be to disappoint the audience. To touch upon it at all, would, I fear, be taking an obvious risk of offending some section of American opinion. If there ever was a moment at which silence might be regarded as golden, it seems to me that, so far as I am concerned, that moment is the present, in relation to any public utterances in the United States.[173]

Staying in the background was difficult for the president but doing so promised the legislation he had sought since the previous spring. Pittman and Majority Leader Barkley knew full well the debate in Congress would take time—four or five weeks or more—as they had agreed to Senate Minority Leader Charles McNary's request that all proposed amendments would receive full attention and an up or down vote.[174] The anti-interventionist senators took full advantage. Working out of Johnson's office, they "carefully planned their speaking schedules on the floor with each sharing oratorical responsibilities."[175]

In response to the rising political temperature, Roosevelt and Hoover chose to stay in the background, attempting to determine the outcome by playing puppet master. But their political ambitions, regardless of their silence, were never far from the mind of either man—Roosevelt pretending he was not seeking a third term and Hoover pretending he was not seeking the Republican nomination. As September became October, Hoover's stealth campaign for the Republican nomination, which had shown such promise a month earlier, floundered. In Los Angeles, a revolt was underway over his *Republican Circles* efforts to influence delegate selection rather than leaving the choice to local politicians.[176]

The dissatisfaction in LA was quickly handled in part because Senator Johnson voiced no objection to an uncommitted delegation, but a few weeks later, Roosevelt's invitation to Landon and Knox to attend the embargo repeal session at the Willard presaged trouble, as it signaled that they headed the Republican Party, not Hoover.[177] This was a direct challenge to his leadership and his moves to secure the nomination. Hoover and his loyalists lobbied California Republicans drawn to Landon or Taft or attracted to New York City district attorney Thomas E. Dewey's rising star to stick with sending an uncommitted delegation to the convention in Philadelphia. At the opportune moment in a brokered convention, uncommitted California delegates would be in position to lead a charge for Hoover. Trouble was brewing on the East Coast as well. New York Republicans cheered reformer Ken Simpson's broadsides that there should be no going back to Hoover, the Liberty League, or "reactionary influences of the past."[178] Stubborn opposition to Hoover's nomination was but one facet of rising difficulties. The good news that *Republican Circles* was making headway in Utah was tempered by the news that money was running out. "There was a real likelihood that unless additional sources of funds were found, the Circles movement might collapse by the middle of November and with it, Hoover's stealth campaign."[179]

On October 4, Hoover returned to the Waldorf after the first game of the World Series to dine and spend the evening with Rickard. Hoover was usually ebullient after watching an exciting baseball game—America's game, he'd proclaimed—and that day the Yankees had defeated the Cincinnati Reds 2 to 1 in the bottom of the ninth, but for Rickard it was a long evening. He found the Chief "very glum and depressed and not communicative."[180] This was surprising, as his meeting that morning and two days earlier with William Honnold, a wealthy engineer and backer who had run the New York office of the Commission for Relief in Belgium in World War I, had likely solved *Republican Circles*' short-term funding problem.[181] Other loyal backers who pitched in to support *Circles* included another engineer, Harvey Mudd, as well as California oil executive A. C. "Bert" Mattei and breakfast cereal king W. K. Kellogg.[182] But the doom-and-gloom atmosphere that pervaded the Waldorf apartment was over not money but the release the day before of an interview with Roy Howard, head of United Press International and the Scripps-Howard newspaper chain. Hoover was invested heavily in the hope that the interview, in which he elaborated in detail his argument about why the Allies would win and why "we must keep out of the war," would bolster his efforts to return to center stage, but he worried it would "not cause [the] sensation he expected."[183] Two days before the interview, Hoover again called Lindbergh, seeking confirmation of his position. It was perfect timing on Hoover's part, for Lindbergh was "working on a new radio address 'Neutrality and War,'" thinking thorough his own position, though he was unsure whether he would deliver the speech.[184] Hoover wanted confirmation that he was on solid ground in asserting that the Maginot Line could withstand a German attack and that the German air force could not defeat the British fleet. Lindbergh agreed but warned that "he should be careful in saying what the result would be of a conflict between the British fleet and German Air Force . . . as that was something we knew very little about—that aviation people tended to be overenthusiastic and naval people too conservative."[185] Hoover listened but stuck with his contention that in an extended battle the British fleet would prevail. If Britain and France did not defeat Germany, then a worst-case scenario was a stalemate, a long war of attrition that would be, as Hitler predicted, a *Kartoffelkrieg*—a "potato war" with little combat and most deaths resulting from starvation. Hoover had changed his mind, for when the Germans invaded Poland, he had predicted a catastrophe, holding that the conflict in Europe would be a long, barbarous war of attrition that would destroy Europe, inflict enormous causalities, and give way to twenty-five years of impoverishment, a *Götterdämmerung*.[186]

Remaining true to his strategy of not directly entering the debate, Hoover mentioned embargo repeal nowhere in the Howard interview, but few readers would miss the obvious conclusion. If it were all but certain that the Allies could not lose, there was no reason for repeal. Hoover warned that Americans needed to ignore the waves of propaganda designed to stir them to action, to remain vigilant in staving off dangerous emotions that undermine reason and create a war fever or war party. Hoover remembered the drums of war sounded by yellow press journalists after the battleship *Maine* exploded in Havana Harbor in 1898, sparking the Spanish-American War, and the cries for intervention when a German submarine torpedoed the passenger ship *Lusitania* in May 1915. "We need," he asserted, "to keep cool."[187]

Hoover's worries, however, that the interview had flopped were premature. The Scripps-Howard chain owned dozens of newspapers with a huge readership and heralded the anti-interventionists' cause. The chain's flagship paper, the *New York World-Telegram*, featured it prominently; as a bonus, the *New York Herald Tribune* did so as well. The interview was successful in keeping his name before the public and establishing him as a leading voice of the anti-interventionists. Hoover's cadre of close political advisors, as well as Alan Fox, his pollster in 1936 and 1939–1940, and men like former Arizona governor Thomas Campbell and Nebraska Supreme Court chief justice Robert Simmons, concurred that the way forward for his crypto-candidacy was to increase his speeches, to garner newspaper coverage, and to place articles in prominent large-circulation magazines like the *Saturday Evening Post*, *Collier's*, and *Liberty Magazine*, warning against intervention and promoting relief.[188] In this way, the Hoover team hoped to create a buzz, a persistent drumbeat that would push politicos, columnists, commentators, and the media to speculate on his candidacy or predict or support his entering the race despite denials that he was running.[189] It was a classic Hoover tactic. He would not publicly put himself forward but would be called from the crowd to serve. He shared with Roosevelt a desire to be drafted by his party.

The indefatigable Hoover's case of the blues lasted no more than one or two days. Reinvigorated, he wrote Leland W. Cutler on October 5 that he was "in day and night conferences with a great many national leaders over the very dangerous situation into which we are drifting over neutrality legislation."[190] But despite Hoover's banished blues and his renewed efforts to win support for his restrictive plan of repeal, his strategy of relying on others to carry his flag was not working. By avoiding the issue of embargo repeal in his Howard interview, he had squandered an opportunity. To win support for his proposal and garner the political capital he sought, he had to put himself forward and be his own gonfalonier. But despite acknowledging this fact, he continued to vacillate. Earlier in the day, before he wrote to Cutler expressing his newfound determination, he again met with Lindbergh over lunch. Hoover, still unsure about going public again, sought affirmation by reading parts of the speech he was writing, one that would directly challenge Roosevelt. Lindbergh agreed with what Hoover read: that restricting offensive weapons "would be an excellent policy for us to adopt in this particular situation, even though I can see the arguments that will be made against it, and they are numerous."[191] Lindbergh revealed that he, too, had been undecided about giving a second speech but had made up his mind to go ahead and would include a proposal to restrict offensive weapons. Hoover was pleased to win Lindbergh's support for his solutions, as the flyer was a powerful voice, one outside the Hoover orbit who claimed to be apolitical, an anti-interventionist who shared a distrust and dislike of Roosevelt.[192] As Hoover remained convinced that the debate in Congress would deadlock, Lindbergh's support had the potential to swing public opinion in his direction and possibly pressure some in Congress to support his restrictions.

Having decided to go public, two days later, on October 7, Hoover arranged a luncheon strategy session at the Harvard Club that included Lindbergh, Castle, Columbia University professor Carl W. Ackerman, and several other prominent Republicans. After introductions, the discussion centered on Roosevelt's neutrality bill and on the worsening European crisis before turning to the order of business. The Chief read the speech he intended to make, which met with approval. The consensus of the group was that to obtain maximum impact he should deliver it a week or so before the final Senate vote, thought likely to occur toward the end of the month. But to find space in the cacophony of voices clamoring for or against the Roosevelt bill, voices that would reach fever pitch in days just before the final vote, he should release his plan soon and, if possible, induce a Democratic senator to offer it as an amendment on the floor of the Senate. Doing so would guarantee wide distribution and press coverage, stir debate, and hopefully elicit support. No one in the strategy session warned that knowledge of a Hoover/Lindbergh collaboration would bring attacks accusing both of being soft on fascism, Lindbergh due to his acceptance of a Nazi civilian medal and Hoover because he had met Hitler and dined at Hermann Göring's estate.

That evening, Rickard and Arthur Hyde, Hoover's former secretary of agriculture, stopped by the Waldorf to pick up Hoover, then headed for cocktails to J.P. Morgan partner Thomas Lamont's elegant mansion, called by the *New York Times* "the best house on the best block" in the city.[193] On the way, Hoover confided to Rickard and Hyde the good news that Lindbergh and Eddie Rickenbacker, famous flyer, World War I ace, and Congressional Medal of Honor recipient, would support his plan. Rickenbacker was an effective "Keep Us Out of War" voice and had fervently made his case a week earlier on the NBC Blue Network.[194] The Chief, having taken the advice offered by those at the luncheon meeting, told Rickard that perhaps Democratic Massachusetts senator Walsh might be "induced to introduce it . . . and meantime . . . get 5 or more other Senators to back his plan."[195] Walsh was a good choice, as his relationship with Roosevelt was poor and he had been an anti-imperialist and anti-interventionist throughout his long political career.[196] After cocktails at Lamont's, the four went on to the Century Club for dinner. It is doubtful that Hoover shared any of his "good news" at the table that evening, for while Lamont was a friend, he was also good friends with FDR and was working hard to bring about an embargo repeal with no restrictions: no cash and carry, no curbs on American shipping, and no restrictions on American loans.[197] Nor would Lamont cheer Hoover's newfound ally Charles Lindbergh. After the Lone Eagle's talk on September 15, Lamont had written his daughter that the speech was "dreadful."[198] Hoover was aware that anything said that evening would likely make its way to the White House. There is no record of the conversation, but perhaps Hoover wished he had skipped dinner and was instead at Yankee Stadium watching the Bronx Bombers beat the Reds for the third game in a row.

Hoover chose Tuesday morning October 10 to release his proposal for amending the neutrality laws to the press, select members of Congress, and a list of those who had solicited his advice.[199] One of those select members was Senator Walsh, with whom he had already discussed the neutrality issue and who might agree to speak in its favor on the Senate floor.[200] In his embargo repeal proposal, Hoover argued that restricting the sale of offensive weapons was fair to any two sides in a conflict, was a neutrality policy, and, more important, would "keep on the side of humanity as against barbarism in war."[201] "There is a moral question here," he stressed, "that reaches to the heart of American instinct for decency." As to bombers, poison gas, and submarines, Hoover refused to believe that the United States would become a merchant of death—that it would "ever sell this kind of weapon to anybody at any time anywhere, whether they be neutral or countries at war."[202] Hoover had no evidence that Roosevelt had any intention of selling poison gas or submarines, but bombers would likely be sold without reservation. For Hoover, his proposal would prevent that from happening and would reinforce the law of war specified in the Hague and Geneva Conventions, although his arguments did not mention them by name. If accepted, he concluded, "with some tightening of the provisions as to cash and the danger zones, the other parts of the bill are in my view constructive."[203] The agonizing was over; Hoover had entered the fray. The following day, he learned that Lindbergh also had made up his mind and would again address the nation on Friday evening.[204] Hoover's press release on Tuesday and Lindbergh's speech on Friday might land a one-two punch to Roosevelt's plans for repeal.[205]

Hoover's October offensive continued: that evening he spoke to a large General Pułaski Memorial Day rally held at the 165th Regiment Armory in Manhattan, the opening event of Polish Week at the New York World's Fair.[206] Hoover was pleased to receive the invitation, as he had decided it was time to come forward publicly in support of Poland, and this was also a chance to refurbish his image as "the Great Humanitarian." Political motives aside, Hoover was proud of the part he had played in Polish independence and his helping hand in stabilizing the new nation inflicted with famine, disease, and war. Just a year before, on a return to Poland during which he was enthusiastically greeted and showered with awards, he found "a nation transformed, regenerated," but now it had once again been brutally attacked, its territory divided. The crowd of fifteen thousand Polish American admirers and loyal supporters were aware of his commitment to their country and looked forward to a message of hope, for they had endured the agony of watching their former country destroyed in five weeks. The last units of the Polish army had capitulated but a week earlier on October 5 near the town of Kock in eastern Poland. After a half dozen speakers, including New York mayor Fiorello La Guardia and Polish ambassador Jerzy Potocki, Hoover was introduced and "greeted with a prolonged ovation."[207] Pleased with his reception, he did not disappoint his audience, warming to a topic that evoked his passion.[208] He was at his best, delivering a rousing speech that opened with "The spirit of a great race does not die from oppression. Poland is not dead. Poland will rise again. There is more to nations than their soil, their cities, their wealth, and even their governments. There is a soul in a great people."[209] This message of hope was exactly what the audience needed to hear, and they responded enthusiastically, interrupting frequently with applause.

Toward the end of his speech, he concluded, "Our immediate task is to do what we can to alleviate the lot of the suffering and the homeless. For that a temporary organization has been created to do what it can. With them are leading Americans of Polish descent. That body merits your generous support."[210] But Hoover chose caution, as his evasive appeal did not disclose that the "temporary organization" mentioned was the Commission for Polish Relief (CPR) and that he had already transferred $25,000 to Paul Super and Jimmy Brown in Bucharest, where the relief operation had made considerable headway. His audience was aware of the news generated by the fast-acting CPR, though few knew it was a Hoover relief organization. Many of those in attendance were also aware of or involved in the efforts of small Polish churches and clubs as well as large organizations in New York, Chicago, Buffalo, Pittsburgh, Detroit, and Cleveland, all hard at work raising money through concerts, art fairs, auctions, dances, bake sales, raffles, carnivals, roller derbies, and bingo nights. The amount of money raised by the smaller groups was often not large but collectively could result in tens of thousands of dollars. The Legion of Young Polish Women, organized in Chicago on September 2, had by Puławski Day raised over $2,000.[211] The Polish Pavilion at the Fair was an ongoing source of larger amounts of money, with attractions such as art shows, Polish music, and folk dancing; a second building that featured a restaurant and bar drew in thousands each day. Polish Week promised additional contributions. The pavilion became a highly visible bastion of Polish independence and a defiant symbol of Polish patriotism, although the building conveyed a bizarre, almost macabre quality, as all reality behind the proud, futuristic exhibits had ceased to exist. Among the temples of propaganda, for Poland, like Czechoslovakia, "the World of Tomorrow" had already become a nightmare.[212]

The Pułaski Day celebration announced that funds collected that evening would go to the Polish Relief Fund, but how the fund, an amalgam of three Chicago-based Polish organizations, would allocate the money was becoming a source of major disagreement. The fund, overseen by Francis Swietlik, was an ardent supporter of Roosevelt, the New Deal, and American Red Cross (ARC) policy on relief to Poland. Maksymilian Węgrzynek, editor-owner of the New York Polish newspaper *Nowy Świat*, favored the CPR as the more effective and more hands-on of the two organizations.[213] Polish Americans, the donor base, were overwhelmingly Democrats loyal to the administration who shared Swietlik's point of view. The disagreement between the New York and Chicago Poles would fester for years, but because they compromised early on, both the CPR and the Red Cross received funds. Hoover was fortunate that for the time being, his ongoing clash with Roosevelt and Davis over Red Cross relief policy remained undetected by the press and unrevealed by the White House, as it would have surely complicated the issue.

Hoover's refusal to step out and take ownership of the CPR in his Pułaski Day address was warranted, for not only did this act protect the largest source of relief money, but it also looked as if aid to the Polish refugees in Romania, Hungary, and Lithuania would soon come to an end. Negotiations with the Nazis for permission to send aid to those in what had been Poland were in the beginning stages and, importantly, it was to those Poles that the CPR intended to send the most aid and for the longest time. But those negotiations might go nowhere, and even if the Germans agreed to a relief program of some kind, the British blockade could nullify the effort. Despite the dangers of failure, in October, Polish Relief still held out the tantalizing possibility of Hoover achieving the publicity and the accolades he sought. To harvest that publicity, he had to downplay, even deny, any presidential aspirations. Hoover could take satisfaction in his Pułaski Day address. The New York press, reporting on the rally, printed the highlights of his speech: he had recounted and affirmed his commitment to Poland and established himself as a leading advocate for aid to those devastated by the Nazi conquest.

By midweek, on October 12, Hoover's embargo repeal plan received extensive coverage. The *New York Times* and many other newspapers reported the "Hoover Plan" on their front pages. Vandenberg, a senator with whom Hoover had frequently disagreed, thought the plan a good idea and called Hoover asking that he put his proposal in legislative form. Hoover demurred. He lacked the knowledge and staff, he said, to correctly draw up an amendment. Vandenberg replied, "I shall see what can be done at this end of the line" and said that he had put Hoover's proposal in the *Congressional Record*.[214] But a handful of senators and enthusiasts aside, the response from fellow Republicans and anti-interventionists was tepid. As Lindbergh foresaw, many viewed the distinction between offensive and defensive weapons as nothing more than a hat trick.[215] From hard-line anti-interventionists, from the sons of wild jackasses, Hoover would get no support—only questions and evasions. Borah commented, "The first thing that occurs to me is, how can it be made feasible?"[216] Nye damned the proposal with faint praise, agreeing "in principle with Mr. Hoover's suggestion."[217] William Allen White wrote to Hoover that he agreed offensive weapons should be embargoed, but he did not say so publicly, as it contradicted the position of his Non-Partisan Committee for Peace through Revision of the Neutrality Law.[218]

A different Allen, fellow Republican Allen Dulles, was quick to respond, penning a letter to the *New York Times* on October 12, claiming, "No one has worked more sincerely or more effectively for the limitation of armaments than Herbert Hoover."[219] But Dulles continued by arguing the proposal was flawed. Citing his experience as legal advisor to the American delegation at the 1932–1933 General Disarmament Conference, he pointed out that the technical commissions for air, land, and naval armaments that struggled with the question for over a month ended in "complete disagreement."[220] The attempt to define and then restrict offensive weapons failed. Dulles argued that it was not the weapon but the intent of the user. While this was true, Dulles ignored that it was also true that the weapon's design limited its use—pursuit planes could not be used as long-range bombers; submarines were limited as surface ships. Dulles further argued that aggressor nations already possessed quantities of offensive weapons, and threatened nations needed offensive weapons to defend themselves. Nowhere in his letter did he address the issue of poison gas. Seeing himself as a realist, a pragmatist, he avoided one of Hoover's key points: the moral culpability in selling implements of war that would likely be used to kill women and children.

Castle immediately came to Hoover's defense, writing to the *New York Times* a few days later, "Mr. Dulles seems to miss the point of the proposal. The emphasis of the plan," he pointed out, "is on the humanitarian rather than on the offensive-defensive aspect. It does not pretend to be technical. Instead of seeking international agreements, it searches the conscience of our own people. Do we want, for example, to sell Japan the planes which may be used to bomb the hospitals and crowded cities of China? I do not believe that the American people want to have any share, however indirect, in these tragedies."[221] Castle concluded that while the United States should give "all unofficial assistance possible to France and England, this aid to be such that we shall not ourselves become involved in the war, we should be taking a stand on the side of decency and morality that ought to receive the enthusiastic support of all Americans and indeed of right-thinking people of all nations."[222]

Democrats were firm in their rejection. Senator Jimmy Byrnes of South Carolina, a Roosevelt insider, announced that he was glad to see Hoover come out for repeal of the arms embargo but said, "I don't see how you are going to draw a distinction between the gun that shoots in self-defense and the gun that shots in aggression."[223] Pittman flippantly remarked that Hoover was "piddling around with immaterialities."[224]

Between the Dulles and Castle letters came the second nationwide address of the Lone Eagle. It was a short speech of fifteen minutes in which Lindbergh cleared away any question as to his stance on repeal, arguing neutrality was essential if America was to avoid war. "I do not believe that repealing the arms embargo would assist democracy in Europe, because I do not believe this is a war for democracy. This is a war over the balance of power in Europe—a war brought about by the desire for strength on the part of Germany and the fear of strength on the part of England and France."[225] Lindbergh's obsession with racial strength, his understanding of nation as biological, bordered on the mystical: "Our bond with Europe is a bond of race and not of political ideology.... It is the European race we must preserve; political progress will follow. Racial strength is vital, politics a luxury. If the white race is ever seriously threatened, it may then be time for us to take our part in its protection, to fight side by side with the English, French, and Germans, but not with one against the other for our mutual destruction."[226] To many of his listeners' surprise, Lindbergh singled out Canada for endangering the hemisphere by declaring war against Germany in support of Great Britain. Toward the end of his speech, without mentioning Hoover's name, he called for the embargo of offensive weapons, defending his position through analogy: "No one says that we should sell opium because it is difficult to make a list of narcotics."[227]

Like Lindbergh's first speech, the second was cheered by anti-interventionists and criticized by those opposed to embargoing offensive weapons. Major General John F. O'Ryan weighed in, claiming Lindbergh's plan for repeal "will not stand analysis," and Democratic Michigan senator Prentiss M. Brown chastised Lindbergh's remarks on Canada as a "gratuitous insult to a sister nation."[228] During the Senate session on Saturday, October 14, discussion of Lindbergh's words "turned into a free-for-all."[229] It began when Senator Clark of Missouri entered the Lindbergh speech into the record. Pittman, who had prepared a speech in answer to Lindbergh, rose, arguing the impossibility of distinguishing between offensive and defensive weapons. He further challenged Lindbergh's assertion that the war in Europe was a war about balance of power and not about small countries attempting to defend themselves against German and Soviet aggression. Pittman praised Lindbergh's accomplishments in aviation and his patriotism but asserted that his stand against repeal encouraged "the ideology of the totalitarian governments and [was] subject to the construction that he approve[d] of their brutal conquest of democratic countries through war or threat of destruction through war."[230] Pittman suggested that Lindbergh, though perhaps well intentioned, had somehow gotten himself on the wrong side of the issue, that his expertise in aviation lent no credence to his recommendations on how embargo repeal should proceed. Pittman was joined by Barkley and Texas senator Thomas Connelly, who asserted that Lindbergh's proposal was the same as Hoover's, released a week earlier. Connelly condemned them both, stating, "I rather suspect Colonel Lindbergh read Mr. Hoover's statement before he made his."[231] His suspicions were correct, though he did not know Hoover and Lindbergh had met several times, talked with one another on the phone, and coordinated their efforts. Perhaps the FBI knew the extent of the collaboration, but its surveillance of Lindbergh was in the early stages.[232] Midway, Clark heated up the debate by injecting for a second time praise of Lindbergh's speech. He further maddened Connelly by conceding that since "it is impossible to draw a distinction between weapons for offense and defense," the Hoover/Lindbergh proposals could be ignored as "this fact ... is the strongest possible argument for an embargo of all arms."[233] The back-and-forth on the Senate floor lasted throughout the day. Arguments included how the United States became involved in World War I, with propaganda being the cause favored by the anti-interventionists and German attacks on American civilian liners and shipping favored by supporters of repeal, but on this question, as well as on the larger issues, no minds changed.

Dorothy Thompson did not praise Lindbergh's patriotism, remaining convinced that he was a Nazi and savaging his second speech, as she had his first, focusing on what others had not: Lindbergh's racial worldview. But it was Eleanor Roosevelt, using her velvet hammer, who hung the albatross around the neck of one of her husband's top political enemies in her "My Day" column, writing, "We were all interested in Mr. Lippmann's column of a few days ago and in Dorothy Thompson's column today. She sensed in Col. Lindbergh's speech a sympathy with Nazi ideals which I thought existed but could not bring myself to believe was really there."[234] Hurtful criticism came from an unexpected source. Harold Nicolson, a family friend and biographer of Anne Morrow Lindbergh's father, penned for *The Spectator* an attack on Lindbergh's character dripping with condescension.[235] Nicolson contended the aviator's "simplicity [had become] muscle-bound; his virility ideal [had become] not merely inflexible but actually rigid; his self-confidence [had] thickened into arrogance, and his convictions [had] hardened into granite." Attempting a coup de grâce, Nicolson concluded, "To this day he remains a fine boy from the Middle

West.... [H]e is and always will be not merely a schoolboy hero, but also a schoolboy."²³⁶ Anne wrote in her diary, "My breath was knocked out of me by this." For Nicolson, she supposed, it had to be "such a temptation to write that little article, that clever little article, that biting little article. He could do it so well. 'The boy from Minnesota,' all that."²³⁷ The article did Nicolson no honor. He began his diary on September 17 with a matter-of-fact entry: "Write my *Spector* article."²³⁸ But worse to come were threats that arrived in the mail accusing Lindbergh of being a Nazi, claiming, "He will be punished," and another particularly cruel threat that his children would be taken.²³⁹

Amid the uproar over Lindbergh's speech, Hoover took to the airwaves on Friday evening, October 20, in a last attempt to win support for his proposal that the United States sell defensive weapons only.²⁴⁰ He expected rough treatment from those in opposition, writing to Castle,

Hoover delivers his proposal for limited embargo repeal, October 20, 1939 (open source).

"No doubt . . . I will receive volleys from all the Dorothy Thompsons and Walter Lippmanns and Mr. Roosevelt and everybody else of the pro-war party."[241] He had written to Vandenberg a few days earlier of his speech that he did "not expect to change the course of events, but it does seem to me that somebody has got to voice moral standards in this country if we are not to slide down the same barbaric road that Europe trod."[242] Whether weapons could be used every which way, he argued, was not the point. Distinctions could still clearly be made. "Every child in Europe knows its destruction comes from bombing planes and poison gas. Equally, every child knows that pursuit planes, observation planes, searchlights, antiaircraft guns and gas masks are its defense. Every child in Europe can tell these weapons apart."[243] Hoover continued, reiterating what he had learned from his World War I experience and emphasizing the points he had made in his speech ten days ago. "My sympathies are with the allies," he concluded; "nevertheless, my deepest conviction is that America must keep out of this war, and it is in the interest of the whole world if we are to be of any help to rebuild this civilization when the war is over. The most difficult job we have in these months before us is to remain at peace."[244] The Hoover amendment came up for a vote in the Senate on October 26 and was defeated 56 to 36.[245] Vandenberg explained to Hoover that he had done his best to win approval, "but the Administration was so completely in command of the Senate that—as you know—we were unable even to get a vote against the exportation of poison gas (and several Republicans joined in this refusal—God save the mark!)."[246] Other amendments offered suffered the same fate, all being systematically voted down.[247] On October 27, H.R. 306, embargo repeal, was put to a final vote in the Senate and passed 63 to 30. Ironically, that same day, Hoover's *Saturday Evening Post* article titled "We Must Keep Out of War" spilled onto the newsstands and into the mailboxes of three million readers.[248] A week later, the House approved embargo repeal 243 to 181.[249] Senate secretary Halsey, who told Roosevelt on September 7 that the final vote would be roughly 60 to 25, had provided an accurate forecast.[250] The thirty opposition votes, however, were bipartisan: "12 Democrats, 15 Republicans, 2 Farmer-Laborites, and 1 Progressive."[251]

Following the lopsided loss, among the anti-interventionists, recriminations and claims of moral victory proliferated. Senator Charles W. Tobey, a Republican from the Granite State, carped, "You can't lick a steamroller." California senator Johnson claimed the loss felt like being "run over by a truck," while Borah maintained that "it was well to have made the fight," but "if the war should run for any length of time, I do not see how it is possible for us to stay out of it."[252] Vandenberg wrote in his diary,

> This dramatic contest closed tonight in the Senate. We were beaten 63 to 30. But we won a great moral victory. . . . It is going to be much more difficult for F.D.R. to lead the country into war. We have forced him and his Senate group to become vehement in their peace devotions—and we have aroused the country to a peace vigilance which is powerful. . . . Everybody is for "peace." This lip service may last a quite a time. But we have definitely taken sides with England and France. There is no longer any camouflage about it. Repealist Senators speak frankly about it. In the name of "democracy" we have taken the first step, once more, into Europe's "power politics." . . . What "suckers" our emotions make of us![253]

Hoover wrote to Vandenberg that the embargo debate "pretty definitely crystallized the pro-war group as well as the anti-war group. The latter is today in the vast majority, but it is in danger from an emotional invasion at any time." To Senator Walsh, he wrote, "As you and I both know from long experience many a battle is lost, the losing of which contributes to the winning of the war. I am convinced that all of the time this last battle has been in progress we were gaining steadily in our campaign to keep the country out of war."[254] With the defeat, the Hoover/Lindbergh joint effort came to an end, but in that defeat the two friends had established themselves as leading voices opposing intervention, convinced that no matter how loud Roosevelt shouted for peace, his intent was step by step to bring America into the war. The defeat and dismemberment of Poland, which accompanied the seven-week debate on embargo repeal, shocked and horrified most Americans, spurred by publicity surrounding

Roosevelt signs neutrality revision bill, November 4, 1939. From left to right: Senator Pittman, Representative Bloom, Secretary Hull, Vice President Garner, Senator McNary, and Senator Barkley (courtesy of AP Images).

reports from Poland circulated by Hoover and his Commission for Polish Relief. To the surprise of anti-interventionists, vivid reports of refugee suffering worked not to their advantage, but rather to that of those favoring repeal.[255]

On November 3, Roosevelt broke his silence on embargo repeal for the first time since calling Congress into special session in September. He was freed from walking on eggs, as he had gotten the legislation he so badly wanted—decisive victory over the anti-interventionists— though in truth the outcome was never in doubt. When asked whether he was satisfied with the bill, the president verbally checked any celebratory comments, replying, "The most terse way of putting it is that I am very glad that the bill has restored the historic position of the neutrality of the United States." The president's broad smile as he delivered this low-key understatement revealed the relief and satisfaction he felt in the victory.

Hoover, in the aftermath of the great neutrality debate, thought the war would "likely go to bed in the military sense until spring."[256] Whether Hoover was right remained to be seen, but the war with Hitler did enter a twilight zone, a kind of period that the famous German writer Erich Kastner described as "no longer" and "not yet." Thus began what the British called the "Bore War"; Churchill, "the Twilight War"; the French, the *Drôle de guerre*; the Germans, a *Sitzkrieg*; and Senator Borah, the "Phoney War." While all were waiting for Hitler's next move, the Soviets were attempting to do to Finland what they had done to Estonia, Latvia, Lithuania, and Romania—rob them of their sovereignty through partial military occupation. Throughout the fall, Hoover aid through the CPR was reaching Poles in Romania and Hungary, and much progress had been made under very difficult circumstances in Lithuania. In overcoming major obstacles, the CPR distributed 286,093 pounds of clothing and spent $1,375,000 for approximately 150,000 refugees. The challenge was to send aid to those in what remained of Poland, those in the Government General.

William C. McDonald, who had performed heroically during the siege of Warsaw, was among the hundreds of foreigners the German army evacuated to Königsberg after the city surrendered, some by car and others by train. McDonald and those from the US embassy were in the car caravan, accompanied by German officers, making the five-hour drive at night across the war-torn countryside. The trip was purposely made at night so that the Americans looking out the windows could not gauge the damage inflicted by the German army. From Königsberg, McDonald made his way to Geneva to find he had been asked by his business partner and friend, Maurice Pate, to join a CPR team assembling in Berlin. The mission was to persuade the Nazis to allow aid to needy Poles under German occupation. McDonald agreed and arrived in a city much changed from his previous visits. Under the Nazis, the decadence center stage in the Weimar years had given way to a dark, repressive atmosphere that threatened violence. Average Berliners trusted only a closely held few and carefully watched what they said in public, fearing the late-night knock on the door from the ever-present Gestapo. The fear of arrest, torture, and deportment to a concentration camp was omnipresent. The nightly blackouts pitched the city into darkness, making driving and walking risky but a boon to muggers and prostitutes, though Ruth Andreas-Friedrich noted an upside in her diary: "On our way home we see stars over Berlin for the first time—not paling sadly behind gaudy electric signs but sparkling with clear solemnity. The moon cast a milky gleam over the roofs of town. Not a spark of electric light falls on the streets."[257] One advantage of the darkness was that the ubiquitous Nazi propaganda posters could not be seen. McDonald, as required of nearly all foreigners, checked into the Adlon Hotel, where foreign guests were as wary as the average Berliner on the streets. American diplomats and journalists assumed telephone lines were tapped, as were those at the embassy. Rationing, in force since the start of the war, presented difficulties for the chefs at the Adlon, as well as for chefs at the famous Horcher's, but they managed as they catered to the Nazi elite. A cup of real coffee, a drink to which Berliners were addicted, was as rare a find as a diamond on the street. Berliners, undeterred by the war, and in spite of the risks, stumbled through the blackout in pursuit of pleasure at the opera and the movies, filling the city's bars and cafés. Writer Eric Larson described Berlin as a "garden of beasts."[258]

Just before McDonald arrived, the Germans and Soviets adjusted the territorial assignments agreed to in the Nazi-Soviet pact and established new borders. The Soviets increased the size of their holdings by getting the largest share of Polish lands. Western Poland was annexed by the Nazis into the Third Reich, and in the middle portions of Poland, the districts of Kielce, Kraków, Lublin, Lwów, and Warsaw became the concoction generically named the Government General.[259] This new Poland had a population of between thirteen and fourteen million—two and half million were Poles and Jews expelled from the area of Poland annexed to the Reich.[260] From the Soviet areas, tens of thousands fled to the Government General, preferring to risk life under the Nazis rather than the Soviets. For the Nazis, their new geographic creation was a huge labor pool whose inhabitants would over time be worked to death or exterminated. Terror and murder were regular occurrences, with food, goods, money, and property expropriated. Life in the cities proved especially difficult because of war damage, loss of income, rapid inflation, homelessness, and severe crowding caused by the continuous arrival of those who had nothing. The onset of a severely cold winter added to the difficulties threatening urban Poles and Jews with starvation. Many, with the barest of clothing, took to the countryside to forage and to make purchases at highly inflated prices in country markets and from black-market profiteers. "Damn the Germans! Damn the peasants! Damn the black-market profiteers" was a curse commonly heard in Warsaw.[261] Over it all was the iron hand of Hitler's old lawyer, Hans Frank, who ruled this Nazi fiefdom from his comfortable quarters in Kraków's Wawel Castle, leading the Poles on a long journey into night.

The American Friends Service Committee had agreed to support Hoover's CPR relief efforts in the Government General and recruited Homer L. Morris and Howard W. Elkinton, Quakers who were well connected and respected in Berlin, as they had worked in Hoover's German Children's Feeding Program in 1921; both spoke the language and knew the country well. Elkinton had been in Germany the previous year with Quakers attempting to gain the release of Jews arrested after Kristallnacht. Well known to the Gestapo, he was used to being shadowed by plainclothesmen. McDonald, while waiting for them to arrive, worked to develop a relationship with Göring's office, as the two men had a passing acquaintance. The Quakers arrived on October 8 and checked into the Continental Hotel, avoiding the Adlon. Their first stop was the Quakerburo, which would serve as their workplace. The following day, they met McDonald, who eagerly planned for the three of them to leave in the morning by car for Warsaw. Plans were scuttled as permission to enter the Government General was denied. Instead, the authorities in the culture department arranged a series of meetings with the National Socialists Welfare Agency (NSV), which proved elusive and noncommittal. After six days, Morris, his wife Edna, and Elkinton had lost patience and developed serious reservations about working with an organization with close ties to the Nazi Party and army. Morris wrote in his diary, "Apparently the NSV is doing an unusually fine piece of relief work. If we make a favorable report the liberal papers in the U.S.A. will consider that we have sold out to the Nazis, and they will be on our neck. After we have gone this far there is a question as to whether or not we can afford to turn back—to decline the invitation if it comes."[262] Morris and Elkinton, in their first few days in Berlin, grasped the central problem that threatened Hoover and the CPR's goal of aiding Poles in the Government General: "Whether or not it will be possible for us to work in Poland without putting ourselves entirely under the control of the NSV is a grave question."[263] They knew the answer was no. While waiting for an NSV response, the two men conferred for the second time with the International Migration Service working to send Jewish children to America and with representatives of the Jewish International who were still able to send three hundred Jews monthly abroad, a huge drop from the ten thousand a month before the start of the war.[264]

Uncertain any arrangement for aid was possible and convinced that permission to visit Warsaw would not be granted, they packed for a trip to visit a Quaker meeting in north Germany. Morris wrote in his diary, "We felt we had waited as long as we could."[265] Stopping by their office at the Quakerburo, they found, to their surprise, that the mailman had delivered a letter from the NSV granting both permission to feed the Poles and the right of inspection.[266] Morris wrote, "I must confess that I was very much disappointed that the acceptance actually came through."[267] Pleas to headquarters in Philadelphia to go slow and with caution were ignored. Morris reasoned the results would be "the best propaganda agency the Government has ever had. It was a clever move on their part to take us up and they did not miss a trick in doing so."[268] Both men feared the Nazis had no intention of allowing relief, that they were being used for propaganda purposes, as front men for fascism, or, worse, being stalled while the Nazis implemented a murderous occupation. The "garden of beasts" was proving treacherous. Yet even in such a garden, humor survived. In a restaurant, Elkinton ordered coffee, and the waiter replied that "they had only 'Horst Wessel' coffee [made from grain]." Elkinton rejoined, "Well, do you have any 'Kaiser Wilhelm' coffee?" (ersatz coffee made from grain drunk in World War I). Both got a laugh. At another café, the waiter asked whether they had seen the new Nazi salute, "with one hand over eye looking out over the landscape." It means, said the waiter, "Hitler looking for more land."[269] Big smiles all around.

With NSV approval came the promised trip to Warsaw. Morris acidly commented, "If we go we can see only what the government shows us and we will be placed in a position of having to put our stamp of approval on NSV." At midday, on October 17, McDonald and his Quaker colleagues, in a line of vehicles, were off to the Government General, a place no outsiders had been allowed since Warsaw surrendered on September 27. The dark cloud hanging over the trip blackened, as sixty miles south of Lublin the car in which Elkinton was riding struck a curb and flipped over. Thrown from the car, he broke his shoulder blade and sustained a leg fracture. "The accident was inexcusable because there was no car in sight and on a perfectly straight two-lane road. This whole thing is a symbol."[270] Elkinton received emergency treatment at a military hospital in Lublin, and all returned to Berlin, Elkinton by ambulance, where doctors discovered he had also broken his pelvis. After much soul-searching, Morris and McDonald decided to go on to Warsaw. In the dark not far from Łódź, Morris counted a column of 102 wagons loaded with refugees heading for home. Along the route they passed through many damaged towns and villages. As they neared Warsaw in a heavy rain, the road was jammed with "wagons, bicycles, cars and people walking."[271] On reaching their destination, McDonald and Morris had dinner that evening with the American consul, George Haering. For McDonald, it was a reunion with those at the consulate who had survived the siege. Morris stayed the night with Vice Consul Thaddeus Henry Chylinski, who, remaining behind along with his Polish wife to watch over the embassy and its Polish staff, witnessed the German invasion and occupation.

As expected, Morris and McDonald's movements were tightly controlled, shepherded by minders, but the embassy staff invited the American Jewish Joint Distribution Committee (JDC) and the Social Self-Help Committee to meet with them. Morris also was able to connect with Warsaw's Quakers. After a week they returned to Berlin with some of the first independent news about conditions in the Government General, but before sharing their information, they visited Elkinton to find he was mending and would likely soon be out of the hospital. Morris and McDonald's findings were horrific. In Warsaw, they reported, a city of 1.3 million, 35 percent of houses had been totally destroyed, while another 20 percent were severely damaged. The destruction was heaviest in the Jewish and working-class neighborhoods. The Germans estimated fifty thousand had been killed in battle, but no count was made of wounded, injured, or homeless. The NSV claimed to be providing hot soup to roughly 250,000, and 300,000 more received a bread ration.[272] Morris acerbically remarked, "One department shoots people up, another pours food into the tummies of the survivors as a means of gaining goodwill and showing what wonderful humanitarians the Nazis really are."[273] Such NSV assistance was paid for by the city of Warsaw. The cities of Kraków, Kielce, Radom, and Łódź sustained little damage but suffered from failed economies and the huge influx of refugees.

McDonald and Morris conceded that the NSV attempted to feed the hungry but would not feed the Jews that comprised 30 percent of the population. To meet minimum demand, the number of meals per day needed to double. On the open market, clothing was near impossible to obtain, as was milk and cod liver oil, needed by small children and pregnant women. In the bitter cold that had begun to hang over Europe, massive amounts of woolen goods, heavy coats, underwear, and blankets were needed. Those in the Government General were in dire straits. The CPR team reported to New York that avoiding famine required they move quickly.[274] A plan was soon assembled, but attached was the condition that the Germans guarantee that aid reached the intended recipients. Supplies would be shipped, stored, and dispensed by the CPR. Receipts would be required for each item given. There would be no discrimination, and aid would be given to all—Poles, Jews, and other minorities. The Germans would agree not to strip food from the Government General and to import specified deliveries of breadstuff and grain.[275] All Hoover relief organizations demanded accountability to donors as a component of any well-run legitimate operation, but the stringent requirements would also answer skeptics in the United States and Great Britain who saw a cross-blockade feeding program in an enemy country as nothing more than collaboration. Accountability also protected the CPR from political attacks that would certainly be mounted by the Democrats, as the Roosevelt administration was opposed.[276]

The Germans did not warm to the CPR plan, and fruitless discussions took place during the first weeks of November as the NSV insisted any aid be delivered through them. Hans Frank in Kraków and Joachim von Ribbentrop in Berlin dreaded the prospect of a large number of American relief workers traveling throughout the Government General and reporting on what they saw to the outside world. As could be expected, the Germans objected strenuously to feeding Jews. Disregarding the responsibility of an occupying power under the rules of the Geneva Conventions and the Hague agreements and having wrecked Poland, the NSV brazenly argued that the disaster facing their satrapy stemmed from the British and French blockade. Aside from the dubious propaganda value of the argument, the Germans wished to further weaken the blockade, although it was not much of a factor, for they had obviously diminished its effectiveness through their marriage of convenience with the Soviets. The Nazi-Soviet pact opened for Germany trade with Manchukuo and Japan—timber, soybeans, fish.[277] The negotiations with the NSV were deadlocked, as were McDonald's talks with Göring's staff. In the Byzantine bureaucratic world of the Nazis, who would make the decision on relief was a puzzle.

For the CPR, the situation was further complicated when an American Red Cross team of Swift, Chatfield-Taylor, and Nicholson, tailing the CPR, arrived from surveying the needs of Polish refugees in Romania and Hungary. The team asked to survey the medical and relief needs of Poles in the Government General, a request smoothed by the Red Cross donation of $25,000 in medical supplies purchased in Switzerland and Italy.[278] The Red Cross gift was based on genuine concern but was motivated as well by politics, as Hoover was generating a continuous stream of favorable press coverage for effectively rendering aid to Polish refugees in Romania, Hungary, and Lithuania.

The trip approved, the Red Cross team left Berlin on a guided tour in the company of Albrecht Lohmann, a German Foreign Office representative with responsibility for Red Cross affairs and shepherded by a general staff officer. After a week in Warsaw, the facts and figures compiled were largely those reported by the CPR. The teams, however, differed on a major point; the Red Cross thought the winter food supply adequate, while the CPR felt shortages could result in famine. Though it was possible that the Nazis might purposely not distribute food or would ship large quantities back to Germany, no one on either team predicted that result happening. In visiting hospitals, the Red Cross found 4,277 sick and wounded soldiers and 4,770 sick and wounded civilians. Swift cabled Davis, "Urgent need are funds for reconstruction hospitals and repairs biological laboratories, suppliers of blankets, sheets, warm clothing, underwear, shoes, stockings, medication and dressings. Urgent requirements vaccines, quinine, iodine, salicylates, cod liver oil, milk fats. We recommend $300,000."[279] Swift underlined the CPR findings and warned that if the NSV stopped feeding, disaster would follow. He emphasized that the housing situation was critical.

On returning to Berlin, the two teams consulted one another on how to move forward, reaching an agreement that the Red Cross needed greater involvement. Davis answered their request by reminding them of the narrow path he wished the Red Cross to tread. "Amcross unable to assume responsibility for a continuing relief program in Poland. Inclined to limit our aid to medicines, hospital supplies, clothing, and bedding to extent funds are available and conditional upon proper safeguards. Polish contributors deeply mistrustful of German agencies delivering supplies and remittances to Poles."[280] The reference to "proper safeguards" meant, as it did for the CPR, that Red Cross representatives must be present in Poland to assure nondiscriminatory, equitable distribution with accountability. Red Cross delegates could work with the International Committee of the Red Cross, the League of Red Cross Societies, and the Polish or German Red Cross, and Davis cabled Swift, "Association of reliable Poles with relief effort would be most helpful."[281] While Davis professed to be holding the line to emergency aid only, he essentially took the recommendation from the field by granting the lion's share of their request, which was $250,000. Additional funds would come from contributions, but he cautioned that these would not be forthcoming if the Germans interfered with the supplies in any way.

On November 18, after what the Americans considered had been a series of unfettered talks, the Germans balked. "All relief for Polish districts by foreign groups including the Quakers," a German spokesman stated, "must be administered by the Deutsche Rote Kreuz. No foreign organization would be permitted representation in Poland and only under unusual circumstances would special permission be granted to visit Polish areas."[282] Red Cross negotiations foundered on the same rock as had the CPR's. However, contrary to the CPR, the American Red Cross team recommended acceptance of the German conditions, although they were painfully aware that aid given under such circumstances, with little or no American supervision, would be unacceptable to many in the United States. Swift concluded that this was Germany's last offer, and if it was not accepted, the Poles would get no aid at all. "Designation of Deutsche Rote Kreuz as sole administering agency important expression of confidence in whole Red Cross. AmCross should give every consideration this factor in making decision."[283] After thinking over his answer to this uncompromising, blunt statement of conditions, Davis tentatively accepted the German offer. He, too, was convinced that a "provisional" beginning was better than being shut out. If the CPR obtained an agreement and the Red Cross did not, it would prove embarrassing to both the Red Cross and the Roosevelt administration and would include political cost as well. Most Poles voted Democrat, and Davis and the president remained rightly convinced that Hoover wished his relief activities to burnish his presidential candidacy.[284] With Red Cross acceptance, the CPR, fearing being shut out, was now under extreme pressure to do the same. After much internal debate, it, too, reversed its position and tentatively accepted the German conditions, hoping later to gain US supervision. The German foreign office announced on November 22 its conditional approval of the CPR and Red Cross plans.[285]

The prolonged negotiations slowed contributions to Polish relief. Many donors, while pleased with the aid to Poles in the countries bordering Poland, continued to argue over aid to Poles in the Government General. The CPR claimed its request for American representatives and control would be granted, guaranteeing Polish communities that their contribution would not be stolen and those they wished to assist would be.[286] The Red Cross gift of $25,000 to the German Red Cross was unrestricted and was very unpopular with Polish Americans.[287] In fact, the CPR's chances were little better than those of the Red Cross, and it overestimated the weight of its past performance and the clout it may have had with some in the upper echelons of the Nazi hierarchy. Hoover and those in the CPR also saw an advantage in being a private relief agency, more streamlined, more efficient, and more likely to avoid problems made manifest by the US declaration of neutrality. Given the organization's difficulty in raising money, the premature claims of success revealed an attempt to one-up the Red Cross and establish the CPR as the preeminent relief agency to which Polish American societies should contribute.

The Germans, the day after their announcement, softened their position on American representatives in occupied Poland, for if they made no concessions, negotiations might well collapse. Lohmann emphasized that no permanent headquarters could be established in the Government General or in Berlin, but delegates would be permitted to inspect the distribution of relief, gather information, and ascertain ongoing needs. As a further concession, Lohmann added, the German Red Cross would continue to work with the Polish Red Cross to facilitate distribution. Anticipating that an agreement was in hand, McDonald left for the United States to convey a full confidential report to Hoover. Morris was on his way home, and Elkinton had nearly recovered from the car accident. A fresh CPR-AFSC negotiating team composed of two Quakers experienced in relief, Edgar Rhoads and Arthur Gamble, and former US senator Frederic C. Walcott, arriving in Berlin, picked up travel documents and left immediately for Warsaw. The progress made on the relief agreement was imperiled by two outstanding issues. Neither the CPR nor the Red Cross would furnish supplies unless the Germans consented to relief for the Jews, and the issue of American representatives remained unresolved. A breakthrough occurred on November 28. The Nazi consented to nondiscriminatory distribution.[288] All that remained was to decide the details of local inspections.

The American Jewish Joint Distribution Committee had not heard from its operatives in Warsaw since the outbreak of the war on September 1.[289] To find out what was happening to the Jews of Poland, to restart or expand JDC programs, and to increase the chances of Jewish representatives gaining access to the Government General, the JDC allied with the CPR and the Quakers. This was no anomaly, for the three groups had worked closely together during and after World War I. The plan to provide aid called for the relief goods to be consigned to the AFSC, which would then turn them over to the German Red Cross, which would supply the Jewish Self-Help Society and the JDC.[290] In this way, the Germans acted as middlemen, had little or no direct contact with Jewish or Polish relief organizations, and were not involved in aiding those they detested.

November ended with the relief agencies feeling optimistic, but in the first week of December, the Germans had not fulfilled their pledge. A series of harsh exchanges took place between the Germans, the Red Cross, the AFSC, and the CPR. "We are still patiently waiting word from the officials of govt., but it is slow, and we do not think prospects very bright."[291] No progress occurred, but the CPR and Red Cross teams stayed in Berlin in case a breakthrough occurred. The sense of urgency of the American teams increased when in late November the NSV stopped feeding and withdrew.[292] Hunger abounded in the frozen city, and the likelihood of famine greatly increased.

The frustration of the CPR and the American Red Cross was compounded by the polite but unyielding stance of the British toward blockade concessions. In late November, clutching the tentative agreement with the Germans, the relief groups approached the British seeking passage through the Allied blockade. The Ministry of Economic Warfare (MEW) and the Foreign Office had not abandoned their reservations concerning supplies sent to occupied Poland, fearing they would be confiscated by the Germans. The British granted there was no doubt the Polish need was great, and they hoped the United States would help, but it was imperative that Great Britain be assured that distribution would be under "absolute American control." The Foreign Office was not uniformly opposed in principle to aid for Poland and approved relaxing the blockade if it served British war policy. From Washington, Lord Lothian cabled that the CPR "[is] well organized and expects to secure support throughout the country where there is of course a very large Polish population. State Department has confirmed that they regard the commission as first-class and entirely responsible."[293]

If the Roosevelt administration supported aid for Poland, the British government would have to strike a balance between commitments to economic warfare and its desire to avoid alienating the United States. The British approved Red Cross emergency medical aid passing the blockade and agreed the Prize Courts would not seize clothing shipments if the Red Cross and the CPR demonstrated that nothing ended up in German hands.[294] British officials focused their objections on inadequate controls and lack of supervision as a means to avoid compromise. The British neatly avoided a decision by blaming the Germans for the success or failure of any aid program. As MEW had anticipated, the Germans hedged over CPR and ARC demands for supervision of distribution. Since the British refused to relax the blockade until these assurances were obtained, aid already in route to Poland was confiscated by the Royal Navy at Gibraltar. The year ended with the collapse of the effort to provide aid to the Poles in the Government General.

9

In the Jaws of the Soviet Bugbear

Juho Paasikivi and the Finnish delegation arrive in Moscow to "negotiate" the fate of their country, October 16, 1939 (courtesy of Wikimedia Commons; original source: Finnish historian Jukka Nevakivi).

THE FRANKLIN DELANO ROOSEVELT ADMINISTRATION AND THE American public had not recovered from the shock of the fall of Poland and were only beginning to take in the ambiguities of the Twilight War when, in October 1939, a Russo-Finnish crisis appeared on the horizon. The average American knew little of Finland. However, public opinion revealed that Americans were generally in possession of four facts: Finland was near the North Pole, was known for long-distance runners, had a famous composer named Jean Sibelius, and—of paramount importance to Americans—was the only nation that had not defaulted on its World War I debt repayment to the United States.[1] Few knew that the crisis unfolding in Finland had been developing for some time and was part of the larger crisis that had enveloped Europe and much of the world. They were soon to learn much more and be tempted to leap into the struggle between tiny, decent Finland, perceived as a peaceful democracy, and its huge thuggish neighbor, the Soviet Union.

Initially acting on an unofficial basis, the Soviet government had approached the Finns almost a year and a half earlier, on April 14, 1938, right after the Anschluss with Austria. Moscow suggested that the two countries begin a series of top-secret conversations concerning their "mutual defense."[2] Boris Yartsev, the second secretary at the Soviet legation in Helsinki, telephoned the Finnish foreign minister, Rudolf Holsti, and requested that they meet immediately so that he might deliver an important message that had just arrived from Moscow. Holsti, a passionate advocate for democracy who worked for good relations with the Soviet Union, agreed to the meeting, despite Yartsev's disregard of diplomatic protocol and the Finnish government's ignorance of any need for "mutual defense." The Finnish leadership knew from Yartsev's previous activities in Finland that he "represented greater authority than his formal rank signified."[3] They concluded that he was in the NKVD, the Soviet Union's police apparatus, and probably spoke for those close to Joseph Stalin. Thus began a fateful sequence of events.

Later that same day, Yartsev explained to Holsti that the Soviet leadership believed that Adolf Hitler was readying an invasion of Russia. If an attack took place, the Germans would use Finland as a base from which to attack Leningrad and the northern Russian port cities of Murmansk and Archangel. All three cities were close to the Finnish border, and from the Russian perspective, the suburbs of Leningrad extended to the frontier with Finland. This strategic concern was not new to the Bolsheviks, for the vulnerability of these vital ports had been a concern of the infant Communist government in 1917, prior to Finnish independence, and had also been a concern of the tsars before the revolution.[4]

Peter the Great put the Russian view succinctly: "The ladies of St. Petersburg could not sleep peacefully as long as the frontier ran so close to our capital."[5] Since the advent of modern weaponry, Leningrad was within artillery range of Finland; at some points, the distance to the border was no more than twenty miles.[6] The need to defend the city, however, was only one aspect of Soviet interest in Finland. Historically, Russia had been deeply concerned about its defenses and attempted to bolster them through a policy of defense through expansion.[7] If the Soviets extended their frontiers far enough, they could battle an attacker on someone else's territory. This goal was intertwined with a desire to regain the lands lost in World War I and through the Treaty of Brest-Litovsk, which included not only Finland but also eastern Poland, Bessarabia, Ruthenia, Estonia, Latvia, and Lithuania.[8] From April 1938 through May 1939, informal talks between the Finns and the Russians produced no agreements. The Soviets, however, worked assiduously to break up Swedish-Finnish attempts to create a Scandinavian block of neutrals and to keep the Finns diplomatically isolated.[9] Throughout the summer of 1939, Europe was a diplomatic whirlwind from which emerged, to much amazement and disbelief, the Nazi-Soviet pact of August 24.[10] At first, the Finns failed to see that the agreement had profound implications for their future; however, several weeks later it became clear that one of the last pillars of Finnish security had been toppled in Moscow. The Finns had assumed that the Germans would resist any Russian incursions into the Baltic. Although the details of the Nazi-Soviet protocol were secret, a good guess, based on the Soviet occupation of eastern Poland on September 17, was that Finland and its small neighbors to the south had been assigned to the Soviet orbit. Proof that the Finns had correctly interpreted the accord between the two dictators was not long in coming. On September 25, Estonian foreign minister Karl Selter was handed a ready-made defense treaty for immediate signature. The Russian claim to discuss trade was but a way to lure Selter to Moscow. Three days later, under threats of an invasion, the Estonians capitulated and signed the agreement granting the Soviets military bases. The other two Baltic republics, Latvia and Lithuania, succumbed, signing similar ready-made agreements on October 11.[11]

Finland's turn came on October 5, when A. S. Yrjo-Koskinen, the Finnish minister to Moscow, was summoned by Vyacheslav Molotov and told that the Soviet Union wished to resolve its differences with Finland. Eljas Erkko, who had replaced Holsti as Finnish foreign minister, was to journey to the Russian capital. The Finns, of course, were not in the dark as to previous Soviet demands, and they were not unfamiliar with the details of the agreements forced on the Baltic republics, but they assumed that in this round of talks the Soviets would insist on even more concessions. Erkko and his colleagues fully realized that Finland was more isolated than at the time earlier discussions had occurred and therefore was more vulnerable. For the first time during the negotiations, the Finns speculated that military action against their country, particularly a surprise attack, was a possibility. J. K. Paasikivi was chosen by the president and the foreign minister to represent Finland and left for Moscow on October 9. He was a wise choice, as he was a patriot, a hardheaded negotiator dedicated to protecting Finland's interests, and a man who had been involved in Finnish politics as a conservative since its fight for independence in 1919. Max Jakobson, in *Diplomacy of the Winter War*, wrote, "The choice was one of the rare intuitive, or perhaps accidental, strokes of genius that may change a nation's history."[12] Sixty-nine-years old, stocky, and ruddy-faced, he had retired as head of one of Finland's largest banks years earlier.[13] Jakobson maintained, "He possessed a scholarly mind and vast learning in history"; he was also "known for his irascible temper, utterly unable to suffer fools and not above throwing ink wells at subordinates in the bank."[14] These character traits would serve him well in Moscow, as he was not likely to be intimated by Stalin or Molotov when hotboxed for hours late into the night in the Kremlin's Little Corner.

Word of the diplomatic mission to Moscow had spread through Helsinki, and although almost no details were available to the public, the average citizen recognized the gravity of the situation. The city's railroad station filled spontaneously with a large crowd of well-wishers who pushed bouquet after bouquet into the hands of the diplomats while singing the national anthem and the Lutheran hymn "God Is My Castle."[15] As the train passed through towns and villages on its way to Moscow's Finland Station, the diplomats were greeted by singing throngs waving Finnish flags. Back in Helsinki, a partial mobilization was ordered.[16] Finland mobilized reserve units under the pretext of the need for refresher courses. Earlier, on October 6, after having received the Russian summons, the army quietly moved into its forward positions along the Russian border. Finland did all it could to ensure it was not caught flat-footed by the lurking Soviet bear. The party arrived on October 11, with negotiations set to start in the Kremlin the following day at 5:00 p.m.[17] In Helsinki, air raid drills were conducted. The American minister to Finland, H. F. Arthur Schoenfeld, reported to Washington that the Finnish government was likely "prepared to take extreme risks in resisting unwarrantable proposals. The record of Soviet-Finnish relations and the national psychology of the country with its characteristic tenacity and stubbornness . . . promise[d] reckless resistance in that event."[18]

In Washington, Finland was represented by the often difficult and excitable Hjalmar Procopé. Active in Finnish politics in the 1920s, he was a member of the Swedish People's Party, as well as a member of parliament, and served in several diplomatic posts. He arrived in Washington in 1931 as head of the Finnish Paper Mills' Association. Tall, suave, and every inch the Swedish/Finnish aristocrat, he, alongside his American wife, was popular among the dinner and cocktail party crowd of Washington.[19] In the fall of 1939, he worked strenuously to arrange a loan that would allow for the purchase of arms and ammunition in order to strengthen his country's defenses against a possible Russian attack.[20] Procopé, extremely upset on learning of the Russian invasion of Poland on September 17, was sure that Finland was now in the Soviet crosshairs. The Roosevelt administration was predisposed to grant Procopé's request for the loan, but unluckily for Finland the neutrality revision bill was before Congress. Roosevelt, "walking on eggs," would do nothing until the votes had been counted. When Procopé learned from Helsinki that an official Soviet summons had arrived from Moscow, he at once arranged to meet with Cordell Hull. During conversations on October 5 and 7, Procopé, in a highly agitated state, asked that the United States intercede with Russia on Finland's behalf. He claimed that the United States still possessed "some moral influence" over the Soviet Union.[21] Hull was not enthusiastic about this request, for he advocated a policy of attempting to control the spread of the European war and feared a loan would lead to greater US involvement. Hull believed the Russian goal of establishing a cordon sanitaire along the length of its western frontier might well extend the war into the Baltic. The secretary characterized Soviet policy after the series of agreements with Hitler as being "like a catfish lying in the mud waiting for anything to come along."[22] A more accurate metaphor would describe the Soviets, unfettered by the recent agreements with Germany, as a barracuda bent on devouring all the smaller fish placed in its tank. In any event, the secretary refused Procopé's request for assistance, explaining that US intervention "might well aggravate [the dispute] rather than resolve it."[23] Using the American commitment to neutrality and the possibility of damaging the success of the current effort to revise neutrality law, Hull concealed from Procopé another important aspect of his policy: the desire not "to alienate Russia, feeling that at some future time she might veer away from her apparently close relationship to Germany."[24] Roosevelt was in agreement with Hull and eschewed an active policy partially for fear of widening the European war.

Undeterred by Hull's lack of support, Procopé called on Adolf Berle on October 6 and proposed a marvelously devious way by which the United States might assist Finland without directly intervening or without contravening US neutrality. He suggested to Berle that FDR call the US ambassador to the Soviet Union, Laurence Steinhardt, and emphasize that the United States had a "special interest in the fate of Finland, with whom we were particular friends."[25] In his diary Berle remarked, "I made a note of this; because I think there is real value in the idea."[26] Using the telephone would guarantee that the Russians and the Germans would be apprised of the US attitude because both monitored all diplomatic calls. Berle was so taken with the idea that he told Procopé he would discuss it with the president on Monday. Then he added a twist of his own: "I should suggest that he send cable notification in advance to make the telephone appointment—to make perfectly sure the right people listen in."[27] FDR did not telephone Steinhardt. He concluded that an unofficial statement conveying the US position on Finland would lose much of its effect and that America's influence on the main adversaries was already minimal. A public statement might possibly lend force to world public opinion, but, as Berle remarked in reference to US pronouncements on Finland in early December, really all the United States was doing was "making the record."[28]

Nonetheless, Procopé and the Swedish ambassador to the United States, W. Bostrom, were successful in getting Roosevelt "to make the record," and this at a time when Roosevelt was prone to limit foreign involvement and protect the embargo repeal bill in Congress. On October 10, having conferred with both ambassadors, and having received messages from the crown prince of Sweden and the president of Finland, Roosevelt agreed to send a message to the Russians through the American ambassador in Moscow. The president stressed to Bostrom that Hull must concur with the contents of the telegram. Then, speculating on the message's chances of success, he commented that "his influence in Moscow was just about zero."[29] Bostrom, a true diplomat, flatteringly replied that "the President's influence could not be zero anywhere in the world."[30] Early that same afternoon, finally consenting but expecting an evasive response, FDR dictated a rough draft of the message to Judge R. Walton Moore, a counselor at the State Department.

On leaving the White House, Ambassador Bostrom went directly to the office of Jay Pierrepont Moffat at the State Department, asking to be informed "if and when a message was sent," as the Swedes were orchestrating a Scandinavian response to Russian pressure on Finland and the Nordic countries and also wished to deliver notes of a similar nature in Moscow.[31] The goal was to pressure the Soviets, through a demonstration of neutral solidarity, into making more acceptable demands on the Finns, which they could accept and thus avoid war. Judge Moore met with Moffat immediately after Bostrom left. He showed him the Roosevelt draft and emphasized that it must not be sent until Hull had approved the text. Moffat wrote in his diary,

> The Judge and I cleaned up the language a little and awaited the Secretary's return until about two o'clock. It was obvious that the Secretary did not like the idea at all, fearing that for the President to intervene in one case would create a precedent that would come home to plague us. However, in view of the President's commitments the utmost

he could do was to suggest certain drafting changes. The way it worked out was that we sent over two alternative paragraphs for the President's choice. He got the Secretary on the telephone and together they agreed on some wording.[32]

The telegram, addressed to Soviet president Mikhail Kalinin, was sent in the late afternoon of October 11 and was delivered by Steinhardt to Molotov at 3:00 p.m. the following day. The essential part read, "The President expresses the earnest hope that the Soviet Union will make no demands on Finland which are inconsistent with the maintenance and development of amicable and peaceful relations between the two countries, and the independence of each."[33]

The Roosevelt administration calculated that sending the message to Moscow entailed some risk and feared that even this limited intervention would have an adverse effect on Congress and on the votes in favor of neutrality. However, public opinion was solidly behind Finland, and the mounting crisis might help to make the president's case to legislators with an ear for the popular cause. Senators Key Pittman and Thomas Connelly and House Speaker William Bankhead "expressed immediate support of the President when his statement became publicly known."[34] The calculated risk paid big dividends, for the public also staunchly supported Roosevelt's actions. Contrary to Roosevelt and Hull's fears, the message to Kalinin increased support for neutrality legislation as events forced the American public to take more interest in foreign affairs. But the somewhat unexpected results of Roosevelt's limited intervention did not embolden the administration to adopt a more activist foreign policy. Despite strong support for Finland's cause, Roosevelt and his advisors remained cautious and unsure of what action to take if the Soviet-Finnish talks collapsed. The Finns, however, were gratified, the press exuberant, lavishing praise on Roosevelt for his letter and for supporting neutrality and providing hope in a time of crisis.[35] The Finnish president and foreign minister expressed their thanks in messages of appreciation to Roosevelt.[36]

On October 11, when Paasikivi and the Finnish delegation arrived by train in Moscow, *Izvestia* noted the negotiators' low-key reception, as only "minor officials of the People's Commissariat for Foreign Affairs . . .

the staff of the Finnish legation and the Swedish Minister to Moscow [Wilhelm Winther]" awaited them at the station.[37] Stalin and Molotov remained unmoved by the letters from Roosevelt and the Scandinavians, assured that the Soviet Union's size and military strength would prove decisive in any negotiation. The Finnish representatives returned from Moscow with Soviet demands on October 16 to face a resolute cabinet reluctant to compromise. Lengthy discussions ensued, in which it finally became apparent to the government that territorial concessions were necessary. What territory and how much remained a hotly debated subject.[38] The flaw in the nascent Finnish counterproposal was the assumption on which it was predicated. Nearly all the participants in the decision-making process concurred that Stalin would bargain and was unlikely to resort to war to enforce Soviet demands. Both assumptions would prove false. While Stalin and Molotov had not given the Finns an ultimatum, they had stated their minimal demands and did not expect to haggle. As the demands had been widely reported in the Soviet press, Russian prestige was committed.[39] Therefore, even though a major shift in Finnish policy had occurred, it proved far short of Russian expectations. The Finnish government continued to struggle to find a compromise, conceding much from its point of view to satisfy its irreconcilable neighbor.[40]

The Soviet press continuously attacked the Finns as provocateurs and warmongers. Erkko and Prime Minister A. K. Cajander still believed that no Soviet military attack would occur. Paasikivi thought that nothing would happen, whereas Vaino Tanner, a cabinet member and skilled negotiator, and Field Marshal Carl Gustaf Emil von Mannerheim, commander of the army and father of his country, were convinced that hostilities might soon begin. The attacks in the Soviet press were a key factor in deciding whether the Russians would use force, although the Finns interpreted the agitprop barrage as an effort to soften them up before diplomatic negotiations resumed. As Uncle Waldemar, a character in Robert Sherwood's very successful play *There Shall Be No Night* about the Winter War, said, "Do you know what the press in Moscow is saying about us? We're 'that Finnish scum,' we're 'bourgeois bandits,' 'Tools of British imperialism,' 'Fascist's assassins.'... Those words were the advance guard of the Red Army."[41] Mannerheim's opinion carried great weight, as he was the revered father of his country who had come out of retirement to again led the Finnish army. He stood "six feet two, booted and spurred, his height accentuated by a splendid snow-white fur hat and his upper-body breadth by a chestful of decorations from several grateful nations."[42] This impressive array was enhanced by a "cavalry sabre at his hip and a marshall's baton in his white-gloved hand."[43] One of those medals had been awarded to him for fighting Germans as an officer in the tsar's army during World War I; the kaiser had awarded him another later for fighting Russians.[44] Like Józef Piłsudski in Poland, Mannerheim had fashioned an army that defeated the Bolsheviks in a brutal conflict and cemented Finnish independence.

In Washington, Cordell Hull learned of the Soviet abrogation of the Russian nonaggression pact with Finland on the afternoon of November 28, when Ambassador William C. Bullitt telephoned the news from Paris. Bullitt warned that an attack could take place at any time and that "if our government could do anything in the circumstances we had better do it quickly."[45] Pressure had already been applied to the State Department when, earlier in the day, Procopé met with Moffat and suggested that the United States might still prevent war if an offer was made to arbitrate the dispute.[46] Hull cabled Schoenfeld and Steinhardt requesting information and then held a meeting at the department. Those in attendance agreed that some kind of action was imperative. Moffat recorded in his diary,

> Of all the possibilities suggested the one that appealed to us most was a public statement in which we offered our good offices. I had prepared a short draft which was accepted with one or two minor drafting changes. The Secretary [Hull] felt that he must speak to the President, who was on his way by train from Warm Springs to Asheville. Connection was finally made, the President approved, and the statement was given to the press at three o'clock.[47]

The statement handed to the Russians in Moscow read,

This government is following with serious concern the intensification of the Finno-Soviet dispute. It would view with extreme regret any extension of the present area of war and the consequent further deterioration of international relations. Without any way becoming involved in the merits of the dispute, and limiting its interest to the solution of the dispute by peaceful process only, this Government would, if agreeable to both parties, gladly extend its good offices.[48]

The Finns at once agreed to mediation, but, as Roosevelt and Hull had expected, the Russians rejected the US offer. In Helsinki, the government dissolved at the insistence of Tanner, who formed a more broadly based war cabinet. The Finnish leadership hoped that this cabinet reshuffle would induce the Soviets to reopen negotiations.[49] As Finland now had no diplomatic relations with the Soviet Union, the United States again aided the Finns in a minor way by agreeing to convey this information to the Kremlin. The Russians took no notice of the Finnish change of government and attempts to continue negotiations. Late in the afternoon of November 29, Molotov, along with Lavrenty Beria, Nikita Khrushchev, Andrey Zhdanov, Kliment Voroshilov, and Grigory Kulik, ranking members of the dictator's court, joined Stalin in his Kremlin apartment for a meeting concerning the recalcitrant Finns. Early that evening an ultimatum was sent to the Finns. After dinner the meeting continued, with vodka freely flowing. Sometime close to midnight, Stalin settled the issue: "Let's get started tomorrow."[50] Kulik was sent to "command the bombardment."[51] Moscow's Finnish Communist puppet government, created on November 30, 1939, in the border city of Terijoki, anticipated being quickly swept into power by the Red Army. Stalin and his coterie swallowed their own propaganda, believing the workers and peasants of Finland would rise to throw off their bourgeois capitalist repressors and welcome the Russians as liberators.[52] The Soviets estimated it would all be over in twelve to fifteen days. Khrushchev, in his memoirs, wrote that they believed the Finns would fold once the first shots were fired.[53]

Morning brought war in earnest. The Red Army attacked the vaunted Mannerheim Line on the Karelian Isthmus, the Finnish series of fortified positions that blocked the road to Helsinki. This was to be the decisive front throughout the Winter War. To cut Finland in half, the Soviets also attacked at the "waist of Finland," in the regions to the north of Lake Ladoga. In the far north, on the Fisherman's Peninsula, Soviet units drove to the port city of Petsamo.⁵⁴ Helsinki was raided several times on the opening day of the war by Red Air Force light bomber groups that could fly many sorties from their recently garrisoned bases on the outskirts of Tallin, Estonia. Marshall Mannerheim "was having breakfast with his niece's husband, Bjorn Weckmann, at his mansion in Kaivopuisto, Helsinki's fashionable diplomatic district, when they were startled by the sound of bombs."⁵⁵ A lone plane had dropped thousands of leaflets and then five bombs near the Malmi airport. Soon after, "as dawn gave way to full daylight, the morning sky was bright and clear, except to the south, where a large cloud bank had formed in the direction of Estonia. At about 10:30, the forward edge of the clouds suddenly rippled with light as a wedge of nine Russian planes . . . left cover and leveled a run over the capital."⁵⁶ The Russian bombardiers, aiming at a harbor fortress and clusters of ships, miscalculated, missing their targets. Finns walked to air raid shelters, wrote E. B. Elliston, correspondent for the *Christian Science Monitor*: "There was no panic. . . . [P]eople simply stayed at the entrances of the bomb-shelters and gazed skyward at the Soviet apparition."⁵⁷ Circling, the flotilla attacked the central railroad station, again missing, but "thoroughly plastered the huge public square in front of the building killing forty civilians."⁵⁸

As the war in Finland raged on, Roosevelt hurried to return to the capital. His train did not reach Washington, DC, until midday on November 30, though Hull, Moffat, Undersecretary Sumner Welles, Stanley Hornbeck (Far Eastern Desk), and James Dunn (European Desk) spent the morning drafting a protest to the Russians, requesting that they not bomb civilians.⁵⁹ Furious over the Soviet air raids, the president wanted to help the Finns, though he was limited in the action he could or would take. In September, the United States had sent a plea to the German government when Nazi planes ruthlessly attacked Polish cities, targeting the civilian population. Why not send a similar note to the Kremlin? Welles argued that the United States should go beyond sending a note of diplomatic protest and break off relations with the Soviets. To Welles, this action might possibly have the further effect of checking the Japanese and might give second thoughts to the Germans.⁶⁰ Hull, opposed to severing diplomatic relations, argued that it would do no good, although the Tennessean's timidity was based on his commitment to a policy of not alienating the Russians. In his memoirs, Hull explained that his goal was to give the Soviets no ground for complaint about their relationship with the United States, for he "could not but feel that the basic antagonisms between Communist Russia and Nazi Germany were so deep, and Hitler's ambitions boundless, that eventually Russia would come over to the side of the allies. We had to be careful not to push her in the other direction."[61]

Several smaller steps were taken by the Roosevelt administration in support of Finland. On December 1, Roosevelt released a statement to the press condemning the outbreak of hostilities. The president also chose not to exercise his option of implementing the Neutrality Act, and on the following day he extended to the Soviet Union the "moral embargo" already in effect against Japan. Not invoking the Neutrality Act was important for the Finns, for if FDR were "to find a war" and neither belligerent declared one, the cash-and-carry provisions of the law would take effect. Finland would be unable to secure credit in the United States, and any goods purchased would have to be carried in Finnish ships. As Finland essentially had no navy, the Neutrality Act (if invoked) greatly favored the Soviets. This noninvocation did not directly aid Finland, but it allowed the Finns an "opportunity" to buy ammunition and arms in the United States and to attempt to secure loans both private and public.[62]

The moral embargo aimed at Russia was broader in its restrictions than the embargo declared against Japan, as the US government asked manufacturers of airplanes, airplane parts, and aviation fuel not to sell to the Russians.[63] Mining concerns and critical alloy producers were also asked for cooperation on December 15.

Secretary Harold Ickes, evaluating the president's response to the Russo-Finnish crisis and commenting on the extension of the "moral embargo," wrote,

> As he usually does in any international situation when he follows his own bent, the President is acting magnificently. At Cabinet meeting some question was raised about a very rare metal [molybdenum] that is valuable for war purposes. It is such an obscure metal that I had

never heard of it and I did not get the name of it. It appears that we have only ten thousand tons. The President told [Henry] Morgenthau that he wanted him to find some way of keeping this out of the hands of Germany and Russia. Morgenthau's reply was that a sale of it to either would be perfectly legal. The President replied that he did not care whether it was legal or not; he wanted it stopped and he expected Morgenthau to find some way to stop it.[64]

Secretary Ickes may have thought that the president had acted "magnificently," but the hard-pressed Finns were of a different opinion. Since the outbreak of the war in Finland, Procopé had redoubled his efforts to garner support and obtain aid from the administration; however, with the announcement of the moral embargo it was clear that, as with Poland, very little real help would be forthcoming. The Roosevelt administration clung to its policy of walking both sides of the street, the Finnish side sympathetically and the Soviet side out of begrudging necessity. Time would vindicate Roosevelt and Hull's policy, but at the expense of the Finns. The Finns were sincerely grateful for the moral support of Roosevelt and Hull, but aircraft, ammunition, tanks, artillery, money, and all the other types of war materiel were needed to support a modern army.[65] The Mannerheim Line was more myth than reality, and the Finnish army's equipment was antiquated. Finland's weaknesses were recognized by the marshall himself, who wrote on November 6 to G. A. Gripenberg, Finnish minister to Sweden, "We would have needed a least a year's intensive work to be anywhere near ready, but with exception of Germany hardly any country is ever ready. Woe betide the weak—if he is unable to defend himself, he cannot count on help from others."[66]

Hull's policy of not alienating the Russians was not the only obstacle to be overcome if the Finnish government could use the United States as a major source of military and civilian supply. The Roosevelt administration would not assume the aggressive role necessary if the beleaguered nation were to get the $60 million it had requested. Procopé had badgered the State and Treasury Departments about a loan for many months but made no progress.[67] In the shock following the Soviet attack, Hull again advised Roosevelt not to antagonize Congress by pushing for a loan to

Finland. He feared a debate in the House of Representatives would increase isolationist strength, which had decreased due to a public change of mood regarding the worsening world crisis, and that the isolationists would see the loan request for Finland as a first step toward administration requests for huge increases in aid for France and Great Britain—a backdoor to war.[68]

Three other problems loomed large for the Finns: the United States was serious about its neutrality position, the 1940 presidential campaign was rapidly warming up, and the Western European *sitzkrieg* might at any moment become a *blitzkrieg*. The watchword in Washington was caution, and Finland would get little more than moral support and platitudes. Extremely frustrated, as had been the Poles, the Finnish government decided to utilize its close Republican contacts and to accept the liabilities inherent in such a tactical maneuver.

Early on Sunday morning, December 3, 1939, Procopé called Lewis Strauss, a longtime friend of Finland; Strauss was a Kuhn-Loeb Wall Street banker and protege of former president Herbert Hoover. Procopé asked for American assistance in Finland's fight against the Soviet Union.[69] The Finnish minister pleaded in his floridly dramatic style: "I am at the very end of my rope and Finland is near the end of hers. Everywhere I go in Washington—to the State Department, to the Treasury, to the White House, even to the Red Cross, I get sympathy, but nothing more. We can't defend ourselves with sympathy, can you help me at all?"[70] Procopé called Strauss because the Finnish leadership had not forgotten how he had aided the Finns in obtaining their independence in 1919 by befriending Rudolf Holsti, the Finnish representative to London and to the Paris Peace Conference. Holsti had convinced Hoover, and Hoover had convinced President Woodrow Wilson, to support Finland's cause. Writing to Wilson, Hoover had pleaded, "If ever there was a case for helping a people who are making a sturdy fight to get on a basis of liberal democracy, and are asking no charity of the world whatever, this is the case."[71] Wilson was persuaded, and he and Hoover were in turn the principals who secured the recognition of Finnish independence.[72] Strauss was able to render this assistance in 1919 because he was Hoover's private secretary and traveled with the Chief to Europe.

Access to Hoover was rigidly controlled by the young, aggressive, and fiercely competitive Strauss. Holsti was waiting to see Hoover at his London office in the Ritz Hotel when he confronted the obstacle that stood in his way. Strauss later recalled this first meeting: "He dressed as though clothing was an afterthought and peered at the world through spectacles with lenses so thick that they looked as if cut from the bottom of beer bottles."[73] While the representative of an aspiring nation-state that had declared its independence from Russia in 1917, Holsti not only dressed shabbily but also was constantly short of money and lacked contacts with people who could persuade those in power to grant recognition.

Strauss was at once drawn to Holsti and almost immediately became his sponsor. Flush with ration coupons, he often invited the Finn to dine with him. After dinner Holsti held forth on Finnish culture and history and on Finland's desire to escape the domineering Russians. This was a message that Strauss was predisposed to hear, and years later he recalled that he was "completely indoctrinated."[74] This important American loaned his Finnish friend money for decent living quarters and better clothing, but, most important, Strauss arranged for Holsti to meet those with influence.

International recognition was only the first step for Finland, as the fledgling nation needed long-term foreign loans to undertake development and immediate help to alleviate desperate famine. Hoover and Strauss made sure American Relief Administration aid went to Finland, and both men were helpful in securing international loans, credits, and other forms of assistance in Great Britain and the United States.[75] In 1921, Holsti wrote to Strauss and thanked him for his help: "You know perfectly well how much I owe to you; your assistance in London in 1918, and during the Peace Conference at Paris, 1919 will never be forgotten by me nor by the Finnish people, to whom the American relief was of capital importance."[76]

Indeed, in the years between the wars, each new Finnish minister to the United States called on Strauss, and he acted as an advisor on Finnish finance and commercial dealings.[77] Keenly aware of the intensity of America's near schizophrenic response to any involvement in the war in Europe, Strauss devised a scheme for aiding Finland that he thought would appeal to both the public and those in government. Finland would release any funds in its possession that were earmarked for food and relief and use that money to purchase military equipment. Strauss then planned to ask Hoover to form a relief organization like the World War I Commission for Relief in Belgium (CRB) and the existing Commission for Polish Relief (CPR), which would take responsibility for maintaining Finnish food imports and provide money and supplies for Finnish relief.[78] Procopé arrived in New York that same evening, December 3, to work out the details of the plan with Strauss.

Prior to Procopé's arrival, Strauss telephoned Ben Cohen, a close advisor to Roosevelt, and asked how the Finns might borrow money from the United States to buy military equipment. Cohen proposed that with the approval of Jessie Jones, head of the Reconstruction Finance Corporation (RFC), a Finnish corporation might be formed that could borrow money from the Import-Export Bank of the RFC.[79] This suggestion was hardly novel, for it was the way in which aid had earlier been given to Chiang Kai-shek and the Nationalist Chinese.[80] Nonetheless, Procopé was enthusiastic about the release scheme, the RFC loan, and the proposed Hoover relief agency. Jones informed Procopé that he had obtained approval from Roosevelt for a credit of $10 million for the purchase of agricultural commodities and manufactured goods.[81] His country's needs were so great that he was obligated to pursue any plans that promised support—especially if dollars were involved.

That evening, Strauss telephoned Hoover in Palo Alto, California. Hoover at once agreed to head a relief drive and confided to Strauss that he had already concluded that such an undertaking was necessary. The crisis in Finland weighed heavily on his mind, and with the beginning of hostilities on November 30, Hoover had issued a statement to the press that was extracted from a speech given that same day to the Young Republican Club meeting in San Francisco. Hoover remarked, "Civilization struck a new low with the Communist attacks on peaceful Finland. It is a sad day to every decent and righteous man and woman in the world. We are back to the morals and butchery of Ghengis Khan."[82] Later, Hoover wrote that a part of his motivation for undertaking Finnish relief was to persuade the public to support a large loan to Finland and to demonstrate to the American people the Soviet government was a "monster."[83] On December 2, in a second press release, Hoover supported Roosevelt's offer to mediate the Finnish crisis; he also supported the administration's protest against the bombing of unarmed targets but advocated that even stronger measures be taken against the Soviet government: "We should, as was done in Germany, have a routine official to represent us in Moscow and withdraw the dignity of our Ambassador."[84] On the following day, December 4, Donald C. Swatland, another Strauss friend and lawyer, was asked to establish the Finnish Relief Fund (FRF) and the Finnish American Trading Corporation, both of which were quickly incorporated in Delaware.[85] With this accomplished and Procopé's assurance to Hoover that his government approved, Strauss then found office space in the Kuhn-Loeb building for the new Finnish enterprises.

Hoover's motives for accepting this added responsibility were as mixed as they had been for founding the Commission for Polish Relief. The CPR, in early December, was embroiled in the initial stages of negotiations with the Germans and with the British; however, throughout the month of December and on into January 1940, no progress was made. The Polish American community was badly split, and the American public had lost interest in the plight of an occupied, divided country. Much to Hoover's chagrin, his attempt to feed the Poles in the Government General had not engendered an effective relief organization and had produced neither a record of achievement nor the intense media coverage that would provide substance to his presidential ambitions. His opposition to Roosevelt, his alternative suggestions for revising the neutrality laws, and the publicity surrounding the founding and early efforts of the CPR had nonetheless given Hoover's political candidacy a shove. In early December, Hoover's star appeared on the rise, and he was taken more seriously as a presidential candidate than at any time since his 1932 nomination and campaign. Throughout the fall he gained in popularity, and his points went up in the polls.[86]

Aid to Finland was even more attractive to Hoover because of his lack of success in Poland and because many of the elements that stymied the Polish relief effort were absent in the case of Finland. Finland was not occupied by a belligerent power or subject to the restrictions of the Allied blockade; also, the Roosevelt administration did not apply the neutrality laws to the Russo-Finnish War in the first few weeks of the conflict and seemed unlikely to do so. Because the situation in Finland differed radically from that in Poland, the Winter War promised to provide Hoover with vast new opportunities. Both the American and the British publics reacted strongly to the Finnish crisis and then to the Soviet attack with overwhelming support for Finland.[87] Gallup interviews between December 14 and 19 asked, "In the present crisis, are your sympathies with Finland or Russia?"[88] Among respondents, 88 percent picked Finland, 11 percent had no opinion, and 1 percent sympathized with Russia.[89]

Only the Communist Party USA attempted to defend Soviet actions, while the number of fellow travelers diminished considerably.[90] In fact, the entire episode of Russo-Finnish negotiations and the Winter War provided welcome relief to the frustrations generated by the "Phoney War" and seemed, at least momentarily, to provide an opportunity for decisive action in contrast with the complexities of the wider European conflict.[91] This proved to be an illusion, for the Russo-Finnish War was at first politically explosive and threatened to broaden the existing conflict. Nonetheless, Americans vented their pent-up anger over the apparently insoluble European situation by focusing their attention on Finland.[92] Romantics argued that if one had missed the Spanish Civil War, the Winter War offered a second chance for political and moral redemption.[93] For a variety of reasons, Americans rushed to champion Finland's cause, and Herbert Hoover was once more at the head of the crowd.

Moved by humanitarian concern, rabid anticommunism, a need for self-justification, and a desire to be president again, Hoover wasted no time in throwing himself into the Finnish relief drive. The morning after assuring Strauss that he would participate, Hoover drove to San Bernadino for another speaking engagement. On the trip, he thought of two ways to accelerate fund-raising for Finland. Stopping for gas, he telephoned Strauss to suggest that newspapers be asked to solicit relief funds by running free advertisements and that the funds be passed on to banks that would agree to hold the money in free accounts for later transfer to the Finnish Relief Fund.[94] Strauss was quickly able to arrange this service through national banking associations. Advertising commitments were handled through the Associated Press and United Press International. Within several days, over one thousand newspapers had agreed to cooperate.

That same Monday morning, December 4, Hoover telephoned Rickard and asked him to line up management for the Finnish Relief Fund from members of the "old CRB group," many of whom already held positions with the Commission for Polish Relief.[95] This task was greatly simplified by the fact that a large number of former CRB personnel were in New York City for their annual reunion and a meeting of the Belgian American Educational Foundation, a scholarship and exchange program established with money that remained in CRB accounts at the end of World War I. Among those attending were many who considered themselves Hoover minutemen, eager to serve. At an extraordinary meeting, these old Hoover associates elected the Chief chairman of the Finnish Relief Fund, with Edgar Rickard as president and Lewis Strauss as vice president. The board of directors was overwhelmingly composed of talented men who had worked in CRB and included Perrin Galpin, head of the Belgian American Educational Foundation, Raymond Sawtelle, Edwin P. Shattuck, Clare Cory, Sidney Mitchell, and John L. Simpson. Galpin, Sawtelle, and Shattuck were already working with the CPR. The only exception to the rule of prior CRB experience was the appointment of Holger Sumelius.[96] The FRF further obtained the services of John Jay Hopkins, who took over management of the organization, and James P. Selvage, who directed public relations and was a Hoover political advisor. Hopkins later displayed his managerial skills by creating the General Dynamics Corporation.[97] Official Finnish approval was sought by giving an honorary chairmanship to Procopé.[98] Rickard, late in the afternoon, sent a telegram to Hoover telling him, "We incorporated and are all set to go."[99]

Before publicly announcing that the FRF was operating and asking for contributions, Hoover was alerted by Strauss that the Red Cross was about to announce an appeal for Finland. "Clearly worried that the Red Cross would get the jump on him, Hoover released his 'preliminary hint of understanding' to the press that evening."[100] His ingenuity was rewarded.

Near the bottom of page one of the *New York Times* appeared a story headlined "Hoover Will Organize Relief for Finland; Red Cross Appeals for Funds for Its Help."[101] The Red Cross announcement in the *Times* article that it had sent an initial contribution of $25,000 to the Finnish Red Cross did not say that it had done so on December 2. Perhaps Strauss's warning about a Red Cross announcement of a donation was triggered because Norman H. Davis had knowledge that Hoover was planning a relief drive and he didn't want Hoover to get the jump on him. That this might have been the case is fortified by the fact that the Red Cross sweetened the pot with news of the purchase of $10,000 worth of emergency medicines, which were obtained in London by the British Red Cross and flown to Finland, to "be followed immediately by shipments of 50,000 surgical dressings, warm clothing and knitted garments."[102] Wishing to keep its involvement limited by staying behind the scenes, the Red Cross was forced to come forward by public pressure to do something for the Finns and by the threat of a second large-scale Hoover relief campaign. In addition to this largess, the Red Cross sought contributions to aid Finnish war victims. Soliciting contributions, however, was not the same thing as a nationwide fund-raising drive.

Hoover needed clarification; to ascertain Red Cross intentions, on December 7 he telephoned Davis. Using the same passive-aggressive pitch he had employed the previous September concerning aid to Poland, he encouraged Davis to have the Red Cross undertake Finnish relief. Hoover volunteered to have his FRF serve under the Red Cross. Davis responded that the Red Cross still planned only to provide emergency medical aid and limited amounts of clothing to war victims, witnessed by the contribution made on December 2 and one consistent with Red Cross policy. Near the end of the conversation the former president proposed a joint drive to raise money "fifty-fifty," which Davis rejected.[103] Hoover now asked Davis's permission to issue a statement to the effect that the two organizations did not overlap and both were worthy of support.[104] Davis agreed, and the ex-president released a statement pleading for support for Finland and stressing that a spirit of cooperation existed between the relief agencies. "The American Red Cross appeal for funds to furnish medicines, hospital supplies, and many garments will be provided through their chapters. They should be supported. The two funds will cooperate fully," proclaimed Hoover.[105] The Red Cross issued a similar press release but significantly did not mention the FRF by name.[106] A temporary compromise in the Hoover–Red Cross battle had been reached.

Outwardly, cooperation seemed the order of the day. In fact, the two organizations were again competing for a limited number of donations and for the publicity that went along with a successful fund-raising drive in support of a popular cause. To many potential donors, the distinction that each organization provided a different kind of aid was too subtle. In Romania, Hungary, Lithuania, and Poland, the CPR had arrived first and stayed and, in this way, had gained an edge. This circumstance forced the Red Cross to demonstrate commitment by continuing programs that otherwise might have been quietly phased out. When the Winter War erupted, however, the Red Cross was quick to dispatch aid to the Finns with the initial contribution of $25,000 on December 2. As Hoover was informing Americans of his plans to raise funds for the Finns, a Red Cross plane loaded with medical supplies was landing in Helsinki. That the Red Cross had gotten aid to Finland first pleased Norman Davis so much that he gleefully pointed out this coup to Hoover in a telephone conversation on December 7.[107]

Exacerbating the tension between the FRF and the Red Cross was the ongoing Roosevelt-Hoover political rivalry. The gut reaction of FDR and close advisors like Ickes, Davis, and Breckinridge Long to a Hoover Finnish relief drive was that the former president had once again pushed in where he did not belong.[108] Long reported Davis's version of his conversation with Hoover quite differently than had Hoover:

> Norman has been having some difficulty with Herbert Hoover. . . . Hoover wanted to make some agreement with him about division of work and a joint announcement made, but Norman told him that the Red Cross could not agree to a limitation of its activity and couldn't agree with other people to divide work. Hoover is a very insistent person, and he is just itching to get something that will help him politically, but this kind of work ought not to be a political activity. However, I warned Norman that he must be very careful that there should be no evidence

of partisan or personal feeling. He thoroughly sensed that. . . . Having failed in the Polish campaign, Hoover now wants to pick up the Finnish campaign—anything to get in the spotlight again.[109]

Davis did not tell Long, however, that he had agreed to the statement that was released by Hoover on December 8 and that the Red Cross could not accede to Hoover's offer of a joint campaign without redefining its role in relief. Joint campaigns like the one proposed by Hoover had occurred in the past.[110] But if the Red Cross accepted Hoover's offer, it would mean a shift of some magnitude in Roosevelt's foreign policy, something Hoover had been after ever since Davis and Myron Taylor had visited him in September. It was apparent that neither the Red Cross nor Hoover had modified their positions. The Roosevelt administration was unsure of what to do about Finland, for the tremendous public clamor for action was difficult to resist in an election year, but it rejected Hoover's maneuver by sticking with its policy of limited emergency aid, albeit not without manifestations of disarray and disharmony.[111] On December 9, reassured the Red Cross would not undertake a nationwide relief drive, Hoover went public with his newly created Finnish Relief Fund.

What really galled Roosevelt and his advisors was that they could do so little to prevent Hoover from capitalizing on the Finnish crisis. In December and January, it appeared as if Hoover would once again turn his relief activities into votes. As a relief advocate who also was a presidential confidant, Davis was not in an enviable position. His options were severely circumscribed, although he had often participated in formulating administration policy and agreed with it. The dilemma for Davis arose from the fact that the president, who had dodged the Finnish crisis to the best of his ability, expected him to generate coverage for the Red Cross, and by extension for administration policies and for the president, to counteract the avalanche of favorable publicity blanketing Hoover and the Finnish Relief Fund.[112]

The Roosevelt administration's frustration heightened when, against all odds, the Finnish army held out. Early predictions were that a Russian victory would take but one or two weeks. Had the Finns quickly collapsed, becoming a part of the Soviet forward defense ring like their Baltic neighbors, Hoover's relief efforts would have disappeared. Pressure on the White House to do more for the beleaguered Finns increased with each military success. The Finnish army hung on until a peace treaty was signed on March 12, 1940. This remarkable military achievement gave Hoover his chance and Roosevelt his dilemma. The exploits of the Finnish army and the heroism of individual soldiers were headline news that retained the interest of the American public.[113] Hoover's enhanced political potential, based on continued Finnish survival, tempted White House staffers to attempt to "sabotage" him and the relief effort that he had founded.[114]

From the standpoint of Hoover and the leadership of the FRF, it was important to quickly absorb as many Finnish relief groups as possible and to discourage others from forming. The tactic of using the nation's newspapers as collection agencies and campaigning on a nationwide level was partially designed with that end in mind. In this way, the FRF could avoid having the Finnish relief effort move in the same direction as had Polish relief. Several hundred Polish groups were in existence by December 1939, and given their diversity of views, effective coordination proved impossible. Because of the FRF's organizational structure, most funds collected in the United States for relief went either to the Hoover group or to the Red Cross.

The only major exceptions were unsolicited monies, clothing, and food that donors sent to Finnish consulates in major American cities. In the first days of the war, some Americans, in their enthusiasm for the Finnish cause, spontaneously gave to any Finnish organization and especially to the consulates.[115] In New York, Finnish consul general T. O. Vahervouri acknowledged that forty-eight crates of clothing were ready for shipment to Finland and that $13,000 in cash had been given to the Finnish Red Cross and General Relief Fund. By the second week of December, the New York consulate had processed twenty-eight volunteers—ten nurses, one pilot, and seventeen able-bodied men—for service in the Finnish army.[116] As the number of volunteers increased, the Finnish government sent them in small groups to Finland on Swedish and Norwegian ships for training, or they were referred to other volunteer groups forming in the United States and Great Britain. The first fifty Finnish volunteers

American volunteers leave for Finland, December 9, 1939 (open source).

preparing to sail on the Swedish liner *Gripsholm* on December 9, 1939, brought with them eighty-six crates and trunks of clothing and blankets for the Finnish Red Cross. All were eligible to volunteer, as none were American citizens and so did not violate the US law that prohibits citizens from serving in foreign armies. Demonstrating their esprit de corps, they posed for group photographs dockside and aboard ship. One boisterously claimed that he aimed "to pull off Stalin's mustache."[117] Three days later, a larger group of three hundred volunteers set sail.

Both the FRF and the Roosevelt administration struggled with the problem of how to spend the money given for the Finns. Finland needed arms and ammunition much more urgently than it needed relief funds. Yet raising money to purchase war material for another nation at war was hardly neutral. Any purchase of war material for Finland risked the wrath of the anti-interventionists. Public opinion eventually substantially supported loaning money to the Finns in some indirect and convoluted fashion to buy arms, but that support did not come until the Winter War was all but over. A Gallup and Fortune Poll taken the day before Finland capitulated to Russia on March 11 asked the 58 percent who had responded yes to loaning money for nonmilitary supplies, "Would you approve or disapprove of letting Finland raise money for her war against Russia by selling bonds to Americans?"[118] Of this group, 58 percent voiced approval, while 28 percent disapproved.[119] Five weeks earlier, on February 6, 39 percent had approved of loans for arms and 61 percent had disapproved.

The question of selling arms to the Finns posed a different problem for Hoover than it did for Roosevelt: How could Hoover support military aid to Finland and not to Great Britain or France, even if it were of a "defensive character"? Writers like John Steinbeck and Theodore Dreiser went even further and asked, rhetorically, where Hoover was during the Spanish Civil War, when the aggressors were Fascist Italy and Nazi Germany.[120] Hoover, like Neville Chamberlain, whom he greatly admired, failed to comprehend the revolutionary, venal, and barbarous nature of European fascism.[121] He failed to perceive the vast difference between the Germany of World War I and the Germany of World War II. "Hoover saw no imminent danger to America from the Third Reich."[122] The "peacemonger," as Richard Norton Smith called Hoover, had to restrain himself for, in his judgment, the Soviet Union was the greater threat—the greater evil.[123] As Gary Dean Best observed, "It is apparent that those who advocated financial aid to victims of Soviet aggression, and not to victims of German aggression, were practicing a double standard while at the same time they criticized the administration for its double standard where German and Soviet aggression were concerned."[124] Hoover simply could not envision the Soviets as allies: indeed, one of the main reasons he had rejected support for the French was their flirtation with Marxism under Leon Blum.[125]

As neither Russia nor Finland had officially declared war, Roosevelt was able to use his discretion as to whether, under the provisions of the Neutrality Act, the conflict between these two nations constituted a "war." The president attempted to aid Finland without alienating Russia and without taking any political risks. He happily found no war in existence. In this way, the cash-and-carry requirement was avoided. Both countries could buy what they wanted, and both could obtain credit. Neither nation was in violation of the 1934 Johnson Act that prohibited nations in default from selling their bonds abroad, but the Soviet Union was held accountable for debts in America that were incurred by the previous tsarist government. Despite this seemingly favorable decision, Finland remained at a decided disadvantage, for it possessed only a small merchant marine and very few financial assets. The Finnish government needed credit and large loans, as Procopé estimated that the war would cost between $350,000 and $500,000 a day. Russia, one of the world's leading gold-producing countries, simply dug deeper, sending a shipment of bullion to San Francisco to adjust its balance of payments.[126] The Import-Export Bank's $10 million loan further crippled Finland by stipulating it was for civilian needs only. Strauss, however, had coached Procopé on how to get around this prohibition. As a result, the Finnish government, with the help of American citizens, undertook surreptitious, illegal activities to obtain military equipment. The Finnish American Trading Corporation, on the advice of Jessie Jones and with the assistance of Julius Klein, Hoover's past assistant secretary of commerce, Eric Warburg, the son of Strauss's business partner, and Strauss himself, bought $10 million worth of surplus commodities in the United States. This fulfilled the loan agreement, and the items were sold on the London exchange, where, by prearrangement, they were purchased by the Swedes. The Finns then ordered $10 million worth of armaments in America.[127] It is difficult to believe that Strauss had not discussed this strategy with Hoover, for the FRF's original concept was designed to provide indirect military aid by allowing the Finnish government to spend money earmarked for relief and food on armaments.[128]

The FRF and the Finnish American Trading Corporation provided military aid to Finland—one organization indirectly and the other directly. When word of the freewheeling deals being struck reached Rickard, he noted in his diary, "Among other matters at office gave session with Col. Krueger, who tells me of strange things in connection with the Finnish buying. (This has no connection with our show). It looks as if some queer actions were being taken in handling the U.S. Government ten-million-dollar loan to Finland."[129] That evening Rickard dined alone with Hoover in his Waldorf apartment and warned him against "having any participation in the activities of the Finnish Import and Export Co. [the Finnish American Trading Corporation], which Julius Klein has created to take care of purchases for the Finnish Gov't."[130] Rickard's warning that Hoover distance himself from the Finnish American Trading Corporation was well-meaning advice on which Hoover could not possibly act. Rickard's affirmative statement that there was no connection between the FRF and the Finnish American Trading Corporation was false, as the latter was Strauss's implementation of Jessie Jones's suggestion for how to obtain a loan for Finland, and it was in the Kuhn-Loeb office building. Also, Strauss had laid out the original plan to Hoover—having two separate organizations to deal with two aspects of the effort—when he asked him to head the Finnish relief drive. Both organizations were incorporated on the same day in Delaware by Donald Swatland, with Strauss as vice president of the FRF and Rickard as president. Rickard either lacked information or chose to utilize the fiction established by the Hoover people in case of such an eventuality. When the Roosevelt administration found out about the "commodities deal," Secretary Morgenthau approved, as did Jessie Jones, but Hull and Herbert Feis, with implied presidential approval, stipulated that any new loan to Finland would prohibit the Finns from selling commodities to a second or third party.[131]

Money, gifts of various kinds, and clothing donated to the consulates and the Finnish Red Cross were unencumbered by US neutrality restrictions, although it was illegal for foreign governments to solicit money and gifts to send directly to the Finnish army, as were donations from the American Red Cross. Direct contributions from private American citizens and access to the vast resources of the American Red Cross opened for Procopé an array of possibilities to creatively exploit on behalf of his country. Lists requesting emergency medical supplies sent to the American Red Cross by the Finns were padded, allowing the army to stock up on scarce commodities. The Red Cross added $125,000 to its initial $35,000 donation of late December, but an itemized Finnish shopping list totaling $250,000 quickly followed. Norman Davis complained to Hoover during a January 8 telephone conversation that some of the supplies requested by the Finns were "enough for ten years. So what I did," said Davis, "was buy them a complete outfit that would do them for 100,000 wounded soldiers for three months. This assumed that a third of their army will be wounded."[132] Davis did not believe that the Finns would suffer that many casualties, but inflating the numbers allowed them to build limited stockpiles and the Red Cross to do more behind the facade of "emergency aid."

Successful with their first two requests, the insatiable Finns submitted a third. This order topped the $2.5 million mark. Davis observed, "Of course what they are after is a complete medical supply such as an army has, which is not a Red Cross job."[133] The Red Cross did honor one small additional request by sending two American doctors who specialized in fighting typhus, though it was later discovered that no outbreak of typhus had occurred. Nothing stemmed the deluge of Finland's requests for assistance. One asked for sixty thousand blankets for people in hospitals, even though it was clear there were not that many hospitalized in the entire country. However, on only two occasions since 1824 had temperatures reached the lows recorded in the winter of 1939–1940, and the army in the field needed the blankets. The Red Cross did not give the Finns all that they asked for, but it shipped twenty-five thousand blankets, large quantities of which obviously reached soldiers at the front.[134]

Even more enterprising were Procopé's activities on behalf of the Finnish Red Cross. Hoover claimed he knew of $60,000 "they have had out of country," and he claimed that one Finnish relief group contributed $10,000.[135] Another relief group made a direct mail appeal specifically for the Finnish Red Cross. Davis finally called Procopé and pointed out that these activities were illegal and asked him to stop. Procopé claimed he was not aware of the illegality of the mailings and promised to close these fund-raising operations. How much "side money" the Finnish government was able to raise in America remains unknown. It is known that the Finns worked all manner of schemes in their effort to get as much money as possible. In the end, the illegal activities of the Finnish American Trading Corporation and of Procopé were turned against them, as Hoover, the Red Cross, and the State Department began to distance themselves from efforts to raise money and garner supplies. Hoover, while in Washington, DC, to testify before the House Foreign Affairs Committee, pleaded for money to aid Poland and talked with Secretary Hull, who confided, "They do not trust Finnish Ambassador."[136] Hoover concurred, thinking Procopé "a complete liar" who had not been "straight" with him.[137] Hull and Hoover's judgment of Procopé, however, was too harsh, given Finland's desperate situation and American parsimony. Roosevelt might have said of Procopé what Whig president Millard Fillmore said in 1851 of Lajos Kossuth, the Hungarian revolutionary who was welcomed as a hero and used the opportunity to sell bonds to achieve Hungarian independence. Per Fillmore, Kossuth should receive "sympathy, personal respect and kindness, but no departure of our established policy."[138]

A part of Hull's complaint was that the American Red Cross was far more vulnerable to Finnish "raiding" than was the FRF, which had taken organizational steps to maintain tight control through centralization. In Helsinki, an official four-member Finnish committee (Suomen Huolto) was formed on December 27, headed by former prime minister Aimo K. Cajander, who had stepped down from office less than three weeks before. At all times, an American representative served on this committee, acted as a liaison between Finland and the FRF in New York, and helped the Finnish committee with purchasing relief supplies in the United States and throughout the world.[139] The first American to serve was the experienced F. Dorsey Stephens, who came to Finland from Lithuania in January 1940. He was followed by W. Hallam Tuck, who was eventually replaced by another very successful relief coordinator, Robert Van Wyck Maverick.[140] Money collected in the United States was sent to the Cajander Committee, as Suomen Huolto was usually called, and this committee decided what to order, how much, and from where. As other relief organizations came into being, and as requests for aid came to the Hoover Committee from outside the United States, some confusion at first occurred, but the FRF steered all requests for aid back to the Cajander Committee in Helsinki.[141] This neat organizational arrangement to some degree sheltered the FRF from domestic politics, introduced control and accountability, generally outflanked Finnish attempts at independent procurement, and allowed the American FRF operation to concentrate on its main function: raising money. In mid-January, the American Red Cross decided that it also would work exclusively through the Cajander Committee.[142]

The Roosevelt administration had not done much for Finland aside from making a few favorable diplomatic moves, the $10 million loan made by the RFC, and the half million dollars in aid provided by the Red Cross. In the fall of 1939, the Red Cross had combined a membership drive and fund-raising campaign that produced $4 million, especially targeted for emergency war relief, out of a total fund that exceeded $18 million.[143] On January 8, Davis asked Hoover, "Is your money coming in pretty well?" Hoover responded, "Very well," although this was a gross exaggeration. Davis said, "That is good. I want to get some of it."[144] Later in the same conversation, Hoover admitted that the FRF financial picture was not so rosy, carping, "We have 600,000 women and children now on rations ... and it is just keeping me humping."[145] If the Red Cross had a war chest for relief of over $4 million, why ask Hoover for money? After granting the half million dollars in emergency aid to the Finns, the Red Cross hoped to replace the money through contributions, but by early January donations for Finnish relief had slowed to a trickle. The Red Cross did not want to spend additional funds for Finnish relief that would be difficult (if not impossible) to replace, and it did not want to render any aid not of an emergency nature. The Red Cross, therefore, held the $4 million raised in the fall of 1939 in reserve, anticipating renewed warfare on the western front. From Washington, the Roosevelt administration had always viewed the Finnish crisis through the lens of France and Great Britain's war with Germany. Davis, demonstrating real chutzpah, asked Hoover for money to support ongoing aid to Finland without taxing Red Cross funds or violating Red Cross policy.[146]

Within these limits, however, the Roosevelt administration was instrumental in obtaining small quantities of arms for the Finns. Of special importance were a few "almost-modern" fighter planes manufactured by the Brewster Corporation: the highly maneuverable little B-239 "Buffalo."[147] The US Navy had ordered fifty-four Brewsters in 1938, and nine had been assigned to a squadron operating off the USS *Saratoga*. In December 1939, Roosevelt had forty-four of these brand-new fighters declared surplus. The planes were paid for with an Import-Export Bank commodities loan converted into cash in London.[148] Shipped to Sweden, the fighters were assembled by Norwegian mechanics and Brewster Corporation technical representatives and then flown to forward areas by Finnish pilots.[149] Though the "Buffaloes" arrived several weeks after the end of the Winter War, ironically they played a role in the "Continuation War," which Finland fought alongside Germany against the United States' new ally, Soviet Russia. Also in March 1940, after the cessation of hostilities, the Finnish government ordered thirty-two eight-inch howitzers and two hundred 75mm field guns.[150] During the Winter War itself, the Finns, on December 14, bought sixty thousand gas masks; on February 21, an order was placed for sixty million cartridges, 176 machine guns, and spare parts for the Brewster "Buffalos."[151]

It is probable that only the gas masks arrived in Finland before war's end.

10

Finnomania: A Cause Célèbre

The new Hoover accepts a contribution from Popeye to the Finnish Relief Fund (courtesy of HHPLM).

IN THE WEEKS JUST BEFORE CHRISTMAS 1939, AS WAR RAGED ON THREE fronts in Finland, Herbert Hoover generated a flurry of activity in his effort to put together a West Coast branch of the Finnish Relief Fund (FRF). In Pasadena for a meeting of the trustees of the Huntington Library and

Art Gallery, on Friday, December 8, he publicly announced the formation of a Finnish Relief Committee in the City of Angels.[1] The response to his suggestion that newspapers collect donations for the Finns was enthusiastically embraced by the fourth estate, which produced an avalanche of favorable publicity. Hoover was delighted—this was exactly what he wanted. Overnight, Finnish relief had become a cause célèbre. Volunteers on both coasts rushed to Finland's cause and contributions began to pour in.[2] Given Hoover's disappointment in raising large amounts of money for Polish relief from a narrow base, he determined that a huge, splashy, star-studded, Hollywood-style campaign calculated to "sweep America off its feet" was the solution to raising big money fast. One of the first large contributions, vindicating his judgment, came directly to the Hoover home in Palo Alto from Sonja Henie, Norwegian champion skater and film star, who donated $1,000.[3] Fund-raising events proliferated on West Coast social calendars after Hoover lined up classical conductor Werner Janssen, who agreed to stage a Los Angeles concert on December 29 that featured the world-renowned Finnish composer Jean Sibelius, who had been sent to America to do what he could for his country. The young conductor telephoned the great composer, inviting him to stay with him in his home.[4]

San Franciscans, not to be outdone by their Los Angeles rivals, planned a Finnish relief ball for that same Monday evening, December 29, and put eight thousand tickets on sale. Working intently over the weekend, Hoover, ably assisted by his minutemen of relief, created a diverse organization that included a women's division, a youth division, a labor division, a sports committee under pugilist Gene Tunney, an entertainment division headed by Helen Hayes, and even an authors' division chaired by writer Fannie Hurst.[5] Movie mogul Merian Cooper used his connections to round up some of Hollywood's most glamorous stars, and James Selvage, Hoover's publicity man back in New York, was successful in recruiting leading actors and actresses from Broadway to the Finnish cause.

On December 11, Hoover called for a nationwide Finland Day on the following Sunday, December 17, and asked churches, newspapers, and state and city officials to use that day to inform their fellow Americans of

Finland's plight and to collect money. Hoover telegraphed all forty-eight governors and the mayors of the country's bigger cities, asking them to make this proclamation.[6] The governors' and mayors' acceptances began to come in, but some key invitees did not respond. Only then did Hoover discover that certain people in Washington disapproved of his efforts on behalf of Finnish relief. The Hoover-Roosevelt antagonism over relief had not abated, but from Hoover's perspective, "the smearing" that had dogged him since 1932 had begun again.[7]

Undeterred, that evening Hoover spoke by telephone to "a mass meeting at Manhattan Center called by the American Committee to Aid Finland."[8] A who's who of speakers at the event included Mayor Fiorello La Guardia, Representatives Bruce Barton and Emanuel Celler, and movie star Joan Bennett; from the American Civil Liberties Union came Roger Baldwin; from the Union Theological Seminary, Dr. Reinhold Niebuhr; from the National Association for the Advancement of Colored People, William Pickens. The American Committee to Aid Finland may have set a record for a relief organization's shortest existence. After listening to Hoover's remarks, the fifteen hundred in attendance agreed that money raised would go to Hoover's Finnish Relief Fund. Baldwin, chairing the event, announced, "The organization will not go on. This is the first, last, and only meeting."[9]

While Hoover orchestrated events from California, in New York the newly formed relief committee moved into emergency office space in the Belgian American Educational Foundation in the Greybar Building on 420 Lexington Avenue and immediately went to work. In need of additional space, the burgeoning relief effort quickly expanded by taking over the entire fourth floor, which swarmed with "myriads of clerks."[10] Underneath the lettering "Belgian American Educational Foundation" on the door of Room 2325, a painter carefully stenciled Finnish Relief Fund, Inc.[11] Inside, Raymond Sawtelle was discussing plans for the drive when both were interrupted by an office boy, who said, "There's a man outside who wants to give some money."[12] Franklin Brown of Dobbs Ferry, New York, handed Sawtelle a check for $25 and received in return receipt no. 1. Brown said he thought his donation was "the best way to discourage people and those countries who think that their might makes them incontestably right."[13] Due to donors like Brown, the FRF became a wellspring of grassroots support that grew rapidly, but later that day the formal opening of the headquarters occurred when the famous mapmaker Otto Lindberg posed for photographers as he handed Sawtelle, FRF treasurer, a donation. From the first day the pace was frenetic and the hours extremely long. Edgar Rickard, whose own workload was doubled, described the daily routine: "Some of the staff work until 3 A.M. clearing correspondence, as typical of all Hoover organizations everyone keen to do a good clean job and not let any work hangover."[14] A few days later, Rickard complained, "Have always considered Saturday morning at the office a particular personal privilege time to clear up various somewhat secondary matters, but not so in these days of Finnish relief, as no let up at all, including staff luncheon."[15]

Before honoring Hoover's request to declare Sunday, December 17, as Finland Day or signing on with the FRF, several Democratic governors checked with the White House. The advice given was not to cooperate with the Hoover group, although at least four of the governors ignored the White House suggestion and supported the relief drive.[16] Between December 12 and 14, columnists like Raymond Clapper and Drew Pearson and reporters like Doris Fleeson and Arthur Krock broke stories emanating from the White House concerning Hoover and the FRF.[17] One story asserted that Hoover had contacted Hjalmar Procopé and pushed the embarrassed Finnish minister into accepting his help. The accusation that received the most press was that Hoover had "snubbed" FDR in September 1939 by turning down the directorship of a war emergency relief post and that, additionally, Hoover had demanded that Norman Davis be fired as director of the American Red Cross. The September encounters that the two rivals had carefully kept from the press had been leaked. The sources had distorted what had occurred to imply that the Red Cross was providing all the aid necessary for Finnish war victims and that Hoover, unable to cooperate or to stand aside, saw his chance to upstage the Red Cross and the administration and use the popularity of Finland's cause to launch a presidential campaign. With the leak, the Hoover-Roosevelt disagreements over relief would be aired in public.

Hoover did not immediately respond to these stories. He had stayed in California not only to organize the West Coast branch of the FRF but also to allow time for the relief movement to gather momentum. As the publicity campaign crested, Hoover flew from California to New York, like an angel of mercy, to take over the directorship of the FRF. On his arrival at the newly opened New York Municipal Airport–La Guardia Field, Hoover's official press release played up the supposed drama of the event: "Mr. Hoover arrived at 9:10 last night from his home in Palo Alto, California to take personal charge of the money and to plan how the funds shall be spent in Finland. Accompanying him on the Transcontinental and Western Airlines plane *Sky Century* was Mayor La Guardia, who joined the former President in Chicago to discuss the fund campaign."[18] Reporters who met the plane deluged Hoover with questions, not about his plans for the FRF, but rather about the rift with Davis and the Red Cross. Although his arrival amid a swirl of controversy somewhat diminished the planned effect of Hoover's "entrance," he was quick to counterattack. He insisted, "There is no friction between the two bodies. Anybody who says there is, is only trying to make trouble."[19] The former president and the mayor had little time for the press, as they were whisked across town to Madison Square Garden to speak to a rally sponsored by the American Jewish Congress and Jewish Labor Committee.

The large crowd, judged to be twenty thousand, gathered to protest the treatment of Jews by Nazi Germany, to show support for Finland, and to rally "the moral forces of the world against Hitlerism and Stalinism."[20] Unsure whether he could wind up his activities in California to arrive in New York in time to speak, Hoover had prereleased a copy of his remarks, but it did not dampen his listeners' enthusiasm, who cheered his castigation of Hitler and Stalin. The "bestialities visited upon the people of Jewish faith" were an outrage, as was the brutal attack on Finland, "and today, hundreds of thousands of Catholics and Protestants as well as Jews are homeless and helpless before the forces of unbridled evil. Happily," he noted, "we are not yet so accustomed to the sight of blood or the cries of the defenseless that our sense of justice has been dulled or the well-spring of our pity run dry. I fervently hope an all-wise Providence will speed the day when these dreadful scenes may be removed from the world."[21] La

Guardia and Hoover were followed by a bevy of speakers that included Alf Landon from Topeka, Kansas, and prominent leaders in the Jewish community, like Dr. Stephen S. Wise, president of the American Jewish Congress, and William L. Green, president of the American Federation of Labor (AFL). Other speakers and celebrities in attendance included New York mayor La Guardia, New York congressmen Bruce Barton and Emanuel Celler, movie actress Joan Bennett, Roger Baldwin of the American Civil Liberties Union, and Reinhold Niebuhr of the Union Theological Seminary.[22] The audience approved a resolution affirming American neutrality and supported Franklin Roosevelt's moral embargo of the Soviet Union but asked the president to formally condemn the aggressions of the Germans and Soviets and to aid in every way the Jews of Poland and the people of Finland. The sponsors announced that money raised that evening, if sufficient, would be shared with Hoover's Finnish Relief Fund. The heavy police presence proved unnecessary, as Communist Party members, who supported Stalin's line on the war in Finland, did not show up to protest.[23] The rally benefited Hoover, as he had shored up Jewish support for the Commission for Polish Relief (CPR) and for the FRF. Perhaps of greater importance was the possibility that Hoover would receive support for the FRF from organized labor—a bipartisan coalition of frenemies was brewing in support of European relief. On December 17, Wise forwarded a check for $500, Hoover's share of the donations from the rally.[24]

The question of whether Hoover had forced himself on the Finnish government or whether it had asked for his help needed to be answered. Acting as a fire brigade, Lewis Strauss and his partner Eric Warburg resolved it rapidly. Warburg was already deeply involved in aiding Finland, as he had helped to arrange the commodities exchange deal in London. He cabled Risto Ryti, prime minister of Finland, on December 13, requesting that Ryti send an urgent cable to Hoover confirming the Finnish request for aid. Warburg, demonstrating chutzpah, went so far as to write the essential sections of the prime minister's statement: "Would appreciate urgent cable message from you to hotel waldorf astoria new york about as follows quote people of Finland rejoice that our friend of so many years is again heading a movement for our distressed people unquote . . . if you could add any words as to needs it would be helpful here regards."[25] On the following morning, December 14, Hoover had in his hands an official confirmation of Finnish support for and approval of the FRF in time for the opening of his New York press conference. The heart of the telegram, with the influence of Eric Warburg clearly present, read, "people of Finland rejoice very much that you, Mr. President, known by people of Finland as their cordial friend since decennaries, is again heading a movement for our distressed people."[26] The message, as requested, went on to stress an urgent need. The people of Finland needed every material and moral assistance that possibly could be given.[27]

The Hoover-Roosevelt-Davis controversy continued to rage in the columns and opinion pages of America's newspapers. Doris Fleeson reported, "The story of the great refusal was told to this correspondent last night [December 14] by an unimpeachable source."[28] "Unimpeachable" source or not, the specific charge of Hoover's refusal leveled by the White House proved easy to refute and lent credit to Hoover's denial, providing him with a club to counter other White House accusations. The most difficult charge to defend was that Hoover's real interest in the relief campaign was the establishment of a base for another presidential run—especially since the charge was partially true. The Roosevelt administration's attempt to "smoke out" Hoover the candidate and impugn his motives was well timed and intended to inflict maximum damage. Through it all, the former president countered the charges, but he was also busy preparing for a second mass rally planned for December 20 at Madison Square Garden. Helen Hayes and Gladys Swarthout arrived at the FRF headquarters for publicity pictures. Hayes, in what looked like the office side room, did several different poses holding a "Let's Help Finland" poster.

But the *St. Louis Post-Dispatch* continued to question Hoover's motives in a December 20 editorial that read in part, "Mr. Hoover's emotional appeals on behalf of Finland do not ring true. They sound dangerously like presidential politics. In 1932, Mr. Hoover accused Mr. Roosevelt of playing politics with human misery. If he is not careful, someone is going to make the same accusation against him."[29] The White House, gratified that this particular story had not died, revealed the level of frustration experienced by Roosevelt and his inner circle in their effort to contain

Hollywood movie star Helen Hayes (courtesy of FRF Records, Hoover Institution Library and Archives).

Hoover by their reaction to the editorial. Across the top of the *Post-Dispatch*, a White House staffer wrote for FDR to see, "Ain't this a sock in the puss for Herbie the Hooter."[30]

The *Post-Dispatch*, in its comments about Hoover, all but discovered that relief and politics were inseparable. Regardless of any political dimensions in Hoover's relief activities, his emotional appeal to aid Finland was valid, as the country was desperately in need of military equipment and civilian relief. Russian bombers displaced thousands, destroying their homes and cities, and the Finnish government had evacuated tens of thousands more from the combat zones along the Finno-Russian border.[31] As a precaution, young children and the old were evacuated in early November, but when the war began, the evacuations dramatically increased. One of the last to leave the Karelian Isthmus was fourteen-year-old Lempi Kähönen and her family, who lived a few miles behind the Mannerheim Line. Evacuated shortly after Christmas, she recalled in her memoir, *Sisu*

Mother, "It had snowed a little during the day and the temperature was twenty degrees. About seven in the evening, a breathless messenger arrived at the house. 'You have to leave now and be on your way as soon as possible. You can take your livestock with you. They are to be driven to the railroad station.' That was seven kilometers away."[32] As dawn broke, the train was fully loaded, with no room for the horses or men, who were sent back to their villages. The train, packed with women, children, and cows, set off for an unknown destination somewhere in western Finland. On arrival, they and thousands like them needed everything. Martha Gellhorn wrote admiringly of the Lotta Svard, "an organization of 200,000 women from all over Finland," formed in 1918 during Finland's war of independence from the Soviets, which assisted and cared for the evacuees.[33] She wrote for her huge *Collier's* audience, "They are firemen; they collect the food and clothing for the homeless, they manage the mail service of the army in the field; they cook and sew for the soldiers at the front and are Red Cross nurses; and throughout the country they stand watches in the observation posts and give air-raid warnings."[34]

Refugees leave Karelia, late March 1940; note that the man in the front of the sled is rubbing snow on the child's nose to prevent frostbite (open source).

Hoover, without real evidence, attributed the leaks and attacks to Norman Davis. Furious, he discussed how to counter this "sock in the puss" with Rickard, Strauss, Selvage, and Perrin Galpin, Hoover proteges and FRF staffers, on the eve of his arrival in New York. As an agreement with Davis and the Red Cross had already been reached on December 7, Hoover observed that he was "beginning to be suspicious that Norman [was] not playing the game."[35] The next day, December 14, at a press conference, Hoover brought with him the cable from Prime Minister Ryti and a $5,000 check from Greta Garbo. Again, asked about trouble with the Red Cross, he lashed out, "There is not a word of truth in the whole story."[36] Then pounding on the desk, he stressed, "Let's make one thing clear. It's a great pity that people start out to poison the wells of human charity. That sort of stuff is an injury to the Finnish people. It is an injury to the American Red Cross. It doesn't hurt me."[37] Hoover went on to reiterate that the FRF and Red Cross missions were different, and he described Davis as a "very able citizen, and no one, so far as I know, has suggested that he be deposed. I would be the first to oppose it."[38]

In Washington, DC, reporters badgered Stephen Early, the president's press secretary, for more information. Shortly after the Hoover press conference, Early attempted to explain Roosevelt's part in the September effort to persuade Hoover to accept a position in charge of European relief. As Davis did not report back to the president, explained the press secretary, the president was forced to conclude that Hoover was uninterested in his offer.[39] Actually, Davis had contacted Roosevelt, told him that Hoover was coming for the Red Cross meeting in Washington, and requested an appointment to convey the details of his earlier meeting with the former president. When Davis met with Roosevelt, he discouraged the president from pursuing the idea of bringing Hoover into the administration, although another source, likely Bernard Baruch, informed Roosevelt that Hoover's plan was excellent and that he would put relief before politics.[40] In any event, a straightforward offer was never made.

Lawrence Richey, Hoover's personal secretary, responded at once to Early's version of these events, touching off a two-day "battle of the secretaries."[41] Richey countered that Hoover had recommended the

Red Cross take charge of and greatly expand general relief and that the scheme to send refugees to Central Africa—a plan that the White House helped to develop—had been torpedoed by the outbreak of war, not by a Hoover pullout.[42] The fact that Hoover spurned the Roosevelt "feeler" because the Red Cross refused to adopt his relief policies was not mentioned. The president and ex-president continued their antagonism by trading half-truths. Hoover and his associates blamed the ruckus on Norman Davis, but Davis released a statement that squared with Hoover's correspondence in September 1939 and with his letters to Hoover in December. If Davis was attempting to discredit the FRF or to expand the role of the Red Cross, he was obviously being pushed by the White House. Letters from Democratic officials inquiring whether to support Finland Day were passed to Davis with the obvious implication they might be of use in his disputes with Hoover.[43] John Callan O'Laughlin, editor of the *Army-Navy Times*, whose lengthy weekly reports to Hoover were quite sound, explained, "To aid the Democratic candidate, whomever he may be, the President is leading the smear of Republican possibilities. This will account to you for the statements of Early and Davis regarding your Finnish relief activity."[44] For O'Laughlin, presidential politics was at the bottom of it all. On Friday, December 15, at another late-night dinner at the Waldorf, Rickard, Richey, and Hoover decided to call up the columnists who broke the story and "tell them Davis had not been playing ball."[45] To squelch the administration's accusations, Hoover sent Richey to Washington to release his correspondence with Davis. To Rickard, he affirmed his commitment "to make a big drive for funds and squarely face Red Cross opposition."[46] Hoover and Davis talked by telephone on Saturday morning, and Hoover recorded the conversation. Rickard was led to claim that the transcript "shows Norman Davis has not been quite square...which surprises me, but not Lewis Strauss, who has suspected him all along as his record with bankers is bad."[47]

The FRF organizers, including Hoover, remained convinced that Davis was the source of journalists' stories. This allegation was difficult to prove, though the result for Davis was that both Hoover and FDR were upset with the longtime diplomat. Harold Ickes observed,

Herbert Hoover has been making quite a play of marshalling relief for Finland and, of course, the newspapers have all fallen for it. The President remarked at Cabinet that Norman Davis had let Hoover get away with this. Norman Davis is president of the Red Cross, and the Red Cross has been supplying all of the civilian needs in Finland since the invasion of that country by Russia. Chatfield-Taylor was in Poland when the war broke out in Finland, and he flew at once to the latter country and has been there ever since as the representative of the Red Cross. Nevertheless, Hoover is getting all the headlines on Finnish relief. Naturally the Administration does not like this, but it has not been able to counter-act so far. The President said that what Norman Davis needed was a good publicity man and that he was trying to find one for him.[48]

By December 18, Davis's troubles were further compounded, as Rickard, describing his status in the Hoover camp and with the Community Chest, recorded, "Important meeting with H.H., George Vincent, Gerard Swope, Allan Burns to discuss relations with Red Cross and Community Chest, all sore at Norman Davis."[49]

Over the weekend, the national media came to the rescue of Hoover and the FRF.[50] Typical was the response from *New York Sun* columnist Dave Boone: "The 1939 pettiness prize goes to the folks who are smearing Herbert Hoover's part in the relief drive to aid Finland. It's a new low even in the political arena. Hoover was a big name in international charities before his critics were even moderately well-known. . . . [I]f there's anything smaller than heaving rocks into a relief drive, you name it."[51] Damage to the FRF was minimal; the Democrats had failed in their effort to discredit Hoover and force him to announce his presidential ambitions.[52]

Hoover's campaign for the nomination remained a hushed affair, and he stuck to his strategy of increasing his popularity through "good works" and of keeping as many Republican candidates in the race as possible. Strauss complied, asking influential wealthy Republicans to support Hoover and at the same time to help others pursue the party's presidential nomination.[53] When Senator Arthur Vandenberg of Michigan faltered in Wisconsin, Hoover encouraged him to stay in the race.[54] In Ohio many Republicans thought Hoover had suggested to John Bricker, the governor, that he become a vice presidential candidate and that the two might have made some kind of political agreement.[55] If a large number of Republican candidates stayed in the field, no one would gather enough delegate strength to either build momentum or control the convention. When Frank Gannett, the newspaper magnate from Buffalo, New York, sought advice on how to set up a presidential campaign, Hoover asked Rickard to help him. The Gannett campaign soon suffered a blow when in January William Borah died, as "the publisher was reported to have expected vigorous support from the Idaho Senator for his campaign."[56] "American has lost a real man," said Gannett. "I had the honor of his friendship and confidence, and I shall treasure it a priceless memory."[57] The anti-interventionists suffered a blow as well, as Borah was a leading voice determined to deter Roosevelt and keep America out of war.

Hoover believed that people in need of relief should be helped as soon as possible; this view partially accounts for his torrid pace, although he was also motivated by his political ambition and competition and controversies with the American Red Cross. He loved the excitement and drama of a big organizational push and the sense of accomplishment that came with successfully tackling a tough job, something that began with him during his years in China. The big Madison Square Garden rally on December 20 drew twenty thousand people on a cold rainy night to cheer the Finns. Opera singer and stage and film star Gladys Swarthout sang the national anthem, followed by speeches from politicians, labor leaders, and journalists. Many in the audience must have marveled to see such a strange collection of bedfellows. Hoover, Dorothy Thompson, B. K. Wheeler, and Matt Woll from the AFL came together on the same platform for Finnish relief. Hoover warmed the hearts of all, holding a check for $6 sent by the *Gallup* (New Mexico) *Independent*, of which $1, the editor wrote, "was contributed in pennies by the children of Finnish-American miners in the section."[58] Hoover concluded, "Every decent person in the world is praying to God tonight that these brave people shall yet be saved from this tide. And the world today witnesses one of these heroic stands for freedom of men that comes but a few times in the centuries. It is a star illuminating the No-Man's-Land of Civilization. Its glow will light the minds of men and give hope to liberty for centuries to come."[59] With the holidays underway, one of the year's last events was the *New York Daily Mirror*'s sponsorship of a preview of the Folies Bergère for the Finnish war victims.[60] The first months of the New Year were packed with events for Finnish relief. Rickard summed up the year in his diary on New Year's Eve, revealing much about the man with whom he had worked so closely for so long:

> Until the Finnish Relief was started H.H. has been most restless. The Finnish Relief Fund gave him an outlet for his great administrative ability and untiring energy and there is no question he ended the year in far better spirits and in good health and he meets his audiences and his contacts cheerfully and with enormous confidence. He is aware that he has neglected everything in his desire to get the attention of the American public, and his investments have suffered because he will not delegate authority to me or to his boys [sons] to take action on the market when there seems to be an opportunity.[61]

It was Finnish military success, heavily reported in newspapers and magazines and on the nation's airwaves, that drove the success of the FRF. Almost miraculously, the Finnish army held the Mannerheim Line on the Karelian Isthmus, the decisive front and the key to Finnish success, as well as the lightly defended Far North near Petsamo. At the waist of Finland, where the Soviets launched a two-pronged attack designed to divide the country, the Finns inflicted a series of startling reversals on the Red Army. Near Suomussalmi, between December 27 and 29, the Finns counterattacked and destroyed the Soviet 163rd Rifle Division composed of about fourteen thousand men. The battle lasting over two weeks left five thousand Russian dead on the battlefield. The temperature continued to plunge, hovering around forty degrees below zero in the first week of the new year. Finnish units, flush with victory at Suomussalmi, now turned to the Soviet 44th Division, a first-line unit largely composed of Ukrainians strung out on the Raate Road. The Finns, chopping the column into segments like cordwood (*Motti* tactics), systematically destroyed the division.

Red Army soldiers "poorly equipped for arctic combat . . . had not been trained to fight in deep snow."[62] Strung out in columns, road bound, the Finns in the surrounding woods ensured they could not light fires for warmth or to cook without being shot. Tanks struggling or unable to maneuver were vulnerable to a homemade weapon made world famous by the Finns. Bottles, usually beer, schnapps, or vodka, filled with kerosene or gasoline had a rag or even a newspaper stuffed in the neck to act as a wick. Christened "Molotov cocktails," mocking the Soviet foreign minister, these poor man's antitank weapons wielded by individual soldiers set Russian track vehicles and trucks ablaze.

Journalists raced to send their stories of these stunning military successes, which in turn triggered a second, larger wave of reporters who rushed to Finland to witness David bringing down the stumbling colossus. But contrary to expectations, there was little to report directly because the Finns refused to allow journalists to visit an active front and because of a policy of strict censorship. All were housed in the "Germanic Black Forest" atmosphere of Helsinki's Kamp Hotel, described by journalist Edward Ward as follows:

> Newspaper men, agency men, photographers, representatives of newsreels throng its corridors and rooms at all hours of the day and night. You hear I don't know how many different languages, and how on earth the staff and particularly the telephone girls manage to cope with the situation is more than I can understand. A big room on the first floor is set aside as a Press Room, which is used as a sort of common-room by Englishmen, Frenchmen, Belgians, Americans, Scandinavians, oh, and almost any other nationality you like to think of, who meet . . . there, particularly every evening to receive the official communiques.[63]

Helsinki was not Bucharest. No fast express trains whisked the rich and famous to the Finnish capital. Air raid warnings and the blackout dampened the experience. The Finns, however, despite their reputation for living in a cold, grey city, were proud of their modern style of architecture and had been counting on showing Finland to the world in the coming Summer Olympics. The award-winning Finnish Pavilion at the New York World's Fair showcased the designs of Alvar Aalto and was festooned with an array of posters touting Finland's lakes and forests. Inside, the staff, often dressed in Finnish costumes, was hard at work booking travel packages for the coming summer events. Finland expected a throng of visitors, but the war would likely force the Olympic Committee to move the event to another city or cancel.[64] The magnificent stadium begun in 1934 had been completed a year earlier. The fine pieces of Finnish architecture were not accessible, and the journalists were largely confined to the Kamp, becoming bored with keeping each other company. Due to these circumstances, much of the information written about the Winter War was inaccurate, fantastic, exaggerated, and repetitive. Despite journalistic difficulties, some of the reportage was well written and exciting, of course becoming grist for the mill of Hoover's Finnish relief efforts and those of the American Red Cross.[65] By mid-December, Martha Gellhorn was fed up, the hotel was running out of liquor, and there was no way to get to the front. Fuel was also running low, and the hotel was always cold. Her early human-interest stories, especially on Finland's first days of war, followed by a run of illustrated articles that appeared regularly in *Collier's*, were keenly followed by a huge reading audience.[66] Frank Hayne, an American military attaché, "noticed a lovely blonde sitting quietly at a corner table in the Kamp restaurant."[67] He walked to her table, they introduced themselves, and he asked whether she would like to be evacuated on a flight out. Gellhorn's loud response was an immediate "Christ, yes," as she jumped up. Hayne told her to go pack. "She was back in five minutes carrying only her pajamas and whiskey bottle."[68] Gellhorn's time in Finland was over. She considered herself a war correspondent, and there was nothing more to do.

In America, while waiting on Hitler, the public thrilled to Finnish success and was captivated by soldiers in their white capes. These ghost soldiers, who invisibly skimmed across the snow-covered ground and across frozen lakes in temperatures forty degrees below zero, brought death to the trapped Ivans hunkered down, cold and hungry. Interviews with pathetic, half-starved captured Russian soldiers and letters home found by Finns on the dead helped to build the myth of the war. Individual Finnish soldiers and valiant nurses were lionized; odes were penned to Finnish bravery and patriotism. The Czechs did not fight, and the Poles, who valiantly defended Warsaw, were defeated, but David, defeating the Red Goliath, captured the American imagination, touching off Finnomania.

In Great Britain, stories by Virginia Cowles in the Sunday *London Times* and later the BBC broadcasts by Edward Ward were popular, while in the United States the enterprising British reporter Geoffrey Cox, determined to escape the claustrophobic Kamp Hotel, partnered with Barbara Alving, who wrote for the Swedish newspaper *Dagens Nyheter*.[69] Credentialed by the Finnish Foreign Office, the two journalists, without permission from the press office, "got aboard the train the next Sunday morning and headed north," enabling them to end up on the Lapland front to report the Finnish success in blunting the Russian effort to cut across the narrow neck of Finland and reach the Swedish border, the Battle of Pelkosenniemi.[70] Cox's reporting, some of the best from the Winter War, was available a year later in his book *The Red Army Moves*. A great impact was made on the US public by a fine piece done by W. L. White (son of William Allen White) on a live CBS report from Helsinki, the day after Christmas. Describing a bomb raid and artillery barrage on a city somewhere in Finland (the exact location was censored), White graphically told of a working-class soldier, home from the front for only three hours on Christmas Day, having coffee with his wife and aged mother when their small wooden home took a direct hit. White added that the neighborhood was much like the one below the tracks in the second ward in Emporia, Kansas, where he "used to carry papers."[71] He continued,

> The bomb tore off his mother's arms setting fire to the house. They had taken her to the hospital when we got there the poor soldier and his wife were trying to save from the flames their little store of furniture, carrying out a Singer sewing machine with the family album on top of it. And we saw a child's new Christmas doll lying half crushed under the heel of a fireman as he sprayed a hose on the ruins of another little cottage. The bombing continued all day and that night two more houses burned. A loud bomb, which you may have heard, landed just outside the studio in the middle of my Christmas afternoon broadcast and I am

glad to be back in Helsinki where there are still hot baths and still fewer bombs and from where I can bring you a more general and less personal picture of this war. Returning you now to Columbia in New York, it was a lively Christmas.[72]

This broadcast and the one that preceded it touched Americans deeply. In the large holiday audience that evening was Robert Sherwood, who was so moved by White's story that he undertook to write a play based on the Winter War. The result, *There Shall Be No Night*, was produced on Broadway. Sherwood contributed the royalties from the play to the FRF—a donation of almost $2,000—and collected a Pulitzer Prize for himself.[73] One of the amazing stories, which remained out of reach of the horde of journalists and would only emerge in the aftermath, was that of sniper Simo Häyhä, whose accomplishments with his iron-sight rifle made him a legend. Often working alone and at night, Häyhä, in just under one hundred days, killed 542 Russian soldiers, a world record that still stands today. "On December 21, 1939, Simo shot what would prove to be his highest daily tally of kills on record—25 confirmed kills."[74] Near war's end on March 6, Häyhä was shot in the face by a Russian sniper. He survived, though maimed, and lived a long and honored life, passing away at age ninety-seven.

Buoyed by Finnish military success and the attendant international media coverage, Hoover began the new year with renewed commitment, and in January and February 1940 he went all out to bring success to the faltering Finnish relief drive. Journalists took note of the ex-president's revitalized spirits. Artist and writer S. J. Woolf remarked that when he had met Hoover, first at a portrait and interview session when he was secretary of commerce and again later when he was president, he had found him "cold and forbidding. His handshake was flaccid, and he had an annoying habit of avoiding the eyes of the person with whom he was speaking. He displayed little humor and at all times seemed ill at ease. Although he was always courteous, he wore an armor of remoteness that nothing apparently could penetrate. It was difficult to imagine him as a humanitarian."[75]

When Woolf arrived at the headquarters of the FRF in January 1940, he was surprised to find "a kindly, beneficent man who [spoke] with horror of the hardships of war; whose voice trembled as he talked of the suffering of humanity, and whose eyes, although almost lost under their heavy lids, looked straight at the listener."[76] Tom Wolf, a National Education Association correspondent, also noted the Hoover transformation: "In 1932 Herbert Clark Hoover . . . was a pale, tired, oldish man with an austere aloofness—a lukewarm handshake, an indefinite gaze, and an almost dour expression. Today this same Herbert Hoover . . . flashes a warm smile on a positively ruddy face. He peers straight into your eyes as he warmly pumps your hand. He looks easily 10 years younger."[77]

Hendrik Willem Van Loon, a well-known Dutch American writer who helped organize the Finnish relief rally in Madison Square Garden on December 20 and who was a great admirer of Roosevelt, was consternated to find himself on a program with Hoover, a man he had castigated when he was president. Despite his strong antipathy for Hoover, Van Loon stuck with the FRF, and he, too, came to see a marked change. "H.H. is so completely different from the man we remember as the rather sour-pussy President. . . . [C]onsidering the foul smearing he suffered as Great White Father, it is surprising to see such an agreeable and cheerful personage."[78]

Indicative of the change was the comic character Popeye, who, "blow me down," turned out for Finnish relief. Right before Popeye went into Hoover's office for photos, Selvage, all too aware of the difficulties of getting an appealing photo of his boss, said, "Now look. Get the Chief in a good humor. Make him laugh. He said, 'What would he say if I stuck out my hand and said, 'Hi y'a, Herbert?' I said, 'He'd love it.' When the Chief stood up to have his picture taken, and just as they got ready to flash, Popeye said, 'Hi y'a Herb,' in his big Popeye voice. Well, the Chief broke out into a big smile."[79] The photo appeared in two leading New York newspapers and *Life* magazine, achieving a wide circulation. Those who saw it smiled as well. Later that same day, a photo of musical and theater star Gertrude Lawrence, wearing a huge pair of mittens and posing as the auctioneer of watercolors by well-known artist Ben Silbert, also managed to coax a big smile from Hoover. Lou Henry Hoover, on seeing the snapshot, remarked "that it was the best picture ever taken of her husband, with a rare look of spontaneous mirth on his face."[80] The Gertrude Lawrence photo Lou so admired was taken at one of the new year's first successes: an auction on January 4 of fourteen watercolor scenes of Finland brought in $3,015.[81]

In response to this "new" Hoover and his redoubled efforts, Hollywood stars, sports legends, politicians, members of the social elite, and Finns in native costume flocked to the standard of the FRF.[82] The Great Humanitarian's renewed commitment, however, was not divorced

Gertrude Lawrence auctions watercolors by well-known artist Ben Silbert (courtesy of Queens Borough Public Library, Archives, *New York Herald Tribune*, Photo Morgue Collection).

from the reality that both the CPR and the FRF drives were stalled. For the CPR to be successful, an agreement with the Germans and the British was necessary.[83] For the FRF to be successful, Hoover needed only to raise substantial amounts of money, not an easy task: though contributions in large numbers steadily came into the FRF, Hoover found their amounts disappointingly small.

The American public overwhelmingly sympathized with the Finns, and the public and the news media had not lost interest in the story. The ex-president estimated that he had only about sixty days in which to find solutions to these problems.[84] At risk was the success of the relief drives and the success of Hoover's campaign for the presidency. His commitment was such that he used his own money, a loan, to float the CPR and the FRF as he developed a plan designed to obtain huge cash donations to underwrite both relief organizations.[85]

In this interim period, he returned to his earlier strategy of conducting an intensive publicity campaign to increase cash flow. The probability that a renewed publicity campaign would raise more money and would boost Hoover's presidential chances was heightened because the basis of support for Finland continued to broaden and the new Hoover had much more appeal. A big step forward occurred when organized labor officially endorsed the FRF in January 1940.[86] Hoover realized that the Finnish cause had "rallied to his support," as Rickard wrote in his diary, "many otherwise inimical groups."[87] Hoover nonetheless tended to back away from courting a new constituency that played little role in the Republican nomination process and was unlikely to produce many votes in the general election, even though Rickard advised that "he should tackle the labor situation in his speeches. It would take courage but people like that. This labor support of Finnish relief may bring the contact he has been looking for."[88]

Blue- and white-collar Americans raised large amounts of money for Finnish relief, but it was upper-crust society that raised the most money and generated more publicity. One of the largest single contributions came from John D. Rockefeller Jr., who gave $100,000 ($2,022,647 in current dollars) when directly approached by Hoover.[89] On March 11, 1940, *Time* magazine observed, "By last week, a U.S. citizen who had neither danced, knitted, orated, played bridge, bingo, banqueted or just shelled out for Finland was simply nowhere socially."[90] America's elite devised endless theme parties, events, and games to help Hoover and the Finns. The posh New York East Side Regency Club sponsored a bridge tournament appropriately called "Bridge to Finland." The club's vice president, Mrs. T. Charles Farrelly, told a *New York Herald Tribune* reporter that the members staunchly backed Finland and that they would "do anything for Mr. Hoover."[91] Taking a cue from the Regency event, hostesses throughout the country threw parties at which the guests played bridge for Finland, while in Palm Beach, Florida, on an exclusive estate, a "Little World's Fair for Finnish Relief" was a "smash."[92]

Younger socialites turned the rooms of the chichi club Cog Rouge into the "Arctic Circle" and invited John Barrymore as the guest of honor. The society highlight of the season, however, was an evening at the "Help Finland Cabaret" at which Mrs. Cornelius Vanderbilt received a cake made from ice and the distinguished Dr. Alexander Hamilton Rice performed the "Boomps-a-Daisy" with chorus girls from the Broadway hit *Hellzapoppin*. At an auction held later that same evening, the notorious playboy Tommy Manville, heir to his father John Manville's asbestos fortune, accompanied by "two blondes swathed in ermine and orchids," paid $500 cash for a De Beers diamond.[93]

Several of the most famous Hollywood stars were photographed with Hoover on January 14 at a luncheon held at the famous Algonquin Hotel to plan theater benefits for Finnish relief. Actor and producer John Golden and actress Ruth Gordon escorted Hoover in a taxi to the luncheon where, Golden reported, the reticent ex-president "listened to our chatter, most of it made up of superlatives and affectionate phrases: 'It was magnificent sweetheart, you murdered them,' and on and on."[94] Hoover turned to Golden and asked, "What words do you theater folks use when you really mean it?"[95] Golden didn't answer, but Gordon whispered she thought Hoover disapproved of the lavish use of superlatives. Another suggested Hoover didn't understand them. "Nonsense," Golden replied. "I'll bet a dollar to fifty cents that Mr. Hoover catches the habit and will be calling Tallulah Ducky before the breast of chicken."[96] The bet was unresolved, but Golden concluded he was right when the photographers brought in copies of the pictures for all to sign. "It had not exactly carried him away, it's true, but still, right there in his own clear handwriting, was the ex-Presidential sentiment: 'With the affection of Herbert Hoover.'"[97]

For another society ball auction held at the Roosevelt Hotel, Paulette Goddard donated a nightgown in which she had slept; Dorothy Lamour, one of her old sarongs; Gladys Swarthout, a hat that she had worn in her first stage appearance; Lana Turner, a lock of her hair; and Greta Garbo, a pair of her evening gloves.[98] Special showings of *Gone with the Wind* were very popular, and "Help Finland Movie Days," held nationwide on the

Tallulah Bankhead, Hoover, Helen Hayes, and Katherine Hepburn lunch at the Algonquin Hotel to plan Finnish relief activities (courtesy of Queens Borough Public Library, Archives, *New York Herald Tribune*, Photo Morgue Collection).

weekend of February 17 and 18, produced $25,000.[99] A "tin can brigade" of Finnish women dressed in native costume collected money in the lobbies of Broadway theaters for three weeks in February, and well-known performers from the cast of *The Taming of the Shrew* sold specially printed programs at each performance. Alfred Lunt, the famous producer, made the first contribution to actress Gertrude Lawrence, and these two events raised over $6,000.[100] Soliciting contributions and sponsoring fundraising events in New York theaters represented a victory in itself, for the actors and actresses of the theater world were involved in a "winter war" of their own. The Theatre Arts Committee, a front organization for radicals and Communists, sided with the Soviets and led a furious "fight against benefit performances for the Finnish Fund," although in the end this was a largely unsuccessful effort.[101]

The flurry of activities for the Finns was briefly interrupted when Dorothy Canfield Fisher, a friend of Eleanor Roosevelt, a well-known, prolific writer, and an advocate for children who had brought Montessori education to America, met for two hours with Hoover at the Waldorf on the afternoon of January 18. Fisher headed the Children's Crusade for Children, which came into being to address the concerns of Eleanor and many in her circle that child refugees were in need of help wherever they might be. When Missy Meloney, in September, suggested to Eleanor that Hoover be brought into the administration, the First Lady thought it a good idea and emphasized that something needed to be done for refugee children. After Hoover made clear that he would not explore the White House feelers extended through Norman Davis, Eleanor, disappointed, continued to search for ways to aid these children and continued to recommend that Hoover be placed in charge of relief, remaining aware that her husband and Davis had no intention of bringing Hoover into the administration. She feared that dozens of relief organizations would be launched that would overlap one another, be generic in their approach, and compete for donations from a confused public. Hoover shared her concerns, continuing to recommend that the Red Cross undertake the task, knowing full well it would not do so. Roosevelt's refusal to expand the role of the Red Cross left the relief issue unresolved. As result, organizations were registering with the State Department at an alarming rate. Eleanor, not to be deterred, continued to advocate for a specialized organization that aided refugee children worldwide.

In October, the novel idea of rising money for refugee children from children in American public schools had emerged. Fisher wrote to a few notables detailing the plan and asking them to serve on a jury that would award the money raised to various established relief agencies. Fisher's friend Eleanor, Monsignor Ryan, and William Allen White "all replied almost by return mail."[102] One of the notables asked to serve as a jury member was Lou Henry Hoover, who did not respond until December 2. Declining, she explained that she could not participate in any "particular movement" and apologized for such a late response, concluding, "With the hope that this enterprise will meet with the great success which it deserves."[103] The Hoovers likely had decided to reject Fisher's offer, as it complicated fund-raising for the FRF and CPR, and its close association with the White House had the potential to give Hoover's political opposition in the Republican Party an issue.

Fisher paid little heed to the refusal and proceeded to build a bipartisan organization of enthusiastic supporters. The plan was to conduct a mite-box campaign in the school systems in the last week of April. Then, in mid-January, Fisher was stunned to learn that Hoover was planning a mite-box campaign in schools for Finnish children in the first weeks of February. The public school systems rarely approved classroom fund-raising, seeing it as an unfair burden on children, many of whom themselves lacked necessities. Fisher rightly feared that the Hoover plan threatened the Children's Crusade, for if Hoover obtained permission and conducted a school drive, permission for a second drive a few months later would almost certainly be refused. If, however, Hoover's mite-box campaign were rejected, it was most unlikely that the Fisher campaign would be approved. Her solution was to meet Hoover to explain the dangers if both their organizations proceeded as planned, as both would likely fail. She arrived at the Hoover apartment in the Waldorf eager to resolve the problem but harbored the suspicion that Hoover had gotten the idea of a mite-box campaign in schools from the material sent to Lou Henry. According to Fisher, in a letter to Monsignor Ryan, she explained the dilemma to Hoover, adding,

> I also ventured to remind him that Mrs. Hoover had known of our plan since October. Mr. Hoover made no answer to this, but said that he would withdraw his plan for an attempt at school-room mite-box collections, only on the condition that our Jury of award will pledge themselves in advance to apportion twenty-five per cent of the money collected by the Children's Crusade, to Finnish children. I replied that this would be entirely against our promise to leave them independent. He merely repeated that only on that condition would he give the orders to desist from the attempt of a hasty organization of class-room collection for the Finnish Relief Fund. I made no comment on this, I think no comment is needed.[104]

Fisher acknowledged she had no choice but to agree, asking that Ryan consent to Hoover's fait accompli. Whether Hoover had gotten the idea of a public school mite-box campaign from the Fisher material is unknown, and, surprisingly, there is no record of correspondence between Hoover or his wife with Fisher, nor is there a memo of conversation or recollections in the Rickard Diary or in other oral history interviews. Nevertheless, Fisher reported her meeting with Hoover as jarring and was deeply resentful of being forced to comply with his demands. To Eleanor, in strictest confidence, she wrote, "I fear that this is worse than what might occur from a mere chance crossing of wires."[105] She continued,

> I've had a good deal of experience, and I'm not easily shocked, but I was really horrified by the tone of the interview with Mr. Hoover. And I feel I ought to give you my personal impression that it would be, in my judgment dangerous in the extreme to entrust to him in his present state of neurotic bitterness and hate, any large responsibility for steering or managing American generosity and charity. Confusion and waste of effort, such as you foresaw, bad as that is, would I feel, be better than what might result if Mr. Hoover were head of any large co-ordinating committee.[106]

Eleanor responded emphatically to her friend, "I am not surprised at your interview with Mr. Hoover and, of course, will agree with the promise. I have come reluctantly to the same conclusion that it would be impossible for him to do a coordinated job which should be done impartially and without bitterness. I am very sorry for him, as I think it must make his life a very bitter thing."[107] Like Eleanor and Ryan, the other four jurors also agreed. Hoover, having loaned money to the struggling FRF and the CPR, saw an opportunity for increased revenues and moved aggressively. Hoover had conceded a potential source of income, gambling that the Children's Crusade would be successful but aware that any payouts were months away. He may have seen his offer as a quid pro quo, and knowing he had levered a Roosevelt-backed charity surely brought a smile to his face. The tone of the meeting is unknown and may have been as Fisher described, but it may have been the result of how badly she had been stung by Hoover's demands. Regardless, the flap was significant, as it signaled the end of any hopes Eleanor harbored of Hoover becoming an administration czar of relief. The view of the new happy, smiling Hoover was everywhere in the press, but for Fisher and Eleanor, Hoover had revealed to them his same old ugsome self. The enmity between the Roosevelts and the Hoovers remained in force.

Of all the multifarious branches of the FRF, the sports division was one of the most successful, bringing in over $700,000 in an astonishing variety of ways. In Florida, spring training was suspended for a day while Tampa hosted a big-league All Star baseball game that yielded $21,296. Joe Williams, sportswriter for the *New York World-Telegram*, obviously swept up in the emotion of the event, wrote,

> The field and stands were liberally sprayed with bunting and flags. It was a strange, unfamiliar touch; the blue elongated cross of Finland against a field of white. All over the grounds Finnish flags fluttered proudly beneath the Stars and Stripes.... [T]he tempo of play and fervor of the crowd reached from palm-fringed Plant Field to gun-shelled Helsinki. Tampa and its neighboring cities did themselves proud in supporting the most elaborate ball game in the history of the South.[108]

The Southwest Conference played five exhibition football games that raised $25,000, and in rural Tennessee a children's basketball game netted $5.60.[109] Throughout the month of March, the sports blitz continued. The young world champion of tennis, Don Budge, played and defeated veteran star Bill Tilden.[110] Paavo Nurmi, a record miler, and Taisto Maki, a record two-miler and soldier just returned from the Karelian front, commenced a national tour and ran against outstanding American greats like Glen Cunningham of Kansas, who had won a medal in the 1936 Olympic Games.[111] March went out like a lion when on March 29 Joe Louis fought Johnny Paycheck.[112] These exciting sports events added over $50,000 to the FRF total.

To help Hoover raise as much money as possible, Finland sent many of its celebrities to America, in addition to Jean Sibelius.[113] One of the more interesting fund-raising projects was the creation of a large four-color lithograph map of Finland, designed by Otto G. Lindberg, one of that nation's finest mapmakers. The FRF sold one hundred thousand through its fifty state committees.[114] After the Finnish capitulation on March 12, the sports activities and the $5,000 donation of Thomas J. Watson, chief executive officer of IBM, helped sustain the relief drive.[115] Of note was a $1,000 gift from Father Charles Coughlin, a $6,765 contribution collected in the territory of Alaska, and twenty-five cents sent to the Finnish Legation by three black prisoners in the South along with an offer to serve in the Finnish army. They expectantly wrote, "You can write to us in care of the Sheriff, and we'll be here."[116]

In February, Hoover finally concluded that no matter how successful his relief drives were, they could not adequately raise the amounts of money necessary to aid Poland and Finland. He admitted the limits of volunteerism and called for government appropriations, as he had during World War I. To secure funding for his relief agencies, Hoover testified before Sol Bloom's House Committee on Foreign Affairs on February 29, recommending a congressional expenditure of $50 million. This was the first time the ex-president had visited Washington since the 1933 inauguration, and he made sure that FDR was out of town in order to avoid a call at the White House.[117] As Congress pondered Hoover's proposals and those of others attempting to secure funds for Finland, at least six separate bills were introduced in the Senate and the House. As the publicity campaign of the FRF reached its height, a controversy surfaced over whether Finland was better served by sending civilian or military aid.[118]

Roosevelt, on March 1, approved a $20 million loan for Finland but did not include 186 requested airplanes and other military equipment.

Public opinion polls repeatedly showed that a majority of Americans favored government loans to Finland, but only a minority of Americans favored loans to buy arms. A smaller but outspoken number organized to raise money to fulfill the Finns' military needs, an area of involvement consciously avoided by the FRF and the Roosevelt administration. General John F. O'Ryan headed Fighting Funds for Finland (FFF), founded on February 2, 1940. O'Ryan proclaimed,

> I question the realism of those who would withhold their aid from the men of Finland, young and old, who in battle, are defending so gallantly and effectively their families and their country. They need additional aircraft, weapons and military stores. If they are not supported in a timely way and generous manner they may go down in a hurricane of violence and destruction, which will leave little to be rescued or salvaged. Armed aggression on the loose can be convincingly dealt with only by adequate and effective gun fire, meaning all that this term implies.[119]

The O'Ryan organization mounted a nationwide campaign with a goal of raising $10 million.[120] A popular list told what military equipment a donation could buy: fifty cents would purchase a pair of socks, $75 a 100-pound bomb or a submachine gun; for the well heeled, $125,000 bought a bomber. Often the donors included comments, which the organization published. From Louisville, Kentucky, came "I enclose a check for $50.00 which I trust can be used to drop bombs on the Russians." From a woman in Brooklyn who sent a check for $10: "This is what I have been waiting for for a long time." From Orleans, Massachusetts: "Dollars for Finland now may save American blood later." From Washington, DC, came a check for $500, and Robert, from Louisiana, sent thirty cents along with the comment "All luxuries are unknown but poor as I am I want to help where I can, so send this mite."[121] At the end of January, Dorothy Thompson, speaking in New Jersey, came out forcefully for arming the Finns: "We should stop being hypocrites: Finland does not need wheat and food. She needs pursuit planes and guns. Dead men don't eat. Actually, the relief we send her is being traded for guns."[122] While this was not quite true, Thompson, well connected with members of the Roosevelt administration, may have picked up some knowledge of the activities of the Finnish American Trading Corporation and the commodity swap that put $10 million in cash in the hands of the Finns to buy military equipment. Two other groups were working to obtain arms in favor of the Finns: Wings over Finland and Airplanes for Finland. The FRF reported that in the rush to militarily aid the Finns, at least nine other newly formed organizations flooded the relief field.[123] The organizations advocating military aid, a loud vocal minority, had a decided and widespread effect on public opinion and on the fund-raising efforts of the FRF and the American Red Cross, although the Red Cross had difficulty raising money for Finnish relief throughout the first quarter of 1940.[124] As the Arms for Finland groups grew and became more visible, their effect was to coalesce the opposition and those who were undecided.

Many Americans believed that loans to belligerents were among the key factors that had brought about eventual US intervention in World War I. Surely that lesson had been learned! Loans for arms and ammunition called up memories of the "ammunition makers" thesis, which, in turn, recalled the long emotional and intellectual struggle America had gone through in the 1920s and 1930s in a collective effort to explain the war and to find rational solutions that would prevent another world calamity. On January 14, six peace organizations, including the American Friends Service Committee (AFSC), which was allied with the FRF, released a statement vigorously opposing US loans of charitable gifts for military equipment. These groups warned, "It is the camel's nose under the tent [and] will be followed speedily by requests for loans to Britain and France."[125]

Other Americans were cognizant of the argument that Hoover's Commission for Relief in Belgium (CRB) was partially responsible for American entry into World War I through its fund-raising publicity (propaganda) by creating an emotional, pro-Allied mood in the country that was the beginning of the end of neutrality. Ironically, Hoover himself, in 1938 and 1939, warned against just such an eventuality if the United States aided Britain and France.[126] Anti-interventionists, pacifists, and critics were to point this out when Hoover founded the CPR and later the FRF. Opposition to Finnish relief on the grounds that it was a first step to involvement also came from the editorial pages of the *Denver Post*, *St. Louis Post-Dispatch*, and *Richmond Times Dispatch*.[127]

A majority of Americans, however, were so outraged by the Russian invasion of Finland that they took one careful step forward on "the dangerous road that led to war" and approved of small loans restricted to purchases of nonmilitary supplies and equipment. It was not clear that Congress would follow this slight majority and enact the necessary legislation. Cordell Hull and Roosevelt concurred that Finland should receive restricted loans but hoped to convince Congress to take leadership and shepherd the bills through the House and Senate.[128] All knew that even in committee the loan proposals would instantly run into anti-interventionists' opposition. Recognizing the potential volatility of the issue, harboring questions and concerns, and noting that the White House was ducking the issue, most members of Congress hung back and refused to get out in front on the issue. Senators Millard Tydings of Maryland and Prentiss Brown of Michigan and Representative John Dingell of Michigan were exceptions who spoke out in support of Fighting Funds for Finland.[129]

In the first week of March, after eight weeks of rancorous debate, Congress finally increased the capital of the Import-Export Bank by $100 million, with $20 million supposedly earmarked for the Finns. *Time* magazine commented, "The scene in the House was an odd mixture of cowardice, confusion and misunderstanding. To beat around the bush of last autumn's Neutrality Act, the loan was restricted to non-military supplies."[130] *Time* might have added that by increasing the capital of the Import-Export Bank, Congress had made money available but had forced the decision as to which countries would receive loans and the amounts back on the Roosevelt administration. Once Congress had acted, Roosevelt, Henry Morgenthau, and Jones took whatever minimal political risks were involved and quickly approved the $20 million in restricted credits for Finland.[131]

Procopé was disappointed with the loan, for throughout January and February he had often spoken out publicly for direct military aid to Finland, while privately he continued to ardently lobby the Roosevelt administration; however, his speeches pleading for direct military assistance did more harm than good.[132] The Finnish minister's relationship with Hoover further deteriorated, as he argued that the FRF should raise money for arms, or at least officially sanction the efforts of Fighting Funds for Finland and other like-minded organizations. Hoover called Procopé and "beg[ged] him to issue a statement clearly defining the difference between our job [FRF] and military equipment."[133]

The Finnish minister was not alone on this issue, as some of the leadership and many of the rank-and-file members of the FRF, FFF, and Wings over Finland called for a united effort of those engaged in raising money for the Finnish cause. Hoover's representatives in Finland, Hallam Tuck and Dorsey Stephens, called Roosevelt's secretary, Pa Watson, from Helsinki and pushed hard for Roosevelt to approve military aid.[134] Two members of the Florida leadership of the FFF cabled the national headquarters in New York City: "Cannot General O'Ryan join with Hoover organization and manage the contributions for defense? Hoover need only authorize contributors to mark their cheques 'For Defense.' This is so obviously the efficient method that we can hardly believe Hoover cannot be persuaded to agree. However, if separate organization is necessary, we pledge our earnest active support to Fighting Funds for Finland."[135]

The attempt of some in the FRF and FFF to bring about a united campaign failed, for Hoover realized that unification would further weaken his own organization's endeavors. He did agree on February 15 to a compromise, accepting, though not soliciting, funds for any purpose and agreeing to maintaining separate organizations, but he did not announce this publicly.[136] Substantial damage had already been caused by O'Ryan and the founders of separate groups that felt compelled to raise money for military equipment. Tragically, these new organizations were created to address an insoluble problem. Civilian aid for Finland released funds that could be spent on armaments, but even with money, loans, and credit, the Finns could still not obtain what they needed.

The United States, France, Great Britain, and other countries had contracts with American manufacturers for almost everything being produced, and production was still far behind.[137] The French had placed huge preemptive orders that met with avid support from Ambassador William C. Bullitt.[138] If the Finns got substantial numbers of aircraft, 150 fighters and 36 fast twin-engine bombers, and other first-line equipment, then the United States, France, and Great Britain would lose out.[139] At the very least, delivery took six months to a year following the date of order. Procopé clearly understood this grim equation and tried to persuade Morgenthau and Hull to step aside and let the Finns buy. The Roosevelt administration could not realistically do this; although Morgenthau recommended it, the State Department, the army, and the navy declined, because public opinion opposed arms deals and because a large number of people, including themselves, thought that the country needed first and foremost to strengthen its own inadequate defenses.[140]

The Roosevelt administration brazenly attempted to obtain aircraft by pressuring Great Britain and France to give from their share of US production what the Finns wanted, but these countries faced the same dilemma, especially France, which had attempted to compensate for its own negligence in aircraft production by placing huge and unrealistic orders in the United States.[141] The British sold the Finns several hundred hand-me-down aircraft, including Gloster Gladiators, Lysanders, Blenheim Bombers, and a few up-to-date Hurricanes, but no nation awaiting American aircraft would yield to the Finns their place in line. Without such a sacrifice, nothing was available for Finland. Even if O'Ryan raised $10 million for arms and aircraft, it would be of no immediate help. Fighting Funds for Finland and Wings over Finland merely provided their creators and supporters with the psychological illusion that they were aiding the Finnish army in the field. Finland could not hold out long enough for effective Western military aid to reach the front. The Finns would get Sweden to assemble and fly the American-made Brewsters to Finland. Robert Winston marveled at the hodgepodge of aircraft parked on the Trollhätten runway waiting to be ferried to the Finns. Next to the British planes were camouflaged Fiats shipped from Italy, as well as French Morane and Kolhoven fighters.[142]

The Finnish government's reaction to this desperate situation was to instruct Procopé to advocate that Washington provide arms. In response, the Finnish ambassador attempted to use the FFF in a last-ditch effort to sway public opinion in favor of his country's military needs, hoping to obtain access to existing stocks and/or a place at the head of the arms production line. The result of this flurry of activity, coupled with Procopé's "crossover," divided the relief groups and eroded the base of support for Finland. The specter of military equipment purchases invigorated those opposed to arm sales. Several labor groups newly won to the FRF immediately backed out, and over fifty large daily newspapers were strongly opposed to the sale of arms.[143] Many of those newspapers had supported the FRF editorially and collected money, but they either changed their minds or concluded that the Finnish effort was dangerous and threatened to lead to intervention.[144] Of course, anti-interventionists, pacifists, and religious groups like the AFSC were opposed to raising funds for arms, and they no longer wholeheartedly supported the FRF. In spring 1940, those who gave money to aid Finland generally gave to the FRF, but the organization's hold on contributions was weakened by the creation of new relief programs, Procopé's outspoken demands for arms, and Hoover's decision to accept all donations. Despite Hoover's determined efforts to help Finland maintain the fragile relief coalition, the movement splintered. In December 1939, the Winter War had caused the United States to move closer to intervention, but a more thorough understanding of what support for Finland entailed occurred in February and March 1940. Confronted with hard choices, Hoover, the Roosevelt administration, and the majority of America's citizenry rejected any direct involvement in or support of the war. The ranks of the interventionists, so swollen over the winter, by spring experienced large numbers of desertions resulting in an affirmation for continued neutrality. Americans wanted Finland to win the war if nothing more than encouragement and cheerleading were required.

Finnomania ended with the capitulation of Finland on March 12. After 105 days of war, exhausted and out of nearly everything, the Finns accepted a peace dictated by Moscow. The price of their stubborn resistance was twenty-five thousand dead, fifty-five thousand wounded, the eastern portion of Karelia, territory farther north near Salla, a handful of small islands in the Gulf of Finland, and a Russian naval base on the Hanko Peninsula. Hoover declared the peace agreement "another sad day for civilization. The Finns have made a heroic defense that will live for all time, but the odds were insuperable."[145] He and O'Ryan from the FFF pledged that the drive to aid Finland would continue. In the days after the surrender, the Finnish need grew exponentially as 470,000 Karelians chose to evacuate what was now Russian territory. Most took were able to take very few of their belongings with them. Many farmers, some forty thousand, took their livestock and, on leaving, set their homes and barns ablaze.[146]

Hoover, in his all-out effort to aid the Finns, had not forgotten the Poles. The ex-president continued to search for ways to feed those in the Government General and to breathe new life into the Commission for Polish Relief to sustain support of Polish refugees in Romania, Hungary, and Lithuania. Since December 1939, the CPR had been paralyzed by a German refusal to allow American aid to enter the Government General, by Great Britain's refusal to allow food through the blockade without adequate American supervision, and by debilitating and rancorous debates in the Polish-American community over the question of how and by whom Poland should or could be aided. Neither Hoover nor the American Red Cross, nor the AFSC, nor the Mennonite Church had ever suspended negotiations with the Ministry of Economic Warfare in London or with the Germans in Berlin and Kraków.[147] In fact, Hoover and Hugh Gibson, a member of the CPR and the first US minister to Poland, worked directly through Hans Thomsen, the chargé d'affaires in the German embassy in Washington, DC, and on January 7, 1940, they submitted a comprehensive plan, modeled on the CRB, which envisioned feeding all of the inhabitants of the Government General.[148]

In February 1940, after six weeks of procrastination, it appeared that the Germans would agree to allow strict American control and accountability of relief supplies on a nonsectarian basis. The turnaround was partially due to a Vatican broadcast that threatened the Nazi propaganda line by accusing the Germans of atrocities in Poland. In Washington, Senator Vandenberg wrote an open letter to the president, insisting he do more to persuade Berlin to allow American aid.[149] Encouraged, Hoover and the Red Cross reasoned that the British would agree to pass limited amounts of food through the blockade once the Germans had met

British objections.[150] The Germans cautiously relented and, on February 20, allowed the four petitioning American relief agencies access to the Government General.[151] It looked as if, after four and a half months of tedious haggling, aid to the needy in Warsaw would begin to flow.

While working through the final details of his feeding program with the British and the Germans, Hoover attempted to reunite the Polish American community by creating a new umbrella organization named the Paderewski Fund.[152] The goal was to raise $1 million in honor of the eightieth birthday of Ignacy Paderewski, Poland's first prime minister and a world-renowned pianist, which was November 6, 1940, and then give that money to CPR to purchase supplies.[153] The fund, headed by Colonel William "Wild Bill" Donovan, would be nationwide in scope and would last only twelve weeks.[154] Hoover proteges like Hugh Gibson, Lewis Strauss, Herbert L. Satterlee, and Charlotte Kellogg served on the fund's board of directors, but a major effort at bipartisan support netted the endorsements of Eleanor Roosevelt and Herbert Lehman.[155] Thomas Watson, who contributed generously to the FRF, also helped establish the Paderewski Fund with a donation of $5,000. This effort at unification was essential, for a reunited Polish American community with broad-based bipartisan political support would also be more effective in pressuring the administration and Congress to grant aid for Poland, and it would assure that the American Red Cross would stay in the field. Continuing to use traditional public relations techniques, Hoover trumpeted Poland's cause at a mass meeting held in Madison Square Garden on the night of March 12. This event and other "Polish Nights" held across the country made the Paderewski Fund a success, but the amount raised was insignificant compared to Poland's need.[156]

Additional aid for Poland was to a degree dependent on Hoover's success with the FRF. Whenever possible, Hoover attempted to harness the popularity of the Finnish cause on behalf of Poland and to create and utilize any "humanitarian spill over." US aid for Finland, both private and public, was obviously a lever that could be used to attempt to produce aid for Poland. In his strategy to obtain government funding for relief programs, Hoover linked the needs of Poland and Finland, thus potentially expanding the base of support that existed in Congress. Before appearing

Drawing by Maxfield Parrish for Polish relief (courtesy of HHPLM).

before the House Committee on Foreign Affairs on February 29, Hoover asked the Polish government-in-exile and the British and the French to each contribute $5 million to keep the CPR going. He wished to show that he and the Allied governments were doing everything possible to feed the starving and to demonstrate that the movement to aid Poland was international and deserved US support.[157]

The British and the French were lukewarm toward contributions to the CPR and at once recognized that if they contributed, the blockade would be pierced and the precedent for feeding captive populations established. Nevertheless, the governments of Neville Chamberlain and Édouard Daladier took the proposal under advisement and decided that with adequate safeguards, to ensure that the Poles received the food, they would approve.[158] Breckinridge Long reported that Lord Lothian stated "his government did not want to say 'no' again to the American government."[159] The Polish government was enthusiastic about the Hoover plan and theoretically agreed to donate $5 million, but, already stretched for money, they asked the Allied governments to intervene with the Romanians and secure the release of Polish gold still held in Bucharest.[160] In the meantime, the Polish government-in-exile contributed $1 million to Hoover and the CPR.[161]

The ex-president testified on Capitol Hill before the Bloom Committee that funds were necessary for Finland. He noted that the Finns needed additional government loans; he emphasized the Finnish situation was a simple one when compared with the problems confronting the CPR in its efforts to reach the needy in Poland. Speaking out strongly for relief for the Poles, he advocated a program that would partially feed approximately seven million people. By early spring, Hoover estimated that the crisis would be at hand and would last until the fall harvest—if that harvest was substantial. If it were not, then the need would be a continuing one. He stated, "All together, by drastic calculations we arrive at a rough calculation of forty or fifty million dollars to carry the Poles over another twelve months. We are not suggesting that all that burden fall on the United States. I have no doubt that somewhere between ten and twenty million dollars would represent a fair share from the United States."[162]

Hoover received a warm reception from the Bloom Committee. He was a surprise witness, for Speaker William Bankhead supposedly did not know he was in Washington or that Sol Bloom was holding hearings on Polish relief bills.[163] This is somewhat surprising, as Robert McCormick and Maurice Pate had testified on the two preceding days and Hoover had met with Hull the day before his congressional appearance.[164] Regardless, the Speaker, like most of the Congress, was opposed to a commitment of this magnitude, aware that it posed a potential threat to US neutrality.

After slipping into Washington and "storming the hill," Hoover turned to resolving the last outstanding issue with the Germans: how many American representatives would be permitted to enter the Government General to supervise and account for the distribution of aid. The Germans did not specify a number when they approved the Hoover feeding plan, though the implication was that only one American would be issued a visa.[165] Finding the limitation to be unacceptable and knowing that it would be equally unacceptable to the British, Hoover decided to ask for fifteen representatives.[166] During the first week of March, the German consul in Chicago called Hoover and explained that any American representatives was entitled to assistants and that the number might be three or four.[167] Given that the Germans would agree to only a small number of representatives, Hoover asked that the CPR assistants be stationed in Danzig, Kraków, and Lublin, as well as in Warsaw.[168] This arrangement was acceptable to Hoover and just might be acceptable to the British, for it was necessary that the CPR not be bottled up in Warsaw.

As the details of the feeding plan were worked out with the Germans point by point, more good news reached the CPR. On March 1, the British released Red Cross supplies that had long been held in Genoa and Gibraltar for shipment to the Government General. Later that month, a Red Cross team surveyed relief needs in Lublin. Nicholson and Taylor were two of the first outsiders to visit Jewish neighborhoods and reported that, overall, five hundred thousand people needed food.[169] Yet, despite this progress, on March 21 a setback revealed the German desire to isolate the Government General and cover up its acts of ruthless murder and exploitation.

The Nazis insisted that US Consul George J. Haering and Vice Consuls Carl Birkeland and William R. Morton leave Warsaw, as had all other foreign diplomats. Hull asked the Germans to allow the consuls to look after the 532 American citizens still in Poland.[170] Among this group were American Jews like Mary Berg and her family, who were stranded and living in deplorable conditions.[171] The German Foreign Office refused Hull's request. The diplomats' expulsion occurred at a critical time, as Jerzy Potocki had just asked Hull to support relief work in Poland, the British had relaxed the blockade, and Congress was still conducting hearings on the proposed $10 million appropriation for direct aid to Poland.[172]

Expulsion of the American consuls tended to confirm suspicions already held by the Roosevelt administration, the Congress, and the British and to provide an additional reason for not supporting a mass-feeding program. Ironically, the most damage done to Hoover's feeding proposal was through his own success in obtaining the promise of large financial contributions from the French, British, and Polish governments. Both the State Department and the Congress were loath to participate in a relief effort as partners with countries that were at war with Germany. "Mixing money" seemed clearly an unneutral act and further complicated the already sensitive issue of American control and accountability.[173]

By late March, the signs were plain that Congress would not fund a comprehensive aid program for Poland. The administration and the public had reaffirmed the nation's commitment to neutrality by refusing to provide arms or significant aid for Finland. The renewed effort to aid Poland, which Hoover had purposely linked to the immensely popular "aid Finland" movement, suffered the same fate. However, the persistent Hoover considered the defeat of his proposals for Poland and Finland not final but a temporary setback. Hoover recognized and counted on support for feeding the Poles that existed within the Roosevelt administration. Norman Davis and the American Red Cross saw the feeding scheme as a follow-up to their rendering of emergency assistance.[174] Hoover struggled to find substantial funding and to increase support for his feeding proposals. If the money could be found, voices in the administration might be raised. In April, two American Red Cross shipments of medical supplies worth $250,000 passed through the British blockade and were eventually distributed in the Government General.[175] In the climate of political safety engendered by the end of the Russo-Finnish War, the Red Cross greatly increased its aid to Finland for rebuilding and for the resettlement of Karelian refugees.

Spring brought cherry blossoms to Washington, but April also brought the Germans to Denmark and Norway, bringing the "Phoney War" to a jarring end. The waiting for Hitler was over. Whether the conquest of the two Nordic countries was the beginning or the end of Hitler's aspirations was immaterial; the battle for the West was underway. Hoover expressed shock at the war's renewal, though he had predicted it would be so after the defeat of the Poles. Food shipments, if any, would now have to be shipped to Genoa or Lisbon. Still, Hoover might have succeeded in establishing an American-directed mass-feeding program in Poland with little or no government funding. This possibility was revived in late April, when the Vatican wrote to the State Department declaring that it wished to send relief to the Poles through the CPR. However, the Roosevelt administration did not answer the papal inquiry until May 28 and did not inform the CPR until June 18, 1940.

Unaware of what might have been missed, Hoover could take some satisfaction in the fact that additional funds would be forthcoming to his relief organizations—specifically, 25 percent—from the hardball deal he had struck with Dorothy Canfield Fisher. The Children's Crusade for Children had successfully conducted its mite-can campaign throughout American schools from April 22 to April 30. The program was extremely popular. Roosevelt, persuaded by Eleanor, stepped up, giving a nationwide address and posing for photos of himself, along with three children, receiving a publicity poster from popular and impressively famous American illustrator Norman Rockwell. American schoolchildren dropped fourteen million pennies into the mite-cans that totaled $137,000 (2,833,672).[176] Patience was required on Hoover's part, as the funds were not dispersed to the relief agencies until August.

For Hoover, the lull in relief activities provided time to turn to politics and the pursuit of the nomination he badly wanted.[177] Publicly he continued to deny his ambition, but privately, as Rickard confided in his diary,

Roosevelt receives Children's Crusade for Children painting from famous artist Norman Rockwell (courtesy of Getty Images).

"there seemed to pour from his lips a torrent of plans, Republican nomination that he had sorely neglected. Regardless of his lapse, it was a calculations, accusations and schemes to keep his name before the public"; later in March, Rickard noted that Hoover "is constantly weighing his chance for nomination and has results of a poll of midwest and eastern papers, which show 50% of republican papers mark him down as the best of candidates to handle problem in Washington."[178] The recognition of the new Hoover, plus the favorable press coverage of his twin relief efforts, had bolstered his image and in April persuaded a growing number of editors and columnists to write favorably about his candidacy. Drew Pearson and Robert Allen of the *Washington Merry-Go-Round* wrote, "While Dewey, Taft, Vandenberg and other GOP hopefuls are making newspaper headlines, a shadowy figure is moving quietly and determinedly behind the scenes."[179] Hoover, undercover, they stated, "has both hands deep in the Republican pie." The *New York Herald Tribune* crowed, "Hoover Seen as Only Choice to Carry on Liberal Democracy."[180] Hoover advisor Jim Selvage summarized the Hoover strategy:

> It seems to some of us here that the time has come, or will come early in May, to begin to activate the demand for the Chief [Hoover] which we know is there, and almost on every side you hear today that he is the ablest man and should be in the White House, coupled with the silly follow up, "but he can't be elected." That is the thing that must be broken down and we have the feeling that if we concentrate our fire over a period of six or seven weeks before the convention, that a grass-roots demand can be built that will catch fire.[181]

Potentially, if all went well, support would come from the western delegations.[182] To secure the nomination, Hoover stuck with his view (held since the previous September) that the forthcoming convention would be divided and many of the delegates' commitment to the aspirants was weak. His judgment was supported by delegate counts in April reporting that Dewey had 290, Taft 266, Vandenberg 114, and others 296, with 35 doubtful.[183] The delegate poll and Hoover seemed to take little account of the candidacy of Wendell Willkie, an anti–New Deal Democrat turned Republican, who was making headway with Wall Street and big business Republicans. To turn the tide in his favor, Hoover calculated that a great speech was in order, one mirroring that of the young Nebraskan, William Jennings Bryan, whose "Cross of Gold" speech at the 1896 Democratic Convention swept him to the nomination.[184] The break would come, Hoover predicted, on the third ballot, as the dithering delegates realized he was the right man with the right experience for the job.[185] But Hoover's willow-o'-the-wisp strategy ignored some of his weaknesses, chief among them being that the Chief was not a dynamic speaker—certainly no leather-lunged orator like William Jennings Bryan. He would not set the stage for his speech by glad-handing delegates, working the Philadelphia convention for votes. His personality was in many ways unsuited for the presidency. He had been unable to overcome the belief that it was wrong for a man to seek a job, even one he wanted badly; rather, the job should seek out the man. Hoover's behavior toward his candidacy in 1939–1940 remained in line with his past behavior in 1936 and his shadow candidacy in the contest for the 1920 Republican nomination. He pushed his associates hard to support him, but he refused to get out front—to toss his hat in the ring—remaining the man behind the curtain.[186] While his chances remained slim, if things broke in the right way, it was just possible he still might grasp his dream.

After Hitler's invasion of Norway, the wait for Hitler's next move was a short one. On May 10, a massive assault on the Low Countries and France was underway. Hoover reacted to the shocking hurricane of events: "We are passing through the most serious moment in the history of the world since the year 410 A.D.—the year of the fall of the Roman Empire and the capture of Rome by the barbaric king, Alaric."[187] In response, Hoover, while opposed to any military intervention, advocated that the United States "arm to the teeth." The selection of Winston Churchill as Britain's wartime prime minister on the day of the invasion immediately ended any possibility of supplies passing through the blockade or of Great Britain contributing money for Polish relief.[188] Churchill intended a strict blockade as a necessary step in defending his island nation. Gibson cabled Hoover at once, informing him of a decided change in attitude at Whitehall. According to Gibson, the British were determined to prevent general relief for Poland, not to relax the blockade, not feed the overrun countries, and not to grant money to relief organizations involved in aiding overrun countries. "Attitudes toward blockade and distressed populations were characterized by toughness unknown in the last war. Antagonism to relief even in unofficial circles on the ground were: (a) hard-boiled belief that suffering populations will exert definite pressure on Germany, (b) belief that current German behavior in Poland such they cannot permit foreigners freedom of movement."[189] The former ambassador to Poland made three other important points: the British and French governments were "weak and in no mood to take courageous action on relief"; the Polish government-in-exile was divided and vacillating on the relief issue; and, finally, the British proposed new and impossible conditions that would have to be met by the Hoover group before any further aid was rendered.[190] Audaciously, the British claimed that these bureaucratic entanglements had been erected by the French, a claim their stricken ally denied. The nine-month struggle to feed the inhabitants and refugees in the Government General collapsed, and the possibility that Finland would be considered inside the blockade imperiled relief efforts there.

Hoover was not surprised by this turn of events, for he and Churchill had differed over blockade policy since the First World War. Despite philosophical and moral differences, Hoover appreciated the grave situation faced by Churchill. "He came to office when practically all Western Europe had fallen before Hitler's onslaught. Great Britain was in the greatest danger of her entire history. In the preservation of his country, Mr. Churchill was serving the cause of freedom for the whole world. I admired him for his constancy to that purpose, his courage, and his abilities."[191] But deep divisions existed between the two men over how war should be conducted, and Hoover would not relent on his plans to undertake a cross-blockade feeding setup. The days of working with the more amenable Chamberlain government were over.

Despite these serious reversals, Hoover fought on for Poland and Finland. The CPR continuously struggled to make large purchases within the blockade. Occasionally they were successful in Holland, Norway, Lithuania, Bulgaria, Romania, and the Soviet Union. The soup kitchens in the Government General remained open.[192] The refugees and interned Polish soldiers in Romania, Hungary, and Lithuania continued to receive aid. Nonetheless, the task of raising money to support these efforts was further complicated by their loss of front-page coverage. Human interest stories concerning need, reconstruction, and resettlement were relegated to the back pages of American dailies, if mentioned at all. The focus was on the tumultuous events brought on by the battle for Norway, the attack on the Low Countries, and the French and British armies' attempt to halt the German advance.

The defeat of Holland and Belgium guaranteed that Hoover would champion the need to expand his humanitarian relief efforts and to continue his crusade for cross-blockade feeding operations. His immediate concern, of course, was to feed the hungry but also, and just as important, to establish a firm principle in international law that it was illegal to include food on any blockade list. Hoover, having fed the Belgians in the First World War, remained active in postwar reconstruction and in exchange scholarships through the Belgian American Education Foundation. To save the imperiled nations of Holland and Belgium from looming food shortages, Hoover acted quickly. On May 13, the day before the Dutch surrendered, he created the Queen Wilhelmina Fund. The Belgian army was still in the field and the Germans, campaigning amid a beautiful warm spring, were not yet in Brussels when Hoover, on May 16, formed a new Commission for Belgian Relief.[193] He did not organize a French relief organization, as he (along with most observers) could not imagine that France would so rapidly fold in the face of the German onslaught. A protracted struggle resulting in a long war seemed the likely outcome. But adding Holland and Belgium to the countries he was already aiding complicated Hoover's existing mission, which was already hampered by obstacles that he had only temporarily overcome.

By the end of May and into June, Hoover, along with his fellow Americans, witnessed from their sheltered vantage point between two oceans the drama of Prime Minister Winston Churchill's desperate trips to the continent in an effort to keep the French in the war, while at the same time rescuing his trapped army from the beaches of Dunkirk—a military defeat the eloquent prime minister transformed into a symbolic victory.[194] It was all but certain that the unthinkable was happening: one the largest armies in the world was going down to defeat, resulting in a geopolitical earthquake, as France was a worldwide empire. The former president closely followed the catastrophe, but it was necessary that he pay attention to advancing his candidacy, as the five-day Republican Convention in Philadelphia was three weeks away. May proved a cruel month for Hoover's plans, as Gallup released a series of polls revealing a political reality that collided with the views held by Hoover and his advisors. Either Roosevelt or Hull, one poll showed, would beat any of the Republican candidates. Another indicated that Dewey had achieved a lead over Taft, making his nomination seem likely.[195] Surprisingly, Gallup's

May 31 poll, conducted between May 18 and May 23, showed only 10 percent of Republicans favoring Willkie. Hoover's internal polls conducted by Alan Fox had widely missed the mark. The ambitious Hoover realized the only option left was a great speech, the only road to the direct challenge of Roosevelt for which he had lusted since his stinging defeat in 1932. Rickard wrote that he spent Sunday "engrossed" in its preparation, working with the journalist George Sokolsky in "amending the introduction."[196] Aides pushed Hoover to grab the reins, to send a team to Philadelphia to establish a headquarters, to plan convention floor demonstrations. However, Hoover refused. He did toy with the idea of encouraging "Draft Hoover Clubs," though he must have known some were already in existence. The Butte County Draft Herbert Hoover Club, headquartered in Chico, California, on May 20, petitioned delegates to the national convention to vote for Hoover, and the Palo Alto club had been active for some time.[197] By May 29, however, Rickard thought he might be getting through to Hoover, "who now for the first time acknowledges a big surge for Willkie among his own supporters."[198] To his dismay, more delegates were daily moving to the Willkie camp from all quarters. It seemed a Hoosier tornado was brewing. That same day, William Star Meyer, a longtime associate, commented in his diary that Hoover "looked more worn and weary than at any time since I saw him in Palo Alto in June 1933."[199]

For the past nine months, Hoover, now well into his sixties, had maintained a brutal schedule. *World Astrology Magazine* warned, "Saturn is not only in his sixth house of health, but is ruler of it, indicating that he is inclined to work hard without thinking of any return. This year he should think of his own welfare, especially where health is concerned."[200] Three days later, on June 1, Hoover sought solace, recuperation, and a chance to think about his speech by going fishing. He and Fred Walcott, a former senator and Polish relief commissioner, drove to Schenob Creek in Massachusetts for two days of trout fishing.[201] On his return, refreshed, Hoover lunched with Dewey on June 4, who improbably claimed that he had four hundred delegates. A week later, the cocky New Yorker noticed that, like Hoover's supporters, many from his camp had also defected to Willkie.[202] Rickard, frustrated, pleaded with Hoover and Larry

Richey, the former president's secretary, "to realize that they have no plans for handling the situation."[203] The following day, he again tried to "discuss Philadelphia arrangements. H.H. says he has a swarm of volunteer workers who will be in Philadelphia, but I want to know who is the boss?"[204] Hoover continued to make no plans for the convention. Rickard explained that he was "absorbed in his speech which is getting altogether too long and labored. He does not seem inclined to accept suggestions yet asks for them. He is tired and goes to be early, and I am home to try and reason out some plan of action."[205] Offers for floor demonstrations following his speech, offers of banners, buttons, and campaign paraphernalia to boost his chances, were all rejected. Mark Sullivan, a journalist and longtime friend, dined with Hoover a few days later and listened as he read his speech aloud, suggesting only a few changes.[206] Hoover remained engrossed in his speech and continued to believe, in the face of an imposing body of contrary evidence, that the convention had within its midst a host of crypto-delegates loyal to his cause.

But lightning struck on June 20. Roosevelt, four days before the opening of the Republican Convention, exhibited his talent for timing by moving to put his own house in order and simultaneously splinter his Republican opposition. He had for some time wished to remove his troublesome secretary of war, Harry H. Woodring. Woodring, with the support of General George Marshall and General Hap Arnold, persistently opposed the president on sending military supplies to the embattled British in an effort not to further weaken an already poorly equipped army.[207] As the anti-interventionist secretary learned, to his surprise, the president was committed to "all aid short of war." Roosevelt offered his troublesome secretary a golden parachute, but Woodring turned down an appointment as governor of Puerto Rico.[208] In the cabinet reshuffle, Roosevelt sent his secretary of the navy, Charles Edison, off to run for the governorship of New Jersey. Emulating Churchill, Roosevelt brought two prominent internationalist Republicans into his cabinet, thereby creating what he termed a "war cabinet." Frank Knox, publisher of the *Chicago Daily News*, who had been Alf Landon's running mate in 1936, stepped in as secretary of the navy, and the distinguished Henry Stimson, who had served as President William Taft's secretary of war and President

Hoover's secretary of state, accepted the appointment to head the War Department. Republicans were horrified, but Roosevelt now had a united front against the anti-interventionists in both political parties and solid support for a policy of aiding Great Britain. For Hoover, the cabinet change was disastrous, as from this point forward the blockade would become an anchor in the growing Anglo-American alliance. While the Republican appointments were not unexpected, Hoover was equally upset by a bipartisan foreign policy, given his continued opposition to all things Roosevelt.[209] As if the ex-president did not have enough to deal with, the Belgian leadership equivocated over what to do about Hoover's relief proposal and their growing concern that the food shortage in their country would worsen. Ambassador Robert van der Straten-Ponthoz, recognizing that Belgium had little to lose, finally seized the initiative. Acting on his own, he accepted Hoover's offer of food aid for his beleaguered country.[210]

In an atmosphere of growing uncertainty, on June 24, just four days after Roosevelt had coopted Stimson and Knox, the Republicans opened their convention in Philadelphia.[211] Hoover's hour was at hand. On Tuesday evening, the second night of the convention, he was to speak at 9:30. The auditorium was overflowing, the galleries packed.[212] Things started poorly. Hoover, wearing a favored blue suit, made his way to the podium too soon and missed the signal from the television camera, the first broadcast of a political event.[213] After a huge ovation, the chairman, Joseph Martin, introduced the former president, and a short demonstration occurred. During the demonstration, Hoover reverting to one of his oldest habits, standing with his hand in his pocket.[214] "Ladies and Gentlemen of the Republican National Convention: We are here faced with the task of saving America for free men."[215] What followed was a slashing attack on Roosevelt's domestic and foreign policy—the gospel according to Palo Alto. Unfortunately, to those toward the back of the hall and in the galleries, Hoover's speech was inaudible. However, the huge radio audience and those few souls squinting at their television sets were able to hear it all. Hoover, shortly after leaving the podium, came to believe the problem with the sound system was that the microphone had been tampered with. Strauss and Richey agreed and set out to investigate.[216] Speculations as to tampering aside, Hoover's speech failed to ignite the expected boom; even if the speech been perfectly audible in the hall, it is unlikely that it would have secured the nomination. Some newspapers and columnists were excited by the speech. The *San Francisco Chronicle*, carrying the headline "Hoover Speech Rocks Convention," maintained that it was "the most powerful and incisive address of his entire political career."[217] The Democratic take on Hoover's speech was quite different: "Connoisseurs of political hara-kari thrilled when the GOP unveiled Herbert Hoover for a prime-time radio address to a national audience. Democratic strategists regarded Hoover's quadrennial appearance at a Republican convention as electoral reinsurance for victory in November."[218]

To complicate matters, Wendell Willkie supporters filled the convention balconies and kept up a steady drum beat of "WE WANT WILLKIE," scuppering any enthusiastic demonstrations for opposing candidates. To the chagrin of hopefuls Vandenberg, Taft, and Dewey, the delegates nominated the dark horse candidate as their standard bearer on the sixth ballot. Republicans turned to Willkie, who possessed an abundance of energy coupled with a charismatic personality, as they desperately wanted to win the election and would not nominate has-beens or any of the young greenhorns in the party. Hoover, licking his wounds after his loss, told the press, "I am going fishing; I'm not going to talk politics now."[219] The plush Ahwanee Hotel, a massive stone edifice in Yosemite National Park, a place the couple loved, was just the right choice for him and his wife Lou Henry to achieve a speedy recovery.[220] Later Hoover pledged his support to the maverick from Indiana even though his ideas on foreign policy generally mirrored Roosevelt's. Privately, he gibed to close associates that the Hoosier was an outsider with a "grab bag mind."[221] After Willkie's nomination, Hoover continued to push privately to secure food for hungry Europeans, as he wished to keep the issue out of the forthcoming campaign.[222] His strategy could change depending on the Democratic candidate and the outcome of the general election, but despite his low regard for Willkie, any Republican was better than four more years of "that man's" New Deal.

Would Roosevelt break with tradition and seek a third term? It is doubtful, regardless of near-endless speculation, that the ghost of

George Washington much affected the Squire of Hyde Park. When the Democratic Convention opened on July 15 in Chicago, the big question had still not been publicly answered, though the president had quietly done much to ensure that the pledged delegates would grant him the nomination. At a Young Democrats Convention in Pittsburgh, a delegate yelled out, "It is not for Roosevelt to tell us that he wants a third term, but it is rather for us to tell Roosevelt that we want a third term."[223] "The Sphinx," as the press had dubbed the elusive president, had successfully and sometimes deceitfully dodged the question for two years. On the eve of the convention, Roosevelt shared his desire to again be nominated with his trusted circle, and even then, he disingenuously claimed that only if offered the nomination would he accept.[224] If assiduously courted by the delegates, how could he possibly refuse? Subterfuge aside, FDR wanted a third term in which, as commander in chief, he could orchestrate American preparedness for a war he wished to avoid, though he doubted that would be possible.[225]

The president sent Harry Hopkins (his trusted aide and former leader of the Works Progress Administration) and his wife Eleanor to Chicago to quietly orchestrate the president's wish to head the ticket once more.[226] Alben Barkley, the convention's permanent chairman and the senate majority leader from Kentucky, began his Tuesday evening address shortly after 9:00 p.m. to a convention bored, confused, and eager for direction. Midway through his speech, Barkley departed from his text and simply said, "FRANKLIN DELANO ROOSEVELT." A tumultuous twenty-five-minute demonstration broke out in favor of again nominating the president.[227] Barkley ended his speech by reading a message from Roosevelt telling the delegates that they were free to vote for any candidate they chose.[228] Momentarily, a sense of bewilderment pervaded the convention, and then a deep voice boomed from a microphone in the basement of the convention hall, bellowing out repeatedly, "WE WANT ROOSEVELT, WE WANT ROOSEVELT." The voice belonged to Thomas D. Garry, superintendent of sewers. The delegates took up the chant, "WE WANT ROOSEVELT, EVERYBODY WANTS ROOSEVELT, THE WORLD NEEDS ROOSEVELT," as many again flooded onto the convention floor.[229] The suspenseful drama played out so long by Roosevelt was over. The precedent set by George Washington had been cast aside; Roosevelt would be nominated for a third term. The following evening, the president was officially awarded the prize he so desired while Superintendent Garry, who had triggered the delegate explosion, achieved lasting fame as "the voice from the sewers."[230] The city bosses and many in the party balked at the president's selection of Secretary of Agriculture Henry Wallace as his running mate, a man who had a reputation among many as too far left and a crackpot due to his interest in the occult. The stubborn Roosevelt held out and, as usual, got his way.[231] The president wanted Wallace, an Iowan and an outstanding progressive secretary of agriculture, as a farm belt insurance policy to counter any Willkie appeal, given the Republican's roots back home in Indiana.

With FDR's and Willkie's securement of their party's nominations, Hoover ruminated about his future. His political career now over, he knew electoral vindication was not to be his. He came to understand that though he was many party members' favorite Republican, and a leading spokesman for Republican principles, the party saw him as unelectable. Now sixty-six years old, the Chief "would never again hear *Hail to the Chief* played for him."[232] Freed from presidential politics and basically ignored by the Willkie campaign, the political pariah from Palo Alto redirected his need to be useful and remain onstage into searching for ways to render aid to hungry Europeans. Holding a deep belief in the essential rightness of a European feeding plan, it became his obsessive task, one that would be even more difficult if Willkie failed to defeat Roosevelt.[233]

The diminution of the relief campaign brought personal disappointment to Hoover, but his campaigns for Polish and Finnish relief had been very successful. Between December 1939 and May 1941, Finland received $3.5 million in aid from the FRF and more than $2.3 million in direct aid from the American Red Cross[234] By any measure, it was an amazing achievement. The largest amount of Red Cross aid was provided in the year following the end of the Winter War. Emergency aid rendered to Polish refugees and to Poles in the Government General, with small amounts, helped thousands of sick and wounded. The CPR spent $3 million on aid to the Government General and to Polish refugees and, if successful in obtaining the

Romanian gold, would add another $3 million to its coffers.[235] The Roosevelt administration attempted to minimize US aid to Finland and Poland to conserve its economic and political resources for support of Great Britain and France. Yet Hoover could take pride that in his battle with Davis, the Red Cross, and Roosevelt; he had forced them to spend far more money and time than intended.

The tens of thousands of Polish soldiers still interned in Romania, Hungary, and Lithuania received CPR support, but what was their fate? In Bucharest in January 1941, the Iron Guard Legionnaires overthrew the government of Ion Antonescu. The large number of internees in three camps in southern Romania were all returned to Nazi control in the Government General. In June 1941, the Soviets took full control of Lithuania and began mass deportation. Polish soldiers held in four large camps in the north of the country were sent to forced labor camps in Siberia. Those interned in Hungary fared much better. In 1944, when the Soviets occupied the country, many made their way back to Poland, while some, having made a home for themselves, stayed. For those who escaped to the west, and to other locations around the world, both soldiers and civilians, starting over was fraught with difficulties, but Poles succeeded in becoming proud citizens of their adopted countries. For those trapped in the bloodlands, the outcome was more than often tragic.

Conclusion

Herbert Hoover's battles with Roosevelt over feeding Europe and going to war were not over. He would tell the story of the National Committee on Food for the Small Democracies in his book *An American Epic*. He likely favored the chapters on his relief efforts that highlighted a more than two-year struggle with Franklin Roosevelt and Winston Churchill. As he later wrote in his magnum opus, *Freedom Betrayed*, he was making his case against Roosevelt "more pungent." But the story he decided not to tell—the story of the nine-month battle starting in September 1939 and ending in June 1940—was ultimately the only success Hoover had in bending Roosevelt's foreign policy in support of his goals. After all, the president possessed enormous power and control of both houses of Congress. Any battle Hoover chose to wage stood little chance of success. It is unclear whether he understood what he had accomplished, though it was during this period that Hoover was effective in rendering aid and his teams on the ground led or worked with other relief agencies in difficult circumstances. Hundreds of thousands of Poles were fed, clothed, and housed. The persistent efforts of Charlotte Kellogg in organizing the Commission for Polish Relief (CPR) and conducting negotiations with the State Department, the flight across Poland of Paul Super and Clare Hollingworth just ahead of the Germans, their imaginative work with Jimmy Brown in Romania and Hungary, and Gilbert Redfern's twenty-seven months in Vilnius were the most difficult and challenging of the CPR relief programs. Exciting stories, yes, and the old man in a hurry, working ferociously night after night in the Waldorf tower, left out all this and more. The people who came forward and volunteered, Hoover's minutemen of relief, were citizens of varied backgrounds and extraordinary accomplishments. Many were successful in business and more than generous with their time and money. Hoover, committed to volunteerism, must have taken great satisfaction in the achievements of his colleagues and partners. However, if he had told the story, it would have been a statistical rendition. It was not that he did not acknowledge the dramatic underlying tale, but he believed the numbers were the story. Ironically, Hoover's opportunity to aid Poland and Finland was dependent on Hitler and Stalin. The pact between the two dictators opened the door. Aid to Polish refugees and to the Government General was possible because Hitler, after conquering Poland, stopped campaigning, creating a six-month space tagged the "Phoney War" by Senator William Borah. The Finns, holding back the Soviet invasion for one hundred days and signing a peace agreement that largely left their country intact, opened a second door for Hoover to provide aid.

The ex-president would continue to speak out against American entry into the European war and to oppose Roosevelt's moves to defend America by aiding the Allies, seeing them not as a defense but as the road to war. In my view, though the battle was heated, Hoover and Roosevelt, along with many other Americans, were closer together then they could imagine. In the nine-month period here under investigation, the terms *interventionist* and *anti-interventionist* mean little. A small number, both in and out of government, advocated for immediate American military intervention, and few argued the country should not intervene under any circumstances. The question so hotly debated was how best to protect the United States and avoid going to war. Most on both sides of the argument were anti-interventionists, including Hoover and Roosevelt. The oft-argued line that the foxlike Roosevelt understood that America would finally have to go to war, to make the world safe for democracy, is a myth. The president was a reluctant belligerent. The decision on war was not made by the United States; it was a decision made in Tokyo and Berlin. Even after Pearl Harbor, Roosevelt was slow to accept the enormity of what was necessary to win. After Pearl Harbor, Hoover supported the war effort but stuck to his humanitarian principles, arguing that the conflict should be conducted within rules set forth in the Geneva and Hague Conventions. He spoke against total war, opposing the bombing of enemy cities and insisting that it was wrong to use food as a weapon of war. Hoover was not alone in his effort and garnered significant support here and in Great Britain, though he stood no chance of putting distance between Roosevelt and Churchill.

Significantly, the first nine months of the war defined the parameters of the rest of the seventeen-month debate, revealing the central question posed to a neutral nation, thousands of miles distant from the unfolding battlefields, a nation soured by the result of its participation in World War I and what followed. The question was what should be done in response to the Nazi invasion of Poland and the Soviet invasion of Finland. The American approach was timid but prudent. Rancorous debates aside, the overwhelming majority of the American people and their representatives in Congress, while shaken by what was happening in Poland and Finland, wished to do what they could. That did not include going to war for either country. The British and French came dangerously close to militarily intervening in Finland but at the last minute stepped back.

A central question asked in this historical period, regarding what measures should be taken when larger and more powerful countries launch unwarranted attacks on smaller neighbors, is very much with us. The dilemma posed by the 2022 Russian invasion of Ukraine echoes the choices posed in 1939. Humanitarian aid, yes, and support for refugees, yes. But the question of military aid, what kind and how much, is a topic of hot debate, as it was regarding Finland. Assisting the Ukrainians in defense of their country without becoming directly involved, incurring the risks inherent in a proxy war, or triggering a wider European war is a tightrope act. History has returned with a vengeance. Hanging over the decisions concerning Ukraine is a new geopolitical reality, a close working relationship between Russia and China that mirrors the Hitler-Stalin pact of August 1939. Future options on Ukraine are shaped by that reality. An understanding of the intense debate between interventionists and anti-interventionists in the first year of war does not prove a guide on choices about the course of action to be made today, but it provides an understanding of the choices America made in very similar circumstances and why, thus expanding the range of our existential choices.

A second question asked in 1939 was what it would mean for the country if America did go to war. For the interventionists, it was a chance to correct the mistakes made after World War I. Their view posited that America had been the makeweight in the war and had failed to use power effectively at Versailles. If the United States had joined the League of Nations, the aggressions of the 1930s might have been prevented. The war was an opportunity to step up and get it right, to take our rightful place in the world and move toward Woodrow Wilson's belief in collective security. Hoover's view was very different. Entering into the great game of European politics was an endless, tireless game that could not be won. History taught Hoover that the European past was one of a continuous rise and fall of contending powers. Hoover learned from World War I that war was the great enlargement of government, an expansion of powers that curbed civil rights. While the internationalists, who won the battle, have been right about the benefits, Hoover and the anti-interventionists have been right that the cost is extraordinary. The mood in America under Joe Biden and his last two predecessors has been retreatism: come home, America; the burden is too great.

Hoover vs. Roosevelt captures those two men's sharp disagreements. Those disagreements, however, rested on shared foundational values. Both had a deep abiding belief in the democratic experiment and in America's potential, buttressed by a faith in the judgment of the average citizen. Both, as Americanists, were of independent mind, tempered by the idealism of Woodrow Wilson. Neither was rigidly ideological. They saw the path forward quite differently, and both embraced the mission articulated by John Winthrop on that spring day in Holland in 1630: "Wee shall be as a city upon a hill, the eies of all people are uppon us." The contenders, Hoover and Roosevelt, differed on what that city was to be. Getting there was a clenched-fist political battle that both relished.

Notes

Foreword

1. Wilson, *Herbert Hoover*, 274.
2. Best, *The Life of Herbert Hoover*, 465.
3. See, for example, Adler, *The Isolationist Impulse*; Jonas, *Isolationism in America*; Cole, *Roosevelt and the Isolationists*; Doenecke, *Storm on the Horizon*; Kupchan, *Isolationism*.
4. Carpenter, "The Dissenters." See also Doenecke, *Not to the Swift*.
5. Hoover, *An American Epic*, vol. 4.

Introduction

1. Neil MacNeil, Oral History Interview (OHI), Second Session, May 7, 1967, Herbert Hoover Presidential Library and Museum (HHPLM), West Branch, Iowa, 48, 58–59.
2. Hu-Hua and Hoo Loo were the Chinese names given Hoover and his wife by their servants in Tientsin.
3. Hoover, *The Memoirs of Herbert Hoover: Years of Adventure, 1874–1920*.
4. Hoover, *The Memoirs of Herbert Hoover: The Cabinet and the Presidency*; Hoover, *The Memoirs of Herbert Hoover: The Great Depression, 1929–1941*.
5. Historian George Nash carefully edited and published the long-withheld manuscript in 2011. See Nash, *Freedom Betrayed*.
6. Smith, "On the Outside Looking In," 146.
7. MacNeil, OHI, Second Session, 31–33.
8. See Hoover, *The Ordeal of Woodrow Wilson*.
9. Hoover, *An American Epic*, 4:113.
10. Barry, *Rising Tide*, 412; Percy, *Lanterns on the Levee*, 249–269.
11. Saul Bellow interview, "My Agonies over Writing," *Telegraph Magazine*, October 3, 1975.

12. Nash, *The Crusade Years*. The majority of the chapter titles in this memoir began with "The Crusade Against Collectivism."

13. Pickett, *For More Than Bread*, 83.

Chapter 1: The End of All Wars

1. On the Declaration of London, see Cox, *Hunger in War and Peace*, 20–28.
2. Burner, *Herbert Hoover*, 82.
3. Ibid.
4. Hoover, *An American Epic*, 2:302; Bane and Lutz, *The Blockade of Germany after the Armistice*.
5. Hoover, *The Ordeal of Woodrow Wilson*, 157.
6. De Wiart, *Happy Odyssey*, 128.
7. Gilbert, *The First World War*, 395.
8. See quote in Cox, *Hunger in War and Peace*, 242. Historian Martin Gilbert gave an estimate of 762,106. See Gilbert, *Churchill*, 256.
9. Ibid.
10. Hoover, *An American Epic*, 1:viii.
11. James, *Winston S. Churchill*, 3:2684.
12. Dallas, *1918*, 445.
13. Ibid.
14. See Steiner, *The Lights That Failed*.
15. Douhet, *The Command of the Air*; Hippler, *Bombing the People*.
16. On casualty figures, see "German Bombing of Britain, 1914–1918," Wikipedia, https://en.wikipedia.org/wiki/German_bombing_of_Britain,_1914–1918 (accessed January 20, 2020); Charlton, *The Air Defense of Britain*; Kennett, *The First Air War*.
17. Stanley Baldwin, "A Fear for the Future (1932)," Wikisource, en.wikisource.org/wiki/A_Fear_For_The_Future (accessed November 16, 2019).
18. Ibid.
19. Rennell, "The Blitz 70 Years On."
20. See Henig, *The Peace That Never Was*; Pedersen, *The Guardians*.
21. Junod, *Warrior without Weapons*, 120.
22. Mencken, *From a Mencken Chrestomathy*, 148–152.
23. Cudahy, *The Armies March*, 208.
24. Ibid., 209.
25. Calvocoressi, Wint, and Pritchard, *Total War*, 513.

NOTES

26. Pieter Serrien, "Bombing of Mortsel," http://pieterserrien.be/english/bombing-of-Mortsel (accessed August 29, 2018); Serrien, *Tranen over Morstel*, 22.

27. Chen, "Bombing of Cities in France and Low Countries 1 Jul 1940–7 May 1945."

28. Examples include Grayling, *Among the Dead Cities*; Overy, *The Bombers and the Bombed*. The German playwright Rolf Hochhuth condemned the bombing campaign in *Soldiers*, as did Jörg Friedrich in *The Fire*; Süss, *Death from the Skies*; Moore, *Bombing the City*.

29. See Orwell, "As I Please."

30. See Roberts, *The Storm of War*, 429. For an evenhanded overview, see Hansen, *Fire and Fury*.

31. See Detzer, *Appointment on the Hill*, 225–252; Vining, *Friend of Life*, 295; Swanberg, *Norman Thomas*, 258–276. On the British side of the Atlantic, see discussion of morality and bombing and the role of George Bell (the bishop of Chichester) in Messenger, *"Bomber" Harris and the Strategic Bombing Offensive*, 209–211; Probert, *Bomber Harris*, 193, 339–340; Bell, *The Church and Humanity*, 129–141; Brittain, *England's Hour*; Brittain, *Testament of Experience*.

32. See Brittain, "Massacre by Bombing."

33. Black, *A Cause for Our Times*, 3.

34. See Bell, "Peace Movements."

35. C. E. M. Joad, "A Pacifist's Conversion," *The Listener*, September 12, 1940, 385.

36. "'Stop Bombing Us': Primate's Appeal to Allies Reported on Belgian Radio," *Catholic Herald*, May 26, 1944.

37. Olson, *Those Angry Days*.

38. Quoted in Olson, *Those Angry Days*, xviii.

39. See Nash, *Freedom Betrayed*, 199.

40. Libby, *To End War*, 150.

41. Whyte, *Hoover*, 564.

42. Fiedler, *303 Squadron*, xxiii.

43. Olson, *Those Angry Days*, xx.

44. Watt, "Roosevelt and Neville Chamberlain," 201–202.

45. Nash, *Freedom Betrayed*, 204.

46. Patterson, *Mr. Republican*, 197.

47. Knowles, *The Poems of Wilfred Owen*, 60.

48. See Chamberlain, *America's Second Crusade*.

Chapter 2: The Contenders: Hoover and Roosevelt

1. Alonzo Field, White House Chief Butler, OHI, July 24, 1970, HHPLM, 18.
2. Weinstein, *The Eddie Cantor Story*, 86.
3. Ibid., 85.
4. Scharnhorst, *Mark Twain*, 317.
5. On the "new conservatism," see Whyte, *Hoover*, 550–574.
6. Freidel, "Hoover and FDR," 136.
7. Nash, *The Life of Herbert Hoover*, 3:428.
8. See Walch and Miller, *Herbert Hoover and Franklin D. Roosevelt*, 5–6, and letter with Hoover handwritten notations in PPI-Roosevelt, Franklin, HHPLM.
9. Dunne, *Mr. Dooley's Philosophy*.
10. Beschloss, *Presidents of War*, 362.
11. Welles, *The Time for Decision*, 3.
12. Hoover, *The Ordeal of Woodrow Wilson*, viii.
13. Wert, "Hoover's Brush with the Boxers," 42.
14. Hoover, *The Memoirs of Herbert Hoover*, 1:53.
15. Ibid.
16. Lou Henry Hoover to Evelyn Wright Allan, no date, circa August 1, 1900, Evelyn Wright Allan Papers, HHPLM.
17. Lou Henry Hoover to Mary Austin, no date, circa 1916, Mary Austin Papers, Box 11, Huntington Library, San Marino, California.
18. "Lord Byron Quote," iz Quotes, http://izquotes.com/quote/359924 (accessed April 22, 2018).
19. From FDR's log of his summer 1918 European trip. See Dallek, *Franklin D. Roosevelt*, 67–68.
20. Brands, *Traitor to His Class*, 118.
21. See Picchi, *The Five Weeks of Giuseppe Zangara*; Burns, *Roosevelt*, 147.
22. Brands, *Traitor to His Class*, 278.
23. Moley, *After Seven Years*, 139.
24. Picchi, *The Five Weeks of Giuseppe Zangara*, 191.
25. Perkins, *The Roosevelt I Knew*, 15.
26. "George Canning Quotes," BrainyQuote, https://brainyquote.com/quotes/george_channing_183459 (accessed April 22, 2018).
27. See https://www.digitalhistory.uh.edu/disp_textbook.cfm?smtID=3&psid=3918 (accessed January 6, 2020).
28. Emerson, *The Collected Works of Ralph Waldo Emerson*, 1:52.
29. See Jordan, *American Warlords*, xiv; Kimball, *The Juggler*, 3.

30. Herbert Hoover, "A Call to American Reason," Chicago, June 29, 1941, in *Addresses upon the American Road, 1940–1941*, 93–94.

31. Dallek, *Franklin D. Roosevelt*, 342.

32. Dallek, *Franklin D. Roosevelt and American Foreign Policy*, 186.

33. See Smith, "Herbert Hoover and the Third Way," in Walch, *Uncommon Americans*, 249–261.

34. See Houck, *FDR and Fear Itself*.

35. Fisher, July 31, 1971, OHI, 15.

36. Colton, *Memoirs of Ethan T. Colton, Sr., 1872–1952*.

37. Noonan, *What I Saw at the Revolution*, 210.

38. Smith, *An Uncommon Man*, 22.

39. Wert, *For the Love of the Game*.

40. Wert, *Hoover the Fishing President*.

41. Adams, *My Camera in Yosemite Valley*.

42. See Ashworth, *Agrarians and Aristocrats*, 66–67.

43. Chevalier, *Society, Manners and Politics in the United States*, 283, 282. Also see Schaff, *America*, 29; Huntington, *Who Are We?*, 69–75.

44. See introductory essay by Richard Norton Smith in Mayer, *Dining with the Hoover Family*.

45. Whyte, *Hoover*, 135.

46. http://satchelpaige.com/quote2.html (accessed September 7, 2019).

47. Helen d'Oyle Sioussat, November 2, 1969, OHI, HHPLM.

48. Ibid.

49. Mr. and Mrs. Allan Campbell, November 30, 1971, OHI, HHPLM, 4.

50. Pevsner, *Pioneers of Modern Design*, 29–32.

51. Ibid.

52. Ibid.

53. Ibid.

54. Ibid.

55. See Kanigel, *The One Best Way*; Lloyd, *Aggressive Introvert*, 62–63.

56. Nash, *The Life of Herbert Hoover*, 3:291.

57. May Bradford Shockley, January 21, 1970, OHI, HHPLM, 11.

58. Ibid.

59. Clements, *Hoover, Conservation and Consumerism*, 62.

60. Joseph C. Green, November 22, 1967, OHI.

61. Cather, "Roll Call on the Prairies," in Berg, *World War I and America*, 570.

62. See "American Relief Administration," Wikipedia, http://en.wikipedia.org/wiki/American_Relief_Administration (accessed October 9, 2018). See also Patenaude, *The Big Show in Bololand*; Smith, *The Russia Job*.

63. Dray, *The Fair Chase*.
64. Lou Henry Hoover to Philippi Harding, July 7, 1921, Correspondence File, Lou Henry Hoover Papers, HHPLM.
65. Olson and Cloud, *Those Angry Days*, xv.
66. See Cole, *Roosevelt and the Isolationists*, 6.
67. Ibid., 5.
68. Ward, *A First-Class Temperament*, xv.
69. See Kimball, *The Juggler*, 7.
70. Burns, *Roosevelt*, 371.
71. Kimball, *The Juggler*, 35.
72. Ibid.
73. Stolberg, "The Decider," *New York Times*, December 24, 2006.
74. Lehrman, *Churchill, Roosevelt, and Company*, 3.
75. Starling, *Starling of the White House*, 309–311.
76. Tate Family Papers, LC.
77. Sherwood, *Roosevelt and Hopkins*, 114.
78. Smith, *FDR*, 162.
79. Lehrman, *Churchill, Roosevelt and Company*, 10. Anna's comment was reported in Henry Wallace's diary and later confirmed by her.
80. See Persico, *Franklin and Lucy*; Ward, *Closest Companions*.
81. See Golway, *Frank and Al*.
82. Biddle quoted in Olson and Cloud, *Those Angry Days*, 63.
83. Lou Henry Hoover to Allen Hoover, February 1933, Allen Hoover Papers, HHPLM.
84. Whyte, *Hoover*, 529.
85. Quoted in Freud, *Civilization and Its Discontents*, 67–68.
86. For a detailed accounting of the negotiations and the signing of this nefarious agreement, see Watt, *How War Came*, 447–478; Moorhouse, *The Devils' Alliance*; Read and Fisher, *The Deadly Embrace*, 246–259; Nekrich, *Pariahs, Partners, Predators*; Weinberg, *Germany and the Soviet Union, 1939–1941*, 65–75. For the text of pact and secret protocol, see US Department of State, *Documents on German Foreign Policy*, 7:245–247.

Chapter 3: *The Liars' League: The World Turned Upside Down!*

1. See Caquet, *The Bell of Treason*; Taylor, *Munich*; Faber, *Munich, 1938*; MacDonogh, *1938, Hitler's Gamble*.

2. Maser, *Hitler's Letters and Notes*, 367.

3. "The Triumph of Hitler: Nazis Take Czechoslovakia," The History Place, https://historyplace.com/worldwar2/triumph/tr-czech.htm (accessed December 30, 2019).

4. On public reaction, see Henderson, *Failure of a Mission*, 208–233; Kennan, *From Prague after Munich*, 80–87.

5. The British government had come to a consensus on Hitler's untrustworthiness prior to his march on Prague. See Watt, *How War Came*, 106–108.

6. For public opinion in Great Britain, see Bouverie, *Appeasement*, 298–304; Eatwell, "Munich, Public Opinion, and Popular Front," 122–139; C. N. Trueman, "Public Opinion and Appeasement in 1938," History Learning Site, November 3, 2019, https://www.historylearningsite.co.uk/world-war-two/causes-of-ww2/public-opinion-and-appeasement-in-1938 (accessed January 12, 2020).

7. Hamby, *For the Survival of Democracy*, 407–408; Baldwin, *The Crucial Years*, 61–62; Murray, *The Change in the European Balance of Power*, 283–309. For the British public's reaction to the dismemberment of the Czechoslovakian state, see Overy, *The Twilight Years*, 347–362; Gallup, *The Gallup International Public Opinion Polls*, 1:17–19. For analysis of American public opinion, see Philip E. Jacob, "Influences of World Events on U.S. Neutrality," *Public Opinion Quarterly* 4, no 1 (March 1940): 48–65. Jacob maintains that Hitler's violation of the Munich Agreement did not have that much effect on US opinion. Opinion did shift, but the cumulative effect of events after Munich was the cause.

8. Rees, *WWII behind Closed Doors*, 13.

9. See Bouverie, *Appeasement*. Two excellent books on Chamberlain are Fuchser, *Neville Chamberlain and Appeasement*, 75; Rock, *Chamberlain and Roosevelt*, 164. Also see Callahan, *Churchill*, 50–51; Harvey, *The Diplomatic Diaries of Oliver Harvey*, 261; Kirkpatrick, *The Inner Circle*, 152; Charmley, *Chamberlain and the Lost Peace*; Colvin, *The Chamberlain Cabinet*; Stewart, *Burying Caesar*. More recent biographies include Self, *Neville Chamberlain*; Crozier, *Neville Chamberlain*.

10. Fuchser, *Neville Chamberlain and Appeasement*, 181.

11. James, *"Chips,"* 185–186.

12. Bouverie, *Appeasement*, 323.

13. Cienciala, *Poland and the Western Powers*, 207–237; Cienciala, "Poland in British and French Policy in 1939." Also see Fuchser, *Neville Chamberlain and Appeasement*, 184–187; Callahan, *Churchill*, 51. The French reaction to the events in 1938 and 1939 is well covered by Shirer, *The Collapse of the Third Republic*, 498–560; Sherwood, *Georges Mandel and the Third Republic*, 211–251; Reynaud, *In the Thick of the Fight*, 177–233.

14. See Jeansonne, *Herbert Hoover*, 322; Nash, *Freedom Betrayed*, xxix.
15. *The German White Paper: Full Text of the Polish Documents Issued by the Berlin Foreign Office*.
16. Gellman, *Secret Affairs*, 195.
17. Nash, *Freedom Betrayed*, 133.
18. See Watt, "Roosevelt and Neville Chamberlain," 200.
19. Ronald Lindsay to Foreign Office (FO), 12 September 1938, *Documents on British Foreign Policy*, series III, II, No. 841, quoted in Watt, "Roosevelt and Neville Chamberlain," 200.
20. See "Roosevelt Presidential Press Conference," in *Complete Presidential Press Conferences of Franklin D. Roosevelt*, 13:237–239; Dallek, *Franklin D. Roosevelt*, 340.
21. Prazmowski, "Poland," 161.
22. Watt, *How War Came*, 433.
23. Gunther, *Inside Europe*, 427.
24. Watt, *How War Came*, 433.
25. For the quotation, see Read and Fisher, *The Deadly Embrace*, 70.
26. See Steiner, *The Triumph of the Dark*, 1031. On the state of the German economy, see Tooze, *The Wages of Destruction*, 285–325.
27. Rees, *WWII behind Closed Doors*, 18.
28. Friedländer, *Nazi Germany and the Jews*, 1:17.
29. See Kershaw, *Hitler, 1936–1945*, 194–195.
30. Stalin, *Report on the Work of the Central Committee to the XVIIIth Congress of the Communist Party of the Soviet Union*, 16.
31. Hoffman, *Hitler Was My Friend*, 102.
32. See Rossi, *The Russo-German Alliance*, 37; Read, *The Devil's Disciples*, 568.
33. Hoffman, *Hitler Was My Friend*, 102.
34. Kotkin, *Stalin*, 663.
35. Bohlen, *Witness to History*, 82.
36. Moorhouse, *The Devils' Alliance*, 5; Ulam, in *Stalin*, 508–509, claims the idea of a nonaggression pact was Ribbentrop's.
37. Montefiore, *Stalin*, 310–311.
38. Ibid., 25.
39. See Bloch, *Ribbentrop*, 248. Also see Weitz, *Hitler's Diplomat*, 209–213.
40. Moorhouse, *The Devils' Alliance*, 26.
41. Ibid., 28.
42. Bohlen, *Witness to History*, 83.
43. Gafencu, *Last Days of Europe*, 226.

44. Montefiore, *Stalin*, 311.
45. Weitz, *Hitler's Diplomat*, 911.
46. Moorhouse, *The Devils' Alliance*, 40.
47. See Hoffman, *Hitler Was My Friend*, 109.
48. Rossi, *The Russo-German Alliance*, 42.
49. Montefiore, *Stalin*, 311–312.
50. Gisevius, *To the Bitter End*, 365.
51. Dallek, *Franklin D. Roosevelt and American Foreign Policy*, 196.
52. Hull, *The Memoirs of Cordell Hull*, 1:657.
53. See Bohlen, *Witness to History*, 68–83; Herwarth, *Against Two Evils*, 140–167.
54. Berle and Jacobs, *Navigating the Rapids*, 245.
55. Hoover, "Shall We Send Our Boys to Foreign Wars?" 12–13, 137–139.
56. Nash, *Freedom Betrayed*, 150.
57. Hoover, *An American Epic*, 4:xiv.
58. Fuchser, *Neville Chamberlain and Appeasement*, 186.
59. Churchill, *The Second World War*, 394.
60. Macmillan, *Winds of Change*, 548–549. Opponents in Parliament called Eden and his followers the "Glamour Boys." See Eden, *The Reckoning*, 36.
61. James, *"Chips,"* 208.
62. Ibid., 208.
63. Ibid., 209.
64. See Corum, *The Roots of Blitzkrieg*, 170–171; Nekrich, *Pariahs, Partners, Predators*, 120–122.
65. See Reynaud, *In the Thick of the Fight*, 232–233.
66. Jędrzejewicz, *Diplomat in Berlin*, 566.
67. Polonius, *I Saw the Siege of Warsaw*, 14.
68. For details of the partitions in 1793 and 1795, see Wandycz, *The United States and Poland*, 26–57; Davies, *God's Playground*, 81–162. For details on the 1939 partition, see Read and Fisher, *The Deadly Embrace*, 246–259.
69. Polonius, *I Saw the Siege of Warsaw*, 14.
70. Ibid., 14.
71. Gorodetsky, *The Maisky Diaries*, 219.
72. Herwarth, *Against Two Evils*, 173–174.
73. See Leonhard, *Betrayal*, 22.
74. Ibid., 23.
75. Hoffman, *Hitler Was My Friend*, 103.
76. Read, *The Devil's Disciples*, 569.

77. For an overview of the refugee work and aid provided by the American National Red Cross (ANRC) and by other relief organizations, see Curti, *American Philanthropy Abroad*; Dulles, *The American Red Cross*; Korson, *At His Side*; Marrus, *The Unwanted*; Proundfoot, *European Refugees*; Victor Weybright, "Altruism at Armageddon," *Survey Graphic* 29 (1940): 373–377, 415; ANRC, *Annual Report, 1940*. Additionally, see Sumner Welles to European Missions, April 30, 1940, State Department Decimal File (SDDF) 840.48/3569A, Record Group (RG) 59, National Archives and Records Administration (NARA), Washington, DC.

78. Korson, *At His Side*, 3–5; Isserman, *A Rabbi with the American Red Cross*, 19–21. For a synopsis of the Red Cross Mission and the organization's relationship with foreign Red Cross societies, see John G. Winant Papers, Box 4, Post Records, RG 84, Washington National Record Center, Suitland, Maryland.

79. Korson, *At His Side*, 3–5; Isserman, *A Rabbi with the American Red Cross*; Dulles, *The American Red Cross*. The AFSC worked in Spain during the civil war and with Spanish refugees who had fled to other countries (especially France) and was actively aiding Jewish refugees from Nazi Germany. See Jones, *Through Loyalist and Insurgent Spain*; Jones, *Swords into Ploughshares*, 293–318; Kershner, *One Humanity*, 19–21; Kershner, *Quaker Service in Modern War*; Pickett, *For More Than Bread*; Wilson, *In the Margins of Chaos*, 184–255. For the pre–World War II work of the JDC, see Bauer, *My Brother's Keeper*; for his later work on WWII JDC activities, see Bauer, *American Jewry and the Holocaust*. The Unitarian Service Committee helped refugees from Czechoslovakia after Munich and then expanded their work during the war. See Di Figlia, *Roots and Visions*; *Newsweek* 19 (April 6, 1942): 60–61. For China, see Schoppa, *In a Sea of Bitterness*, as well as the worldwide activities of the Mennonites in Unruh, *In the Name of Christ*.

80. Norman H. Davis, "Memorandum Concerning a War Emergency in Which the United States Is Not Engaged," August 28, 1939, SDDF 840.48/2952.

81. Ibid.

Chapter 4: War

1. Wegierski, *September 1939*, 26.
2. Patterson, *Between Hitler and Stalin*, 142.
3. De Wiart, *Happy Odyssey*, 155.
4. Super, *Twenty-Five Years with the Poles*, 202.
5. Ibid., 202.

6. See Halder, *The Halder War Diary*; Höhne, *Canaris*, 347; Rossino, *Hitler Strikes Poland*, 9.

7. Russell, *Berlin Embassy*, 35.

8. Wegierski, *September 1939*, 27; Neugebauer, *The Defence of Poland*, 93.

9. See Bethell, *The War Hitler Won*, 1–13. Early-morning attacks on Katowice and Kraków are well reported in Hollingworth, *The Three Weeks' War in Poland*, 16–24, as is the commencement of the war in Maitland, *European Dateline*, 43–52. For an excellent recounting of military operations, see Zaloga and Madej, *The Polish Campaign, 1939*; Rossino, *Hitler Strikes Poland*, 58–87; Neugebauer, *The Defence of Poland*.

10. Nash, *Freedom Betrayed*, 151.

11. Hollingworth, *Frontline*, 15.

12. Patterson, *Between Hitler and Stalin*, 144–145.

13. Korwin-Rhodes, *The Mask of Warriors*, 8–9.

14. Moorhouse, *First to Fight*, 18–19.

15. Cannistraro, Wynot, and Kovaleff, *Poland and the Coming of the Second World War*, 97.

16. Monika Sieradzka, "WWII: Poland Marks 80 Years Since First Bombs Fell on Wielun," DW, August 31, 2019, https://www.dw.com/en/wwii-poland-marks-80-years-since-first-bombs-fell-on-wielun/a-50161482 (accessed January 24, 2020).

17. See Łukasiewicz, *Diplomat in Paris*, 272–273.

18. Italian "attempts" to bring about an international conference can be found in Ciano, *The Ciano Diaries, 1939–1943*, 136–138, and in the biography of the British ambassador to Italy, Sir Percy Loraine. See Waterfield, *Professional Diplomat*, 238–347.

19. Stewart, *Burying Caesar*, 379–380; Gilbert, *Winston S. Churchill*, 5:1106. The Polish ambassador called Lord Halifax shortly after 10:00 a.m.; see Raczynski, *In Allied London*, 25.

20. Quote appears in Cosgrove, *Churchill at War*, 32. A detailed account of these events can also be found in Parkinson, *Peace for Our Time*, 195–226.

21. Amery, *My Political Life*, 3:324.

22. Stewart, *Burying Caesar*, 383–384; Aster, *1939*, chap. 24.

23. Dilks, *The Diaries of Sir Alexander Cadogan*, 211; Cosgrove, *Churchill at War*, 33–34; Gates, *End of an Affair*, 3–7; Henderson, *Failure of a Mission*, 292–293; Parkinson, *Peace for Our Time*, 195–226.

24. Shirer, *The Collapse of the Third Republic*, 515.

25. Ibid., 514.
26. Brittain, *England's Hour*, 8.
27. MacLeod, *Neville Chamberlain*, 276.
28. Reston, *Deadline*, 74.
29. Dugdale, *Baffy*, 150.
30. For British reaction to the start of war, see Charman, *Outbreak 1939*, 153, 157–256; Ball, *The Last Days of the Old World*; Brittain, *England's Hour*, 2–3; Brittain, *Testament of Experience*, 213–214; Panter-Downes, *London War Notes, 1939–1945*, 3–4; Seth, *The Day the War Broke Out*; Turner, *The Phony War*, 445. For reaction in Berlin, see Mosely, *On Borrowed Time*, 445; Parkinson, *Peace for Our Time*, 220; Shirer, *The Rise and Fall of the Third Reich*, 198–202. For France, see Shirer, *The Collapse of the Third Republic*, 514.
31. Cooper, *Old Men Forget*, 258.
32. Maitland, *European Dateline*, 50; Shachtman, *The Phony War, 1939–1940*, 57.
33. Bullitt, *For the President, Personal and Secret*, 368–369; Brownell and Billings, *So Close to Greatness*, 239.
34. Asquith, *Margot Asquith's Great War Diary*, 13. Also see Reynolds, *The Long Shadow*, 243–276.
35. Stargardt, *The German War*, 30.
36. Klemperer, *I Will Bear Witness*, 306–307.
37. Gorodetsky, *The Maisky Diaries*, 221.
38. Burns, *Roosevelt*, 394.
39. Alsop and Kintner, *American White Paper*, 58–60.
40. Ibid., 58.
41. Hull, *The Memoirs of Cordell Hull*, 1:671.
42. *The Public Papers and Addresses of Franklin D. Roosevelt: War and Neutrality*, 8:454.
43. Roosevelt, *This I Remember*, 207.
44. Ibid.
45. Roosevelt, *My Day*, 141; Howarth, *August 1939*, 244.
46. *Complete Presidential Press Conferences of Franklin D. Roosevelt*, 14:133.
47. Bland, Ritenour, and Wunderlin, *The Papers of George Catlett Marshall*, 2:46.
48. Roosevelt, *FDR*, 915–917.
49. Ibid.
50. D'Este, *Eisenhower*, 250.
51. See Hoover's early pronouncements on avoiding war, "Shall We Send Our Youth to War" and "We Must Keep Out," in Hoover, *Further Addresses upon the*

American Road, 116–128, 139–157. For Hoover's comment, see Public Statement File, September 1, 1939, Herbert Hoover Papers (HHP), HHPLM. Also see Hal Elliott Wert, "Years of Frustration: Herbert Hoover and World War II," in Walch, *Uncommon Americans*, 209–223.

52. "Broadcast on Outbreak of European War," San Francisco, September 1, 1939, Herbert Hoover Special Collections: Articles, Addresses and Public Statements, 1915–1964, HHP, HHPLM.

53. Ibid.

54. Roosevelt, *F.D.R.*, 916.

55. Brittain, *England's Hour*, 8.

56. Tanner, "W. H. Auden's 'September 1, 1939'—Fifty Years Later."

57. Wyndham, *Love Lessons*, 10.

58. Wiser, *The Twilight Years*, 226–227.

59. Mullen, *Lightening Man*.

60. James, *"Chips,"* 265.

61. Harvey, *The Diplomatic Diaries of Oliver Harvey*, 316; Parkinson, *Peace for Our Time*, 224–226. Also see Shachtman, *The Phony War*, 63–65, for more detail on the British debate over what or where to attack or even if an attack was warranted.

62. Harvey, *The Diplomatic Diaries of Oliver Harvey*, 316.

63. Gates, *The End of an Affair*, 18–20; Shachtman, *The Phony War*, 66–67; Shirer, *The Collapse of the Third Republic*, 520–530.

64. Miller, *War at Sea*, 17–20.

65. Van der Vat, *The Atlantic Campaign*, 4–6.

66. For stories of those aboard the *Athenia* and their rescue, see Carroll, *Athenia Torpedoed*.

67. Ibid., 5.

68. Callie, "Sinking of the *Athenia*," WW2 Memories, July 29, 2011, http://ww2memories.wordpress.com/2011/07/29/sinking-of-the-athenia (accessed October 13, 2018).

69. See Goebbels, *The Goebbels Diaries*, 25.

70. See Blair, *Hitler's U-Boat War*, 69.

71. On immediate implementation of the blockade, see Medlicott, *The Economic Blockade*, 1:63. On the Dutch steamer as the first blockade case, see Alexander Kirk, Charge d'Affaires, American Embassy Berlin, to Cordell Hull, telegram, "Summary of German Press," September 5, 1939, SDDF 740.00112 European War (EW), 1939/45.

72. Lord Lothian to Cordell Hull, telegram, September 10, 1939, SDDF 740.00112 EW, 1939/45.
73. Brock, *Nor Any Victory*, 10–11.
74. Ibid., 14.
75. Shachtman, *The Phony War*, 74.

Chapter 5: Crushed

1. De Wiart, *Happy Odyssey*, 155.
2. De Wiart, *Happy Odyssey*, 64.
3. Hollingworth, *The Three Weeks' War in Poland*, 75.
4. Ibid., 155. De Wiart offered this advice on September 24.
5. Hollingworth, *The Three Weeks' War in Poland*, 20.
6. Wegierski, *September 1939*, 33.
7. Moorhouse, *First to Fight*, 19.
8. Rossino, *Hitler Strikes Poland*, 58–87.
9. Zaloga and Madej, *The Polish Campaign, 1939*, 116–144.
10. Super, *Twenty-Five Years with the Poles*, 203.
11. See Dorman, "Poland August/September 1939," Special Collection Library, University of Wisconsin, Milwaukee.
12. Ibid.
13. Ibid., 154; Juliette Bretan, "'Pakty i Fakty': The Last-Ever Polish Interwar Cabaret Revue," https://pl/en/article/pakty-i-fakty-thelast-ever-polish-interwar-cabaret-review (accessed March 19, 2020).
14. Earle, *Blackout*, 147.
15. Ibid., 148.
16. Brzezinski, *Isaac's Army*, 7.
17. Ibid.
18. Showalter, *Hitler's Panzers*, 88; Mosier, *The Blitzkrieg Myth*, 62–78.
19. Hollingworth, *The Three Weeks' War in Poland*, 27.
20. Polonius, *I Saw the Siege of Warsaw*, 37.
21. See Citino, *Blitzkrieg to Desert Storm*, 28–30. The Wehrmacht corrected mistakes made in Poland, produced larger tanks with larger guns, and proved just how effective combined arms warfare (Blitzkrieg) could be seven months later in the battle for France.
22. Ibid., 29.
23. "U.S. Military Aide Back from Berlin," *New York Times*, November 30, 1939, 11. Black's comments to the *Times* stirred controversy as he asserted, "I do not believe any of the atrocity stories."

24. Wegierski, *September 1939*, 42.

25. Ibid., 43.

26. See Weigel, *Witness to Hope*, 41.

27. Ibid., 53. Lolek was a nickname bestowed by family when Karol when a child.

28. Maitland, *European Dateline*, 50; Shachtman, *The Phony War, 1939–1940*, 57.

29. Super, *Twenty-Five Years with the Poles*, 203.

30. Polonius, *I Saw the Siege of Warsaw*, 34–35.

31. Hollingworth, *Frontline*, 20.

32. Ibid.

33. Patterson, *Between Hitler and Stalin*, 152.

34. Ibid., 153.

35. Ibid., 161.

36. Ibid., 152.

37. Hollingworth, *The Three Weeks' War in Poland*, 27.

38. Collier, *The Warcos*, 6–7.

39. Ibid.

40. Patterson, *Between Hitler and Stalin*, 155.

41. Super, *Twenty-Five Years with the Poles*, 203–204.

42. Ibid., 204.

43. Ibid.

44. Ibid.

45. Ibid.

46. Korwin-Rhodes, *The Mask of Warriors*, 19. For a detailed accounting of the gold, see nbp.pl/en/publikacje/bankoteka_4_September_2014_internet.pdf (accessed April 6, 2020).

47. Ibid.

48. "The Wartime Fate of the Polish Gold," *Bankoteka*, Special Issue, September 4, 2014, nbp.pl/en/publikacje/bankoteka_4_September_2014_internet.pdf (accessed April 30, 2020).

49. Super, *Twenty-Five Years with the Poles*, 206.

50. Ibid., 3.

51. Hoover, *The Memoirs of Herbert Hoover*, 1:356; Cornebise, *Typhus and the Doughboys*.

52. See Snyder, *Bloodlands*, 1–20.

53. Davies, *God's Playground*.

54. Super, *Twenty-Five Years with the Poles*, 12.

55. Ibid., 13.
56. Ibid., 25.
57. See Davidowicz, *From That Place and Time*, 164–185.
58. Super, *Twenty-Five Years with the Poles*, 207.
59. Ibid., 208.
60. Ibid.
61. Ibid., 210.
62. Ibid., 211.
63. Ibid., 213.
64. Ibid.
65. Biddle to Secretary of State Cordell Hull, September 5, 1939, telegram 124.60C/89, *Foreign Relations of the United States, 1938*, Vol. 2, 1956, 674.
66. J. Crang, "Escape from Poland, WWII Memories and History," War Illustrated, http://ww2momories.wordpress.com/2011/08/24/how-we-escaped-from-Poland (accessed October 11, 2018).
67. Biddle, *Poland and the Coming of the Second World War*, 113.
68. Patterson, *Between Hitler and Stalin*, 167.
69. Snippets from Margaret Thompson's diary are found at Boyce Thompson, "Margaret Thompson Biddle's Furs Barely Escaped the Bombs in Poland," Thompson Family History, https://thompsongenealogy.com/2010/05/margaret-thompson-biddles-furs-barely-escaped-the-bombs-in-poland (accessed April 21, 2020).
70. Earle, *Blackout*, 146.
71. Thrasher, "The Well-Tempered Diplomat," 73.
72. *Life* 7, no. 16 (October 16, 1939): 29.
73. Walser, "War Comes to Warsaw."
74. Crang, "Escape from Poland."
75. Biddle, *Poland and the Coming of the Second World War*, 130–132.
76. Ibid., 131; Crang, "Escape from Poland."
77. See Brzezinski, *Isaac's Army*, 19.
78. *Wywołać wika z lasu* (to call the wolf from the forest) is an old peasant proverb for disaster. See Piotrowski, *Vengeance of the Swallows*, 8.
79. Quote by Otto Tolischus, *New York Times*, September 11, 1939, in Collier, *The Warcos*, 6.
80. Biddle, *Poland and the Coming of the Second World War*, 116.
81. Brownell and Billings, *So Close to Greatness*, 205.
82. Rosenman, *The Public Papers and Addresses of Franklin D. Roosevelt*, 8:454.
83. Biddle, *Poland and the Coming of the Second World War*, 117.

84. Stanley Baldwin, "A Fear for the Future (1932)," Wikisource, http://en.wikisource.org/wiki/A_Fear_For_The_Future (accessed November 16, 2019); Junod, *Warrior without Weapons*, 120.
85. Calvocoressi, Wint, and Pritchard, *Total War*, 513.
86. Spiegel, *Renia's Diary*, 37. Three years later, Renia escaped the liquidation of the Przemyśl ghetto but a few days later was discovered and shot.
87. Garrett, *Of Fortunes and War*, 83.
88. Biddle, *Poland and the Coming of the Second World War*, 120.
89. Ibid., 123.
90. Ibid., 121.
91. See Thompson, "Margaret Thompson Biddle's Furs."
92. Bryan, *Warsaw*, 16.
93. Ibid.
94. Ibid., 17.
95. Ibid., 13.
96. Ibid., 14.
97. Ibid., 18.
98. Olson and Cloud, *A Question of Honor*, 66.
99. Salter, *Flight from Poland*, 72.
100. Bryan, *Warsaw*, 19.
101. See Langbart, "We Found Ourselves Living in the Midst of a Battlefield."
102. Bryan, *Warsaw*, 31.
103. Langbart, "We Found Ourselves Living in the Midst of a Battlefield."
104. Bryan, *Warsaw*, 20.
105. Ibid., 22.
106. Polonius, *I Saw the Siege of Warsaw*, 151–152.
107. Ibid., 152.
108. Ibid., 153.
109. Ibid., 161.
110. Ibid., 161–162.
111. Janiszewska, *The Colors of War*, 5.
112. Hollingworth, *Frontline*, 26.
113. Zamoyska-Panek, *Have You Forgotten?*, 34.
114. Ibid., 35.
115. Ibid.
116. Hollingworth, *The Three Weeks' War in Poland*, 68.
117. Biddle, *Poland and the Coming of the Second World War*, 126.
118. See Sosabowski, *Freely I Served*, 37.

119. Rossino, *Hitler Strikes Poland*, 186.
120. Biddle, *Poland and the Coming of the Second World War*, 128.
121. Ibid., 128–129.
122. Crang, "Escape from Poland."
123. Beck, *Final Report*, 218–220.
124. Biddle, *Poland and the Coming of the Second World War*, 133.
125. Hollingworth, *The Three Weeks' War in Poland*, 59.
126. Ibid., 67.
127. Thrasher, "The Well-Tempered Diplomat," 87.
128. Biddle, *Poland and the Coming of the Second World War*, 137.
129. Hollingworth, *The Three Weeks' War in Poland*, 71.
130. Ibid., 70.
131. Ibid., 71.
132. Ibid., 66–67.
133. Ibid., 56–57.
134. Ibid., 50.
135. Ibid., 17–18.
136. Garrett, *Of Fortunes and War*, 38–39.
137. Ibid., 39–40.
138. There is body of literature on the Fields, their association with the Unitarian Universalist Service Committee, the BCRC, and the rescue operations run out of Prague. See Marton, *True Believer*; Di Figlia, *Roots and Visions*, 22–52; Joukowsky, *Defying the Nazis*; Subak, *Rescue and Flight*; Brinson and Malet, *Exile in and from Czechoslovakia during the 1930s and 1940s*.
139. Garrett, *Fortunes and War*, 45.
140. Ibid., 42.
141. Ibid., 36.
142. Tomasz Targański, "Zaleszczyki, przedwojenny kurort z dramatyczną historią w tle," *Polityka*, September 12, 2017, https://polityka.pl/tygodnikpolityka/historis/1719128,1,zaleszczyki-przedwojenny-kurot-z-dramatyczna-historia-w-tle.read (accessed May 17, 2020).
143. Sapieha, *Polish Profile*, 309.
144. Ibid., 315.
145. Ibid., 317.
146. Biddle, *Poland and the Coming of the Second World War*, 145–146.
147. Ibid., 148–149.
148. Bryan, *Warsaw*, 16.

149. Moorhouse, *First to Fight*, 208–209; Rossino, *Hitler Strikes Poland*, 99; Westermann, *Hitler's Police Battalions*, 128. Moorhouse estimates that over a three-day period, six hundred Jews were murdered.
150. See Thompson, "Margaret Thompson Biddle's Furs."
151. Ibid.
152. Hollingworth, *The Three Weeks' War in Poland*, 87.
153. Ibid., 88.
154. Ibid., 90–91.
155. Moorhouse, *First to Fight*, 211.
156. Patterson, *Between Hitler and Stalin*, 370.
157. Hollingworth, *The Three Weeks' War in Poland*, 97.
158. Biddle, *Poland and the Coming of the Second World War*, 154.
159. Patterson, *Between Hitler and Stalin*, 173.
160. Ibid.
161. Ibid., 175.
162. Prażmowska, *Britain and Poland*, 11.
163. Patterson, *Between Hitler and Stalin*, 175.
164. Biddle, *Poland and the Coming of the Second World War*, 156.
165. Earle, *Blackout*, 114–115.
166. Biddle, *Poland and the Coming of the Second World War*, 156; Hollingworth, *The Three Weeks' War in Poland*, 98.
167. Hollingworth, *The Three Weeks' War in Poland*, 98.
168. Ibid., 102.
169. Bussgang, "Haunting Memories," 238.
170. Hollingworth, *The Three Weeks' War in Poland*, 105.
171. Patterson, *Between Hitler and Stalin*, 178.
172. Bussgang, "Haunting Memories," 238.
173. Salter, *Flight from Poland*, 190.
174. Hollingworth, *The Three Weeks' War in Poland*, 102.
175. Ibid., 107. There is disagreement about what time the heads of the government and military crossed the bridge.
176. Patterson, *Between Hitler and Stalin*, 178.
177. Hollingworth, *The Three Weeks' War in Poland*, 108.
178. Patterson, *Between Hitler and Stalin*, 179.
179. Patterson, *Between Hitler and Stalin*, 180; Mirowicz, *Edward Rydz-Śmigły*, 304.
180. Bussgang, "Haunting Memories," 239.
181. Hollingworth, *The Three Weeks' War in Poland*, 108.

182. Ibid., 108–109.
183. Ibid.
184. Hollingworth, *Frontline*, 43.
185. Hollingworth, *The Three Weeks' War in Poland*, 148–149.
186. Ibid.
187. Ibid., 109
188. Ibid., 111.

Chapter 6: The Rapprochement That Failed: The Battle over Aid Begins

1. *Time*, September 11, 1939.
2. Rosenman, *The Public Papers and Addresses of Franklin D. Roosevelt*, 8:464–473.
3. Israel, *The War Diary of Breckinridge Long*, 1.
4. Ibid., 2–3.
5. Ibid.
6. Berle and Jacobs, *Navigating the Rapids*, 250.
7. Ibid.
8. Ibid.
9. Hull, *The Memoirs of Cordell Hull*, 1:675.
10. Berle and Jacobs, *Navigating the Rapids*, 251.
11. Ickes, *The Secret Diary of Harold L. Ickes*, 2:712.
12. Ibid., 713.
13. Ibid., 712.
14. Ibid.
15. Hull, *The Memoirs of Cordell Hull*, 1:675.
16. Rasmussen, "On Labor Day Weekend 1939."
17. Ibid.
18. Rosenman, *The Public Papers and Addresses of Franklin D. Roosevelt*, 8:463.
19. Ibid.
20. *Time*, September 11, 1939; "President Wilson's Declaration of Neutrality," World War I Document Archive, http://wwi.lib.byu.edu/index.php/President_Wilson%27s_Declaration_of_Neutrality (accessed September 17, 2020). Also see Knock, *To End All Wars*, 34–35.
21. Ibid., 463–464.
22. Roosevelt, *FDR*, 916.
23. Berle and Jacobs, *Navigating the Rapids*, 252.

24. Gellman, *Secret Affairs*; Berle and Jacobs, *Navigating the Rapids*, 245.
25. Ickes, *The Secret Diary of Harold L. Ickes*, 2:715.
26. Blum, *Years of Urgency*, 87.
27. Blum, *Years of Urgency*, 95–96.
28. Hull, *The Memoirs of Cordell Hull*, 1:678. For more on Hull and neutrality, see Cole, *Roosevelt and the Isolationists*, 319–330; Dallek, *Franklin D. Roosevelt and American Foreign Policy*, 199–232; Langer and Gleason, *The Challenge to Isolation*, 1:201–235.
29. Farnham, *Roosevelt and the Munich Crisis*.
30. Hull, *The Memoirs of Cordell Hull*, 1:673–674; "A Proclamation of Neutrality of the United States Issued Pursuant to General International Law," Proclamation No. 2348, September 5, 1939, in Rosenman, *The Public Papers and Addresses of Franklin D. Roosevelt*, 8:464–473. For the best account of the formation of the "Special Division," see Corbett, *Quiet Passages*, 1–24.
31. See www.fdrlibrary.marist.edu/daybyday/daylog-september-1-1939 (accessed August 8, 2020).
32. On newspapers read per day, see White, *F.D.R. and the Press*, 77; quote in Ickes, *The Secret Diary of Harold L. Ickes*, 2:717.
33. Walch and Miller, *Herbert Hoover and Franklin D. Roosevelt*, 170.
34. Eleanor Roosevelt to Marie Meloney, September 10, 1939, Eleanor Roosevelt Papers (ERP), Series 100, Franklin D. Roosevelt Library (FDRL), Hyde Park, New York.
35. Eleanor Roosevelt to Bernard Baruch, September 10, 1939, ERP, Series 100, FDRL; Eleanor Roosevelt to Meloney, September 10, 1939.
36. Eleanor Roosevelt to Meloney, September 10, 1939.
37. Galloway, "The Public Life of Norman H. Davis," 143, 149.
38. Cole, *Roosevelt and the Isolationists*, 65–66.
39. Dulles, *The American Red Cross*, 345.
40. Hooker, *The Moffat Papers*, 263–264.
41. Ibid.
42. Berle and Jacobs, *Navigating the Rapids*, 252.
43. Ickes, *The Secret Diary of Harold L. Ickes*, 2:717.
44. Ibid.
45. Ibid.
46. Ibid., 718.
47. Edgar Rickard Diary, September 8, 1939, HHPLM.
48. Patenaude, *Big Show in Bololand*, 65.

49. Nash, *The Life of Herbert Hoover*, 2:364.

50. Fisher, July 31, 1971, OHI, 9–11; Best, *Herbert Hoover*, 1:121.

51. Charlotte Kellogg to Perrin Galpin, September 17, 1939, Box 32, Polish Relief, Paderewski Fund for Polish Relief, 1939–1940, HHP, Hoover Institution (HI).

52. Smith, "On the Outside Looking In," 143.

53. See Whyte, *Hoover*, 565.

54. "Our Documents: Franklin Roosevelt's Address Announcing the Second New Deal," October 31, 1936, FDRL.

55. Hoover Memorandum of Conversation, September 11, 1939, Post-Presidential Individual (PPI), HHPLM.

56. It is not known whether Taylor knew that Eleanor wanted Hoover to head a "new relief agency."

57. Ibid.

58. Ibid.

59. Barry, *Rising Tide*.

60. Ibid.

61. Smith, *An Uncommon Man*, 274; Memorandum of a Conversation with Myron Taylor, December 11, 1939, PPI, HHPLM; undated Hoover memorandum of the Taylor meeting, National Committee on Food for the Small Democracies Records, Box 61, Hoover Institution Archives (HIA).

62. Whyte, *Hoover*, 524.

63. Picchi, *The Five Weeks of Giuseppe Zangara*, 131–140.

64. Smith, *An Uncommon Man*, 164.

65. Starling, *Starling of the White House*, 306.

66. Fischer, July 31, 1971, OHI, 30; Brown, December 6, 1966, OHI, 2–3.

67. Smith, *An Uncommon Man*, 164.

68. Rickard Diary, September 11, 1939.

69. Ibid.

70. "Hoover Diary," Box 113, 186, Folder 2, HHP, HI.

71. Ibid.

72. Ibid.

73. For supposed fears of the Congress and the Republican leadership, see John Callan O'Laughlin to Hoover, September 23, 1939, Box 113, Folder 2, HHP, HI.

74. Hoover, *Further Addresses upon the American Road*, 134–135.

75. Myers, *The Foreign Policies of Herbert Hoover, 1929–1933*, 159.

76. See https://20012009.state.gov/r/pa/ho/time/id/16326.htm#:~:text=Since %20calls%20for%20a%20cessation,Japanese%20might%20impose%20upon%20 China (accessed November 1, 2020).

77. Best, *The Life of Herbert Hoover*, 117.

78. See Nash, *Freedom Betrayed*, xciii, n. 78.

79. Eleanor Roosevelt to Maria "Missy" Meloney, September 17, 1939, ERP, Series 100, FDRL.

80. Memoranda, Central Committee Meeting, September 18, 1939, Central Committee Meetings, 1935–1944, Box 110–114, Decimal File 900.6, ANRCR, RG 200, NARA, Washington, DC.

81. Ibid.

82. Hoover to Norman H. Davis, September 15, 1939, American Red Cross, Group 3, 900.02: Finnish Relief Fund, Box 1316, RG 200, NARA; PPI-Davis, September 15, 1939, HHP, HHPLM.

83. Rickard Diary, September 14, 1939.

84. Ibid.

85. *New York Daily News*, September 14, 1939.

86. Berle and Jacobs, *Navigating the Rapids*, 255.

87. Edwin Watson, Memorandum for the President, September 15, 1939, Official File 115, Box 1, Herbert Hoover, 1939–1945, FDRL.

88. Memoranda, Central Committee Meeting, September 18, 1939.

89. Norman Davis, memorandum of telephone conversation with Hoover on September 19, 1939, PPI-Davis, HHP, HHPLM.

90. Memoranda, Central Committee Meeting, September 18, 1939.

91. Ibid.

92. Ibid.

93. Ibid.

94. Ibid.

95. See Hoover, *An American Epic*, 4:1–3; Lerski, *Herbert Hoover and Poland*, 42; McCoy, "Herbert Hoover and Foreign Policy," 401–425; Herbert Hoover's correspondence with Norman Davis, PPI-Davis, HHP, HHPLM.

96. Long, *The War Diary of Breckenridge Long*, 12–13.

97. See Hinshaw, *Herbert Hoover*, 117; Lyons, *Herbert Hoover*, 118.

98. *YMCA Bulletin*, n.s. 16, no. 4 (1938), PPS, HHPLM.

99. Hoover to Super, April 27, 1938, Foreign Service Poland, 1938, American Friends Service Committee Archives (AFSCA).

100. Smith, *An Uncommon Man*, 251–258; Best, *Herbert Hoover*, 1:103.

101. For aid to Polish refugees in Romania, Hungary, Lithuania, Latvia, and German-occupied Poland, see Davis, "Informal Report," November 4, 1939, State Department Decimal File (SDDF) 840.48/300.

102. Berle and Jacobs, *Navigating the Rapids*, 255–256.

103. Kellogg to Galpin, September 17, 1939, HI.

104. Ibid.

105. Ibid.

106. Ibid.

107. Ibid.

108. Ibid.

109. Ibid.

110. Davis, Memorandum of Conversation with Eleanor and Franklin Roosevelt, September 17, 1939, Civilian Relief, European Theater of Operations, General Plans, Policies and Programs, 900.62/01, ANRCR, RG 200, NARA.

111. Ibid.

112. Ibid.

113. Ibid.

114. Ibid.

115. Ibid.

116. Ibid.

117. Ibid.

118. Lord Lothian to FO, telegram, September 18, 1939, FO 371/22882, C14069/13545/49, British National Archives (BNA), Kew Gardens, London; Bullitt to Roosevelt, telegram, September 16, 1939, SDDF 740.00112, EW 1939/75, RG 59, NARA.

119. Nash, *Freedom Betrayed*, xxxvi.

120. Rosenman, *The Public Papers and Addresses of Franklin D. Roosevelt*, 8:515.

121. Eleanor Roosevelt to Marie "Missy" Meloney, September 17, 1939, ERP, Series 100, FDRL.

122. Ibid.

123. Eleanor Roosevelt to Martha Gellhorn, September 27, 1939, ERP, Series 100, FDRL.

124. Eleanor Roosevelt to Meloney, October 8, 1939, ERP, Series 100, FDRL.

125. Nash, *Freedom Betrayed*, xxxvi.

126. Memoranda, Central Committee Meeting, September 18, 1939.

127. See Hoover calendar, September 19, 1939.

128. Rickard Diary, September 19, 1939.

129. Ibid.

130. Ibid., September 20, 1939.

131. Hoover to Davis, September 20, 1939, PPI-Davis, HHP, HHPLM.

132. Davis to Hoover, September 22, 1939, American Red Cross Correspondence, 1933–1934, Box 21, PPSF, HHP, HHPLM.

133. Davis to Hoover, September 27, 1939, American Red Cross Group 3, File 900.02, Finnish Relief Fund, Box 1316, RG 200, NARA.

134. Moffat to Kellogg, September 20, 1939, Polish Relief, Box 45, State Department, Washington, DC, 1939–1940, HI.

135. Ibid.

136. Ibid.

137. Hoover to Davis, September 24, 1939, PPI-Davis, HHP, HHPLM.

138. "Hoover Diary," Hoover note to himself, Folder 2, Box 113, 202, HHP, HI.

139. For quotation, see "We Must Keep Out," in Hoover, *Further Addresses upon the American Road*, 152. Hoover summed up his reasons in "We Must Stay Out," which first appeared in the *Saturday Evening Post*, October 27, 1939.

140. Hoover, *An American Epic*, 4:2.

141. Schmidt, "Hoover's Reflections on the Versailles Treaty," 61–86.

142. Whyte, *Hoover*, 223.

143. Smith, *An Uncommon Man*, 92.

144. Keynes, *The Economic Consequences of the Peace*.

145. See Hinshaw, *Herbert Hoover*, 117; Lyons, *Herbert Hoover*, 118.

146. Hoover, *An American Epic*, 4:2.

147. See letterhead of the Commission for Polish Relief (CPR), November 15, 1939, Box 387, PPI-Mrs. Vernon Kellogg, HHP, HHPLM.

148. See Diana Souhami, *Edith Cavell*.

149. "Hugh S. Gibson," Wikipedia, https://en.wikipedia.org/wiki/Hugh_S._Gibson (accessed January 3, 2021).

150. Ibid. Also see Grew, *Turbulent Era*, 76–77.

151. Nash, *Freedom Betrayed*, xxxvii.

152. Wert, "Years of Frustration," in Walch, *Uncommon Americans*, 211.

153. "News Bulletin No. 2," CPR, October 29, 1939, FO371/24103, W16631/13884/48, BNA.

154. Kellogg to Hoover, November 15, 1939, Box 387, PPI-Mrs. Vernon Kellogg, HHP, HHPLM.

155. News Bulletin No. 2, CPR, October 29, 1939, FO371/24103, W16631/13884/48, BNA.

Chapter 7: Rescue in Romania, Hungary, and Lithuania

1. Manning, *The Balkan Trilogy*, 107.
2. Hollingworth, *Frontline*, 45.
3. Sebastian, *Journal, 1935–1944*, 240.
4. Waldeck, *Athene Palace*, 16.
5. Patterson, *Between Hitler and Stalin*, 180.
6. Easterman, *King Carol, Hitler and Lupescu*, 186–188.
7. Waldeck, *Athene Palace*, 40–41.
8. Cowles, *Looking for Trouble*, 270.
9. Ibid., 271.
10. Manning, *The Balkan Trilogy*, 116.
11. Patterson, *Between Hitler and Stalin*, 191.
12. Salter, *Flight from Poland*, 95–98.
13. "Rumanian Prime Minister Shot Dead in the Street," *Sarasota-Herald Tribune*, September 21, 1939. Also see Sebastian, *Journal, 1935–1944*, 239, and Sturdza, *The Suicide of Europe*, 148–149.
14. Breckinridge Long Diary, Box 5, 224, Breckinridge Long Papers, MD, LC and *The Moffat Papers*, 268–269.
15. Ibid.
16. Waldeck, *Athene Palace*, 58; Salter, *Flight from Poland*, 97.
17. Sebastian, *Journal, 1935–1944*, 239–240.
18. Long Diary, September 24, 1939, 224–225.
19. Patterson, *Between Hitler and Stalin*, 181.
20. Łukasiewicz, *Diplomat in Paris, 1936–1939*, 349; Patterson, *Between Hitler and Stalin*, 181.
21. Clifford Norton was counselor to the British Embassy in Poland.
22. Łukasiewicz, *Diplomat in Paris, 1936–1939*, 343.
23. Coutouvidis, "Government-in-Exile."
24. Kapronczay, *Refugees in Hungary*, footnote 33, 54.
25. "Escape Route," Poland in Exile, 2008, http://www.polandinexile.com/escape.html (accessed February 24, 2021).
26. Garliński, *The Enigma War*, 45; Kippenhahn, *Code Breaking*, 178–179.
27. Garlinski, *The Enigma War*, 56.
28. Ibid.
29. *New York Times*, September 21, 1939, 16.
30. Super to E. E. Barnett, September 21, 1939, Poland, Correspondence and Reports, 1939, Kautz family YMCA Archives.

Notes

31. Super, *Twenty-Five Years with the Poles*, 213.
32. Super to E. E. Barnett, September 21, 1939, Poland, Correspondence and Reports, 1939; *New York Times*, September 21, 1939, 16.
33. Super, *Twenty-Five Years with the Poles*, 216.
34. Patterson, *Between Hitler and Stalin*, 190; Beck, *Final Report*, photographs between 246 and 247.
35. Super, *Twenty-Five Years with the Poles*, 217.
36. Ibid.
37. Bio, File C, James W. Brown, Kautz Family YMCA Archives.
38. James W. Brown to Frank V. Slack, September 12, 1939, Brown, James, Correspondence, Kautz Family YMCA Archives; Hollingworth, *The Three Weeks' War in Poland*, 147.
39. Brown to Slack, September 12, 1939.
40. Ann Cardwell or Ann Su Cardwell (pen name of Margaret Super), "The American YMCA's New Work—Polish Refugees in Romania," ND, circa Fall 1939, Super, Margaret, Articles, Letters, Polish Relief, CPR, HI.
41. Super, *Twenty-Five Years with the Poles*, 218.
42. Ann Cardwell, "The American YMCA's New Work—Polish Refugees in Romania," November 4, 1939, Super, Margaret, Articles, Letters, Polish Relief, CPR, HI.
43. Hollingworth, *The Three Weeks' War in Poland*, 147.
44. Ibid.
45. Abel Dairy, September 27, 1939, Vol. 6, 194.
46. Frank V. Slack, "Memorandum to the Staff," Poland, Correspondence and Reports, 1939, Kautz Family YMCA Archive and Super to D. A. Davis, October 3, 1939, Paul W. Super Correspondence, World Alliance of YMCAs, Geneva, Switzerland.
47. Super to Davis, October 3, 1939.
48. Ibid.
49. Super, *Twenty-Five Years with the Poles*, 219.
50. Ibid.
51. Super to Barnett, September 30, 1939, Poland, Correspondence and Reports, Kautz Family YMCA Archives.
52. Super to Davis, October 3, 1939.
53. Super, *Twenty-Five Years with the Poles*, 222.
54. Natalie Slivici, a YW staffer to Ruth Frances Woodsmall, General Secretary for the World YMCA, September 30, 1939, Poland, Correspondence and Reports, 1939, Kautz Family YMCA Archives.

55. Ernest Hemingway, "A Clean Well-Lighted Place," *The Complete Short Stories of Ernest Hemingway* (New York: Scribner, 2003), 288–291.

56. "Extract from a Letter from Paul D. Sturge," London, October 13, 1939, Polish Committee, AFSCA; Wilson, *In the Margins of Chaos*, 257.

57. Arthur Sweetser, League of Nations to Norman Davis, October 12, 1939, Norman H. Davis Papers (NDP), MSS, LC. Attached "Report by Dr. R Gautier on His Mission to Roumania, Hungary, and Yugoslavia," October 3, 1939, NDP, MSS, LC.

58. Natalie Slivici to Ruth Frances Woodsmall, September 30, 1939.

59. nbp.pl/en/publikacje/bankoteka_4_September_2014_internet.pdf, 8 (accessed April 6, 2020).

60. Jędrzejewicz, *Poland in the British Parliament*, 1:368.

61. Ibid., 1:149.

62. Hollingworth, *The Three Weeks' War in Poland*, 150.

63. Ibid., 151.

64. Super, *Twenty-Five Years with the Poles*, 224.

65. Hollingworth, *The Three Weeks' War in Poland*, 152.

66. Super, *Twenty-Five Years with the Poles*, 246–247.

67. Hoad, *The Eagle's Child*, 13–32.

68. Super, *Twenty-Five Years with the Poles*, 247.

69. Hollingworth, *The Three Weeks' War in Poland*, 152.

70. Super, *Twenty-Five Years with the Poles*, 224.

71. Ibid.

72. Ibid.

73. Hollingworth, *The Three Weeks' War in Poland*, 152.

74. "Shipments of Food to Hungry Poland," *The Monthly Future* 1, no. 6 (June 1940), 40; "Interim Report of the CPR," November 28, 1940, SDDF 840.48/4432; and Bertha Anne Peet, "How Polish Relief Works," *The Commonweal* 33, no. 12 (July 12, 1940), 242–244.

75. "News Bulletin No. 3," CPR, November 10, 1939, PPS-Poland-Relief, HHP, HHPLM.

76. Maurice Pate to Paul Super, October 25, 1939, Poland, Correspondence and Reports, 1939, Kautz Family YMCA Archives.

77. Jürgen Järvik, "Imaginary Budapest," Grande Flânerie, October 2016–March 2017, https://grandeflanerie.com/imaginarybudapest/ (accessed April 5, 2021).

78. Montgomery, *Hungary: The Unwilling Satellite*.

79. Kapronczay, *Refugees in Hungary*, 40–41.

80. Anna Kołakowska, "Hungarians towards the German Aggression on Poland," Przystanek Historia (Next Stop History), October 19, 2020, http://przystanekhistoria.pl/pa2/tematy/english-content/75481,Hungarians-towards-the-Geman-agression-on-Poland.html (accessed April 11, 2021).

81. Kapronczay, *Refugees in Hungary*, 41; "Poland in Exile—Evacuation Routes, 1939–1940," http://polandinexile.com/escape.html (accessed January 21, 2021); "The Long, Long Trail of Misery: Refugees from Poland and How They Are Being Helped," *The World's Children* XX, no. 1 (December 1939): 8–9.

82. Moorhouse, *First to Fight*, 212.

83. Patterson, *Between Hitler and Stalin*, 18; Biddle to Roosevelt, November 10, 1939, President's Secretary's File (PSF), Box 65, Poland, July–December 1939, FDRL; Patterson, *Between Hitler and Stalin*, 181.

84. Kołakowska, "Hungarians towards the German Aggression on Poland."

85. Jerzy Kirszak, "Biographies: Kazimierz Sosnkowski," Józef Piłsudski Institute of America, https://www.pilsudski.org/en/about-us/history/biographies/56-kazimierz-sosnkowski (accessed April 11, 2021).

86. Kołakowska, "Hungarians towards the German Aggression on Poland."

87. Super, *Twenty-Five Years with the Poles*, 260.

88. Super to Pate, telegram, October 26, 1939, Poland, Correspondence and Reports, 1939, Kautz Family YMCA Archives.

89. "John Flournoy Montgomery," Wikipedia, https://en.wikipedia.org/wiki/John_Flournoy_Montgomery (accessed April 15, 2021).

90. Ibid.

91. Quoted in Frank, *Discussing Hitler*, 15–16.

92. See Montgomery, *Hungary: The Unwilling Satellite*, and Frank, *Discussing Hitler*.

93. Super, *Twenty-Five Years with the Poles*, 261.

94. Dyboski to D. A. Davis, October 10, 1939, Poland, Correspondence and Reports, 1939, Kautz Family YMCA Archives.

95. Super to Davis, October 23, 1939, Paul W. Super Correspondence, World Alliance of YMCAs, Geneva; Super, *Twenty-Five Years with the Poles*, 261–262.

96. Super, *Twenty-Five Years with the Poles*, 269.

97. Pate to Super, cable, October 20, 1939, Poland, Correspondence and Reports, 1939, Kautz Family YMCA Archives.

98. Super, *Twenty-Five Years with the Poles*, 266.

99. Ibid.

100. Pate to Super, October 24, 1939, Poland, Correspondence and Reports, 1939, Kautz Family YMCA Archives.

101. Ibid.
102. Ibid.
103. Super to Pate, October 26, 1939, Poland, Correspondence and Reports, 1939, Kautz Family YMCA Archives.
104. Super to Pate, October 27, 1939.
105. Super to Tracy Strong, October 22, 1939, Correspondence, World Alliance of YMCAs, Geneva.
106. Super, *Twenty-Five Years with the Poles*, 267.
107. Ibid.
108. Ibid.
109. Margaret Super to Eleanor Roosevelt, September 26, 1939, in Bernard Baruch to ER correspondence, Box 680, Series 100, ERP, FDRL.
110. Norman H. Davis to Roosevelt, October 25, 1939, American Red Cross File, Roosevelt Papers, FDRL.
111. Slack to J.E. Manley, Poland, Correspondence and Reports, 1939, Kautz Family YMCA Archives.
112. Clarence Pickett Diary, November 14, 1939, AFSC Archive.
113. Eleanor Roosevelt, "My Day," *New York World-Telegram*, November 14, 1939, PPI-Mrs. Vernon Kellogg, Box 387, HHP, HHPLM.
114. Pate to Eleanor Roosevelt, November 17, 1939, Box 698, Series 100, ER Papers, FDRL.
115. Ibid.
116. Super to Strong, October 22, 1939.
117. Super, *Twenty-Five Years with the Poles*, 267.
118. Davis to Roosevelt, October 25, 1939, Swift-Taylor cable attached, American Red Cross File, Roosevelt Papers, FDRL.
119. Eleanor Roosevelt to Bernard Baruch, November 2, 1939, Box 680, Series 100, ERP, FDRL.
120. Slack to Manley, November 16, 1939.
121. In writing my first articles on Polish Relief in Romania and Hungary, I corresponded with Salamon-Racz. Salamon-Racz to author, May 22, 1991.
122. Davis to Eleanor Roosevelt, November 4, 1939, Box 685, Series 100, ERP, FDRL.
123. Lord Lothian to FO, telegram, September 18, 1939, FO 371/22882, C14069/13545/49; Bullitt to Roosevelt, telegram, September 16, 1939, SDDF, 740.00112 European War (EW) 1939/75.
124. Breckinridge Long Diary, November 9, 1939, Manuscript Division, Library of Congress.

125. Super to Slack, November 7, 1939, Poland, Correspondence and Reports, 1939, Kautz Family YMCA Archives.

126. Ibid.

127. Ibid.

128. Super, *Twenty-Five Years with the Poles*, 264.

129. Wilson, *In the Margins of Chaos*, 260–261.

130. H.D. Watson to Foreign Office, October 26, 1939, FO 371/24103, W16125/13884/48, British National Archives.

131. Hollingworth, *The Three Weeks' War in Poland*, 152–153.

132. Hollingworth, *Frontline*, 46.

133. Hollingworth, *The Three Weeks' War in Poland*, 155.

134. Ibid., 155–156.

135. Ibid., 158.

136. Ibid.

137. Garrnett, *Of Fortunes of War*, 99–115.

138. Hollingworth, *The Three Weeks' War in Poland*, 162.

139. Ibid.

140. Ibid.

141. Super, *Twenty-Five Years with the Poles*, 244.

142. Ibid.

143. Ibid., 240.

144. D. A. Davis to Super, November 21, 1939, World Alliance of YMCAs.

145. Ibid., 246.

146. Ibid.

147. Super to Davis, October 17, 1939, Poland, Correspondence and Reports, 1939, Kautz Family YMCA Archives.

148. Super, *Twenty-Five Years with the Poles*, 241–242.

149. Ibid., 243.

150. "The Polish Relief Fund, Activities to the End of 1939," Polish Reference, Box 39, Polish Relief Fund, London, 1940, Hoover Institution.

151. Brown to American Minister Mott, December 31, 1939, Poland, Correspondence and Reports, 1939, Kautz Family YMCA Archives.

152. Super, *Twenty-Five Years with the Poles*, 273.

153. Super to Davis and Strong, January 28, 1940, Paul W. Super Correspondence, World Alliance of YMCAs.

154. Šeinius, *Raudonasis Tvanas*, 2–3.

155. Norem, *Timeless Lithuania*, 149.

156. Redfern to CPR, April 17, 1941, Poland Relief, Box 40, Redfern, Gilbert, Correspondence 1941, HI. Whether Redfern made the remark that morning that he later wrote to Pate in his summation of CPR activities in Vilnius is unknown.

157. "Demographic History of the Vilnius Region," Wikipedia, https://en.wikipedia.org/wiki/Demographic_history_of_the_Vilnius_region (accessed July 4, 2021). Figures vary. The most reliable data is from the 1931 census, but by 1939 the Lithuanian population had grown from 1 percent to perhaps 6 percent. In 1939, the Jewish community may have constituted 40 percent of the population.

158. Kruk, *The Last Days of the Jerusalem of Lithuania*.

159. "We shall not rest until Vilnius is ours! [mes be Vilniaus nenurimsim!]" See Balkelis, "War, Conflict and the Refugee Crisis in Lithuania, 1939–1940," 468.

160. "Jurgis Alekna," Enciklopedija Lietuvai ir pasauliui (Encyclopedia for Lithuania and the world), https://lietuvai.lt/wiki/Jurgis_Alekna (accessed August 24, 2021).

161. Steve Danko, "The Rasos Cemetery in Vilnius, Lithuania," *Steve's Genealogy Blog*, November 3, 2007, https://stephendanko.com/blog/1875 (accessed August 1, 2021).

162. Norem, *Timeless Lithuania*, 160.

163. Naujokaitis, "Lithuania and the Soviet Union, 1939–1940," 1–14.

164. Ibid., 4.

165. Ibid., 2.

166. Ibid.

167. Ibid.

168. Ibid., 5.

169. *New York Times*, October 12, 1939, 3.

170. Šeinius, *Raudonasis Tvanas*, 16.

171. Tracy Strong, World Alliance of YMCAs, "Visit from February 26–March 2, 1940," Chronological Appendix on Polish Refugees (October 1939 to October 1942) with General Index, 39–44, ANRCR, 1935–1964, RG 200, NARA.

172. Ibid., 39.

173. Šeinius, *Raudonasis Tvanas*, 17.

174. Ibid.

175. Redfern, *The Tragedy of Vilna*, 2, Commission for Polish Relief (CPR), December 15, 1939, Poland, Correspondence and Reports, 1939, Kautz Family YMCA Archives.

176. Šeinius, *Raudonasis Tvanas*, 16.

177. Ibid., 18.

Notes

178. Koper and Stańczyk, *Ostatnie Lata Polskiego Wilna*.

179. See Balkelis, "War, Ethnic Conflict and the Refugee Crisis in Lithuania," 465; enclosure to Dispatch no. 608 (diplomatic), dated November 3, 1939, from American Legation at Kaunas, Lithuania, on the subject of Report of Mr. I. Seinius of the Lithuanian Red Cross, SDDF 840.48/3051, NA; Witold Zahorski to E. E. Barnett, November 12, 1939, Poland, Correspondence and Reports, 1939, Kautz Family YMCA Archives.

180. "Evacuation Routes 1939–1949," at "Escape Routes," polandinexile.com, http://polandinexile.com/escape.html (accessed August 21, 2021).

181. Šeinius, *Raudonasis Tvanas*, 18.

182. Alfred Wiener, "Conditions in Poland under Russian Domination, Winter 1939–1940, Hardships for the Population," March 27, 1941, Folder 815, Joint Distribution Committee Archive (JDCA), Joint Distribution Committee (JDC).

183. Ibid.

184. Gilbert Redfern, *Broken Families*, CPR, December 15, 1939, Polish Relief, Redfern, Gilbert Correspondence, HI.

185. Redfern, *The Tragedy of Vilna*.

186. By the end of the year, the CPR had sent $25,000. The clothing was a contribution from the Polish National Council of New York. See "News Bulletin No. 4," November 22, 1939, and "News Bulletin No. 5," December 29, 1939, Committees and Organizations, CPR, 1939, AFSCA.

187. "Informal Report by Norman H. Davis, Chairman of the American Red Cross, Regarding Relief for Polish Refugees," November 4, 1939, SDDF 840.48/3009, NA.

188. Redfern to Pate, January 17, 1939, Letter No. 6, Polish Relief, Box 40, HI.

189. For the Committee, Dr. Maria Petrusewicz, Report of Mr. I. Seinius of the Lithuanian Red Cross, October 30, 1939, Enclosure to Dispatch no. 608 (Diplomatic), November 3, 1939, American Legation Kaunas, Lithuania, SDDF 840.48/3051.

190. "War Activities of the JDC, Poland and Refugees from Poland, January 11, 1940," *Poland Publicity Bulletin* No. 5, Folder 812, JDCA, JDC. This bulletin was distributed to the JDC membership and others in the United States detailing the tragic events transpiring in Poland. The bulletin wished to make ongoing Nazi atrocities more widely known.

191. "News from All Over the World," *Jewish Telegraphic Agency* 6, no. 98, December 1, 1939, Jewish Telegraphic Agency bulletins, 1939, Box 23, Polish Relief, HI.

192. "News Bulletin No. 6," CPR, February 10, 1940, SDDF 840.48/3310. Also see Wilson, *In the Margins of Chaos*, 256–291; Hollingworth, *The Three Weeks' War in Poland*, 147–155, 165; "The Severe Winter of 1939–40," Netweather Community, November 7, 2006, https://www.netweather.tv/forum/topic/33839-the-severe-winter-of-1939-40.

193. Balkelis, "War, Ethnic Conflict and the Refugee Crisis in Lithuania," 466.

Chapter 8: Embargo Repeal, Politics, and Negotiations in the Garden of Beasts

1. See Langer and Gleason, *The Challenge to Isolation*, 16.
2. FDR to Norman Hapgood, August 28, 1935, in Roosevelt, *F.D.R.*, 1:504–505.
3. Ickes, *The Secret Diary of Harold L. Ickes*, 2:446.
4. Hansen, "Flashback"; Tucker, "The Legacy of the Brown Condor."
5. Harris, *African-American Reactions to War in Ethiopia*, 38.
6. Ibid., 93.
7. Quoted in Moorehead, *Gellhorn*, 107.
8. Eleanor Roosevelt to Martha Gellhorn, June 24, 1937, CER, Series 100, Eleanor Roosevelt Papers (ERP), FDRL.
9. Janet Somerville, "The Friendship of Eleanor Roosevelt and Martha Gellhorn," *Hazlitt*, February 12, 2018, https://hazlitt.net/longreads/friendship-eleanor-roosevelt-and-martha-gellhorn (accessed September 27, 2021); Martha Gellhorn to Eleanor Roosevelt, July 8, 1937, CER, Series 100, ERP, FDRL.
10. Smith, *American Relief Aid and the Spanish Civil War*, 2. Also see Gallup, *The Gallup Poll*, 1:49.
11. Mitter, *Forgotten Ally*, 98–108, 124–144; Harmsen, *Shanghai 1937*.
12. Philip E. Jacob, "Influences of World Events on U.S. 'Neutrality' Opinion," *Public Opinion Quarterly* 4, no. 1 (March 1940): 53.
13. Dallek, *Franklin D. Roosevelt and American Foreign Policy*, 148.
14. For the speech, see Rosenman, *The Public Papers and Addresses of Franklin D. Roosevelt*, 8:406–411.
15. Ibid., 406, 408.
16. Langer and Gleason, *The Challenge to Isolation*, 19.
17. Barkley, *That Reminds Me*, 168.
18. Ibid.
19. Dallek, *Franklin D. Roosevelt and American Foreign Policy*, 148.

20. Farnham, *Roosevelt and the Munich Crisis*, 135–138.

21. Blum, *Years of Urgency*, 2:48.

22. Figure from Gary Evans, "The Nanking Atrocity: Still and Moving Images 1937–1944," ResearchGate, June 15, 2014, https://www.researchgate.net/figure/Filmed-images-of-baby-Ping-Mei-Source-LOOK-Magazine_fig3_273513763.

23. Dallek, *Franklin D. Roosevelt and American Foreign Policy*, 199.

24. Ibid., 172.

25. Gelderman, "Point-to-Point Navigation," 6.

26. A series of polls on neutrality, aid for the Allies, and American participation in the war can be found in Cantrill and Struck, *Public Opinion*, 1074–1081, 1156–1163, and 1185–1189. See also Gallup, *The Gallup Poll*, 178–188. Some information from these polls and on public opinion on these issues can be found in Dallek, *Franklin D. Roosevelt and American Foreign Policy*, 201; Schneider, *Should America Go to War?*.

27. Gallup, *The Gallup Poll*, 149.

28. Dallek, *Franklin D. Roosevelt and American Foreign Policy*, 188–190; Smith, *FDR*, 188.

29. Dallek, *Franklin D. Roosevelt and American Foreign Policy*, 187; Hull, *The Memoirs of Cordell Hull*, 645.

30. Ibid., 189.

31. Ibid., 191.

32. See Israel, *Nevada's Key Pittman*, 165–166.

33. Glad, "Personality, Role Strains, and Alcoholism," 18–32; Glad, "Medical and Political Behavior," in *Key Pittman*, 280–281.

34. *Complete Presidential Press Conferences of Franklin D. Roosevelt*, 13–14:86–87.

35. McFarland and Roll, *Louis Johnson and the Arming of America*, 83.

36. *New York Times*, August 30, 1939, 3.

37. Rosenman, *The Public Papers and Addresses of Franklin D. Roosevelt*, 8:457.

38. Ibid., 8:460–464. Hull, admitting he was not neutral, advised against the inclusion of this statement in FDR's speech. See Hull, *The Memoirs of Cordell Hull*, 1:676.

39. Hull, *The Memoirs of Cordell Hull*, 1:674–675.

40. Langer and Gleason, *The Challenge to Isolation*, 201.

41. Ibid.

42. Brands, *Traitor to His Class*, 532.

43. Vandenberg, *The Private Papers of Senator Vandenberg*, 2–3.

44. Memo from Stephen Early to FDR, September 7, 1939, in Roosevelt, *F.D.R., His Personal Letters*, 918.

45. Israel, *Nevada's Key Pittman*, 167–168; Bloom, *The Autobiography of Sol Bloom*, 236–237.
46. Connelly, *My Name Is Tom Connelly*, 228.
47. Dallek, *Franklin D. Roosevelt and American Foreign Policy*, 201.
48. Cole, *Roosevelt and the Isolationists*, 321.
49. See Cole, *Roosevelt and the Isolationists*, 323, 325, and 327, on repeal of embargo as a boon to the economy. On the slowdown of mobilization, see Dallek, *Franklin D. Roosevelt and American Foreign Policy*, 203. The mobilization story is well told in McFarland and Roll, *Louis Johnson and the Arming of America*, and Eiler, *Mobilizing America*.
50. Nichols, "The Middle West and the Coming of World War II," 136.
51. Doenecke, *Storm on the Horizon*, 18, 21.
52. Dallek, *Franklin D. Roosevelt and American Foreign Policy*, 203.
53. Cole, *Roosevelt and the Isolationists*, 325.
54. McKenna, *Borah*, 88–89.
55. Felsenthal, *Alice Roosevelt Longworth*, 144.
56. "William E. Borah, Main Biography Page," law2.imkc.edu/faculty/projects/ftrails/haywood/Hay_BBOR.HTM.
57. Borah, "Retain the Arms Embargo: It Helps Keep Us Out of War," September 14, 1939, *Vital Speeches of the Day*, 741–743; *New York Times*, September 16, 1939, 1.
58. Langer and Gleason, *The Challenge to Isolation*, 220; Guinsburg, *The Pursuit of Isolationism in the United States Senate from Versailles to Pearl Harbor*, 213.
59. Cole, *Roosevelt and the Isolationists*, 144.
60. Ibid.
61. Olson, *Those Angry Days*, 66–67.
62. Ibid.
63. Ibid.
64. See Lower, *A Bloc of One*, 6.
65. Ibid., 22.
66. Ibid.
67. Ibid., 323.
68. "Burton Kendall Wheeler," *Time*, April 15, 1940, 21–22, quoted in Johnson, *Political Hell-Raiser*, 242.
69. Ibid., 238.
70. Ibid., 225.
71. Ibid., 224.

72. Olson, *Those Angry Days*, 63.

73. "'Quarantine' Speech at Chicago, Ill.," in Rosenman, *The Public Papers and Addresses of Franklin D. Roosevelt*, 8:406–411.

74. Johnson, *Political Hell-Raiser*, 237. For the full address, see Burton K. Wheeler, "Foreign Policy and Neutrality," April 15, 1939, *Vital Speeches of the Day*, 406–407.

75. "'Quarantine' Speech at Chicago, Ill."

76. Jackson, *That Man*, 105.

77. L. M. Bailey to Dear Fellow American, September 16, 1939, Cordell Hull Papers, Library of Congress, Manuscript Division (LCMD).

78. *New York Times*, September 21, 1939; *Life* 7, no. 14 (October 2, 1939): 12–13; Divine, *The Illusion of Neutrality*, 297–298.

79. *New York Times*, September 21, 1939, 16.

80. Ibid.

81. *Life*, October 2, 1939, 11.

82. *New York Times*, September 22, 1939, 16.

83. Colonel Charles A. Lindbergh, "Let Us Look to Our Own Defense," September 15, 1939, *Vital Speeches of the Day*, 5:751–752.

84. Ibid.

85. Ibid.

86. Entry for August 23, 1939, in Lindbergh, *The Wartime Journals of Charles A. Lindbergh*, 245; Olson, *Those Angry Days*, 69.

87. Olson, *Those Angry Days*, 71.

88. Entry for September 14, 1939, in Lindbergh, *The Wartime Journals of Charles A. Lindbergh*, 254–256.

89. Entry for September 15, 1939, in ibid., 256–258. Also see Berg, *Lindbergh*, 396–397.

90. Entry for September 15, 1939, in ibid., 257–258.

91. See Charles, *J. Edgar Hoover and the Anti-interventionists*, 39–42; Charles and Rossi, "FBI Political Surveillance and the Charles Lindbergh Investigation."

92. *North to the Orient* in 1935 and *Listen! The Wind* in 1938 were both best sellers.

93. Lindbergh, *War Within and Without*, 58.

94. Dorothy Thompson, "Col. Lindbergh and Propaganda," *On the Record*, *New York Herald Tribune*, September 20, 1939; "Lindbergh's 'Inclination toward Fascism' Cited by Dorothy Thompson," *Jewish Telegraphic Agency*, September 21, 1939; Olson, *Those Angry Days*, 77–79; Peter Kurth, *American Cassandra*, 312–313; Berg, *Lindbergh*, 397.

95. *New York Times*, September 15, 1934, 15. Also see Dorothy Thompson, *Let the Record Speak*.

96. Her fifty-page essay, "The Wave of the Future," was published in October 1940.

97. Lindbergh, *War Within and Without*, 59.

98. Entry for September 23, 1939, in Ickes, *The Secret Diary of Harold L. Ickes*, 3:20.

99. Entry for September 20, 1939, in William R. Castle Diary, Houghton Library, Harvard University, Cambridge, Massachusetts.

100. De Sales, *The Making of Yesterday*, 66–67.

101. Warren, *Radio Priest*, 186.

102. Ibid.

103. "Father Coughlin (x) Strict Neutrality and No Cash and Carry," Old Time Radio Downloads, September 17, 1939, https://www.oldtimeradiodownloads.com/historical/father-coughlin/father-coughlin-39-09-17-x-strict-neutrality-and-no-cash-and-carry.

104. See Weinstein, *The Eddie Cantor Story*, 130–134.

105. Hoover to Castle, September 14, 1939, William R. Castle Papers (WCP), Box 24, HHPLM.

106. Jeansonne, *Herbert Hoover*, 322.

107. Best, *Herbert Hoover*, 1:126–127.

108. Ibid.

109. Ibid.

110. Ibid.

111. Ibid.

112. Entry for September 12, 1939, in Rickard Diary; also see Hoover to Castle, September 14, 1939, WCP, Box 24, HHPLM.

113. Ibid.

114. Castle to Hoover, September 19, 1939, WCP, Box 24, HHPLM.

115. First quote from Castle to Hoover, September 19, 1939, WCP; second quote from the Castle Diary, September 19, 1939, Houghton Library, Harvard University.

116. Jeansonne, *Herbert Hoover*, 223–224.

117. McCoy, *Landon of Kansas*, 419.

118. "Senators Express Varying Opinions," *New York Times*, October 21, 1939, 16.

119. Alsop and Kintner, *American White Paper*, 75.

120. Smith, *Thomas E. Dewey and His Times*, 277.

121. Cole, *Roosevelt and the Isolationists*, 322; Cole, *Charles A. Lindbergh and the Battle against American Intervention in World War II*, 142–153; Jeans, *American Isolationists*, 7.

122. McKenna, *Borah*, 349.

123. McCoy, *Landon of Kansas*, 419.

124. Alsop and Kintner, *American White Paper*, 75.

125. *New York Times*, September 21, 1939, 16.

126. Best, *Herbert Hoover*, 1:132.

127. Nash, *Freedom Betrayed*, xxxvi.

128. For Hoover on bipartisanship and Roosevelt's idea of a "War Cabinet," see Hoover to Senator Charles W. Tobey, September 27, 1939, PPI, HHP, HHPLM; Best, *Herbert Hoover*, 1:132–133.

129. White to Knox, September 23, 1939, William Allen White Papers, LCMD.

130. Alsop and Kintner, *American White Paper*, 76.

131. Berle and Jacobs, *Navigating the Rapids*, 257.

132. Ibid., 257–258.

133. Ibid., 258.

134. *New York Times*, September 22, 1939, 17.

135. Ibid., 18.

136. See minutes of the Philadelphia Committee meeting on the night of August 19, 1939. "Philadelphia Committee for the Defense of Constitutional Rights and Thomas Blisard, September 1939," Temple University Libraries, https://digital.library.temple.edu/digital/collection/p16002coll31/id/1937.

137. Ibid.

138. Ibid.

139. "Luther Patrick," Wikipedia, https://en.wikipedia.org/wiki/Luther_Patrick.

140. *New York Times*, September 22, 1939, 18. Also see Jeansonne, *Women of the Far Right*, 123–124.

141. Devine, *The Illusion of Neutrality*, 297; Hull, *The Memoirs of Cordell Hull*, 684.

142. Rosenman, *The Public Papers and Addresses of Franklin D. Roosevelt*, 8:515.

143. See Cole, *Roosevelt and the Isolationists*, 319–330; Dallek, *Franklin D. Roosevelt and American Foreign Policy*, 200–204; Hull, *The Memoirs of Cordell Hull*, 1:676; Langer and Gleason, *The Challenge to Isolation*, 1:201–203.

144. Rosenman, *The Public Papers and Addresses of Franklin D. Roosevelt*, 8:516.

145. Alsop and Kintner, *American White Paper*, 77.

146. Rosenman, *The Public Papers and Addresses of Franklin D. Roosevelt*, 8:512.
147. Ibid., 520–521.
148. Rickard Diary, September 20, 1939.
149. *New York Times*, August 13, 1939.
150. Hoover to Colonel Charles A. Lindbergh, September 20, 1939, PPI, HHP, HHPLM.
151. Lindbergh, *The Wartime Journals of Charles A. Lindbergh*, 260. Lindbergh's diary is the only source of what transpired in their conversation. Hoover apparently made no memo of the conversation.
152. Ibid.
153. Ibid.
154. Ibid.
155. Ibid.
156. Ibid.
157. James B. Howell to Herbert Hoover, September 13, 1939, PPI, HHP, HHPLM.
158. Rickard Diary, September 21, 1939.
159. Best, *Herbert Hoover*, 1:125.
160. Frederick J. Libby, Executive Secretary, National Council for Prevention of War, to Herbert Hoover, September 21, 1939, PPI, HHP, HHPLM.
161. *New York Times*, October 2, 1939, 9.
162. Jeansonne, *Women of the Far Right*, 61.
163. Ibid.
164. *New York Times*, September 27, 1939, 25; Jeansonne, *Women of the Far Right*, 60–62.
165. Jeansonne, *Women of the Far Right*, 62.
166. See Johnson, *William Allen White's America*, 515–519; Cole, *Roosevelt and the Isolationists*, 321; Doenecke, *Storm on the Horizon*, 60. For opposition to amendment of neutrality laws, see Cole, *America First*, 8–16; Cole, *Charles A. Lindbergh and the Battle against American Intervention in World War II*, 70–77; Schneider, *Should America Go to War?*, 26–36.
167. White to Hoover, telegram, October 2, 1939, PPI, White, William Allen, Correspondence, 1936–1941, Box 252, HHP, HHPLM.
168. *New York Times*, October 4, 1939, 13.
169. Dulles and Fish, *Can America Stay Neutral?*.
170. Israel, *Nevada's Key Pittman*, 168.
171. Entry for September 27, 1939, in Ickes, *The Secret Diary of Harold L. Ickes*, 3:21–22.

172. Dallek, *Franklin D. Roosevelt and American Foreign Policy*, 202; Langer and Gleason, *The Challenge to Isolation*, 1:229.

173. Mackenzie King to John D. Rockefeller, October 13, 1939, Rockefeller Family, Record Group III, 2H, Friends and Relatives, Rockefeller Archive Center, Pocantico Hills, New York.

174. Cole, *Roosevelt and the Isolationists*, 327.

175. Ibid.

176. See Ben Allen to Jacob Allen, September 9, 1939, 5, PPI, HHP, HHPLM; Best, *Herbert Hoover*, 1:116.

177. On Johnson, see Smith, *An Uncommon Man*, 270.

178. Quoted in Smith, *Thomas E. Dewey and His Times*, 290.

179. Jacob Allen to Herbert Hoover, September 14, 1939; Ben Allen to James B. Howell, September 7, 1939; Herbert Hoover to James B. Howell, September 14, 1939, PPI, HHP, HHPLM; Best, *Herbert Hoover*, 1:131–132.

180. Rickard Diary, October 4, 1939.

181. On money, see Best, *Herbert Hoover*, 1:132; on Honnold and Hoover, see Nash, *The Life of Herbert Hoover*, 2:271–272.

182. James B. Howell to Herbert Hoover, September 12, 1939, PPI, HHP, HHPLM.

183. For the first quote, see Roy W. Howard, "Hoover Says Allies Can't Lose, Wants No 'War Party' in U.S.," September 4, 1939, *New York Herald Tribune*, Articles, Addresses and Public Statements, 2542, HHP, HHPLM; Rickard Diary, October 4, 1939.

184. Entry for October 1, 1939, in Lindbergh, *The Wartime Journals of Charles A. Lindbergh*, 267.

185. Entry for October 2, 1939, in ibid., 267.

186. See press release by Hoover, September 1, 1939, Public Statement File, HHP, HHPLM.

187. Howard, "Hoover Says Allies Can't Lose."

188. Best, *Herbert Hoover*, 1:123–129; on the Fox polls, see Smith, *An Uncommon Man*, 270–271.

189. Best, *Herbert Hoover*, 1:141–142, 147.

190. Hoover to Leland W. Cutler, October 5, 1939, PPI, HHP, HHPLM.

191. Entry for October 5, 1939, in Lindbergh, *The Wartime Journals of Charles A. Lindbergh*, 270.

192. Ibid., 271.

193. Rickard Diary, October 7, 1939; *New York Times*, July 12, 2009. The Lamont House address was 107 E. 70th St.

194. "Broadcast by Captain Eddie Rickenbacker America's Ace of Aces during the World War," September 26, 1939, WJZ-NBC Blue Network, Rockefeller Family, Record Group III 2 Q, World Affairs, Box 36, Folder 304, Rockefeller Archives Center, Poncantico Hills, New York.

195. Rickard Diary, October 7, 1939.

196. "David I. Walsh," Wikipedia, https://en.wikipedia.org/wiki/David_I._Walsh.

197. Lamont, *The Ambassador from Wall Street*, 445.

198. Ibid., 444.

199. "Memorandum on Neutrality Bill Sent to Several Senators, Congressmen and Others," October 11, 1939, Articles, Addresses and Public Statements, 1915–1964, HHPLM.

200. Hoover to Walsh, October 10, 1939, PPI, HHP, HHPLM.

201. "Hoover Proposes a New Neutrality Plan Prohibiting the Sale of 'Terrorizing' Arms," *New York Times*, October 1, 1939, 1.

202. "Memorandum on Neutrality Bill Sent to Several Senators, Congressmen and Others."

203. Ibid.

204. "Lindbergh to Talk Again on Repeal of Embargo," *New York Times*, October 12, 1939, 1.

205. Whether Hoover and Lindbergh planned to closely follow one another is unknown, but it was quite possible, as Hoover did much of his business on the telephone and likely talked with Lindbergh several times; unfortunately, no telephone logs were kept.

206. Program of Events, Polish Week, October 10th–15th, 1938, Polish-American Participation Committee, Inc., New York World's Fair, Polish Relief, Polish Museum of America, Chicago.

207. *New York Times*, October 12, 1939, 19, Clipping File, HHP, HHPLM.

208. "Hoover Predicts Poland's Rebirth," *New York Times*, October 12, 1939.

209. Herbert Hoover, "The Spirit of Poland," in *Further Addresses upon the American Road*, 227–230; "Rise of Poland as Free Nation Seen by Hoover," *Christian Science Monitor*, October 12, 1939, Clipping File, HHP, HHPLM.

210. Ibid.

211. See http://www.lib.luc.edu/specialcollections/exhibits/show/lypw.

212. For a general description of some of the fair's pavilions, see Schactmann, *The Phony War*, 3–4; *Official Catalogue of the Pavilion at the World's Fair in New York, 1939*.

213. Wegrzynek published an open letter to F. X. Swietlik on the front page of *Nowy Świet* in 1941 that reviewed the history of the disagreements. See Polish

Relief, *Nowy Świat*, 1941, Box 39, HI. On Swietlik's support for Roosevelt and the Red Cross, see J. Gordon Hylton, "Francis Swietlik, Marquette Law School, and Polish War Relief," Marquette University Law School Faculty Blog, October 18, 2010, https://law.marquette.edu/facultyblog/2010/10/francis-swietlik-marquette-law-school-and-polish-war-relief. For a sketch of Swietlik and history of Rada, see https://archives.lib.umn.edu/repositories/6/resources/3893.

214. See letters from Hoover to Vandenberg, October 12; Vandenberg to Hoover, October 13; and Hoover to Vandenberg, October 17, 1939, PPI, HHP, HHPLM.

215. Entry for October 5, 1939, in Lindbergh, *The Wartime Journals of Charles A. Lindbergh*.

216. *New York Times*, October 12, 1939, 16.

217. Ibid.

218. White to Hoover, October 11, 1939, William Allen White Papers, LCMD; White to Hoover, telegram, October 23, 1939, PPI, HHP, HHPLM.

219. Allen W. Dulles, "The Hoover Arms Proposal," *New York Times*, October 12, 1939, 25.

220. Ibid.

221. W. R. Castle, "Hoover Proposal Approved," *New York Times*, October 16, 1939, William Castle Papers, Articles and Speeches, August–September 1939, Box 31, HHPLM.

222. Ibid.

223. *New York Times*, October 12, 1939, 16.

224. Ibid.

225. Colonel Charles A. Lindbergh, Aviator, "What Our Decision Should Be: Our Policy Must Be as Clear as Our Shore Lines," October 13, 1939, *Vital Speeches of the Day*, 4:57–59.

226. Ibid.

227. Ibid.

228. "Lindbergh Thesis Disputed by O'Ryan," *New York Times*, October 15, 1939, 45.

229. "Lindbergh Speech Assailed in Senate," *New York Times*, October 15, 1939, 1.

230. "Text of Pittman's Reply to Lindbergh," *New York Times*, October 15, 1939, 45.

231. "Lindbergh Speech Assailed in Senate," 45; Pearson and Allen, "The Washington Merry-Go Round," *Boston Transcript*, October 19, 1939, Clipping File, HHP, HHPLM.

232. Charles, *J. Edgar Hoover and the Anti-interventionists*, 41.
233. "Lindbergh Speech Assailed in Senate," 45.
234. See column dated October 19, 1939, in Roosevelt, *My Day*.
235. See *New York Times*, October 22, 1939, 29; Nicolson, *Dwight Morrow*.
236. *New York Times*, October 22, 1939, 29; Max Wallace, *The American AXIS*, 210–211.
237. Lindbergh, *War Within and Without*, 65–66.
238. Nicolson, *Diaries and Letters*, 2:34.
239. Lindbergh, *War Within and Without*, 64.
240. *New York Times*, October 21, 1939, 1, 6.
241. Castle to Hoover, October 20, 1939, PPI, HHP, HHPLM.
242. Hoover to Vandenberg, October 17, 1939, PPI, HHP, HHPLM.
243. See "Broadcast Transcript," Articles, Addresses, and Public Statements, HHP, HHPLM; *New York Times*, October 21, 1939, 1, 6.
244. Ibid.
245. Smith, *An Uncommon Man*, 277; Rickard Diary, October 26, 1939.
246. Vandenberg to Hoover, November 6, 1939, PPI, HHP, HHPLM.
247. See Doenecke, *Storm on the Horizon*, 65–66.
248. Beverly C. Tomek, "Saturday Evening Post," Encyclopedia of Greater Philadelphia, 2015, https://philadelphiaencyclopedia.org/archive/saturday-evening-post.
249. Cole, *Roosevelt and the Isolationists*, 329–330.
250. Memo from Stephen Early to FDR, September 7, 1939, in Roosevelt, *F.D.R., His Personal Letters*, 918.
251. Cole, *Roosevelt and the Isolationists*, 329.
252. First quote in Doenecke, *Storm on the Horizon*, 66; second quote in Cole, *Roosevelt and the Isolationists*, 330.
253. See entry for October 27, 1939, in Vandenberg, *The Private Papers of Senator Vandenberg*.
254. Hoover to Vandenberg, November 7, 1939; Hoover to Walsh, November 1, 1939, PPI, HHP, HHPLM.
255. Langer and Gleason, *The Challenge to Isolation*, 1:244–246.
256. Hoover to O'Laughlin, November 6, 1939.
257. Large, *Berlin*, 320.
258. Larson, *In the Garden of Beasts*.
259. Republic of Poland, Ministry of Foreign Affairs, *German Occupation of Poland*. See Jan Tomasz Gross, *Polish Society Under German Occupation*, and, also by Gross, *Revolution from Abroad*.

NOTES

260. Davies, *God's Playground*, 2:441–447.

261. Gross, *Polish Society under German Occupation*, 50–51; Yisreal Gutman, *The Jews of Warsaw, 1939–1943*, 25–27. Also see "Rations in Poland," William J. Donovan Papers, and "Polish Relief Organization Meeting," American National Red Cross, December 7, 1939, ANRCDF 900.02 Political Organizations.

262. Diaries, Letters, and Memoranda of Homer and Edna W. Morris as Commissioners to Germany for the American Friends Service Committee (AFSC), 1939, AFSC Foreign Service, AFSCA, 44.

263. Ibid., 44.

264. Ibid., 45.

265. Ibid., 47.

266. "News Bulletin No. 1," October 20, 1939, FO 371/24104, W17041/13884/48, BNA.

267. Diaries, Letters and Memorandum of Homer L. Morris and Edna W. Morris as Commissioners to Germany, 1939, 47.

268. Ibid., 48.

269. Ibid., 47.

270. Ibid., 50; "News Bulletin No. 1," October 20, 1939, CPR, FO 371/24104, BNA.

271. Diaries, Letters and Memorandum of Homer L. Morris and Edna W. Morris as Commissioners to Germany, 1939, 54.

272. "News Bulletin No. 2," October 29, 1939, CPR, FO 371/24104, W17041/13884/48.

273. Ibid., 56.

274. MacDonald to Pate, October 26, 1939, PPI, HHP, HHPLM; "A Partial Report of Homer L. and Edna W. Morris," September 14–October 27, 1939, AFSCA.

275. Ibid.

276. Homer L. Morris to Dr. Hilgenfeldt, Director of the NSV, October 26, 1939, Foreign Service Poland, AFSCA.

277. Read and Fisher, *The Deadly Embrace*, 442.

278. "Informal Report by Norman Davis," November 4, 1939, State Department Decimal File (SDDF) 840.48/3009, NA.

279. Ibid.

280. Davis to Swift, Chatfield-Taylor, and Nicholson, telegram, November 11, 1939, SDDF 840.48/3016.

281. Ibid.

282. Davis to Swift, Chatfield-Taylor, and Nicholson, telegram, November 18, 1939, SDDF 840.48/3023, and "American Red Cross War Relief in Europe, September 1-December 6, 1939," December 8, 1939, SDDF 840.48/3095.

283. Ibid., and series of telegrams between Davis and Swift, Chatfield-Taylor, and Nicholson, November 22, 1939, SDDF 840.48/3032.

284. See Lothian's detailed report on the politics of relief to Halifax, telegram, December 16, 1939, FO 371/24105, W18809/13884.48, BNA.

285. Pienkos, *For Your Freedom Through Ours*, 82–83.

286. Davis to Swift, Chatfield-Taylor, and Nicholson, telegram, November 11, 1939, SDDF 840.48/3016; Rickard Diary, January 7, 1940.

287. "American Red Cross War Relief in Europe," September 1–December 8, 1939, SDDF 840.48/3095.

288. Ibid.

289. Bauer, *American Jewry and the Holocaust*.

290. "Report on Poland, 1939–1945," Folder 817, Joint Distribution Committee Archive; "Interim Report of the CPR," November 29, 1940, SDDF 840.48/4432.

291. See McCormick to Thomsen, January 9, 1940, SDDF 840.48/3354, and series of telegrams, Davis to Swift, Chatfield-Taylor, and Nicholson, February 1, 1940; Hull to Kirk, February 1, 1940; and Moffat to Kirk, February 1, 1940, SDDF 840.48/3232.

292. Edgar Rhoads to Edith Rhoads, December 3, 1939, Committees and Organizations, CPR, 1939, AFSCA; Elkinton to Morris, telegram, December 2, 1939, AFSC, Foreign Service Poland, 1939, AFSCA; "Polish Relief Organization Meeting," December 7, 1939, Polish Relief Organizations, Box 1322, ANRCDF 900.02.

293. Lothian to FO, telegram, No. 745 (R), November 10, 1939, FO 371/24103, W16537/13884/48, and later that same day, telegram, No. 746, November 10, 1939, FO 371/24103, W16631/13884/48, BNA.

294. MEW to FO, November 16, 1939, FO 371/24104, W16888/13884/48, BNA.

Chapter 9: In the Jaws of the Soviet Bugbear

1. Sobel, *The Origins of Interventionism*, 67.

2. See Tanner, *The Winter War*, 3–24; Mannerheim, *The Memoirs of Marshall Mannerheim*, 293–321; Jakobson, *The Diplomacy of the Winter War*, 7–11;

Gripenberg, *Finland and the Great Powers*, 1–54; Van Dyke, *The Soviet Invasion of Finland, 1939–40*, 1–34.

3. Jakobson, *The Diplomacy of the Winter War*, 3–4.
4. Edwards, *The Winter War*, 28–29.
5. Jakobson, *The Diplomacy of the Winter War*, 14.
6. Engle and Paananen, *The Winter War*, 10.
7. Dallin, *Soviet Russia's Foreign Policy*, 113–114.
8. See Pirinen, *A History of Finland*.
9. Jakobson, *The Diplomacy of the Winter War*, 60–61; Mannerheim, *The Memoirs of Marshall Mannerheim*, 295–303; Upton, *Finland, 1939–1940*, 18–21; Polvinen, "Finland in International Politics."
10. Read and Fisher, *The Deadly Embrace*; Moorhouse, *The Devils' Alliance*.
11. Van Dyke, *The Soviet Invasion of Finland*, 10–14. Also see Scott, *Duel for Europe*, 62–89; Schuman, *Night over Europe*, 387–396.
12. Jakobson, *The Diplomacy of the Winter War*, 107.
13. Sander, *The Hundred Day Winter War*, 33.
14. Ibid., 108.
15. Mannerheim, *The Memoirs of Marshall Mannerheim*, 310.
16. Van Dyke, *The Soviet Invasion of Finland*, 16–17. Also see Schwartz, *America and the Russo-Finnish War*, 6.
17. Tanner, *The Winter War*, 25.
18. Ibid.
19. Sander, *The Hundred Day Winter War*, 57.
20. On Procopé's character and frenetic efforts to obtain a loan for his country, see Berle and Jacobs, *Navigating the Rapids*, 255, 263, and 275; Sobel, *The Origins of Interventionism*, 73–74; Hull, *The Memoirs of Cordell Hull*, 1:978; Hooker, *The Moffat Papers*, 282–283; Rickard Diary, February 29, 1940; Blum, *Years of Urgency*, 129–132; Raymond Clapper, *New York World-Telegram*, December 2, 1939.
21. Hull, *The Memoirs of Cordell Hull*, 1:702; *Foreign Relations of the United States [FRUS], 1939*, 1:959–961.
22. Hull, *The Memoirs of Cordell Hull*, 1:702; Dallek, *Franklin D. Roosevelt and American Foreign Policy*, 208.
23. Hull, *The Memoirs of Cordell Hull*, 1:702; *FRUS, 1939*, 1:960–961.
24. Ibid.
25. Berle and Jacobs, *Navigating the Rapids*, 263–264.
26. Ibid., 264.
27. Ibid.
28. Ibid., 273.

29. Hull, *The Memoirs of Cordell Hull*, 1:702–703; Hooker, *The Moffat Papers*, 269–271; Berle and Jacobs, *Navigating the Rapids*, 264–265; Dallek, *Franklin D. Roosevelt and American Foreign Policy*, 208–209.
30. Hull, *The Memoirs of Cordell Hull*, 1:702–703.
31. Hooker, *The Moffat Papers*, 271; Jakobson, *The Diplomacy of the Winter War*, 112–113.
32. Berle and Jacobs, *Navigating the Rapids*, 264–265.
33. *FRUS, 1939*, 1:967.
34. Schwartz, *America and the Russo-Finnish War*, 7.
35. Ibid., 8.
36. Ibid.
37. *FRUS, 1939*, 1:968.
38. Ibid.
39. Jakobson, *The Diplomacy of the Winter War*, 123–124.
40. Ibid.
41. Sherwood, *There Shall Be No Night*, 49.
42. Edwards, *The Winter War*, 19.
43. Ibid.
44. Ibid., 21.
45. Hull, *The Memoirs of Cordell Hull*, 1:705; Bullitt, *For the President, Personal and Secret*, 388.
46. Langer and Gleason, *The Challenge to Isolation*, 327.
47. Hooker, *The Moffat Papers*, 279.
48. *Department of State Bulletin* (December 2, 1939), 1:609–610.
49. Jakobson, *The Diplomacy of the Winter War*, 161.
50. Montefiore, *Stalin*, 327–328.
51. Ibid.
52. Engle and Paananen, *The Winter War*, 1 and 3; Hooton, *Stalin's Claws*, 109.
53. Khrushchev, *Khrushchev Remembers*, 135–136.
54. Combat histories include Sander, *The Hundred Day Winter War*; Chew, *The White Death*; Trotter, *A Frozen Hell*; Engle and Paananen, *The Winter War*; Edwards, *The Winter War*; Van Dyke, *The Soviet Invasion of Finland*.
55. Sander, *The Hundred Day Winter War*, 44.
56. Trotter, *A Frozen Hell*, 48.
57. Elliston, *Finland Fights*, 217.
58. Trotter, *A Frozen Hell*, 48.
59. Hooker, *The Moffat Papers*, 280.
60. Ibid. Also see Langer and Gleason, *The Challenge to Isolation*, 332; Sobel, *The Origins of Interventionism*, 90.

61. Hull, *The Memoirs of Cordell Hull*, 1:707; Drew Pearson and Robert S. Allen, "Washington Merry-Go-Round," *San Francisco Chronicle*, December 7, 1939, Clipping File, December 1–9, HHP, HHPLM.

62. Dallek, *Franklin D. Roosevelt and American Foreign Policy*, 209; Sobel, *The Origins of Interventionism*, 95.

63. Hull, *The Memoirs of Cordell Hull*, 1:707; Langer and Gleason, *The Challenge to Isolation*, 331.

64. Ickes, *The Secret Diary of Harold L. Ickes*, 3:75.

65. Mannerheim, *The Memoirs of Marshall Mannerheim*, 324–325.

66. Jägerskiöld, *Mannerheim*, 109.

67. Blum, *Years of Urgency*, 2:129–132; Morgenthau Diary, Vol. 198, June 22, 1939, 168–169, FDRL; Papers of Henry J. Morgenthau Jr., FDRL; Hjalmar Procopé to Cordell Hull, December 28, 1939, Official File (OF) 434, Box 1, FRP, FDRL.

68. Hull, *The Memoirs of Cordell Hull*, 2:707–708.

69. Strauss, *Men and Decisions*, 60–70; Pfau, *No Sacrifice Too Great*, 60–61; Hoover, *An American Epic*, 4:10.

70. Strauss, *Men and Decisions*, 66.

71. Hoover to Wilson, April 26, 1919, in Hoover, *An American Epic*, 3:34–35.

72. Pfau, *No Sacrifice Too Great*, 20–21.

73. Strauss, *Men and Decisions*, 61.

74. Ibid., 17.

75. Ibid., 61–62, 65.

76. Pfau, *No Sacrifice Too Great*, 21.

77. Strauss, *Men and Decisions*, 12.

78. Ibid., 66.

79. Ibid. Also see Jones, *Fifty Billion Dollars*, 222–223.

80. Jones, *Fifty Billion Dollars*, 221–222; O'Laughlin to Hoover, December 9, 1939, PPI, HHP, HHPLM.

81. Jones to Roosevelt, December 9, 1939, OF 643, Box 3, Reconstruction Finance Corporation, FDRP, FDRL; Pfau, *No Sacrifice Too Great*, 61.

82. Hoover, Press Statement, November 30, 1939, No. 2558, Articles, Addresses, and Public Statements, HHP, HHPLM.

83. Nash, *Freedom Betrayed*, xxxvii.

84. Hoover, Press Statement, December 2, 1939, No. 2564, Articles, Addresses, and Public Statements, HHP, HHPLM.

85. Strauss, *Men and Decisions*, 66–67; Rickard Diary, December 4 and 5, 1939.

86. See Harlan Miller, "Over the Coffee," *Des Moines Register*, November 6, 1939; Howard Vincent O'Brien, "All Things Considered," *Chicago Daily News*, November 6, 1939; Raymond Clapper, November 10, 1939, *San Francisco News*; Charles N. Wheeler, "Hoover and Dewey in 1940 Is Dream of Admirers," *Chicago Daily News*, November 16, 1939; Drew Pearson and Robert S. Allen, "The Washington Merry-Go-Round," *Washington Star*, October 27, 1939, and Charles G. Ross, "Hoover Seen Receptive to Nomination," *Washington Star*, October 27, 1939, Clipping File, HHP, HHPLM.

87. For US support for Finland, see George V. Denny Jr., "What's Your Opinion: What Aid for Finland?" *Current History* 51, no. 7 (March 1940): 42–44; "What the Finns Won," *Collier's* 105, no. 15 (April 13, 1940): 82; "The Attack on Finland," *Christian Century* 66, no. 50 (December 13, 1939), 1534–1535; "U.S. Government Aids Finland: Hoover Organizes Relief for Finland," *Scholastic* 35, no. 13 (December 18, 1939): 5.

88. See poll released on December 31, 1939, in Gallup, *The Gallup Poll*, 197.

89. Ibid.

90. Sobel, *The Origins of Interventionism*, 70–71; Hicks, *Where We Came Out*; Brown, *The Fabulous Lunts*, 283–288; "Russia, Finland and the U.S.A.," *Propaganda Analysis Bulletin* 3, no. 8 (April 30, 1940), Emil Hurja Papers, FDRL. For the Communist perspective, see "Murder at Bargain Prices," *Daily Worker*, December 21, 1939, Clipping File, HHP, HHPLM; Citrine, *My Finnish Diary*.

91. Nevakivi, *The Appeal That Was Never Made*, 62–95; Clark, *Three Days to Catastrophe*; Krosby, *Finland, Germany, and the Soviet Union*.

92. Sobel, *The Origins of Interventionism*, 68–69; "Editorials on Financial Aid for Finland, December–January 1940," *Washington Star*, OF 434c, Box 1, Finnish Russian War and War Relief, 1939–1940, FDRP, FDRL; Address of Frank Knox, January 12, 1940, Box 143, Miscellaneous Printed Matter, Hurja Papers, FDRL.

93. Citrine, *My Finnish Diary*; Langdon-Davies, *Finland*, 1–3.

94. Strauss, *Men and Decisions*, 66–67.

95. Rickard Diary, December 4, 1939.

96. Rickard Diary, December 4 and 5, 1939; Strauss, *Men and Decisions*, 67; Hoover, *An American Epic*, 4:11.

97. Strauss, *Men and Decisions*, 67.

98. *New York Times*, December 9, 1939.

99. Rickard Diary, December 5, 1939.

100. Nash, *Freedom Betrayed*, xxxviii.

101. *New York Times*, December 6, 1939, 1.

102. Ibid.

103. Finnish Relief Fund, circa December 15 or 16, PPI, HHP, HHPLM.

104. Ibid. Also see Smith, *An Uncommon Man*, 277–278.

105. "National Appeal for Finnish Relief," Press Statement, December 8, 1939, No. 2567, Articles, Addresses and Public Statements, HHP, HHPLM; *New York Times*, December 8, 1939.

106. Press releases, December 9 and 10, 1939, OF 124, Box 2, American Red Cross 1939, FDRP, FDRL; Ernest J. Swift and Wayne Chatfield Taylor to Davis, December 1, 1939, State Department Decimal File (SDDF) 840.48/3054; American Red Cross Bulletin, No. 4, War Relief, December 8, 1939, SDDF 840.48/3095.

107. Finnish Relief Fund, undated and unsigned, circa December 15, 1939, PPI; American Red Cross Correspondence, 1933–44, PPSF, HHP, HHPLM; Hoover "Diary," December 7, 1939, HHP, Box 145, HIA; entry for December 7, in Israel, *The War Diary of Breckinridge Long*, 40.

108. Israel, *The War Diary of Breckinridge Long*, 40; Ickes, *The Secret Diary of Harold L. Ickes*, 3:95–96.

109. Ibid.

110. Finnish Relief Fund, undated and unsigned, circa December 15, 1939, PPI; American Red Cross Correspondence, 1933–44, PPSF, HHP, HHPLM.

111. Langer and Gleason, *The Challenge to Isolation*, 334.

112. Ickes, *The Secret Diary of Harold L. Ickes*, 3:95–96.

113. For Finnish Army success, see Sander, *The Hundred Day Winter War*; Trotter, *A Frozen Hell*; Chew, *The White Death*.

114. Rickard Diary, December 31, 1939; Walter Lippmann, "Today and Tomorrow," *New York Herald Tribune*, December 16, 1939, Clipping File, HHP, HHPLM.

115. *New York Herald Tribune*, December 14, 1939, Clipping File, HHP, HHPLM.

116. On clothing dropped off at consulates, see *New York Herald Tribune*, December 12, 1939, Clipping File, HHP, HHPLM; on volunteers, see *New York Times*, December 7, 1939, and *New York Herald Tribune*, December 14, 1939, Clipping File, HHP, HHPLM.

117. *New York Times*, December 10, 1939, 48.

118. "Gallup and Fortune Polls," *Public Opinion Quarterly* (June 1940): 358–359.

119. Ibid.

120. "Russia, Finland and the U.S.A.," *Propaganda Analysis Bulletin*, 2.

121. Smith, *An Uncommon Man*, 271–272; Best, *Herbert Hoover*, 1:122–124, 144.

122. Jeansonne, *Herbert Hoover*, 324.

123. Smith, *An Uncommon Man*, 271–272; Best, *Herbert Hoover*, 1:122–124.

124. Best, *Herbert Hoover*, 1:144; *New Republic* 103, no. 1 (January 29, 1940): 132.

125. Best, *Herbert Hoover*, 1:122.

126. Synopsis of a conversation between B. M. Cochran and Procopé in Cochran to Morgenthau, Morgenthau Diary, Vol. 235, January 12, 1940, 136–150, FDRL. On Soviet gold, see Senator John G. Townsend, "U.S. Helps Reds More Than Finns," press release, January 27, 1940, Box 141, "Finnish Relief 1940," Hurja Papers, FDRL. For a complete list of exports to the Soviet Union from November 1939 through January 1940, see D. W. Bell to FDR, Morgenthau Diary, Vol. 240, February 13, 1940, 183–185.

127. Strauss, *Men and Decisions*, 66; Jakobson, *The Diplomacy of the Winter War*, 193–194; Blum, *From the Morgenthau Dairies*, 2:130; Erich Warburg to Riksbanken, Stockholm, "Telegram," December 7, 1940, Box 51, Strauss/Warburg Correspondence, Strauss Papers, HHPLM.

128. Strauss, *Men and Decisions*, 66.

129. Rickard Diary, January 15, 1940.

130. Ibid.

131. Ibid. Also see Morgenthau Diary, Vol. 236, January 17, 1940, 210, and January 18, 1940, 222.

132. Blum, *Years of Urgency*, 2:129–132; Morgenthau Diary, Vol. 198, June 22, 1939, 168–169; Papers of Henry J. Morgenthau Jr., FDRL; Hjalmar Procopé to Cordell Hull, December 28, 1939, OF 434, Box 1, FRP, FDRL.

133. Ibid.

134. Ibid.

135. Ibid.

136. Rickard Diary, February 27, 1939; Hooker, *The Moffat Papers*, 282–283.

137. Ibid.

138. HIF, "The Aftermath of 1848," Hungary Foundation, August 11, 2014, https://www.hungaryfoundation.org/the-aftermath-of-1848/.

139. "Report to American Donors, December 1939–January 1940," 23, Finnish Relief Fund, PPSF, HHP, HHPLM; "Civilian Relief Committee Named by Finnish Premier," January 8, 1940, No. 2591, Articles, Addresses and Public Statements, HHP, HHPLM.

140. Ibid.

141. Ibid. Also see "Hoover/Davis Transcript of Telephone Conversation," January 8, 1940, PPI, HHP, HHPLM.

142. PPI, HHP, HHPLM.

143. Hoover to Davis, circa January 10, 1940, PPI, HHP, HHPLM; *New York World-Telegram*, December 15, 1939, Clipping File, HHP, HHPLM.

144. "Hoover/Davis Transcript of Telephone Conversation," January 8, 1940.

145. Ibid.

146. Ibid.

147. Liikkanen, *Fighter over Finland*, 191–193; Winston, *Aces Wild*, 1–20; Schwartz, *America and the Russo-Finnish War*, 25.

148. Strauss, *Men and Decisions*, 68.

149. Ibid. Also see Winston, *Aces Wild*, 1–28; Berle Diary, December 20, 1939, Box 211, Berle Papers, FDRL.

150. Engle and Paananen, *The Winter War*, 155; Jakobson, *The Diplomacy of the Winter War*, 196.

151. Schwartz, *America and the Russo-Finnish War*, 25.

Chapter 10: Finnomania: A Cause Célèbre

1. "Hoover Plea for Finns Voiced," *Pasadena Star News*, December 8, 1939, Clipping File, HHP, HHPLM.

2. *New York Times*, December 9, 1939.

3. *Palo Alto Times*, December 11, 1939, Clipping File, HHP, HHPLM.

4. *New York Times*, December 11, 1939, and *Berkeley Gazette*, December 12, 1939, Clipping File, HHP, HHPLM.

5. *San Francisco Examiner*, December 12, 16, and *New York Herald Tribune*, December 12, 1939, Clipping File, HHP, HHPLM.

6. Ibid.

7. See Ashum Brown, *Providence Journal*, December 17, 1939, Clipping File, and Frank Kent, *Los Angeles Times*, December 28, 1939, Finnish relief, PPSF, HHPLM.

8. *New York Times*, December 11, 1939, 2, 9.

9. *New York Times*, December 12, 1939, 16.

10. Rickard Diary, January 11, 1940.

11. *New York Times*, December 9, 1939, 2, 5.

12. Ibid.

13. *New York Times*, December 11, 1939, 2, 9.

14. Rickard Diary, January 13, 1940.

15. Ibid.

16. Paul Mallon, "The News Behind the News," *Chicago Herald American*, December 16, 1939, Clipping File.

17. *New York Times* and *New York Herald Tribune*, December 14, 1939; Raymond Clapper, *San Francisco News*, December 15, 1939; Drew Pearson, *Boston Transcript*, December 15, 1939; Doris Fleeson, *New York World-Telegram*, December 15, 1939; Arthur Krock, *New York Times*, December 15, 1939, Clipping File, HHP, HHPLM.

18. *New York Times* and *New York Herald Tribune*, December 14, 1939; press release, Addresses, Articles and Public Statements, No. 2562, HHP, HHPLM.

19. Ibid.

20. *New York Times*, December 14, 1939, 1, 8; *New York Journal-American*, December 14, 1939, Clipping File, HHP, HHPLM.

21. Ibid.

22. *New York Times*, December 11, 1939.

23. *New York Times*, December 14, 1939, 1, 8.

24. "$500 Donated to Finnish Relief Fund by Sponsors of Garden Protest Rally," *Jewish Telegraphic Agency*, December 17, 1939, https://www.jta.org/archive/500-donated-to-finnish-relief-fund-by-sponsors-of-garden-protest-rally.

25. Warburg to Ryti, telegram, December 13, 1939, Strauss/Warburg Correspondence, Box 51, Strauss Papers, HHPLM.

26. Ryti to Hoover, telegram, December 14; Hoover to Ryti, December 14; and Warburg to Ryti, December 15, 1939, Strauss/Warburg Correspondence, Box 51, Strauss Papers, HHPLM.

27. Ibid.

28. Fleeson, *New York World-Telegram*.

29. *St. Louis Post-Dispatch*, December 20, 1939, OF434c, Box 1, Finnish Russian War and War Relief,'39–'40, Roosevelt Papers, FDRL.

30. Ibid. Sobel, in *The Origins of Interventionism*, wrote that Roosevelt scribbled, "Ain't that a sock in the snoot for Herbie the Hoot," across an editorial by Walter Lippmann in his column *Today and Tomorrow* in the December 14, 1939, issue of the *New York Herald Tribune*.

31. Finnish Relief Fund, Report to American Donors, December 1939–July 1940, PPSF, HHP, HHPLM.

32. Kähönen-Wilson, *Sisu Mother*, 10.

33. Gellhorn, "Death in the Present Tense," 14–15, 46.

34. Ibid.

35. Rickard Diary, December 13, 1939.

36. Press remarks on New York arrival, press release, December 14, 1939, Addresses, Articles and Public Statements, No. 2575; *New York Journal-American*, December 15, 1939, Clipping File, HHP, HHPLM.

37. Ibid.

38. Ibid.

39. Ibid.

40. Smith, *An Uncommon Man*, 278–279.

41. *New York Journal-American*, December 15, 1939, Clipping File, HHP, HHPLM.

42. Ibid.

43. See Sioux City, Iowa, mayor David F. Loepp to Steve Early, December 14, 1939; Early to Loepp, December 15, 1939, OF434c, Box 1, Finnish Russian War and War Relief, '39–'40, Roosevelt Papers, FDRL.

44. O'Laughlin to Hoover, December 16, 1939, PPIF, HHP, HHPLM.

45. Rickard Diary, December 15, 1939.

46. Ibid.

47. Rickard Diary, December 16, 1939; transcript of telephone conversation, December 16, 1939, PPI-Davis, HHP, HHPLM.

48. Ickes, *The Secret Diary of Harold L. Ickes*, 3:95–96.

49. Rickard Diary, December 18, 1939.

50. See Paul Mallon, *Chicago Herald American*, December 16, 1939; Ashum Brown, *Providence Journal*, December 17, 1939; *New York Post*, December 15, 1939, Clipping File; Frank Kent, *Los Angeles Times*, December 28, 1939, Finnish Relief, PPSF, HHP, HHPLM.

51. "Dave Boone Says," *New York Sun*, December 18, 1939, Clipping File, HHP, HHPLM.

52. Best, *Herbert Hoover*, 1:129, 149–150.

53. See Strauss to Hoover, February 14, 1940, PPI, HHP, HHPLM.

54. Best, *Herbert Hoover*, 1:149–150.

55. Ibid., 1:146–147.

56. *New York Times*, January 20, 1940, 9.

57. Ibid.

58. *New York Daily Mirror*, December 21, 1939, Clipping File, HHP, HHPLM.

59. Addresses, Articles and Public Statements, No. 2587, HHP, HHPLM.

60. *New York Daily Mirror*, December 21, 1939, Clipping File, HHP, HHPLM.

61. Rickard Diary, December 31, 1939.

62. Merridale, *Ivan's War*, 58.

63. Ward, *Dispatches from Finland*, 18–19.

64. The committee had already moved the Olympics from Tokyo to Helsinki, but the spread of war forced cancellation there as well. There were no 1940 Olympics.

65. See Sander, *The Hundred Day Winter War*, 7–9; Elliston, *Finland Fights*, 261–262; White, "I Saw It Happen," 153–164; "Russia, Finland and the U.S.A.," *Propaganda Analysis Bulletin*, 7–10.

66. See Cowles, *Looking for Trouble*, 283–332; Gellhorn, "Slow Boat to War," 10–12–45; Gellhorn, "Blood on the Snow," *Collier's*, 9–11; Gellhorn, "Bombs from a Low Sky," 12–14, 41; Gellhorn, "Fear Comes to Sweden," 20–22; Gellhorn, "Death in the Present Tense," 14–16, 46.

67. Rollyson, *Nothing Ever Happens to the Brave*, 145.

68. Ibid.

69. Cox, *The Red Army Moves*, 60–61.

70. Ibid., 63–66.

71. W. L. White, "Today in Europe," CBS Nightly Reports from Helsinki, December 26, 1939.

72. Ibid.

73. Sherwood, *There Shall be No Night*; Brown, *The Worlds of Robert E. Sherwood*.

74. Saarelainen, *The White Sniper*, 29.

75. Woolf, "Mr. Hoover Tackles Another Relief Job."

76. Ibid.

77. Wolf, "Meet the 'New' Hoover," *National Education Association Newspaper*, January 1940, Finnish Relief, PPSF, HHP, HHPLM.

78. Van Loon, *The Story of Hendrik Willem Van Loon*, 340.

79. James P. Selvage, February 22, 1967, OHI, HHPLM.

80. Selvage, OHI; Smith, *An Uncommon Man*, 280.

81. *New York Times*, January 5, 1940, 2.

82. For examples of the array of celebrities who came out in support of the FRF, see press release, Finnish Relief Fund, January 27–30, 1940, Box 140, Press Clippings, '39–'40, Hurja Papers, FDRL; Hoover to Theatre Managers, January 23, 1940, Box 141, Finnish Relief 1940, Hurja Papers, FDRL; "Russia, Finland and the U.S.A.," *Propaganda Analysis Bulletin*, 5–7.

83. Transcript of Telephone Conversation, January 8, 1940, PPI-Davis, HHP, HHPLM.

84. Hoover to Davis, January 10, 1940, PPI, HHP, HHPLM; Wolf, "Meet the 'New' Hoover."

85. Transcript of Telephone Conversation, January 8, 1940, PPI-Davis, HHP, HHPLM.

86. See William Green and Mathew Woll to National and International Unions, January 11, 1940, Box 141, Finnish Relief Misc., Hurja Papers, FDRL; "Help Finland," brochure, National Labor Committee and Finnish Relief, January 11, 1940, Reprint File, HHP, HHPLM.

87. Rickard Diary, December 31, 1939.

88. Ibid.

89. Rickard Diary, February 19, and February 27, 1940.

90. "War and Peace," *Time* 35, no. 11 (March 11, 1940), 22.

91. "Russia, Finland and the U.S.A.," *Propaganda Analysis Bulletin*, 6.

92. *New York Herald Tribune*, March 12, 1940; *New York Times*, March 9, 1940, Finnish Relief, PPSF, HHP, HHPLM.

93. "Russia, Finland, and the U.S.A.," *Propaganda Analysis Bulletin*, 6.

94. John Golden, "When Herbert Hoover Met Broadway," *Baltimore Sun*, June 7, 1953, Freeview clippings.

95. Ibid.

96. Ibid.

97. Ibid.

98. Ibid. See also *Washington Star*, January 14, 1940, Finnish Relief, PPSF, HHP, HHPLM and *New York Times*, February 29, 1940, 2.

99. *New York Herald Tribune*, January 15, 1940; *New York Times*, March 4, 1940, Finnish Relief, PPSF, HHP, HHPLM.

100. *New York Times*, February 3 and 4, 1940; *New York Post*, March 4, 1940, Finnish Relief, PPSF, HHP, HHPLM.

101. *San Francisco Chronicle*, April 10, 1940, Finnish Relief, PPSF, HHP, HHPLM.

102. See Dorothy Canfield Fisher to Monsignor Ryan, January 20, 1940, Series 100, ERP, FDRL.

103. Ibid.

104. Ibid.

105. Dorothy Canfield Fisher to Eleanor Roosevelt, January 21, 1940, Series 100, ERP, FDRL.

106. Ibid.

107. Eleanor Roosevelt to Dorothy Canfield Fisher, January 24, 1940, Series 100, ERP, FDRL.

108. Joe Williams, "All Stars Dish Up World Series Thrills," *New York World-Telegram*, March 19, 1940; *World-Telegram*, March 18, 1940; *World-Telegram*,

April 14, 1940; *New York Herald Tribune*, March 12, 1940, Finnish Relief, PPSF, HHP, HHPLM.

109. *New York Herald Tribune*, March 12, 1940; *New York World-Telegram*, April 14, 1940, Finnish Relief, PPSF, HHP, HHPLM.

110. *New York Times*, March 11, 1940, Finnish Relief, PPSF, HHP, HHPLM.

111. On the races, see *New York Daily Mirror*, March 8, 1940; *New York Herald Tribune*, March 8, 1940; on Washington race, see Milton M. Brown to Emil Hurja, February 29, 1940, Box 141, Finnish Relief Misc., Hurja Papers, FDRL.

112. *New York Herald Tribune*, March 12, 1940, Finnish Relief, PPSF, HHP, HHPLM.

113. *New York World-Telegram*, March 5, 1940, Finnish Relief, PPSF, HHP, HHPLM.

114. Ibid.

115. *New York Herald Tribune*, March 18, 1939.

116. On Coughlin's donation, see "Russia, Finland and the U.S.A.," *Propaganda Analysis Bulletin*, 7. On Alaska contribution, see *Juneau Daily Alaskan Empire*, ca. March 15, 1940, Box 141, Finnish Relief 1940, Hurja Papers, FDRL. On jailhouse volunteers, see Drew Pearson and Robert S. Allen, "Washington Merry-Go-Round," *New York Mirror*, March 7, 1940, Finnish Relief, PPSF, HHP, HHPLM.

117. Draft of press release, Herbert Hoover Collection, Box 153, HIA; article by John C. Henry, February 29, 1940, *Washington Star*, Hoover Collection, Box 107 HIA; Leonard Lyons, "The Lyons Den," *New York Post*, March 4, 1940, Finnish Relief, PPSF, HHP, HHPLM.

118. See US Congress, House Committee on Ways and Means, H.R. 7630, 76th Congress, 3rd Session, January 3, 1940, and Senate Committee on Banking and Currency, S. 3069, 76th Congress, 3rd Session, January 8, 1940. For loan approval, see press release, Jessie Jones, March 1, 1940, Morgenthau Diary, Vol. 244, 98. For requested fighters and bomber, see Morgenthau Diary, Vol. 246, 69–70, FDRL; B. M. Cochran to Morgenthau, March 7, 1940, Morgenthau Diary, Vol. 246, 39.

119. Earl Fredrickson, "Fighting Funds," *The Northman*, March 8, 1940, Seattle, Washington, 8, Finnish Relief, PPSF, HHP, HHPLM.

120. "U.S. Helps the Finns," *Life*, February 19, 1940; "War and Peace," *Time* 35, no. 11 (March 11, 1940).

121. "Report of Major-General John F. O'Ryan, National Chairman, May 27th, 1940," MSS B 46, Box 4, Folder 1, Benjamin Franklin Riter Papers, Utah State Historical Society, Salt Lake, City, UT.

122. "Ms. Thompson Urges U.S. Help Finns Buy Arms," January 30, 1940, *New York Herald Tribune*, Finnish Relief Fund, O'Ryan, J. F., Fighting Funds for Finland, Box 15c, Misc., HIA.

123. "Pros and Cons of Appeal to American Charity for Purchase of Arms for Finland," February 1940, Box 141, Finnish Relief, 1940, Hurja Papers, FDRL.

124. Ibid.

125. *Washington Star*, January 14, 1940, Finnish Relief, PPSF, HHP, HHPLM.

126. Best, *Herbert Hoover*, 1:131.

127. "The Pros and Cons of Appeal to American Charity for Purchase of Arms for Finland," Hurja Papers, FDRL.

128. Blum, *Years of Urgency*, 2:131; Morgenthau Diary, Vol. 234, January 10, 1940, 256–258.

129. Press release, Radio Address of Hon. Millard Tydings, February 16, 1940; "Aid to Finland, February 19, 1940," *Congressional Record*, 76th Congress, 3rd Session, Box 139, Finland 1940, Hurja Papers; Press release, Address of Senator Prentiss M. Brown, NBC National Radio Forum, February 26, 1940, Box 141, Finnish Relief Misc. Hurja Papers, FDRL.

130. "War and Peace," *Time* 35, no. 11 (March 11, 1940).

131. Morgenthau Diary, Vol. 244, March 1, 1940, 98.

132. Rickard Diary, January 27, 1940, February 1, 1940, and February 29, 1940; Morgenthau Diary, Vol. 246, March 7, 1940, 39; Berle Diary, Box 211, March 26, 1940, A. A Berle Papers, FDRL.

133. Rickard Diary, February 1 and 29, 1940.

134. Telephone transcript, Tuck to Watson, January 17, 1940, Box 1, Finland, '40–'45, OF434, Roosevelt Papers, FDRL.

135. F. N. Huntington-Wilson and A. D. Turnbull to Fighting Funds for Finland, January 30, 1940, Finnish Relief, PPSF, HHP, HHPLM.

136. Rickard Diary, February 15, 1940; *New York Herald Tribune*, February 20, 1940, Finnish Relief, PPSF, HHP, HHPLM.

137. "America's Mass Shipments of Planes to the Allies May Decide War's Outcome," *Life* 8, no. 2 (January 8, 1940): 11–15.

138. Brownell and Billings, *So Close to Greatness*, 223–253.

139. See Morgenthau Diary, Vol. 245, March 5, 1940, 223–231; Mannerheim to Procopé, telegram, March 1, 1940, Morgenthau Diary, Vol. 246, March 7, 1940, 51–52.

140. Morgenthau Diary, Vol. 245, March 5, 1940, 223–231; Vol. 246, March 11, 1940, 218–219.

141. "America's Mass Shipment of Planes to the Allies May Decide War's Outcome"; Brownell and Billings, *So Close to Greatness*, 224–229.

142. Winston, *Aces Wild*, 47–48; Engle and Paananen, *The Winter War*, 153–157.

143. "Pros and Cons of Appeal to American Charity for Purchase of Arms for Finland," February 1940, Hurja Papers, FDRL.

144. Ibid.

145. "Hoover Saddened by Finn Peace," *San Francisco Examiner*, March 14, 1949, Clipping File, HHP, HHPLM.

146. See "Finland's Need for Aid to Survive Stressed by Red Cross in Appeal," *New York Times*, March 22, 1940.

147. British, Red Cross, and CPR negotiations with the Germans in the State Department Decimal File. See Pate to Rhoads, December 27, 1939, SDDF 840.48/3114; Earl of Drogheda (MEW) to Herschel V. Johnson, January 26, 1940, SDDF 840.48/3312; Davis to Nicholson, February 1, 1940, and Moffat to Kirk, February 1, 1940, SDDF 840.48/3232; Drogheda to Johnson, February 6, 1940, SDDF 840.48/3049; Hull to Kirk, February 7, 1940, SDDF 840.48/3248; Kirk to Hull, February 9, 1940, SDDF 840.48/3265; Hull to Pittman, February 15, 1940, SDDF 840.49/3305.

148. Hoover, *An American Epic*, 4:8; Chauncey McCormick to Hans Thomsen, January 9, 1940, SDDF 840.48/3354; *New York Times*, February 19, 1940; Addresses, Articles and Public Statements, No. 2649, HHP, HHPLM.

149. *New York Herald Tribune*, February 25, 1940, Reprint File, HHP, HHPLM; Davis to Nicholson, February 1, 1940, SDDF 840.48/3232; Thomsen to McCormick, February 20, 1940, SDDF 840.48/3354.

150. *New York Herald Tribune*, April 13, 1940, Poland Relief, PPSF, HHP, HHPLM.

151. *New York Times*, February 21, 1940, Poland Relief, PPSF, HHP, HHPLM; Thomsen to Chauncey McCormick, February 20, 1940, SDDF 840.48/3354; Breckinridge Long to Hull, February 27, 1940, SDDF 840.48.3420.

152. *New York Times*, February 26, 1940; *New York Herald Tribune*, February 26, 1940, Poland Relief, PPSF, HHP, HHPLM.

153. Ibid. See also newsletters of the Paderewski Fund, PPSF, HHP, HHPLM.

154. Ibid.

155. Ibid.

156. Souvenir Program, Polish Relief Mass Meeting, March 12, 1940, Reprint File, HHP, HHPLM.

157. McCormick to Thomsen, January 7, 1940, SDDF 840.38/3354; *New York Times*, February 19, 1940, Addresses, Articles and Public Statements, No. 2639, HHP, HHPLM.

Notes

158. "Memorandum of Conversation," Lothian to Long, March 22, 1940, SDDF 840.48/3439.

159. Ibid.

160. "Memorandum of Conversation," Potocki and Long, March 22, 1940, SDDF 840.48/3248; for Polish enthusiasm, see Taylor to Swift, March 17, 1940, SDDF 840.48/3478.

161. "Memorandum of Conversation," Lothian and Long, March 6, 1940, SDDF 840.48/3439; "Memorandum of Conversation," Potocki and Long, March 22, 1940, SDDF 840.48/3248.

162. For testimony, see Addresses, Articles and Public Statements, No. 2644, HHP, HHPLM, and attached article, *Washington Star*, February 29, 1940. See also *Washington Times Herald*; *Washington Post*, March 1, 1940, Poland Relief, PPSF, HHP, HHPLM; (Little Rock) *Arkansas Gazette*, March 1, 1940, OF 115, Box 1, Herbert Hoover, RP, FDRL.

163. "Memorandum of a Conversation," Bankhead and Long, March 1, 1940, SDDF 840.48/3349 1/2.

164. McCormick to Hull, March 5, 1940, SDDF 840.48/3354.

165. Thomsen to McCormick, February 20, 1940, SDDF 840.48/3345; McCormick to Hull, March 5, 1940, SDDF 840.48/3354.

166. "Memorandum of Conversation," Potocki and Long, February 27, 1940, SDDF 840.48/3370.

167. Ibid.

168. Ibid.

169. Lothian to McCormick, March 1, 1940, SDDF 840.48/3354; *New York Times*, February 21, 1940, Poland Relief, PPSF, HHP, HHPLM; *New York Herald Tribune*, February 25, 1940, Reprint File, HHP, HHPLM. On Red Cross survey of needs, see *New York Times*, March 19, 1940, Poland Relief, PPSF, HHP, HHPLM.

170. *New York Herald Tribune*, March 21, 1940, Poland Relief, PPSF, HHP, HHPLM.

171. Berg, *Warsaw Ghetto*, 24–29.

172. *New York Herald Tribune*, March 21, 1940, Poland Relief, PPSF, HHP, HHPLM.

173. "Memorandum of a Conversation," Lothian and Long, March 6, 1940, SDDF 840.48/3478.

174. Taylor to Swift, March 27, 1940; Swift to Long, April 1, 1940, SDDF 840.48/3478.

175. Taylor to Davis, April 15, 1940, SDDF 840.48/3462.

176. "Canfield Report to Young Americans," November 1940, Series 100, ERP, FDRL.

177. Smith, *An Uncommon Man*, 269–270. See also McCoy, *Landon of Kansas*, 235–236.

178. Rickard Diary, December 31, 1939, and March 10, 1940.

179. Drew Pearson and Robert S. Allen, "Hoover Toils Quietly behind the Scenes to Wipe Out Stigma of 1932 Defeat," *Washington Merry-Go-Round*, April 2, 1940, Clipping File, HHP, HHPLM.

180. "Republican Foreign Policy: Hoover Seen as Only Choice to Carry on Liberal Democracy," *New York Herald Tribune*, April 9, 1940, Clipping File, HHP, HHPLM.

181. James Selvage to William Gross, April 19, 1940, HHP, HHPL.

182. Jeansonne, *Herbert Hoover*, 333; Best, *Herbert Hoover*, 123, 151–152.

183. Paul Mallon, "Dewey's Chances at Convention," News Behind the News, *San Francisco Chronicle*, April 1940, Clipping File, HHP, HHPLM.

184. Nash, *Freedom Betrayed*, xliii–xliv; Best, *Herbert Hoover*, 159–163.

185. Rickard Diary, April 15, 1940.

186. Nash, *Freedom Betrayed*, xliii.

187. *New York Times*, May 26, 1940, 15. FDR described the conquest of Western Europe in spring 1940 as a "hurricane of events." See Olson, *Those Angry Days*, 97.

188. Gibson to Hoover, May 10, 1940, SDDF 840.48/3553; Hoover, *An American Epic*, 4:17–21.

189. Gibson to Hoover, May 10, 1940, SDDF 840.48/3553.

190. Ibid.

191. Hoover, *An American Epic*, 4:17.

192. "Interim Report of the CPR," November 29, 1940, SDDF 840.48/4432. For purchase in Soviet Union, see following series of dispatches: Steinhardt to FDR, Hull, and Welles, February 24, 1941, SDDF 840.48/4714; Steinhardt to FDR, Hull, and Welles, February 28, 1941, SDDF 840.48/4722; and Steinhardt to Hull, March 10, 1941, SDDF 840.48/4756.

193. Best, *The Life of Herbert Hoover*, 136.

194. See Hastings, *Winston's War*, 23–49, and Hugh Sebag-Montefiore, *Dunkirk*.

195. See Gallup polls, May 2, 8, 12, 15, 17, 20, and 31 and June 5, in Gallup, *The Gallup Polls*, 221–224, 227.

196. Rickard Diary, May 20, 1940.

197. *Palo Alto Times*, June 8, 1940, Clipping File, HHP, HHPLM.

198. Rickard Diary, May 29, 1940.
199. Quoted in Best, *The Life of Herbert Hoover*, 138.
200. "Herbert Hoover," *World Astrology Magazine*, May 1940, Clipping File, HHP, HHPLM.
201. Wert, *Hoover the Fishing President*, 271–272.
202. Rickard Diary, June 4, 1940.
203. Ibid., June 12, 1940.
204. Ibid., June 13, 1940.
205. Ibid., June 16, 1940.
206. Ibid., June 18, 1940.
207. See McFarland, *Harry H. Woodring*, 209–234.
208. Ibid., 229.
209. Best, *The Life of Herbert Hoover*, 142.
210. See "Memorandum of Conversation," van der Straten-Ponthoz and Moffat, May 14, 1940, SDDF 840.48/3618, and "Memorandum of Conversation," van der Straten-Ponthoz, Georges Theunis (Belgian Ambassador at Large), and Joseph E. Davies, June 1, 1940, SDDF 840.48/3753.
211. Moe, *Roosevelt's Second Act*, 162–169; Dunn, *1940*, 101–120; and Best, *Herbert Hoover*, 160–162.
212. "Hoover Speech Rocks Convention," *San Francisco Chronicle*, June 26, 1940, Clipping File, HHP, HHPLM.
213. Best, *The Life of Herbert Hoover*, 145.
214. Ibid., 145.
215. Hoover, "Republican National Convention, Philadelphia, Pennsylvania, June 25, 1940," in *Addresses upon the American Road, 1940–1941*, 205–223.
216. See Best, *Herbert Hoover*, 162–163; Smith, *An Uncommon Man*, 284–285; and Nash, *Freedom Betrayed*, xliv. See also Strauss to Hoover, July 8, 1940; Strauss to Hoover, July 23, 1940; and Hoover to Strauss, August 26, 1940, PPI, HHP, HHPLM.
217. "Hoover Speech Rocks Convention," *San Francisco Chronicle*, June 26, 1940.
218. Smith, *FDR*, 454.
219. "Hoover Off to Fish, Rules Out Politics," *New York Times*, June 29, 1940, Clipping File, HHP, HHPLM.
220. "Hoover Comes Home to Fish," *Palo Alto Times*, July 1, 1940, Clipping File, HHP, HHPLM.
221. Smith, *An Uncommon Man*, 288. On his coolness toward Willkie, see Ray Tucker, "Washington Whirligig," July 2, 1940, PPI, HHP, HHPLM.

222. See McCoy, "Herbert Hoover and Foreign Policy," 404; Hoover, *An American* Epic, 4:22.

223. *New York Times*, June 22, 1940.

224. On Roosevelt's decision to run, one of the best sources remains Sherwood's *Roosevelt and Hopkins* (see 176–179).

225. Smith, *FDR*, 456.

226. Sherwood, *Roosevelt and Hopkins*, 176–179.

227. Dunn, *1940*, 137.

228. Smith, *FDR*, 460.

229. Davis, *FDR*, 597.

230. *Time*, July 29, 1940.

231. Smith, *FDR*, 461.

232. See Wert, *Hoover the Fishing President*, 274.

233. Hoover was not alone in his concerns for the hungry in Europe, as supporters of aid to Poland, Finland and France continued to agitate for assistance throughout the spring and summer of 1940. See Victor Weybright, "Sympathy Is Not Enough," *Survey Graphic* 29, no. 4 (April 1940): 212–216, 265–269, and Weybright, "Altruism at Armageddon," *Survey Graphic* 29, no. 7 (July 1940): 373–377, 415.

234. "Report to American Donors, December 1939–July 1940," Finnish Relief, PPSF, HHP, HHPLN, and audit figures from December 6, 1939, to December 31, 1946, in Report, Deloitte, Plender, Griffiths and Co. to Herbert Hoover, January 10, 1947, Finnish Relief, PPSF, HHP, HHPLM; "Report of the Treasury Department, Department of Agriculture and the American Red Cross, April 30, 1941," PF 124, American Red Cross, July–December 1940, RPM 1940, FDRL; and Berle to Hull and Welles, October 25, 1940, SDDF 840.48/4481.

235. Hoover, *An American Epic*, 4:7.

BIBLIOGRAPHY

Books

Adams, Ansel. *My Camera in Yosemite Valley.* Boston: Houghton Mifflin, 1949.

Adler, Selig. *The Isolationist Impulse: Its Twentieth Century Reaction.* New York: Abelard-Schuman, 1957.

Agar, Herbert. *The Saving Remnant: An Account of Jewish Survival.* New York: Viking Press, 1960.

Albion, Robert G., and Jennie B. Pope. *Sealanes in Wartime.* New York: W. W. Norton, 1942.

Alsop, Joseph, and Robert Kitner. *American White Paper: The Story of American Diplomacy and the Second World War.* New York: Simon and Schuster, 1940.

Archer, Laird. *Balkan Journal: An Unofficial Observer in Greece.* New York: W. W. Norton, 1944.

Ashworth, John. *Agrarians and Aristocrats: Party Political Ideology in the United States, 1837–1846.* London: Boydell and Brewer, 1983.

Asquith, Margot. *Margot Asquith's Great War Diary, 1914–1916: The View from Downing Street.* Edited by Michael and Eleanor Brock. New York: Oxford University Press, 2014.

Aster, Sidney. *1939: The Making of the Second World War.* New York: Simon and Schuster, 1973.

Baldwin, Hanson W. *The Crucial Years, 1939–1941.* New York: Harper and Row, 1976.

Ball, Adrian, *The Last Days of the Old World.* London: Frederick Muller, 1963.

Bane, Suda Lorena, and Ralph Haswell Lutz. *The Blockade of Germany after the Armistice, 1918–1919.* Stanford, CA: Stanford University Press, 1942.

Barkley, Alben. *That Reminds Me.* Garden City, NY: Doubleday, 1954.

Barry, John M. *Rising Tide: The Great Mississippi Flood of 1927 and How It Changed America.* New York: Simon and Schuster, 1997.

Bauer, Yehuda. *American Jewry and the Holocaust: The American Jewish Joint Distribution Committee, 1939–1945*. Detroit, MI: Wayne State University Press, 1981.

———. *My Brother's Keeper*. Philadelphia: Jewish Publication Society of America, 1974.

Beaton, Cecil. *The Years Between: Diaries 1939–44*. New York: Holt, Rinehart and Winston, 1965.

Beck, Jozef. *Final Report: Diplomatic Memoirs of Colonel Jozef Beck Former Foreign Minister of Poland*. New York: Robert Speller and Sons, 1957.

Beir, Robert L. *Roosevelt and the Holocaust: A Rooseveltian Examines the Policies and Remembers the Times*. Fort Lee, NJ: Barricade Books, 2006.

Belgian American Educational Foundation. *The Belgian Campaign and the Surrender of the Belgian Army, May 10–28, 1940*. New York: Belgian American Educational Foundation, 1941.

Bell, A. C. *A History of the Blockade of Germany, 1914–1918*. London: His Majesty's Stationary Office, 1937.

Bell, George K. A. *The Church and Humanity, 1939–1945*. London: Longmans, Green, 1946.

Bell, Henry McGrady. *Land of Lakes*. London: Robert Hale, 1950.

Berg, A. Scott. *Lindbergh*. New York: G. P. Putnam's Sons, 1998.

———, ed. *World War I and America: Told by the Americans Who Lived It*. New York: Library of America, 2017.

Berg, Mary. *Warsaw Ghetto: A Diary*. New York: L. B. Fischer, 1945.

Berghahn, Marion. *German-Jewish Refugees in England: The Ambiguities of Assimilation*. New York: St. Martin's Press, 1984.

Berle, Beatrice, and Travis Beal Jacobs, eds. *Navigating the Rapids, 1918–1971*. New York: Harcourt Brace Jovanovich, 1973.

Berry, R. Michael. *American Foreign Policy and the Finnish Exception: Ideological Preferences and Wartime Realities*. Jyvaskyla: Gummerus Oy Kirjapaino, 1987.

Beschloss, Michael. *Presidents of War: The Epic Story, from 1807 to Modern Times*. New York: Crown, 2018.

Best, Gary Dean. *Herbert Hoover: The Postpresidential Years, 1933–1945*. Vol. 1. Stanford, CA: Hoover Institution Press, 1983.

———. *Herbert Hoover: The Postpresidential Years, 1946–1964*. Vol. 2. Stanford, CA: Hoover Institution Press, 1983.

———. *The Life of Herbert Hoover: Keeper of the Torch, 1933–1964*. New York: Palgrave Macmillan, 2013.

Bethell, Nicholas, *The War Hitler Won: The Fall of Poland, September 1939*. New York: Holt, Rinehart and Winston, 1973.

Bibliography

Biddle, Anthony Joseph Drexel. *Poland and the Coming of the Second World War: The Diplomatic Papers of A. J. Drexel Biddle, Jr., United States Ambassador to Poland, 1937–1939*, edited by Philip V. Cannistraro, Edward D. Wynot, and Theodore P. Kovaleff. Columbus: Ohio State University Press, 1976.

Bishop, Alan, and Y. Aleksander Bennett, eds. *War Chronicle: Vera Brittain's Diaries, 1939–1945*. London: Victor Gollancz, 1989.

Black, Maggie. *A Cause for Our Times: Oxfam—the First 50 Years*. London: Oxford University Press, 1992.

Blair, Clay. *Hitler's U-Boat War: The Hunters, 1939–1942*. New York: Random House, 1996.

Bland, Larry I., Sharon R. Ritenour, and Clarence E. Wunderlin, Jr., eds. *The Papers of George Catlett Marshall*. Baltimore, MD: Johns Hopkins University Press, 1986.

Bloch, Michael. *Ribbentrop: A Biography*. New York: Crown, 1992.

Bloom, Sol. *The Autobiography of Sol Bloom*. New York: G. P. Putnam's Sons, 1948.

Blum, John Morton. *Years of Urgency, 1938–1941: From the Morgenthau Diaries*. Boston: Houghton Mifflin, 1965.

Bohlen, Charles. *Witness to History, 1929–1969*. New York: W. W. Norton, 1973.

Bond, Brian, ed. *Chief of Staff: The Diaries of Lieutenant-General Sir Henry Pownall, 1933–1940*. Vol. 1. London: Leo Cooper, 1972.

———, ed. *Chief of Staff: The Diaries of Lieutenant-General Sir Henry Pownall, 1940–1944*. Vol. 2. London: Leo Cooper, 1974.

Bonney, Therese. *Europe's Children*. New York: Rhode Publishing, 1943.

Bouverie, Tim. *Appeasement: Chamberlain, Hitler, Churchill, and the Road to War*. New York: Tim Duggan Books, 2019.

Brands, H. W. *Traitor to His Class: The Privileged Life and Radical Presidency of Franklin D. Roosevelt*. New York: Random House, 2008.

Brandt, Karl. *Management of Agriculture and Food in the German-Occupied and Other Areas of Fortress Europe*. Stanford, CA: Stanford University Press, 1953.

Braun, Connie. *The Steppes Are the Color of Sepia: A Mennonite Memoir*. Vancouver, Canada: Ronsdale Press, 2008.

Breitman, Richard, and Alan M. Kraut. *American Refugee Policy and European Jewry, 1933–1945*. Bloomington: Indiana University Press, 1987.

Breitman, Richard, Alan M. Kraut, Barbara McDonald Stewart, and Severin Hochberg, eds. *Refugees and Rescue: The Diaries and Papers of James G. McDonald, 1932–1935*. Bloomington: Indiana University Press, 2007.

———, eds. *Refugees and Rescue: The Diaries and Papers of James G. McDonald, 1935–1945*. Bloomington: Indiana University Press, 2009.

Brinson, Charmian, and Marian Malet, eds. *Exile in and from Czechoslovakia during the 1930s and 1940s.* New York: Rodopi, 2009.
Brittain, Vera. *England's Hour.* New York: Macmillan, 1941.
———. *Testament of Experience.* London: Victor Gollancz, 1957.
Brock, Ray. *Nor Any Victory.* New York: Reynal and Hitchcock, 1942.
Brown, Jared. *The Fabulous Lunts.* New York: Atheneum, 1986.
Brown, John Mason. *The Worlds of Robert E. Sherwood.* New York: Harper and Row, 1965.
Brownell, Will, and Richard N. Billings. *So Close to Greatness: A Biography of William C. Bullitt.* New York: Macmillan, 1987.
Browning, Christopher R. *Ordinary Men: Reserve Police Battalion 101 and the Final Solution in Poland.* New York: Harper Perennial, 1992.
Bryan, Julien. *Siege: Photographs and a Dramatic Narrative of Personal Experience.* New York: Doubleday, Doran, 1940.
———. *Warsaw: 1939 Siege, 1959 Warsaw Revisited.* Warsaw: Polonia Publishing House, 1959.
Brzezinski, Matthew. *Isaac's Army: A Story of Courage and Survival in Nazi-Occupied Poland.* New York: Random House, 2012.
Bullitt, Orville H., ed. *For the President, Personal and Secret: Correspondence between Franklin D. Roosevelt and William C. Bullitt.* Boston: Houghton Mifflin, 1972.
Bullock, Alan. *Hitler and Stalin: Parallel Lives.* New York: Alfred A. Knopf, 1992.
Burdick, Charles, and Hans-Adolf Jacobsen, eds. *The Halder War Diary, 1939–1942.* Novata, CA: Presidio, 1988.
Burner, David. *Herbert Hoover: A Public Life.* New York: Alfred A. Knopf, 1979.
Burns, James MacGregor. *Roosevelt: The Lion and the Fox.* New York: Harcourt, Brace, 1956.
Butler, J. R. M. *Grand Strategy, September 1939–June 1941.* Vol. 2. London: Her Majesty's Stationary Office, 1971.
Callahan, Raymond A. *Churchill: Retreat from Empire.* Wilmington, DE: Scholarly Resources, 1984.
Calvocoressi, Peter, Guy Wint, and John Pritchard. *Total War.* New York: Pantheon, 1989.
Cantrill, Hadley, and Mildred Struck, eds. *Public Opinion, 1935–1946.* Princeton, NJ: Princeton University Press, 1951.
Caquet, P. E. *The Bell of Treason: The 1938 Munich Agreement in Czechoslovakia.* New York: Other Press, 2018.
Cardwell, An Su. *Poland and Russia.* New York: Sheed and Ward, 1944.
Carlgren, W. M. *Swedish Foreign Policy during the Second World War.* New York: St. Martin's Press, 1977.

Carr, William. *Arms, Autarky and Aggression.* New York: W. W. Norton, 1972.
Carroll, Francis M. *Athenia Torpedoed: The U-Boat Attack That Ignited the Battle of the Atlantic.* Annapolis, MD: Naval Institute Press, 2012.
Casey, Lord. *Personnel Experience, 1939–1946.* New York: David McKay, 1962.
Castle, Alfred L. *Diplomatic Realism: William R. Castle, Jr., and American Foreign Policy, 1919–1953.* Honolulu: Samuel N. and Mary Castle Foundation, 1999.
Chamberlain, William Henry. *America's Second Crusade.* Chicago: Regnery, 1950.
Chandler, Andrew. *George Bell, Bishop of Chichester: Church, State, and Resistance in the Age of Dictatorship.* Grand Rapids, MI: William R. Eerdmans, 2016.
Charles, Douglas M. *J. Edgar Hoover and the Anti-interventionists: FBI Political Surveillance and the Rise of the Domestic Security State, 1939–1945.* Columbus: Ohio State University Press, 2007.
Charlton, Lionel. *The Air Defense of Britain.* London: Penguin, 1938.
Charman, Terry. *Outbreak 1939: The World Goes to War.* London: Virgin Books, 2009.
Charmley, John. *Chamberlain and the Lost Peace.* Chicago: Ivan R. Dee, 1989.
Chevalier, Michael. *Society, Manners and Politics in the United States: Being a Series of Letters on North America.* Boston: Weeks, Jordan, 1839.
Chew, Allen F. *The White Death.* East Lansing: Michigan State University Press, 1971.
Churchill, Winston S. *The Second World War: The Gathering Storm.* Boston: Houghton Mifflin, 1948.
Chylinski, Thaddeus. *Poland under Nazi Rule, 1939–1941: A Report by Thaddeus Chylinski, American Vice-Consul in Warsaw.* Independently published by Donna B. Gawell, 2019.
Ciano, Galeazzo. *The Ciano Diaries, 1939–1943.* New York: Doubleday, 1946.
Cienciala, Anna M. *Poland and the Western Powers.* London: Routledge and Kegan Paul, 1968.
Cisek, Janusz. *Polish Refugees and the Polish American Immigration and Relief Committee.* Jefferson, NC: McFarland, 2006.
Citino, Robert M. *Blitzkrieg to Desert Storm: The Evolution of Operational Warfare.* Lawrence: University Press of Kansas, 2004.
Citrine, Walter. *My Finnish Diary.* London: Penguin Books, 1940.
Clark, Douglas. *Three Days to Catastrophe.* London: Hammond, 1966.
Clements, Kendrick A. *Hoover, Conservation and Consumerism: Engineering the Good Life.* Lawrence: University Press of Kansas, 2000.
———. *The Life of Herbert Hoover: Imperfect Visionary, 1918–1928.* New York: Palgrave Macmillan, 2010.

Clifford, J. Gary, and Samuel R. Spencer Jr. *The First Peacetime Draft*. Lawrence: University Press of Kansas, 1986.
Cole, Wayne S. *America First: The Battle against Intervention, 1940–1941*. Madison: University of Wisconsin Press, 1953.
———. *Charles A. Lindbergh and the Battle against American Intervention in World War II*. New York: Harcourt Brace Jovanovich, 1974.
———. *Roosevelt and the Isolationists, 1932–1945*. Lincoln: University of Nebraska Press, 1983.
Collier, Richard. *The Warcos: The War Correspondents of World War II*. London: Weidenfeld and Nicolson, 1989.
Collingham, Lizzie. *The Taste of War: World War II and the Battle for Food*. New York: Penguin Press, 2012.
Collum, Danny Duncan, ed. *African Americans in the Spanish Civil War: "This Ain't Ethiopia, but It'll Do."* New York: G. K. Hall, 1992.
Colton, Ethan Theodore. *Memoirs of Ethan T. Colton, Sr., 1872–1952*. New York: Historical Resources and Library Committee, National Board of Young Men's Christian Associations, 1969.
Colville, John. *Winston Churchill and His Inner Circle*. New York: Wyndham Books, 1981.
Colvin, Ian. *The Chamberlain Cabinet*. New York: Taplinger, 1971.
Committee of the Polish Air Force. *Destiny Can Wait: The History of the Polish Air Force in the Second World War*. London: Heineman, 1949.
Conant, Jennet. *The Irregulars: Roald Dahl and the British Spy Ring in Wartime Washington*. New York: Simon and Schuster, 2008.
Connelly, Tom. *My Name Is Tom Connelly*. New York: Crowell, 1954.
Coogan, John W. *The End of Neutrality*. Ithaca, NY: Cornell University Press, 1981.
Cook, Blanche Wiesen. *Eleanor Roosevelt: The War Years and After, 1939–1962*. Vol. 3. New York: Viking, 2016.
Cooper, Duff. *Old Men Forget*. New York: E. P. Dutton, 1954.
Corbett, P. Scott. *Quiet Passages*. Kent, OH: Kent State University Press, 1987.
Cornebise, Alfred E. *Typhus and Doughboys: The American Polish Typhus Relief Expedition, 1919–1921*. Newark: University of Delaware Press, 1982.
Corum, James S. *The Roots of Blitzkrieg: Hans von Seeckt and German Military Reform*. Lawrence: University Press of Kansas, 1992.
Cosgrove, Patrick. *Churchill at War*. London: Collins, 1974.
Cowles, Virginia. *Looking for Trouble*. New York: Harper and Brothers, 1944.
Cox, Geoffrey. *Countdown to War: A Personal Memoir of Europe, 1938–1940*. London: Hodder and Stoughton, 1990.

———. *The Red Army Moves.* London: Victor Gollancz, 1941.

Cox, Mary. *Hunger in War and Peace: Women and Children in Germany, 1914–1924.* Oxford: Oxford University Press, 2019.

Crossland, James. *Britain and the International Committee of the Red Cross, 1939–1945.* New York: Palgrave Macmillan, 2014.

Crozier, Andrew. *Neville Chamberlain.* London: Hodder Arnold, 2010.

Cudahy, John. *The Armies March.* New York: Charles Scribner's Sons, 1941.

Curti, Merle. *American Philanthropy Abroad.* New Brunswick, NJ: Rutgers University Press, 1963.

Curtis, Anna L. *The Quakers Take Stock.* New York: Island Press, 1944.

Dallas, Gregor. *1918: War and Peace.* London: John Murray, 2000.

Dallek, Robert. *Franklin D. Roosevelt: A Political Life.* New York: Viking, 2017.

———. *Franklin D. Roosevelt and American Foreign Policy, 1932–1945.* New York: Oxford University Press, 1979.

Dallin, Alexander. *German Rule in Russia, 1941–1945: A Study of Occupation Policies.* London: Macmillan, 1957.

Dallin, David J. *Soviet Russia's Foreign Policy, 1939–1942.* New Haven, CT: Yale University Press, 1942.

Dalton, Hugh. *The Fateful Year: Memoirs, 1931–1935.* 3 Vols. London: Frederick Muller, 1957.

Davidowicz, Lucy S. *From That Place and Time: A Memoir, 1938–1947.* New Brunswick, NJ: Rutgers University Press, 2008.

Davies, Norman. *God's Playground: A History of Poland.* 2 Vols. New York: Columbia University Press, 1984.

———. *Trail of Hope: The Anders Army, an Odyssey across Three Continents.* Oxford: Osprey, 2015.

Davies, Tegla A. *Friends Ambulance Unit: The Story of the F.A.U. in the Second World War, 1939–1946.* London: George Allen and Unwin, 1947.

Davis, Kenneth S. *FDR: Into the Storm, 1937–1940.* New York: Random House, 1993.

D'Este, Carlo. *Eisenhower: A Soldier's Life.* New York: Henry Holt, 2002.

De Sales, Raoul de Roussy. *The Making of Yesterday.* New York: Reynal and Hitchcock, 1947.

De Wiart, Sir Adrian Carton. *Happy Odyssey: The Memoirs of Lieutenant-General Sir Adrian Carton De Wiart.* Yorkshire, UK: Pen and Sword, 2018.

Demetriades, Phokion. *Shadow over Athens.* New York: Rinehart, 1946.

Des Jardins, Julie. *American Queenmaker: How Missy Meloney Brought Women into Politics.* New York: Basic Books, 2020.

Detzer, Dorothy. *Appointment on the Hill.* New York: Henry Holt, 1948.

Di Figlia, Ghanda. *Roots and Visions: The First Fifty Years of the Unitarian Universalist Service Committee.* Boston: Unitarian Universalist Service Committee, 1990.

Diamond, Hanna. *Fleeing Hitler: France 1940.* New York: Oxford University Press, 2007.

Dilks, David. *The Diaries of Sir Alexander Cadogan, 1938–1945.* London: Cassell, 1971.

Divine, Robert A. *The Illusion of Neutrality.* Chicago: University of Chicago Press, 1962.

———. *Second Chance: The Triumph of Internationalism in America during World War II.* New York: Atheneum, 1967.

Doenecke, Justus D. *In Danger Undaunted: The Anti-interventionist Movement in 1940–1941 as Revealed in the Papers of the America First Committee.* Stanford, CA: Hoover Institution Press, 1990.

———. *Not to the Swift: The Old Isolationists in the Cold War Era.* Lewisburg, PA: Bucknell University Press, 1979.

———. *Storm on the Horizon: The Challenge to American Intervention, 1939–1941.* Lanham, MD: Rowman & Littlefield, 2000.

Donat, Alexander. *The Holocaust Kingdom.* New York: Holt, Rinehart and Winston, 1963.

Dorian, Emil. *The Quality of Witness: A Romanian Diary, 1937–1944.* Philadelphia: Jewish Publication Society of America, 1982.

Douglas, Charles M. *J. Edgar Hoover and the Anti-interventionists: FBI Political Surveillance and the Rise of the Domestic Security State, 1939–1945.* Columbus: Ohio State University Press, 2007.

Douhet, Guilio. *The Command of the Air.* New York: Coward-McCann, 1942.

Dray, Philip. *The Fair Chase.* New York: Basic Books, 2018.

Duffy, James P. *Lindbergh and Roosevelt: The Rivalry That Divided America.* Chicago: Regnery, 2010.

Dugdale, Blanche. *Baffy: The Diaries of Blanche Dugdale, 1936–1947.* Edited and translated by Norman Rose. London: Vallentin-Mitchell, 1973.

Dulles, Allen W., and Hamilton Armstrong Fish. *Can America Stay Neutral?* New York: Harper and Brothers, 1939.

Dulles, Foster Rhea. *The American Red Cross: A History.* New York: Harper and Brothers, 1950.

Dunant, Henri. *A Memory of Solferino.* Washington, DC: American Red Cross, 1959.

Dunn, Dennis J. *Caught between Roosevelt and Stalin: America's Ambassadors to Moscow.* Lexington: University of Kentucky Press, 1998.

Dunn, Susan. *1940: FDR, Willkie, Lindbergh, Hitler—the Election amid the Storm.* New Haven, CT: Yale University Press, 2013.

Dunne, Finley Peter. *Mr. Dooley's Philosophy.* New York: R. H. Russell, 1902.

Earle, Hubert P. *Blackout: The Human Side of Europe's March to War.* Philadelphia: J. B. Lippincott, 1939.

Easterman, A. L. *King Carol, Hitler, and Lupescu.* London: Victor Gollancz, 1942.

Eccles, David. *By Safe Hand: Letters of Sybil and David Eccles, 1939–42.* London: Bodley Head, 1983.

Eden, Anthony. *The Reckoning: The Memoirs of Anthony Eden, Earl of Avon.* Boston: Houghton Mifflin, 1965.

Edwards, Robert. *The Winter War: Russia's Invasion of Finland, 1939–1940.* New York: Pegasus Books, 2008.

Edwards, Ruth Dudley. *Victor Gollancz: A Biography.* London: Victor Gollancz, 1987.

Egan, Eileen. *Catholic Services: The Beginning Years, for the Life of the World.* New York: Catholic Relief Services, 1988.

———. *For Whom There Is No Room: Scenes from the Refugee World.* New York: Paulist Press, 1995.

Eiler, Keith E. *Mobilizing America: Robert P. Patterson and the War Effort, 1940–1945.* Ithaca, NY: Cornell University Press, 1997.

Einzig, Paul. *Economic Warfare.* London: Macmillan, 1940.

El Greco: Loan Exhibition for the Benefit of the Greek War Relief Association, January 17 to February 15, 1941. New York: Art Aid Corporation, 1941.

Elliston, H. B. *Finland Fights.* Boston: Little, Brown, 1940.

Emerson, Ralph Waldo. *The Collected Works of Ralph Waldo Emerson.* Volume 1: *Nature, Addresses, and Lectures.* Introductions and notes by Robert E. Spiller. Cambridge, MA: Belknap Press, 1971.

Engelking, Barbara, and Jacek Leociak. *The Warsaw Ghetto: A Guide to the Perished City.* New Haven, CT: Yale University Press, 2009.

Engle, Eloise K., and Lauri Paananen. *The Winter War.* New York: Charles Scribner's Sons, 1973.

Epp, Marlene. *Women without Men: Mennonite Refugees of the Second World War.* Toronto: University of Toronto Press, 2000.

Etkind, Alexander. *Roads Not Taken.* Pittsburgh, PA: University of Pittsburgh Press, 2017.

Evans, Richard J. *The Third Reich at War.* New York: Penguin Press, 2009.

Faber, David. *Munich, 1938: Appeasement and World War II.* New York: Simon and Schuster, 2008.

Farnham, Barbara Rearden. *Roosevelt and the Munich Crisis: A Study of Political Decision-Making*. Princeton, NJ: Princeton University Press, 1997.

Felsenthal, Carol. *Alice Roosevelt Longworth*. New York: G. P. Putnam's Sons, 1988.

Ferguson, Niall. *The Pity of War: Explaining World War I*. New York: Basic Books, 1999.

Fiedler, Arkady. *303 Squadron: The Legendary Battle of Britain Fighter Squadron*. Los Angeles, CA: Aquila Polonica, 2010.

———. *Squadron 303: The Polish Fighter Squadron with the R.A.F.* New York: Roy Publishers, 1943.

Fighting the Russians in Winter. Leavenworth Papers, no. 5. Leavenworth, KS: Combat Studies Institute, US Command and General Staff College, 1981.

Firsoff, V. A. *Ski Track on the Battlefield*. New York: A. S. Barnes, 1943.

Forsythe, David P. *The Humanitarians: The International Committee of the Red Cross*. Cambridge: Cambridge University Press, 2005.

Frank, Matthew. *Making Minorities History: Population Transfers in Twentieth-Century Europe*. New York: Oxford University Press, 2017.

Frank, Tibor, ed. *Discussing Hitler: Advisers of U.S. Diplomacy in Central Europe, 1934–1941*. Budapest: Central European University, 2003.

Freud, Sigmund. *Civilization and Its Discontents*. New York: W. W. Norton, 1961.

Friedländer, Saul. *Nazi Germany and the Jews, The Years of Persecution, 1933–1939*. Vol. 1. New York: HarperCollins, 1997.

Friedrich, Jörg. *The Fire: The Bombing of Germany, 1940–1945*. New York: Columbia University Press, 2008.

Fry, Varian. *Surrender on Demand: The Dramatic Story of the Underground Organization Set Up by Americans in France to Rescue Anti-Nazis from the Gestapo*. New York: Random House, 1945.

Fuchser, Larry William. *Neville Chamberlain and Appeasement: A Study in the Politics of History*. New York: W. W. Norton, 1982.

Gafencu, Grigore. *Last Days of Europe: A Diplomatic Journey*. New Haven, CT: Yale University Press, 1948.

Gallup, George H., ed. *The Gallup International Public Opinion Polls, Great Britain, 1937–1975*. New York: Random House, 1976.

———, ed. *The Gallup Poll: Public Opinion, 1935–1971*. New York: Random House, 1972.

Garlinski, Józef. *The Enigma War: The Inside Story of the German Enigma Codes and How the Allies Broke Them*. New York: Charles Scribner's Sons, 1979.

Garrett, Patrick. *Of Fortunes and War: Clare Hollingworth, First of the Female War Correspondents*. London: Thistle Publishing, 2015.

Bibliography

Gates, Eleanor M. *End of an Affair*. Berkeley: University of California Press, 1981.

Geer, Andrew. *Mercy in Hell: An American Ambulance Driver with the Eighth Army*. New York: McGraw-Hill, 1943.

Gelfand, Lawrence E., ed. *Herbert Hoover: The Great War and Its Aftermath, 1914–23*. Iowa City: University of Iowa Press, 1974.

Gellhorn, Martha. *The Face of War*. New York: Grove Press, 2018.

Gellman, Irwin F. *Secret Affairs: Franklin Roosevelt, Cordell Hull, and Sumner Welles*. Baltimore: Johns Hopkins University Press, 1995.

Gemie, Dharif, Fiona Reid, and Laure Humbert. *Outcast Europe: Refugees and Relief Workers in an Era of Total War, 1936–48*. New York: Continuum, 2012.

Georgakas, Dan, and Charles C. Moskos, eds. *New Directions in Greek American Studies*. New York: Pella Publishing, 1991.

Gilbert, Martin. *Churchill: A Life*. New York: Henry Holt, 1991.

———. *The Churchill War Papers: Never Surrender, May 1940–December 1940*. 3 Vols. New York: W. W. Norton, 1995.

———. *The First World War: A Complete History*. New York: Henry Holt, 1994.

———. *Winston S. Churchill*. Vol. 5: *The Prophet of Truth, 1922–1939*. Boston: Houghton Mifflin, 1977.

———. *Winston S. Churchill*. Vol. 6: *Finest Hour, 1939–1941*. Boston: Houghton Mifflin, 1983.

Gisevius, H. B. *To the Bitter End*. London: Jonathan Cape, 1948.

Główczewski. Jerzy. *The Accidental Immigrant: A Memoir*. New York: Xlibris Corporation, 2007.

Gnyś, Stefan. *First Kills: The Illustrated Biography of Fighter Pilot Władysław Gnyś*. Philadelphia: Casemate, 2017.

Gnyś, Władek. *First Kill: A Fighter Pilot's Autobiography*. London: William Kimber, 1981.

Goebbels, Joseph. *The Goebbels Diaries, 1939–1941*. Edited and translated by Fred Taylor. New York: G. P. Putnam's Sons, 1983.

Gold, Mary Jane. *Crossroads Marseilles, 1940: A Memoir*. Garden City, NY: Doubleday, 1980.

Goldman, Stuart D. *Nomonhan, 1939: The Red Army Victory That Shaped World War II*. Annapolis, MD: Naval Institute Press, 2012.

Gole, Henry G. *Exposing the Third Reich: Colonel Truman Smith in Hitler's Germany*. Lexington: University of Kentucky Press, 2013.

Golway, Terry. *Frank and Al: FDR, Al Smith and the Unlikely Alliance That Created the Modern Democratic Party*. New York: St. Martin's Press, 2018.

Gorham, Deborah. *Vera Brittain: A Feminist Life*. Oxford: Blackwell, 1996.

Gorodetsky, Gabriel, ed. *The Maisky Diaries: Red Ambassador to the Court of St. James's, 1932–1943.* New Haven, CT: Yale University Press, 2015.

Grayling, A. C. *Among the Dead Cities: The History and Moral Legacy of the WWII Bombing of Civilians in Germany and Japan.* New York: Walker, 2006.

Grew, Joseph C. *Turbulent Era: A Diplomatic Record of Forty Years, 1904–1945.* Boston: Houghton Mifflin, 1952.

Gripenberg, G. A. *Finland and the Great Powers: Memoirs of a Diplomat.* Lincoln: University of Nebraska Press, 1965.

Gross, Irena Grudzińska, and Jan Tonasz Gross. *War through Children's Eyes.* Stanford, CA: Hoover Institution Press, 1981.

Gross, Jan Tomasz. *Polish Society under German Occupation: The Generalgouvernement, 1939–1944.* Princeton, NJ: Princeton University Press, 1979.

———. *Revolution from Abroad: The Soviet Conquest of Poland's Western Ukraine and Western Belorussia.* Princeton, NJ: Princeton University Press, 1988.

Grove, William R. *War's Aftermath: Polish Relief in 1919.* New York: House of Field, 1940.

Guinsburg, Thomas N. *The Pursuit of Isolationism in the United States Senate from Versailles to Pearl Harbor.* New York: Garland, 1982.

Gunther, John. *Inside Europe.* New York: Harper and Brothers, 1940.

Gutman, Yisreal. *The Jews of Warsaw, 1939–1943.* Bloomington: University of Indiana Press, 1989.

Guttmann, Allen. *American Neutrality and the Spanish Civil War.* Lexington, MA: D. C. Heath, 1963.

Gyllenhaal, Lars, and Lennart Westberg. *Swedes at War: Willing Warriors of a Neutral Nation, 1914–1945.* Bedford, PA: Aberjona Press, 2010.

Halder, Franz. *The Halder War Diary, 1939–1942.* Edited by Charles Burdick and Hans-Adolf Jacobsen. Novato, CA: Presidio, 1988.

Hamby, Alonzo L. *For the Survival of Democracy: Franklin Roosevelt and the World Crisis of the 1930s.* New York: Free Press, 2004.

Hampton, Janie. *How the Girl Guides Won the War.* London: Harper Press, 2011.

Hansen, Randell. *Fire and Fury: The Allied Bombing of Germany, 1942–1945.* New York: NAL Caliber, 2008.

Harmsen, Peter. *Shanghai 1937: Stalingrad on the Yangtze.* Philadelphia: Casemate, 2013.

Harris, Joseph E. *African-American Reactions to War in Ethiopia, 1936–1941.* Baton Rouge: Louisiana State University Press, 1994.

Harvey, John, ed. *The Diplomatic Diaries of Oliver Harvey.* London: Collins, 1970.

———. *The War Diaries of Oliver Harvey.* London: Collins, 1979.

Haskell, Arnold L., ed. *Ballet—to Poland: A Gala Performance on Aid of the Polish Relief Fund.* London: Adam and Charles Black, 1940.

Hassel, Ulrich von. *The Ulrich von Hassell Diaries: The Story of the Forces against Hitler inside Germany.* London: Frontline Books, 2011.

Hastings, Max. *Winston's War: Churchill, 1940–1945.* New York: Alfred A. Knopf, 2010.

Hawley, Ellis W., ed. *Herbert Hoover as Secretary of Commerce, 1921–1928: Studies in New Era Thought and Practice.* Iowa City: University of Iowa Press, 1974.

Helger, Bengt. *Ravitaillement de la Grèce: Pendant L'Occupation 1941–1944 et pendant les Premiers Cinq Mois aprés la Liberation.* Athens: Societe Hellenique D'Editions, 1949.

Henderson, Neville. *Failure of a Mission.* New York: G. P. Putnam's, 1940.

Henig, Ruth. *The Peace That Never Was: A History of the League of Nations.* London: Haus, 2019.

Herwarth, Hans von. *Against Two Evils.* New York: Rawson Wade, 1981.

Hickey, Donald R. *The War of 1812: A Forgotten Conflict.* Campaign-Urbana: University of Illinois Press, 2012.

Hicks, Granville. *Where We Came Out.* New York: Viking Press, 1954.

Hilberg, Raul, Stanislaw Staron, and Josef Kermisz, eds. *The Warsaw Diary of Adam Czerniakow.* New York: Stein and Day, 1979.

Hinshaw, David. *An Experiment in Friendship: A Study of Quaker Relief Work.* New York: G. P. Putnam's Sons, 1947.

———. *Herbert Hoover: American Quaker.* New York: Farrar, Straus, 1950.

Hinsley, F. H. *British Intelligence in the Second World War.* 3 Vols. London: Her Majesty's Stationary Office, 1979.

Hionidou, Violetta. *Famine and Death in Occupied Greece, 1941–1944.* Cambridge: Cambridge University Press, 2006.

Hippler, Thomas. *Bombing the People: Guilio Douhet and the Foundation of Air-Power Strategy, 1884–1939.* Cambridge: Cambridge University Press, 2013.

Hoad, Edith E. *The Eagle's Child.* Raleigh, NC: Lilu.com, 2011.

Hoare, Samuel, Viscount Templewood. *Nine Troubled Years.* London: Collins, 1954.

Hochhuth, Rolf. *Soldiers: An Obituary for Geneva.* New York: Grove Press, 1968.

Hoffman, Heinrich. *Hitler Was My Friend: The Memoirs of Hitler's Photographer.* London: Frontline Books, 2011.

Höhne, Heinz. *Canaris: Hitler's Master Spy.* New York: Doubleday, 1979.

Holli, Melvin G. *The Wizard of Washington: Emil Hurja, Franklin Roosevelt, and the Birth of Public Opinion Polling.* New York: Palgrave, 2002.

Hollingworth, Clare. *Frontline.* London: Jonathan Cape, 1990.

———. *The Three Weeks' War in Poland*. London: Duckworth, 1940.
———. *There's a German Just behind Me*. London: Secker and Warburg, 1942.
Hondros, John Louis. *Occupation and Resistance: The Greek Agony, 1941–44*. New York: Pella Publishing, 1983.
Hooker, Nancy Harvison, ed. *The Moffat Papers: Selections from the Diplomatic Journals of Jay Pierrepont Moffat, 1919–1943*. Cambridge, MA: Harvard University Press, 1956.
Hooton, E. R. *Stalin's Claws: from the Purges to the Winter War: Red Army Operations before Barbarossa, 1937–1941*. Pulborough, UK: Tattered Flag Press, 2013.
Hoover, Herbert. *Addresses upon the American Road, 1933–1938*. New York: Charles Scribner's Sons, 1938.
———. *American Individualism*. Garden City, NY: Doubleday Page, 1922.
———. *An American Epic: Famine in Forty-Five Nations*. Vol. 2: *Organization behind the Front, 1914–1923*. Chicago: Henry Regnery, 1960.
———. *An American Epic: Famine in Forty-Five Nations*. Vol. 3: *The Battle on the Front Line, 1914–1923*. Chicago: Henry Regnery, 1961.
———. *An American Epic: Famine in Forty-Five Nations*. Vol. 4: *The Guns Cease Killing and the Saving of Life from Famine Begins, 1939–1963*. Chicago: Henry Regnery, 1964.
———. *Further Addresses upon the American Road, 1938–1940*. New York: Charles Scribner's Sons, 1940.
———. *The Memoirs of Herbert Hoover*. Vol. 1: *The Years of Adventure: 1874–1920*. New York: Macmillan, 1951.
———. *The Memoirs of Herbert Hoover*. Vol. 2: *The Cabinet and the Presidency, 1920–1932*. New York: Macmillan, 1952.
———. *The Memoirs of Herbert Hoover*. Vol. 3: *The Great Depression, 1929–1941*. New York: Macmillan, 1952.
———. *The Ordeal of Woodrow Wilson*. New York: McGraw-Hill, 1958.
Horak, Stephan. *Poland and Her National Minorities, 1919–39*. New York: Vantage Press, 1961.
Horowitz, David A. *Beyond Left and Right: Insurgency and the Establishment*. Urbana: University of Illinois Press, 1997.
Howarth, Stephen. *August 1939: The Last Four Weeks of Peace*. San Francisco, CA: Mercury House, 1989.
Howson, Gerald. *Arms for Spain: The Untold Story of the Spanish Civil War*. New York: St. Martin's Press, 1998.
Hull, Cordell. *The Memoirs of Cordell Hull*. Vol. 1. New York: Macmillan, 1948.
Huntington, Samuel P. *Who Are We? The Challenges to America's National Identity*. New York: Simon and Schuster, 2004.

Hutchinson, John F. *Champions of Charity: War and the Rise of the Red Cross.* Boulder, CO: Westview Press, 1996.

Hyde, H. Montgomery. *The Quiet Canadian: The Secret Service Story of Sir William Stephenson.* London: Hamish Hamilton, 1962.

Ickes, Harold L. *The Secret Diary of Harold L. Ickes.* Vol. 2: *The Inside Struggle.* New York: Simon and Schuster, 1954.

———. *The Secret Diary of Harold L. Ickes.* Vol. 3: *The Lowering Clouds, 1939–1941.* New York: Simon and Schuster, 1954.

Insh, George Pratt. *The War-Time History of the Scottish Branch, British Red Cross Society.* Glasgow, Scotland: Jackson, Son, 1952.

Iranek-Osmecki, K. *He Who Saves Lives.* New York: Crown Publishers, 1971.

Israel, Fred L. *Nevada's Key Pittman.* Lincoln: University of Nebraska Press, 1963.

———. *The War Diary of Breckinridge Long: Selections from the Years 1939–1944.* Lincoln: University of Nebraska Press, 1966.

Isserman, Ferdinand M. *A Rabbi with the American Red Cross.* New York: Whittier Books, 1958.

Jackson, Robert H. *That Man: An Insider's Portrait of Franklin D. Roosevelt.* New York: Oxford University Press, 2003.

Jacobs, Travis B. *America and the Winter War, 1939–1940.* New York: Garland, 1981.

Jägerskiöld, Stig. *Mannerheim: Marshall of Finland.* Minneapolis: University of Minnesota Press, 1986.

Jakobson, Max. *The Diplomacy of the Winter War.* Cambridge, MA: Harvard University Press, 1957.

James, Robert Rhodes, ed. *"Chips": The Diaries of Sir Henry Channon.* London: Weidenfeld, 1993.

———, ed. *Winston S. Churchill: His Complete Speeches, 1897–1963.* Vol. 3: *1914–1922.* New York: Chelsea House, 1974.

Janiszewska, Aleksandra, ed. *The Colors of War: The Siege of Warsaw in Julien Bryan's Color Photographs.* Warsaw: Karta Center, 2010.

Jaworski, Pawel. *Dreamers and Opportunists: Polish-Swedish Relations during the Second World War.* Stockholm: Södertörn Academic Studies, 2019.

Jeans, Roger B. *American Isolationists: Pro-Japan Anti-interventionists and the FBI on the Eve of the Pacific War, 1939–1941.* Lanham, MD: Rowman & Littlefield, 2021.

Jeansonne, Glen. *Herbert Hoover: A Life.* New York: New American Library, 2016.

———. *Women of the Far Right: The Mothers' Movement and World War II.* Chicago: University of Chicago Press, 1996.

Jędrzejewicz, Włacław, ed. *Diplomat in Berlin, 1933–1939: Papers and Memoirs of Józef Lipski, Ambassador of Poland.* New York: Columbia University Press, 1968.

———, ed. *Diplomat in Paris, 1936–1939: Memoirs of Juliusz Łukasiewicz, Ambassador of Poland.* New York: Columbia University Press, 1970.

———. *Piłsudski: A Life for Poland.* New York: Hippocrene Books, 1982.

———. *Poland in the British Parliament, 1939–1945.* 3 vols. New York: Józef Piłsudski Institute of America, 1945.

Johnson, Marc C. *Political Hell-Raiser: The Life and Times of Senator Burton K. Wheeler of Montana.* Norman: University of Oklahoma Press, 2019.

Johnson, Walter. *The Battle against Isolation: The Story of America's Greatest Battle—Which Can Either Wreck or Save World Peace.* Chicago: University of Chicago Press, 1944.

———, ed. *Selected Letters of William Allen White.* New York: Henry Holt, 1947.

———. *William Allen White's America.* New York: Henry Holt, 1947.

Johnstone, Andrew. *Against Immediate Evil: American Internationalists and the Four Freedoms on the Eve of World War II.* Ithaca, NY: Cornell University Press, 2014.

Jolluck, Katherine R. *Exile and Identity: Polish Women in the Soviet Union during World War II.* Pittsburgh: University of Pittsburgh Press, 2002.

Jonas, Manfred. *Isolation in America, 1935–1941.* Ithaca, NY: Cornell University Press, 1966.

Jones, Jesse. *Fifty Billion Dollars: My Thirteen Years with the RFC, 1932–1945.* New York: Macmillan, 1951.

Jones, Mary Hoxie. *Swords into Ploughshares: An Account of the American Friends Service Committee, 1917–1937.* New York: Macmillan, 1937.

Jones, Sylvester. *Through Loyalist and Insurgent Spain: The Journal of Sylvester Jones, December 1936–January 1937.* Philadelphia: Spanish Child Feeding Mission of the American Friends Service Committee, 1937.

Jordan, Jonathan W. *American Warlords: How Roosevelt's High Command Led America to Victory in World War II.* New York: NAL Caliber, 2015.

Joukowsky, Artemis. *Defying the Nazis: The Sharp's War.* Boston: Beacon Press, 2016.

Junod, Dr. Marcel. *Warrior without Weapons: The Story of Ten Years of Service in the International Red Cross.* New York: Macmillan, 1951.

Jutikkala, Eino, and Kauko Pirinen. *A History of Finland.* New York: Praeger, 1971.

Kähönen-Wilson, Lempi. *Sisu Mother.* St. Cloud, MN: North Star Press, 2002.

Kanigel, Robert. *The One Best Way: Frederick Winslow Taylor and the Enigma of Efficiency.* New York: Viking, 1997.

Kapronczay, Karoly. *Refugees in Hungary: Shelter from the Storm during World War II*. Toronto-Buffalo: Matthias Corvinus, 1999.

Karamanos, Georgios. *Lest We Forget That Noble and Immortal Nation . . . Greece*. New York: Athenian Press, 1943.

Kean, Hilda. *The Great Cat and Dog Massacre*. Chicago: University of Chicago Press, 2017.

Kennan, George F. *From Prague after Munich*. Princeton, NJ: Princeton University Press, 1968.

Kennedy, Robert M. *The Campaign in Poland (1939)*. Washington, DC: US Government Printing Office, 1956.

Kennett, Lee. *The First Air War, 1914–1918*. New York: Free Press, 1999.

Kershaw, Ian. *Hitler, 1936–1945: Nemesis*. New York: W. W. Norton, 2000.

Kershner, Howard E. *One Humanity*. London: Sheppard Press, 1944.

———. *Quaker Service in Modern War: Spain and France, 1939–1940*. New York: Prentice-Hall, 1950.

Keynes, John Maynard. *The Economic Consequences of the Peace*. New York: Harcourt, Brace and Howe, 1920.

Khrushchev, Nikita Sergeevich. *Khrushchev Remembers*. Boston: Little, Brown, 1972.

Kimball, Warren F., ed. *Churchill and Roosevelt*. 3 vols. Princeton, NJ: Princeton University Press, 1984.

———. *Forged in War: Roosevelt, Churchill, and the Second World War*. New York: William Morrow, 1997.

———. *The Juggler: Franklin Roosevelt as Wartime Statesman*. Princeton, NJ: Princeton University Press, 1991.

Kinzer, Stephen. *The Brothers: John Foster Dulles, Allen Dulles, and Their Secret World War*. New York: St. Martin's Griffin, 2013.

Kippenhahn, Rudolf. *Code Breaking: A History and Explanation*. New York: Overlook Press, 2000.

Kirkpatrick, Ivone. *The Inner Circle*. New York: St. Martin's Press, 1959.

Kirszak, Jerzy. *General Kazimierz Sosnkowski, 1885–1969*. Warsaw: Instytut Pamieci Narodowej, 2012.

Klassen, Peter J. *A Homeland for Strangers: An Introduction to Mennonites in Poland and Prussia*. Fresno, CA: Center for Mennonite Brethren Studies, 1989.

Kleczkowski, Stefan. *Poland's First 100,000: The Story of the Rebirth of the Polish Army, Navy and Air Force after the September Campaign, Together with a Biographical Note about Its Creator General Sikorski*. London: Hutchison [ca. 1941].

Klemperer, Victor. *I Will Bear Witness: A Diary of the Nazi Years, 1933–1941*. New York: Random House, 1998.

Knock, Thomas J. *To End All Wars: Woodrow Wilson and the Quest for a New World Order*. New York: Oxford University Press, 1992.

Knowles, Owen, ed. *The Poems of Wilfred Owen*. London: Wadsworth Poetry Library, 1994.

Knowles, Sebastian D. G. *A Purgatorial Flame: Seven British Writers in the Second World War*. Philadelphia: University of Pennsylvania Press, 1990.

Kochanski, Halik. *The Eagle Unbowed: Poland and the Poles in the Second World War*. Cambridge, MA: Harvard University Press, 2012.

Koper, Sławomir, and Tomasz Stańczyk. *Ostatnie Lata Polskiego Wilna* [*The last years of Polish Vilna*]. Warsaw: Fronda, 2002.

Korbonski, Stefan. *The Jews and the Poles in World War II*. New York: Hippocrene Books, 1989.

Korson, George. *At His Side: The Story of the American Red Cross Overseas in World War II*. New York: Coward-McCann, 1945.

Korwin-Rhodes, Marta. *The Mask of Warriors: The Siege of Warsaw, September 1939*. New York: Libra Publications, 1964.

Kotkin, Stephen. *Stalin: Waiting for Hitler, 1929–1941*. New York: Penguin Press, 2017.

Kraus, Hertha. *International Relief in Action, 1914–1943: Selected Records, with Notes*. Scottdale, PA: Herald Press, 1944.

Krosby, Peter. *Finland, Germany, and the Soviet Union, 1940–1941*. Madison: University of Wisconsin Press, 1968.

Kruk, Herman. *The Last Days of the Jerusalem of Lithuania: Chronicles from the Vilna Ghetto and the Camps, 1939–1944*. New Haven, CT: Yale University Press, 2002.

Kupchan, Charles A. *Isolationism: A History of America's Efforts to Shield Itself from the World*. New York: Oxford University Press, 2020.

Kurth, Peter. *American Cassandra: The Life of Dorothy Thompson*. Boston: Little, Brown, 1990.

Lamont, Edward M. *The Ambassador from Wall Street: The Story of Thomas W. Lamont, J. P. Morgan's Chief Executive*. Lanham, MD: Madison Books, 1994.

Langdon-Davies, John. *Finland*. London: George Routledge, 1940.

Langer, William L., and S. Everett Gleason. *The Challenge to Isolation, 1937–1940*. New York: Harper and Brothers, 1952.

Large, David Clay. *Berlin*. New York: Basic Books, 2000.

Larson, Erik. *In the Garden of Beasts: Love, Terror, and an American Family in Hitler's Berlin*. New York: Crown, 2011.

Lehrman, Lewis E. *Churchill, Roosevelt and Company: Studies in Character and Statecraft.* Guilford, CT: Stackpole Books, 2017.
Leiser, Clara. *Refugee: The Personal Account of Two "Aryan" Germans Whom Nazi Brutality Failed to Crush.* New York: Prentice Hall, 1940.
Lemkin, Raphaël. *Axis Rule in Occupied Europe: Laws of Occupation, Analysis of Government, Proposals for Redress.* Washington, DC: Carnegie Endowment for International Peace, 1944.
Leonhard, Wolfgang. *Betrayal: The Hitler-Stalin Pact of 1939.* New York: St. Martin's Press, 1989.
Lerski, George J. *Herbert Hoover and Poland: A Documentary History of a Friendship.* Stanford, CA: Hoover Institution Press, 1977.
Lerski, George "Jur." *Poland's Secret Envoy, 1939–1945.* New York: Bicentennial Publishing Corporation, 1988.
Libby, Frederick J. *To End War: The Story of the National Council for Prevention of War.* Nyack, NY: Fellowship Publications, 1969.
Liekis, Sarunas. *1939: The Year That Changed Everything in Lithuanian History.* Amsterdam: Brill, 2010.
Liikkanen, Eino. *Fighter over Finland.* London: MacDonald, 1963.
Lindbergh, Anne Morrow. *War Within and Without: Diaries and Letters, 1939–1944.* New York: Harcourt, Brace and Jovanovich, 1980.
———. *The Wave of the Future: A Confession of Faith.* New York: Harcourt, Brace, 1940.
Lindbergh, Charles A. *The Wartime Journals of Charles A. Lindbergh.* New York: Harcourt, Brace and Jovanovich, 1970.
Lipsett, Alexander. *Famine Stalks Europe.* New York: Craft Union Publishers, 1941.
Lloyd, Craig. *Aggressive Introvert: Herbert Hoover and Public Relations Management, 1912–1932.* Columbus: Ohio State University Press, 1972.
Lochery, Neill. *Lisbon: War in the Shadows of the City of Light, 1939–1945.* New York: Public Affairs, 2011.
Lochner, Louis P. *Herbert Hoover and Germany.* New York: Macmillan, 1960.
Long, Breckinridge. *The War Diary of Breckinridge Long.* Selected and edited by Fred L. Israel. Lincoln: University of Nebraska Press, 1966.
Lowenheim, Francis, Harold D. Langley, and Winfred Jonas. *Roosevelt and Churchill.* New York: Saturday Review Press, 1975.
Lower, Richard Coke. *A Bloc of One: The Political Career of Hiram W. Johnson.* Stanford, CA: Stanford University Press, 1993.
Lowrie, Donald A. *The Hunted Children.* New York: W. W. Norton, 1963.

Lubrich, Oliver. *Travels in the Reich, 1933–1945: Foreign Authors Report from Germany*. Chicago: University of Chicago Press, 2010.

Luick-Thrams, Michael. *Out of Hitler's Reach: The Scattergood Hostel for European Refugees, 1939–43*. Mason City: Iowa Community Action Coalition, 1996.

Lukacs, John. *The Duel, 10 May–31 July 1940: The Eighty-Day Struggle between Churchill and Hitler*. New York: Ticknor and Fields, 1990.

———. *Five Days in London, May 1940*. New Haven, CT: Yale University Press, 1999.

Lukas, Richard. *Forgotten Holocaust: The Poles under German Occupation, 1939–1944*. Lexington: University of Kentucky Press, 1986.

Lunde, Henrik. *Finland's War of Choice: The Troubled German-Finnish Coalition in World War II*. Philadelphia: Casemate, 2011.

Lyons, Eugene. *Herbert Hoover: A Biography*. Garden City, NY: Doubleday, 1964.

MacDonald, Florence. *For Greece a Tear: The Story of the Greek War Relief of Canada*. Fredericton, Canada: University of New Brunswick Press, 1954.

MacDonogh, Giles. *1938, Hitler's Gamble*. London: Constable, 2009.

Mackrell, Judith. *The Correspondents: Six Women Writers on the Front Lines of World War II*. New York: Doubleday, 2021.

MacLeod, Iain. *Neville Chamberlain*. New York: Atheneum, 1962.

Macmillan, Harold. *Winds of Change, 1914–1939*. New York: Harper and Row, 1966.

Maiolo, Joseph. *Cry Havoc: How the Arms Race Drove the World to War, 1931–1941*. New York: Basic Books, 2010.

Maitland, Patrick. *European Dateline*. London: Quality Press, 1941.

Maloney, John. *Let There Be Mercy: The Odyssey of a Red Cross Man*. New York: Doubleday, Doran, 1941.

Mannerheim, Carl Gustaf Emil. *The Memoirs of Marshall Mannerheim*. New York: E. P. Dutton, 1954.

Manning, Olivia. *The Balkan Trilogy*. New York: Penguin Books, 1988.

Maramorosch, Karl. *The Thorny Road to Success: A Memoir*. Bloomington, IN: iUniverse, 2014.

Marino, Andy. *A Quiet American: The Secret War of Varian Fry*. New York: St. Martin's Press, 1999.

Marrus, Michael R. *The Unwanted: European Refugees in the Twentieth Century*. New York: Oxford University Press, 1985.

Marton, Kati. *True Believer: Stalin's Last American Spy*. New York: Simon and Schuster, 2016.

Maser, Werner. *Hitler's Letters and Notes*. New York: Harper and Row, 1973.

Mather, Sir Carol. *Aftermath of War: Everyone Must Go Home.* London: Brassey's, 1992.
Matson, Robert W. *Neutrality and Navicerts: Britain, the United States, and Economic Warfare, 1939–1940.* New York: Garland, 1994.
Matzen, Robert. *Dutch Girl: Audrey Hepburn and World War II.* Pittsburgh, PA: Good Knight Books, 2019.
Mayer, Arno J. *Why Did the Heavens Not Darken?* New York: Pantheon Books, 1990.
Mayer, Dale C. *Dining with the Hoover Family.* West Branch, IA: Herbert Hoover Presidential Library, 1991.
McCleary, Rachel M. *Global Compassion: Private Voluntary Organizations and U.S. Foreign Policy since 1939.* New York: Oxford University Press, 2009.
McClelland, Grigor. *Embers of War: Letters from a Quaker Relief Worker in War-Torn Germany.* London: British Academic Press, 1997.
McCoy, Donald R. *Landon of Kansas.* Lincoln: University of Nebraska Press, 1966.
McDonald, James G. *Advocate for the Doomed: The Diaries and Papers of James G. McDonald, 1932–1935.* Edited by Richard Breitman, Barbara McDonald Stewart, and Severin Hochberg. Bloomington: Indiana University Press, 2007.
———. *Refugees and Rescue: The Diaries and Papers of James G. McDonald, 1935–1945.* Edited by Richard Breitman, Barbara McDonald Stewart, and Severin Hochberg. Bloomington: Indiana University Press, 2009.
McFarland, Keith D. *Harry H. Woodring: A Political Biography of FDR's Controversial Secretary of War.* Lawrence: University Press of Kansas, 1975.
McFarland, Keith D., and David L. Roll. *Louis Johnson and the Arming of America.* Bloomington: Indiana University Press, 2005.
McJimsey, George. *Harry Hopkins.* Cambridge, MA: Harvard University Press, 1987.
McKenna, Marian C. *Borah.* Ann Arbor: University of Michigan Press, 1961.
McMeekin, Sean. *Stalin's War: A New History of World War II.* New York: Basic Books, 2021.
McSheery, James E. *Stalin, Hitler, and Europe.* 2 Vols. Cleveland, OH: World Publishing, 1968.
Medlicott, W. N. *The Economic Blockade.* 2 Vols. London: Her Majesty's Stationary Office, 1952.
Mencken, H. L. *From a Mencken Chrestomathy: His Own Selection of His Choicest Writings.* New York: Vintage, 1982.
Merridale, Catherine. *Ivan's War: Life and Death in the Red Army, 1939–1945.* New York: Henry Holt, 2006.

Messenger, Charles. *"Bomber" Harris and the Strategic Bombing Offensive, 1939–1945*. New York: St. Martin's Press, 1984.
Mezynski, Kazimierz. *From the History of Mennonites in Poland*. Warsaw: Akademia Rolnicza w Warszawie, 1975.
Miller, Lawrence, *Witness for Humanity: A Biography of Clarence E. Pickett*. Wallingford, PA: Pendle Hill Publications, 1999.
Miller, Nathan. *War at Sea: A Naval History of World War II*. New York: Scribner, 1995.
Minny, R. J. *The Private Papers of Hore-Belisha*. London: Collins, 1960.
Mirowicz, Ryszard. *Edward Rydz-Śmigły: A Political and Military Biography*. Edited and translated by Gregory P. Dziekonski. University of Washington Libraries, 2012. https://digital.lib.washington.edu/researchworks/bitstream/handle/1773/22699/Rydz-Smigly.pdf?sequence=1.
Mitter, Rana. *Forgotten Ally: China's World War II, 1937–1945*. Boston: Houghton, Mifflin, Harcourt, 2013.
Moe, Richard. *Roosevelt's Second Act: The Election of 1940 and the Politics of War*. New York: Oxford University Press, 2013.
Moley, Raymond. *After Seven Years*. New York: Harper and Brothers, 1939.
Montefiore, Simon Sebag. *Stalin: The Court of the Red Tsar*. New York: Alfred A. Knopf, 2004.
Montgomery, John Flournoy. *Hungary: The Unwilling Satellite*. New York: Devin-Adair Company, 1947.
Moore, Aaron William. *Bombing the City: Civilian Accounts of the Air War in Britain and Japan, 1939–1945*. Cambridge: Cambridge University Press, 2018.
Moore, Bob. *Victims and Survivors: The Nazi Persecution of the Jews in the Netherlands, 1940–1945*. London: Arnold, 1997.
Moorehead, Caroline. *Dunant's Dream: War, Switzerland and the History of the Red Cross*. New York: Carroll and Graf, 1999.
———. *Gellhorn: A Twentieth-Century Life*. New York: Henry Holt, 2003.
Moorhouse, Roger. *The Devils' Alliance: Hitler's Pact with Stalin, 1939–1941*. New York: Basic Books, 2014.
———. *First to Fight: The Polish War, 1939*. London: Bodley Head, 2019.
Mosely, Leonard. *On Borrowed Time*. New York: Random House, 1969.
Mosier, John. *The Blitzkrieg Myth: How Hitler and the Allies Misread the Strategic Realities of World War II*. New York: HarperCollins, 2003.
Muir, Peter. *War without Music*. New York: Charles Scribner's Sons, 1940.
Mullen, Thomas. *Lightning Men*. New York: 37 Ink, 2017.
Munch-Petersen, Thomas, ed. *Scandinavia during the Second World War*. Minneapolis: University of Minnesota Press, 1983.

Murray, Williamson. *The Change in the European Balance of Power, 1938–1939*. Princeton, NJ: Princeton University Press, 1984.

Myers, William Starr. *The Foreign Policies of Herbert Hoover, 1929–1933*. New York: Charles Scribner's Sons, 1940.

Naimark, Norman M. *Fires of Hatred: Ethnic Cleansing in Twentieth-Century Europe*. Cambridge, MA: Harvard University Press, 2001.

Nash, George H., ed. *The Crusade Years, 1933–1945: Herbert Hoover's Lost Memoir of the New Deal Era and Its Aftermath*. Stanford, CA: Hoover Institution Press, 2013.

———, ed. *Freedom Betrayed: Herbert Hoover's Secret History of the Second World War and Its Aftermath*. Stanford, CA: Hoover Institution Press, 2011.

———. *The Life of Herbert Hoover*. Vol. 1: *The Engineer, 1874–1914*. New York: W. W. Norton, 1983.

———. *The Life of Herbert Hoover*. Vol. 2: *The Humanitarian, 1914–1917*. New York: W. W. Norton, 1988.

———. *The Life of Herbert Hoover*. Vol. 3: *Master of Emergencies, 1917–1918*. New York: W. W. Norton, 1996.

Nash, Lee, ed. *Herbert Hoover and World Peace*. Lanham, MD: University Press of America, 2010.

———. *Understanding Herbert Hoover: Ten Perspectives*. Stanford, CA: Hoover Institution Press, 1987.

Nazi Conspiracy and Aggression, International Military Trails, Nurnberg. Vol. 6. Washington, DC: US Government Printing Office, 1946.

Neiberg, Michael. *The Home to War: How the First World War Created Modern America*. New York: Oxford University Press, 2016.

Nekrich, Aleksandr M. *Pariahs, Partners, Predators: German-Soviet Relations, 1922–1941*. New York: Columbia University Press, 1997.

Nenye, Vesa, Peter Munter, and Toni Wirtanen. *Finland at War: The Winter War, 1939–1930*. New York: Osprey, 2015.

Neugebauer, M. Norwid, *The Defence of Poland (September 1939)*. London: M. I. Kolin, 1942.

Nevakivi, Jukka. *The Appeal That Was Never Made*. Montreal: McGill-Queen's University Press, 1976.

Nicholas, Lynn H. *Cruel World: The Children of Europe in the Nazi Web*. New York: Alfred A. Knopf, 2005.

Nicolson, Harold. *Diaries and Letters*. Vol. 2: *The War Years, 1939–1945*. New York: Atheneum, 1967.

———. *Dwight Morrow: A Biography*. New York: Harcourt, Brace, 1935.

Nicolson, Nigel, ed. *Diaries and Letters: The War Years, 1939–1945*. Vol. 2. New York: Atheneum, 1967.

Noonan, Peggy. *What I Saw at the Revolution: A Political Life in the Reagan Era*. New York: Random House, 1990.

Norem, Dr. Owen J. C. *Timeless Lithuania*. Chicago: Amerlith Press, 1943.

Olson, Lynne, and Stanley Cloud. *A Question of Honor: The Kosciuszko Squadron, Forgotten Heroes of World War II*. New York: Alfred A. Knopf, 2003.

———. *Those Angry Days: Roosevelt, Lindbergh, and America's Fight over World War II, 1939–1941*. New York: Random House, 2013.

Overy, R. J. *The Bombers and the Bombed: Allied Air War over Europe, 1940–1945*. New York: Viking, 2014.

———. *The Nazi Economic Recovery, 1932–1938*. London: Macmillan, 1982.

———. *The Twilight Years: The Paradox of Britain between the Wars*. New York: Viking, 2009.

Panter-Downes, Mollie. *Letter from England*. Boston: Little, Brown, 1940.

———. *London War Notes, 1939–1945*. New York: Farrar, Straus and Giroux, 1971.

Parkinson, Roger. *Peace for Our Time*. New York: David McKay, 1972.

———. *Summer, 1940: The Battle of Britain*. New York: David McKay, 1977.

Patenaude, Bertrand M. *The Big Show in Bololand: The American Relief Expedition to Soviet Russia in the Famine of 1921*. Stanford, CA: Stanford University Press, 2002.

Patmore, Derek. *Balkan Correspondent*. New York: Harper and Brothers, 1941.

Patterson, Archibald L. *Between Hitler and Stalin: The Quick Life and Secret Death of Edward Smigly-Rydz Marshall of Poland*. Indianapolis: Dog Ear Publishing, 2010.

Patterson, James T. *Mr. Republican: A Biography of Robert A. Taft*. Boston: Houghton Mifflin, 1972.

Pedersen, Susan. *Eleanor Rathbone and the Politics of Conscience*. New Haven, CT: Yale University Press, 2004.

———. *The Guardians: The League of Nations and the Crisis of Empire*. New York: Oxford University Press, 2017.

Percy, William Alexander. *Lanterns on the Levee*. Baton Rouge: Louisiana State University Press, 1973.

Perkins, Charles, ed. *Children of the Storm: Childhood Memories of World War II*. Osceola, WI: MBI Publishing, 1998.

Perkins, Frances. *The Roosevelt I Knew*. New York: Viking Press, 1946.

Persico, Joseph E. *Franklin and Lucy: President Roosevelt, Mrs. Rutherfurd, and Other Remarkable Women in His Life*. New York: Random House, 2008.

Persson, Sune. *Escape from the Third Reich: The Harrowing True Story of the Largest Rescue Effort Inside Nazi Germany.* New York: Sky Horse Publishing, 2009.

Petrov, Richard. *The Bitter Years: The Invasion and Occupation of Denmark and Norway.* New York: William Marrow, 1974.

Pevsner, Nikolaus. *Pioneers of Modern Design.* New York: Viking Penguin, 1975.

Pfau, Richard. *No Sacrifice Too Great.* Charlottesville: University of Virginia Press, 1984.

Picchi, Blaise. *The Five Weeks of Guiseppe Zangara: The Man Who Would Assassinate FDR.* Chicago: Academy Chicago Publishers, 1998.

Pickett, Clarence E. *For More Than Bread: An Autobiographical Account of Twenty Years' Work with the American Friends Service Committee.* Boston: Little, Brown, 1953.

Pienkos, Donald. *For Your Freedom through Ours: Polish American Efforts on Poland's Behalf, 1863–1991.* Boulder, CO: East European Monographs, 1991.

———. *One Hundred Years Young: A History of the Polish Falcons of America, 1887–1987.* Boulder, CO: East European Monographs, 1987.

———. *P.N.A. Centennial History of the Polish National Alliance of the United States of North America.* Boulder, CO: East European Monographs, 1984.

Pimlott, Ben. *Hugh Dalton.* London: Jonathan Cape, 1985.

Piotrowski, Tadeusz. *Genocide and Rescue in Wołyń.* Jefferson, NC: McFarland, 2000.

———. *Poland's Holocaust: Ethnic Strife, Collaboration with Occupying Forces and Genocide in the Second Republic, 1918–1947.* Jefferson, NC: McFarland, 1998.

———, ed. *The Polish Deportees of World War II: Recollections of Removal to the Soviet Union and Dispersal throughout the World.* Jefferson, NC: McFarland, 2004.

———. *Vengeance of the Swallows: Memoirs of a Polish Family's Ordeal.* Jefferson, NC: McFarland, 1995.

Pirinen, Kauko. *A History of Finland.* New York: Praeger, 1971.

Polonius, Alexander. *I Saw the Siege of Warsaw.* Glasgow, UK: William Hodge, 1941.

Polosky, Anthony. *Politics in Independent Poland, 1927–1939.* New York: Oxford University Press, 1972.

Potocki, Jan-Roman, and H. Vivian Reed. *Amerykanie w Polsce/Americans in Poland, 1919–1947.* Warszawa: Dom Sportkań z Historia, 2019.

Prażmowska, Anita. *Britain and Poland, 1939–1943: The Betrayed Ally.* Cambridge: Cambridge University Press, 1995.

Preston, Thomas Hildebrand. *Before the Curtain.* London: John Murray, 1950.

Probert, Henry. *Bomber Harris: His Life and Times*. London: Greenhill Books, 2001.

Proudfoot, Malcolm J. *European Refugees, 1939–52: A Study in Forced Population Movement*. Evanston, IL: Northwestern University Press, 1956.

Pruszynski, Xavier. *Poland Fights Back: From Westerplatte to Monte Cassino*. New York: Roy Publishers, 1944.

Pula, James S. *Polish Americans: An Ethnic Community*. New York: Twayne, 1995.

Raczynski, Count Edward. *In Allied London: The Wartime Diaries of the Polish Ambassador*. London: Weidenfeld and Nicolson, 1962.

Randall, William Sterne. *Unshackling America: How the War of 1812 Truly Ended the American Revolution*. New York: St. Martin's Press, 2017.

Rappleye, Charles. *Herbert Hoover in the White House: The Ordeal of the Presidency*. New York: Simon and Schuster, 2017.

Read, Anthony. *The Devil's Disciples: Hitler's Inner Circle*. New York: W. W. Norton, 2004.

Read, Anthony, and David Fisher. *The Deadly Embrace: Hitler, Stalin, and the Nazi-Soviet Pact, 1939–1941*. New York: W. W. Norton, 1988.

Redfern, Gilbert. *The Tragedy of Vilna*. New York: Commission for Polish Relief, 1939.

Rees, Laurence. *WWII behind Closed Doors: Stalin, the Nazis and the West*. New York: Pantheon Books, 2008.

Republic of Poland, Ministry of Foreign Affairs. *German Occupation of Poland: Polish White Book*. New York: Greystone Press, 1941.

Reston, James. *Deadline: A Memoir*. New York: Random House, 1991.

Reynaud, Paul. *In the Thick of the Fight: The Testimony of Paul Reynaud, 1930–1945*. New York: Simon and Schuster, 1955.

Reynolds, David. *The Creation of the Anglo-American Alliance, 1937–1941*. Chapel Hill: University of North Carolina Press, 1982.

———. *The Long Shadow: The Legacies of the Great War in the Twentieth Century*. New York: W. W. Norton, 2014.

Reynolds, David, Warren F. Kimball, and Alexander O. Chubarian. *Allies at War: The Soviet, American, and British Experience, 1939–1945*. New York: Palgrave Macmillan, 1994.

Riess, Curt, ed. *They Were There: The Story of World War II and How It Came About by America's Foremost Correspondents*. Garden City, NY: Garden City Publishing, 1945.

Roberts, Andrew. *Masters and Commanders: How Four Titans Won the War in the West, 1941–1945*. New York: Harper Perennial, 2008.

Bibliography

———. *The Storm of War: A New History of the Second World War*. New York: Harper Perennial, 2012.

Roberts, Geoffrey. *Stalin's Wars: From World War to Cold War, 1939–1953*. New Haven, CT: Yale University Press, 2008.

———. *The Unholy Alliance: Stalin's Pact with Hitler*. Bloomington: Indiana University Press, 1989.

Rock, William R. *Chamberlain and Roosevelt: British Foreign Policy and the United States, 1937–1940*. Columbus: Ohio State University Press, 1988.

Roll, David L. *The Hopkins Touch: Harry Hopkins and the Forging of the Alliance to Defeat Hitler*. New York: Oxford University Press, 2013.

Rollyson, Carl. *Nothing Ever Happens to the Brave: The Story of Martha Gellhorn*. New York: St. Martin's Press, 1990.

Roosevelt, Eleanor. *My Day, 1939–1945*. New York: Pharos Books, 1989.

———. *This I Remember*. New York: Harper and Brothers, 1949.

Roosevelt, Elliott, ed. *F.D.R.: His Personal Letters, 1928–1945*. 2 Vols. New York: Duell, Sloan and Pearce, 1950.

Roosevelt, Franklin D. *Looking Forward*. New York: John Day, 1933.

———. *On Our Way*. New York: John Day, 1934.

Rose, N. A., ed. *Baffy: The Diaries of Blanche Dugdale, 1936–1947*. London: Vallentin-Mitchell, 1973.

Rosen, Robert N. *Saving the Jews: Franklin D. Roosevelt and the Holocaust*. New York: Thunder's Mouth Press, 2006.

Rosenman, Samuel I., ed. *The Public Papers and Addresses of Franklin D. Roosevelt*. Vol. 8: *War—and Neutrality*, 1939. New York: Macmillan, 1941.

———. *Working with Roosevelt*. New York: Harper and Brothers, 1952.

Rossi, A. *The Russo-German Alliance, 1939–1941*. Boston: Beacon Press, 1951.

Rossino, Alexander B. *Hitler Strikes Poland: Blitzkrieg, Ideology, and Atrocity*. Lawrence: University Press of Kansas, 2003.

Rudnicki, General K. S., DSO. *The Last of the War-Horses*. London: Bachman and Turner, 1974.

Russell, William. *Berlin Embassy*. New York: Carroll and Graf, 2005.

Rygg, A. N. *American Relief for Norway: A Survey of American Relief Work for Norway during and after the Second World War*. Chicago: Arnesen Press, 1947.

Saarelainen, Tapio M. *The White Sniper: Simo Häyhä*. Philadelphia: Casemate, 2016.

Salter, Cedric. *Flight from Poland*. London: Faber and Faber, 1940.

Sander, Gordon F. *The Hundred Day Winter War: Finland's Gallant Stand against the Soviet Army*. Lawrence: University Press of Kansas, 2013.

Sapieha, Virgilia. *Polish Profile.* Garden City, NY: Garden City Publishing, 1942.
Schactmann, Tom. *The Phony War.* New York: Harper and Row, 1982.
Schaff, Philip. *America: A Sketch of Its Political, Social and Religious Character.* Cambridge, MA: Harvard University Press, 1961.
Scharnhorst, Gary. *Mark Twain: The Complete Interviews.* Tuscaloosa: University of Alabama Press, 2006.
Schneider, James. *Should America Go to War? The Debate over Foreign Policy in Chicago, 1939–1941.* Chapel Hill: University of North Carolina Press, 1989.
Schoonmaker, Nancy, and Doris Fielding Reid, eds. *We Testify.* New York: Smith and Durrell, 1941.
Schoppa, R. Keith. *In a Sea of Bitterness: Refugees During the Sino-Japanese War.* Cambridge, MA: Harvard University Press, 2011.
Schuman, Frederick L. *Night over Europe.* New York: Alfred A. Knopf, 1941.
Schwartz, Andrew J. *America and the Russo-Finnish War.* Washington, DC: Public Affairs Press, 1960.
Scott, John. *Duel for Europe.* Boston: Houghton Mifflin, 1942.
Scott, William R. *Sons of Sheba's Race: African-Americans and the Italo-Ethiopian War, 1935–1941.* Bloomington: Indiana University Press, 1993.
Sebag-Montefiore, Hugh. *Dunkirk: Fight to the Last Man.* Cambridge, MA: Harvard University Press, 2006.
Sebastian, Mihail. *Journal, 1935–1944: The Fascist Years.* Chicago: Ivan R. Dee, 2000.
Seib, Philip. *Broadcasts from the Blitz: How Edward R. Murrow Helped Lead America into War.* Washington, DC: Potomac Books, 2007.
Šeinius, Ignas. *Raudonasis Tvanas* [*The red tide*]. New York: Talka, 1953.
Self, Robert. *Neville Chamberlain: A Biography.* London: Ashgate, 2006.
———, ed. *The Neville Chamberlain Diary Letters.* Vol. 4: *The Downing Street Years, 1934–1940.* London: Ashgate, 2005.
Senn, Alfred Eric. *Lithuania 1940: Revolution from Above.* Amsterdam: Rodopi, 2007.
Serrien, Pieter. *Tranen over Mortsel: De laatste getuigen over het zwaarste bombardment ooit in Belgie.* Antwerpen: Davidsfonds, Uitgeverij, 2018.
Seth, Ronald. *The Day the War Broke Out.* London: Neville Spearman, 1963.
Sevadson, Jørgen. *Britain and Denmark: Political, Economic and Cultural Relations in the 19th and 20th Centuries.* Charlottenlund, DK: Museum Tusculanmum Press, 2003.
Shachtman, Tom. *The Phony War, 1939–1940.* New York: Harper and Row, 1982.

Shedd, Clarence Prouty, ed. *History of the World's Alliance of Young Men's Christian Associations*. London: S.C.P.K., 1955.
Sherwood, John M. *Georges Mandel and the Third Republic*. Stanford, CA: Stanford University Press, 1970.
Sherwood, Robert E. *Roosevelt and Hopkins*. New York: Harper and Brothers, 1952.
———. *There Shall Be No Night*. New York: Charles Scribner's Sons, 1941.
Shirer, William L. *The Nightmare Years, 1930–1940*. Boston: Little, Brown, 1984.
———. *The Rise and Fall of the Third Reich*. New York: Simon and Schuster, 1960.
Showalter, Denis. *Hitler's Panzers: The Lighting Attacks That Revolutionized Warfare*. New York: Berkley Caliber, 2009.
Sidney, Marion C. *The Allied Blockade of Germany, 1914–1916*. Westport, CT: Greenwood Press, 1973.
Smith, Douglas. *The Russia Job: The Forgotten Story of How America Saved the Soviet Union from Ruin*. New York: Farrar, Straus and Giroux, 2019.
Smith, Eric R. *American Relief Aid and the Spanish Civil War*. Columbia: University of Missouri Press, 2013.
Smith, Gaddis. *American Diplomacy during the Second World War, 1941–1945*. New York: John Wiley, 1965.
Smith, Geoffrey S. *To Save a Nation: American Countersubversives, the New Deal, and the Coming of World War II*. New York: Basic Books, 1973.
Smith, Jean Edward. *FDR*. New York: Random House, 2007.
Smith, Richard Norton. *Thomas E. Dewey and His Times*. New York: Simon and Schuster, 1982.
———. *An Uncommon Man: The Triumph of Herbert Hoover*. New York: Simon and Schuster, 1984.
Snyder, Timothy. *Bloodlands: Europe between Hitler and Stalin*. New York: Basic Books, 2010.
Sobel, Robert. *The Origins of Interventionism*. New York: Bookman Associates, 1960.
Solberg, Richard W. *As between Brothers: The Story of Lutheran Response to World Need*. Minneapolis: Augsburg Publishing House, 1957.
Sosabowski, Maj. Gen. Stansilaw. *Freely I Served*. Nashville: Battery Press, 1982.
Souhami, Diana. *Edith Cavell*. London: Quercus Books, 2010.
Spiegel, Renia. *Renia's Diary: A Young Girl's Life in the Shadow of the Holocaust*. London: Ebury Press, 2019.
Sprague, Martina. *Swedish Volunteers in the Russo-Finnish Winter War, 1939–1940*. Jefferson, NC: McFarland, 2010.

Stafford, David. *Roosevelt and Churchill: Men of Secrets*. Woodstock, NY: Overlook Press, 1999.

Stahel, David. *The Battle for Moscow*. Cambridge: Cambridge University Press, 2015.

Stalin, Joseph. *Report on the Work of the Central Committee to the XVIIIth Congress of the Communist Party of the Soviet Union*. London: Red Star Books, 1978.

Stargardt, Nicholas. *The German War: A Nation under Arms, 1939–1945*. New York: Basic Books, 2015.

Starling, Edmund W. *Starling of the White House: The Story of the Man Whose Secret Service Detail Guarded Five Presidents from Woodrow Wilson to Franklin D. Roosevelt*. New York: Simon and Schuster, 1946.

Starr, S. Frederick. *Against Two Evils: Memoirs of a Diplomat-Soldier during the Third Reich*. London: Collins, 1981.

Steiner, Zara. *The Lights That Failed: European International History, 1919–1933*. New York: Oxford University Press, 2005.

———. *The Triumph of the Dark: European International History, 1933–1939*. New York: Oxford University Press, 2011.

Stenehjem, Michele Flynn. *An American First: John T. Flynn and the America First Committee*. New Rochelle, NY: Arlington House Publishers, 1976.

Stewart, Graham. *Burying Caesar: The Churchill-Chamberlain Rivalry*. New York: Overlook Press, 1999.

Stoler, Mark A. *Allies and Adversaries: The Joint Chiefs of Staff, the Grand Alliance, and U.S. Strategy in World War II*. Chapel Hill: University of North Carolina Press, 2000.

Strauss, Lewis. *Men and Decisions*. New York: Doubleday, 1962.

Strode, Hudson, *Finland Forever*. New York: Harcourt, Brace, 1941.

Sturdza, Michael. *The Suicide of Europe: Memoirs of Prince Michael Sturdza, Former Foreign Minister of Rumania*. Boston: Western Lands, 1968.

Subak, Susan Elizabeth. *Rescue and Flight: American Relief Workers Who Defied the Nazis*. Lincoln: University of Nebraska Press, 2010.

Super, Paul. *Twenty-Five Years with the Poles*. Trenton, NJ: Paul Super Memorial Fund, White Eagle Printing, 1948.

Surface, Frank M., and Raymond L. Bland. *American Food in the World War and Reconstruction Period: Operations of the Organizations under the Direction of Herbert Hoover, 1914–1924*. Stanford, CA: Stanford University Press, 1931.

Süss, Dietmar. *Death from the Skies: How the British and Germans Survived Bombing in World War II*. Oxford: Oxford University Press, 2011.

Swanberg, W. A. *Norman Thomas*. New York: Charles Scribner's Sons, 1976.

Sword, Edward Roland. *The Diary and Dispatches of a Military Attaché in Warsaw, 1938–1939.* London: Polish Cultural Foundation, 2001.

Szkola Polska w Osiedlu Santa Rosa: Sprawozdanie z Dzialalnosci za Okres od 16 Sierpnia 1943 do 30 Kwietnia 1944. Leon, Mexico: Delegatura Ministerstwa Wyznan Religunych i Oswiecenia Publicznego w Meksyku, 1944.

Tanner, Vaino. *The Winter War.* Stanford, CA: Stanford University Press, 1957.

Taylor, Fred, ed. and trans. *The Goebbels Diaries, 1939–1941.* New York: G. P. Putnam's Sons, 1983.

Taylor, Telford. *Munich: The Price of Peace.* Garden City, NY: Doubleday, 1979.

Terraine, John. *A Time of Courage: The Royal Air Force in the European War, 1939–1945.* New York: Macmillan, 1985.

Thiessen, Edna Schroeder, and Angela Showalter. *Life Displaced: A Mennonite Woman's Flight from War-Torn Poland.* Kitchener, Canada: Pandora Press, 2000.

Thomas, Evan. *Ambulance in Africa.* New York: D. Appleton-Century, 1943.

Thompson, Dorothy. *Let the Record Speak.* Boston: Houghton Mifflin, 1939.

Tierney, Dominic. *FDR and the Spanish Civil War: Neutrality and Commitment in the Struggle That Divided America.* Durham, NC: Duke University Press, 2007.

Tooze, Adam. *The Wages of Destruction: The Making and Breaking of the Nazi Economy.* New York: Viking, 2007.

Trotter, William R. *A Frozen Hell: The Russo-Finnish War of 1939–1940.* Chapel Hill, NC: Algonquin Books, 1991.

Turner, Barry. *Waiting for War: Britain, 1939–1940.* London: Icon Books, 2019.

Turner, E. S. *The Phony War.* New York: Random House, 1969.

Tuuninen, Pasi. *Finnish Military Effectiveness in the Winter, 1939–1940.* London: Palgrave Macmillan, 2018.

Ulam, Adam B. *Stalin: The Man and His Era.* New York: Viking Compass, 1973.

Unruh, John D. *In the Name of Christ: A History of the Mennonite Central Committee and Its Service, 1920–1951.* Scottsdale, PA: Herald Press, 1952.

Upton, Anthony F. *Finland, 1939–1940.* Newark: University of Delaware Press, 1974.

US Department of State. *Documents on German Foreign Policy.* Washington, DC: US Government Printing Office, 1957.

Vail, Margaret. *Yours Is the Earth.* Philadelphia: J. B. Lippincott, 1944.

Van der Vat, Dan. *The Atlantic Campaign: World War II's Great Struggle at Sea.* New York: Harper and Row, 1988.

Van Dyke, Carl. *The Soviet Invasion of Finland, 1939–40.* London: Frank Cass, 1997.

Van Loon, Gerard Willem. *The Story of Hendrik Willem Van Loon.* Philadelphia: J. B. Lippincott, 1972.

Vanberg, Bent. *For So Many . . . for So Few: The Norwegian–North American Aid to Norway during World War II.* Minneapolis: Sons of Norway Heritage Productions, n.d.

Vandenberg, Arthur H., Jr., ed. *The Private Papers of Senator Vandenberg.* Boston: Houghton Mifflin, 1952.

Vincent, Paul. *The Politics of Hunger: The Allied Blockade of Germany, 1915–1919.* Athens: Ohio University Press, 1985.

Vining, Elizabeth Gray. *Friend of Life: The Biography of Rufus M. Jones.* Philadelphia: J. B. Lippincott, 1958.

Walch, Timothy, ed. *Uncommon Americans: The Lives and Legacies of Herbert and Lou Henry Hoover.* Westport, CT: Praeger, 2003.

Walch, Timothy, and Dwight M. Miller, eds. *Herbert Hoover and Franklin D. Roosevelt: A Documentary History.* Westport, CT: Greenwood Press, 1998.

Waldeck, R. G. *Athene Palace: Hitler's "New Order" Comes to Romania.* Chicago: University of Chicago Press, 2013.

Wallace, Max. *The American AXIS: Henry Ford, Charles Lindbergh and the Rise of the Third Reich.* New York: St. Martin's Griffin, 2003.

Wancerz-Gluza, Alicja, and Agnieszka Knyt. *Rumuński Azyl: Losy Polaków 1939–1945.* Warszawa: Ośrodek "Karta": Dom Spotkań z Historią, 2009.

Wandycz, Piotr. *The United States and Poland.* Cambridge, MA: Harvard University Press, 1980.

Ward, Edward. *Dispatches from Finland: January–April 1940.* London: Bodley Head, 1940.

Ward, Geoffrey C. *A First-Class Temperament: The Emergence of Franklin Roosevelt, an Intimate Portrait of the Private World, Personal Ordeal, and Public Triumph of the Man Who Became FDR.* New York: Harper and Row, 1989.

———. *Closest Companions: The Unknown Story of an Intimate Friendship Between Franklin Roosevelt and Margaret Suckley.* Boston: Houghton Mifflin, 1995.

Warner, Oliver. *Marshall Mannerheim and the Finns.* London: Weidenfeld and Nicolson, 1967.

Warren, Donald. *Radio Priest: Charles Coughlin, the Father of Hate Radio.* New York: Free Press, 1996.

Washington, Pat Beauchamp. *Eagles in Exile.* London: Maxwell, Love, 1941.

Waterfield, Gordon. *Professional Diplomat.* London: John Murray, 1973.

Watt, Donald Cameron. *How War Came: The Immediate Origins of the Second World War, 1938–1939.* New York: Pantheon Books, 1989.

Weber, Ronald. *The Lisbon Route: Entry and Escape in Nazi Europe.* Lanham, MD: Ivan R. Dee, 2011.

Wegierski, Dominik. *September 1939.* Edinburgh: Riverside Press, 1940.

Weigel, George. *Witness to Hope: The Biography of Pope John Paul II, 1920–2005.* New York: Harper Perennial, 2005.

Weinberg, Gerhard L. *Germany and the Soviet Union, 1939–1941.* Leiden: E. J. Brill, 1954.

Weinstein, David. *The Eddie Cantor Story: A Jewish Life in Performance and Politics.* Waltham, MA: Brandeis University Press, 2017.

Weitz, John. *Hitler's Diplomat: The Life and Times of Joachim von Ribbentrop.* New York: Ticknor and Fields, 1992.

Welles, Benjamin. *Sumner Welles: FDR's Global Strategist.* New York: St. Martin's Press, 1997.

Welles, Sumner. *The Time for Decision.* New York: Harper and Brothers, 1944.

Werner, Emmy E. *Through the Eyes of Innocents: Children Witness World War II.* Boulder, CO: Westview Press, 2000.

Wert, Hal Elliott. *Hoover the Fishing President: Portrait of the Private Man and His Life Outdoors.* Mechanicsburg, PA: Stackpole Books, 2020.

Wertheim, Stephen. *Tomorrow the World: The Birth of U.S. Global Supremacy.* Cambridge, MA: Harvard University Press, 2020.

Westermann, Edward B. *Hitler's Police Battalions: Enforcing Racial War in the East.* Lawrence: University Press of Kansas, 2005.

White, Graham J. *F.D.R. and the Press.* Chicago: University of Chicago Press, 1979.

Whyte, Kenneth. *Hoover: An Extraordinary Life in Extraordinary Times.* New York: Alfred A. Knopf, 2017.

Wilson, Francesca M. *In the Margins of Chaos: Recollections of Relief Work in and between Three Wars.* New York: Macmillan, 1945.

Wilson, John Hoff. *Herbert Hoover: Forgotten Progressive.* Boston: Little, Brown, 1975.

Wilson, Roger C. *Quaker Review: An Account of the Relief Work of the Society of Friends, 1940–1948.* London: George Allen and Unwin, 1952.

Wilson, Theodore A. *The First Summit: Roosevelt and Churchill at Placentia Bay 1941.* Boston: Houghton Mifflin, 1969.

Winston, Robert A. *Aces Wild.* New York: Holiday House, 1941.

Wiser, William. *The Twilight Years: Paris in the 1930s.* New York: Carroll and Graf, 2000.

Woods, Randell Bennett. *A Changing of the Guard: Anglo-American Relations, 1941–1945.* Chapel Hill: University of North Carolina Press, 1990.

Wortman, Marc. *1941: Fighting the Shadow War, a Divided America in a World at War.* New York: Atlantic Monthly Press, 2016.

Wriggins, Howard. *Picking Up the Pieces from Portugal to Palestine: Quaker Refugee Relief in World War II*. Lanham, MD: University Press of America, 2004.
Wuorinen, John H. *Finland and World War II, 1939–1944*. New York: Ronald Press, 1948.
Wyman, David S. *Paper Walls: America and the Refugee Crisis, 1938–1941*. Amherst: University of Massachusetts Press, 1968.
———. *A Race against Death: Peter Bergson, America, and the Holocaust*. New York: New Press, 2002.
Wyndham, Joan. *Love Lessons: A Wartime Diary*. London: Virago, 2001.
Wynot, Edward D., Jr. *Polish Politics in Transition: The Camp of National Unity and the Struggle for Power, 1935–1939*. Athens: University of Georgia Press, 1974.
Zaloga, Steven, and Victor Madej. *The Polish Campaign, 1939*. New York: Hippocrene Books, 1985.
Zamoyska-Panek, Christine. *Have You Forgotten? A Memoir of Poland, 1939–1945*. New York: Doubleday, 1989.
Zamoyski, Adam. *The Forgotten Few: The Polish Air Force in the Second World War*. New York: Hippocrene Books, 1995.
Zimmerman, Joshua D. *The Polish Underground and the Jews, 1939–1945*. Cambridge: Cambridge University Press, 2017.

Articles and Chapters

"Ambassador Biddle Flees Poland after Race against Death from German Warplanes." *Life* 7, no. 16 (October 16, 1939): 29.
Anuskewicz, Maj. Benjamin T. "Relief for Poland: How American Funds and Food Are Used to Aid the Needy in That Unhappy Country." *Current History* 51 (June 1940): 40–41.
Baldwin, Stanley. "A Fear for the Future (1932)." Wikisource, https://en.wikisource.org/wiki/a-fear-the-future (accessed November 16, 2019).
Balkelis, Tomas. "War, Ethnic Conflict and the Refugee Crisis in Lithuania, 1939–1940." *Contemporary European History* 16, no. 4 (2007): 461–477.
Beaumont, Joan. "Starving for Democracy: Britain's Blockade of and Relief for Occupied Europe, 1939–1945." *War and Society* 8, no. 2 (October 1990): 57–82.
Bell, P. M. H. "Peace Movements." In *The Origins of World War Two: The Debate Continues*, edited by Robert Boyce and Joseph A. Maiolo, 273–285. New York: Palgrave Macmillan, 2003.
Brittain, Vera. "Massacre by Bombing." *Fellowship* 10, no. 3, part 2 (March 1944): 49–64.

Bussgang, Julian. "Haunting Memories." In *We Shall Not Forget! Memories of the Holocaust*, edited by Carole Garbuny Vogel. Lexington, MA: Temple Isaiah, 1994.

Callahan, Raymond. "Opinion: Churchill and the Erosion of British Power: A Subject of Debate." *Finest Hour* 57 (August 1987): 19.

Castle, Alfred L. "William L. Castle and Opposition to U.S. Involvement in an Asian War, 1939–1941." *Pacific Historical Review* 54, no. 3 (August 1985): 337–351.

Cather, Willa. "Roll Call on the Prairies." In *World War I: Told by Americans Who Lived It*, edited by A. Scott Berg, 568–576. New York: Library of America, 2007. Originally in *Red Cross Magazine* (1919).

Charles, Douglas M., and John P. Rossi. "FBI Political Surveillance and the Charles Lindbergh Investigation, 1939–1944." *The Historian* 59, no. 4 (Summer 1997): 831–847.

Chen, Peter C. "Bombing of Cities in France and the Low Countries, 1 Jul 1940–7 May 1945." World War II Database, https://www2db.com/battle-spec.php?battle_id=318 (accessed August 29, 2018).

Cienciala, Anna M. "Poland in British and French Policy in 1939: Determination to Fight or Avoid War." *Polish Review* 34, no. 3 (Fall 1989): 199–226.

Corell, John T. "The Cloud over Lindbergh." *Air Force Magazine* (August 2014): 76–82.

Coutouvidis, J. "Government-in-Exile: The Transfer of Polish Authority Abroad in September 1939." *Review of International Studies* 10 (1984): 285–296.

Delzell, Charles F. "Pius XII, Italy, and the Outbreak of War." *Journal of Contemporary History* 2, no. 4 (October 1967): 137–161.

Doenecke, Justus D. "American Anti-interventionist Tradition: A Bibliographic Essay by Justus Doenecke." Online Library of Liberty. http://oll.libertyfund.org/pages/american-anti-interventionist-tradition-a-bibliographical-essay-ny-justus-doenecke.

———. "The Anti-interventionism of Herbert Hoover." *Journal of Libertarian Studies* 8, no. 2 (Summer 1987): 311–340.

———. "U.S. Policy and the European War, 1939–1941." *Diplomatic History* 19, no. 4 (Fall 1995): 669–698.

Eatwell, Roger. "Munich, Public Opinion, and Popular Front." *Journal of Contemporary History* 5, no. 4 (1971): 122–139.

Fai-Podlipnik, Judith. "Hungary's Relationship with Poland and Its Refugees during World War II." *East European Quarterly* 34, no. 1 (March 2002): 63–78.

"The Fate of Poland." *Christian Century* 56, no. 38 (September 20, 1939): 1127–1129.

Fels, Bradley. "'Whatever Your Heart Dictates and Your Pocket Permits': Polish-American Aid to Polish Refugees during World War II." *Journal of American Ethnic History* 22, no. 2. (Winter 2003): 3–30.

Frankl, Michal. "'Exhausted, Frozen and Only Half Alive': The Suwałki No Man's Land." We Refugees Archive. https://en.we-refugees-archive.org/chapters/the-suwalki-no-mans-land (accessed May 4, 2022).

Freidel, Frank. "Hoover and FDR: Reminiscent Reflections." In *Understanding Herbert Hoover: Ten Perspectives*, edited by Lee Nash, 125–140. Stanford, CA: Hoover Institution Press, 1987.

Galloway, J. M. "The Public Life of Norman H. Davis." *Tennessee Historical Quarterly* 27, no. 2 (Summer 1968): 142–156.

Gelderman, Carol. "Point-to-Point Navigation: Franklin Delano Roosevelt, 1933–1945." Chap. 1 in *All the Presidents' Words: The Bully Pulpit and the Creation of the Virtual Presidency*. New York: Walker, 1997.

Gellhorn, Martha. "Blood on the Snow." *Collier's* 105, no. 3 (January 20, 1940): 9–11.

———. "Bombs from a Low Sky." *Collier's* 105, no. 4 (January 27, 1940): 12–13, 41.

———. "Death in the Present Tense." *Collier's* 105, no. 6 (February 10, 1940).

———. "Fear Comes to Sweden." *Collier's* 105, no. 6 (February 3, 1940).

———. "Slow Boat to War." *Collier's* 105, no. 1 (January 6, 1940).

George, James H., Jr. "Another Chance: Herbert Hoover and World War II Relief." *Diplomatic History* 16, no. 2 (July 1993): 389–407.

Glad, Betty. "Medical and Political Behavior." In *Key Pittman: The Tragedy of a Senate Insider*, 280–281. New York: Columbia University Press, 1986.

———. "Personality, Role Strains, and Alcoholism: Key Pittman as Chairman of the Senate Foreign Relations Committee." *Politics and the Life Sciences* 7, no. 1 (August 1988): 18–22.

Hansen, John Mark. "Flashback: Black Chicagoan John C. Robinson Fought Italy's Fascists as Commander of Ethiopia's Air Force." *Chicago Tribune*, July 2, 2021.

Harrison, E. D. R. "Caton de Wiart's Second Military Mission to Poland and the German Invasion of 1939." *European History Quarterly* 41, no. 4 (2011): 609–633.

Hershberger, Guy F. "Historical Background to the Formation of the Mennonite Central Committee." *Mennonite Quarterly Review* 44, no. 3 (July 1970): 213–244.

Himmelberg, Robert F. "Hoover's Public Image, 1919–20: The Emergence of a Public Figure and a Sign of the Times." In *Herbert Hoover: The Great War and Its Aftermath, 1914–23*, edited by Lawrence E. Gelfand, 207–232. Iowa City: University of Iowa Press, 1974.

Hoover, Herbert. "Feed Hungry Europe." *Collier's* 106 (November 23, 1940): 12, 69, 70–72.

———. "Our Foreign Relations." *American Voters Digest*, January–March 1941.

———. "Shall We Send Our Boys to Foreign Wars?" *American Magazine* (August 1939).

Janicki, David. "The British Blockade during World War I: The Weapon of Deprivation." *Inquiries Journal/Student Pulse* 6 (2014): 1–22.

Janowsky, Oscar I. "More Minorities—More Pawns." *Survey Graphic* 27, no. 11 (November 1939): 668–672, 704.

Kennedy, G. "Neville Chamberlain and the Strategic Relations with the US during His Chancellorship." *Diplomacy and Statecraft* 13, no. 1 (2002): 95–120.

Kyrou, Alexandros K. "Ethnicity as Humanitarianism: The Greek American Relief Campaign for Occupied Greece, 1941–1944." In *New Directions in Greek American Studies*, edited by Dan Georgakas and Charles C. Moskos, 111–128. New York: Pella Publishers, 1991.

———. "Operation Blockade: Greek American Humanitarianism during World War II." In *Greece's Pivotal Role in World War II and Its Importance to the U.S. Today*, edited by Eugene T. Rossides, 109–127. Washington, DC: American Hellenic Institute Foundation, 2001.

Langbart, David A. "We Found Ourselves Living in the Midst of a Battlefield." *American Diplomacy*. April 2018. https://americandiplomacy.web.unc.edu/2018/04/we-found-ourselves-living-in-the-midst-of-a-battlefield.

Lawler, Justus George. "Terror Bombing: Shattering the Immunity of Civilians Has Become the Very Definition of Terrorism." *American Magazine* (August 28, 2006). https://www.americamagazine.org/issue/581/bookings/terror-bombing.

Majewski, Marcin. "Polish Refugees in Câmpiling-Muşcel during World War II." *Archiva Moldaviae* 9 (2017): 235–243.

Martindale, C. C., SJ. "The Poles Remain." *The Commonweal* 31, no. 14 (January 26, 1940): 300–302.

Matson, Robert W. "The U.S. Response to the Finnish-Soviet Winter War, November 30, 1939–March 12, 1940." Paper given at "World War II, 1939: A 50-Year Perspective" conference, Siena College, Loudonville, NY, June 1–2, 1989.

McCoy, Donald R. "Herbert Hoover and Foreign Policy, 1939–1945." In *Herbert Hoover Reassessed*, compiled by Mark O. Hatfield. Washington, DC: US Government Printing Office, 1981.

Nash, George H. "The 'Great Enigma' and the 'Great Engineer': The Political Relationship of Calvin Coolidge and Herbert Hoover." In *Calvin Coolidge and the Coolidge Era: Essays on the History of the 1920s*, edited by John Earl Haynes, 167–169. Washington, DC: Library of Congress, 1998.

Naujokaitis, Sigita, ed. and trans. "Lithuania and the Soviet Union, 1939–1940: The Fateful Years—Memoirs by Juozas Urbšys." *Lituanas: Lithuanian Quarterly Journal of Arts and Sciences* 34, no. 2 (Summer 1989): 1–14.

Nichols, Jeannette. "The Middle West and the Coming of World War II." *Ohio State Archeological and Historical Quarterly* 62, no. 2 (April 1953): 122–145.

Orwell, George. "As I Please." *Tribune*, May 9, 1944.

Pankhurst, Richard. "Italian Fascist War Crimes in Ethiopia: A History of Their Discussions, from the League of Nations to the United Nations, 1936–1949." *Northeast African Studies* 6, no. 1–2 (1999): 83–140.

Peet, Betha Anne. "How Polish Relief Works: How American Ingenuity and Charity Have Tackled a Task of Mercy." *The Commonweal* 32, no. 12 (July 12, 1940): 242–244.

Peszke, Michael Alfred. "The Forgotten Campaign: Poland's Military Aviation in September 1939." *Polish Review* 39, no. 1 (1994): 51–72.

———. "Poland's Preparation for World War 2." *Military Affairs, Journal of the American Military Institute* 43 (1979): 18–24.

"Poll—Herbert Hoover Gains Significantly." *Pathfinder*, April 13, 1940.

Polvinen, Tuomo. "Finland in International Politics." *Scandinavian Journal of History* 2 (1977): 107–122.

Prazmowski, Anita J. "Poland." In *The Origins of World War Two: The Debate Continues*, edited by Robert Boyce and Joseph A. Maiolo. New York: Palgrave Macmillan, 2003.

"The Press, Cartwheel Girl." *Time* 33, no. 24 (June 12, 1939): 46–49.

Rasmussen, Frederick N. "On Labor Day Weekend 1939, the War Begins." *Baltimore Sun*. September 6, 2009.

"Relief Agencies Meet War Crisis." *News and Notes* (Council of Jewish Federations and Welfare Funds, New York) 67 (May 9, 1941): 5–8.

Rennell, Tony. "The Blitz 70 Years On: Carnage at the Café de Paris." *Mail Online*. April 9, 2010. https://www.dailymail.co.uk/femail/article-1264532/The-blitz-70-years-Carnage-Caf-Paris.html.

Rich, John F. "Aftermath in Poland." *Survey Graphic* 23, no. 12 (December 1939): 740–741.

Schmidt, Royal J. "Hoover's Reflections on the Versailles Treaty." *Herbert Hoover: The Great War and Its Aftermath, 1914–23*, edited by Lawrence E. Gelfand, 61–86. Iowa City: University of Iowa Press, 1979.

Schwarz, Benjamin. "The Right Stuff." *Los Angeles Times*. September 20, 1998. https://benjaminschwarz.org/1998/09/20/the-right-stuff/.

Serrien, Pieter. "Bombing of Mortsel." http://pieterserrien.be/enlish/bombing-of-Mortsel (accessed August 29, 2018).

Smith, Richard Norton. "On the Outside Looking In: Herbert Hoover and World War II." *Prologue* 26, no. 3 (Fall 1994).

Stolberg, Sheryl Gay. "The Decider." *New York Times*. December 24, 2006.

Tanner, Stephen L. "W. H. Auden's 'September 1, 1939': Fifty Years Later." In *World War II: A Fifty Year Perspective on 1939*, edited by Robert W. Hoeffner. Loudonville, NY: Siena College Research Institute Press, 1992.

"Testimony of Estonia's Foreign Minister Karl Selter, 1938–1939." *Litaunas: Lithuanian Quarterly Journal of Arts and Sciences* 14, no. 2 (Summer 1968): 1–6.

Thompson, Dorothy. "Escape in a Frozen World." *Survey Graphic* 28, no. 2 (February 1939): 93–96, 168–169.

Thrasher, Edward J. "The Well-Tempered Diplomat: Reminiscences of the United States Foreign Service, 1938–1967." Association for Diplomatic Studies and Training Foreign Affairs Oral History Project, 1994. Library of Congress. https://tile.loc.gov/storage-services/service/mss/mfdip/2004/2004thr01/2004thr01.pdf.

Trueman, C. N. "Public Opinion and Appeasement in 1938." History Learning Site. July 3, 2015. https://www.historylearningsite.co.uk/world-war-two/causes-of-ww2/public-opinion-and-appeasement-in-1938 (accessed November 3, 2019).

Tucker, Phillip Thomas. "The Legacy of the Brown Condor." *Selamta Magazine* (March–April 2016): 56–61.

Tuttle, William M., Jr. "Aid-to-the-Allies Short-of-War versus American Intervention, 1940: A Reappraisal of William Allen White's Leadership." *Journal of American History* 56, no. 4 (March 1970): 840–858.

Usdin, Steve. "When a Foreign Government Interfered in a U.S. Election—to Reelect FDR." *Politico Magazine*, January 16, 2017, https://www.politico.com/magazine/story/2017/01/when-a-foreign-government-interfered-in-a-us-electionto-reelect-fdr-214634.

Von Wedel, Lt. Col. "The German Campaign in Poland." *Monthly Future* 3, no. 2–3 (February–March 1941): 8–13.

Walch, Timothy. "The Ordeal of a Biographer: Herbert Hoover Writes about Woodrow Wilson." *Prologue* 40, no. 3 (Fall 2008): 12–19.

Walser, Ray. "War Comes to Warsaw: September 1939." *Foreign Service Journal*, September 2019, https://afsa.org/war-comes-warsaw-september-1939.

Watt, Donald. "Roosevelt and Neville Chamberlain: Two Appeasers." *International Journal* 28, no. 2 (1973): 185–204.

Wert, Hal. "Hoover's Brush with the Boxers." *History Today* 61, no. 9 (September 2011): 36–43.

Wert, Hal E. "Military Expediency, the 'Hunger Winter,' and Holland's Belated Liberation." In *Victory in Europe 1945: From World War to Cold War*, edited by Arnold A. Offner and Theodore A. Wilson. Lawrence: University Press of Kansas, 2000.

Wert, Hal Elliott. "Flight and Survival: American and British Aid to Polish Refugees in the Fall of 1939." *Polish Review* 34, no. 3 (1989): 227–248.

———. "Hoover, Roosevelt and the Politics of Aid to Finland during the Winter War, 1939–1940." In *World War II: A Fifty Year Perspective on 1939*, edited by Robert W. Hoeffner, 89–112. Loudonville, NY: Siena College Research Institute Press, 1992.

———. "U.S. Aid to Poles under Nazi Domination, 1939–1940." *The Historian* 57, no. 3 (Spring 1995): 511–524.

———. "Years of Frustration: Herbert Hoover in World War II." In *Uncommon Americans: The Lives and Legacies of Herbert and Lou Henry Hoover*, edited by Timothy Walch, 209–224. Westport, CT: Praeger, 2003.

Weybright, Victor. "Altruism at Armageddon." *Survey Graphic* 29, no. 7 (July 1940): 373–377, 415.

———. "Sympathy Is Not Enough." *Survey Graphic* 29, no. 4 (April 1940): 212–216, 265–269.

White, W. L. "I Saw It Happen." In *Zero Hour*, by Stephen Vincent Benét, Erika Mann, McGeorge Bundy, William Lindsay White, Garrett Underhill, and Walter Millis. New York: Farrar and Rinehart, 1940.

Woolf, S. J. "Mr. Hoover Tackles Another Relief Job." *New York Times Magazine*, January 21, 1940.

Pamphlets

Clarke, R. W. B. *Britain's Blockade*. Oxford Pamphlets on World Affairs 38. Oxford: Clarendon Press, 1940.

Hetherington, William. *Swimming against the Tide: The Peace Pledge Union Story, 1934–2009*. London: Peace Pledge Union Peaceworks, 2009.
Horst, Irvin B. *A Ministry of Goodwill: A Short Account of Mennonite Relief, 1939–1949*. Akron, PA: Mennonite Central Committee, 1950.
Houck, Davis. *FDR and Fear Itself: The First Inaugural Address*. College Station: Texas A&M University Press, 2002.
Hourmouzios, S. L. *Starvation in Greece*. London: Harrison & Sons, 1943.
Medlicott, W. N. *The Coming of War in 1939*. London: Routledge and Kegan Paul, 1963.
Norway Thanks You: To the American Relief for Norway from Nasjonaljelpen, Norway. Oslo: Th. Larsen [ca. 1948].
Wilson, Roger. *Relief and Reconstruction: Notes on Principles Involved in Quaker Relief Service*. Pendle Hill Pamphlet 22. Wallingford, PA: Society of Friends [ca. 1944].

Papers and Archives

Adolf A. Berle Papers, Franklin D. Roosevelt Presidential Library and Museum (FDRL), Hyde Park, NY
American Friends Service Committee Archives (AFSCA), Philadelphia, PA
American Jewish Joint Distribution Committee, New York, NY
Arthur Schoenfeld Papers, Schoenfeld Private Family Papers, Washington, DC
Arthur Bliss Lane Papers, Sterling Library, Yale University, New Haven, CT
Belgian American Education Foundation Records, HHPLM
Benjamin Franklin Riter Papers, Utah State Historical Society, Salt Lake City, UT
Bernard H. Fraser Papers, HHPLM
Breckinridge Long Diary, Breckinridge Long Papers, Library of Congress Manuscript Division (LCMD), Washington, DC
Charlotte Hoffman Kellogg Papers, Hoover Institute (HI), Stanford, CA
Chauncey McCormick Papers, Newberry Library, Chicago, IL
Chester W. Wright Papers, Wayne State University, Detroit, MI
Chicago Daily News, Clipping File, HHPLM
Clarence Pickett Journals, AFSCA
Colonel Edward Mandell House Diaries, House Papers, Yale University, New Haven, CT
Cordell Hull Papers, LCMD

Correspondence, Statistics, Newspaper Clippings Relating to the Finnish Relief Fund in Buffalo and Erie County, 1940, Buffalo and Erie County Public Library, Buffalo, NY
Edgar Rickard Papers, HHPLM
Eleanor Roosevelt Papers, FDRL
Emil Hurja Papers, FDRL
Ernest Lindley Papers, Spencer Research Library, University of Kansas, Lawrence, KS
Francis X. Swietlik, Clippings, Marquette University Library, Milwaukee, WI
Franklin D. Roosevelt Papers, FDRL
George Meany Memorial Archives, Silver Springs, MD
Henry A. Wallace Diaries, University of Iowa, Iowa City, IA
Henry L. Stimson Papers, Sterling Library, Yale University, New Haven, CT
Henry Morganthau Diaries, FDRL
Herbert Hoover Papers, HHPLM
Herbert Hoover Papers, HI
Homer L. Morris and Edna W. Morris Diaries, AFSCA
Hugh S. Gibson Collection, HHPLM
Hugh S. Gibson Papers, HI
Jay Pierrepont Moffat Diaries, Harvard University, Cambridge, MA
Joel T. Boone Collection, HHPLM
John Callan O'Laughlin Collection, HHPLM
John Callan O'Laughlin Papers, LCMD
John G. Winant Papers, Family Holdings
John G. Winant Papers, Post Records, RG84, National Archives, College Park, MD
Kellogg-Dickie Papers, Stirling Library, Yale University, New Haven, CT
Kemp Malone Papers, Sheridan Libraries, Johns Hopkins University, Baltimore, MD
Key Pittman Papers, LCMD
Larry Richey Papers, HHPLM
Leopolis Collection of the Museum of Independence, Warsaw, Poland
Lewis Strauss Papers, HHPLM
Lincoln MacVeagh Diary, Mudd Library, Princeton University, Princeton, NJ
Lou Henry Hoover Papers, HHPLM
Maria Mattingly Meloney Papers, Butler Library, Columbia University, New York, NY
Mary Austin Papers, Huntington Library, San Marino, CA
Maurice Pate Papers, Mudd Library, Princeton University, Princeton, NJ

Bibliography

Narodowe Archiwun Cyfrowe, Warsaw, Poland
Neil MacNeil Papers, HHPLM
New York Herald Tribune
New York Times
Nicholas Roosevelt Papers, George Arents Research Library, Syracuse University, Syracuse, NY
Ossolineum, Wrocław, Poland
Paul H. Appleby Papers, George Arents Research Library, Syracuse University, Syracuse, NY
Perrin Comstock Galpin Papers, HI
Richard L. Wilson Papers, HHPLM
Robert A. Taft Papers, LCMD
Roy Howard Papers, LCMD
Thomas W. Lamont Papers, Baker Library, Harvard Business School, Cambridge, MA
Utah State Historical Society, Salt Lake City, UT
Vannevar Bush Papers, LCMD
Varian Fry Papers, Butler Library, Special Collections, Columbia University, New York, NY
Wayne S. Cole Papers, HHPLM
William Allen White Papers, LCMD
William Green Papers, George Meany Memorial Archives, Silver Springs, MD
William J. Donovan Papers, US Army Military Institute, Carlisle Barracks, PA
William L. White Papers, Kansas Collection, Spencer Research Library, University of Kansas, Lawrence, KS
William R. Castle Diary, Houghton Library, Harvard University, Cambridge, MA
William R. Castle Papers, HHPLM
Willian Hallam Tuck Papers, HHPLM

Primary Sources

Annual Report, 1927–1928, American National Red Cross.
Complete Presidential Press Conferences of Franklin D. Roosevelt, intro. by Jonathan Daniels. 25 Vols. New York: Da Capo Press, 1972.
The German White Paper: Full Text of the Polish Documents Issued by the Berlin Foreign Office. New York: Howell, Soskin, 1940.
Official Catalogue of the Pavilion at the World's Fair in New York, 1939. Warsaw: Polish Government Publication, 1939.

Videos and Film

Bryan, Julien. *Siege: 1940 Academy Award-Nominated Newsreel.* Los Angeles, CA: Aquila Polonica, 2009.

Dissertations and Master's Theses

Burkholder, Harold L. "U.S. Quandry: United States Neutrality v. Aid to Finland during the Winter War." PhD diss., Shippensburg State College, 1970.

Campbell, Patrick E., Jr. "What Would Be the Harm? Soviet Rule in Eastern Poland, 1939–1941." MA thesis, Ohio University, 2007.

Carpenter, Ted Galen. "The Dissenters: American Isolationists and Foreign Policy, 1945–1954." PhD diss., University of Texas, 1980.

Fels, Bradley. "That Poland Might Be Free: Polish-American and Polish Efforts to Gain American Support for Poland during the Second World War." PhD diss., University of Kansas, 2001.

Hopkins, Ryan Patrick. "The Historiography of the Allied Bombing Campaign of Germany." MA thesis, East Tennessee State University, 2008.

Kent, Wesley. "Drugi Potop: The Fall of the Second Polish Republic." MA thesis, Georgian Southern University, 2013.

Mulvihill, Peggy. "The United States and the Russo-Finnish War." PhD diss., University of Chicago, 1964.

Porfireanu, Emma. "Between Expectation and Hesitation: Romanian-American Relations, 1938–1940." MA thesis, University of Nebraska, Omaha, 1997.

Raymond, Matthew. "Kazimierz Sosnkowski: The Polish Army and Political State Building, 1905–1944." PhD diss., Ohio State University, 1994.

Wasell, F. F. "Attitudes of the Various Polish-American Organizations toward American Foreign Policy Affecting Poland." MA thesis, Columbia University, 1946.

Wert, Hal Elliott. "Specter of Starvation: Hoover, Roosevelt and American Aid to Europe, 1939–1941." PhD diss., University of Kansas, 1991.

Index

Aalto, Alvar, 345
Abel, Theodore, 185–86, 201, 226
Ackerman, Carl W., 274
Adams, Ansel, 34
Adams, Phelps, 76
Admiral Graf Spee, 82
AFSC. *See* American Friends Service Committee
Agricola, Georgius, 41
aid to refugees: as backdoor to conflict, 21–22, 360–61; cooperation of agencies in, 200, 207–8, 214–23, 226, 277; early attempts at, 124–25, 134–35; grassroots efforts, 277; requirements for organizations, 292–94. *See also* Commission for Polish Relief; Finnish Relief Fund; Polish refugees
Airplanes for Finland, 360
airpower, 14–15, 90, 185
Alekna, Jurgis, 228–29, 231, 235
Allen, Robert, 372
Alsop, Corrine Robinson, 45
Alving, Barbara, 347
Ambassador Hotel, Bucharest, 199
America First Movement, 22
American Committee to Aid Finland, 333
American Friends Service Committee (AFSC): and bombing, 20; Peace Section, 253; and World War I aid, 14
American Jewish Joint Distribution Committee (JDC), 184, 236, 291, 296–97
American Red Cross (ARC), 63–64; and CPR, 145–88, 215–21, 278, 296; and early days of war, 151; and Finland, 318–21, 328; and FRF, 334–35, 340; Hoover and, 165–66, 169–70, 178; and Hungary, 215–18; and negotiations on relief mission, 293–94, 365; and Poland, 370–71; and Vilnius, 235–36
American Relief Administration (ARA), 3, 4, 12, 39, 40*f*, 97, 180, 314
American Socialist Party, 20
Amery, Leo, 71–72
Andreas-Friedrich, Ruth, 288
Anglo-Polish Fund, 208
anti-interventionists: and early days of war, 76–78; and embargo, 249, 272–76; historiography of, ix–x; Hoover and, 258–60; Lindbergh and, 254–55; and loans, 360–61; motivations of, 258; National League for the Limitations of Armament, 11*f*; organizations of, 253–54, 267; and Pearl Harbor, 386–88; personnel, 20, 249–53; Roosevelt and, 261–62; support for, 148; term, ix; 386
anti-Semitism: Coughlin and, 258; in Poland, 100
appeasement, 50
ARA. *See* American Relief Administration
ARC. *See* American Red Cross
Arnold, Hap, 255, 378
Asquith, H. H., 73
Asquith, Margot, 73
Athenee Palace Hotel, Bucharest, 191–92
Athenia, SS, 80–81
Atlantic, Battle of, 80–82
Auden, W. H., 78
Austin, Warren, 261

497

Baldwin, Roger, 333, 336
Baldwin, Stanley, 15, 106, 244
Bankhead, Tallulah, 353*f*
Bankhead, William, 306, 369
Barkley, Alben, 243, 270, 281–82, 286*f*, 381
Barnett, E. E. "Gene," 201–2
Barrymore, John, 352
Barton, Bruce, 333, 336
Baruch, Bernard, 25, 340
baseball, Hoover and, 34, 271
Baudot, Anatole de, 37
BCRC. *See* British Committee for Refugees from Czechoslovakia
Beck, Jadwiga, 198
Beck, Józef, 52, 103, 132–33, 134, 138, 198, 224; and evacuation, 119–20, 127, 135
Beck, Maria, 119–20, 138
Belgian American Educational Foundation, 318
Belgium, 8, 375–76, 379; conditions in, 17–19; food aid during World War I, 11–12
Bell, George, 20
Bellow, Saul, 7
Bennett, Joan, 333, 336
Berg, Mary, 370
Beria, Lavrenty, 309
Berle, Adolf, 59, 146–47, 150, 304; and embargo, 263–64; and neutrality, 155, 156*f*
Berle, Beatrice, 147
Berlin, Germany, 287–88, 290–91
Berlin, Isaiah, 43
Bessarabia, 56, 190
Best, Gary Dean, ix, 324
Biddle, Anthony Joseph Drexel, Jr., 69, 70*f*; and early days of war, 74, 107, 133–34; and evacuation, 103–8, 116–19, 121, 126–29, 128*f*, 131–33, 135–36; and Polish government in exile, 194; in Romania, 191–92, 195
Biddle, Francis, 46
Biddle, Margaret, 103–4, 108, 129–30; and evacuation, 121, 131, 136; in Romania, 191–92, 195

bipartisanship, Hoover and, 159
Birkeland, Carl, 370
Black, Percy, 89, 402n23
Black Americans, and Ethiopia, 240
Black Eagle, 82
blackout, 73, 101, 127, 288
Blisard, Thomas A., 264
blockade, and food aid, 17–18, 293, 297, 365–66, 368–69, 374; Hoover and, 164; international law and, 376; in World War I, 12–14
bloodlands, 99
Bloom, Sol, 245, 248, 286*f*, 358, 369
Boettiger, Anna, 45
Bohlen, Charles, 57, 59
bombing: controversy over, 18–21, 244; Hoover and, 164; in Polish invasion, 70–71, 87, 96, 107–8, 111–12, 116, 120, 123–24, 129; Roosevelt on, 75, 106, 191; strategic, 17
Bonnet, Georges, 71
Boone, Dave, 342
Borah, William, 243, 249–51, 261–62, 279, 285, 343
Bostrom, W., 305
Brauchitsch, Walther von, 83*f*
Bricker, John, 343
British: and Battle of Atlantic, 80–82; and Battle of Britain, 374–75, 378–79; and blockade, 297, 368–69; and declaration of war, 73, 90–92; and early days of war, 79–80; and Finland, 362; and German expansion, 50–51; and Nazi-Soviet pact, 60–61; and Poland, 52–53, 120; and war, 84
British Committee for Refugees from Czechoslovakia (BCRC), 124–25, 224
Brittain, Vera, 20, 72, 78
Brock, Ray and Mary, 82
Brown, Franklin, 333
Brown, James W., 198, 199–200, 209, 226, 277
Brown, Mollie, 34
Brown, Prentiss M., 281, 361
Brown, Sally, 203

Index

Brunel, Robert, 219
Bryan, Julien, 70*f*, 108–10, 112, 113*f*, 114, 129
Bryan, William Jennings, 373
Buchanan, Pat, 33
Bucharest, Romania, 103, 129, 190–92, 194, 204
Budapest, Hungary, 209–10
Budge, Don, 358
Bulgaria, 121
Bullitt, William C., 51, 134, 151; and early days of war, 74, 75, 106; and Finland, 308, 363
Bunge, Hilda, 184
Bush, George W., 43
business practices, Hoover and, 35–36
Bussgang, Julian, 136, 139
Byrnes, Jimmy, 280
Byron, George Gordon, Lord, 29

Cajander, Aimo K., 307, 328
Călinescu, Armand, 192–93, 264
Calvocoressi, Peter, 18
Campbell, 150
Campbell, Allan, 36
Campbell, Thomas, 273
camps, refugee, 212; conditions in, 206–7, 223; for interned soldiers, 204–7, 205*f*
Canada, 151, 155, 270, 281
Canaris, Wilhelm, 53
Cantor, Eddie, 26, 258
Capper, Arthur, 267
Caragea, Catherine, 207–8
Cardwell, Ann Su, 100, 203. *See also* Super, Margaret
Carol, king of Romania, 133, 190, 193, 227
Carol's Dyke, 190
Carpenter, Ted Galen, ix
cash-and-carry policy, 240–87
Castle, William, 255, 257, 259–61, 274, 280
Cather, Willa, 39
Cavell, Edith, 183
celebrities, and Finland, 331–44, 331*f*, 338*f*, 349–50, 352–54, 353*f*, 357–58

Celler, Emanuel, 333, 336
Cermak, Anton, 30, 161
Chamberlain, Neville, 50, 60, 71–73
Channon, Henry "Chips," 50, 60–61, 79
Charanov, Nikolai, 118–19
Chatfield-Taylor, Wayne, 216–17, 293–94, 342
Chevalier, Michel, 35
children. *See* women and children
Children's Crusade for Children, 354–57, 371, 372*f*
Child Welfare Society, 200
China, 243, 387; Hoovers in, 2, 28–29
Christie, Agatha, 195
Churchill, Winston, 12–13, 81, 374–75, 376; and early days of war, 60, 71, 73; and Hoover, 171
Chylinski, Thaddeus Henry, 291
Clapper, Raymond, 252, 334
Clark, Champ, 267, 281–82
class, and FRF support, 351–52
Clemenceau, Georges, 180
Clements, Kendrick A., 39
Codreanu, Corneliu, 193
Cohen, Ben, 315
Colbern, William H., 129, 135
Cole, Wayne S., 41–42, 153
Colin, Rene, 17–18
Colten, Ethan T., 33
Commission for Belgian Relief, 376
Commission for Polish Relief (CPR), 277, 351, 365; and ARC, 145–88, 215–21, 278, 296; effectiveness of, 287, 382–83; establishment of, 173, 180; and FRF, 336; and negotiations on relief mission, 278–98; organization of, 186–87; personnel of, 180–86, 188
Commission for Relief in Belgium (CRB), 3, 4, 12, 39, 157, 180; and war, 360–61
Committee to Aid the Refugees, 234
Committee to Defend America by Aiding the Allies, 22
Communism/Communists, 32; and Finland, 317, 354; Hitler and, 53; Hollingworth and, 125, 224; and pact, 62

499

Connelly, Thomas, 248, 282, 306
conservatism, Hoover and, 26
consulates, and donations for Finland, 322
Continuation War, 330
Coolidge, Calvin, 38, 159
Cooper, Duff, 73
Cooper, Merian, 185, 332
Cortesi, Phillippe, 121
Cory, Clare, 318
Coughlin, Charles, 258, 259f, 267–68, 358
Cowles, Virginia, 191–92, 347
Cox, Geoffrey, 347
CPR. *See* Commission for Polish Relief
Crang, J., 104, 119
CRB. *See* Commission for Relief in Belgium
Cross, Lillian, 30
cryptographers, Polish, 196–98
Csáky, István, 210
Cudahy, John, 17–18
Cunningham, Glen, 358
Curie, Marie, 178
Czechoslovakia, 49–50

Daladier, Edouard, 51
Darrow, Clarence, 250
Davis, John K., 110
Davis, Malcolm, 226
Davis, Norman H., 63–64, 99; and ARC, 169–70, 221; and CPR, 173–75, 218; and early days of war, 151; and Finland, 320, 326–27, 341–42; and Gibson, 183; and Hoover, 152–54, 160, 165–68, 177, 319, 340–41; and negotiations on relief mission, 294; and Poland, 370
Declaration of London, 12
Deering, William, 182
defense spending, Roosevelt and, 244–47
Denmark, 371
Dennis, Lawrence, ix
de Sales, Raoul de Roussy, 257
Detzer, Dorothy, 20
Deutschland, 82
Dewey, Thomas E., 158, 271, 372–73, 376–77, 380

De Wiart, Adrian Carton, 12, 84–85
Dingell, John, 361
displaced persons. *See* aid to refugees; refugees
Dix, Otto, 23, 24f
Dodd, William, 32
Doenecke, Justus D., ix–xiii
Dom Polski, 200
Donovan, William "Wild Bill," 366
Douhet, Giulio, 14–15
Dreiser, Theodore, 324
Drymmer, Helena, 227
Dugdale, Blanche, 73
Dulles, Allen, 268–69, 279–80
Dunkirk, 376
Dunn, James, 310
Dunne, Finley Peter, 27
Dyboski, Stefania, 215
Dyboski, Tadeusz, 94, 101, 215

Earle, George, 21–22
Earle, Hubert, 134
Early, Stephen, 147, 340
economic issues, 3, 26, 47; and early days of war, 76–77; Hoover and, 31, 38; Roosevelt and, 31–32
Edison, Charles, 76–77, 157, 378
education, relief efforts as, 9
Eichelberger, Clark, 268
Eisenhower, Dwight, 77
election of 1932, 26
election of 1938, 159
election of 1940, 6–7; cabinet and, 156–57; and Finland, 313; Long on, 221; Republican nomination for, 158, 270–71, 273, 278–79, 316, 337–38, 341–43, 371–80
Elkinton, Howard W., 289–92
Ellis, Richard, 204
Elliston, E. B., 310
embargo provision of neutrality laws, repeal of, 240–87, 286f; vote on, 284–85
Emerson, Ralph Waldo, 31
Emisarski, Jan, 212
engineering, Hoover and, 36–37

Index

enigma machines, 196–98
Erkko, Eljas, 302, 307
Estonia, 167; Nazi-Soviet pact and, 56; Soviet Union and, 230, 301
Ethiopia, 240–41

Fala (dog), 46*f*
Farrelly, T. Charles, Mrs., 352
fascism, 32, 268; Hoover and, 274, 324; Lindbergh and, 257, 282
Feis, Herbert, 326
Fellowship of Reconciliation, 253
Field, Hermann, 124
Fígas, Justin, 226
Fighting Funds for Finland, 361–62
Finland, 167, 287, 299–330, 371; American volunteers and, 322–23, 323*f*; army of, 299–330, 344–45, 362–64; capitulation of, 364–65; conditions in, 338–39, 339*f*, 345–48; Nazi-Soviet pact and, 56; Strauss and, 184. *See also* Winter War
Finnish American Trading Corporation, 316, 325–27
Finnish Relief Fund (FRF), 316, 318–44, 350–59; and Children's Crusade, 354–57; effectiveness of, 382–83; federal money and, 358–59, 368–70; personnel of, 333–34; West Coast branch, 331–32
Fish, Hamilton, 261, 269
Fisher, Dorothy Canfield, 354–57
Fleeson, Doris, 334, 337
Fleischen, Adolf, 225
food aid: in Romania, 203, 209; in Vilnius, 236*f*; in World War I, 11–14. *See also* blockade
Forman, Harrison, 87
Fox, Alan, 273, 377
Fox, George, 45
France, 51, 374; and blockade, 368; and early days of war, 79–80; food aid during World War I, 11–12; Hoover and, 324; and Nazi-Soviet pact, 61; and Poland, 52–53, 120; and Polish government in exile, 194–96, 228; surrender of, 376

Franco, Francisco, 241
Frank, Hans, 289, 293
Fraser, Bernard, 188
FRF. *See* Finnish Relief Fund
fund-raising, 8; and aid negotiations, 294–96; celebrities and, 331–44, 331*f*, 338*f*; and CPR versus ARC, 166; and Finland, 320, 332, 350–59; Hoover and, 277; issues in, 219, 221–22, 358–59; Super and, 103, 142, 215–17, 221–22; and Vilnius, 235–36

Gallup, George, 247
Galpin, Perrin, 163, 172
Gamble, Arthur, 296
Gamelin, Gustave, 61, 72, 79
Gannett, Frank, 158, 343
Garbo, Greta, 340, 353
Garner, John Nance, 286*f*
Garrett, Patrick, 125
Garry, Thomas D., 381–82
Gellhorn, Martha, 176, 241, 339, 346
Geneva Convention, 11, 15
German Children's Feeding Program, 12–14, 14*f*
Germany: and atrocities, 117, 122; and declaration of war, 73–74; and expansion, 49–64, 288, 371; and Hungary, 212; and Nazi-Soviet nonaggression pact, 47–48, 53–64, 119; and negotiations on relief mission, 278–98, 365, 369; and Poland, 65–82, 88–89, 92–93, 131; and refugees, 237–38; and Romania, 190–92; and start of World War II, 17–24; and World War I, 11–15
Gibson, Hugh, 27, 33, 163, 183–84, 365–66, 374–75
Gillette, Guy M., 254
Goddard, Paulette, 353
Goebbels, Joseph, 62–63, 81
Goering, Hermann, 92, 289
Golden, John, 352–53
Gordon, Ruth, 352
Government General (Poland), 288–89, 291, 369–71, 375

501

Great Depression, 3, 26, 31
Greece, 22
Green, William, 39, 336
Greene, Hugh Carleton, 93, 130, 132, 139, 193
Greenwood, Arthur, 71–72
Grew, Joseph C., 184
Grey, Jenny, 34
Grey Samaritans, 97–98, 97*f*
Grigorcea, Gheorghe, 134
Gripenberg, G. A., 312
Gunther, Franklin Mott, 131
Gunther, John, 52

Hackworth, Green H., 155
Haering, George, 291, 370
Hague Conventions, 11–12, 15
Halifax, Edward Wood, earl of, 266
Haller, József, 97
Halsey, Ed, 248, 284
Hanauer, Alice, 184
Hanky, Robin, 67
Harding, Warren, 38, 159
Hartigan, John, 187
Harvey, Oliver, 79
Hayek, Friedrich, 38
Hayes, Helen, 332, 337, 338*f*, 353*f*
Häyhä, Simo, 348
Hayne, Frank, 346
Heine, Heinrich, 47
Helsinki, Finland, 345–46, 348
Hemingway, Ernest, 241, 258
Henie, Sonja, 332
Henle, Ray, 2
Hepburn, Katherine, 353*f*
Herwarth, Johnny, 59
Herwarth, Pussi, 62
Hewel, Walther, 54
Hibbard, Fred, 131
Hiss, Donald, 42
Hitler, Adolf, 32, 49*f*, 81, 185–86; and Communists, 53; and expansion, 49–50; and pact, 47–48, 54, 56; and Poland, 66
Hoare, Reginald, 208
Hoffman, Heinrich, 54, 56–57

Hollingworth, Clare, 68*f*, 84, 86, 209; character of, 137; and direct aid, 222–25; and invasion of Poland, 67–68, 90–93, 114–15, 120, 122–23, 128, 130, 132, 137–38; and refugee rescues, 124–25; and Romania, 139, 142–43, 193, 201, 205–8
Hollywood: Cooper and, 185; and Finland, 331*f*, 332–33, 336–37, 338*f*, 349–50, 352–54, 353*f*
Holmes, Oliver Wendell, 42
Holsti, Rudolf, 300, 313–14
Honnold, William, 271
Hoover, Herbert, 1*f*, 5*f*, 25*f*, 35*f*, 37*f*, 353*f*; and *Athenia*, 81; background of, 25–29, 32–41; character of, 33–34, 36–39, 262–63, 348–49, 373–74; and Children's Crusade, 355–57; and early days of war, 77–78; and embargo, 258–60, 266–68, 272–76, 283–85, 283*f*; and Finland, 313–21, 331*f*, 362, 364–65, 368–69; later years, 382–83, 385–88; and military aid, 324–26; motivations of, 221; and Nazi-Soviet pact, 59–60; and neutrality, 163–64; and nomination, 270–71, 273, 278–79, 316, 337–38, 341–43, 371–80; and Poland, 98–99, 239*f*, 276–77, 365–68; principles of, 11–12, 31; reputation of, ix, 25–26, 47, 171, 180; and suspicion, 47, 161–62, 176–77, 340; and war, 386–88; as writer, 1–5, 13. *See also* Roosevelt–Hoover relationship
Hoover, J. Edgar, 255
Hoover, Lou Henry, 28, 41, 47, 161, 162, 349–50, 355, 380
Hoover-Stimson Doctrine, 164
Hopkins, Harry, 45, 381
Hopkins, John Jay, 318
Hornbeck, Stanley, 310
Horthy, Miklós, 214
House, Edward, 180
Howard, Roy, 272
Hubicki, Stefan, 215
Hudson, Hendrik, 102
Hughes, Charles Evan, 174

Hughes, Noël Evelyn. *See* Norton, Peter
Hull, Cordell: and early days of war, 74–75; and embargo repeal, 243, 245, 263–64, 286*f*; and Finland, 303–5, 308, 310–11, 312–13, 326; and Germany, 370; and loans, 361; and Nazi-Soviet pact, 57; and neutrality, 146–47, 150–51, 155, 156*f*; and nomination, 376
Hungarian-Polish Society, 215
Hungarian Red Cross, 210, 215
Hungarian YMCA/YWCA, 215
Hungary, 22, 102, 383; refugees in, 136, 202, 209–12; rescue efforts in, 189–238
Huntington, George S., Mrs., 75
Hurst, Fannie, 332
Hyde, Arthur, 275

Ickes, Harold, 147–48, 156, 240, 257, 269; and Finland, 311–12, 320; and Hoover, 341–42
Ickes, Jane, 148
idealism, Hoover and, 28
Illaová, Mlle., 224–25
Ingalls, Laura, 268
International Committee of the Red Cross, 178–79, 219–20, 294
International Migration Service, 290
interventionists, 387–88; term, 386
Iron Guard, Romania, 192–93
isolationists, ix, 262. *See also* anti-interventionists
Italy, 240–41
Ivens, Joris, 241

Jackson, Robert, 147, 253
Jackson, Zaidee, 192
Jakobson, Max, 302
Janssen, Werner, 332
Japan, 55
JDC. *See* American Jewish Joint Distribution Committee
Jenkins, Douglas, Jr., 110
Jewish Self-Help Society, 297
Jews: aid negotiations on, 292–93, 296; among Polish refugees, 106–7, 136; diaspora of, 22, 290; and FRF, 336; in Poland, 296–97; treatment of, 117, 129, 288; in Vilnius, 229, 235, 237–38
Joad, C. E. M., 20
John Paul II. *See* Wojtyła, Karol Józef
Johnson, Hiram, ix, 249, 251–52, 261, 271, 285
Johnson, Howard, 258
Johnson, Ken "Snakehips," 15
Johnson, Louis A., 76, 147, 246
Jones, Jessie, 315, 325, 326, 361
Jones, Rufus, 20
journalists. *See* media
Joyce, James, 78–79
Junod, Marcel, 15–16, 106

Kähönen, Lempi, 338–39
Kalinin, Mikhail, 306
Kamp Hotel, Helsinki, 345–46
Kant, Immanuel, 55
Kastner, Erich, 287
Kellogg, Charlotte, 157–59, 172–73, 182*f*, 366; and establishment of CPR, 177–79, 181, 187–88
Kellogg, Vernon, 157
Kellogg, W. K., 271
Kennard, Howard, 73, 90, 107, 120, 128, 132, 135
Kennedy, Joseph, 148
Keynes, John Maynard, 38, 171, 180
Khrushchev, Nikita, 309
King, Mackenzie, 151, 155, 270
Kirk, Alexander, 67
Kitchener, Herbert, earl of, 12
Klein, Julius, 325
Klemperer, Eva, 74
Klemperer, Victor, 73–74
Klepper, Jochen, 73
Knox, Frank, 156–57, 262, 268, 378
Knut Nelson, 80
Konapacka, Halina, 96
Kościuszko, Tadeusz, 171, 188
Kossuth, Lajos, 328
Kraków, Poland, 86, 89, 124
Krock, Arthur, 171, 334

Krueger, Joseph, 188, 325
Krzemieniec, Poland, 107, 115, 118, 120
Kubicz, Stanley, 110
Kulik, Grigory, 309
Kullmann, G., 125
Kun, Béla, 209
Kuty, Poland, 128, 131

labor unions, and FRF, 351
La Follette, Philip, 41
La Follette, Robert, 267
La Guardia, Fiorello, 277, 333, 335–36
Lamont, Thomas, 275
Landon, Alf, 156–57, 262, 268, 378
Lansing, Robert, 147
Larson, Eric, 288
Latvia: Nazi-Soviet pact and, 56; refugees in, 136; Soviet Union and, 230, 301
Lawrence, Gertrude, 349, 350f, 354
League of Nations, 15, 27, 164, 166
League of Nations Union (LNU), 124–25
League of Red Cross Societies, 235–36, 294
Legion of Young Polish Women, 277
LeHand, Marguerite "Missy," 45
Lehman, Herbert, 366
Lemp, Fritz-Julius, 80–81
Lewis, Fulton J., 2, 255
Libby, Frederick J., 20, 21
Lindberg, Otto G., 334, 358
Lindbergh, Anne Morrow, 257
Lindbergh, Charles, 254–55, 256f; critics of, 257, 275, 281–82; and embargo, 272, 274, 276, 280–83; and Hoover, 266–67
Lindsay, Ronald, 244
Lipkowska, Magdalena, 69, 96
Lipski, Józef, 61
Lithuania, 8, 22, 383; refugees in, 136; rescue efforts in, 189–238; Soviet Union and, 301. See also Vilnius
LNU. See League of Nations Union
loans to Finland, 300, 314–15, 325, 359–64; public support for, 359
Lohmann, Albrecht, 293–94, 296

Long, Breckinridge, 146, 193, 221, 320–21, 368
Longworth, Alice Roosevelt, 250
Loos, Adolf, 37
Lord Mayor of London Relief Fund, 208
Lothian, Philip Kerr, marquess of, 150–51, 297–98, 368
Lotta Svard, 339
Louis, Joe, 358
Lower, Richard Coke, 251–52
Lubieńska, Teresa, 88
Lubieński, Michael, 138
Lublin, Poland, 94, 100
Łukasiewicz, Juliusz, 71, 155
Lunt, Alfred, 354

MacArthur, Douglas, 77
MacCracken, Henry Noble, 188
Macmillan, Harold, 60
MacNeil, Neil, 4
Maisky, Ivan, 62, 74
Maitland, Patrick, 130
Majewska, Włada, 225
Maki, Taisto, 358
management: Hoover and, 38–39, 187–88; Roosevelt and, 42–43
Manion, Clarence, x
Mannerheim, Carl Gustaf Emil von, 307–8, 310, 312
Mannerheim Line, 309, 312, 338, 344
Manville, Tommy, 352
marriage: Hoover and, 41; Roosevelt and, 45–46
Marshall, George, 76, 378
Martin, Evangeline "Vannie," 34
Martin, Joseph, 262, 379
mathematicians, Polish, 196–98
Mattei, A. C. "Bert," 271
Mayenburg, Ruth von, 62
McCormick, Chauncey, 182–83, 188
McCormick, Robert A., 182, 369
McDonald, William C., 110, 112, 142, 165, 187; and aid negotiations, 287–96
McIntire, Ross, 147, 148
McNary, Charles, 270, 286f

McQuatters, Eugenia, 104
media: and anti-interventionists, 273, 361; and Czechoslovakia, 50; and evacuation from Poland, 109–10, 114–15, 119, 130–32, 135–36; and Finland, 317–18, 322, 332, 334–35, 345, 347; and fundraising, 375; and Hoover on embargo, 279; and military support, 364; and Republican nomination, 337–38, 341, 372–73, 380
Meloney, Marie Mattingly "Missy," 152, 153*f*, 177–78, 181, 354
Mencken, H. L., 16
Meyer, William Star, 377
Mika, Andzia, 113*f*
Mika, Kazimiera, 112, 113*f*
Mikoyan, Anastas, 62
military support: for Britain, 378–79; for Finland, 324–27, 329–30, 358–60, 362–64; for Poland, 120; for Ukraine, 387. *See also* war materiel
Miller, Bunny, 2
Minthorn, Henry, 34
Mises, Ludwig von, 38
Mitchell, Sidney, 318
Mizwa, Stephen, 188
Moffat, Jay Pierrepont, 155, 179, 305–6
Moley, Raymond, 30
Molotov, Vyacheslav, 55, 57, 58*f*, 230, 302, 309
Molotov cocktails, 345
molybdenum, 311–12
Montgomery, John Flournoy, 212, 214
Monzie, Anatole, 72
Moore, Aaron William, 19
Moore, R. Walton, 305
Morgan, J. P., 187
Morgenthau, Henry, 150, 217, 244, 312, 326, 361
Morris, Edna, 289
Morris, Homer L., 289–92
Morton, William R., 121, 129–30, 370
Mościcki, Ignacy, 68, 105, 138, 194
Mott, John R., 98
Mudd, Harvey, 271

Murray, Columba P., Jr., 188
Mussolini, Benito, 71, 241
Mutual Assistance Treaty, 230

National Committee on Food for the Small Democracies (NCFSD), 4–5, 385
National Council for Prevention of War, 20, 253, 267
National Keep America Out of War Committee, 253–54
National League for the Limitations of Armament, 11*f*
National Socialists Welfare Agency, 289–90, 292
Nazi-Soviet nonaggression pact, 47–48, 53–64, 119, 288; codicil to, 231; and Finland, 301; reactions to, 57–64
NCFSD. *See* National Committee on Food for the Small Democracies
Netherlands, 81, 374–76
Neutrality Acts, 145–51, 145*f*, 166–67, 175–76; embargo provision, repeal of, 240–87, 286*f*; Hoover and, 163–64; and loans, 361; and Winter War, 311, 317, 324–27
Nicholson, James T., 293–94, 369
Nicolson, Harold, 282–83
Niebuhr, Reinhold, 333, 336
Nieuw Amsterdam, 82
Noël, Léon, 107, 120, 195
Noel-Buxton, N. E., 208
Non-Partisan Committee for Peace through Revision of the Neutrality Law, 268
nonrecognition, Hoover and, 164
Noonan, Peggy, 33
Norem, Owen J. C., 228, 231, 235
Normandie, 150
Norton, Clifford, 122, 195
Norton, Peter, 122–32, 195, 222–24
Norway, 80, 371
Nurmi, Paavo, 358
Nye, Gerald P., 243, 249, 251, 279

O'Donovan, Dermod, 204, 206–7, 227
Okay (dog), 104, 121, 195
O'Laughlin, John Callan, 341
Olson, Lynn, 41
Olympics, 96, 444n64
Ordonówna, Hanka, 66
Orient Express, 195
Orwell, George, 19
O'Ryan, John F., 281, 359, 362, 365
Osnos, Martha, 88
outdoors: Hoover and, 34, 35*f*, 40, 377, 380; Roosevelt and, 43–44
Owen, Wilfred, 23

Paasikivi, J. K., 302, 306–7
Paderewski, Ignacy, 98, 171, 366
Paderewski Fund, 366
Page, Walter Hines, 183
Paige, Satchel, 36
Panay, 243
Parrish, Maxfield, 367*f*
Pate, Maurice, 165, 183, 187, 209, 287, 369; and CPR versus ARC, 218
Patrick, Luther A., 264–65
Patterson, Cissy, 250
Paycheck, Johnny, 358
Peace Pledge Union, 20
Pearl Harbor, 386
Pearson, Drew, 334, 372
Pelenyi, John, 147
Perkins, Frances, 27, 31
Peter the Great, 301
Petrowski, John, 110
Petrusewicz, Maria, 234–35, 236
Phantom Train, 105, 107, 119
Philadelphia Committee for the Defense of Constitutional Rights, 264
Pickens, William, 333
Pickett, Clarence E., 8, 20, 218
Piłudski, Józef, 52, 84, 134, 171, 185, 229
Ping Mei, 244
Pittman, Key, 246, 248, 269–70, 280, 281, 286*f*, 306
Pius XII, 21
Poland: Anglo-French support for, 51–53, 71–73, 79–80; army of, 86–87, 125–26, 131, 140*f*–41*f*, 210–12, 211*f*; conditions in, 16, 100, 285–86, 291–92, 375; effects of invasion in, 83–143; evacuation of government of, 93–96, 101–6, 116–20, 125–26, 137; government in exile, 134, 138–39, 193–96; Hoover and, 171–72, 365–68; invasion of, 65–82, 83*f*; and Nazi-Soviet pact, 56, 61, 288; Vilnius, 228–35; World's Fair and, 276–78
Polish Red Cross, 109, 234
Polish refugees, aid to, 5–7, 86, 93, 126–27, 134–35, 383; costs of, 175, 202, 227; early attempts at, 86, 88, 94, 100–101, 111; Hoover and, 37*f*, 162–63; negotiations with Nazis on, 278–98; Roosevelt and, 221; waves of, Super on, 226–27. *See also* Commission for Polish Relief
Polish Relief Fund, 208, 236, 278
Polish soldiers, interned, 189*f*, 202, 204–5, 205*f*, 206–7, 383
Polish-Soviet War, 99
Polish YMCA, 188, 225
Polonius, Alexander, 61–62, 90, 110–12
Południca, 90
Popeye, 331*f*, 349
Potocka, Joseph, 88
Potocki, Jerzy, 51, 154–55, 170–71, 239*f*, 277
Potulicki, Count, 105
Procopé, Hjalmar, 167, 303–5, 308, 312, 315, 361–62, 263; and aid, 318, 327–28, 334–35; and credit, 325
Prugar-Ketling, Bronisław, 211
public opinion: and election of 1940, 376–77; and Finland, 306, 317, 322, 324, 333–34, 351–52; and Jews, 335; and loans, 359; and military support, 364; and war, 247, 258, 260

Quakers: and aid negotiations, 289–92, 296; American Friends Service Committee, 14, 20, 253; British team, 204, 208, 215, 223; Hoover and, 33; principles of, 12

Index

Queen Mary, 150–51
Queen Wilhelmina Fund, 376

Raczkiewicz, Władysław, 101, 194
Raczyński, Edward, 71, 155, 208
Radziwill, Charles, 84
Radziwill, Isabella, 115
Rapallo Treaty, 61
Raskin, Willie, 258
Reconstruction Finance Corporation, 315
Red Cross. *See* International Committee of the Red Cross; *specific country*
Redfern, Gilbert, 187, 228, 231, 234, 235–36, 238
Reed, Daniel A., ix
Reed, John, 191
refugees: as bombing targets, 106, 116, 123–24; conditions of, 143, 206–7, 223; exploitation of, 196; number of, 179, 202; rescue efforts, 189–238. *See also* aid to refugees; Polish refugees
Regnery, Henry, 5, 5*f*
Reifenstahl, Leni, 117, 118*f*
Rejewski, Marian, 196–98
Remarque, Erich Maria, 23
Republican Party: and election of 1940, 158, 270–71, 273, 278–79, 316, 337–38, 341–43, 371–80; and neutrality laws, 163–64
Reynaud, Paul, 61
Reyntiens, Ynès, 183
Rhoads, Edgar, 296
Ribbentrop, Joachim von, 52, 54–57, 58*f*, 59, 293
Rice, Alexander Hamilton, 352
Richey, Lawrence, 161–62, 163, 340–41, 377–78, 379
Richtofen, Wolfran von, 70
Rickard, Edgar: and FRF, 318, 325–26, 334; and Hoover, 157, 159, 163, 165, 275, 344, 371–72; and Lindbergh, 266; and nomination, 377–78; and relief, 177; and Roosevelt, 267, 351
Rickenbauer, Eddie, 275
Roberts, Andrew, 19

Robinson, John C., 240
Rockefeller, John D., Jr., 270, 351
Rockwell, Norman, 371, 372*f*
Roey, Jozef-Ernest van, 19, 20–21
Rogers, Will, 26
Romance, Viviane, 66
Romania, 22, 103, 129–31, 133, 383; conditions in, 190; crossing into, 134–39, 140*f*–41*f*; rescue efforts in, 189–238
Romanian Red Cross, 200
Romanian YMCA, 198
Roosevelt, Eleanor, 44; and aid, 173–74, 217; and Children's Crusade, 354–57, 371; and CPR, 219–21; and early days of war, 75, 79, 147; and Hoover, 152, 165, 176–77; and Lindbergh, 282; and Paderewski Fund, 366; and Spanish Civil War, 241; and third term, 381
Roosevelt, Franklin, Jr., 27
Roosevelt, Franklin Delano, 25*f*, 46*f*; and aid, 22, 221; and ARC, 175; background of, 29–33, 41–47; and bombing, 75, 106, 191; and cabinet reshuffle, 157; character of, 6, 31, 41–43, 45–46; and Children's Crusade, 371, 372*f*; and communications, 32, 214; and early days of war, 51–52, 74–77, 106; and embargo repeal, 240, 243–47, 261–65, 286–87, 286*f*; and Finland, 310, 320–22, 324–25, 329–30; and loans, 361; and Nazi-Soviet pact, 57; and neutrality proclamation, 145–51, 145*f*, 149–50, 166–67; reputation of, 47; and third term, 269, 376–77, 380–82; and war, 23, 378–79
Roosevelt, Theodore, 27, 43, 251
Roosevelt–Hoover relationship, 2–3, 7, 9, 23–27, 44–45, 262; and aid debate, 151–52, 157–60; and Finland, 320–21, 334; and meetings, 153–54; security issues and, 161–62
Rose, W. J., 208
Rosenman, Samuel I., 42, 263, 264
Różycki, Jerzy, 196–98

Russell, William, 67
Russia, Ukraine and, 387. *See also* Soviet Union
Ryan, Monsignor, 355–56
Rydz, Edward Śmigły, 68–69, 83*f*, 84, 85*f*, 92, 127, 133–34, 138–39
Ryti, Risto, 336

Salamon-Racz, Tamas, 221
Salter, Cedric, 137
sanctions, Hoover and, 164
Sapieha, Virgilia, 126–27
Saratoga, USS, 329
Satterlee, Herbert L., 187, 366
Save the Children Fund, 200, 207–8, 210, 215, 223–24
Sawtelle, Raymond, 333
Schlesinger, Arthur, Jr., 21
Schoenfeld, H. F. Arthur, 303, 308
Schulenburg, Friedrich-Werner von der, 55
Schulze, Peggy, 104, 108, 121
Schulze, Richard, 56
Sebastian, Mihail, 190, 194
Šeinius, Ignas, 228–29, 233
Selassie, Haile, 240–41
Selter, Karl, 167, 301
Selvage, James P., 318, 332, 373
Shakespeare, William, 50
Shattuck, Edwin P., 318
Shaw, Arch, 163, 165
Sherwood, Robert, 307, 348
Sibelius, Jean, 332, 358
Siegfried Line, 79
Sikorski, Władysław, 134, 194–96
Silbert, Ben, 349, 350*f*
Sima, Horia, 193
Simmons, Robert, 273
Simpson, John L., 318
Simpson, Ken, 271
Sioussat, Helen d'Oyle, 36
Składkowski, Felicjan, 68, 132, 134, 138, 194
Slack, Frank V., 201–2, 218
Śmigły-Rydz, Edward. *See* Rydz, Edward Śmigły

Smith, Al, 46
Smith, Richard Norton, 324
Smith, Truman, 255
Soboniewski, Stephan, 136–37
Social Self-Help Committee, 291
Society of Friends. *See* Quakers
Sokolsky, George, 377
Sosabowski, Stansilaw, 116–17
Sosnkowski, Kazimierz, 131, 167, 211–12, 213*f*
Soviet Union: army of, conditions in, 232, 345; and Finland, 287, 299–330, 364–65; and Hungary, 209; and Lithuania, 383; and Nazi-Soviet nonaggression pact, 47–48, 53–64, 119; and Polish invasion, 102, 133–34, 172–73, 195–96, 288; and Polish-Soviet War, 99; refugees in, 136; and Vilnius, 228–35
Spanish Civil War, 241, 324
Spanish Earth (film), 241, 242*f*
Spiegel, Boruch, 105
Spiegel, Renia, 106–7, 405n86
sports, Finland and, 357–58
St. Catherine's Crib, 207
Stalin, Joseph, 49*f*; and Baltics, 230; and Finland, 309; Hoover on, 60; and pact, 53–57, 58*f*; and Poland, 195; and Yartsev, 300
Stark, Harold R., 76
Starling, Edmund W., 162
Starzyński, Stephan, 109
Steinbeck, John, 34, 324
Steinhardt, Laurence, 304, 308
Stephens, F. Dorsey, 187, 228, 231, 328, 362
Stephens, Zora, 187
Stimson, Henry, 147, 263, 268, 378
Stokes, Dick, 20
Straja Tarii, 200
Straten-Ponthoz, Robert van der, 379
Strauss, Lewis, 184–85, 313–15; and FRF, 318, 325, 326, 336; and nomination, 379; and Paderewski Fund, 366
Strong, Tracy, 232

Suckley, Margaret "Daisy," 46
Sullivan, Mark, 163, 378
Suomen Huolto, 328
Super, Margaret: and Eleanor Roosevelt, 217; and evacuation, 94, 96, 100–102; and Hoover, 171–72; in Hungary, 209–10; in Romania, 198–99, 203, 209, 227–28. *See also* Cardwell, Ann Su
Super, Paul, 95*f*, 111, 200, 226; and Caragea, 207–8; and cooperating agencies, 219–22, 226; and evacuation, 93–94, 96–97, 100–103; and fundraising, 103, 142, 215–17, 221–22, 277; and Hoover, 171–72; in Hungary, 209–10, 212–17; in interwar Poland, 98–100; and outbreak of war, 66, 88; in Romania, 198–99, 201–3, 209, 227–28
Sutter, Hans, 89
Swarthout, Gladys, 337, 343, 353
Swatland, Donald C., 316, 326
Sweden, 305
świetlica, 225; term, 204
Swietlik, Francis, 278
Świętochowski, Zbigniew, 69
Swift, Ernest J., 216–17, 220, 293–95
Switzerland, 121–22
Szembek, Jan, 107

Taber, John, x
Taft, Robert A., ix, 23, 372–73, 376, 380
Tănase, Maria, 192
Tanner, Vaino, 307
Taylor, Arthur, 99
Taylor, Frederick Winslow, 37–38
Taylor, Myron, 154, 157, 159, 160–61, 165, 220, 369
technology: Hoover and, 36–37, 40; and warfare, 14
Theatre Arts Committee, 354
Thomas, Lowell, 2, 22
Thomas, Norman, 20
Thomas-Zaleska, Marta, 85*f*
Thompson, Boyce, 103–4
Thompson, Dorothy, 75, 257, 282, 343, 359–60

Thomsen, Hans, 365
Thrasher, Edward J., 120–21
Thwaites, John Anthony, 67, 90, 114–15, 124, 131, 138
Tilden, Bill, 358
Tobey, Charles W., 266, 285
Tomara, Sonia, 130, 132
total war, 18–19
Trianon, Treaty of, 210
Trippe, Juan, 267
Truman, Harry, x, 4–5
Trypka, Aloisy, 102, 200, 226
Tuck, W. Hallam, 184, 362
Tunney, Gene, 332
Turner, Lana, 353
Twain, Mark, 26
Tweedsmuir, John Buchan, baron, 269
Tydings, Millard, 361
Tyszler, Jan, 70

Ukraine, xi, 99, 133, 387
Urbšys, Juozas, 230

Vahervouri, T. O., 322
Vandenberg, Arthur, 158, 247–48, 279, 284, 285, 342; and nomination, 365, 372–73, 380
Vanderbilt, Cornelius, Mrs., 352
van de Velde, Henry, 37
Van Loon, Hendrik Willem, 349
Versailles, Treaty of, 180–81
Villa, Pancho, 185
Vilnius, 228–35, 233*f*, 236*f*
Voroshilov, Kliment, 309
Vorys, John M., 245

Walcott, Frederic C., 185–86, 187, 296, 377
Waldeck, R. G., 191
Wallace, Henry, 32, 150, 382
Walsh, David, 267, 275
war: devastation of, 14–16, 18–19; Hoover and, 29, 161; laws of, 11–12, 14–16, 386–87; Roosevelt and, 29–30
Warburg, Eric, 325, 336–37

Ward, Edward, 345, 347
War Food Administration, 3, 4, 39
war materiel: Anglo-French provision of, 79; for Finland, 323–24, 362–64; repeal of embargo on, 239–87. *See also* military support
War Resisters League, 253
Warsaw, Poland, 68–70, 87, 291–92; siege of, 110–12, 113*f*, 114
Watson, Edwin "Pa," 147, 167, 362
Watson, Thomas J., 358, 366
Weckmann, Bjorn, 310
Wegierski, Dominik, 65, 86
Węgrzynek, Maksymilian, 202, 278
Welles, Sumner, 28, 52, 147, 155, 156*f*, 157, 310
Wenda, Zygmunt, 138
Wheeler, Burton K., 243, 249, 252–53, 343
White, Case, 89
White, W. L., 347
White, William Allen, 22, 263, 268, 279, 355
Whitlock, Brad, 163
Wieluń, Poland, 69–70, 117
Williams, Joe, 357
Willkie, Wendell, 373, 377, 380
Wilson, Francesca, 204, 223
Wilson, Joan Hoff, ix
Wilson, Woodrow, 147, 149, 166, 313; Hoover and, 3, 4; influence of, 27–28
Wings over Finland, 360, 362
Winston, Robert, 362
Wint, Guy, 18
Winter War, 299–330, 344–45, 362–65
Winther, Wilhelm, 307
Winthrop, John, 31, 388
Wise, Stephen S., 336
Wojtyła, Karol Józef (John Paul II), 89–90, 91*f*
Wolf, Tom, 349
Woll, Matt, 343
women and children: aid mechanisms for, 226–27; Caragea and, 207–8;

evacuation from Poland, 105–6; in Vilnius, 235
Women's International League for Peace and Freedom, 20, 253
Women's National Committee to Keep the U.S. Out of War, 268
Wood, Kingsley, 79
Woodring, Harry H., 76, 157, 255, 378
Woolf, S. J., 348–49
World Peace Commission, Methodist Church, 253
World's Fair, 146, 276–78, 345–46
World War I, 11–14, 27; and anti-interventionists, 23; causes of, 360–61; Hoover and, 29, 31; Roosevelt and, 29
World War II: early days of, 65–82; Hitler and Stalin and, 49–64; and laws of war, 16; lull in, 287; preliminaries of, 17–24; US and, 386–87
Wright, Frank Lloyd, 37
Wrszlacki, Jan, 105, 119
Wyndham, Joan, 78

Yartsev, Boris, 300
YMCA, 94; and funding, 221–22; in Hungary, 215; organizing for aid, 100–103; in Poland, 97–100, 188, 225; in Romania, 198
Young, Loretta, 66
Yrjo-Koskinen, A. S., 302
YWCA, 215, 227

Zagórsky, Ignacy, 234–35, 236
Zaleszczyki, Poland, 125–26, 128, 130
Zamoyska-Panek, Christine, 116
Zamoyski family, 115–16
Zangara, Giuseppe, 30, 161
Zhdanov, Andrey, 309
Zhukov, Georgy, 55
Zum Schwarzer Adler (hotel), 130
Zygalski, Henryk, 196–98